Phil Edmonston

LEMON-AID

2009|2010

USED CARS and TRUCKS

Phil Edmonston

LEMON-AID

2009|2010

USED CARS and TRUCKS

DUNDURN PRESS

TORONTO

Editing: Andrea Douglas, Andrea Battiston
Design: Jack Steiner, Cheryl Hawley, Carol Anderson
Printer: Webcom

1   2   3   4   5   13   12   11   10   09

 Conseil des Arts du Canada   **Canada Council for the Arts**    Canadä   **ONTARIO ARTS COUNCIL CONSEIL DES ARTS DE L'ONTARIO**

We acknowledge the support of the Canada Council for the Arts and the Ontario Arts Council for our publishing program. We also acknowledge the financial support of the Government of Canada through the Book Publishing Industry Development Program and The Association for the Export of Canadian Books, and the Government of Ontario through the Ontario Book Publishers Tax Credit program, and the Ontario Media Development Corporation.

Care has been taken to trace the ownership of copyright material used in this book. The author and the publisher welcome any information enabling them to rectify any references or credits in subsequent editions.
J. Kirk Howard, President

Printed and bound in Canada.
www.dundurn.com

Dundurn Press
3 Church Street, Suite 500
Toronto, Ontario, Canada
M5E 1M2

Gazelle Book Services Limited
White Cross Mills
High Town, Lancaster, England
LA1 4XS

Dundurn Press
2250 Military Road
Tonawanda, NY
U.S.A. 14150

CONTENTS

KEY DOCUMENTS

Lemon-Aid is a feisty owner's manual that has no equal anywhere. We don't want you stuck with a lemon, or to wind up paying for repairs that are the automaker's fault and are covered by secret "goodwill" warranties. That's why we are the only book that includes many hard-to-find, confidential, and little-known documents that automakers don't want you to see.

In short, we know you can't win what you can't prove.

The following charts, documents, and service bulletins are included in this index so that you can stand your ground and be treated fairly. Photocopy and circulate whichever document will prove helpful in your dealings with automakers, dealers, service managers, insurance companies, or government agencies. Remember, most of the hundreds of summarized service bulletins outline repairs or replacements that should be done for free.

Introduction

THE DETROIT BIG THREE, OR "BEG" THREE

Part One

GET THE BEST FOR LESS

Part Two

GETTING A REFUND

Part Three

1980–2006 LEMONS AND CHERRIES

SMALL CARS

MEDIUM CARS

LARGE CARS

LUXURY CARS

SPORTS CARS

SPORT-UTILITY VEHICLES AND PICKUP TRUCKS

THE DETROIT BIG THREE, OR "BEG" THREE

Only 10 Percent of New Vehicles Are Lemons

Out of 100 vehicles, we're apt to build 10 that are as good as any that Toyota has ever built, 80 that are okay and 10 that cause repeat problems for our customers.

ROBERT LUTZ, FORMER PRESIDENT,
CHRYSLER U.S.
CHRYSLER TIMES, JULY 17, 1995

1

WHY DREAD A HYBRID?

$8,000 (U.S.) BATTERY PACK
BATTERY DISPOSAL?
ELECTROCUTION DURING ACCIDENTS
EXPENSIVE
50% DEPRECIATION AFTER 3 YEARS
HIGH INSURANCE RATES
$30,000 FOR A PRIUS
FUEL SAVINGS OFF BY 40%
DEALER-ONLY SERVICE

A BETTER IDEA: A 2005 HONDA CIVIC ($9,000)...LEAVES $21,000 FOR FUEL!

A replacement battery pack is now estimated to cost about $5,000 (U.S.).

Detroit automakers are dying from self-inflicted wounds. Chrysler, Ford, and GM will not survive with their present company structures, despite the $50 billion bailout they received from the American and Canadian governments earlier this year.

Bad news for Detroit is good news for car buyers. New- and used-car prices have plummeted. Large trucks and SUVs became almost as cheap as toasters last year because of soaring fuel costs. And even now that fuel prices have dropped by almost 75 percent, vehicle prices remain in the basement. This is the time to buy.

For example, a 2006 all-equipped Yukon Denali (a *Lemon-Aid* rated Average buy) that sold for $63,645 can now be bought for only $23,000. At the other end of the vehicle spectrum, a fuel-frugal 2006 Ford Focus ZX5 SES four-door hatchback (also rated Average) that listed new for $21,800 can now be picked up for $9,000. Incidentally, I have used the 2006 model year as an example because it was a watershed year for across-the-board safety and quality improvements in most cars, vans, SUVs, and trucks.

The 2006 Tahoe (above), Yukon, and Escalade are the best large SUVs that GM builds. Buy one at almost one-third its original price.

The 2006 Ford Focus (above) and later models are good buys; earlier models are manure.

Interestingly, cars and trucks that are currently coming off three- and five-year leases have added to the savings possible when buying used. Dealers gave these vehicles inordinately high buy-back residual values, resulting in owners dumping the vehicles at the end of their leases to buy more-affordable choices. This trend has created a glut of reliable, overpriced vehicles that dealers can't sell without massive discounting.

But there is a serious downside to purchasing a new or used car or truck now, and for the fore-seeable future. Credit will remain tight, perhaps forcing you to come up with the cash. Some dealers will likely go out of business, so you will have to take additional time to shop around. Having fewer dealers also creates servicing and parts supply problems. And leasing new or used vehicles will become much more difficult now that Chrysler has abandoned leasing and Ford and GM have cut back on the models they will lease.

Savvy buyers can easily overcome the preceding obstacles. Here are five ways to snap up a bargain and save money as we head into a depression, highlighted by mass bankruptcies in the auto sector:

1. Buy a vehicle that's relatively uncomplicated and easy to service, and that has been sold in large numbers over a decade or so. This will ensure that independent garages can provide service and parts, because many parts suppliers and dealers will have shut their doors.
2. Stay away from European cars, vans, and SUVs. Their dealership networks are already very thin, their parts are incredibly expensive and hard to find, and few garages will invest in the expensive diagnostic equipment needed to service their relatively complicated emissions and fuel-delivery systems. The old axiom that there is a right way, a wrong way, and a European way to troubleshoot a car still holds true.
3. Don't buy a hybrid or a diesel. They're failure-prone, complicated to service, and dealer-dependent, and they don't provide the fuel economy or savings they hype. Furthermore, with gas as cheap as it is, there really isn't an imperative to complicate your life with a complex piece of machinery. (Diesel complexity comes from emissions regulations that require the use of cleaner-burning engines and fuel.)
4. Don't buy most Chrysler or Dodge models, with the exception of a well-inspected minivan or Jeep Wrangler or Liberty. Chrysler is the weakest of the Detroit automakers, most of its products are infected with serious safety- and performance-related defects, and its automatic transmissions, brakes, and AC units are practically biodegradable. They are no bargains at any price.
5. Don't buy any vehicle that requires an extended warranty. It's likely warranties will be worthless when a company shuts down. And, as cash gets scarce, automakers and dealers will find more reasons to deny warranty coverage.

Lemon-Aid's 2009–10 Improvements

As Canada's automotive market and consumers' buying habits change, the annual *Lemon-Aid* guides change as well. In this year's used-vehicle guide, we discuss used cars and minivans as well as used SUVs, pickups, and vans, whereas, during the past decade, we treated them in separate guides. Owner reports of safety defects and failures are better summarized this year, and, as usual, the listing of "secret" warranty extensions has been updated (for example, see the GM, Honda, and Subaru bulletins, following):

GENERAL MOTORS SPECIAL COVERAGE (INSTRUMENT PANEL CLUSTER)

BULLETIN NO.: 07187B   DATE: SEPTEMBER 9, 2008

VEHICLES AFFECTED: 2003–04 Cadillac Escalade, Escalade ESV, Escalade, and EXT; Chevrolet Avalanche, Silverado, Suburban, and Tahoe; GMC Sierra, Yukon, and Yukon XL

SYMPTOM: The instrument panel (IP) cluster gauges may stick, flutter, or not work at all. This may cause inaccurate fuel gauge and speedometer readings.

CORRECTIVE ACTION: Replace the instrument panel cluster at no charge to the customer for a period of 7 years or 70,000 miles [112,600 km], regardless of ownership.

HONDA PAINT WARRANTY EXTENSION

BULLETIN NO.: 08-031   DATE: MAY 21, 2008

VEHICLES AFFECTED: 2003–05 Odysseys with peeling "Midnight Blue Pearl" paint

SYMPTOM: The paint may discolour and crack, before peeling away.

CORRECTIVE ACTION: Repaint the vehicle's horizontal (flat) surfaces and recessed areas around the glass or the sliding doors at no charge to the customer. This warranty extension is valid for a period of 7 years, regardless of mileage or ownership.

SUBARU WHEEL BEARINGS WARRANTY EXTENSION

BULLETIN NO.: 03-58-08   DATE: APRIL 30, 2008

VEHICLES AFFECTED: 2005–06 Legacy Outback

SYMPTOM: Rear wheel bearings may produce a whining noise.

CORRECTIVE ACTION: Replace rear wheel bearings at no charge to the customer. This warranty extension is valid for a period of 8 years or 100,000 miles [160,900 km], regardless of ownership.

Finally, we have updated our jurisprudence and complaint tactics (see Part Two).

For almost 40 years, our overall goal has been to help you buy the safest, most reliable car or truck for the least amount of money and with a minimum of fear and loathing. This year's edition continues that tradition.

Phil Edmonston
February 2009

Part One

GET THE BEST FOR LESS

Buy a Pair of Gloves

What's the difference between a $30,000 car and one that costs $50,000? A lot of wasted money, according to Stephan Sharf, a former Chrysler Corp. manufacturing executive. Sharf says all the amenities like heated steering wheels and leather seats just don't add up to that extra $20,000. He suggests it would be better to buy a pair of gloves and forgo the heated steering wheel. If it's prestige you're looking for, he says, "it would be cheaper and make more sense to buy $20 cigars."

STEPHAN SHARF
"GLITZ AND GLAMOUR"
WARD'S AUTOWORLD, APRIL 1, 1999

4

Guaranteed to get you from 30 to 60...er, thousand...with the stroke of a pen.

Plenty of Used Bargains

Buying a new or used car, truck, or van is partly the buying of an illusion. We want to look good. We want to save money. And we don't want to be left on the highway, waiting for a tow truck. That's not a lot to ask for, yet most buyers *do* get stuck with the 80 percent of vehicles that GM car czar Bob Lutz calls "okay," or the 10 percent of vehicles that are problems.

However, finding a used vehicle that's "as good as any that Toyota has ever built," without paying a high Toyota price, takes a little extra effort. But there are plenty of good models available, if you know what to look for.

Both Hyundai's Elantra and its Kia subsidiary's Sorento mid-sized SUV were much improved from 2007 on—after Hyundai hired away Toyota engineers who were carrying briefcases full of Toyota's internal quality control documents.

Used Sales Are Popular

Dealers make more money selling used vehicles than they make selling new cars and trucks, because they aren't under the manufacturer's thumb and prices are more easily manipulated. (With used vehicles, there are no such things as manufacturer's suggested retail prices, high floor plan interest rates, reduced commissions, and warranty chargebacks.) Used-car buyers are often more trusting and reasonable than new-car shoppers, and they experience simpler, quicker transactions, without all the add-on charges and options to deal with when buying new. This explains why 20–23 percent of consumers replace their vehicles each year, with only one-third buying another vehicle from a private owner and almost two-thirds buying through a dealer.

Dealers get their vehicles from fleets, lessees, wholesalers, trade-ins, and private sales. Chrysler, GM, and Ford dealers generally have an abundance of "young" used vehicles for sale, while dealers selling import brands are chronically short of product because owners keep these vehicles three to four years longer. Interestingly, the majority of private sales comprise vehicles six years or older, while independent used car dealers get most of their profit from selling vehicles that are six to 10 years old or are nearly new.

There are more than 19 million cars on Canada's roads, and they're all used. The transformation from new to used occurs as soon as the sales contract is signed, creating a huge pool of less-expensive used vehicles for buyers to choose from and making it much easier to get a discount through smart haggling.

What Canadians buy, however, is quite different from what Americans buy. For example, we are more conservative in the types and sizes of vehicles we buy, with

> **VEHICLES THAT WILL LAST 15 YEARS OR MORE**
>
> Ford Ranger and Escape
> Honda Accord and Civic
> Jeep Wrangler and YJ
> Mazda 323 and 626, B-Series trucks, Miata, and Protegé
> Nissan Frontier and Sentra
> Toyota Camry, Corolla, Tacoma, T100, and Tercel

51 percent of Canadians opting for small cars. Minivans are also more popular north of the border, and they don't carry the soccer mom stigma fuelling American crossover wagon sales. Canadians also don't care if a car hails from Oakville, Ontario, or Oaxaca, Mexico, as long as it's cheap and reliable. Finally, we're reluctant to trade in a vehicle that suits our needs just because it's old. In fact, almost 51 percent of Canadians keep cars and trucks nine years or more, 50 percent of the vehicles purchased 15 years ago are still on the road today, and one-quarter of light trucks are still on the road after 20 years of operation, according to Toronto-based auto consultant Dennis DesRosiers.

The Honda Civic is Canada's favourite small car. In the States, it's the larger Toyota Camry that rules the small-car roost. Downsized SUVs—such as the Subaru Forester, the Honda CR-V, and the Toyota RAV4—make up almost half of our small-car market but account for only one-quarter of the sales south of the border. As far as minivans go, we believe that less is more and, therefore, favour small imports over Detroit's unreliable front-drives and rear-drive gas hogs.

Despite higher fuel costs, Canadians are still in love with their cars. Back in the '70s, the average car racked up 160,000 km before it was dropped off at the junkyard. In the '90s, the average car reached 240,000 km before it was recycled. Nowadays, new models are expected to see 300,000 km before they're discarded.

And most cars and minivans are more reliable than ever before (with a few Detroit exceptions). One Canadian Automobile Association (CAA) ownership survey revealed that less than 10 percent of Canadians who owned cars five years old or younger got rid of them because of reliability problems or high maintenance costs.

Far more common reasons for selling a car five years old or younger were as follows: 43 percent were sold because the lease had expired, 30 percent of owners said they just wanted a change, and 21 percent felt the vehicle no longer met their requirements. Only 22 percent of survey participants who owned vehicles six to 10 years old got rid of them due to reliability problems.

There are lots of reasons why it's a great time to buy a used car or truck—as long as you stay away from some of the rotten products. Fortunately, there's not as much late-'70s and early-'80s junk out there as there once was, and 2006 and later models are safer and come loaded with extra convenience and performance features, like standard electronic stability control (ESC), increased crashworthiness, and safer front and side full-torso airbags. Additionally, there are a lot of cheap vehicles to choose from as sellers compete with lower new-car prices, and a growing off-lease inventory.

But dealers aren't giving anything away, although fuel-efficient, three-year-old small cars are selling at about one-half of their original price, and aren't likely to depreciate much more over the next few years. Smart shoppers are buying downsized vehicles or going to the South Koreans to keep costs manageable. Rather than getting a Ford Focus or Buick LeSabre, buyers are opting for family sedans, crossover wagons like the Mazda5, and small cars from Daewoo, Hyundai, and Kia.

But lower fuel consumption and cheaper prices aren't the only factors to consider. Vehicle quality and dependability are equally important. Sure, you can prance around telling your friends how you "stole" that five-year-old Chrysler Caravan, GM Venture/Montana, or Ford Windstar/Freestar—until you have to spend $3,500 for engine or transmission work (or both, in GM's case). Granted, some of the junk is fairly well known, and vehicles are safer now; however, many Detroit models are loaded with nonessential convenience and performance features that fail around the fifth year of ownership. Chief among these are navigation systems, adaptive cruise control, ABS brakes, and sunroofs.

Luxury Lemons

But let's not just pick on Ford, GM, and Chrysler. European automakers make their share of lemons as well. For example, J.D. Power and Associates has consistently ranked Mercedes' quality as worse than average. If, however, you have been a steady reader of *Lemon-Aid* since 1991, you've been wary of Mercedes' poor quality for over a decade and probably saved money buying a Lincoln Town Car or Toyota Avalon instead. BMW owners have proven to be some of the most satisfied with their cars' overall dependability when compared with most other European makes, including Audi, Volkswagen, and Volvo.

Lincoln's front-drive Continental (a failure-prone Taurus in disguise) and Mercedes' unreliable early entry-level cars and SUVs are proof positive that there's absolutely no correlation between safe, dependable transportation and the amount of money a vehicle costs. In fact, almost the opposite conclusion could be reached with front-drive Ford and GM luxury cars. Rear-drive Lincolns and Cadillacs, however, have always performed well after many years. Recently introduced Chrysler luxury rear-drives, like the 300 and Magnum, that once sold at a premium are now piling up on dealers' lots due to their reputation as gas-guzzlers. It's hard to believe, but a used 2008 Chrysler 300 Touring that originally sold for $31,895 is now worth barely $19,000. The opposite is true of Japanese luxury cars: Models that originally sold for $25,000 to $35,000 retain more of their value and are far better buys used than are most new luxury cars costing twice as much. Again, J.D. Power and *Consumer Reports* (*CR*) confirm this fact.

Three Decades of Hits and Misses

Hits

Acura—Integra, CL Series
Chrysler—Avenger, Colt, 2004 and later minivans, 2000 and later Neons, PT Cruiser, Sebring, Stealth, and Tradesman vans (invest in an extended warranty for the automatic transmission)

Ford—Crown Victoria, Econoline, Escape, 1991 and later Escorts, Grand Marquis, Mustang, and Ranger
GM—Aveo, Camaro, Enclave, Escalade, Express, Firebird, Outlook, Rainier, Savana, Tahoe, Vandura, and Yukon
Honda—Accord, Civic, CR-V, Element, Fit, Odyssey, and Pilot
Hyundai—Accent, Elantra, Santa Fe, Tiburon, Tucson, and Veracruz
Lincoln—Mark series and Town Car
Mazda—323, 626, Mazda3, Mazda5, Mazda6, Miata, Protegé, and Tribute
Nissan—Sentra and Versa
Suzuki—Aerio, Esteem, Forenza, Swift, and Verona
Toyota—Avalon, Camry, Corolla, Cressida, Echo, Sienna, RAV4, Tercel, and Yaris
VW—Beetle Convertible

Misses

Chrysler—Intrepid, LHS, early Neons, New Yorker, and Sprinter
Daewoo—All early models built before 2004, when GM upgraded the lineup
Ford—Aerostar, Contour, Explorer, F-150, 2003 and later Focus, Mystique, Sable, Taurus, Tempo, Topaz, and Windstar/Freestar
GM—Astre, Catera, Cimarron, Fiero, Firenza, J-body cars, Lumina/Montana/Trans Sport/Venture, Vega, and X-body cars
Hyundai—Excel, Pony, pre-2006 4-cylinder Sonatas, and Stellar
Infiniti—G20
Jaguar—All models
Kia—Rio, Sedona, Sephia, Sorento, Spectra, and 2006 and earlier Sportages
Lada—All models
Land Rover—All models
Lincoln—Continental front-drive
Mercedes-Benz—190, C-Class, and M series
Merkur—All models
Nissan—240Z, 250Z, 260Z, pre-2005 Altimas, B210, and Quest
Saab—All models
Saturn—L-Series, ION, Relay, S-Series, and VUE
Suzuki—Samurai and X-90
Toyota—Previa
VW—Eurovan, Passat, and Rabbit

Note in the list above how many so-called premium luxury brands have fallen out of favour and have been orphaned by shoppers and then abandoned by the auto-makers themselves. Their hapless owners are left with practically worthless, unreliable cars that can't be serviced properly.

Also, keep in mind that some Japanese makes from Toyota, Honda, Mazda, and Nissan have had a resurgence of engine and transmission problems, in addition to an apparent overall decline in reliability. For example, Nissan engineers have worked overtime during the past few years to correct Altima, Maxima, Quest, and Titan glitches, and Toyota's new Tundra pickup has serious drivetrain and suspension problems. As they capture more of the market share, it seems the Asian automakers are coasting on their earlier reputations and cutting quality, thereby committing the same mistake Detroit did years ago. Nevertheless, they are still far ahead of the American automakers in terms of quality control and publicly disclosing "goodwill" extended warranties.

Chrysler on the Brink

Chrysler was bought recently by Cerberus, a private equity investor firm that also bought a controlling interest in GMAC Financial Services. Now called Chrysler LLC, the automaker no longer publicly discloses its financial reports; however, the company says it is teetering on the brink of bankruptcy, despite American government assistance worth almost $20 billion. Head office administrators, dealers, and suppliers are running for the hills while flashing "I'm all right, Jack" smiles. They know that Chrysler's new owner doesn't know beans about running an auto company and that the true target of the purchase was money-making—now money-losing—Chrysler Financial.

So does this mean you should steer clear of all Chrysler products?

No, but you have to be careful. Hold on to your Jeep or your Chrysler minivan, or buy one if the price is tempting. Residual values will definitely drop, but this will hurt you less the longer you keep the vehicle, and servicing won't be much of a problem due to the large number of independent garages that can fix Chrysler cars and trucks using the tons of available generic parts. However, recent-model trucks, vehicles equipped with diesel engines, and the Crossfire, with its mixture of Chrysler and Mercedes parts, will likely have serious servicing problems.

Jeep's four-door Wrangler is a bestseller that will easily survive Chrysler's suicide.

As far as warranty rights are concerned, it's unclear what Cerberus' liability will be with used Chryslers that have some of their original warranties left. Of course, selling dealers can be named as codefendants, but if the dealer shuts down, you may be left without recourse. Small claims court, with its quick case turnover and $10,000–$25,000 claim threshold, is your best bet for getting compensation before all assets disappear.

Top Six Safety and Reliability Problems

In spite of the hand-wringing over Chrysler's takeover by Cerberus and the possible auctioning off of Ford and General Motors divisions (think Volvo, Saab, and Hummer), I have little sympathy for these automakers. Their wounds are self-inflicted. And they were warned repeatedly over the past three decades, by *Lemon-Aid* and by independent journalists, that the dangerous junk they were selling and their cheapskate warranty handouts would lead to their downfall.

Over the past decade, many quality issues have afflicted major auto manufacturers, but these are the top six: Chrysler's biodegradable automatic transmissions, Ford's fires and Firestone tire blowouts, General Motors' engine head gasket failures, all Detroit automakers' poorly performing diesel engines, and Ford's leaking tire valve stems imported from China.

I've spent almost 40 years battling automakers and dealers who lie through their teeth as they try to convince customers, financial analysts, and journalists that their vehicles are well made and that the "few" defects reported are caused mainly by the proverbial nut behind the wheel, poor maintenance, or abusive driving. That's why the auto industry has such a lousy reputation—car owners know better. The average Canadian either has personally experienced the lying, cheating, and stealing that's so rampant at all levels of the automotive manufacturing and marketing processes or knows someone who has.

Chrysler Automatic Transmissions

For almost two decades, practically all models in Chrysler's lineup have had disposable automatic transmissions. What adds insult to injury, though, is that Chrysler regularly stiffs its customers with transmission repair bills that average about $3,000—about half the average vehicle's worth after five years—when the warranty expires. Since this is far less than what a new car or minivan would cost, most owners pay the bill and then hop onto the transmission merry-go-round, replacing the same transmission at regular intervals. Go ahead, ask any transmission shop.

Ford Fires and Firestone Tires

Flaming Fords

Imagine sleeping soundly while your car or truck catches fire in the garage below you.

This has happened to dozens of fire victims who are part of a massive voluntary recall, affecting 16 million Ford vehicles, to fix a defective cruise-control deactivation switch that can cause a vehicle to catch fire—even when the engine is shut off, the key is taken from the ignition, and the vehicle is parked in your garage. Over 559 spontaneous fires have been reported to the National Highway Traffic Safety Administration (NHTSA).

The $20 switch was used from 1992 to 2003 to shut off the cruise control when the brakes are applied. Known as a "brake pressure switch," it connects to the brake master cylinder and cruise-control system. An electric current passes through the switch continuously, causing it to overheat and ignite the brake fluid, even while the vehicle is parked.

Ford admits that its lawyers have settled out of court "a number" of fire claims (estimated to be in the hundreds) linked to the cruise-control switch. Its own internal documents show that the same switch is used on 16 million cars, SUVs, trucks, minivans, and vans.

Ford is voluntarily recalling the vehicles listed in the table below due to another factory screw-up that can lead to vehicle fires. Its engineers found that if brake fluid leaks through the speed-control deactivation system into the speed-control system's electrical components, those components may corrode, which can lead to overheating and may start a fire at the switch. This condition may occur at any time, even if the speed control is not in use or if the vehicle is parked. (For more information, call 1-888-222-2751, toll-free, or visit *www.ford.com*.)

SPEED-CONTROL SYSTEM RECALL

TRUCKS	CARS
1997–2002 Expedition	1992–98 Town Car
1998–2002 Navigator	1992–98 Crown Victoria
2002–03 Blackwood	1992–98 Grand Marquis
1993–96 Bronco	1993–98 Mark VIII
2000–03 Excursion	1993–95 Taurus SHO automatic
1992–2003 Econoline E-150, E-250, E-350	1994 Capri
1996–2003 Econoline E-450	
2002–03 Econoline E-550	
1998–2002 Ranger	
1998–2001 Explorer/Mountaineer	
2001–02 Explorer Sport, Sport Trac	
2003–04 F-150 Lightning	
1993–2003 F-Series	
1995–2002 F-53 Motorhome	

Note: Diesel-engine-equipped vehicles are excluded.

Parts for the speed-control system recall are now available for passenger cars and trucks only. For affected cars and trucks, Ford will install a fused jumper harness between the speed-control deactivation switch and the speed-control mechanism. This jumper harness acts as a circuit breaker, eliminating the electrical current at the switch if the switch becomes shorted. For the other vehicles, dealers will perform an interim repair to disable the speed-control system until the time when the part necessary to complete the repair becomes available.

That's right. Ford customers will not be able to use the speed-control feature until the part is finally replaced. Because the electric circuit to the speed control deactivation switch is always alive, refraining from using the speed-control system will have no effect on the overheating switch. However, Ford *does* suggest that owners *not* park an affected vehicle in a garage until the entire repair has been completed.

Sleep tight!

Tire blowouts are especially deadly with SUVs and pickups because these vehicles have a high tendency to roll over.

Firestone tires

Firestone tire blowouts that led to Ford Explorer roll-overs weren't an aberration; they were a microcosm of the denial of responsibility and the high-powered lobbying that goes on throughout the auto industry when it is found to be both irresponsible and dishonest. When the tires started shredding in South America and the Middle East, and injuries and deaths from Ford Explorer rollovers started to mount, Ford used a secret warranty program to pay off Explorer owners. When the media discovered the cover-up, Ford lied to both customers and officials, saying either that the company wasn't aware of the tire failures or that it was all Firestone's fault. Both excuses were shot down in subsequent probes carried out in Saudi Arabia and Venezuela.

The Venezuelan federal Institute for the Defense and Education of the Consumer and the User (INDECU) recommended in September 2000 that both Firestone and Ford face criminal charges for their roles in creating and using defective tires that had led to at least 47 deaths in that country since 1998.

General Motors Engines

Afflicting most of GM's lineup since 1994, intake manifold gasket failures cause engine oil or coolant leaks and can cost from $1,000 to $5,000 to repair if the engine is overheated. Following *Lemon-Aid's* prodding, GM began paying off owners' claims in 1999 under a 7-year/160,000 km secret warranty extension.

GM's stubborn refusal to accept blame and pay all owners' claims led to one of the largest class actions ever brought against an automaker in Canada. Seeking $1.2 billion (CDN) in damages, the lawsuit was filed in Toronto on June 20, 2006, by Stevensons LLP on behalf of an estimated 400,000 owners of 1995 through 2004 model-year vehicles equipped with 3.1L, 3.4L, 3.8L, or 4.3L engines. (Stevensons LLP: Colin Stevenson, 416-599-7900, and Harvin Pitch, Counsel, 416-865-5310. *Kenneth David Stewart v. General Motors of Canada Limited and General Motors Corporation*; Ontario Superior Court of Justice; Court File No. 06-CV-310082PDI; June 20, 2006; Amended Statement of Claim.) By August 2008, these lawsuits were settled for up to $800 per claimant. Affected owners should go to *www.gmcanadianclassaction.ca* to claim compensation.

This cheap engine gasket may bankrupt GM.

Here's the "smoking gun" confidential service bulletin, supplied by *Lemon-Aid*, that will cost GM millions in engine claim payouts:

Diesel Defects

All three Detroit manufacturers are having injector problems with their newest diesel engines. Ford and GM are covering repair costs through a variety of "good-will" programs, and Chrysler is using its seven-year warranty to authorize repair refunds on 2002 through 2004 models.

Nevertheless, J.D. Power's 2004 Vehicle Dependability Study found that Ford and Chevrolet diesel pickups were worse performers than similar gas models, while Dodge and GMC trucks were better overall. Owners of Volkswagen diesels reported up to twice as many engine problems as did owners of VWs that burn gas.

Chrysler

Although Chrysler's Cummins engine has been the most reliable diesel sold by American automakers, it also has had some serious manufacturing flaws, involving lift-pump failures that compromise injector-pump performance. Here's how independent mechanic Chuck Arnold (*chuck@thepowershop.com*) describes the problem:

> The Cummins 24-valve injector pumps will not live without an adequate lift pump fuel supply. These pumps are totally fuel-lubricated and cooled. Without excess fuel flow for cooling and lubrication, these injector pumps die if asked to pull heavy loads. Four out of the last ten lift pumps purchased by the PowerShop have been bad. Two new pumps would not pump enough to prime the system and start the truck. Two others would not supply enough fuel to maintain pressure under load conditions. Cummins needs to improve quality control on their lift pumps and Dodge should investigate moving the lift pump to inside the fuel tank where cavitation and engine heat can't lead to failure over time. [Unfortunately], the Dodge-recommended lift pump tests do not find marginal performing pumps.

Arnold ends with these comments:

> Low fuel pressure is very dangerous because it is possible for the engine to run very well right up to the moment of failure. There may be no symptom of a problem at all before you are walking. If you notice extended cranking before startup of your Cummins 24-Valve engine you should get your lift pump checked out fast. Addition of fuel lubricant enhancing additives to every tank of fuel may minimize pump damage and extend pump life. Finally, Cummins and Bosch should re-engineer their injector pump to make it less sensitive to low-fuel-pressure-induced failure. Existing safety systems designed to limit performance or signal engine trouble need to be redesigned to work when fuel pressure is inadequate so that very expensive injector pumps are not destroyed without warning.

Incidentally, Chrysler's "Customer Satisfaction Notification No. 878" authorized the free replacement of lift pumps in some 2000 and 2001 Dodge pickups.

Ford

F-Series 2003 and 2004 model-year trucks equipped with the 6.0L Power Stroke diesel engine were so badly flawed that they couldn't be fixed, forcing Ford to buy back over 500 units. Wary customers are snapping up Ford's earlier 7.3L diesels, which are apparently more reliable, though less powerful (275 hp versus 325 hp). Power Strokes have a history of fuel injectors that leak into the crankcase, and, on the 7.3L diesel, water can leak into the fuel tank, causing the engine to seize. Other glitches affect the turbocharger, the fuel injection control pressure sensor, and the engine control software.

One Ford dealer mechanic has seen it all:

> You name it, we've seen it. Oil "blowing" into the cooling system (fortunately, not the other way around), numerous running problems, tubes blowing off the turbos, and oil leaks. We had one truck with 8 miles [13 km] on it that we had to pull the engine on. It was a truck going to Hertz, so it wasn't a big deal to the customer, Ford owned [it] anyway, but still, it was a new truck coming off the autohauler sounding like it had a 5 hp air compressor running under the hood and a dead skip.

> We're pulling heads off of a 6.0 now with 4,000 miles [6,400 km] on it. All these problems I've mentioned are on trucks with less than 20,000 miles [32,000 km]. My diesel tech constantly wishes that since they had worked all the kinks out of the 7.3, Ford would have kept it. So far, we've had six buybacks. The one we're pulling the heads off of now will be the next. Before this, I only had one buyback, in four years.

After years of stonewalling and rejecting *Lemon-Aid*'s criticism and owners' refund claims for faulty 6.0L diesel truck engines, Ford now agrees that its engines were crap and has demanded that the supplier of these engines, International Engine Group, pay the automaker compensation for the defective diesels. Ironic, isn't it? Ford is now doing to International what many angry owners of Power Stroke 6.0L-diesel-equipped trucks threatened to do to Ford. And, as in the Ford Explorer/Firestone tire debacle, neither company will admit guilt, or even apologize to owners, for their shoddy product.

Ford Power Stroke: A "Power Joke?"

The 6-liter Power Stroke diesel V8, built by a unit of Navistar for Ford, commands nearly half the U.S. market for diesel pickups. But a raft of problems and repeat trips to dealerships for repairs has left some owners upset, threatening Ford's efforts to rebuild a reputation for quality vehicles.

Soon after the new engines went on sale in November in heavy-duty Ford pickups and the Ford Excursion sport-utility vehicle, owners started reporting problems. Among the costliest is fuel seeping into the engine's oil supply in amounts large enough to ruin the engine. Other complaints included engines that ran roughly or stalled, lack of power at low speeds and harsh shifts.

JUSTIN HYDE
REUTERS, AUGUST 20, 2003

General Motors

GM's diesel engine failures primarily affect the 6.6L Duramax engine, which has been plagued by persistent oil leaks and excessive oil burning, and by defective turbochargers, fuel injection pumps, and injectors, causing seized engines, chronic stalling, loss of power, hard starts, and excessive gas consumption. To its credit, GM has a Special Policy program that extends the warranty to 11 years on injection pumps installed in 1994–2002 models. GM also extended the fuel injector's warranty coverage for owners of 2001 and 2002 Duramax 6600–equipped pickup trucks. Another program, Special Policy #04039, was set up in June 2004, giving additional warranty protection for seven years from the date the vehicle was placed into service, or for 330,000 km (200,000 miles)—whichever comes first.

Cracked, Leaking Tire Stems

Just when you thought Ford had learned its lesson from the hundreds of millions of dollars it paid out for faulty Firestone tires causing Ford Explorer rollovers over a decade ago, the automaker repeats its error. This time, it's cracked, leaking tire valve stems imported from China. Made by Topseal, a subsidiary of the Baolong Automotive Corporation, these stems were used on many of Ford's 2007 model vehicles—including the Ford Explorer. NHTSA has recorded dozens of complaints from car owners, like the following from the owner of a 2007 Ford Explorer with factory tires:

> Approximately May or early June 2008 my vehicle Low Tire Pressure light came on. I discovered a cracked valve stem causing [a] leak. Dealer repaired and attempted to file [a] road hazard claim.... Approximately Aug. 08, 2008 [the] Low Pressure indicator again came on. Discovered another cracked stem leaking air on a different tire. Vehicle mileage was approximately 34,700 [55,840 km]. Repaired at dealer on Aug. 09, 2008 for a fee.... On Sept. 30, 2008 I read [a] news report about Dill valve stem issue (NHTSA action number: PE08036). Inspected tires—and discovered [the] same splitting of valve stems as depicted in news article and Dill Air Controls web site on the other two remaining original equipment tires. Dealer replaced both valve stems...for a fee. Removed valve stems with no additional damage and returned to me.... Spare tire visually inspected and found no visible defects on stem. Spare is mounted under vehicle with valve facing up against underbody protecting stem from elements. Ford statement to news media indicates that Ford's position is that their original equipment is not subject to [the] same issue.... I find that all 4 original equipment valve stems exhibited [the] same cracking defect as [the] Dill recall. Stems replaced on Oct. 01, 2008 show "07 tr414 030" and "08 tr414 018" and both have a triangular logo. As all 4 stems were replaced, the only original valve cap I have came from the spare tire and displays "Topseal," the numbers "317" and "630" and what appears to be the same triangular logo as is on the valve stems.

Although Ford lies through its corporate teeth and says leaking tire stems is not a safety issue, Explorer rollover hearings almost a decade ago proved that any variation in an Explorer's tire pressure could easily cause the vehicle to roll over.

Faced with this danger, owners of Fords and other vehicles manufactured from late 2005 through 2008 should get their tire stems inspected and replaced if they were made by Topseal. Also, if you have bought a replacement tire or valve stem, you should check out where it comes from.

The cost of the replacement should be borne jointly by the selling dealer and Ford of Canada after they are notified by registered letter that a refusal of the claim will mean a quick trip to small claims court. Lawsuits have already been filed against several tire retailers and Dill Air Controls Products LLC, the North Carolina–based distributor of Topseal valves to retail tire stores and other distributors. These lawsuits should be airtight winners (pun intended), inasmuch as Dill has admitted liability on its website at *www.dillaircontrols.com/tovalvesteminstallers.html*:

> We are diligently investigating concerns raised regarding how certain snap-in valve stems produced overseas in the second half of 2006 withstand exposure to high ozone

levels. If you replace one valve stem for being cracked, we recommend replacing all four valve stems on the vehicle.

Four Decades of Lies and Litigation

Think of bad cars of the '60s, and the Ralph Nader–targeted Chevrolet Corvair comes to mind. Yet by the time Nader's bestselling book *Unsafe at Any Speed* came out in 1965, the car's handling had been substantially improved. No, what killed the Corvair were GM's lies and cover-ups, and their stalking of Nader, who was a scheduled witness at upcoming Senate hearings on auto safety in February 1967.

"The requirement of a just social order," Nader told the senators, "is that responsibility shall lie where the power of decision rests. But the law has never caught up with the development of the large corporate unit. Deliberate acts emanate from the sprawling and indeterminable shelter of the corporate organization. Too often responsibility for an act is not imputable to those whose decision enables it to be set in motion."

Following Nader's testimony, GM President James M. Roche reluctantly admitted, after many denials, that his company—without his knowledge—had hired a private eye to peer into Nader's personal life by questioning over 50 of his friends and colleagues. Roche apologized twice to the Senate Committee and Nader, and gave this assurance: "It will not be our policy in the future to undertake investigation of those who speak or write critically of our products."

GM then agreed to a $425,000 out-of-court settlement of Nader's lawsuit against the company for invasion of privacy. That money was subsequently used to finance many of Nader's non-profit public-interest groups, including the Center for Auto Safety, an organization that effectively forces automakers to correct safety defects and cease fraudulent activities.

Dishonest practices, poor quality control, and a reckless disregard for public safety have always been a part of the automobile industry. When I founded the Automobile Protection Association in Montreal in the fall of 1969, American Motors was giving out free television sets with its new cars, and the TVs lasted longer than the Eagle (Ford gave free Dell computers to 2005 Focus buyers). Volkswagen had a monopoly on hazardous and poorly heated Beetles and, later, self-starting Rabbits. Ford was churning out disintegrating cars and trucks, and was denying that it had a secret "J-67" warranty to cover rust repairs. Chrysler's entire product line was rain-challenged—stalling and leaking in wet weather because of misaligned body panels and faulty ballast resistors, distributor caps, and rotors. Later on, the company's automatic transmissions would laughingly be called "biodegradable" by some independent car journalists.

Japanese and European cars imported into Canada during the '70s were unreliable rustbuckets, yet they got a toehold in the North American car market because the Big Three's products were worse—and they still are. Seizing the opportunity, foreign automakers smartened up within a remarkably short period of time. They quickly began building reliable and durable cars and trucks, and offering them fully loaded and reasonably priced.

Meanwhile, American automakers continued pumping out dangerous and unreliable junk throughout the '90s—including GM's Chevy Vega, Firenza, and Fiero, as well as early Saturns, Cavaliers, Sunbirds, and the Lumina/Trans Sport minivan; Chrysler's Omni, Horizon, Dynasty, Imperial, Concorde, Neon, and post-'90 minivans; and Ford's Pinto, Bobcat, Tempo, Topaz, Taurus, Sable, Contour, Mystique (Mistake?), Merkur, Bronco, Explorer, and Windstar. Not surprisingly, sales continued to nosedive.

Then, in the early '90s, Detroit got a second chance to prove itself. The minivan carved out a popular new marketing niche, and American SUVs such as the Ford Explorer were piling up profits. But, as Micheline Maynard makes crystal clear in *The End of Detroit* (Doubleday, 2004), the American auto industry's arrogance disconnected its products from reality, and by focusing mainly on high-profit trucks and SUVs, Detroit abandoned average car buyers to the Japanese and the South Koreans.

American automakers lost the knack for making quality machines three decades ago, when they became more interested in the deal than in the product. Suppliers of high-quality components were often rewarded with increased demands for price cuts and with sudden changes in specifications. Quality dropped, and owner loyalty shifted to Asian automakers that used identical suppliers but treated them better.

Today, the Detroit automakers' quality control is still below average when compared with Japanese and South Korean automakers. Where the gap is particularly noticeable is in engine, automatic transmission, airbag, and anti-lock brake reliability, as well as fit and finish. And, according to *Consumer Reports*, Chrysler is the worst of a bad lot.

 You can reduce your risk of buying a lemon by getting a used vehicle rated as "Recommended" in this guide—one that has some of its original warranty still in effect. This protects you from some of the costly defects that are bound to show symptoms shortly after your purchase. The warranty allows you to make one final inspection before it expires, and requires both the dealer and the automaker to compensate you for all warrantable defects found at that time, even though they may not be fixed until after the warranty expires.

Why Smart Canadians Buy Used

We buy used vehicles simply because new cars are too expensive. According to the Royal Bank of Canada (RBC), the average Canadian's take-home income hasn't kept pace with the rising costs of purchasing and owning a new vehicle. Read on to learn five more reasons why Canadians increasingly prefer to buy used vehicles rather than new ones.

1. Less Initial Cash Outlay, Slower Vehicle Depreciation, "Secret" Warranty Repair Refunds, and Better and Cheaper Parts Availability

New-vehicle prices have been pummelled by record-breaking industry losses during 2008. Still, Dennis DesRosiers estimates the average new-vehicle price to be around $30,000. Insurance is another wallet buster, costing about $2,500 a year for young drivers. In 2007, CAA calculated that once you add financing costs, maintenance, taxes, and a host of other expenses, the yearly outlay for a medium-sized car is over $8,252, or 36.7 cents/km; trucks or SUVs may run you about 10 cents/km more. Of course, these figures aren't as high for 2009 due to lower vehicle and fuel costs. For a comprehensive, though depressing, comparative analysis of all the costs involved over one- to 10-year periods, access Alberta's consumer information website at *www.agric.gov.ab.ca/app24/costcalculators/vehicle/getvechimpls.jsp.*

Used vehicles aren't sold with $1,600–$2,000 transport fees or $495 "administration" charges, either. And you can legally avoid paying some sales tax when you buy privately. That's right: You'll pay at least 10 percent less than the dealer's price, and you may avoid the federal Goods and Services Tax (GST) that applies in some provinces to dealer sales only.

Depreciation savings

If someone were to ask you to invest in stocks or bonds guaranteed to be worth less than half their initial purchase value after three to four years, you'd probably head for the door.

But this is exactly the trap you're falling into when you buy a new vehicle that will likely lose 60 percent of its value after three years of use (minivans and other specialty vehicles, like sport-utilities and trucks, depreciate more slowly). Here's how that would work out in Ontario (above right).

When you buy used, the situation is altogether different. That same vehicle can be purchased four years later, in good condition and with much of the manufacturer's warranty remaining, for less than half its original cost. Look at what happens to the price (below right).

COST OF A NEW VEHICLE

Purchase price (2008 Honda Accord V6 EX-L Sedan)	$35,000
Federal GST (5 percent)	$1,750
Provincial tax (8 percent)	$2,800
Total price	**$39,550**

COST OF A USED VEHICLE

Purchase price (2004 Honda Accord V6 EX-L Sedan, four years old, 80,000 km)	$14,000
No GST (if sold privately)	—
Provincial tax (8 percent)	$1,120
Total price	**$15,120**

In this example, the 2004 Accord buyer saves $21,000 on the selling price, pays no federal GST, hands over only $1,120 in provincial taxes, and gets a reliable, guaranteed set of wheels. Furthermore, the depreciation hit will be negligible in the ensuing years.

Secret warranty refunds

Almost all automakers use secret "goodwill" warranties to cover factory-related defects long after a vehicle's original warranty has expired. This creates a huge fleet of used vehicles that are eligible for free repairs.

We're not talking about merely a few months' extension on small items. In fact, some free repairs—like those related to Mercedes engine sludge and GM diesel engines—are authorized up to 10 years or more as part of "goodwill" programs. Still, most secret warranty extensions hover around the five- to seven-year mark and seldom cover vehicles exceeding 160,000 km (100,000 miles). This benchmark includes engine and transmission defects affecting the Detroit automakers, Honda, Hyundai, Lexus, and Toyota.

Incidentally, automakers and dealers claim that there are no "secret" warranties, since they are all published in service bulletins. Although this is technically correct, have you ever tried to get a copy of a service bulletin? Or—if you did manage to get a copy—did the dealer or automaker say the benefits are applicable only in the States? Pure weasel speak!

Parts

Used parts can have a surprisingly long lifespan. Generally, a new gasoline-powered car or minivan can be expected to run with few problems for at least 200,000–300,000 km (125,000–200,000 miles) in its lifetime, and a diesel-powered vehicle can easily double those figures. Some repairs will crop up at regular intervals, and, along with preventive maintenance, your yearly running costs should average about $1,000. Buttressing the argument that vehicles get cheaper to operate the longer you keep them, the U.S. Department of Transportation (DOT) points out that the average vehicle requires one or more major repairs after every five years of use. Once these repairs are done, however, the vehicle can then be run relatively trouble-free for another five years or more, as long as the environment isn't too hostile. In fact, the farther west you go in Canada, the longer owners keep their vehicles—an average of 10 years or more in some provinces.

Time is on your side in other ways, too. Three years after a model's launching, the replacement parts market usually catches up to consumer demand. Dealers stock larger inventories, and parts wholesalers and independent parts manufacturers expand their output.

Used replacement parts are unquestionably easier to come by after this three-year point through bargaining with local garages, carefully searching auto wreckers' yards, or looking on the Internet. And a reconditioned or used part usually costs one-third to one-half the price of a new part. There's generally no difference in the quality of reconditioned mechanical components, and they're often guaranteed for as long as, or longer than, new ones. In fact, some savvy shoppers use the ratings in Part Three of this guide to see which parts have a short life and then buy those parts from retailers who give lifetime warranties on their brakes, exhaust systems, tires, batteries, and so on.

Buying from discount outlets or independent garages, or ordering through mail-order houses, can save you big bucks (30–35 percent) on the cost of new parts and another 15 percent on labour when compared with dealer charges. Mass merchandisers like Costco are another good source of savings; they cut prices and add free services and lifetime warranties (on brakes, mufflers, and transmissions).

Body parts are a different story. Although car company repair parts cost 60 percent more than certified generic aftermarket parts, buyers would be wise to buy only original equipment manufacturer (OEM) parts supplied by automakers in order to get body panels that fit well, protect better in collisions, and have maximum rust resistance, says *Consumer Reports* magazine. Insurance appraisers often substitute cheaper, lower-quality aftermarket body parts in collision repairs, but *Consumer Reports* found that 71 percent of those policyholders who requested OEM parts got them with little or no hassle. The magazine suggests that consumers complain to their provincial Superintendent of Insurance if OEM parts aren't provided.

With some European models, you can count on a lot of aggravation and expense caused by the unacceptably slow distribution of parts and by the high markup. Because these companies have a quasi-monopoly on replacement parts, there are few independent suppliers you can turn to for help. And junkyards, the last-chance repository for inexpensive car parts, are unlikely to carry foreign parts for vehicles that are more than three years old or are manufactured in small numbers.

Finding parts for Asian and domestic cars and trucks is no problem because of the large number of vehicles produced, the presence of hundreds of independent suppliers, the ease with which relatively simple parts can be interchanged from one model to another, and the large reservoir of used parts stocked by junkyards.

2. Insurance Costs Less

The price you pay for insurance can vary significantly, not only between insurance companies but also within the same company, over time. But one thing does remain constant: The insurance for used vehicles is a lot cheaper than new-car coverage, and through careful comparison shopping, insurance premium payouts can be substantially reduced.

Beware of "captive" brokers

Although the cost of insurance premiums for used cars is often one-third to one-half the cost the premiums you would pay for a new vehicle, using the Internet

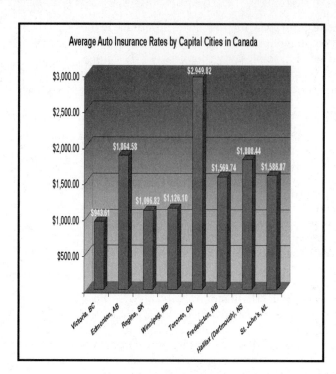

Average Auto Insurance Rates by Capital Cities in Canada

$3,000.00

$2,500.00

$2,000.00

$1,500.00

$1,000.00

$500.00

$2,949.82

$1,864.58

$1,096.82 $1,126.10

$1,569.74

$1,808.44

$1,586.87

$943.61

Victoria, BC
Edmonton, AB
Regina, SK
Winnipeg, MB
Toronto, ON
Fredericton, NB
Halifax (Dartmouth), NS
St. John's, NL

to find the lowest auto insurance quote and accepting a large deductible are critical to keeping premiums low.

A Consumers' Association of Canada's (CAC) national study on auto insurance rates, released July 19, 2005, found that consumers in Ontario paid 45 percent more for their auto insurance than B.C. drivers did. The average auto insurance rate in Ontario was $2,383, while in B.C., it was $1,324. The CAC blamed the high costs on Ontario insurance brokers that, they say, may actually be fronts for a handful of affiliated insurers to offer non-competitive rates.

Use InsuranceHotline.com

One effective agency that tracks the lowest premiums is InsuranceHotline.com. It has created a watchdog service to alert drivers to the changes in their insurance rates. For $20 per year, the agency will automatically rerun members' profiles to ensure that they always know which insurer has the lowest rate from its database of 30 insurance companies (representing over 80 percent of the written premiums in Canada).

Surprisingly, some of the vehicles with the poorest reliability, durability, and fuel economy ratings, such as GM's Hummer, have good insurance rates. Additionally, if you are ticketed or have one accident, your premiums can almost quadruple. When rates for a 2006 Hummer and a 2006 Honda Civic were calculated, the Civic driver saved only $49 compared to the Hummer premium. But add a police ticket and accident to the equation, and the Civic owner could pay over $2,500 more (see chart below).

INSURANCE PREMIUMS COMPARISON

MODEL	NO CLAIMS		ONE TICKET & ONE ACCIDENT	
	LOW	HIGH	LOW	HIGH
Hummer	$1,651	$3,138	$2,812	$8,769
Honda Civic	$1,602	$3,125	$2,812	$11,271

Here are some other *InsuranceHotline.com* findings:

- A family car under $35,000 can cost more to insure than one over $35,000.
- SUVs under $35,000 don't always cost more to insure than a family car or a small luxury model.
- Luxury cars mean luxury premiums, costing on average about $500 more annually to insure than family cars, SUVs, muscle cars, or hybrids.
- Hybrids' fuel savings can be wiped out by higher-cost insurance premiums that rival what you would pay to insure a muscle car.

3. Defects Can't Hide

You can easily avoid any nasty surprises by having your choice of used vehicle checked out by an independent mechanic (for $85–$100) before you purchase. This examination protects you against any hidden defects the vehicle may have. It's also a tremendous negotiating tool, since you can use the cost of any needed repairs to bargain down the purchase price.

It's easier to get permission to have the vehicle inspected if you promise to give the seller a copy of the inspection report should you decide not to buy it. If you still can't get permission to have the vehicle inspected elsewhere, walk away from the deal, no matter how tempting the selling price. The seller is obviously trying to put something over on you. Ignore the standard excuses that the vehicle isn't insured, that the licence plates have expired, or that the vehicle has a dead battery.

4. You Know the Past, Present, and Future

Smart customers can easily run an Internet history check on a vehicle and its owners through CarProof ($50) and then read through *Lemon-Aid* to get answers to the following questions before signing a contract: What did the vehicle first sell for, and what is its present insured value? Who serviced it? Has it had accident repairs? Are parts easily available? How much of the original warranty or repair warranties are left? Does the vehicle have a history of costly performance-related defects? What free repairs are available through "goodwill" warranty extensions? (See "Secret Warranties/Internal Bulletins/Service Tips" in Part Three.)

5. Justice is Cheap and Easy

Lawyers win, regardless of whether you win or lose. And you're likely to lose more than you'll ever get back using the traditional court system in a used-car dispute.

But, if you're just a bit creative, you'll discover there are many federal and provincial consumer-protection laws that go far beyond whatever protection may be offered by the standard new-vehicle warranty. Furthermore, buyers of used vehicles don't usually have to conform to any arbitrary rules or service guidelines to get this protection.

Let's say you do get stuck with a vehicle that's unreliable, has undisclosed accident damage, or doesn't perform as promised. Fortunately, small claims courts have a jurisdiction limit of $10,000–$25,000—more than enough to cover the cost of repairs, or compensate you if the vehicle is taken back. That way, any dispute between buyer and seller can be settled within a few months, without lawyers or excessive court costs. Furthermore, you're not likely to face a battery of lawyers standing in for the automaker and dealer in front of a stern-faced judge. You may not even have to face a judge at all, since many cases are settled through court-imposed mediators at a pretrial meeting that's usually scheduled a month or two after filing.

Choosing Safe "Wheels"

Looking through Part Three can help you make a list of safe and reliable buys you can consider, before you leave the house.

The best indicator of a car's overall safety is NHTSA's front, side, and rollover crashworthiness ratings, applicable to most vehicles made over the past several decades and sold in North America. You will then want to compare NHTSA scores with ratings from the Insurance Institute for Highway Safety (IIHS), which crashes vehicles at a higher speed and at an offset angle, more common in collisions than the head-on scenario. Results from these two bodies are posted for each model rated in Part Three.

2008 Smart Fortwo: Front- and side-impact results and rollover findings are worrisome.

However, there are many other national and international testing agencies that you may consult, and they can be found at *www. crashtest.com/netindex.htm*. This site shows the results of early crash tests of cars that were sold in Australia, Europe, and Japan and that are just now coming to the North American market. Take the Mercedes Smart Car as an example: Nowhere in Mercedes' or Chrysler's sales brochures did I see a reference to the Smart's unimpressive "Acceptable" frontal crash test rating for early models, or any mention that during the 2008 Fortwo's side impact test, the driver-side door unlatched and opened. A door opening during a side-impact crash increases the likelihood of occupant ejection and of massive injuries or death.

Of course, no one expects to be in a collision, but NHTSA estimates that every vehicle will be in two accidents of varying severity during its lifetime. So why not put the averages on your side?

At right are the European-sourced Smart Car's crashworthiness ratings from European New Car Assessment Program (Euro NCAP) tests carried out in 2008. Later, American NCAP tests found that rollover prevention, a category not tested in Europe, was only average and front- and side-impact protection were problematic.

Reliable, Cheap, and "Green" Buys

Consider these important points when making your choice:

- The 19 million cars and light-duty trucks on Canada's roads today are responsible for 12 percent of the nation's greenhouse gas emissions.
- Nationwide, 5,000 deaths per year are attributed to smog pollutants, which alone cost the Ontario economy $10 billion in health care costs and business losses, according to the Ontario Medical Association.
- By purchasing a used vehicle, you are already doing a lot for the environment by not adding to the vehicle population. Nevertheless, in choosing a fuel-efficient, safe small car, you are also protecting your life and your wallet.

Here are *Lemon-Aid*'s picks of the top environmentally friendly, reliable, and cheap used cars, SUVs, trucks, and vans.

Chrysler Neon—Year 2000 and later models are dirt cheap, peppy, and fuel-frugal
Ford Focus—2005–07s are more reliable and fuel-efficient; earlier buys are poison
Ford Escape/Mazda Tribute—A gas-saver; Escape Hybrid is outstanding but pricey
GM Aveo—A cheap, sometimes problematic Daewoo fuel-sipper
Honda Civic—A reliable fuel miser; pricey, but worth it
Honda Fit—A good-performing minicar; 2009s get power and interior upgrades
Honda Odyssey—Better engineered and better performing than Toyota's Sienna; no price-haggling
Hyundai Accent—Cheap with good fuel economy, but not-so-great acceleration
Hyundai Elantra/Tiburon—Reliable, cheap, roomy, and fair gas mileage
Hyundai Tucson—Reliable and versatile, but horsepower may be overstated
Mazda5—A mini-minivan that carries six passengers and burns fuel like a compact car
Nissan Sentra—Reasonably priced, reliable, and average fuel economy
Nissan Versa—A reliable "jumbo shrimp"; roomy and hoards fuel, though a bit pricey

Suzuki Aerio, Accent, and Swift—Cheap, cheap, and cheap; urban dwellers
Toyota Corolla—Reliable, spacious, comfortable, but pricey
Toyota Echo—Economical and bland, but reliable and cheaper than a Yaris
Toyota Yaris—Not as refined as a Honda Fit or Nissan Versa

Note: We don't recommend gas-electric engine hybrids (except for the Ford Escape Hybrid SUV), such as the Toyota Prius, Honda Insight (no longer sold), or Civic Hybrid. Their fuel economy can be 40 percent worse than the automakers' reports, their long-term reliability is unknown, battery replacement costs may be $3,000, their retail prices are almost double what an Echo would cost, and the resale value for a 2001 Prius that originally sold for $29,990 (CDN) is a disappointing $7,000. Hmm…let's see: $7,000 minus $3,000 for a battery pack... Yikes!

By the way, a 2001 Toyota Solara SE that originally sold for $2,000 *less* than a 2001 Prius is now worth $500 *more* than the Prius.

Fuel Economy Fantasies

Consumer Reports has discovered what *Lemon-Aid* has known for the past several decades: The mileage promised on car stickers is grossly inflated, sometimes by as much as 40 percent. *CR* says that hybrids alone account for fuel consumption discrepancies that average 12.0 L/100 km (19 mpg) worse than the city-driving rating given by the U.S. Environmental Protection Agency and Transport Canada.

But Chrysler, Ford, GM, Honda, Lexus, and Toyota don't tell the average buyer that their so-called fuel-frugal hybrids and ethanol-friendly or diesel-powered vehicles are simply high-tech, feel-good PR machines that often don't hold their values as well as conventionally powered comparable models. Not only are the costs of running vehicles equipped with special engines and alternate fuels much higher than advertised, but poor reliability and higher servicing costs also give these green vehicles a decidedly lemony flavour.

Yet most public environmental protection groups and government agencies, seconded by the major automobile clubs, genuflect whenever the hybrid, ethanol, or diesel alternative is proposed.

Once again, we have to be wary of the lies. Toyota, for example, seldom mentions the fact that its hybrid battery packs can cost about $3,000 (U.S.) to replace, or that *Automotive News, Car and Driver,* and Edmunds have also found that diesel and hybrid fuel consumption figures can be 30–40 percent more than advertised.

What about ethanol? After all, the federal Conservative government committed $2 billion in incentives for ethanol, made from wheat and corn, and for biodiesel in its 2007 budget. The Canadian Renewable Fuels Association says ethanol is "good for the environment," a position echoed by the Manitoba and Saskatchewan governments, which emphasize that ethanol "burns cleaner" than gasoline.

Hogwash! Environment Canada's own unpublished research says ethanol "burns no cleaner than gasoline."

Scientists at Environment Canada studied four vehicles of recent makes, testing their emissions in a range of driving conditions and temperatures. "Looking at tailpipe emissions, from a greenhouse gas perspective, there really isn't much difference between ethanol and gasoline," said Greg Rideout, head of Environment Canada's toxic emissions research. The study was broadcast by CBC on March 30, 2007, and can be found at *www.cbc.ca/canada/manitoba/story/2007/03/30/ ethanol-emissions.html?ref=rss#skip300x250.*

Scientists found no statistical difference between the greenhouse gas emissions of regular unleaded fuel and 10 percent ethanol blended fuel. Although they did note a reduction in carbon monoxide, a pollutant that forms smog, emissions of some other gases, such as hydrocarbons, actually increased under certain conditions.

Other drawbacks of ethanol: It's hard to find (there are only two outlets in all of Canada), it eats fuel line and gas tank components, it performs poorly in cold climates, it gives you 25–30 percent less fuel economy than gasoline, and it adds to world hunger (one person can be fed for a year with the crop used to produce one SUV fill-up of ethanol).

Smart drivers should continue to ignore automaker gas-saving hype, hunker down, and keep their paid-for, reliable, gas-guzzling used vehicles, because the depreciation savings will more than offset the increased cost of fuel.

Courts Blast Fuel Economy Lies

Car owners, panicked over soaring fuel prices in early 2008, were being scammed by retailers with bogus gas-saving devices and additives, while salespeople and automakers lied about the fuel economy of the vehicles they sold.

Fortunately, Canadian courts are cracking down on lying dealers who use false gas consumption figures to sell their cars. Ontario's revised *Consumer Protection Act, 2002* (*www.e-laws.gov.on.ca/html/statutes/english/elaws_statutes_02c30_e.htm*), for example, lets consumers cancel a contract within one year of entering into the agreement if a dealer makes a false, misleading, deceptive, or unconscionable representation. This includes false fuel economy claims.

Dealers cannot make the excuse that they were fooled or that they were simply providing data supplied by the manufacturer. The law clearly states that both parties are jointly liable, and therefore the dealer is *presumed* to know the history, quality, and true performance of what is sold.

Fuel economy misrepresentation can lead to a contract's cancellation if the dealer gives a higher-than-actual figure, even if they claim it was an innocent misrepresentation, according to the precedent-setting decision in *Sidney v. 1011067 Ontario Inc. (c.o.b. Southside Motors)*. In *Sidney*, the buyer was awarded $11,424.51 plus prejudgment interest because of a false representation made by the defendant regarding fuel efficiency. The plaintiff claimed that the defendant advised him that the vehicle could run 800–900 km per tank of fuel, when in fact the maximum distance was only 500 km per tank.

This consumer victory is particularly important as fuel savings are misrepresented by everyone from automakers to sellers of ineffective gas-saving gadgets who make outlandishly false fuel economy claims.

When and Where to Buy

When to Buy

In the fall, dealer stocks of quality trade-ins and off-lease returns are at their highest level, and private sellers are moderately active. Prices are higher, but a greater choice of vehicles is available. In winter, prices decline substantially, and dealers and private sellers are generally easier to bargain with because buyers are scarce and weather conditions don't present their wares in the best light. In spring and summer, prices go up a bit as private sellers become more active and increased new-car rebates bring in more trade-ins.

Private Sellers

Private sellers are your best source for a cheap and reliable used vehicle because you're on an equal bargaining level with a vendor who isn't trying to profit from your inexperience. A good private sale price would be about 5 percent *more* than the rock-bottom wholesale price, or approximately 20 percent *less* than the retail price advertised by local dealers. You can find estimated wholesale and retail prices in Part Three.

Remember, no seller, be it a dealer or a private party, expects to get his or her asking price. As with price reductions on home listings, a 10–20 percent reduction on the advertised price is common with private sellers. Dealers usually won't cut more than 10 percent off their advertised price.

Buying with Confidence

No matter whom you're buying a used vehicle from, there are a few rules you should follow to get the best deal.

First, have a good idea of what you want and the price you're willing to pay. If you have a preapproved line of credit, that will keep the number crunching and extra fees to a minimum. Finally, be resolute and polite, but make it clear that you are a serious buyer and won't participate in any "showroom shakedowns."

Here's a successful real-world technique used by Kurt Binnie, a frequent *Lemon-Aid* tipster:

High-Tech Help

Imagine the surprise of the used-car salesman when I pulled out my BlackBerry and did a VIN search right in front of him using Carfax. Threw him right off balance. Carfax results for Ontario vehicles give a good indication, but not the complete MTO [Ministry of Transportation, Ontario] history. I bought the UVIP [Used Vehicle Information Package]...before closing the deal. For the car I ended up buying, I didn't even tell the sales staff that I was running the VIN while I was there. I was able to see it wasn't an auction vehicle or a write-off. This technique should work with pretty much any WAP [Wireless Application Protocol] enabled phone.

Kurt's letter goes on to describe how he avoids negotiations with sales staff and managers. He figures out the price he's willing to pay beforehand, using a combination of book values and the prices listed at *www.autotrader.ca*. He then test-drives the vehicle, runs the VIN through his BlackBerry, and then makes a point-blank, one-time offer to the dealer. He has also found that used-car staff often have no knowledge about the vehicles on their lots beyond their asking price, and they make no distinction between cars manufactured early or late in the model year. An alert buyer could get a car built in August 2002 for the same price as one from September 2001, since they're both used 2002 cars.

Primary Precautions

As a buyer, you should get a printed sales agreement, even if it's just handwritten, that includes a clause stating that there are no outstanding traffic violations or liens against the vehicle. It doesn't make a great deal of difference whether the car will be purchased "as is" or certified under provincial regulation. A vehicle sold as safety certified can still turn into a lemon or be dangerous to drive. The certification process can be sabotaged if a minimal number of components are checked, the mechanic is incompetent, or the instruments are poorly calibrated. "Certified" is not the same as having a warranty to protect you from engine seizure or transmission failure. It means only that the vehicle met the minimum safety standards on the day it was tested.

Make sure the vehicle is lien-free and has not been damaged in a flood or written off after an accident. Flood damage can be hard to see, but it impairs ABS, power steering, and airbag functioning (making deployment 10 times slower).

Canada has become a haven for rebuilt U.S. wrecks. Write-offs are also shipped from provinces where there are stringent disclosure regulations to provinces where there are lax rules or no rules at all.

If you suspect your vehicle is flood-damaged, a rebuilt wreck from the States, or was once a taxi, there's a useful Canadian search agency called CarProof that can quickly give you a complete history of any vehicle within a day.

CarProof (www.carproof.com)

Operating out of London, Ontario, CarProof's services cost $34.95, $49.95, or $59.95, plus GST, per report. Information requests can be completed overnight online. Contact the company through its website, or if you prefer to talk, call 519-675-1415.

In most provinces, you can do a lien and registration search yourself, but it's hardly worth the effort considering the low cost and comprehensive nature of CarProof's services.

If a lien does exist, you should contact the creditor(s) listed to find out whether any debts have been paid. If a debt is outstanding, you should arrange with the vendor to pay the creditor the outstanding balance, or agree that you can put the purchase price in a trust account to pay the lender. If the debt is larger than the purchase price of the car, it's up to you to decide whether you wish to complete the deal. If the seller agrees to clear the title personally, make sure that you receive a written relinquishment of title from the creditor before transferring any money to the seller. Make sure the title doesn't show an "R" for "restored," since this indicates that the vehicle was written off as a total loss and may not have been properly repaired.

Even if all documents are in order, ask the seller to show you the vehicle's original sales contract and a few repair bills in order to ascertain how well it was maintained. The bills will show you if the odometer was turned back and will also indicate which repairs are still guaranteed. If none of these can be found, leave. If the contract shows that the car was financed, verify that the loan was paid. If you're still not sure that the vehicle is free of liens, ask your bank or credit union manager to check for you. If no clear answer is forthcoming, look for something else.

Don't Pay Too Much

Used prices for large and mid-sized cars, trucks, and SUVs have tumbled because new prices have been slashed due to huge inventories and a sour economy. But this price drop hasn't been as severe with small cars and trucks, mini-minivans, downsized SUVs, or wagon crossovers. Their prices on the used-car market are relatively stable and are expected to stay that way through the summer, even though fuel costs are down 50 percent for 2009.

But prices won't stay steady for long. This summer, we'll see an intensified discount war spearheaded by Chrysler LLC, as its Cerberus owners begin selling Chrysler piece by piece to avoid bankruptcy. The automaker is close to shutting down due to poor sales, plummeting residual values, unpaid car loans, tight credit, and leasing cutbacks. Looking for immediate cash, Chrysler LLC will continue to trim its dealer body, fire assembly-line workers, pare many poorly selling models from its 2009–10 lineup, slash retail prices, and team up with Fiat. Ford and GM will certainly follow suit, while South Korean and Japanese automakers will likely slash their prices and offer attractive leasing deals.

As prices for new vehicles go into freefall, used-car sellers will cut prices even more to attract customers who might consider buying new. In effect, we are moving into "perfect storm" conditions, where the buyer will be king and dealerships will be turned into flea markets.

If you'd like to save even more when buying used, consider these tips:

- Choose a vehicle that's five years old or more and has a good reliability and durability record. Don't buy an extended warranty that may become worthless. The money you save from the extra years' depreciation and lower insurance premiums will make up for some additional maintenance costs.
- Look for discounted off-lease vehicles with low mileage and a good reputation.
- Buy a vehicle that's depreciated more than average simply because of its bland styling, unpopular colour (dark blue, white, and champagne are out; silver is in), lack of high-performance features, or discontinuation.
- Buy a cheaper twin or rebadged model like a fully loaded Camry instead of a Lexus ES, a Toyota Matrix in lieu of a Pontiac Vibe, or a Plymouth Voyager instead of a Dodge Caravan.
- Buy a fully equipped gas hog. Your $30,000 savings on a large SUV or pickup will pay the gas bill many times over, and the vehicle can be easily resold a few years down the road, with only moderate depreciation.

Price Guides

The best way to determine the price range for a particular model is to read the *Lemon-Aid* values found in Part Three. From there, you may wish to get a free second opinion by accessing Vehicle Market Research International's (VMR) Canadian Used Car Prices at *www.vmrcanada.com*. It is one of the few free sources that list wholesale and retail values for used cars in Canada. The site even includes a handy calculator that adjusts a vehicle's value according to model, mileage, and options.

Black Book and *Red Book* price guides, found in most libraries, banks, and credit unions, can also be helpful. But accessing their information for free on the Internet takes a little insider knowledge. To access the *Canadian Black Book* values, simply copy the following URL into your web browser: *www.canadianblackbook. com/prv/auth.cfm?token=AB04DC39ZKL01.*

Now, if you want to use the *Canadian Red Book Vehicle Valuation Guide*, which seems more attuned to Quebec and Ontario sales, you can order single copies of their used car and light truck wholesale and retail price guide for $16.95 at *www. canadianredbook.com/default2.asp* (an annual subscription costs $95, plus Ontario provincial sales tax, if applicable). There are no restrictions as to who may subscribe.

You may also go to *Auto Trader* magazine's website at *www.autotrader.ca* to see at what prices other Canadians are trying to sell your chosen vehicle.

Don't be surprised to find that many national price guides have an Eastern Ontario and Quebec price bias. They often list unrealistically low prices compared with what you'll see in the eastern and western provinces and in rural areas, where good used cars are often sold for outrageously high prices or are simply passed down through the family for an average of eight to 10 years. Other price guides may list prices that are much higher than those found in your region. Consequently, use whichever price guide lists the highest value when selling your trade-in or negotiating a write-off value with an insurer. When buying, use the guide with the lowest values as your bargaining tool.

Cross-Border Sales

Shopping in the States for a used car or truck won't save you much money with Canadian prices so low. But if you spy a rare bargain, here's what to do:

1. Check with Ottawa to see if the used vehicle you covet can be imported into Canada (call the Registrar of Imported Vehicles (RIV) at 1-888-848-8240, or visit their website at *www.riv.ca*).
2. Take a trip across the border to scout out what is available from all dealers. Compare your findings with what's offered by Canadian cross-border brokers.
3. Verify if the price is fair, once taxes and transport charges are considered.

Hire a broker or deal directly with the dealer. Be wary of private sellers, because your legal rights may be more limited in cross-border transactions.

Rental and Leased Vehicles

Next to buying privately, the second-best choice for getting a good used vehicle is a rental company or leasing agency. Due to our slumping economy, Budget, Hertz, Avis, and National are selling, at cut-rate prices, vehicles that have one to two years of service and approximately 80,000–100,000 km on the odometer. These rental companies will gladly provide a vehicle's complete history and allow an independent inspection by a qualified mechanic of the buyer's choice, as well as arrange for competitive financing.

Rental vehicles are generally well maintained, sell for a few thousand dollars more than privately sold vehicles, and come with strong guarantees, like Budget's 30-day money-back guarantee at some of its retail outlets (including three in B.C.). Rental-car companies also usually settle customer complaints without much hassle so as not to tarnish their images with rental customers.

Rental agencies tend to keep their stock of cars on the outskirts of town near the airport (particularly in Alberta and B.C.) and advertise in the local papers. Sales are held year-round as inventory is replenished. Late summer and early fall are usually the best times to see a wide selection because the new rentals arrive during this time period.

Vehicles that have just come off a three- or five-year lease are much more competitively priced than rentals, generally have less mileage, and are usually as well maintained. You're also likely to get a better price if you buy directly from the lessee, rather than going through the dealership or an independent agency. But remember that you won't have the dealer's leverage to extract post-warranty "goodwill" repairs from the automaker.

Repossessed Vehicles

Repossessed vehicles frequently come from bankrupt small businesses or subprime borrowers who failed to make their finance payments. They are usually found at auctions, but finance companies and banks sometimes sell them as well. Canadian courts have held that financial institutions are legally responsible for defects found in what they sell, so don't be at all surprised by the disclosure paperwork that will be shoved under your nose. Also, as with rental car company transactions, the combination of these companies' deep pockets and their abhorrence of bad publicity means you'll likely get your money back if you make a bad buy. The biggest problem with repossessed sport-utilities and pickups is that they may have been damaged by off-roading or neglected by their financially troubled owners. Although you rarely get to test-drive or closely examine these vehicles, a local dealer may be able to produce a vehicle maintenance history by running the VIN through their manufacturer's database.

New-Car Dealers

New-car dealerships aren't bad places to pick up good used cars or trucks. Prices are 15–20 percent higher than those for vehicles sold privately, but rebates and zero percent financing plans have trimmed used prices dramatically. Plus, dealers are insured against selling stolen vehicles or vehicles with finance or other liens owing. They also usually allow prospective buyers to have the vehicle inspected by an independent garage, offer a much wider choice of models, and have their own repair facilities to do warranty work. Also, if there's a possibility of getting post-warranty "goodwill" compensation from the manufacturer, your dealer can provide additional leverage, particularly if the dealership is a franchisee for the model you have purchased. Finally, if things do go terribly wrong, dealers have deeper pockets than private sellers, so there's a better chance of winning a court judgment.

"Certified" vehicles

The word "certified" doesn't mean much. Ideally, it tells us the vehicle has undergone some reconditioning that was monitored by the manufacturer. Of course, some dealers don't do anything but slap a "certified" sticker on the car and then inflate the selling price. Sometimes, an auto association will certify a vehicle that has been inspected and has had the designated defects corrected. In Alberta, the Alberta Motor Association (AMA) will perform a vehicle inspection at a dealer's request. On each occasion, the AMA gives a written report to the dealer that identifies potential and actual problems, required repairs, and serious defects.

Used-car leasing

It isn't a good idea to lease either new or used vehicles. Leasing has been touted as a method of making the high cost of vehicle ownership more affordable, but don't you believe it. Leasing is generally costlier than an outright purchase, and, for most people, the pitfalls far outweigh any advantages. If you must lease, do so for the shortest time possible and make sure the lease is close-ended (meaning that you walk away from the vehicle when the lease period ends). Also, make sure there's a maximum mileage allowance of at least 25,000 km per year and that the charge per excess kilometre is no higher than 8–10 cents.

Used-Car Dealers

Used-car dealers usually sell their vehicles for a bit less than what new-car dealers charge. However, their vehicles may be worth a lot less because they don't get the first pick of top-quality trade-ins. Many independent urban dealerships are marginal operations that can't invest much money in reconditioning their vehicles, which are often collected from auctions and new-car dealers reluctant to sell the vehicles to their own customers. And used-car dealers don't always have repair facilities to honour the warranties they do provide. Often, their credit terms are easier (but more expensive) than those offered by franchised new-car dealers.

That said, used-car dealers operating in small towns are an entirely different breed. These small, often family-run businesses recondition and resell cars and trucks that usually come from within their communities. Routine servicing is usually done in-house, and more complicated repairs are subcontracted out to specialized garages nearby. On one hand, these small outlets survive by word-of-mouth advertising and wouldn't last long if they didn't deal fairly with local townsfolk. On the other hand, their prices will likely be higher than elsewhere due to the better quality of their used vehicles and the cost of reconditioning and repairing what they sell under warranty.

Auctions

First of all, make sure it's a legitimate auction. Many are fronts for used-car lots where sleazy dealers put fake ads in complicit newspapers, pretending to hold auctions that are no more than weekend selling sprees.

Furthermore, you'll need lots of patience, smarts, and luck to pick up anything worthwhile. Government auctions—places where the mythical $50 Jeeps are sold—are fun to attend but highly overrated as places to find bargains. Look at the odds against you: It's impossible to determine the condition of the vehicles put up for bid, prices can go way out of control, and auction employees, professional sellers, their relatives, and their friends usually pick over the good stuff long before you ever see it.

To attend commercial auctions is to swim with the piranhas. They are frequented by "ringers" who bid up the prices, and by professional dealers who pick up cheap, worn-out vehicles unloaded by new-car dealers and independents. There are no guarantees, cash is required, and quality is apt to be as low as the price. Remember, too, that auction purchases are subject to provincial and federal sales taxes, the auction's sales commission (3–5 percent), and, in some cases, an administrative fee of $75–$100.

If you are interested in shopping at an auto auction, remember that certain days are reserved for dealers only, so call ahead. You'll find the vehicles locked in a compound, but you should have ample opportunity to inspect them and, in some cases, take a short drive around the property before the auction begins.

The Internet

The Internet is the worst place to buy a used car. You don't know the seller, and you know even less about the car. It's easy for an individual to sell a car they don't own, and it's even easier to create a virtual dealership, with photos of a huge inventory and a modern showroom, when the operation is likely made up of one guy working out of his basement.

Rating systems are unreliable too. Ratings from "happy customers" may be nothing but ploys—fictitious postings created by the seller to give out five-star ratings and the appearance that the company is honest and reliable.

If you must use the Internet, get the seller's full name and a copy of their driver's licence, plus lots of references. Then go see the vehicle, take a road test, and have a mechanic verify if the car is roadworthy and able to pass a safety inspection.

Although you take an even bigger risk buying out of province or in the States, there are a few precautions you can take to protect yourself. First off, compare shipping fees with a Canadian automobile transporter like Hansen's (*www.lhf.com/ebay*), and put your money into an escrow account until the vehicle is delivered in satisfactory condition.

If the car is located in the United States, print out the tips found on eBay's website at *pages.ebay.ca/ebaymotors/explained/checklist/howtobuyUS.html*. The website takes you through each step in detail and will tell you if the vehicle is admissible in Canada and what the likely modification requirements are. If the vehicle needs modification, you should check with a mechanic for an estimate. You will also need to get a recall clearance letter from the dealer or automaker in order to pass federal inspection. Additional information can be obtained from the RIV (Tel: 1-888-848-8240; Website: *www.riv.ca*).

Canadian car sales websites

- *AMVOQ.ca*—Quebec used-car classifieds
- *AutoHunter.ca*—Alberta used-car classifieds
- *Autonet.ca*—New and used cars and trucks, new-car dealers, new-car prices, and reviews
- *AutoTrader.ca*—Used-car classifieds from all across Canada
- *BuySell.com*—Classifieds from all across Canada
- eBay Motors Canada (*www.eBay.ca*)—The premiere site for used cars located anywhere in the world
- North American Automobile Trade Association (*www.naata.org*)—This trade association lists dealers and brokers who will help you find a new or used cross-border bargain
- *RedFlagDeals.com*—A compendium of shopping tips, as well as advice on dealing with the federal and provincial governments. Read the thread at *www.redflag-deals.com/forums/showthread.php?t=481415* to learn how a *Victoria News* editor was fired for publishing a favourable article about cross-border car buying.
- Used Cars Ontario (*www.usedcarsontario.com*)—Used-car classifieds for major cities in Ontario, with links and articles

U.S. car sales websites

- *AutoTrader.com*—New- and used-car classifieds
- *Cars.com*—Ditto, except there's an "Advanced Search" option
- *CarsDirect.com*—One of the largest car-buying sites
- eBay Motors U.S. (*www.eBay.com*)—Similar to the Canadian site
- *Edmunds.com*—Lots of price quotes and articles
- The Big Lot! (*www.thebiglot.com*)—Another large car-buying site

Financing Choices

You shouldn't spend more than 30 percent of your annual gross income on the purchase of a new or used vehicle. By keeping the initial cost low, there is less risk to you, and you may be able to pay mostly in cash. This can be an effective bargaining tool to use with private sellers, but dealers are less impressed by cash sales because they lose their kickbacks from the finance companies.

Credit Unions

A credit union is the best place to borrow money for a used car at competitive interest rates and with easy repayment terms. In fact, credit unions are jumping into car financing as the major automakers pull back. You'll have to join the credit union or have an account with it before the loan is approved. You'll also probably have to come up with a larger down payment.

Banks

Banks are always leery of financing used cars, but they generally charge rates that are competitive with what dealers offer. As of January 2009, the interest rates provided by Canadian financial institutions on a three-year, $15,000 car loan were as listed in the chart below.

In your quest for a bank loan, keep in mind that the loan officer will be impressed by a prepared budget and sound references, particularly if you seek out a loan before choosing a vehicle. If you don't have a pre-approved loan, it wouldn't hurt to buy from a local dealer, since banks like to encourage businesses in their area.

The Internet offers help for people who need an auto loan and want quick approval but don't want to face a banker. Used-car buyers can post a loan application on a bank's website, such as TD Canada Trust's (*www.tdcanadatrust.com/lending/autoloan.jsp*), even if they don't have an account. Scotiabank offers a great Automotive Centre website with resources for car buyers (*www.scotiabank.com/cda/content/0,1608,CID520_LIDen,00.html*); however, you have to contact a branch to apply for a loan.

INTEREST RATES FOR A THREE-YEAR, $15,000 CAR LOAN	
Bank of Montreal	9.65 %
Bank of Nova Scotia	7.75 %
Caisses Desjardins	8.85 %
CIBC	8.25 %
COMTECH Credit Union	5.99 %
Ontario Civil Service Credit Union	5.65 %
Royal Bank	8.35 %
TD Canada Trust	9.50 %
Source: *Canoe.ca*	

Dealers

Dealer financing isn't the rip-off it once was, but still be watchful for all the expensive little extras the dealer may try to pencil into the contract, because, believe it or not, dealers make far more of a profit on used-car sales than on new-car deals. Don't write them off for financing, though—they can finance your purchase at rates that compete with those of banks and finance companies, because they agree to take back the vehicle if the creditor defaults on the loan. Some dealers mislead their customers into thinking they can get financing at rates far below the prime rate. Actually, the dealer jacks up the base price of the vehicle to compensate for the lower interest charges. As bank and other financing choices dry up in some areas, a credit union or cash may be your only alternatives.

Dealer Scams

Most dealer sales scams are so obvious, they're laughable. But like the "Nigerian lost fortune" email scams, enough stupid people get sucked in to make these dealer deceptions profitable.

One of the more common tricks is to not identify the previous owner because the vehicle was used commercially, was problem-prone, or had been written off as a total loss after an accident. It's also not uncommon to discover that the mileage has been turned back, particularly if the vehicle was part of a company's fleet. Your best defence? Demand the name of the vehicle's previous owner and then run a VIN check through CarProof as a prerequisite to purchasing it.

It would be impossible to list all the dishonest tricks employed in used-vehicle sales. As soon as the public is alerted to one scheme, crooked sellers use other, more elaborate frauds. Nevertheless, under industry-financed provincial compensation funds, buyers can get substantial refunds if defrauded by a dealer.

Here are some of the more common fraudulent practices you're likely to encounter.

Evading Sales Tax by Trimming the Price

Here's where your own greed will do you in. In a tactic used almost exclusively by small, independent dealers and some private sellers, the buyer is told that he or she can pay less sales tax by listing a lower selling price on the contract. But what if the vehicle turns out to be a lemon, or the sales agent has falsified the model year or mileage? The hapless buyer is offered a refund on the fictitious purchase price indicated on the contract. If the buyer wanted to take the dealer to court, it's quite unlikely that he or she would get any more than the contract price. Moreover, both the buyer and dealer could be prosecuted for making a false declaration to avoid paying sales tax.

Phony Private Sales ("Curbsiders")

Individual transactions account for about three times as many used-vehicle sales as dealer sales, and crooked dealers get in on the action by posing as private sellers. Called "curbsiders," these scammers lure unsuspecting buyers through lower prices, cheat the federal government out of the GST, and routinely violate provincial registration and consumer protection regulations. Bob Beattie, executive director of the Used Car Dealers Association of Ontario, *www.ucda.org*, once estimated that about 20 percent of so-called private sellers in Ontario are actually curbsiders. Dealers in large cities like Toronto, Calgary, and Vancouver believe curbsiders sell half of the cars advertised in the local papers. This scam is easy to detect if the seller can't produce the original sales contract or show repair bills made out over a long period of time in his or her own name. You can usually identify a car dealer in the want ads section of the newspaper—just check to see if the same telephone number is repeated in many different ads. Sometimes you can trip up a curbsider by requesting information on the phone, without identifying the specific vehicle. If the seller asks you which car you are considering, you know you're dealing with a curbsider.

Legitimate car dealers claim to deplore the dishonesty of curbsider crooks, yet they are their chief suppliers. Dealership sales managers, auto auction employees, and newspaper classified ad sellers all know the names, addresses, and phone numbers of these thieves but don't act on the information. Newspapers want the ad dollars, auctions want the action, and dealers want someplace they can unload their wrecked, rust-cankered, and odometer-tricked junkers with impunity. Talk about hypocrisy, eh?

Curbsiders are particularly active in Western Canada, importing vehicles from other provinces where they were sold by dealers, wreckers, insurance companies, and junkyards (after having been written off as total losses). They then place private classified ads in B.C. and Alberta papers, sell their stock, and then import more.

Buyers taken in by these scam artists should sue both the seller and the newspaper that carried the original classified ad in small claims court. When just a few cases are won in court and the paper's competitors play up the story, the practice will cease.

"Free-Exchange" Privilege

Dealers get a lot of sales mileage out of this deceptive offer. The dealer offers to exchange any defective vehicle for any other vehicle in stock. What really happens, though, is that the dealer won't have anything else selling for the same price and so will demand a cash bonus for the exchange—or you may get the dubious privilege of exchanging one lemon for another.

"Money-Back" Guarantee

Once again, the purchaser feels safe in buying a used car with this kind of guarantee. After all, what could be more honest than a money-back guarantee? Dealers using this technique often charge exorbitant handling charges, rental fees, or mechanical repair costs to the customer who's bought one of these vehicles and then returned it.

"50/50" Guarantee

This can be a trap. Essentially, the dealer will pay half of the repair costs over a limited period of time. It's a fair offer if an independent garage does the repairs. If not, the dealer can always inflate the repair costs to double their actual worth and then write up a bill for that amount (a scam sometimes used in "goodwill" settlements). The buyer winds up paying the full price of repairs that would probably have been much cheaper at an independent garage. The best kind of used-vehicle warranty is 100 percent with full coverage for a fixed term, even if that term is relatively short.

"As Is" and "No Warranty"

These phrases are pure bluff, whether used in a dealer or private sale. Sellers try to use these clauses much like parking lot owners or coat checkers at restaurants do when they claim they have no responsibility to indemnify your losses. In fact, when you pay for a custodial service or a used vehicle, the commission the seller of that service or product receives requires that you be protected.

Remember, every vehicle carries a provincial legal warranty protecting you from misrepresentation and the premature failure of key mechanical or body components. Nevertheless, sellers often write "as is" or "no warranty" in the contract in the hope of dissuading buyers from pressing legitimate claims.

Generally, when "as is" has been written into the contract or bill of sale, it usually means that you're aware of mechanical defects, you're prepared to accept the responsibility for any damage or injuries caused by the vehicle, and you're agreeing to pay all repair costs. However, the courts have held that the "as is" clause is not a blank cheque to cheat buyers, and must be interpreted in light of the seller's true intent. Was there an attempt to deceive the buyer by including this clause? Did the buyer really know what the "as is" clause could do to his or her future legal rights? It's also been held that the courts may consider oral representations ("parole evidence") as an expressed warranty, even though they were never written into the formal contract. So, if a seller makes claims as to the fine quality of the used vehicle, these claims can be used as evidence. Courts generally ignore "as is" clauses when the vehicle has been intentionally misrepresented, when the dealer is the seller, or when the defects are so serious that the seller is presumed to have known of their existence. Private sellers are usually given more latitude than dealers or their agents.

Odometer Fraud

Who says crime doesn't pay? It most certainly does if you turn back odometers for a living in Canada.

Estimates are that each year close to 90,000 vehicles with tampered odometers reach the Canadian marketplace—at a cost to Canadians of more than $3.56 million. This is about double the incidents one would expect based on a 2002 U.S. National Highway Traffic Safety Administration study that pegs odometer fraud at 450,000 vehicles annually. NHTSA estimates that half of the cars with reset odometers are relatively new high-mileage rental cars or fleet vehicles.

Obviously, gangs of odometer scammers ply their trade in Canada because it seems as if no one cares what they do, and the average resale value of a doctored car can be boosted by thousands of dollars, or 10 cents profit for each mile erased from the odometer. Moreover, electronic digital odometers make tampering child's play for anyone with a laptop computer, or anyone who has sufficient skill to simply replace the dashboard's instrument panel.

Think: When was the last time you heard of a dealership being charged with odometer fraud? Probably a long time ago, if at all. And what is the punishment for those dealers convicted of defrauding buyers? Not jail time or loss of their franchises. More than likely, it'll be just a small fine.

Misrepresentation

Used vehicles can be misrepresented in a variety of ways. A used airport commuter minivan may be represented as having been used by a Sunday school class. A mechanically defective sports car that's been rebuilt after several major accidents may have plastic filler in the body panels to muffle the rattles or hide the rust damage, heavy oil in the motor to stifle the clanks, and cheap retread tires to eliminate the thumps. Your best protection against these dirty tricks is to have the vehicle's quality completely verified by an independent mechanic before completing the sale. Of course, you can still cancel the sale if you learn of the misrepresentation only after taking the vehicle home, but your chances of successfully doing so dwindle as time passes.

> I'm finding it difficult finding a reasonably priced used car in the Toronto area. Many of the ads for private sales here turn out to be dealers or mechanics selling cars pretending to be private persons. Also, the prices are ridiculously inflated. Your books are a great read and have made me at least slow down and ask questions. For example, I almost got caught in a lease the other day and pulled out at the last minute. All this advertising had me believe there would be zero down, zero delivery, etc. until I found out there would be a $350 lease acquisition fee and a $250 admin. fee and all kinds of other charges, some legitimate such as licensing. However, my zero down turned into a whopping $1,200!

Private Scams

A lot of space in this guide has been used to describe how used-car dealers and scam artists cheat uninformed buyers. Of course, private individuals can be dishonest, too. In either case, protect yourself at the outset by keeping your deposit small and by getting as much information as possible about the vehicle you're considering. Then, after a test drive, you may sign a written agreement to purchase the vehicle and give a deposit of sufficient value to cover the seller's advertising costs, subject to cancellation if the automobile fails its inspection. After you've taken these precautions, watch out for the following private sellers' tricks.

Vehicles That Are Stolen or Have Finance Owing

Many used vehicles are sold privately without free title because the original auto loan was never repaid. You can avoid being cheated by asking for proof of purchase and payment from a private seller. Be especially wary of any individual who offers to sell a used vehicle for an incredibly low price. Check the sales contract to determine who granted the original loan, and call the lender to see if it's been repaid. Place a call to the provincial Ministry of Transportation to ascertain whether the car is registered in the seller's name. Find out if a finance company is named as beneficiary on the auto insurance policy. Finally, contact the original dealer to determine whether there are any outstanding claims.

In Ontario, all private sellers must purchase a Used Vehicle Information Package at one of 300 provincial Driver and Vehicle Licence Issuing Offices, or online at *www.mto.gov.on.ca/english/dandv/vehicle/used.htm*. This package, which costs $20, contains the vehicle's registration history in Ontario; the vehicle's lien information (i.e., if there are any liens registered on the vehicle); the fair market value on which the minimum tax payable will apply; and other information such as consumer tips, vehicle safety standards inspection guidelines, retail sales tax information, and forms for bills of sale.

In other provinces, buyers don't have easy access to this information. Generally, you have to contact the provincial office that registers property and then pay a small fee for a computer printout that may or may not be accurate. You'll be asked for the current owner's name and the car's VIN, which is usually found on the driver's side of the dashboard.

There are two high-tech ways to get the goods on a dishonest seller. First, have a dealer of that particular model run a vehicle history check through the automaker's online network. This will tell you who the previous owners and dealers were, what warranty and recall repairs were carried out, and what other free repair programs may still apply. Second, you can use CarProof (*www.carproof.com*) to carry out a background check.

Wrong Registration

Make sure the seller's vehicle has been properly registered with provincial transport authorities; if it isn't, it may be stolen, or you could be dealing with a curbsider.

Summary: Pinching Your Pennies

You can get a reliable used car or minivan at a reasonable price—it just takes some patience and homework. Avoid potential headaches by becoming thoroughly familiar with your legal rights, as outlined in Part Two, and by buying a vehicle recommended in Part Three. The following is a summary of the steps to take to keep your level of risk to a minimum.

1. Keep your present vehicle at least 10 years. Don't get panicked over high fuel costs—depreciation is a greater threat to your pocketbook.
2. Sell to a dealer if the reduction in GST and PST on your next purchase is greater than the potential profit of selling privately.
3. Sell privately if you can get at least 15 percent more than what the dealer offered.
4. Buy from a private party, rental car outlet, or dealer (in that order).
5. Use an auto broker to save time and money, but pay a set fee, not a commission.
6. Buy only a *Lemon-Aid* recommended three- to five-year-old vehicle with some original warranty left that can be transferred.
7. Carefully inspect front-drive vehicles that have reached their fifth year. Pay particular attention to the engine intake manifold and head gasket, CV joints, steering box, and brakes. Make sure the spare tire and tire jack haven't been removed.

8. Buy a full-sized, rear-drive delivery van and then add the convenience features that you would like (seats, sound system, etc.) instead of opting for a more-expensive, smaller, less-powerful minivan.
9. Don't buy an extended warranty, because many of these warranty providers may be headed for bankruptcy.
10. Have repairs done by independent garages that offer lifetime warranties on brakes, exhaust systems, and automatic transmissions.
11. Install used or reconditioned parts; demand that original parts be used for accident repairs.
12. Keep all the previous owner's repair bills to facilitate warranty claims and to let mechanics know what's already been replaced or repaired.
13. Upon delivery, adjust mirrors to reduce blind spots and adjust head restraints to prevent your head from snapping back in the event of a collision. On airbag-equipped vehicles, move the seat backward more than half its travel distance and sit at least 30 cm away from the airbag housing.
14. Ensure that the side airbags include head protection.
15. Make sure that both the dealer and automaker have your name in their computers as the new owner of record. Ask for a copy of your vehicle's history, which is stored in the same computer. Get a $25 Internet download or data disc of all your vehicle's service bulletins from ALLDATA. This will keep you current as to the latest secret warranties, recalls, and troubleshooting tips for correcting factory screw-ups.

2

Part Two
GETTING A REFUND

Car designers are just going to have to come up with an automobile that outlasts the payments.

ERMA BOMBECK
AUTHOR AND HUMOURIST

In *Prebushewski v. Dodge City Auto (1985) Ltd. and Chrysler Canada Ltd.*, the Supreme Court ordered Chrysler to pay $25,000 in punitive damages for denying a Saskatoon Dodge Ram owner's refund request.

Broken Promises

Used cars can turn out to be bad buys for two reasons: Either they were misrepresented or they are afflicted with defects that make them unreliable or dangerous to drive. Misrepresentation is relatively easy to prove; you simply have to show the vehicle doesn't conform to the oral or written sales representations made before or during the time of purchase. These representations include sales brochures and newspaper, radio, and television ads.

Private sales can easily be cancelled if the vehicle's mileage has been turned back, if accident damage hasn't been disclosed, or if the seller is really a dealer in disguise. Even descriptive phrases like "well-maintained," "driven by a woman" (is this meant to be a positive or negative feature?), or "excellent condition" can get the seller into trouble if misrepresentation is alleged.

Defects are usually confirmed by an independent garage examination that shows either that the deficiencies are premature, factory-related, or not maintenance-related or that they were hidden at the time of purchase. It doesn't matter if the vehicle was sold new or used. In fact, most of the small claims court victories against automakers relating to defective paint, engines, and transmissions were won by owners who sued both the seller and the automaker.

Think of *Lemon-Aid* as your legal arsenal. Here's 38 years' worth of information on strategy, tactics, negotiation tools, and jurisprudence you may cite to hang tough and get an out-of-court settlement, or to win your case without spending a fortune on lawyers and research.

Warranties

Used-car and truck defects are covered by two warranties: the *expressed* warranty, which has a fixed time limit, and the *implied*, or *legal*, warranty, the application of which is entirely up to a judge's discretion.

Expressed

The expressed warranty given by the seller is often full of empty promises, and it allows the dealer and manufacturer to act as judge and jury when deciding whether a vehicle was misrepresented or is afflicted by defects they'll pay to correct. Rarely does it provide a money-back guarantee.

Some of the more familiar lame excuses used in denying expressed warranty claims are "You abused the car," "It was poorly maintained," "It's normal wear and tear," "It's rusting from the outside, not the inside," and "It passed the safety inspection." Ironically, the expressed warranty sometimes says there is no warranty at all, or that the vehicle is sold "as is." Fortunately, courts often throw out these exclusions by upholding two legal concepts:

1. The vehicle must be fit for the purpose for which it was purchased.
2. The vehicle must be of merchantable quality when sold.

Not surprisingly, sellers use the expressed warranty to reject claims, while smart plaintiffs ignore the expressed warranty and argue for a refund under the implied warranty instead.

Implied

The implied warranty ("of fitness") is your ace in the hole. As clearly stated in the under-reported Saskatchewan decision *Maureen Frank v. General Motors of Canada Limited* (see page 62), in which the judge declared that paint discoloration and peeling shouldn't occur within 11 years of the purchase of the vehicle, the implied

EXPRESSED WARRANTY "WEASEL WORDS"

For any damage and/or breakdown resulting from freezing, rust or corrosion, water or flood, acts of god, salt, environmental damage, chemicals, contamination of fluids, fuels, coolants or lubricants.

For any breakdown caused by misuse, abuse, negligence, lack of normal maintenance, or improper servicing or repairs subsequent to purchase. For any breakdown caused by contaminants resulting from your failure to perform recommended maintenance services, or failure to maintain proper levels of lubricants and/or coolants, or failure to protect your vehicle from further damage when a breakdown has occurred or failure to have your vehicle towed to the service facility when continued operation may result in further damage. Continued operation includes your failure to observe warning lights, gauges, or any other signs of overheating or component failure, such as fluid leakage, slipping, knocking, or smoking, and not protecting your vehicle by continuing to drive creating damage beyond the initial failure.

For any repair or replacement of any covered part if a breakdown has not occurred or if the wear on that part has not exceeded the field tolerances allowed by the manufacturer.

For loss of use, time, profit, inconvenience, or any other consequential loss and any consequential damage to a non-covered part that results from a breakdown.

When the responsibility for the repair is covered by a manufacturer and/or dealer customer assistance program.

For any pre-existing condition known to you or for any breakdown occurring before coverage takes effect or prior to the contract purchase date.

warranty is an important legal principle. It is solidly supported by a large body of federal and provincial laws, regulations, and jurisprudence, and it protects you primarily from hidden defects that may be either dealer- or factory-related. But the concept also includes misrepresentation and a host of other scams.

This warranty also holds dealers to a higher standard of conduct than private sellers because, unlike private sellers, dealers and auto manufacturers are presumed to be aware of the defects present in the vehicles they sell. That way, they can't just pass the ball to the previous owner and then walk away from the dispute.

Dealers are also expected to disclose defects that have been repaired. For instance, in British Columbia, provincial law (the *Motor Dealer Act*) says that a dealer must disclose damages that cost more than $2,000 to fix. This is a good law to cite in other jurisdictions.

In spite of all your precautions, there's still a 10 percent chance you'll buy a lemon, says Runzheimer International. It confirms that one out of every 10 vehicles produced by the Detroit automakers is likely to be a lemon (a figure also cited by GM VP Bob Lutz—see Part One).

Why the implied warranty is so effective

- It establishes the concept of reasonable durability (see "How Long Should a Part or Repair Last?"), meaning that parts are expected to last for a reasonable period of time, as stated in jurisprudence, judged by independent mechanics, or expressed in extended warranties given by the automaker in the past (7–10 years/160,000 km for engines and transmissions).
- It covers the entire vehicle and can be applied for whatever period of time the judge decides.
- It can order that the vehicle be taken back, or a major repair cost be refunded:

> I wanted to let you and your readers know that the information you publish about Ford's paint failure problem is invaluable. Having read through your "how-to guide" on addressing this issue, I filed suit against Ford for the "latent" paint defect. The day prior to our court date, I received a settlement offer by phone for 75 percent of what I was initially asking for.

- It can order that plaintiffs be given compensation for supplementary transportation, inconvenience, mental distress, missed work, screwed-up vacations, insurance paid while the vehicle was in the repair shop, repairs done by other repairers, and exemplary, or punitive, damages in cases where the seller was a real weasel.
- It is often used by small claims court judges to give refunds to plaintiffs "in equity" (out of fairness), rather than through a strict interpretation of contract law.

How Long Should a Part or Repair Last?

How do you know when a part or service hasn't lasted as long as it should and whether you should seek a full or partial refund? Sure, you have a gut feeling based on the use of the vehicle, the way you maintained it, and the extent of work that was carried out. But you'll need more than emotion to win compensation from garages and automakers.

You can definitely get a refund if a repair or part lasts beyond its guarantee but not as long as is generally expected. You'll have to show what the auto industry considers to be "reasonable durability," however.

This isn't all that difficult if you use the following conservative benchmarks that automakers, mechanics, and the courts have recognized over the years:

REASONABLE PART DURABILITY

ACCESSORIES

Air conditioner	7 years
Cruise control	5 years/100,000 km
Power doors, windows	5 years
Radio	5 years

BODY

Paint (peeling)	7–11 years
Rust (perforations)	7–11 years
Rust (surface)	5 years
Water/wind/air leaks	5 years

BRAKE SYSTEM

Brake drum	120,000 km
Brake drum linings	35,000 km
Brake rotor	60,000 km
Brake calipers/pads	30,000 km
Master cylinder	100,000 km
Wheel cylinder	80,000 km

ENGINE AND DRIVETRAIN

CV joint	6 years/160,000 km
Differential	7 years/160,000 km
Engine (diesel)	15 years/350,000 km
Engine (gas)	7 years/160,000 km
Motor	7 years/112,000 km
Radiator	4 years/80,000 km
Transfer case	7 years/160,000 km
Transmission (auto.)	7 years/160,000 km
Transmission (man.)	10 years/250,000 km
Transmission oil cooler	5 years/100,000 km

EXHAUST SYSTEM

Catalytic converter	5 years/100,000 km or more
Muffler	2 years/40,000 km
Tailpipe	3 years/60,000 km

IGNITION SYSTEM

Cable set	60,000 km
Electronic module	5 years/80,000 km
Retiming	20,000 km
Spark plugs	20,000 km
Tune-up	20,000 km

SAFETY COMPONENTS

Airbags	life of vehicle
ABS brakes	7 years/160,000 km
ABS computer	10 years/160,000 km
Seatbelts	life of vehicle

STEERING AND SUSPENSION

Alignment	1 year/20,000 km
Ball joints	10 years/160,000 km
Coil springs	10 years/160,000 km
Power steering	5 years/80,000 km
Shock absorber	2 years/40,000 km
Struts	5 years/80,000 km
Tires (radial)	5 years/80,000 km
Wheel bearing	3 years/60,000 km

VISIBILITY

Halogen/fog lights	3 years
Sealed beam	2 years
Windshield wiper	5 years

Much of the above table's guidelines are extrapolated from the terms of automaker payouts to dissatisfied customers within the past three decades, and from Chrysler's original seven-year powertrain warranty, applicable from 1991 to 1995 and then reapplied in 2001. Other sources for this table are:

- Ford and GM transmission warranties, which are outlined in their secret warranties

- Ford, GM, and Toyota engine "goodwill" programs, which are laid out in their internal service bulletins
- Court judgments where judges have given their own guidelines as to what constitutes reasonable durability

Airbags

Airbags usually carry a lifetime warranty. Chrysler confirmed as much in its replacement program for 1999 minivan airbags (go to NHTSA's website at *www-odi.nhtsa.dot.gov/cars/problems/recalls/recallsearch.cfm* and search for Campaign ID Number 04V480000). The admission below can serve as a handy benchmark as to how long one can expect these components to last.

Any personal injuries or interior damages caused by airbag deployment are covered by your accident insurance policy. However, if the airbag fails to deploy, or there is a sudden deployment for no apparent reason, the automaker and the dealer should be held jointly responsible for all injuries and damages caused by the failure.

Inadvertent deployment may occur after passing over a bump in the road or slamming the car door, or, in some Chrysler minivans, simply by putting the key in the ignition. This happens more often than you might imagine, judging by the hundreds of recalls and thousands of complaints recorded on NHTSA's website.

Your car's data recorder (see page 71) can be used to prove that the airbag, brakes, or throttle control failed prior to an accident. Simply hook a computer up and then download the data from your vehicle's "black box." This will likely lead to a

---

NHTSA CAMPAIGN ID NUMBER: 04V480000

Make: DODGE **Model:** CARAVAN **Year:** 1999 **Manufacturer:** DAIMLERCHRYSLER CORPORATION
NHTSA CAMPAIGN ID Number: 04V480000 **Mfg's Report Date:** OCT 05, 2004 **Component:** AIRBAGS
Potential Number Of Units Affected: 955,344
SUMMARY: On certain minivans, the driver's airbag may become disabled due to a failure of the clockspring, which is located in the hub of the steering wheel.
CONSEQUENCE: This condition will manifest itself through illumination of the airbag warning lamp, and could eventually result in a driver's airbag open circuit if the part is not replaced in a reasonable amount of time.
REMEDY: Dealers will replace the clockspring assembly on all covered vehicles with 70,000 miles [112,650 km] or less. For those vehicles with more than 70,000 miles [112,650 km], DaimlerChrysler will offer an extended lifetime warranty, under which it will replace the clockspring at no charge if it fails. DaimlerChrysler will also reimburse owners who have paid to have the clockspring replaced on their vehicles. The recall began on October 12, 2004. Owners should contact DaimlerChrysler at 1-800-853-1403.
NOTES: DaimlerChrysler Recall No. D17. Customers can contact the National Highway Traffic Safety Administration's auto safety hotline at 1-888-dash-2-dot (1-888-327-4236).

Almost all vehicles have a data recorder.

more-generous settlement from the two parties and will prevent your insurance premiums from being jacked up.

Emissions Components

Car companies have got themselves into hot water repeatedly over the years for refusing to replace emissions parts free of charge. These parts are covered by the emissions warranty. The warranty was set up by automakers with the approval of the U.S. Environmental Protection Agency (EPA), which also monitors the warranty. Canada has approved the same warranty, but leaves enforcement up to the States and the courts. Ford and Chrysler have both been fined by the EPA for violating the warranty's provisions, and have entered into consent agreements to respect owner warranty rights (see "Emissions-Control Warranties" on page 58).

Use the manufacturer's emissions warranty as your primary guideline for the expected durability of high-tech electronic and mechanical pollution-control components, such as powertrain control modules (PCMs) and catalytic converters. Look first at your owner's manual for an indication of which parts on your vehicle are covered. If you don't come up with much information, ask the auto manufacturer for a list of specific components covered by the emissions warranty. If you're stonewalled, invest $26.95 (U.S.) in an ALLDATA service bulletin subscription (1982–2008 models). Or you can avoid the ALLDATA fee by accessing bulletin numbers and titles at *www.alldatadiy.com/recalls*, or NHTSA's free service bulletin summary at *www-odi.nhtsa.dot.gov/cars/problems/tsb* (search for the complete bulletin by its number or by the car model and year).

Contact the Right People

Before we go any further, let's get one thing straight: A telephone call to a service manager or automaker usually won't get you much help. Auto manufacturers and their dealers want to make money, not give it back. Customer service advisors are paid to *apply* the warranty policy; don't expect them to *make* policy due to your claim's extenuating circumstances.

To get action, if you suspect a secret warranty applies or that your vehicle has a factory-related defect, you have to kick your claim upstairs, where the company representatives have more power. This can usually be accomplished by sending your claim to the legal affairs department (typically found in Ontario). It should be a registered letter, fax, or email—something that creates a paper trail and gets attention. What's more, that letter must contain the threat that you will use the implied warranty against the dealer and manufacturer and cite convincing jurisprudence to win your small claims court action in the same region where that business operates.

Following are two sample complaint letters that show you the type of ammunition you'll need in order to invoke the implied warranty to get a refund for a bad car or ineffective repairs.

USED VEHICLE COMPLAINT LETTER/FAX/EMAIL

WITHOUT PREJUDICE

Date: _____

Name: _____

Please be advised that I am dissatisfied with my used vehicle, a (state model), for the following reasons:

1. _____

2. _____

3. _____

4. _____

5. _____

In compliance with the provincial consumer protection laws and the "implied warranty" set down by the Supreme Court of Canada in *Donoghue v. Stevenson, Wharton v. GM*, and *Sharman v. Ford Canada*, I hereby request that these defects be repaired without charge. This vehicle has not been reasonably durable and is, therefore, not as represented to me.

Should you fail to repair these defects in a satisfactory manner and within a reasonable period of time, I shall get an estimate of the repairs from an independent source and claim them in court, without further delay. I also reserve my right to claim up to $1 million for punitive damages, pursuant to the Supreme Court of Canada's February 22, 2002, ruling in *Whiten v. Pilot*.

I have dealt with your company because of its honesty, competence, and sincere regard for its clients. I am sure that my case is the exception and not the rule.

A positive response within the next five (5) days would be appreciated.

(signed with telephone number, fax number, or email address)

SECRET WARRANTY CLAIM LETTER/FAX/EMAIL

WITHOUT PREJUDICE

Date: _____
Name: _____

Please be advised that I am dissatisfied with my vehicle, a _____, bought from you on _____.

It has had the following recurring problems that I believe are factory-related defects, as confirmed by internal service bulletins sent to dealers, and are covered by your "goodwill" policies:

1. _____

2. _____

3. _____

If your "goodwill" program has ended, I ask that my claim be accepted nevertheless, inasmuch as I was never informed of your policy while it was in effect and should not be penalized for not knowing it existed.

I hereby formally put you on notice under federal and provincial consumer protection statutes that your refusal to apply this extended warranty coverage in my case would be an unfair warranty practice within the purview of the above-cited laws.

Your actions also violate the "implied warranty" set down by the Supreme Court of Canada (*Donoghue v. Stevenson* and *Longpre v. St. Jacques Automobile*) and repeatedly reaffirmed by provincial consumer protection laws (*Lowe v. Chrysler, Dufour v. Ford du Canada*, and *Frank v. GM*).

I have enclosed several estimates (my bill) showing that this problem is factory related and will (has) cost $_____ to correct. I would appreciate your refunding me the estimated (paid) amount, failing which, I reserve the right to have the repair done elsewhere and claim reimbursement in court without further delay. I also reserve the right to claim up to $1 million for punitive damages, pursuant to the Supreme Court of Canada's February 22, 2002, ruling in *Whiten v. Pilot*.

A positive response within the next five (5) days would be appreciated.

(signed with telephone number, fax number, or email address)

Send a claim letter to both the seller (if they're a dealer) and the automaker to let them work out together how much they will refund to you. Make sure you keep plenty of copies of the complaint and indicate how you can most easily be reached.

Unfair contract clauses

Don't let anyone tell you that contracts are iron-clad and cannot be broken. In fact, unfair sales contracts can be cancelled anytime by a judge, even though corporate lawyers spend countless hours making sure their clients are well protected with one-sided standard-form contracts. Judges look upon these agreements, called "contracts of adhesion," with a great deal of skepticism. They know these loan documents, insurance contracts, and automobile leases grant consumers little or no bargaining power. So when a dispute arises over terms or language, provincial consumer protection statutes require that judges interpret these contracts in the way most favourable to the consumer. Simply put, ignorance can sometimes be a good defence.

Hearsay

Judges in civil courts in common-law provinces have considerable latitude in allowing hearsay evidence if it's introduced properly. But it is essential that printed evidence and/or witnesses (relatives are not excluded) be available to confirm that a false representation actually occurred, that a part is failure-prone, or that its replacement is covered by a secret warranty or internal service bulletin alert. If you can't find an independent expert, introduce this evidence through the auto-maker reps and dealership service personnel who have to be at the trial anyhow. They know all about the service bulletins and extended warranty programs cited in *Lemon-Aid* and will probably contradict each other, particularly if they are excluded from the courtroom prior to testifying. Incidentally, you may wish to have the court clerk send a subpoena requiring the deposition of the documents you intend to cite, all warranty extensions relevant to your problem, and other lawsuits filed against the company for similar failures. This will make the fur fly in Oshawa, Oakville, and Windsor, and will likely lead to an out-of-court settlement. Sometimes, the service manager or company representative will make key admissions if questioned closely by you, a court mediator, or the trial judge. Here are some questions to ask: Is this a common problem? Do you recognize this service bulletin? Is there a case-by-case "goodwill" plan covering this repair?

Automakers often blame owners for having pushed their vehicle beyond its limits. Therefore, when you seek to set aside the contract or get repair work reimbursed, it's essential that you get an independent mechanic or your co-workers to prove the vehicle was well maintained and driven prudently.

Reasonable diligence

When asking for a refund, keep in mind the "reasonable diligence" rule that requires that a suit be filed within a reasonable amount of time after the purchase, which usually means less than a year. Because many factory-related deficiencies take years to appear, the courts have ruled that the reasonable diligence clock starts clicking only after the defect is confirmed to be manufacturer- or dealer-related (powertrain, paint, etc.). For powertrain components like engines and transmissions, this allows you to make a claim for up to seven years after the vehicle was originally put into service, regardless of whether it was bought new or used. Body failures like paint delamination (see *Frank v. GM*) are reimbursable for up to 11 years. If there have been negotiations with the dealer or the automaker, or if either the dealer or the automaker has been promising to correct the defects for some time or has carried out repeated unsuccessful repairs, the deadline for filing the lawsuit can be extended.

Extra, punitive damages

Yes, you can claim for hotel and travel costs or compensation for general inconvenience. Fortunately, when legal action is threatened—usually through small claims court—automakers quickly up their out-of-court offer to include most of the owner's expenses because they know the courts will be far more generous. For example, a British Columbia court's decision gave $2,257 for hotel and travel costs, and then capped it off with a $5,000 award for "inconvenience and loss of enjoyment of their luxury vehicle," to a motorist who was fed up with his lemon Cadillac (see *Wharton v. Tom Harris Chevrolet Oldsmobile Cadillac Ltd. and General Motors of Canada Limited*; B.C. Supreme Court, Vancouver; 1999/12/02; Docket C982104). In the *Sharman v. Ford* case (see page 95), the judge gave the plaintiff $7,500 for "mental distress" caused by the fear that his children would fall out of his 2000 Windstar equipped with a faulty sliding door.

As of March 19, 2005, the Supreme Court of Canada confirmed that car owners can ask for punitive, or exemplary, damages when they feel the seller's or the automaker's conduct has been so outrageously bad that the court should protect society by awarding a sum of money large enough to dissuade others from engaging in similar immoral, unethical conduct. I call this the "weasel-whacker" law. In *Prebushewski v. Dodge City Auto (1985) Ltd. and Chrysler Canada Ltd.* (2001 SKQB 537; QB1215/99JCS), the plaintiff got $25,000 in a judgment handed down December 6, 2001, in Saskatoon. The award followed testimony from Chrysler's expert witness that the company was aware of many cases where daytime running lights shorted and caused 1996 Ram pickups to catch fire. The plaintiff's truck had burned to the ground, and Chrysler refused the owner's claim, saying it had fulfilled its expressed warranty obligations, in spite of its knowledge that fires were commonplace. The plaintiff sued on the grounds that there was an implied warranty that the vehicle would be safe. Justice Rothery gave this stinging rebuke in his judgment against Chrysler and its dealer:

Not only did Chrysler know about the problems of the defective daytime running light modules, it did not advise the plaintiff of this. It simply chose to ignore the plaintiff's requests for compensation and told her to seek recovery from her insurance company. Chrysler had replaced thousands of these modules since 1988. But it had also made a business decision to neither advise its customers of the problem nor to recall the vehicles to replace the modules. While the cost would have been about $250 to replace each module, there were at least one million customers. Chrysler was not prepared to spend $250 million, even though it knew what the defective module might do.

Counsel for the defendants argues that this matter had to be resolved by litigation because the plaintiff and the defendants simply had a difference of opinion on whether the plaintiff should be compensated by the defendants. Had the defendants some dispute as to the cause of the fire, that may have been sufficient to prove that they had not willfully violated this part of the *Act*. They did not. They knew about the defective daytime running light module. They did nothing to replace the burned truck for the plaintiff. They offered the plaintiff no compensation for her loss. Counsel's position that the definition of the return of the purchase price is an arguable point is not sufficient to negate the defendants' violation of this part of the *Act*. I find the violation of the defendants to be willful. Thus, I find that exemplary damages are appropriate on the facts of this case.

In this case, the quantum ought to be sufficiently high as to correct the defendants' behaviour. In particular, Chrysler's corporate policy to place profits ahead of the potential danger to its customers' safety and personal property must be punished. And when such corporate policy includes a refusal to comply with the provisions of the *Act* and a refusal to provide any relief to the plaintiff, I find an award of $25,000 for exemplary damages to be appropriate. I therefore order Chrysler and Dodge City to pay: Damages in the sum of $41,969.83; Exemplary damages in the sum of $25,000; Party and party costs.

Warranty Rights

The manufacturer's or dealer's warranty is a written legal promise that a vehicle will be reasonably reliable, subject to certain conditions. Regardless of the number of subsequent owners, this promise remains in force as long as the warranty's original time/kilometre limits haven't expired. Tires aren't usually covered by car manufacturers' warranties; they're warranted instead by the tiremaker on a pro-rated basis. This isn't such a good deal, because the manufacturer is making a profit by charging you the full list price. If you were to buy the same replacement tire from a discount store, you'd likely pay less, without the prorated rebate.

But consumers have gained additional rights following Bridgestone/Firestone's massive recall in 2001 of its defective ATX II and Wilderness tires. Because of the confusion and chaos surrounding Firestone's handling of the recall, Ford's 575 Canadian dealers stepped into the breach and replaced the tires with any equivalent tires they had in stock, no questions asked. This is an important precedent that tears down the traditional wall separating tire manufacturers from automakers in product liability claims. In essence, whoever sells the product can now be held liable for damages. In the future, Canadian consumers will have an easier time holding the dealer, the automaker, and the tire manufacturer liable, not just for recalled products but also for any defect that affects the safety or reasonable durability of that product.

This is particularly true now that the Supreme Court of Canada (*Winnipeg Condominium v. Bird Construction* [1995] 1 S.C.R. 85) has ruled that defendants are liable in negligence for any designs that result in a risk to the public's safety or health. In doing so, the Supreme Court reversed a long-standing policy and provided the public with a new cause of action that had not existed before in Canada.

Other Warranties

In the U.S., safety restraints such as airbags and safety belts have warranty coverage extended for the lifetime of the vehicle, following an informal agreement made between automakers and NHTSA. In Canada, however, some automakers have tried to dodge this responsibility, alleging that they are separate entities, their vehicles are different, and no U.S. agreement or service bulletin can bind them. That distinction is both disingenuous and dishonest and wouldn't likely hold up in small claims court—probably the reason why most automakers relent when threatened with legal action.

 Aftermarket products and services—such as gas-saving gadgets, rustproofing, and paint protectors—can render the manufacturer's warranty invalid, so make sure you're in the clear before purchasing any optional equipment or services from an independent supplier.

How fairly a warranty is applied is more important than how long it remains in effect. Once you know the normal wear rate for a mechanical component or body part, you can demand proportional compensation when you get less than normal durability—no matter what the original warranty says. Some dealers tell customers that they need to have original equipment parts installed in order to maintain their warranty. A variation on this theme requires that the selling dealer does routine servicing—including tune-ups and oil changes (with a certain brand of oil)—or the warranty is invalidated. Nothing could be further from the truth. Canadian law stipulates that whoever issues a warranty cannot make that warranty conditional on the use of any specific brand of motor oil, oil filter, or any other component, unless it's provided to the customer free of charge.

Sometimes dealers will do all sorts of minor repairs that don't correct the problem, and then after the warranty runs out, they'll tell you that major repairs are needed. You can avoid this nasty surprise by repeatedly bringing your vehicle to the dealership before the warranty ends. During each visit, insist that a written work order include the specific nature of the problem, as you see it, and a statement that this is the second, third, or fourth time the same problem has been brought to the dealer's attention. Write this down yourself, if need be. This allows you to show a pattern of non-performance by the dealer during the warranty period and establishes that the problem is both serious and chronic. When the warranty expires, you have the legal right to demand that it be extended on those items consistently reappearing on your handful of work orders. *Lowe v. Fairview Chrysler* (see page 92) is an excellent judgment that reinforces this important principle. In another lawsuit, *François Chong v. Marine Drive Imported Cars Ltd. and Honda Canada Inc.* (see page 91), a Honda owner forced Honda to fix his engine six times—until they got it right.

A retired GM service manager suggested another effective tactic to use when you're not sure that a dealer's warranty "repairs" will actually correct the problem for a reasonable period of time after the warranty expires. Here's what he says you should do:

> When you pick up the vehicle after the warranty repair has been done, hand the service manager a note to be put in your file that says you appreciate the warranty repair, however, you intend to return and ask for further warranty coverage if the problem reappears before a reasonable amount of time has elapsed—even if the original warranty has expired. A copy of the same note should be sent to the automaker.... Keep your copy of the note in the glove compartment as cheap insurance against paying for a repair that wasn't fixed correctly the first time.

Extra-Cost Warranties

If predicted bankruptcies occur, supplementary warranties will be worthless. At best, payouts will be parsimonious. Supplementary warranties providing extended coverage may be sold by the manufacturer, the dealer, or an independent third party and are automatically transferred when the vehicle is sold. They cost between $1,500 and $2,000 and are usually a waste of money. You can protect yourself better by steering clear of vehicles that have a reputation for being unreliable or expensive to service (see Part Three), and using the threat of small claims courts when factory-related trouble arises. Don't let the dealer pressure you into deciding right away.

Generally, you can purchase an extended warranty any time during the period in which the manufacturer's warranty is in effect or, in some cases, shortly after buying the vehicle from a used-car dealer. An automaker's supplementary warranty will likely cost about a third more than warranties sold by independents. And in some parts of the country, notably B.C., dealers have a quasi monopoly on selling warranties, with little competition from the independents.

Dealers love to sell extended warranties, whether you need them or not, because dealer markup represents up to 60 percent of the warranty's cost. Out of the remaining 40 percent comes the sponsor's administration costs and profit margin, calculated at another 15 percent. What's left to pay for repairs is a paltry 25 percent of the original amount. The only reason that automakers and independent warranty companies haven't been busted for this Ponzi scheme is that only half of the car buyers who purchase extended service contracts actually use them.

It's often difficult to collect on supplementary warranties because independent companies frequently go out of business or limit the warranty's coverage through subsequent mailings. Provincial laws cover both situations. If the bankrupt warranty company's insurance policy won't cover your claim, take the dealer to small claims court and ask for repair costs and the refund of the original warranty payment. Your argument for holding the dealer responsible is a simple one: By accepting a commission to act as an agent of the defunct company, the dealer took on the obligations of the company as well. As for limiting the coverage after you have bought the warranty policy, this is illegal, and it allows you to sue both the dealer and the warranty company for a refund of both the warranty and the repair costs.

Emissions-Control Warranties

These little-publicized warranties can save you big bucks if major engine or exhaust components fail prematurely. They come with all new vehicles and cover major components of the emissions-control system for up to 8 years/130,000 km, no matter how many times the vehicle is sold. Unfortunately, although owner's manuals vaguely mention the emissions warranty, most don't specify which parts are covered. The U.S. Environmental Protection Agency has intervened on several occasions with hefty fines against Chrysler and Ford and ruled that all major motor and fuel-system components are covered. These include fuel metering, ignition spark advance, restart, evaporative emissions, positive crankcase ventilation, engine electronics (computer modules), and catalytic converters, as well as hoses, clamps, brackets, pipes, gaskets, belts, seals, and connectors. Ford's comprehensive guidelines as to what the emissions warranty covers and for how long can be found at *www.fordvehicles.com/assets/pdf/2007warranty.pdf*.

Unlike the United States, Canada has no governmentally defined list of parts that must be covered. Nevertheless, Environment Canada and the Canadian Vehicle Manufacturers' Association (CVMA) do have a Memorandum of Understanding that says emissions warranties will be identical on both sides of the border (see *www.ec.gc.ca/CEPARegistry/participation/LEV_MOU_E.pdf*).

Many of the confidential technical service bulletins listed in Part Three show parts failures that are covered under the eight-year emissions warranty, even though motorists are routinely charged for their replacement.

Make sure to get your emissions system checked out thoroughly by a dealer or an independent garage before the emissions warranty expires and before having the vehicle inspected by provincial emissions inspectors. In addition to ensuring you pass provincial tests, this precaution could save you up to $1,000 if both your catalytic converter and other emissions components are faulty.

Furthermore, go to NHTSA's website (at *www-odi.nhtsa.dot.gov/cars/problems/ recalls/recallsearch.cfm*) to look for service bulletins acknowledging that a problem exists or emissions warranties that have been extended through manufacturer

recall settlements with the federal government. Then ask that your vehicle's component be covered by a similar extended warranty. Unfortunately, few car owners know about these warranty extensions because automobile manufacturers, in connivance with their dealers, keep them secret.

Psst..."Secret" Warranties Are Everywhere

Automakers are reluctant to make free repair programs public because they feel that doing so would weaken confidence in their product and increase their legal liability. The closest they come to an admission is sending a "goodwill policy," "product improvement program," or "special policy" technical service bulletin (TSB) to dealers or first owners of record. Consequently, the only motorists who find out about these policies are the original owners who haven't changed their addresses or leased their vehicles. The other motorists who get compensated for repairs are the ones who read *Lemon-Aid* each year, staple TSBs to their work orders, and yell the loudest.

Remember, vehicles on their second owners and repairs done by independent garages are included in these secret warranty programs. Large, costly repairs, such as blown engines, burned transmissions, and peeling paint, are often covered. Even mundane little repairs, which can still cost you a hundred bucks or more, are frequently included in these programs. If you have a TSB but you're still refused compensation, keep in mind that secret warranties are an admission of manufacturing negligence. Here are a few examples of secret warranties that may save you thousands of dollars. More extensive listings are found in Part Three's model ratings.

Acura

2001–03 3.2 CL; 1999–2003 TL; 2004–05 TSX

Problem: Breakage of the rear stabilizer bar link. **Warranty coverage:** Honda will replace both stabilizer bar links under a "goodwill" warranty extension that was confirmed in TSB #05-015, issued June 24, 2005.

Acura/Honda

1999–2003 Acura CL and TL; Honda Accord, Prelude, and Odyssey models

Problem: Defective automatic transmission and torque converter. **Warranty coverage:** This "goodwill" warranty extension was confirmed in the August 4, 2003, edition of *Automotive News*. Honda will fix or replace the transmission free of charge up to 7 years/160,000 km (100,000 mi.), whether owners bought their vehicle new or used. The company will also reimburse owners who already paid for the repair.

Audi

2002–06 S4 and A6 equipped with 2.7L turbocharged V6 engines

Problem: Defective auxiliary coolant pump leaks coolant from the pump body. When the pump fails, the coolant light will come on, warning that continued driving could cause serious engine damage. **Warranty coverage:** VW will install a Repair Kit free of charge up to 7 years/160,000 km. See TSB #05-05, published October 28, 2005.

Audi, Chrysler, Mercedes-Benz, Saab, Toyota, and VW

1997–2004 Audi A4; 1999–2002 Chrysler models equipped with a 2.7L V6; 1998–2002 Mercedes-Benz vehicles; 1998–2003 Saab 9-3 and 9-5 models; 1997–2002 Toyota and Lexus vehicles with 2.2L 4-cylinder or 3.0L V6 engines; and 1997–2004 VW Passat

Problem: Engine sludge. **Warranty coverage:** Varies; usually 7–10 years/160,000 km. Automakers can't automatically deny this free repair because you don't have proof of all of your oil changes, unless they can show that the sludge was caused by a missed oil change (which, according to independent mechanics, is impossible to do). Remember, the warranty has been extended to fix a factory-related problem that occurs despite regular oil changes. That's why it's the automaker's responsibility.

Service bulletins, press releases, and dealer memos are all admissions of responsibility. From there, the legal doctrine of "the balance of probabilities" applies. To wit, a defect *definitely* causes engine sludge, while a missed oil change *may* cause engine sludge. Therefore, it is more probable that the defect caused the sludge.

Once the sludge condition is diagnosed, the dealer and automobile manufacturer are jointly liable for all corrective repairs plus additional damages for your inconvenience, your loss of use or the cost of a loaner vehicle, and the cost to replace the oil. The automaker's owner notification letter may not have gone out to Canadian owners, since it is not required by any Canadian recall or by statute. If a letter goes out, it is usually sent only to first owners of record. And in the case of Chrysler's engine, no customer notification letters have been sent to anyone.

Some automakers say owners must use a special, more-expensive oil to prevent sludge. This after-sale stipulation is illegal and can also provide owners with a reason to ask for damages, or even a refund, since it wasn't disclosed at the time of sale. All of the letter restrictions and decisions made by the dealer and the manufacturer can easily be appealed to the small claims court, where the sludge letter is powerful proof of the automaker's negligence.

Chrysler, Ford, General Motors, and Asian Automakers

All years, all models

Problem: Faulty automatic transmissions that self-destruct, shift erratically, gear down to "limp mode," are slow to shift in or out of Reverse, or are noisy. **Warranty coverage:** If you have the assistance of your dealer's service manager, or some internal service bulletin that confirms the automatic transmission may be defective (such as the bulletin below), expect an offer of 50–75 percent (about $2,500) if you threaten to sue in small claims court. Acura, Honda, Hyundai, Lexus, and Toyota coverage varies between seven and eight years.

> I've just been told that I need my fourth transmission on my '96 Town & Country minivan with 132,000 miles [212,000 km] on it. I've driven many cars well past that mileage with only *one* transmission. The dealer asked Chrysler, who said they

---

CHRYSLER TRANSMISSION DELAYED ENGAGEMENT

BULLETIN NO.: 21-004-05   DATE: JANUARY 22, 2005

OVERVIEW: This bulletin involves replacing the front pump assembly in the transmission and checking the Transmission Control Module (TCM) for the latest software revision level.

2004 (CS) Pacifica

2002– 2004 (JR) Sebring Convertible/Sebring Sedan/Stratus Sedan

2003 (KJ) Liberty

2003 (KJ) Cherokee (International Markets)

2002 2004 (LH) 300M/Concorde/Intrepid

2002 2003 (PL) Neon

2002 2003 (PT) PT Cruiser

2002 2003 (RG) Chrysler Voyager (International Markets)

2002 2003 (RS) Town & Country/Caravan/Voyager

2003 (TJ) Wrangler

would not help me. My appeals to Chrysler's customer service department yielded me the same result.... Chrysler split some of the costs with me on the previous rebuilt replacements.

CBC TV's *Marketplace* "Underdogs" series has a segment on people who have successfully taken on Chrysler and other companies for customer service problems. Review the program at *www.cbc.ca/consumers/market/files/services/underdogs.*

All years, all models

Problem: Premature wearout of brake pads, calipers, and rotors. Produces excessive vibration, noise, and pulling to one side when braking. **Warranty coverage:** *Calipers and pads:* "Goodwill" settlements confirm that brake calipers and pads that fail to last 2 years/40,000 km will be replaced for 50 percent of the repair cost; components not lasting 1 year/20,000 km will be replaced for free. *Rotors:* If they last less than 3 years/60,000 km, they will be replaced at half price; replacement is free up to 2 years/40,000 km.

Chrysler, Ford, General Motors, and Honda

All years, all models

Problem: Faulty paint jobs that cause paint to turn white and peel off in horizontal panels. **Warranty coverage:** Automakers will offer a free paint job or

partial compensation for up to six years (no mileage limitation). Thereafter, most manufacturers will offer 50–75 percent refunds on the small claims courthouse's front steps.

In *Maureen Frank v. General Motors of Canada Limited,* the Saskatchewan small claims court judge ruled that paint finishes should last for 11 years, and three other Canadian small claims judgments have extended the benchmark to seven years, to second owners, and to pickups.

Although the automakers' attempts to blame paint delamination on the sun, acid rain, tree sap, bird droppings, and owners' lack of care appear comical at first, professional car washers are not laughing. The International Carwash Association advises its members to inform drivers that the paint defect is due to a poor factory paint job—not the soap or brushes used in car washes (see *www.carwash.com/article.asp?IndexID=6633551,* halfway down the page).

Chrysler

1998–2000 Caravan, Grand Caravan, Voyager, Grand Voyager, and Town & Country

Problem: Defective airbag clock springs cause multiple failures of the electrical system governing other components. **Warranty coverage:** Lifetime coverage up to 110,000 km (70,000 miles).

CHRYSLER RECALL—CLOCK SPRING REPLACEMENT/WARRANTY EXTENSION
DATE: OCTOBER 2004

DEALER SERVICE INSTRUCTIONS FOR SAFETY RECALL D17—CLOCKSPRING/ LIFETIME WARRANTY

1998–2000 Caravan, Grand Caravan, Voyager, Grand Voyager, and Town & Country

IMPORTANT: The clockspring on about 1,290,000 of the above vehicles may lose the electrical connection to the steering wheel mounted electrical components. This could cause the driver's airbag, horn, speed control and/or steering wheel mounted radio controls (if equipped) to be inoperative. An inoperative driver's airbag will not deploy, which can result in increased injury to the driver in a frontal crash.

REPAIR: Vehicles with a failed clockspring or vehicles with 70,000 miles [112,000 km] or LESS, must have the clockspring assembly replaced. Vehicles involved in this recall have a lifetime warranty on the clockspring assembly.

Ford

1992–2004 Aerostar, Focus, Sable, Taurus, and Windstar

Problem: Defective front coil springs may suddenly break, puncturing the front tire and leading to loss of steering control. **Warranty coverage:** Under a "Safety Improvement Campaign" negotiated with NHTSA, Ford will replace *broken* coil springs at no charge up to 10 years/unlimited mileage. The company initially said that it wouldn't replace the springs until they had broken—if you survived to submit a claim, that is—but it relented when threatened with a lawsuit. Since then, customer complaints have trailed off. 1997–98 models that are registered in rust-belt states or in Canada have been recalled for the installation of a protective shield (called a "spring catcher bracket" in the Canadian recall) to prevent a broken spring from shredding the front tire.

1996–2004 F-Series trucks, SUVs, and Windstar vans

Problem: Sudden steering loss due to the premature wear and separation of the steering tie-rod ends. **Warranty coverage:** Presently Ford is advising owners to have their vehicles inspected regularly. If pressed, the dealer will replace the component for free up to 5 years/100,000 km.

Ford/Lincoln

1996–2001 Crown Victoria, Mercury Grand Marquis, and Lincoln Town Car; 1997 Mercury Cougar, Ford Thunderbird, and Ford Mustang; 1998–2001 Mustang; and 2002 Ford Explorer

Problem: Intake manifolds may crack at the coolant crossover, resulting in V8 engine coolant leakage. **Warranty coverage:** For over a decade, *Lemon-Aid* has chided Ford for stonewalling engine intake manifold complaints and hiding the existence of a secret warranty slush fund. And then in late 2005, after some prodding by *Lemon-Aid*, Ford formally granted free engine intake manifold repairs and an extended warranty to Canadian owners. Ford agreed to reimburse money paid for the repair and also to provide a free seven-year retroactive warranty with unlimited mileage. Owners report getting their refund cheques directly from their dealers, a move that speeds up the refund program considerably.

> In mid-January 2006, Ford refunded me 100% ($1,400) for the intake manifold repair carried out on my 1997 Mercury Grand Marquis in October of 2002. The odometer reading at the time of the repair was 144,700 km. Current reading is around 202,500 km.
>
> GREG

General Motors

1995–2004 engine head gasket and intake manifold failures

Problem: The engine may overheat, lose power, burn extra fuel, or possibly self-destruct. Under the best of circumstances, the repair will take a day and cost about $800–$1,000. **Warranty coverage:** If you have the assistance of your dealer's service manager, expect a first offer of 50 percent up to 5 years/100,000 km (about $1,500, if other parts are damaged). GM Canada reached a settlement relating to 17 class actions commenced in Canada in 2006 where it will pay up to $800 for repairs caused by this defect. The lawsuits alleged that the nylon intake manifold gaskets installed in certain GM vehicles were defective. General Motors' lawyers insist that this settlement does not constitute any admission of liability or wrongdoing by GM—a position taken by many corporations that are up to their eyeballs in wrongdoing. (Go to *www.gmcanadiansettlement.ca* to see the terms of the settlement and which vehicles are involved.)

Numerous GM service bulletins obtained by *Lemon-Aid* and used in the previously mentioned class action settlement confirm a pattern of engine intake manifold gasket defects, which have been covered by a 7-year/100,000 km secret warranty since 1996. The most incriminating "smoking gun" GM internal service bulletins below, admit to poor-quality engine intake manifolds. Note that this defect has existed over 10 model years. Imagine how many owners have paid thousands of dollars to fix this problem, which GM admits here is clearly its own fault.

GM ENGINE OIL OR COOLANT LEAK

BULLETIN NO.: 03-06-01-010A   **DATE: APRIL 2003**

ENGINE OIL OR COOLANT LEAK (INSTALL NEW INTAKE MANIFOLD GASKET)

2000–03 Buick Century; 2002–03 Buick Rendezvous; 1996 Chevrolet Lumina APV; 1997–2003 Chevrolet Venture; 1999–2001 Chevrolet Lumina; 1999–2003 Chevrolet Malibu, Monte Carlo; 2000–03 Chevrolet Impala; 1996–2003 Oldsmobile Silhouette; 1999 Oldsmobile Cutlass; 1999–2003 Oldsmobile Alero; 1996–99 Pontiac Trans Sport; 1999–2003 Pontiac Grand Am; 2000–03 Pontiac Grand Prix, Montana 2001–03 Pontiac Aztek with 3.1L or 3.4L V6 engine (VINs J, E–RPOs LGB, LA1)

CONDITION: Some owners may comment on an apparent oil or coolant leak. Additionally, the comments may range from spots on the driveway to having to add fluids.

CAUSE: Intake manifold may be leaking allowing coolant, oil or both to leak from the engine.

CORRECTION: Install a new-design intake manifold gasket. The material used in the gasket has been changed in order to improve the sealing qualities of the gasket. When replacing the gasket, the intake manifold bolts must also be replaced and torqued to a revised specification. The new bolts will come with a pre-applied threadlocker on them.

GM NEW UPPER INTAKE MANIFOLD AND GASKET KITS

BULLETIN NO.: 04-06-01-017   **DATE: MAY 26, 2004**

1995–97 Riviera; 1995–2004 Park Avenue; 1996–2004 Regal; 1997–2004 LeSabre; 1998–99 Lumina; 1998–2004 Monte Carlo; 2000–04 Impala; 1995–96 Ninety-Eight; 1995–99 Eighty-Eight; 1998–99 Intrigue; 1995–2004 Bonneville; 1997–2003 Grand Prix with 3.8L V6 engine

New upper intake manifold and gasket kits have been released. These new kits will provide the dealer with the ability to get exactly what is necessary for a correct repair. In addition some of the gaskets have been updated to a more robust design.

2006–07 Cadillac DTS

Problem: Water leaks inside of the headlight assembly. **Warranty coverage:** GM will modify the headlight assembly free of charge until October 31, 2009.

2003–05 Corvette; 2004–05 Cadillac XLR

Problem: Faulty fuel gauge reads empty when there actually is fuel in the tank. **Warranty coverage:** GM will replace the left fuel-tank level sensor for free up to 5 years/100,000 km.

2005–06 Corvette

Problem: Roof delaminates and separates from the frame. **Warranty coverage:** GM will repair or replace for free the affected roofs.

CUSTOMER SATISFACTION PROGRAM 05112D

Customer Satisfaction Program 05112D addresses all 2005 Corvettes and 2006 through VIN 31106. If a customer has a concern and the VIN is within these break points the bulletin can be used to correct the condition even though the VIN is not listed in VIS. If the VIN is not listed in VIS dealers should use labor operation B2308 and use the time that is supplied in bulletin 05112D.

Roofs that are partially delaminated or debonded can be repaired using the procedure outlined in Bulletin 05112D. When the roof remains attached on one of the four sides it can be repaired and the vehicle placed back into service. Bulletin 05112D outlines this is as a temporary repair until a replacement roof can be obtained. Once a roof is properly repaired with the foam process, tests indicate the roof will not separate from the frame.

2000–03 Buick LeSabre; 2002–06 Buick Rendezvous; 2000–05 Cadillac DeVille; 2003–06 Cadillac CTS; 2004–06 Cadillac SRX; 2005–06 Cadillac STS; 2006 Cadillac DTS; 1997–2002 Venture, Trans Sport/Montana, and Silhouette; 2001–03 Oldsmobile Aurora; 2000–03 Pontiac Bonneville

Problem: Roof rust perforation. **Warranty coverage:** GM will replace, repair, or repaint the roof for free up to 6 years/100,000 km.

GM FRONT/REAR ROOF RUST PERFORATION

BULLETIN NO.: 02-08-67-006B   DATE: MARCH 2003

ROOF PERFORATION (REPLACE ROOF)

1997–2003 Chevrolet Venture; 1997–2003 Oldsmobile Silhouette; 1997–2003 Pontiac TranSport/Montana

IMPORTANT: Implementation of this service bulletin by "GM of Canada" dealers requires prior District Service Manager approval.

CONDITION: Some customers may comment that there is rust forming around the front or rear portion of the roof.

CAUSE: During production, the E-coating (ELPO primer) may have been missed in concealed areas of the front or rear portions of the outer roof panel.

2002–03 Alero, Cavalier, Grand Am, Malibu, and Sunfire

Problem: Transmission shifts erratically, slips, or won't shift due to defective driven sprocket support assembly. **Warranty coverage:** GM will replace the component free of charge up to seven years (TSB #03-07-30-012B; Date: August 22, 2005).

2005 Cobalt and Pursuit

Problem: Inaccurate fuel gauge. **Warranty coverage:** GM will recalibrate the electronic control module (ECM) free of charge (TSB #05-08-49-002A; Date: January 28, 2005).

2005 Malibu, Malibu Maxx, and G6

Problem: Loss of power-steering assist. **Warranty coverage:** Under Special Coverage Adjustment #07126, dated December 3, 2007, GM will replace the failed components free of charge up to 7 years/110,000 km.

2003–06 Saturn Ion

Problem: No-cranks; no-starts. **Warranty coverage:** Owners will be offered free replacement of the body control module, and ignition if necessary (TSB #04-08-45-005C5; Date: December 14, 2005).

2004–05 Saturn Ion Red Line

Problem: Engine camshaft-position-sensor housing-seal failure may cause an oil leak and engine damage. **Warranty coverage:** This Customer Satisfaction Campaign allows for the free replacement of the component without any mileage or prior ownership limitations (TSB #05522; Date: May 6, 2005).

2002–05 Saturn Vue and 2003–04 Ion Quad Coupe

Problem: Faulty CVT automatic transmission. **Warranty coverage:** Special Policy #04020 allows for the free replacement of the VTi automatic transmission, without prior ownership limitations, up to 5 years/125,000 km.

2001–02 Grand Prix, Impala, Monte Carlo, and Regal

Problem: Defective catalytic converters may cause vehicle to lose power or the dash warning light to come on. **Warranty coverage:** The converter warranty is extended to 10 years. Owners will also be reimbursed for previous converter/OBD system repairs or replacements.

2003–06 Vibe

Problem: Rear hatch rust. **Warranty coverage:** GM will refinish, at no charge, the affected hatch area (TSB #05-08-51-002A; Date: December 2, 2005).

Honda

2003–04 Civic

Problem: Inaccurate fuel-gauge reading. **Warranty coverage:** Honda believes the problem occurs due to incorrect software and will replace the gauge assembly free of charge under a "goodwill" program, whether owners bought their vehicles new or used (TSB #05-002; Date: March 4, 2005).

1998–2003 Honda Accord, Odyssey, and Pilot models equipped with 6-cylinder engines

Problem: Defective aluminum engine block. **Warranty coverage:** Repair or replace engine under a "goodwill" program.

2003–04 Honda Accords equipped with 6-cylinder engines

Problem: When turning, either a clunking is heard from the steering or looseness is felt in the steering wheel. **Warranty coverage:** Under a "goodwill" program, Honda will replace the tie-rod ball joints and perform an alignment, free of charge (TSB #05-013; Date: March 25, 2005).

1999–2003 Odyssey and Pilot

Problem: EGR valve contamination or EGR port clogging may cause engine surging or stalling. **Warranty coverage:** Honda will install a new EGR valve and a valve kit under a "goodwill" program applicable up to 8 years/160,000 km (TSB #05-026; Date: July 20, 2005).

Hyundai

1999–2002 Elantra; 1999–2003 Tiburon

Problem: The exhaust manifold may crack, causing the engine to overheat. **Warranty coverage:** Hyundai will inspect and replace any defective exhaust manifold free of charge up to 7 years/160,000 km under Campaign V04, initiated in March 2005.

Toyota

1995–2000 Tacoma and Tundra

Problem: Rust-damaged structural frames. The excessive rusting is caused by inadequate anti-corrosion undercoating applied at the factory. **Warranty coverage:** According to the April 14, 2008, edition of *Automotive News*, Toyota will repair or buy back the affected pickups. Dealers will inspect all affected Tacomas and Tundras, free of charge, and apply an extended 15-year frame-rust warranty. Trucks with minor frame pitting will be repaired for free; trucks with more-serious damage will be bought back at 150 percent of the "excellent" value listed in the U.S.-published *Kelley Blue Book* guide, regardless of the truck's condition.

Free Recall Repairs

Vehicles are recalled for one of two reasons: Either they are potentially unsafe or they don't conform to federal pollution control regulations. Whatever the reason, recalls are a great way to get free repairs—if you know which ones apply to you and you have the patience of Job.

In North America, over half a billion unsafe vehicles have been recalled by automakers for the free correction of safety-related defects since American recall legislation was passed in 1966 (a weaker Canadian law was enacted in 1971). During that time, about one-third of the recalled vehicles never made it back to the dealership for repairs, because owners were never informed, didn't consider the defect to be that hazardous, or gave up waiting for corrective parts.

Subsequent American legislation targets automakers that drag their feet in making recall repairs. Owners on both sides of the border may wish to cite the NHTSA guidelines below for support.

If you've moved or bought a used vehicle, it's smart to pay a visit to your local dealership, give them your address, and get a report card on which recalls, warranties, and free service campaigns apply to your vehicle. Simply give the service advisor the vehicle identification number (VIN)—found on your insurance card, or on your dash just below the windshield on the driver's side—and have the number run through the automaker's computer system. Ask for a computer printout of the vehicle's history (have it faxed to you, if you're so equipped) and make sure you're listed in the automaker's computer as the new owner. This ensures that you'll receive notices of warranty extensions and emissions and safety recalls.

> ### DEALER RECALL RESPONSIBILITY—FOR U.S. AND IPC (U.S. STATES, TERRITORIES, AND POSSESSIONS)
>
> The U.S. *National Traffic and Motor Vehicle Safety Act* provides that each vehicle that is subject to a recall must be adequately repaired within a reasonable time after the customer has tendered it for repair. A failure to repair within 60 days after tender of a vehicle is *prima facie* evidence of failure to repair within a reasonable time. If the condition is not adequately repaired within a reasonable time, the customer may be entitled to an identical or reasonably equivalent vehicle at no charge or to a refund of the purchase price less a reasonable allowance for depreciation. To avoid having to provide these burdensome remedies, every effort must be made to promptly schedule an appointment with each customer and to repair their vehicle as soon as possible.
>
> GM Bulletin No. 00064C, issued September 2002

Regional Recalls

Don't let any dealer refuse you recall repairs because of where you live.

In order to cut recall costs, many automakers try to limit a recall to vehicles in a certain designated region. This practice doesn't make sense, since cars are mobile and an unsafe, rust-cankered steering unit can be found anywhere—not just in certain rust-belt provinces or American states.

For instance, in 2001, Ford attempted to limit to five American states its recall of faulty Firestone tires. Public ridicule of the company's proposal led to an extension of the recall throughout North America.

Common safety defects

Wherever you live or drive, don't expect to be welcomed with open arms when your vehicle develops a safety- or emissions-related problem that's not yet part of a recall campaign. Automakers and dealers generally take a restrictive view of what constitutes a safety or emissions defect and frequently charge for repairs that should be free under federal safety or emissions legislation. To counter this tendency, look at the following list of typical defects that are clearly safety-related. If you experience similar problems, insist that the automaker fix the problem at no expense to yourself, including a car rental.

- Airbag malfunctions
- Corrosion affecting safe operation
- Disconnected or stuck accelerators
- Electrical shorts
- Faulty windshield wipers
- Fuel leaks
- Problems with original axles, driveshafts, seats, seat recliners, or defrosters
- Seat belt problems
- Stalling or sudden acceleration
- Sudden steering or brake loss
- Suspension failures
- Trailer coupling failures

In the U.S., recall campaigns force automakers to pay the entire cost of fixing a vehicle's safety-related defect for any vehicle purchased up to eight years before the recall's announcement. A reasonable period beyond that time is usually a slam dunk in small claims court.

Voluntary recall campaigns, frequently called "Special Service" or "Safety Improvement Campaigns," are a real problem, though. The government doesn't monitor the notification of owners; dealers and automakers routinely deny there's a recall, thereby dissuading most claimants; and the company's so-called fix, not authorized by any governing body, may not correct the hazard at all. Also, the voluntary recall may leave out many of the affected models, or unreasonably exclude certain owners.

Safety Defect Information

If you wish to report a safety defect or want recall info, you may access Transport Canada's website at *www.tc.gc.ca/roadsafety/recalls/search_e.asp*. You can get recall information in French or English, as well as general information relating to road safety and importing a vehicle into Canada. Web surfers can now access the recall database for 1970–2008 model year vehicles, but, unlike NHTSA's website, owner complaints aren't listed, defect investigations aren't disclosed, voluntary warranty extensions (secret warranties) aren't shown, and service bulletin summaries aren't provided. You can also call Transport Canada at 1-800-333-0510 (toll-free within Canada) or 613-993-9851 (within the Ottawa region or outside Canada) to get additional information.

If you aren't happy with Ottawa's treatment of your recall inquiry, try NHTSA's website. It's more complete than Transport Canada's (NHTSA's database is updated daily and covers vehicles built since 1952). You can search the database for your vehicle or tires at *www.nhtsa.dot.gov/cars/problems.* You'll get immediate access to four essential database categories applicable to your vehicle and model year: the latest recalls, current and closed safety investigations, defects reported by other owners, and a brief summary of TSBs.

"Black Box" Data Recorders

If your car has an airbag, it's probably spying on you. And if you get into an accident caused by a mechanical malfunction, you will be glad that it does.

Event data recorders (EDRs) the size of a VCR tape have been hidden near the engine, under the seat, or in the centre consoles of about 30 million airbag-equipped Ford and GM vehicles since the early '90s. Almost all domestic and imported cars now carry them. To find out if your car or truck carries an EDR, read your owner's manual, contact the regional office of your car's manufacturer, or go to *www.harristechnical.com/downloads/cdrlist.pdf.*

The data recorders operate in a similar fashion to flight data recorders used in airplanes: They record data during the last five seconds before impact, including the force of the collision, the airbag's performance, when the brakes were applied, engine and vehicle speed, gas pedal position, and whether the driver was wearing a seat belt.

Getting EDR Data

In the past, automakers have systematically hidden their collected data from government and insurance researchers, citing concerns for drivers' privacy. This argument, however, has been roundly rejected by law enforcement agencies, the courts, and car owners who need the independent information to prove negligence or simply to keep track of how and where their vehicles are driven. Car owners, rental agencies, and fleet administrators are also using EDR data to pin legal liability on automakers for accidents caused by the failure of safety components, such as airbags that don't deploy when they should (or do deploy when they shouldn't) and anti-lock brakes that don't brake.

One handy portable tool for downloading EDR data to any PC is made by the Vetronix Corporation and sells for $2,500 (U.S.). It's presently marketed to accident reconstructionists, safety researchers, law enforcement agencies, and insurance companies as a tool to assess culpability in criminal and civil trials. Car owners who wish to dispute criminal charges, oppose their insurer's decision as to fault, or hold an automaker responsible for a safety device's failure (airbags, seat belts, or brakes) will find this data invaluable—if the data hasn't been wiped clean by the dealer!

A Tool for Parents

One of the scariest days for parents is when their teenager passes the driver's exam. Today there are cell phones, flip-down DVD players, satellites, radios, and other entertainment options to distract even the most seasoned drivers. Teenagers just learning the rules of the road are especially susceptible to these distractions, and even more so when other teens are in the car.

It's now possible to electronically monitor your teenage driver's driving habits and the places he or she visits with a device called the Road Safety RS-1000 On-Board Computer (see *www.techedu.com/RoadSafety_RS-1000.asp*). It is a relatively inexpensive device that plugs into the data recorder and sets off an audible alarm

Electronic monitors are a constant reminder to teens that driving is a privilege that can be taken away if they don't drive safely. No more "he said, she said"!

when the driver exceeds a preset speed limit. The device also uses an accelerometer, similar to those used in automotive testing, to measure vehicle G-forces that are created by aggressive driving. As G-forces become excessive, an audible warning immediately tells the driver to back off. The only way to prevent hearing the audible warning (and feeling the embarrassment when friends are in the vehicle) is to drive safely.

The RS-1000 black box tells you how and when your teen was driving on a second-by-second basis. If you say, "I don't want you speeding on the freeway," and your teen does it anyway, you will know it. If curfew is at midnight and your darling gets home at 1:00 a.m., you will know it. The data is always accessible: Just pop the memory card out of the RS-1000 black box and plug it into your family's computer to display the reports and graphs.

The RS-1000 can be bought through Road Safety International's website. Devices cost $295 (U.S.). For 1996 and newer vehicles, anyone can install the system by simply plugging the on-board computer into the vehicle's OBD-II connector. The device will also work in 1995 and older vehicles, but it will require hard-wire installation by a qualified automotive technician. For more information, contact the company at *rsi@roadsafety.com* or 805-498-9444.

Another useful monitoring gadget is the CarChip Pro (see *www.davisnet.com/drive/products/drive_product.asp?pnum=08226*). It costs $119 (U.S.) and can be used with any PC using Windows 98SE and above.

Free Recorders

You can get a free data recorder as well as up to 25 percent off your car insurance by subscribing to Aviva Canada's Autograph program (*www.avivacanada.com/autograph*). Aviva, an automobile insurance underwriter operating primarily in Ontario, says its Autograph program will reduce drivers' premiums if the monitoring device they attach to their EDR system proves they are safe drivers. And Aviva will throw in the Autograph recording device for free.

Once connected, the Autograph records specific information about a vehicle's use, including speed, distance driven, and time of the day. This information remains in the unit until you choose to download it to your computer. The company then reviews the data and adjusts your premium accordingly. Drivers are given a standard 5 percent discount for agreeing to be part of the program.

Safety Benefits

EDRs are not simply good tools for collecting safety data; they have also had a positive effect on accident prevention. A 1992 study by the European Union, cited by the Canada Safety Council, found that EDRs reduced the collision rate by 28 percent and costs by 40 percent in police fleets where drivers knew that they were being monitored.

The recorders are particularly helpful in getting compensation for accident victims, prompting automaker recalls, and punishing dangerous drivers—even those who happen to be U.S. Congressmen. In January 2004, South Dakota Congressman Bill Janklow was convicted of manslaughter for speeding through a stop sign—his EDR readout proved he was driving faster than the speed limit, although slower than police had estimated.

In October 2003, Montreal police won their first dangerous driving conviction using EDR data (*R. v. Gauthier*; 2003/05/27 QC C.Q. Dossier: 500-01-013375-016; *www.canlii.org/qc/jug/qccq/2003/2003qccq17860.html*). In June 2003, Edwin Matos of Pembroke Pines, Florida, was sentenced to 30 years in prison for killing two teenage girls after crashing into their car at more than 160 km/h (100 mph). The recorder's speed data convicted him. A chronological list of dozens of Canadian and American court cases related to automotive EDRs has been prepared by Harris Technical Services (traffic accident reconstructionists) and is available at *www.harristechnical.com*.

The Art of Complaining

Step 1: Can We Talk?

Not likely. You can try phoning the seller or automaker, but don't expect to get much out of the call. Private sellers won't want to talk with you, and dealer customer service agents will tell you the vehicle was sold "as is." They simply apply the dealership's policy, knowing that 90 percent of complainers will drop their claims after venting their anger.

Still, try to work things out by contacting someone higher up who can change the policy to satisfy your request. In your attempt to reach a settlement, ask only for what is fair and don't try to make anyone look bad.

Speak in a calm, polite manner, and try to avoid polarizing the issue. Talk about cooperating to solve the problem. Let a compromise emerge—don't come in with a rigid set of demands. Don't insist on getting the settlement offer in writing, but make sure that you're accompanied by a friend or relative who can confirm the offer in court if it isn't honoured. Be prepared to act upon the offer without delay so that your hesitancy won't be blamed if the seller or automaker withdraws it.

Service manager help

Service managers have more power than you may realize. They make the first determination of what work is covered under warranty or through post-warranty "goodwill" programs, and they are directly responsible to the dealer and manufacturer for that decision (dealers hate manufacturer audits that force them to pay back questionable warranty decisions). Service managers are paid both to save the dealer and automaker money and to mollify irate clients—almost an impossible balancing act. Nevertheless, when a service manager agrees to extend warranty coverage, it's because you've raised solid issues that neither the dealer nor the automaker can ignore. All the more reason to present your argument in a confident, forthright manner with your vehicle's service history and *Lemon-Aid*'s "Reasonable Part Durability" table on hand (see page 48). Also, bring as many technical service bulletins and owner complaint printouts as you can find from NHTSA's website and similar sources. It's not important that they apply directly to your problem; they establish parameters for giving out after-warranty assistance, or "goodwill."

Don't use your salesperson as a runner, since the sales staff are generally quite distant from the service staff and usually have less pull than you do. If the service manager can't or won't set things right, your next step is to convene a mini-summit with the service manager, the dealership principal, and the automaker's service rep, if he or she represents that make. Regional service representatives are technicians who are regularly sent out by the manufacturer to help dealers with technical problems. By getting the automaker involved, you can often get an agreement where the seller and the automaker pay two-thirds of the repair cost, even though the vehicle was bought used.

Dealers who sell a brand of vehicle used that they don't sell new will give you less latitude. You have to make the case that the vehicle's defects were present at the time of purchase or should have been apparent to the seller, or that the vehicle doesn't conform to the representations made when it was purchased. Emphasize that you intend to use the courts if necessary to obtain a refund—most sellers would rather settle than risk a lawsuit with all the attendant publicity. An independent estimate of the vehicle's defects and repair costs is essential if you want to convince the seller that you're serious in your claim and that you stand a good chance of winning your case in court. Come prepared with an estimated cost of repairs to challenge the dealer who agrees to pay half the repair costs and then jacks up the price 100 percent so that you wind up paying the whole shot.

Step 2: Create a Paper Trail

If you haven't sent a written claim letter, fax, or email, you really haven't complained—or at least, that's the auto industry's mindset. If your vehicle was misrepresented, has major defects, or wasn't properly repaired under warranty, the first thing you should do is give the seller a written summary of the outstanding problems and stipulate a time period within which the seller can fix the vehicle or refund your money. Follow the format of the sample complaint letters on pages 51–52.

Remember, you can ask for compensation for repairs that have been done or need to be done, insurance costs while the vehicle is being repaired, towing charges, supplementary transportation costs such as taxis and rented cars, and damages for inconvenience. If no satisfactory offer is made, ask for mediation, arbitration, or a formal hearing in your provincial small claims court. Make the manufacturer a party to the lawsuit, especially if the emissions warranty, a secret warranty extension, a safety recall campaign, or extensive chassis rusting is involved.

Step 3: Mediation and Arbitration

If the formality of a courtroom puts you off, or you're not sure that your claim is all that solid and don't want to pay legal costs to find out, consider using mediation or arbitration. These services are sponsored by the Better Business Bureau (BBB), the Automobile Protection Association (APA), the Canadian Automobile Association (CAA), and by many small claims courts where compulsory mediation is a prerequisite to going to trial.

Getting Outside Help

Don't lose your case because of poor preparation. Ask government or independent consumer protection agencies to evaluate how well you've prepared before going to your first hearing. Also, use the Internet to ferret out additional facts and gather support (*www.lemonaidcars.com* and its links are good places to start).

Pressure Tactics

You can put additional pressure on a seller or garage, and have fun at the same time, by putting a lemon sign on your car and parking it in front of the dealer or garage, by creating a "lemon" website, or by forming a self-help group. Angry Chrysler and Ford owners, for example, have received sizeable settlements in Canada by forming their own Chrysler Lemon Owners Group (CLOG) and Ford Lemon Owners Group (FLOG).

Use your website, or place a newspaper ad, to gather data from others who may have experienced a problem similar to your own; this can help you set the foundation for a meeting with the automaker, or even for a class action, and it pressures the dealer or manufacturer to settle. Websites are often the subject of news stories, so the media may pick up on yours.

Here's some more advice from this consumer advocate with hundreds of pickets and mass demonstrations under his belt from the past 40 years: Keep a sense of humour, and never break off the negotiations.

Finally, don't be scared off by threats that it's illegal to criticize a product or company. Unions, environmentalists, and consumer groups do it regularly (it's called informational picketing), and the Supreme Court of Canada in *R. v. Guinard* reaffirmed this right in February 2002. In that judgment, an insured posted a sign on his barn claiming the Commerce Insurance Company was unfairly refusing his claim. The municipality of Saint-Hyacinthe, Quebec, told him to take the sign down. He refused, maintaining that he had the right to state his opinion. The Supreme Court agreed.

This judgment means that consumer protests, signs, and websites that criticize the actions of corporations or government cannot be shut up or taken down simply because they say unpleasant things. However, what you say must be true, and your intent must be to inform, without malice.

Safety Failures

Incidents of sudden acceleration and chronic stalling are quite common. However, they are very difficult to diagnose, and individual cases can be treated very differently by federal safety agencies. Sudden acceleration is considered to be a safety-related problem—stalling isn't. Never mind that a vehicle's sudden loss of power on a busy highway puts everyone's lives at risk (as is the case with 2001–05 Toyota and Lexus models). The same problem exists with engine and transmission powertrain failures, which are only occasionally considered to be safety-related. ABS and airbag failures are universally considered to be life-threatening defects. If your vehicle manifests any of these conditions, here's what you need to do:

1. Get independent witnesses to confirm that the problem exists. This includes verification by an independent mechanic, passenger testimony, downloaded data from your vehicle's data recorder, and lots of Internet browsing using *www.lemonaidcars.com* and a search engine like Google as your primary tools. Notify the dealer or manufacturer by fax, email, or registered letter that you consider the problem to be a factory-induced, safety-related defect. Make sure you address your correspondence to the manufacturer's product liability or legal affairs department. At the dealership's service bay, make sure that every work order clearly states the problem as well as the number of previous attempts to fix it. (You should end up with a few complaint letters and a handful of work orders confirming that this is an ongoing deficiency.) If the

dealer won't give you a copy of the work order because the work is a warranty claim, ask for a copy of the order number "in case your estate wishes to file a claim, pursuant to an accident." (This will get the service manager's attention.) Leaving a paper trail is crucial for any claim you may have later on, because it shows your concern and persistence and clearly indicates that the dealer and manufacturer had ample time to correct the defect.

2. Note on the work order that you expect the problem to be diagnosed and corrected under the emissions warranty or a "goodwill" program. It also wouldn't hurt to add the phrase on the work order or in your claim letters that "any deaths, injuries, or damage caused by the defect will be the dealer's and manufacturer's responsibility" since this work order (or letter, fax, or email) constitutes you putting them on formal notice.

3. If the dealer does the necessary repairs at little or no cost to you, send a follow-up confirmation saying that you appreciate the assistance. Also, emphasize that you'll be back if the problem reappears, even if the warranty has expired, because the repair renews your warranty rights applicable to that defect. In other words, the warranty clock is set back to its original position. You won't likely get a copy of the repair bill, because dealers don't like to admit that there was a serious defect present. Keep in mind, however, that you can get your complete vehicle file from the dealer and manufacturer by issuing a subpoena, which costs about $75 (refundable), if the case goes to small claims or a higher court. This request has produced many out-of-court settlements when the internal documents show extensive work was carried out to correct the problem.

4. If the problem persists, send a letter, fax, or email to the dealer and manufacturer saying so, look for ALLDATA service bulletins to confirm that your vehicle's defects are factory-related, and call Transport Canada or NHTSA, or log onto NHTSA's website, to report the failure. Also, contact the Center for Auto Safety in Washington, D.C., at 202-328-7700 or *www.autosafety.org* for a lawyer referral and an information sheet covering the problem.

5. Now come two crucial questions: Should you repair the defect now or later, and should you use the dealer or an independent? Generally, it's smart to use an independent garage if you know the dealer isn't pushing for free corrective repairs from the manufacturer, if weeks or months have passed without any resolution of your claim, if the dealer keeps claiming that it's a maintenance item, or if you know an independent mechanic who will give you a detailed work order showing the defect is factory-related and not a result of poor maintenance. Don't mention that a court case may ensue, since this will scare the dickens out of your only independent witness. A bonus of using an independent garage is that the repair charges will be about half of what a dealer would demand. Incidentally, if the automaker later denies warranty "goodwill" because you used an independent repairer, use the argument that the defect's safety implications required emergency repairs to be carried out by whoever could see you first.

6. Dashboard-mounted warning lights usually come on prior to airbags suddenly deploying, ABS brakes failing, or engine glitches causing the vehicle to stall out. (Sudden acceleration, however, usually occurs without warning.)

Automakers consider these lights to be critical safety warnings and generally advise drivers to immediately have the vehicle serviced to correct the problem (advice that can be found in the owner's manual) when any of the above lights come on. This bolsters the argument that your life was threatened, emergency repairs were required, and your request for another vehicle or a complete refund isn't out of line.

7. Sudden acceleration can have multiple causes, isn't easy to duplicate, and is often blamed on the driver mistaking the accelerator for the brakes or failing to perform proper maintenance. Yet NHTSA data shows that factory-related defects are often the culprit. For example, 1997–2004 Lexus ES 300/330s and Toyota Camrys may have a faulty transmission that may cause engine surging. So how do you satisfy the burden of proof showing that the problem exists and is the automaker's responsibility? Use the legal doctrine called "the balance of probabilities" by eliminating all of the possible dodges the dealer or manufacturer may employ. Show that proper maintenance has been carried out, that you're a safe driver, and that the incident occurs frequently and without warning.

8. If any of the above defects causes an accident, the airbag fails to deploy, or you're injured by its deployment, ask your insurance company to have the vehicle towed to a neutral location and clearly state that neither the dealer nor the automaker should touch the vehicle until your insurance company and Transport Canada have completed their investigation. Also, get as many witnesses as possible and immediately go to the hospital for a check-up, even if you're feeling okay. You may be injured and not know it because the adrenalin coursing through your veins is masking your injuries. A hospital exam will easily confirm that your injuries are related to the accident, which is essential in court or for future settlement negotiations.

9. Peruse NHTSA's online accident database to find reports of other accidents caused by the same failure.

10. Don't let your insurance company settle the case if you're sure the accident was caused by a mechanical failure. Even if an engineering analysis fails to directly implicate the manufacturer or dealer, you can always plead the aforementioned balance of probabilities. If the insurance company settles, your insurance premiums will probably be increased.

Paint and Body Defects

The following tips on making a successful claim apply mainly to paint defects, water and air leaks, and subpar fit and finish, but you can use the same strategy for any other vehicle defect that you believe is the automaker's or dealer's responsibility. If you're not sure whether the problem is a factory-related deficiency or a maintenance item, have it checked out by an independent garage or get a technical service bulletin summary for your vehicle. The summary may include specific bulletins relating to the diagnosis, correction, and ordering of upgraded parts needed to fix your problem.

1. If you know that your vehicle's paint problem is factory-related, take your

vehicle to the dealer and ask for a written, signed estimate. When you're handed the estimate, ask if the paint job can be covered by some "goodwill" assistance. (Ford's euphemism for this secret warranty is "Owner Notification Program" or "Owner Dialogue Program," GM's term is "Special Policy," and Chrysler simply calls it an "Owner Satisfaction Notice." Don't use the term "secret warranty" yet; you'll just make everyone angry and evasive.)

2. Your request will probably be met with a refusal, an offer to repaint the vehicle for half the cost, or (if you're lucky) an agreement to repaint the vehicle free of charge. If you accept the half-cost offer, make sure that it's based on the original estimate you have in hand, since some dealers jack up their estimates so that your 50 percent is really 100 percent of the true cost.

3. If the dealer or automaker has already refused your claim and the repair hasn't been done yet, get an additional estimate from an independent garage that shows the problem is factory-related.

4. If the repair has yet to be done, mail or fax a registered claim to the automaker (and send a copy to the dealer), claiming the average of both estimates. If the repair has been done at your expense, mail or fax a registered claim with a copy of your bill.

5. If you don't receive a satisfactory response within a week, deposit a copy of the estimate or paid bill and claim letter/fax before the small claims court and await a trial date. This means that the automaker/dealer will have to appear, no lawyer is required, and costs should be minimal (under $100). Usually, an informal pretrial mediation hearing with the two parties and a court clerk will be scheduled within a few months, followed by a trial a few weeks later (the time varies among different regions). Most cases are settled at the mediation stage. You can help your case by collecting photographs, maintenance work orders, previous work orders dealing with your problem, and technical service bulletins, and by speaking to an independent expert (the garage or body shop that did the estimate or repair is best, but you can also use a local teacher who teaches automotive repair). Remember, service bulletins can be helpful, but they aren't critical to a successful claim.

Other situations

- If the vehicle has just been repainted or repaired but the dealer says that "goodwill" coverage was denied by the automaker, pay for the repair with a certified cheque and write "under protest" on the cheque. Remember, though, if the dealer does the repair, you won't have an independent expert who can affirm that the problem was factory-related or that it was a result of premature wearout. Plus, the dealer can say that you or the environment caused the paint problem. In these cases, technical service bulletins can make or break your case.

- If the dealer or automaker offers a partial repair or refund, take it. Then sue for the rest. Remember, if a partial repair has been done under warranty, it counts as an admission of responsibility, no matter what "goodwill" euphemism is used. Also, the repaired component or body panel should be just as durable as if it were new. Hence the clock starts ticking from the time of the repair until you reach the original warranty parameter—again, no matter what the dealer's repair warranty limit says.

Very seldom do automakers contest these paint claims before small claims court, instead opting to settle once the court claim is bounced from their customer relations people to their legal affairs department. At that time, you'll probably be offered an out-of-court settlement for 50–75 percent of your claim.

Stand fast, and make reference to the service bulletins you intend to subpoena in order to publicly contest in court the unfair nature of this "secret warranty" program (automakers' lawyers cringe at the idea of trying to explain why consumers aren't made aware of these bulletins)—100 percent restitution will probably follow.

Four favourable paint judgments

Dunlop v. Ford of Canada (No. 58475/04; Ontario Superior Court of Justice, Richmond Hill Small Claims Court; January 5, 2005; Deputy Judge M.J. Winer). The owner of a 1996 Lincoln Town car purchased used in 1999 for $27,000 was awarded $4,091.64. Judge Winer cited the *Shields* decision (following) and gave these reasons for finding Ford of Canada liable:

> Evidence was given by the Plaintiff's witness, Terry Bonar, an experienced paint auto technician. He gave evidence that the [paint] delamination may be both a manufacturing defect and can be caused or speeded up by atmospheric conditions. He also says that [the paint on] a car like this should last ten to 15 years, [or even for] the life of the vehicle....

> It is my view that the presence of ultraviolet light is an environmental condition to which the vehicle is subject. If it cannot withstand this environmental condition, it is defective in my view.

Shields v. General Motors of Canada (No. 1398/96; Ontario Court, General Division; Oshawa Small Claims Court; July 24, 1997; Deputy Judge Robert Zochodne). The owner of a 1991 Pontiac Grand Prix purchased the vehicle used with over 100,000 km on its odometer. Beginning in 1995, the paint began to bubble and flake and eventually peeled off. Deputy Judge Robert Zochodne awarded the plaintiff $1,205.72 and struck down every one of GM's environmental/acid rain/UV rays arguments. Here are the other important aspects of this 12-page judgment that GM did not appeal:

1. The judge admitted many of the technical service bulletins referred to in *Lemon-Aid* as proof of GM's negligence.
2. Although the vehicle already had 156,000 km on it when the case went to court, GM still offered to pay for 50 percent of the paint repairs if the plaintiff dropped his suit.

3. The judge ruled that the failure to protect the paint from the damaging effects of UV rays is akin to engineering a car that won't start in cold weather. In essence, vehicles must be built to withstand the rigours of the environment.
4. Here's an interesting twist: The original warranty covered defects that were present at the time it was in effect. The judge, taking statements found in the GM technical service bulletins, ruled that the UV problem was factory-related, existed during the warranty period, and represented a latent defect that appeared once the warranty expired.
5. The subsequent purchaser was not prevented from making the warranty claim, even though the warranty had long since expired from a time and mileage standpoint and he was the second owner.

Bentley v. Dave Wheaton Pontiac Buick GMC Ltd. and General Motors of Canada (Victoria Registry No. 24779; British Columbia Small Claims Court; December 1, 1998; Judge Higinbotham). This small claims judgment builds on the Ontario *Shields v. General Motors of Canada* decision and cites other jurisprudence as to how long paint should last on a car. If you're wondering why Ford and Chrysler haven't been hit by similar judgments, remember that they usually settle out of court.

Maureen Frank v. General Motors of Canada Limited (No. SC#12 (2001); Saskatchewan Provincial Court; October 17, 2001; Provincial Court Judge H.G. Dirauf). I discuss this case on page 62.

Other paint and rust cases

Whittaker v. Ford Motor Company (1979) (24 O.R. (2d), 344). A new Ford developed serious corrosion problems in spite of having been rustproofed by the dealer. The court ruled that the dealer, not Ford, was liable for the damage for having sold the rustproofing product at the time of purchase. This is an important judgment to use when a rustproofer or paint protector goes out of business or refuses to pay a claim, since the decision holds the dealer jointly responsible.

Martin v. Honda Canada Inc. (March 17, 1986; Ontario Small Claims Court, Scarborough; Judge Sigurdson). The original owner of a 1981 Honda Civic sought compensation for the premature "bubbling, pitting, [and] cracking of the paint and rusting of the Civic after five years of ownership." Judge Sigurdson agreed with the owner and ordered Honda to pay $1,163.95.

Thauberger v. Simon Fraser Sales and Mazda Motors (3 B.C.L.R., 193). This Mazda owner sued for damages caused by the premature rusting of his 1977 Mazda GLC. The court awarded him $1,000. Thauberger had previously sued General Motors for a prematurely rusted Blazer truck and was also awarded $1,000 in the same court. Both judges ruled that the defects could not be excluded from the auto-maker's expressed warranty or from the implied warranty granted by British Columbia's *Sale of Goods Act*.

See also:

- *Danson v. Chateau Ford (1976) C.P.* (Quebec Small Claims Court; No. 32-00001898-757; Judge Lande)
- *Doyle v. Vital Automotive Systems* (May 16, 1977; Ontario Small Claims Court, Toronto; Judge Turner)
- *Lacroix v. Ford* (April 1980; Ontario Small Claims Court, Toronto; Judge Tierney)
- *Marinovich v. Riverside Chrysler* (April 1, 1987; District Court of Ontario; No. 1030/85; Judge Stortini)

Using the Courts
Sue as a Last Resort

If the seller you've been negotiating with agrees to make things right, give him or her a deadline and then have an independent garage check the repairs. If no offer is made within 10 working days, file suit in court. Make the manufacturer a party to the lawsuit only if the original, unexpired warranty was transferred to you; if your claim falls under the emissions warranty, a TSB, a secret warranty extension, or a safety recall campaign; or if there is extensive chassis rusting due to poor engineering.

Choosing the Right Court

You must decide what remedy to pursue; that is, whether you want a partial refund or a cancellation of the sale. To determine the refund amount, add the estimated cost of repairing existing mechanical defects to the cost of prior repairs. Don't exaggerate your losses or claim for repairs that are considered routine maintenance. A suit for cancellation of sale involves practical problems. The court requires that the vehicle be "tendered," or taken back to the seller, at the time the lawsuit is filed. This means that you are without transportation for as long as the case continues, unless you purchase another vehicle in the interim. If you lose the case, you must then take back the old vehicle and pay storage fees. You could go from having no vehicle to having two, one of which is a clunker.

Generally, if the cost of repairs or the sales contract amount falls within the small claims court limit (discussed later), file the case there to keep costs to a minimum and to get a speedy hearing. Small claims court judgments aren't easily appealed, lawyers aren't necessary, filing fees are minimal (about $125), and cases are usually heard within a few months.

Watch what you ask for. If you claim more than the small claims court limit, you'll have to go to a higher court—where costs quickly add up and delays of a few years or more are commonplace.

Small Claims Courts

Crooked automakers scurry away from small claims courts like cockroaches from bug spray, not because the courts can issue million-dollar judgments or force litigants to spend millions in legal fees (they can't), but because they can award sizeable sums to plaintiffs and make jurisprudence that other judges on the same bench are likely to follow.

For example, in *Dawe v. Courtesy Chrysler* (Dartmouth Nova Scotia Small Claims Court; SCCH #206825; July 30, 2004), Judge Patrick L Casey, Q.C., rendered an impressive 21-page decision citing key automobile product liability cases over the past 80 years. He awarded $5,037 to the owner of a new 2001 Cummins-equipped Ram pickup that wandered all over the road; lost power, or jerked and bucked; shifted erratically; lost braking ability; bottomed out when passing over bumps; allowed water to leak into the cab; produced a burnt-wire and oil smell in the interior as the lights would dim; and produced a rear-end whine and wind noise around the doors and under the dash. Dawe had sold the vehicle and reduced his claim to meet the small claims threshold.

There are small claims courts in most counties of every province, and you can make a claim either in the county where the problem happened or in the county where the defendant lives and conducts business. Simply go to the small claims court office and ask for a claim form. Instructions on how to fill it out accompany the form. Remember, you must identify the defendant correctly, and this may require some help from the court clerk or a law student because some automakers name local attorneys to handle suits (look for other recent lawsuits naming the same party). Crooks often change their company's name to escape liability; for example, it would be impossible to sue Joe's Garage (2008) if your contract is with Joe's Garage Inc. (2004).

At this point, it wouldn't hurt to hire a lawyer or a paralegal for a brief walk-through of small claims procedures to ensure that you've prepared your case properly and that you know what objections will likely be raised by the other side. If you'd like a lawyer to do all the work for you, there are a number of law firms around the country that specialize in small claims litigation. "Small claims" doesn't mean small legal fees, however. In Toronto, some law offices charge a flat fee of $1,000 for the basic small claims lawsuit and trial.

Remember that you're entitled to bring to court any evidence relevant to your case, including written documents such as a bill of sale or receipt, contract, or letter. If your car has developed severe rust problems, bring a photograph (signed and dated by the photographer) to court. You may also have witnesses testify, but it's important to discuss witness testimony prior to the court date. If a witness can't attend the court date, he or she can write a report and sign it for representation in court. This situation usually applies to an expert witness, such as an independent mechanic who has evaluated your car's problems.

If you lose your case in spite of all your preparation and research, some small claims court statutes allow cases to be retried, at a nominal cost, in exceptional circumstances. If a new witness has come forward, additional evidence has been discovered, or key documents that were previously not available have become accessible, apply for a retrial. In Ontario, this little-known provision is Rule 18.4 (1).B.

Alan MacDonald, a *Lemon-Aid* reader who won his case in small claims court, gives the following tips on beating Ford (*MacDonald v. Highbury Ford Sales Limited*, Ontario Superior Court of Justice in the Small Claims Court London, June 6, 2000, Court File #0001/00, Judge J. D. Searle):

> In 1999 after only 105,000 km the automatic transmission went. I took [my 1994 Ford Taurus wagon] to Highbury Ford to have it repaired. We paid $2,070 to have the transmission fixed, but protested and felt the transmission failed prematurely. We contacted Ford, but to no avail: their reply was we were out of warranty period. The transmission was so poorly repaired (and we went back to Highbury Ford several times) that we had to go to Mr. Transmission to have the transmission fixed again nine months later at a further $1,906.02....

> My observations with going through small claims court involved the following: I filed in January of 2000, the trial took place on June 1 and the judgment was issued June 6.

> At pretrial, a representative of Ford (Ann Sroda) and a representative from Highbury Ford were present. I came with one binder for each of the defendants, the court, and one for myself (each binder was about 3 inches thick—containing your reports on Ford Taurus automatic transmissions, ALLDATA Service Bulletins, [and extracts from the following websites:] Taurus Transmissions Victims (Bradley website), Center for Auto Safety...Read This Before Buying a Taurus...and the Ford Vent Page....

> The representative from Ford asked a lot of questions (I think she was trying to find out if I had read the contents of the information I was relying on). The Ford representative then offered a 50 percent settlement based on the initial transmission work done at Highbury Ford. The release allowed me to still sue Highbury Ford with regards to the necessity of going to Mr. Transmission because of the faulty repair done by the dealer. Highbury Ford displayed no interest in settling the case, and so I had to go to court.

> For court, I prepared by issuing a summons to the manager at Mr. Transmission, who did the second transmission repair, as an expert witness.... Next, I went to the law school library in London and received a great deal of assistance in researching cases pertinent to car repairs. I was told that judgments in your home province (in my case, Ontario) were binding on the court; that cases outside of the home province could be considered, but not binding, on the judge.

The cases I used for trial involved *Pelleray v. Heritage Ford Sales Ltd.*, Ontario Small Claims Court (Scarborough) SC7688/91 March 22, 1993; *Phillips et al. v. Ford Motor Co. of Canada Ltd. et al*, Ontario Reports 1970, 15th January 1970; *Gregorio v. Intrans-Corp.*, Ontario Court of Appeal, May 19, 1994; *Collier v. MacMaster's Auto Sales*, New Brunswick Court of Queen's Bench, April 26, 1991; *Sigurdson v. Hillcrest Service & Acklands (1977)*, Saskatchewan Queen's Bench; *White v. Sweetland*, Newfoundland District Court, Judicial Centre of Gander, November 8, 1978; *Raiches Steel Works v. J. Clark & Son*, New Brunswick Supreme Court, March 7, 1977; *Mudge v. Corner Brook Garage Ltd.*, Newfoundland Supreme Court, July 17, 1975; *Sylvain v. Carroseries d'Automobiles Guy Inc. (1981)*, C.P. 333, Judge Page; and *Gagnon v. Ford Motor Company of Canada, Limited et Marineau Automobile Co. Ltée. (1974)*, C.S. 422–423.

In court, I had prepared the case, as indicated above, and had my expert witness and two other witnesses who had driven the vehicle (my wife and my 18-year-old son). As you can see by the judgment, we won our case and I was awarded $1,756.52, including prejudgment interest and costs.

Key Court Decisions

The following Canadian and U.S. lawsuits and judgments cover typical problems that are likely to arise. Use them as leverage when negotiating a settlement or as a reference should your claim go to trial. Legal principles applying to Canadian and American law are similar; Quebec court decisions, however, may be based on legal principles that don't apply outside of that province. Nevertheless, you can find a comprehensive listing of Canadian decisions from small claims courts all the way to the Supreme Court of Canada at *www.legalresearch.org/docs/internet3.html* or *www.canlii.org*.

You can find additional court judgments in the legal reference section of your city's main public library or at a nearby university law library. Ask the librarian for help in choosing the legal phrases that best describe your claim. LexisNexis (*www.lexis-nexis.com*) and FindLaw (*www.findlaw.com*) are two useful Internet sites for legal research. Their main drawback, though, is that you may need to subscribe or use a lawyer's subscription to access jurisprudence and other areas of the sites.

Some of the small claims court cases cited in *Lemon-Aid* may not be reported. If that happens, contact the office of the presiding judge named in the decision and ask his or her assistant to send you a copy of the judgment. If the judge or assistant isn't available, ask for the court clerk of that jurisdiction to search for the case file and date referenced in *Lemon-Aid*.

An excellent reference book that will give you plenty of tips on filing, pleading, and collecting your judgment is Judge Marvin Zuker's *Ontario Small Claims Court Practice 2009* (Carswell, 2008). Judge Zuker's book is easily understood by non-lawyers and uses court decisions from across Canada to help you plead your case successfully in almost any Canadian court.

Product Liability

Almost three decades ago, in *Kravitz v. GM* (the first case where I was called as a pro bono expert witness), the Supreme Court of Canada clearly affirmed that automakers and their dealers are jointly liable for the replacement or repair of a vehicle if independent testimony shows that it is afflicted with factory-related defects that compromise its safety or performance. The existence of a secret warranty extension or technical service bulletin also helps prove that the vehicle's problems are the automaker's responsibility. For example, in *Lowe v. Fairview Chrysler* (see page 92), technical service bulletins were instrumental in showing an Ontario small claims court judge that Chrysler's history of automatic transmission failures went back to 1989.

In addition to replacing or repairing the vehicle, an automaker can also be held responsible for any damages arising from the defect. This means that loss of wages, supplementary transportation costs, and damages for personal inconvenience can be awarded. However, in the States, product liability damage awards often exceed millions of dollars, while Canadian courts are far less generous.

Implied Warranty Rulings

Reasonable durability

As outlined near the beginning of the chapter, this is that powerful "other" warranty that they never tell you about. It applies during and after the expiration of the manufacturer's or dealer's expressed or written warranty and requires that a part or repair will last a reasonable period of time. What is reasonable depends in a large part on benchmarks used in the industry, the price of the vehicle, and how it was driven and maintained. Look at the "Reasonable Part Durability" table on page 48 for some guidelines as to what you should expect. Judges usually apply the implied or legal warranty when the manufacturer's expressed warranty has expired and the vehicle's manufacturing defects remain uncorrected.

Chevrier v. General Motors Du Canada (October 18, 2006; Quebec Small Claims Court, Joliette District (Repentigny) No. 730-32-004876-046; Justice Georges Massol). You can get the judgment at *www.canlii.org/fr/qc/qccq/doc/2006/2006qccq1 5312/2006qccq15312.pdf*.

The plaintiff leased and then bought a 2000 Montana minivan. At 71,000 km, the automatic transmission failed and two GM dealers estimated the repairs to be between $2,200 and $2,500. They refused warranty coverage because the warranty had expired after the third year of ownership or 60,000 km of use. The owner repaired the transmission at an independent garage for $1,869 and kept the old parts, which GM refused to examine.

A small claims court lawsuit was filed, and Judge Massol gave the following reasons for ruling against GM's two arguments that (1) there was no warning that a claim would be filed and (2) all warranties had expired:

- GM filed a voluminous record of jurisprudence in its favour, relative to other lawsuits that were rejected because they were filed without prior notice. But the judge reasoned that GM could not plead a "failure to notify," because the owner went to several dealers who were essentially agents of the manufacturer.
- The judge also reasoned that the expiration of GM's written warranty does not nullify the legal warranty set out in articles 38 and 39 of the *Consumer Protection Act*. The legal warranty requires that all products be "reasonably durable," which did not appear to be the case with the plaintiff's vehicle, given its low mileage and number of years of use.

GM was ordered to pay the entire repair costs, plus interest, and the $90 filing fee.

Dufour v. Ford Canada Ltd. (April 10, 2001; Quebec Small Claims Court, Hull; No. 550-32-008335-009; Justice P. Chevalier). Ford was forced to reimburse the cost of engine head gasket repairs carried out on a 1996 Windstar 3.8L engine—a vehicle not covered by the automaker's Owner Notification Program, which cut off assistance after the '95 model year.

Schaffler v. Ford Motor Company Limited and Embrun Ford Sales Ltd. (Ontario Superior Court of Justice; L'Orignal Small Claims Court; Court File No. 59-2003; July 22, 2003; Justice Gerald Langlois). The plaintiff bought a used 1995 Windstar in 1998. Its engine head gasket was repaired for free three years later, under Ford's seven-year extended warranty. In 2002, at 109,600 km, the head gasket failed again, seriously damaging the engine. Ford refused a second repair. Justice Langlois ruled that Ford's warranty extension bulletin listed signs and symptoms of the covered defect that were identical to the problems written on the second work order ("persistent and/or chronic engine overheating; heavy white smoke evident from the exhaust tailpipe; flashing 'low coolant' instrument panel light even after coolant refill; and constant loss of engine coolant"). Judge Langlois concluded that "the problem was brought to the attention of the dealer well within the warranty period; the dealer was negligent." The plaintiff was awarded $4,941 plus 5 percent interest. This judgment included $1,070 for two months' car rental.

John R. Reid and Laurie M. McCall v. Ford Motor Company of Canada (Superior Court of Justice; Ottawa Small Claims Court; Claim No: #02-SC-077344; July 11, 2003; Justice Tiernay). A 1996 Windstar, bought used in 1997, experienced engine head gasket failure in October 2001 at 159,000 km. Judge Tiernay awarded the plaintiffs $4,145 for the following reason:

> A Technical Service Bulletin dated June 28, 1999, was circulated to Ford dealers. It dealt specifically with "undetermined loss of coolant" and "engine oil contaminated with coolant" in the 1996–98 Windstar and five other models of Ford vehicles. I conclude that Ford owed a duty of care to the Plaintiff to equip this vehicle with a cylinder head gasket of sufficient sturdiness and durability that would function trouble-free for

at least seven years, given normal driving and proper maintenance conditions. I find that Ford is answerable in damages for the consequences of its negligence.

Dawe v. Courtesy Chrysler (Dartmouth Nova Scotia Small Claims Court; SCCH #206825; July 30, 2004; Judge Patrick L Casey, Q.C.). "Small claims" doesn't necessarily mean small judgments. This 21-page, unreported Nova Scotia small claims court decision is impressive in its clarity and thoroughness. It applies *Donoghue, Kravitz, Davis, et al.* in awarding a 2001 Dodge Ram owner over $5,000 in damages. Anyone with engine, transmission, and suspension problems or water leaking into the interior will find this judgment particularly useful.

Fissel v. Ideal Auto Sales Ltd. (1991) (91 Sask. R. 266). Shortly after the vehicle was purchased, its motor seized and the dealer refused to replace it, even though the car was returned on several occasions. The court ruled that the dealer had breached the statutory warranties in sections 11 (4) and (7) of the *Consumer Products Warranties Act*. The purchasers were entitled to cancel the sale and recover the full purchase price.

Friskin v. Chevrolet Oldsmobile (72 D.L.R. (3d), 289). A Manitoba used-car buyer asked that his contract be cancelled because of his car's chronic stalling problem. The garage owner did his best to correct it. Despite the seller's good intentions, the *Manitoba Consumer Protection Act* allowed for cancellation.

Graves v. C&R Motors Ltd. (April 8, 1980; British Columbia County Court; Judge Skipp). The plaintiff bought a used car on the condition that certain deficiencies be remedied. They never were, and he was promised a refund, but it never arrived. The plaintiff brought suit, claiming that the dealer's deceptive activities violated the provincial *Trade Practices Act*. The court agreed, concluding that a deceptive act that occurs before, during, or after the transaction can lead to the cancellation of the contract.

Hachey v. Galbraith Equipment Company (1991) (33 M.V.R. (2d) 242). The plaintiff bought a used truck from the dealer to haul gravel. Shortly thereafter, the steering failed. The plaintiff's suit was successful because expert testimony showed that the truck wasn't roadworthy. The dealer was found liable for damages for being in breach of the implied condition of fitness for the purpose for which the truck was purchased, as set out in section 15 (a) of the New Brunswick *Sale of Goods Act*.

Henzel v. Brussels Motors (1973) (1 O.R., 339 (C.C.)). The dealer sold a used car, brandishing a copy of the mechanical fitness certificate as proof that the car was in good shape. The plaintiff was awarded his money back because the court held the certificate to be a warranty that was breached by the car's subsequent defects.

Johnston v. Bodasing Corporation Limited (February 23, 1983; Ontario County Court, Bruce; No. 15/11/83; Judge McKay). The plaintiff bought a used 1979 Buick Riviera that was represented as being "reliable" for $8,500. Two weeks after purchase, the motor self-destructed. Judge McKay awarded the plaintiff $2,318 as compensation to fix the Riviera's defects. One feature of this particular decision is that the trial judge found that the *Sale of Goods Act* applied, notwithstanding the fact that the vendor used a standard contract that said there were no warranties or representations. The judge also accepted the decision in *Kendal v. Lillico (1969)* (2 Appeal Cases, 31), which indicates that the *Sale of Goods Act* covers not only defects that the seller ought to have detected but also latent defects that even his or her utmost skill and judgment could not have detected. This places a very heavy onus on the vendor, and it should prove useful in actions of this type in other common-law provinces with laws similar to Ontario's *Sale of Goods Act*.

General Motors Products of Canada Ltd. v. Kravitz, (1979) (1 S.C.R. 790). The court said the seller's warranty of quality was an accessory to the property and was transferred with it on successive sales. Accordingly, subsequent buyers could invoke the contractual warranty of quality against the manufacturer, even though they did not contract directly with it. This precedent was then codified in articles 1434, 1442, and 1730 of Quebec's *Civil Code*.

Morrison v. Hillside Motors (1973) Ltd. (1981; 35 Nfld. & P.E.I.R. 361). A used car advertised to be in A-1 condition and carrying a 50/50 warranty developed a number of problems. The court decided that the purchaser should be partially compensated because of the ad's claim. In deciding how much compensation to award, the presiding judge considered the warranty's wording, the amount paid for the vehicle, the model year of the vehicle, the vehicle's average life, the type of defect that occurred, and the length of time the purchaser had use of the vehicle before its defects became evident. Although this judgment was rendered in Newfoundland, judges throughout Canada have used a similar approach for more than a decade.

Neilson v. Maclin Motors (71 D.L.R. (3d), 744). The plaintiff bought a used truck on the strength of the seller's allegations that the motor had been rebuilt and that it had 210 hp. The engine failed. The judge awarded damages and cancelled the contract because the motor had not been rebuilt and did not have 210 hp, and the transmission was defective.

Parent v. Le Grand Trianon and Ford Credit (1982) (C.P., 194; Judge Bertrand Gagnon). Nineteen months after paying $3,300 for a used 1974 LTD, the plaintiff sued the Ford dealer for his money back because the car was prematurely rusted out. The dealer replied that rust was normal, there was no warranty, and the claim was too late. The court held that the garage was still responsible. The plaintiff was awarded $1,500 for the cost of rust repairs.

Narbonne v. Glendale Recreational Véhicules (Quebec Small Claims Court; June 2, 2008; Reference: 2008 QCCQ 5325; Judge Richard Landry). Three years after the plaintiff purchased a travel trailer, the manufacturer sent a recall notice to the wrong address. Seven years after that, the vehicle broke down when the recalled part failed. The manufacturer said it had done its part in sending out the recall notice. The judge disagreed, and found the company responsible for the full cost of the repairs, lodging, and $500 for general inconvenience, for a total of $5,792. (A copy of the judgment may be obtained from the Automobile Protection Association at *www.apa.ca*.)

"As is" clauses

Since 1907, Canadian courts have ruled that a seller can't exclude the implied warranty as to fitness by including such phrases as "there are no other warranties or guarantees, promises, or agreements than those contained herein." See *Sawyer-Massey Co. v. Thibault* (1907; 5 W.L.R. 241).

Adams v. J&D's Used Cars Ltd. (1983) (26 Sask. R. 40 Q.B.). Shortly after the plaintiff purchased a car, its engine and transmission failed. The court ruled that the inclusion of "as is" in the sales contract had no legal effect. The dealer breached the implied warranty set out in Saskatchewan's *Consumer Products Warranties Act*. The sale was cancelled, and all monies were refunded.

Leasing

Ford Motor Credit v. Bothwell (December 3, 1979; Ontario County Court, Middlesex; No. 9226-T; Judge Macnab). The defendant leased a 1977 Ford truck that had frequent engine problems, characterized by stalling and hard starting. After complaining for one year and driving 35,000 km, the defendant cancelled the lease. Ford Credit sued for the money owing on the lease. Judge Macnab cancelled the lease and ordered Ford Credit to repay 70 percent of the amount paid during the leasing period. Ford Credit was also ordered to refund repair costs, even though the corporation claimed that it should not be held responsible for Ford's failure to honour its warranty.

Salvador v. Setay Motors/Queenstown Chev-Olds (Hamilton Small Claims Court; Case No.1621/95). The plaintiff was awarded $2,000, plus costs, from Queenstown Leasing. The court found that the company should have tried harder to sell the leased vehicle, and at a higher price, when the "open lease" expired.

Schryvers v. Richport Ford Sales (May 18, 1993; B.C.S.C.; No. C917060; Justice Tysoe). The court awarded $17,578.47, plus costs, to a couple who paid thousands of dollars more in unfair and hidden leasing charges than if they had simply purchased their Ford Explorer and Escort. The court found that this price difference constituted a deceptive, unconscionable act or practice, in contravention of the *Trade Practices Act*, R.S.B.C. 1979, c. 406.

Judge Tysoe concluded that the total of the general damages awarded to the Schryvers for both vehicles would be $11,578.47. He then proceeded to give the following reasons for awarding an additional $6,000 in punitive damages:

Little wonder Richport Ford had a contest for the salesperson who could persuade the most customers to acquire their vehicles by way of a lease transaction. I consider the actions of Richport Ford to be sufficiently flagrant and high handed to warrant an award of punitive damages.

There must be a disincentive to suppliers in respect of intentionally deceptive trade practices. If no punitive damages are awarded for intentional violations of the legislation, suppliers will continue to conduct their businesses in a manner that involves deceptive trade practices because they will have nothing to lose. In this case I believe that the appropriate amount of punitive damages is the extra profit Richport Ford endeavoured to make as a result of its deceptive acts. I therefore award punitive damages against Richport Ford in the amount of $6,000.

See also:

- *Barber v. Inland Truck Sales* (11 D.L.R. (3rd), No. 469)
- *Canadian-Dominion Leasing v. Suburban Super Drug Ltd.* (1966) (56 D.L.R. (2nd), No. 43)
- *Neilson v. Atlantic Rentals Ltd.* (1974) (8 N.B.R. (2d), No. 594)
- *Volvo Canada v. Fox* (December 13, 1979; New Brunswick Court of Queen's Bench; No. 1698/77/C; Judge Stevenson)
- *Western Tractor v. Dyck* (7 D.L.R. (3rd), No. 535)

Repairs: Faulty Diagnosis

Davies v. Alberta Motor Association (August 13, 1991; Alberta Provincial Court; Civil Division; No. P9090106097; Judge Moore). The plaintiff had the AMA's Vehicle Inspection Service check out a used 1985 Nissan Pulsar NX prior to buying it. The car passed with flying colours. A month later, the clutch was replaced and numerous electrical problems ensued. At that time, another garage discovered that the car had been involved in a major accident, had a bent frame and a leaking radiator, and was unsafe to drive. The court awarded the plaintiff $1,578.40 plus three years' interest. The judge held that the AMA set itself out as an expert and should have spotted the car's defects. The AMA's defence—that it was not responsible for errors—was thrown out. The court held that a disclaimer clause could not protect the association from a fundamental breach of contract.

Secret Warranty Rulings

It's common practice for manufacturers to secretly extend their warranties to cover components with a high failure rate. Customers who complain vigorously get extended warranty compensation in the form of "goodwill" adjustments.

François Chong v. Marine Drive Imported Cars Ltd. and Honda Canada Inc. (May 17, 1994; British Columbia Provincial Small Claims Court; No. 92-06760; Judge C.L. Bagnall). Mr. Chong was the first owner of a 1983 Honda Accord with 134,000 km on the odometer. He had six engine camshafts replaced—four under Honda "goodwill" programs, one where he paid part of the repairs, and one via this small claims court judgment.

In his ruling, Judge Bagnall agreed with Chong and ordered Honda and the dealer to each pay half of the $835.81 repair bill for the following reasons:

> The defendants assert that the warranty, which was part of the contract for purchase of the car, encompassed the entirety of their obligation to the claimant, and that it expired in February 1985. The replacements of the camshaft after that date were paid for wholly or in part by Honda as a "goodwill gesture." The time has come for these gestures to cease, according to the witness for Honda. As well, he pointed out to me that the most recent replacement of the camshaft was paid for by Honda and that, therefore, the work would not be covered by Honda's usual warranty of 12 months from date of repair. Mr. Wall, who testified for Honda, told me there was no question that this situation with Mr. Chong's engine was an unusual state of affairs. He said that a camshaft properly maintained can last anywhere from 24,000 to 500,000 km. He could not offer any suggestion as to why the car keeps having this problem.

> The claimant has convinced me that the problems he is having with rapid breakdown of camshafts in his car is due to a defect, which was present in the engine at the time that he purchased the car. The problem first arose during the warranty period and in my view has never been properly identified nor repaired.

Automatic Transmission Failures (Chrysler)

Lowe v. Fairview Chrysler-Dodge Limited and Chrysler Canada Limited (May 14, 1996; Ontario Court, General Division; Burlington Small Claims Court; No. 1224/95). This judgment, in the plaintiff's favour, raises important legal principles relative to Chrysler:

- Technical dealer service bulletins are admissible in court to prove that a problem exists and that certain parts should be checked out.
- If a problem is reported prior to a warranty's expiration, warranty coverage for the problematic component(s) is automatically carried over after the warranty ends.
- It's not up to the car owner to tell the dealer/automaker what the specific problem is.
- Repairs carried out by an independent garage can be refunded if the dealer/automaker unfairly refuses to apply the warranty.
- The dealer/automaker cannot dispute the cost of the independent repair if they fail to cross-examine the independent repairer.
- Auto owners can ask for and win compensation for their inconvenience, which in this judgment amounted to $150.

Court awards quickly add up. Although the plaintiff was given $1,985.94, with the addition of court costs and prejudgment interest, plus costs of inconvenience fixed at $150, the final award amounted to $2,266.04.

Tire Failures: Premature Wear

Blackwood v. Ford Motor Company of Canada Ltd., 2006 (Provincial Court of Alberta, Civil Division; Docket: PO690101722; Registry: Canmore; 2006/12/08; Honourable J. Shriar). This four-page judgment gives important guidelines as to how a plaintiff can successfully claim a refund for a defective tire.

The plaintiff bought a new 2005 Ford Focus. After 10 months and 22,000 km, his dealer said all four tires needed replacing at a cost of $560.68. Both the dealer and Ford refused to cover the expense under the 3-year/60,000 km manufacturer's tire warranty, alleging that the wear was "normal wear and tear." Judge Shriar disagreed and awarded the plaintiff the full cost of the replacement tires, plus the filing fee and costs related to the registered mail and corporate records address check. An additional $100 was awarded for court costs, plus interest on the total amount from the date of the filing.

False Advertising

Misrepresentation

Goldie v. Golden Ears Motors (1980) Ltd (Port Coquitlam; June 27, 2000; British Columbia Small Claims Court; Case No. CO8287; Justice Warren). In a well-written eight-page judgment, the court awarded plaintiff Goldie $5,000 for engine repairs on a 1990 Ford F-150 pickup in addition to $236 court costs. The dealer was found to have misrepresented the mileage and sold a used vehicle that didn't meet Section 8.01 of the provincial *Motor Vehicle Act Regulations* due to its unsafe tires and defective exhaust and headlights.

In rejecting the seller's defence that he disclosed all information "to the best of his knowledge and belief" as stipulated in the sales contract, Justice Warren stated,

> The words "to the best of your knowledge and belief" do not allow someone to be willfully blind to defects or to provide incorrect information. I find as a fact that the business made no effort to fulfill its duty to comply with the requirements of this form.... The defendant has been reckless in its actions. More likely, it has actively deceived the claimant into entering into this contract. I find the conduct of the defendant has been reprehensible throughout the dealings with the claimant.

This judgment closes a loophole that sellers have used to justify their misrepresentation, and it allows for cancellation of the sale and damages if the vehicle doesn't meet highway safety regulations.

MacDonald v. Equilease Co. Ltd. (January 18, 1979; Ontario Supreme Court; Judge O'Driscoll). The plaintiff leased a truck that was misrepresented as having an axle stronger than it really was. The court awarded the plaintiff damages for repairs and set aside the lease.

Seich v. Festival Ford Sales Ltd. (1978) (6 Alta. L.R. (2nd), No. 262). The plaintiff bought a used truck from the defendant after being assured that it had a new motor and transmission. It didn't, and the court awarded the plaintiff $6,400.

Used car sold as new (demonstrator)

Bilodeau v. Sud Auto (Quebec Court of Appeal; No. 09-000751-73; Judge Tremblay). This appeals court cancelled the contract and held that a car can't be sold as new or as a demonstrator if it has ever been rented, leased, sold, or titled to anyone other than the dealer.

Rourke v. Gilmore (January 16, 1928; as found in *Ontario Weekly Notes,* vol. XXXIII, p. 292). Before discovering that his new car was really used, the plaintiff drove it for over a year. For this reason, the contract couldn't be cancelled. However, the appeals court instead awarded damages for $500, which was quite a sum in 1928!

Vehicle not as ordered

Whether you're buying new or used, the seller can't misrepresent the vehicle. Anything that varies from what one would commonly expect, or from the seller's representation, must be disclosed prior to signing the contract. Typical misrepresentation scenarios include odometer turnbacks, undisclosed accident damage, used or leased cars being sold as new, new vehicles that are the wrong colour or the wrong model year, and vehicles that lack promised options or standard features.

Chenel v. Bel Automobile (1981) Inc. (August 27, 1976; Quebec Superior Court, Quebec City; Judge Desmeules). The plaintiff didn't receive his new Ford truck with the Jacob brakes essential for transporting sand in hilly regions. The court awarded the plaintiff $27,000, representing the purchase price of the vehicle less the money he earned while using the truck.

Lasky v. Royal City Chrysler Plymouth (February 18, 1987; Ontario High Court of Justice; 59 O.R. (2nd), No. 323). The plaintiff bought a 4-cylinder 1983 Dodge 600 that was represented by the salesman as being a 6-cylinder model. After putting 40,000 km on the vehicle over a 22-month period, the buyer was given her money back, without interest, under the provincial *Business Practices Act.*

Punitive Damages

Punitive damages (also known as "exemplary damages") allow the plaintiff to get compensation that exceeds his or her losses as a deterrent to those who carry out dishonest or negligent practices. These kinds of judgments have been quite common in the U.S. for almost 50 years, and they sometimes reach hundreds of millions of dollars.

Punitive damages are rarely awarded in Canadian courts and are almost never used against automakers. When they are given out, it's usually for sums less than

$100,000. During the past five years, though, our courts have cracked down on business abuses and awarded plaintiffs amounts varying from $5,000 to $1 million.

- In February 2002, the Supreme Court of Canada let stand an unprecedented million-dollar award against what it called "the insurer from hell." In *Whiten v. Pilot Insurance Co.*, the couple's home burned down and the insurer refused to pay the claim. The jury was so outraged that it ordered the company to pay $345,000 for the loss, plus $320,000 for legal costs and $1 million in punitive damages, making it the largest punitive damage award in Canadian history. The Supreme Court refused to overturn the jury's decision. This judgment scares the dickens out of insurers, who fear that they face huge punitive damage awards if they don't pay promptly.
- In May 2005, the Supreme Court of Canada once again reaffirmed the use of punitive damages in *Prebushewski v. Dodge City Auto (1985) Ltd. and Chrysler Canada Ltd.* (2001 SKQB 537; Q.B. No. 1215). The Court backed the Saskatchewan court's $25,000 punitive damage award against Chrysler, rendered on December 6, 2001, in Saskatoon, which cited egregious violations of provincial consumer protection statutes (see part of the judgment on page 55). The Supreme Court of Canada's confirmation of the judgment can be found at *scc.lexum.umontreal.ca/en/2005/2005scc28/2005scc28.html*.

See also:

- *Vlchek v. Koshel (1988)* (44 C.C.L.T. 314; B.C.S.C., No. B842974).
- *Granek v. Reiter* (Ontario Court, General Division; No. 35/741)
- *Morrison v. Sharp* (Ontario Court, General Division; No. 43/548)
- *Schryvers v. Richport Ford Sales* (May 18, 1993; B.C.S.C., No. C917060; Judge Tysoe)
- *Varleg v. Angeloni* (B.C.S.C., No. 41/301)

Mental distress

Canadian courts have become more generous in awarding plaintiffs money for mental distress experienced when defects aren't repaired properly under warranty. In *Sharman v. Formula Ford Sales Limited, Ford Credit Limited, and Ford Motor Company of Canada Limited*, Justice Shepard of the Ontario Superior Court in Oakville awarded the owner of a 2000 Windstar $7,500 for mental distress resulting from the breach of the implied warranty of fitness, plus $7,207 for breach of contract and breach of warranty. The Windstar's sliding door wasn't secure and leaked air and water after many attempts to repair it. Interestingly, the judge cited the *Wharton* decision as support for his award for mental distress:

> The plaintiff and his family have had three years of aggravation, inconvenience, worry, and concern about their safety and that of their children. Generally speaking, our contract law did not allow for compensation for what may be mental distress, but that may be changing. I am indebted to counsel for providing me with the decision of the British Columbia Court of Appeal in *Wharton v. Tom Harris Chevrolet Oldsmobile*

Cadillac Ltd., [2002] B.C.J. No. 233, 2002 BCCA 78. This decision was recently followed in *T'avra v. Victoria Ford Alliance Ltd.,* [2003] B, CJ No. 1957.

In *Wharton,* the purchaser of a Cadillac Eldorado claimed damages against the dealer because the car's sound system emitted an annoying buzzing noise and the purchaser had to return the car to the dealer for repair numerous times over two and a half years. The trial court awarded damages of $2,257.17 for breach of warranty with respect to the sound system, and $5,000 in non-pecuniary damages for loss of enjoyment of their luxury vehicle and for inconvenience, for a total award of $7,257.17. The Court of Appeal upheld the decision of the trial judge and Levine J.A. spent considerable time reviewing the law, but in particular the law relating to damages for breach of implied warranty of fitness: "The principles applicable to an award of damages for mental distress resulting from a breach of contract were thoroughly and helpfully analyzed in the recent judgment of the House of Lords in *Farley v. Skinner,* [2001] 3 W.L.R. 899, [2001] H.L.J. No. 49, affirming and clarifying the decision of the English Court of Appeal in *Watts v. Morrow,* [1991] I W.L.R. 142 1. Both of those cases concerned a claim by a buyer of a house against a surveyor who failed to report matters concerning the house as required by the contract. In *Watts,* the surveyor was negligent in failing to report defects in the house, and non-pecuniary damages of $6,750 were awarded to each of the owners for the inconvenience and discomfort experienced by them during repairs. In *Farley,* the surveyor was negligent in failing to discover, as he specifically undertook to do, that the property was adversely affected by aircraft noise. The House of Lords upheld the trial judge's award of non-pecuniary damages of $610,000, reversing the Court of Appeal, principally on the grounds that the object of the contract was to provide 'pleasure, relaxation, peace of mind, or freedom from molestation' and also because the plaintiff had suffered physical discomfort and inconvenience from the aircraft noise."

• • •

The reasons for judgment in *Farley* provide a summary and survey of the law as it has developed, in England, to date. They are helpful in analyzing and summarizing the principles derived from *Watts,* which are, in my view, applicable to the case at bar. In summary they are (borrowing the language from both *Watts* and *Farley*):

(a) A contract-breaker is not in general liable for any distress, frustration, anxiety, displeasure, vexation, tension, or aggravation which the breach of contract may cause to the innocent party.

(b) The rule is not absolute. Where a major or important part of the contract is to give pleasure, relaxation or peace of mind, damages will be awarded if the fruit of the contract is not provided or if the contrary result is instead procured.

(c) In cases not falling within the "peace of mind" category, damages are recoverable for inconvenience and discomfort caused by the breach and the mental suffering directly related to the inconvenience and discomfort. However, the cause of the inconvenience or discomfort must be a sensory experience as opposed to mere disappointment that the contract has been broken. If those effects are foreseeably suffered during a period when defects are repaired, they create damages even though the cost of repairs are not recoverable as such.

Application of Law to the Facts of This Case

In the *Wharton* case, the respondent contracted for a "luxury" vehicle for pleasure use. It included a sound system that the appellant's service manager described as "high end." The respondent's husband described the purchase of the car in this way:

"[W]e bought a luxury car that was supposed to give us a luxury ride and be a quiet vehicle, and we had nothing but difficulty with it from the very day it was delivered with this problem that nobody seemed to be able to fix.... So basically we had a luxury product that gave us no luxury for the whole time that we had it."

It is clear that an important object of the contract was to obtain a vehicle that was luxurious and a pleasure to operate. Furthermore, the buzzing noise was the cause of physical, in the sense of sensory, discomfort to the respondent and her husband. The trial judge found it inhibited listening to the sound system and was irritating in normal conversation. The respondent and her husband also bore the physical inconvenience of taking the vehicle to the appellant on numerous occasions for repairs. The inconvenience and discomfort was, in my view, reasonably foreseeable, if the defect in the sound system had been known at the date of the contract. The fact that it was not then known is, of course, irrelevant.

The award of damages for breach of the implied warranty of fitness satisfies both exceptions from the general rule that damages are not awarded for mental distress for breach of contract, set out in *Watts* as amplified in *Farley*.

The justice continued and said at para. 63 "...awards for mental distress arising from a breach of contract should be restrained and modest."

The court upheld the trial judge's award of $5,000 in *Wharton* where the issue was a buzzing in the sound system.

In my view, a defect in manufacture which goes to the safety of the vehicle deserves a modest increase. I would assess the plaintiff's damage for mental distress resulting from the breach of the implied warranty of fitness at $7,500.

Judgment to issue in favour of the plaintiff against the defendants, except Ford Credit, on a joint and several basis for $14,707, plus interest and costs....

Provincial business practices acts and consumer protection statutes prohibit false, misleading, or deceptive representations and allow for punitive damages should the unfair practice toward the consumer amount to an unconscionable representation (see *Canadian Encyclopedic Digest* (3d) s. 76, pp. 140–45). "Unconscionable" is defined as "where the consumer is not reasonably able to protect his or her interest because of physical infirmity, ignorance, illiteracy, or inability to understand the language of an agreement or similar factors." This concept has been successfully used in consumer, environmental, and labour law.

- Exemplary damages are justified where compensatory damages are insufficient to deter and punish. See *Walker et al. v. CFTO Ltd. et al. (1978)* (59 O.R. (2nd), No. 104; Ontario Court of Appeal).
- Exemplary damages can be awarded in cases where the defendant's conduct was "cavalier." See *Ronald Elwyn Lister Ltd. et al. v. Dayton Tire Canada Ltd. (1985)* (52 O.R. (2nd), No. 89; Ontario Court of Appeal).
- The primary purpose of exemplary damages is to prevent the defendant and all others from doing similar wrongs. See *Fleming v. Spracklin* (1921).
- Disregard of the public's interest, lack of preventive measures, and a callous attitude all merit exemplary damages. See *Coughlin v. Kuntz (1989)* (2 C.C.L.T. (2nd); B.C.C.A.).
- Punitive damages can be awarded for mental distress. See *Ribeiro v. Canadian Imperial Bank of Commerce (1992)* (Ontario Reports 13 3rd) and *Brown v. Waterloo Regional Board of Commissioners of Police (1992)* (37 O.R. 2nd).

In the States, punitive damage awards have been particularly generous. Whenever business complains of an "unrestrained judiciary," it trots out a 20-year-old case where an Alabama plaintiff won a multi-million dollar award because his new BMW had been repainted before he bought it and the seller didn't tell him so.

The case was *BMW of North America, Inc. v. Gore* (517 U.S. 559; 116 S. Ct. 1589; 1996). In this case, the Supreme Court cut the damages award and established standards for jury awards of punitive damages. Nevertheless, million-dollar awards continue to be quite common. In the following example, an Oregon dealer learned that a $1 million punitive damages award was not excessive under *Gore* and under Oregon law.

The Oregon Supreme Court determined that the standard it set forth in *Oberg v. Honda Motor Company* (888 P.2d 8; 1996), on remand from the Supreme Court, survived the Supreme Court's subsequent ruling in *Gore*. The court held that the jury's $1 million punitive damages award, 87 times larger than the plaintiff's compensatory damages in *Parrott v. Carr Chevrolet, Inc.* (2001 Ore. LEXIS; 1 January 11, 2001), wasn't excessive. In that case, Mark Parrott sued Carr Chevrolet, Inc. over a used 1983 Chevrolet Suburban under Oregon's *Unlawful Trade Practices Act*. The jury awarded Parrott $11,496 in compensatory damages and $1 million in punitive damages because the dealer failed to disclose collision damage to a new-car buyer.

See also:

- *Grabinski v. Blue Springs Ford Sales, Inc.* (U.S. App. LEXIS 2073; 8th Cir. W.D. MO; February 16, 2000)

1980–2007
LEMONS AND CHERRIES

Pay to Save

People want economy, and they will pay any price to get it.

LEE IACOCCA

NEW YORK TIMES, OCTOBER 13, 1974

No Vehicle Is Defect-Free

No matter if you buy American, Asian, or European, new or used, you are taking on someone else's problems: the dealers' and automakers', or the previous owners'. Fortunately, you saved a bundle buying used and can correct any deficiencies at cheaper, independent shops. Also, used cars don't easily hide their factory-related defects, crashworthiness has likely been tested and retested by a handful of different agencies, and automaker closings will affect them the least.

Vehicles Should Last 10–15 Years

Primarily, you buy used to save money and to have reliable transportation for a decade or more. A good used car or truck should cost you no more than one-third to one-half of its original selling price ($7,500–$15,000) and should be between three and five years old. A "new" used car must meet your everyday driving needs and have high crashworthiness and reliability scores. Annual maintenance should cost no more than the CAA-surveyed average of $800, and the depreciation rate should have levelled off. Parts and servicing costs shouldn't be excessive, as CBC TV's *Marketplace* found to be the case at some dealerships, and servicing shouldn't be given with a shrug or a snarl.

Fuel economy isn't all that important when you are buying used, since all of your other savings should easily compensate for the extra fuel costs. We don't recommend most gas-electric engine hybrids: Their fuel economy can be 40 percent worse than the automakers' reports, their long-term reliability is problematic, their battery replacement costs are estimated to run as high as $3,000 (U.S.) for the Toyota Prius and $6,000 for other makes, their expensive motors are predicted to have a high failure rate due to corrosion, their retail prices are incredibly high, and their eight-year resale values are no better than similar vehicles equipped with conventional engines. Look, again, at a 2001 Toyota Prius that originally sold for $29,990. It is now valued at a disappointing $7,500 (and we're coming up to the expiration of that battery-pack warranty). Compare that to the price of a fully equipped 2001 Camry CE V6, which sells for about the same price—with no $3,000 battery-pack surcharge .

Depreciation Is Your Friend

Cars and trucks are not all born with equal attributes, and they age (depreciate) at different rates. When buying new, you want a reliable model that depreciates slowly; when buying used, consider a vehicle that has prematurely lost much of its value but is still dependable and inexpensive to maintain. Fortunately, there are plenty of the latter on the market due to poor vehicle sales in 2008.

On the other hand, used vehicles that hold their value well after four years won't be bargains now, but they'll have considerable equity in them should you have to sell due to a cash emergency. And, yes, models that depreciate slowly are usually the more dependable vehicles that hold up better in the long run.

During the past year, fluctuating fuel costs, rebates, cut-rate financing, subsidized leasing, and poor quality reputations have depressed the residual values of most American cars and trucks. According to the Automotive Lease Guide (ALG), *www. alg.com*, Detroit-made vehicles that come off lease barely keep 37 percent of their sticker values after three years. As we go through the present recession, values are hovering near 30 percent.

THE 10 BEST AND 10 WORST VEHICLES FOR HOLDING VALUE OVER FIVE YEARS

BEST VALUE-HOLDERS		WORST VALUE-HOLDERS	
1. Volkswagen R32	6. Toyota RAV4*	1. Hyundai Entourage*	6. Kia Rio
2. Jeep Wrangler*	7. Infiniti G35/G37*	2. Chevrolet Malibu Classic*	7. Suzuki Reno
3. BMW MINI Cooper*	8. Dodge Viper*	3. Kia Optima	8. Kia Spectra
4. Toyota Scion xB	9. BMW 1 Series*	4. Suzuki Forenza	9. Chevrolet Uplander
5. Honda CR-V*	10. Nissan Rogue*	5. Hyundai Accent*	10. Lincoln Town Car*

Source: ALG; August 2008.

Lemon-Aid has rated these vehicles highly over the years.

Judging "Quality Ratings"

Lemon-Aid has been giving honest, independent, and dependable auto ratings for almost 40 years by following these simple rules:

- Ratings should be used primarily as a comparative database when the low-ranked or recommended models reappear in different driving tests and owner surveys. The best rating approach is to combine a driving test with an owner's survey of past models (only *Consumer Reports* does this).
- The responses must come from a large owner pool (1.2 million responses from *Consumer Reports* subscribers, for example). Anecdotal responses should then

be cross-referenced, updated, and given depth and specificity through NHTSA's safety complaint prism. Responses must again be cross-referenced through automaker internal service bulletins to determine the extent of the defect over a specific model and model-year range and to alert owners to problems likely to occur. This is how we discovered that millions of GM 1995–2004 cars and minivans had defective engine intake manifold gaskets.

- Rankings should be predicated on important characteristics measured over a significant period of time, unlike Car of the Year contests, owner-perceived values, or J.D. Power–surveyed problems after only three months of ownership.
- Ratings must come from unimpeachable sources. There should be no conflicts of interest due to ties with advertisers or consultants, and no results gathered from self-serving tests done under ideal conditions, like previous years' Transport Canada and U.S. Environmental Protection Agency (EPA) fuel economy tests.
- Tested cars must be bought, not borrowed, and serviced, not pampered as part of a journalists' fleet lent out for ranking purposes. Also, all automakers need to be judged equally (Toyota at one time did not accept weekend car journalist "roundup" tests as valid and refused to lend its vehicles to the events; thus, they were penalized). Automakers must not be members of the ranking body.
- Again, be wary of self-administered fuel economy ratings used by automakers in complicity with the federal government. *Automotive News* recently added its name to the list of skeptics when it found that Honda and Toyota hybrids get 20–40 percent less real-world gas mileage than advertised. The car industry publication discovered that hybrids need to be driven in a particular way in order to be fuel efficient; are penalized by short trips and the use of air conditioning more than ordinary cars; and are affected by colder climates, resulting in increased fuel consumption way beyond what the ratings figures indicate. The EPA has admitted its fuel economy calculations were overestimated and has set up a website at *www.fueleconomy.gov* that contains recalculated figures for 1985–2007 model-year vehicles that will leave you scratching your head.

Definitions of Terms

We rate vehicles on a scale of one to five stars, with five stars being our top ranking. Models are designated as "Recommended," "Above Average," "Average," "Below Average," or "Not Recommended," with the most recent year's rating indicated by the number of stars beside the vehicle's name.

Recommended

We don't give this rating out very often. And we don't believe for one moment that the more you spend, the better or safer the vehicle. For example, most Hondas are as good as Acuras, which cost thousands of dollars more for their luxury cachet. The same is true when you compare Toyota and Lexus. Even more surprising, some luxury makes, such as Jaguar, are "pseudo-luxe," because they are merely dressed-up ordinary Fords sold at a luxury-car price. The extra money only buys you more features of dubious value and newer, unproven technology, such as rear-mounted video cameras and failure-prone electronic gadgetry.

In fact, the simplest choice is often the best buy. Chrysler's minivans and small Jeeps, GM's Camaro and Firebird, and Hyundai's Elantra and Tiburon get positive ratings because they are easy to find, fairly reliable, and reasonably priced—not the case with many overpriced Hondas and Toyotas.

Recommended vehicles don't need optional, extra-cost ($1,000–$2,000) extended warranties, either. Usually, but not always, an extended warranty is advised for those model years that aren't rated Recommended, but you really shouldn't buy these low-rated vehicles in the first place. Still, if you want extra protection, don't buy too much warranty. For example, if the vehicle has a history of powertrain problems, buy the cheaper powertrain warranty only—not the bumper-to-bumper product. Also, invest in only enough extra warranty to get you through the critical fifth year of ownership. When shopping for an extended warranty, don't be surprised to discover that dealers have the market practically sewn up. You can bargain the price down by getting competing dealers to bid against each other; contact them by fax or through their websites. Be careful with extended-warranty companies that aren't backed by major insurers.

Above Average/Average

Vehicles that are given an Above Average or Average rating are good second choices if a Recommended vehicle isn't your first choice, isn't available, or isn't within budget.

Below Average/Not Recommended

Many vehicles are given a Below Average rating by *Lemon-Aid* because we know they will likely be troublesome; however, we also believe their low price and reasonably priced servicing may make them acceptable buys to some do-it-yourselfers. Vehicles given a Not Recommended rating are best avoided altogether, no matter how low the price. They may be attractively styled and loaded with convenience features (like Ford and GM front-drive minivans, for example), but they're likely to suffer from so many durability and performance problems that you will never stop paying for them. Sometimes, however, a Not Recommended model will improve over several model years and garner a better rating (as the Ford Focus and Chrysler minivans have done).

Incidentally, for those owners who wonder how I can stop recommending model years I once recommended, let me be clear: As vehicles age, their ratings change to reflect new information from owners and from service bulletins relating to durability and the automaker's warranty performance. For example, Nissan's Quest, Toyota's Sienna, and BMW's MINI have been downgraded for some years because new service bulletins and additional owner complaints show some disturbing trends in dependability and servicing performance. Unlike Enron and

Nortel stock analysts, I warn shoppers of changes via subsequent editions of *Lemon-Aid* and updates to my website, *www.lemonaidcars.com*.

I do more than simply write about failure-prone cars: Throughout the year, I try to get refunds for buyers who have made the wrong choice. I lobby automakers to compensate out-of-warranty owners, either through formal warranty extension programs or on a case-by-case basis. I also publish little-known lawsuits, judgments, and settlements in *Lemon-Aid* to help car owners win their cases or get a fair settlement without my personal assistance.

Reliability data is compiled from a number of sources, including confidential technical service bulletins; owner complaints sent to me each year by *Lemon-Aid* readers; owners' comments posted on the Internet; and survey reports and tests done by auto associations, consumer groups, and government organizations. Some auto columnists feel this isn't a scientific sampling, and they're quite right. Nevertheless, the results have been mostly on the mark over the past three decades.

Not all cars and trucks are profiled; those that are new to the market or relatively rare may receive only an abbreviated mention until sufficient owner or service bulletin information becomes available. Best and worst buys for each model category (e.g., "Small Cars" or "Medium Cars") are listed in a summary at the beginning of each rating section.

Strengths and Weaknesses

With the Detroit automakers, engine head gasket and automatic transmission failures are omnipresent; South Korean vehicles have weak transmissions; and Japanese makes are mostly noted for their electrical system, brake, door, AC, sound system, and window glitches, though engine and transmission failures have been appearing more frequently, especially with Toyota and Lexus models built during the past five years. Finally, the European automakers are in a high-tech bind: Electronic demons constantly bedevil Audi, BMW, Jaguar, Land Rover, Mercedes, Saab, Volvo, and VW products, making them unreliable and costly to service after only a few years of service; plus, their vehicles are so complicated to understand, diagnose, and service that many mechanics simply throw up their hands in dismay.

As we ride through the present recession, European automakers will be traded like baseball cards, parts suppliers and service centres will dry up, and resale values will nosedive.

Unlike other auto guides, *Lemon-Aid* knows where automotive skeletons are buried and pinpoints potential parts failures, explains why those parts fail, and advises you as to your chances of getting a repair refund. We also give parts numbers for upgraded parts (why replace poor-quality brake pads with the same brand, for example?) and offer troubleshooting tips direct from the automakers' bulletins, so that your mechanic won't replace parts unrelated to your troubles before coming upon the defective component that is actually responsible.

Parts supply can be a real problem. It's a myth that automakers have to keep a supply of parts sufficient to service what they sell, as any buyer of a Cadillac Catera, a front-drive Lincoln Continental, or a Ford Tempo/Topaz will quickly tell you. Additionally, apart from *Lemon-Aid*, there's no consumer database that warns prospective purchasers as to which models are "parts-challenged."

The "Secret Warranties/Internal Bulletins/Service Tips" sections and vehicle profile tables show a vehicle's overall reliability and safety, providing details as to which specific model years pose the most risk and why. This helps you to direct an independent mechanic to check out the likely trouble spots before you make your purchase.

Vehicle History

This section outlines a vehicle's differences between model years, including major redesigns and other modifications.

 ## Safety Summary

Ongoing safety investigations, safety-related complaints, and safety probes make up this section. National Highway Traffic Safety Administration (NHTSA) complaints are summarized by model year, even though they aren't all safety-related. The summary will help you spot a defect trend (like cracked Ford and GM engine intake manifolds and faulty fuel gauges) before a recall or bulletin is issued. You can also prove that a part failure is widespread and factory-related and then use that information for free "goodwill" repairs or in litigation involving accident damage, injuries, or death. NHTSA records indicate that ABS and airbag failures represent the most frequent complaints from car and van owners. Other common safety-related failures concern sudden acceleration, a vehicle rolling away with the transmission in Park, minivan sliding doors either not opening when they should or opening when they shouldn't, and power-assisted windows injuring or even killing children (see *www.kidsandcars.org*).

Several years ago, a Calgary mother left her two-year-old daughter in an idling SUV to run a quick errand. The child was strangled by the power-assisted window. A passerby extricated her from the window and left to call the police. The mother returned and saw what she thought was the child asleep in the rear seat. Almost an hour later, she realized her daughter was dead. Safety researchers know of at least eight other incidents in North America. Yet parents assume the window will retract automatically if a hand or neck is caught in its path. And they make the same false assumption about minivan automatic sliding side doors.

If *Lemon-Aid* doesn't list a problem you have experienced, go to the NHTSA website's database at *www.nhtsa.dot.gov/cars/problems* for an update. Your vehicle may be currently under investigation, or may have been recalled since this year's guide was published.

Automotive News says an estimated 72 percent of the 25 million vehicles recalled in 2005 were fixed, which is an improvement over the earlier 65 percent fix rate. *Lemon-Aid* doesn't list most recalls because there are so many, and the info can be easily obtained from either NHTSA (*www-odi.nhtsa.dot.gov/recalls/recallsearch.cfm*) or Transport Canada (*www.tc.gc.ca/roadsafety/recalls/search_e.asp*). Dealers willingly give out recall info when they run a vehicle history search through their computers, since they hope to snag the extra repair dollars. Just make sure you ask the dealer to also check for a "customer satisfaction program," a "service policy," a "goodwill" warranty extension, or a free emissions warranty service.

Secret Warranties/Internal Bulletins/Service Tips

It's not enough to know which parts on your vehicle are likely to fail. You should also know which repairs will be done for free by the dealer and automaker, even though you aren't the original owner and the manufacturer's warranty has long since expired.

Welcome to the hidden world of secret warranties, found in confidential technical service bulletins (TSBs) or gleaned from owners' feedback.

Over the years, I've grown tired of having service managers deny that service bulletins exist to correct factory-related defects free of charge. That's why I pore over thousands of bulletins each year and summarize or reproduce in *Lemon-Aid* the important ones for each model year, along with improved parts numbers. These bulletins target defects related to safety, emissions, and performance that service managers would have you believe either don't exist or are your responsibility to fix. If you photocopy the applicable service bulletin included in *Lemon-Aid*, you'll have a better chance of getting the dealer or automaker to cover all or part of the repair costs. Bulletins taken from *Lemon-Aid* have also been instrumental in helping claimants win in small claims court mediation and trials (remember, judges like to have the bulletins validated by an independent mechanic or the dealer/automaker witness you are suing).

Service bulletins listed in *Lemon-Aid* cover repairs that may be eligible for expressed or implied warranty coverage in one or more of the following five categories (although the description of the repairs is not always specific):

- Emissions expressed warranty (5–8 years/80,000–130,000 km)
- Safety component expressed warranty (this covers seat belts, ABS, and airbags, and usually lasts from eight years to the lifetime of the vehicle)
- Body expressed warranty (paint: six years; rust perforations: seven years)
- Secret implied warranty (coverage varies from five to 10 years)
- Factory defect/implied legal warranty (depends on mileage, use, and repair cost; may be as high as 11 years, according to GM paint delamination jurisprudence)

Use these bulletins to get free repairs—even if the vehicle has changed hands several times—and to alert an independent mechanic about defects to look for. They're also great tools for getting compensation from automakers and dealer service managers after the warranty has expired, since they prove that a failure is factory-related and, therefore, not part of routine maintenance or caused by a caustic environmental substance such as bird droppings or acid rain. In small claims court, the argument that bird droppings caused a paint problem usually loses credibility when only certain models or certain years are shown to be affected, pointing the finger at the paint process and quality.

Automakers' "bird-poop" defence doesn't explain why birds apparently defecate only on certain model vehicles (Chrysler Caravans, Ford's Taurus and Sable, GM minivans, etc.). Nevertheless, the implied warranty requires that all automakers use the same durability standard or disclose at the time of sale that their vehicles aren't "bird-proofed."

The diagnostic shortcuts and lists of upgraded parts found in many service bulletins make them invaluable in helping mechanics and do-it-yourselfers to troubleshoot problems inexpensively and to replace the correct part the first time. Auto owners can also use the TSBs listed here to verify that a repair was diagnosed correctly, that the correct upgraded replacement part was used, and that the labour costs were fair.

Each annual edition of *Lemon-Aid* begins lists of safety-related failures, crashworthiness scores, service bulletins, and prices at a later model year. If your vehicle, perhaps a 1997 model, isn't included in this year's guide (which provides detailed information on 1999–2007 models), consult an earlier edition.

Getting your own bulletins

Summaries of service bulletins relating to 1982–2008 vehicles can be obtained for free from the ALLDATA or NHTSA websites, but they are worded so cryptically that you really need the bulletins themselves. If you have a vehicle that's off warranty, you should get copies of the hundreds of pages of bulletins applicable to your model year, listing factory-related defects and diagnostic shortcuts. These bulletins can be ordered and downloaded from the Internet through ALLDATA for $26.95 (U.S.) at *www.alldatadiy.com/buy/index.html*. Or you can get the bulletin title for free from ALLDATA and then search for it on the Internet through a search engine such as Google.

Vehicle Profile Tables

These tables cover the various aspects of vehicle ownership at a glance. Included for each model year are the vehicle's original selling price (the manufacturer's suggested retail price, or MSRP), the wholesale and retail prices you can expect to pay, reliability ratings (specific defective parts are listed in the "Strengths and Weaknesses" section), and details on crashworthiness.

Prices

Dealer profit margins on used cars vary considerably—giving lots of room to negotiate a fair price if you take the time to find out what the vehicle is really worth. Three prices are given for each model year: the vehicle's selling price when new, as suggested by the manufacturer; its maximum used price (▲), which is often the starting price with dealers; and its lowest used price (▼), more commonly found with private sellers.

The original selling price is given as a reality check for greedy sellers who inflate prices on some vehicles (mostly Japanese imports, minivans, and sport-utilities) in order to get back some of the money they overpaid in the first place. This happens particularly often in the Prairie provinces and British Columbia.

Used prices are based on sales recorded as of February 2008. Prices are for the lowest-priced standard model that is in good condition with a maximum of 20,000 km for each calendar year. Watch for price differences reflecting each model's equipment upgrades, designated by a numerical or alphabetical abbreviation. For example, L, LX, and LXT usually mean more standard features are included, progressively, in each model. Numerical progression usually relates to engine size.

Prices reflect the auto markets in Quebec and Ontario, where the majority of used-vehicle transactions take place. Residents of Eastern Canada should add 10 percent, and Western Canadians should add at least 15–20 percent to the listed price. Why the higher costs? Less competition, combined with inflated new-vehicle prices in these regions. Don't be too disheartened, though; you'll recoup some of what you overpaid down the road when you sell the vehicle.

Why are *Lemon-Aid*'s prices sometimes lower than the prices found in dealer guides such as the *Red Book*? The answer is simple: Much like a homeowner selling a house, dealers inflate their prices so that you can bargain the price down and wind up convinced that you made a great deal.

I use newspaper classified ads from Quebec, Ontario, and B.C., as well as auction reports, to calculate my used-vehicle values. I then check these figures against the *Red Book* and *Black Book*. I don't start with the *Red Book*'s retail or wholesale figures because their prices are inflated about 10 percent for wholesale/private sales and almost 20 percent for retail/dealer sales (compare the two, and you'll see what I mean). I then project what the value will be by mid-model year, and that lowers my prices further. I'll almost always fall way under the *Red Book*'s value, but not far under the *Black Book*'s prices.

I include a top and bottom price to give you some margin for negotiation as well as to account for the regional differences in prices, the sudden popularity of certain models or vehicle classes, and the generally depreciated value of used vehicles.

Most new cars depreciate 50–60 percent during the first three years of ownership, despite the fact that good-quality used cars are in high demand. On the other hand, some minivans and most vans, pickups, and sport-utilities lose barely 40 percent of their value, even after four years of ownership.

Since no evaluation method is foolproof, check dealer prices with newspaper- and Internet-sourced private classified ads and then add the option values listed on the next page to come up with a fairly representative offer. Don't forget to bargain the price down further if the odometer shows a cumulative reading of more than 20,000 km per calendar year. Interestingly, the value of anti-lock brakes in trade-ins plummeted during the last few years as they became a standard feature on many entry-level vehicles.

It will be easier for you to match the lower used prices if you buy privately. Dealers rarely sell much below the maximum prices; they claim that they need the full price to cover the costs of reconditioning and paying future warranty claims. If you can come within 5–10 percent of this guide's price, you'll have done well.

In the table on the following page, take note that some options—such as paint protector, rustproofing, and tinted windows—have little worth on the resale market, though they may make your vehicle easier to sell.

Reliability

The older a vehicle gets (at five to seven years old), the greater the chance that major components, such as the engine and transmission, will fail as the result of high mileage and environmental wear and tear. Surprisingly, a host of other expensive-to-repair failures are just as likely to occur in new vehicles as in older ones. The air conditioning, electronic computer modules, electrical systems, and brakes are the most troublesome components, manifesting problems early in a vehicle's life. Other deficiencies that will appear early, due to sloppy manufacturing and harsh environments, include failure-prone body hardware (trim, finish, locks, doors, and windows), susceptibility to water leakage or wind noise, and peeling and/or discoloured paint. The following legend shows a vehicle's relative degree of overall reliability; the numbers lighten as the rating becomes more positive.

1	**2**	**3**	**4**	**5**
Unacceptable	Below Average	Average	Above Average	Excellent

Crashworthiness

Some of the main factors weighed in the safety ratings are a model's crashworthiness, its front and rear visibility, and the availability of safety features such as seat belt pretensioners, depowered airbags, airbag disablers, adjustable brake and accelerator pedals, integrated child safety seats, effective head restraints, and assisted stability and traction control.

VALUE OF OPTIONS BY MODEL YEAR

OPTION	1999	2000	2001	2002	2003	2004	2005	2006	2007
Air conditioning	$200	$300	$300	$400	$500	$600	$700	$800	$950
AM/FM radio & CD player	100	100	100	150	175	200	300	500	600
Anti-lock brakes	0	50	100	125	150	175	300	300	400
Automatic transmission	150	200	250	275	300	400	500	700	800
Cruise control	0	50	50	75	100	125	225	300	350
Electric six-way seat	0	50	100	125	150	175	200	400	450
Leather upholstery	50	100	200	225	325	400	500	800	900
Level control (suspension)	0	50	75	100	125	150	250	350	450
Paint protector	50	50	50	50	50	50	50	50	50
Power antenna	0	0	0	0	0	75	75	75	75
Power door locks	0	50	100	125	150	175	200	250	250
Power windows	0	50	100	125	150	175	225	250	250
Rustproofing	0	0	0	0	25	25	50	50	50
Stability control	0	50	100	125	150	175	225	275	300
Sunroof	0	50	50	75	125	150	300	500	500
T-top roof	150	200	300	400	500	700	800	1,000	1,000
Tilt steering	0	50	50	75	75	100	175	250	200
Tinted windows	0	0	0	0	25	50	50	50	50
Tires (Firestone)	–100	–100	–100	–100	–100	–150	–150	–150	–150
Traction control	50	100	125	150	175	275	400	500	500
Wire wheels/locks	50	75	100	125	150	175	275	300	350

Front and side crash protection figures are taken from NHTSA's New Car Assessment Program. For the front crash test, vehicles are crashed into a fixed barrier, head-on, at 57 km/h (35 mph). NHTSA uses star rankings to show the likelihood, expressed as a percentage, of the belted occupants being seriously injured—the higher the number, the greater the protection.

NHTSA's side crash test represents an inter-section-type collision with a 1,368 kg (3,015 lb.) barrier moving at 62 km/h (38.5 mph) into a standing vehicle. The moving barrier is covered with material that has give in order to replicate the front of a car.

NHTSA COLLISION RATINGS: CHANCE OF SERIOUS INJURY

	FRONT	SIDE
5	10% or less	5% or less
4	11% to 20%	6% to 10%
3	21% to 35%	11% to 20%
2	36% to 45%	21% to 25%
1	46% or greater	26% or greater

Note: Two numbers indicate either driver or passenger injury risk (D/P) or front/rear occupant injury risk (F/R).

The Insurance Institute for Highway Safety (IIHS) rates vehicles' frontal offset, side, and head-restraint/rear crash protection as "Good," "Acceptable," "Marginal," or "Poor." Head restraints may be rated for both front- and rear-seat occupants.

In the Institute's 64 km/h (40 mph) frontal offset test, 40 percent of the total width of each vehicle strikes a barrier on the driver's side. The barrier's deformable face is made of aluminum honeycomb, which makes the forces in the test similar to those involved in a frontal offset crash between two vehicles of the same weight, each going just less than 64 km/h.

IIHS's 50 km/h (31 mph) side-impact test is carried out at a slower speed than NHTSA's test; however, the barrier uses a front end that is shaped to simulate the typical front end of a pickup or SUV, which is deemed to give truer results. The Institute also includes the degree of frontal-impact head injury in its ratings.

While many automakers are making improvements, a few are going in the wrong direction. Seat/head restraints in recent Chrysler 300, Kia Amanti, and Nissan Altima tests have earned Marginal ratings, compared with Acceptable ratings for their earlier designs, which were tested in 2004. Furthermore, a disappointingly large number of other models have been rated Poor. They include the Acura TSX, BMW 5 Series, Buick LaCrosse (Allure in Canada) and Lucerne, Cadillac CTS and DTS, Chevrolet Aveo, Honda Accord and Fit, Hyundai Accent, Infiniti M35, Jaguar X-Type, Kia Rio, Mitsubishi Galant, Pontiac Grand Prix, Toyota Avalon and Corolla, and Suzuki Forenza and Reno.

Rollovers

A vehicle's rollover resistance rating is an estimate of its risk of rolling over in a single-vehicle crash, not a prediction of the likelihood of a crash. The lowest-rated vehicles (one star) are at least four times more likely to roll over than the highest-rated vehicles (five stars) when involved in a single-vehicle crash.

Safest Used Cars

Just as with quality, purchase price is no indication of how well a car will protect occupants in a collision. To be included in the list that follows, a vehicle must be fairly cheap, have two frontal crash test ratings and two side crash test ratings, and have earned four- and five-star ratings across the board. In addition, any vehicle meeting our pricing criteria and having five-star ratings across the board, as well as vehicles with three five-star ratings and one four-star rating, were also guaranteed a spot on the list.

Ford—Escape, Mustang
Honda—Accord, Civic, Element
Hyundai—Accent, Elantra
Mazda—Mazda3, Tribute

Mitsubishi—Galant
Nissan—Frontier, Sentra
Suzuki—Aerio
Toyota—Corolla, Echo

"Fender-Bender" Wallet Busters

Crashworthiness is usually defined as how well occupants are protected in different kinds of accidents at various speeds. However, it can also describe the measure of damage sustained by a vehicle in low-speed "fender-bender" collisions. In the IIHS fender-bender chart below, note how the 1981 Ford Escort sustained only $469 in damages, while the 2007 Nissan Maxima required $9,051 in repairs.

BUMPER PERFORMANCE IN LOW-SPEED CRASH TESTS: VEHICLE REPAIR COSTS

	FRONT FULL	FRONT CORNER	REAR FULL	REAR CORNER	TOTAL DAMAGE
Mitsubishi Galant	$2,929	$1,138	$1,048	$1,162	$4,277
Toyota Camry	$ 936	$1,467	$1,480	$1,028	$4,911
Mazda6	$ 978	$1,384	$1,202	$1,397	$4,961
Ford Fusion	$1,620	$ 991	$1,298	$1,121	$5,030
Volvo S40	$2,252	$1,306	$ 802	$1,240	$5,600
Kia Optima	$1,730	$1,534	$1,715	$ 756	$5,735
Saturn Aura	$1,032	$1,152	$3,191	$ 999	$6,374
Nissan Altima	$ 945	$ 969	$3,114	$1,431	$6,459
Chevrolet Malibu	$1,268	$1,610	$2,542	$1,226	$6,646
Subaru Legacy	$3,911	$1,287	$1,122	$1,128	$7,448
Chrysler Sebring	$1,084	$2,061	$3,210	$1,099	$7,454
Hyundai Sonata	$4,312	$1,349	$ 739	$1,165	$7,565
Honda Accord	$3,469	$1,169	$2,767	$ 605	$8,010
Volkswagen Passat	$4,594	$1,544	$ 982	$1,139	$8,259
Pontiac G6	$4,588	$1,183	$1,638	$1,510	$8,919
Volkswagen Jetta	$2,598	$1,223	$3,375	$1,824	$9,020
Nissan Maxima	$4,535	$1,732	$1,787	$ 997	$9,051
1981 Ford Escort	$ 86	$ 0	$ 383	$ 0	$ 469

Note: Sonata repair costs reflect reduced parts pricing, effective January 2007.

Source: IIHS Status Report. Vol. 42, No. 2. March 1, 2007.

Remember, these vehicles were crashed at only 5–10 km/h (3–6 mph)—a brisk walk or run.

SMALL CARS

Electric Car Reality Check

When you are out in the middle of nowhere with an electric vehicle, and you have no back-up powerplant, you are truly, truly screwed. You can't go to the nearest wall outlet and bring back five gallons of electricity.

WWW.AUTOBLOGGREEN.COM

Chevy's 2010 Volt electric vehicle: 70 km and then no juice.

It's a no-brainer that your first line of defence against ever-changing high fuel prices isn't buying a Toyota Prius, a Honda Insight hybrid, or GM's $40,000 2010 Volt electric car. What you want instead is a cheap, small, crashworthy, reliable, and easy-to-repair used car. And, in the bargain, you'll be following the "reduce, reuse, and recycle" environmentalist creed.

Indeed, fuel-frugal 4-cylinder compact cars are primarily for city dwellers who want good fuel economy in the city/highway range of 9.3/5.9 L/100 km (30/48 mpg), easy manoeuvrability in urban areas, a relatively low retail price, and modest depreciation. In exchange, owners must accept a cramped interior that may carry only two passengers in comfort, an engine that can take eons to merge with traffic or pass other cars, and insufficient luggage capacity (hatchbacks, however, make the best use of what room there is). As well, engine and road noise are fairly excessive.

In response to these shortcomings, many cars in this class, such as the Honda Civic and Toyota Echo, have been replaced during the past decade by much larger iterations that rival the size of Honda's early Accord and Toyota's Camry. This upsizing makes room for new "micro" small cars introduced in 2007, like the Honda Fit, Hyundai Accent, and Nissan Versa, which vary in size between Mercedes-Benz's Smart Car and BMW's Mini Cooper.

Safety is a mixed bag, however.

One of the more alarming characteristics of a small car's highway performance is its extreme vulnerability to strong lateral winds, which may make the car difficult to keep on course. On the other hand, crashworthiness is not necessarily compromised by a small size. In fact, evidence suggests that lighter-weight vehicles can be made to be as safe as heavier ones.

In the October 17, 2005, edition of *Automotive News*, Robert Hall, professor emeritus of operations management at Indiana University, said the following:

> In the last 40 years, auto-racing speeds have increased, yet deaths have decreased significantly while the weights of the vehicles have gone down progressively. Why? Crushable fronts that absorb impact, "tubs" that shelter drivers after the entire car has disintegrated, a relocation of the front axle and, yes, crash bags. In this case, lighter is markedly safer.

Granted, the small size of some small, mass-produced vehicles may compromise their crash safety, but not necessarily. Many newer small cars incorporate a body structure that deflects crash forces away from occupants, making these cars more crashworthy than some larger vehicles. The Smart Car is a good example: It offers acceptable, though not impressive, crashworthiness through a well-designed restraint system and the use of a stiff chassis design that minimizes intrusion.

The Smart Car sandwiches its powerplant under the floor—raising the passenger compartment above the impact area in a collision with another passenger car. The powertrain is mounted on a sliding rack to diminish the force of a collision (see *Popular Science*, January 1998, page 82).

"Bargain" Prices

During the past several years, automakers have added features to their small cars that have subsequently driven down the prices of less-refined models. Recent examples of this trend are General Motor's Cavalier and Sunfire, two recent "orphans" that were replaced by the 2005 Cobalt and Pursuit, a European Opel variant; and the Dodge Neon, dropped in favour of the 2007 Caliber. In both cases, the older cars are fairly reliable and can be picked up at fire-sale prices. Furthermore, Ottawa's $2,000 rebates to owners of new fuel-efficient small cars will also spill over into the used market and keep prices low as sellers of used cars compete with lower-priced new offerings.

SMALL CAR RATINGS

Recommended

Honda Civic (1999–2007)
Honda Fit (2007)
Hyundai Elantra (2001–07)
Mazda3 (2006–07)
Nissan Versa (2007)

Suzuki Aerio (2003–07)
Suzuki Swift, Swift+ (2002–07)
Suzuki SX4 (2007)
Toyota Echo (2000–05)

Above Average

Hyundai Accent (2006–07)
Hyundai Elantra (1999–2000)
Mazda3 (2004–05)
Mazda5 (2006–07)
Mazda Protegé (1999–2003)

Nissan Sentra (2007)
Subaru Forester (2003–07)
Suzuki Esteem (1999–2002)
Suzuki Swift, Swift+ (1999–2001)
Toyota Yaris (2006–07)

Average

BMW MINI Cooper (2007)
Chrysler Caliber front-drive (2007)
Chrysler Neon, SX 2.0, SRT4
   (2003–06)
Daewoo/General Motors Aveo, Aveo5,
   Wave (2006–07)
Daewoo/General Motors Optra, Optra5
   (2006–07)
Ford Focus (2005–07)
General Motors Cavalier,
   Sunfire (2003–05)
Hyundai Accent (2004–05; 1999–2000)

Kia Rio, Rio5, Spectra, Spectra5
   (2006–07)
Nissan Sentra (2001–06)
Subaru Forester (1999–2002)
Subaru Impreza (1999–2007)
Subaru Legacy, Outback (1999–2007)
Subaru WRX (2007)
Suzuki Verona (2004–06)
Toyota Corolla (1999–2007)
Toyota/General Motors Matrix/Vibe (2003–07)
Volkswagen diesel models (2005–07)
Volkswagen Golf, Jetta, Cabrio, Eos (2007)

Below Average

BMW MINI Cooper (2002–06)
Chrysler Caliber AWD (2007)
Chrysler Neon (2000–02)
Daewoo/General Motors Aveo, Aveo5,
   Wave (2004–05)
Daewoo/General Motors Optra, Optra5
   (2004–05)
Ford Escort, ZX2 (1999–2000)

General Motors Cavalier, Sunfire (1999–2002)
General Motors ION (2003–07)
General Motors L-Series (2000–05)
General Motors S-Series (1999–2002)
Hyundai Accent (2001–03)
Subaru WRX (2002–06)
Volkswagen diesel models (1999–2004)
Volkswagen Golf, Jetta, Cabrio (1999–2006)

Not Recommended

Chrysler Neon (1999)
Daewoo Lanos, Nubira, Leganza
   (2000–02)
Ford Focus (2000–04)
Honda Civic Hybrid (2003–07)
Honda Insight (2001–06)

Kia Rio, Rio5, Spectra/Sephia, Spectra5
   (2000–05)
Mercedes-Benz Smart Fortwo (2005–07)
Nissan Sentra (1999–2000)

BMW

MINI COOPER ★★★

RATING: Average (2007); Below Average (2002–06). This car will burn you in more ways than one (see "Safety Summary"). With the MINI, you choose performance and "cuteness" over reasonable reliability and cheap, convenient servicing. **"Real" city/highway fuel economy:** *Manual 5-speed: 9.0/6.2 L/100 km. Manual 6-speed: 7.3/5.4 L/100 km. Automatic 6-speed: 7.8/5.9 L/100 km.* **Maintenance/ Repair costs:** Outrageously higher than average (power-steering pump and clutch cost $2,000 and $3,000 each to repair/replace). **Parts:** Expensive and sometimes rare. **Extended warranty:** A good idea. **Best alternatives:** Ford Mustang, Honda Civic Si, Mazda3, and Saturn Sky. Also try the Honda Civic; Hyundai Accent or Elantra; Mazda Protegé; Nissan Sentra; Suzuki Aerio, Esteem, or Swift; and Toyota Corolla, Echo, or Yaris.

Strengths and Weaknesses

The BMW MINI Cooper came to Canada as a 2002 model. It is larger than the classic MINI and weighs almost twice as much: 1,050 kg (2,315 lb.) versus 650 kg (1,433 lb.). The 2007 hatchback was redesigned and given more power and slightly larger dimensions. The convertible's 2002–06 design was carried over unchanged.

Base hatchbacks come with a 118 hp 4-cylinder engine, while S versions are equipped with a turbocharged 172 hp variant. Convertibles feature a standard 115 hp 4-banger, while the S sports a 168 hp version of the same powerplant. A 6-speed manual is standard on most models, but the 2007 adds a 6-speed automatic that replaces the previous year's continuously variable transmission (CVT). 2007 hatchbacks come with front side airbags and side curtain airbags; convertibles are equipped with front side airbags with head and torso protection.

This is a typical, fun-to-drive, small European car that doesn't sacrifice power and handling for fuel economy. Handling is a breeze: The car performs responsibly in all speed ranges with precise steering, minimal body lean, and hardly any front-end noseplow. The 2007 redesign smoothed out the car's choppy ride but made the audio and climate controls more confusing than ever. The ride is a bit harsh, road and engine noise are omnipresent, body glitches are common, and rear interior room and comfort are sadly lacking.

Here is where I disagree with *Consumer Reports'* rating of this car as having above average reliability. It does not. Owner complaints and internal service bulletins point to major performance and safety deficiencies that are obviously factory-related. 2002–07 models are plagued by chronic stalling on the highway, CVT automatic transmission breakdowns, power-steering failures, automatic window electrical shorts, prematurely worn side struts and brake calipers and rotors, constantly cracking windshields, and poor fit and finish and body design (for example, the hood scoop deforms due to heat from the turbo)—as well as expensive servicing and long waits for parts.

 ## Safety Summary

2002—Fire ignited under the dashboard. • Airbag failed to deploy. • Frequent power-steering failures. • Automatic window failures. • Many early automatic transmission, clutch, and cable replacements:

> The automatic transmission of my 2002 MINI Cooper failed while my friend was driving my car. She was on a winding coastal road and the car died on a blind curve, putting her at great danger. Fortunately nobody was hurt. The car was towed to the San Francisco BMW dealership, where I was informed I needed a $8,500 "refurbished" transmission, as the transmission is not even made anymore. Research on line shows that this [is] becoming a frequent problem with "first generation" MINIs with the "CVT" automatic transmission.

2003—CVT transmission and steering failures continue. • Power-steering pump caught fire; in other reported incidents, it simply stops working. • Electrical shorts cause inside lights and gauges to operate erratically. • Power windows open on their own. **2004**—Vent fan in motor caught fire. • More transmission trouble. • Power steering fails:

www.mini2.com has reports of around 1 in 4 vehicles having this pump fail prematurely. I believe an investigation is important due to member reports of fires starting under the hood.

• Manual transmission failure. • Power window doesn't roll down. • Windshield is easily cracked:

> While driving normally a very very small pebble size stone hits underneath the windshield wiper on the passenger's side. The windshield [immediately] spiders all over the window. I've been told all the problems with the BMW windshields were corrected, but I've heard from over 20 fellow MINI owners of random cracking and failures within the first 2,000 miles [3,200 km]!!!

• Brake failure. • Hard to find horn button's "sweet spot." **2005**—Power-steering pump, transmission, clutch, and strut failures continue unabated:

> Complete catastrophic failure of the front passenger strut, strut tower, mount and lower control arm bushing caused by an imperfection on a public, well traveled road. Reports on enthusiast forums of over 216 others suffering the same failure on the same model car and a report in the Sept–Oct 2007 edition of *MC²* magazine citing the need to look for these common flaws on this model car when considering purchasing a used one.

• Car continually loses power when cruising; owner is told the problem is a loose gas cap, but it isn't. • Windshield spontaneously cracks. • Sudden stalling ("limp home" mode) on the highway; DME component needs to be reprogrammed. • Front wheel rubbing noises when turning hard left or hard right. • Lost three out of four lug nuts on the front driver-side wheel. **2006**—Vehicle suddenly stalls on the highway. • Both strut mounts failed. • ABS and DSC systems don't work properly. • Speedometer registers 7 percent faster than the actual speed; odometer registers 1 percent more than the actual mileage. • Passenger-side seatback won't lock in the upright position. • "Mushrooming" struts:

> "Mushrooming" is when the car gets a hard hit and the strut tower pushes up the metal where it is attached to [create] a bubble and damage the alignment. How can the strut tower [make] this damage without damaging the rim first?

• Stalling and then sudden acceleration. • Engine seized after driving through a rain puddle. • Clutch slips at low mileage. • Windshield cracked (stress fracture) while car was parked overnight; many other complaints of cracks, while BMW denies all liability. • Car suddenly veered out of control on the highway when brakes were applied. BMW experts say it was due to brake rotor "unexpected separation." Again, BMW denies all liability. • Plastic fuel tank is easily punctured by road debris. • Tailpipe sticks too far out; driver burned leg when unloading baggage. **2006–07**—Passenger-side airbag disabled when average-sized adult is seated. **2007**—Tailpipe burned leg as driver unloaded packages from the rear; a common hazard with the MINI:

The tailpipes, when hot, apparently protrude enough to cause severe burns to the leg. My 7 year old daughter sustained a serious burn this way when getting something out of the hatchback.

•

After a 30 minute drive, I parked and then pulled something out of the trunk. While reaching in, I burned my left shin on the tailpipe. I showed it a couple of days later to our burn unit director and he told me that it was a functional full thickness burn in an extremely dangerous location (because of the poor blood perfusion to the shin, healing is impaired and infection risk is high). He sent me home from work on antibiotics and I had to be on bed rest with my leg elevated. I spoke to MINI and they suggested that I be careful—as the tailpipe can get hot. I thanked them for the advice and made the following point: Sure, it gets hot.... It's an exhaust tailpipe. However,...it's in the center of a car that requires you to get close in order to pull something out of the trunk. I suggested that BMW issue a recall and adjust the tailpipe so that the first thing the leg hits is the bumper (like most cars). I was told that no change was planned at this time.... It is a very common problem (a simple Google search or [*www. northamericanmotoring.com*] search will show this).

• Engine revs poorly in cold weather. • Ongoing problems with transmission and fuel-pump failures and with windshield stress fractures. • Hood scoop deforms due to extreme heat. • Excessive heat in driver's footwell near the centre pillar. • Dunlop run-flat radial tubeless tires have side wall bubbling.

Secret Warranties/Internal Bulletins/Service Tips

2007—No-crank, no-start. • Free crankcase breather retrofit and engine-cooling-fan fuse replacement. • Cruise control cuts out at 110 km/h. • Automatic transmission fluid leak. • Various drivability complaints. • Crackling noise from tweeters. • An inoperative navigation system may require the replacement of the HIP module under warranty. • Diagnosing and repairing various electrical malfunctions. • Inoperative electric steering lock. • Steering rattles. • Front-end clunking when passing over bumps. • Rear axle knocking. • Water leaks onto the front carpet. • Tailgate hard to open or close. • Fuel gauge brightness fluctuations. • Speedometer buzzes and sunroof squeaks. • Sunroof sunshade opens on its own; sunroof wind noise. • Instrument panel rattle. • Windshield whistling noise.

MINI COOPER PROFILE

	2002	2003	2004	2005	2006	2007
Cost Price ($)						
Cooper	25,200	25,200	22,700	23,500	23,500	23,950
S	29,950	29,950	29,950	30,500	30,600	30,600
Convertible	29,950	29,950	29,950	30,500	30,600	30,600
Used Values ($)						
Cooper ▲	7,500	8,500	9,500	13,000	15,000	17,000
Cooper ▼	6,500	8,000	8,500	12,500	14,500	15,500

S ▲	9,000	11,500	13,000	15,500	19,000	22,000
S ▼	8,000	10,500	12,000	14,500	17,500	20,500
Convertible ▲	—	—	—	17,000	21,000	24,500
Convertible ▼	—	—	—	16,500	20,000	23,000
Reliability	2	2	2	2	3	4
Crash Safety (F)	4	4	4	4	4	—
Side	4	4	4	4	4	—
IIHS Side	—	—	—	—	3	—
Offset	2	2	2	2	2	2
Head Restraints (F)	2	2	2	2	2	3
Rollover Resistance	4	4	4	4	4	—

Chrysler

CALIBER ★★★ / ★★

RATING: *Caliber front-drive:* Average (2007). *Caliber AWD:* Below Average (2007). A quality-challenged underpowered fuel hog that runs in the back of the pack. **"Real" city/highway fuel economy:** Very poor; in the 14.0/15.0 L/100 km range. **Maintenance/Repair costs:** Likely to be higher than average once the warranty expires. Far more serious will be the effects of a possible Chrysler bankruptcy. **Parts:** Easily found and relatively inexpensive. **Extended warranty:** A good idea in case Chrysler leaves you high and dry. **Best alternatives:** The GM Firefly, Metro, Cavalier, or Sunfire (2000 or later); Honda Civic; Hyundai Accent; Mazda Protegé; Suzuki Esteem; and Toyota Corolla, Echo, Tercel, or Yaris.

Strengths and Weaknesses

This small four-door hatchback provides a good view of the road, thanks to its SUV-like raised seats. The ride is acceptable; however, handling is poor, and the noisy 1.8L and 2.4L engines (148 and 172 hp, respectively) lack low-end power for merging with traffic—which would be acceptable if there was a trade-off for good fuel economy, but there isn't. Gas consumption (regular or premium) is quite high for a car this small. Many powertrain and fit and finish problems have been reported in these first-generation models. A more-powerful 280 hp SRT4 has just been launched, but it promises to be troublesome due to first-year factory-related glitches.

Reliability has never been Chrysler's strong suit, and this relatively new vehicle duplicates many of the quality and performance failures of earlier models. Interestingly, the AWD version is much less reliable than the front-drive versions. Nevertheless, expect numerous powertrain defects, like chronic stalling followed by sudden lurching; 4-cylinder engine, tie-rod end, and automatic transmission module failures; an unreliable automatic transmission; poor-quality suspension struts (four replacements in one year); and excessive vibration caused by a defective idler pulley. The air conditioning system is failure-prone and costly to repair. Brake and electrical problems abound. Interior noise is omnipresent, and includes engine rattles, window-crank and door-hinge squeaks, radio-speaker and fender rattles (the fender may be missing a bolt), and windshield snapping. Poor body fits allow for wind and water to enter the car practically everywhere. Paint easily peels off at the car wash, and windshield cracks at the windshield wiper mounting are common.

Crashworthiness is fairly good. NHTSA awarded the 2007 Caliber five stars for front- and side-impact occupant protection and four stars for rollover resistance. IIHS, however, concluded that the Caliber gives only Acceptable side crash protection, although it rated frontal protection as Above Average.

Caliber prices remain competitive due to the large number of unsold new units piling up in dealer inventories. A 2007 base SE will cost $9,000–$10,500, the RT front-drive is valued at $12,000–$13,000, and the RT AWD will cost $14,000–$15,000.

 ## Safety Summary

2007—Airbag failed to deploy. • Constant stalling. • There's an off-idle hesitation when pulling away from a traffic stop. • Tailpipe is cut too short; allows fumes to enter the cabin. • Firestone tire-tread separation; 15-inch Dunlop tire defects. • Premature wheel bearing replacement. • AC/heater produces a nauseating smell when activated. • Excessive highway vibration "cured" only by paying $600 for new aluminum wheels. • Gas-pedal bushing fell out, causing engine to surge. • In another case, the assembly fell under the brake pedal, preventing braking. • ABS failure caused an accident. • Cold, rainy weather prevents the power windows from rolling down. • Automatic door locks can lock you out if you exit the vehicle too close the garage door, for example. • Cold, then hot, water drips onto passengers from the heater core:

> Hot water leaking from under the steering wheel. Husband sustained second and third degree burns.... It was determined that the AC condensation drain hose was clogged with debris which caused hot water to get inside the vehicle.

• If a passenger's head is resting near the door lock button when the door is unlocked, the force of the spring could cause injury. • One cannot drive with the rear windows down without hearing a painful, helicopter-like roar.

Secret Warranties/Internal Bulletins/Service Tips

2007—Poor acceleration and engine ticking require the reflashing of the engine PCM computer. • AC compressor noise or housing damage. • Metallic rattle from liftgate. • Squeaking clutch pedal. • Water leaking from headliner. • Windshield crack diagnosis for warranty approval. **2007–08**—Engine won't start with wireless key feature. • Seat creak or squawk. • Whistling sound from the left side mirror. • Horizontal panel paint etching.

NEON, SX 2.0, SRT4 ★★★

RATING: Average (2003–06); Below Average (2000–02); Not Recommended (1999). A low-quality, fuel-thirsty small car that improved a bit during its last three years on the market. 1999 and earlier models eat engine head gaskets for breakfast and wallets for lunch. **"Real" city/highway fuel economy:** Owners report extremely poor fuel economy in the 19.0/18.0 L/100 km range. **Maintenance/ Repair costs:** Higher than average. **Parts:** Easily found and relatively inexpensive. However, Chrysler is particularly slow in distributing parts needed for safety recall campaigns; waits of several months are commonplace. **Extended warranty:** A good idea for the powertrain if the base warranty has expired. **Best alternatives:** The GM Firefly, Metro, Cavalier, or Sunfire (2000 or later); Honda Civic; Hyundai Accent; Mazda Protegé; Suzuki Esteem; and Toyota Corolla, Echo, Tercel, or Yaris.

Strengths and Weaknesses

A small, noisy car with big quality problems in its first-generation models, the Neon does offer a spacious interior and responsive steering and handling. Nevertheless, it's seriously handicapped by an antiquated, feeble, and fuel-thirsty 3-speed automatic gearbox; a DOHC 4-cylinder 150 hp powerplant that has to be pushed hard to do as well as the SOHC 132 hp engine; and a mushy base suspension.

The 2003 Neon was renamed the SX 2.0 in Canada. It is roomy and reasonably powered for urban use, and later refinements gave it a softer, quieter ride while enhancing the car's handling and powertrain performance.

Chrysler has tried to make its low-end cars more appealing and more profitable by adding high-performance features that quickly lose their value as the vehicle ages. For example, the $26,950 2004 SRT4, equipped with a turbocharged 215 hp 2.4L 4-cylinder engine hooked to a manual 4-speed transmission, now sells for $9,000.

Reliability has always bedevilled the Neon. Owners have reported major powertrain defects characterized by 4-cylinder engine head gasket failures and an unreliable automatic transmission that often slams into gear. The AC system is noted for condenser and compressor failures, there's a plethora of electrical problems, interior noise and water leaks are everywhere, wheels quickly corrode, and the uneven fit and finish is easy to see, along with poor-quality trim items.

2003–06 models continue to have some engine, transmission, and body glitches, but they are less serious than the failures reported on previous models. Engine stalling is a recurrent problem, mostly caused by poorly calibrated computer modules (an 8-year/130,000 km emissions warranty item). Paint delamination continues to afflict these cars:

> I own a 2005 Dodge Neon (Chrysler) and the paint is coming off the car. The dealership says I have to pay for the fix when it is a fact that the vehicle has never been in an accident/collision. How/why would a two year old car lose its paint so fast?

Owners of these newer models also say that when the car is passing through puddles, water is ingested into the engine though the air-intake port (Chrysler will replace the engine when threatened with court action); the automatic transmission shudders when shifting; the AC fails to cool the vehicle adequately; they experience no-starts because of early starter rust-out; there's constant brake squeaking; and the engine noticeably loses power when windows are lowered, the sunroof is opened, or the AC is engaged. They also complain of overall poor fuel economy.

VEHICLE HISTORY: 1999—Depowered airbags. **2000**—A second-generation redesign improves powertrain quality a bit and adds interior room and trunk space. The manual transmission and stereo are upgraded, traction control is offered, and redesigned doors reduce wind noise and water leaks. **2002**—An upgraded automatic transmission (some reliability problems remain, though). **2003**—Neons are renamed SX 2.0 in Canada. New steering wheels, front and rear fascias, and engine mounts to smooth out engine roughness. A taller Fifth gear for the manual transmission. **2004**—High-performance versions get a small 15 hp boost and a limited-slip differential. An optional 4-speed automatic transmission is made available. **2005**—The SRT4 gets a specially tuned sport suspension, improved brakes, and sport seats.

 Safety Summary

All models/years: Fires. • "Inappropriate" airbag deployment, or failure to deploy. • Sudden acceleration. • Chronic stalling. • No-start because of rusted-out starter. • Throttle system failures. • Faulty cruise control. • Steering loss. • Steering locks up when it rains. • Chronic transmission failures and slippage. • Transmission suddenly downshifts to First gear when accelerating at 90 km/h. • ABS brake failures. • Defective brake master cylinder. • Premature front brake pad/rotor wearout. • Excessive vibration. • Small horn buttons are hard to find in an emergency. • Trunk lid or hood may fall. • Headlight switch is a hide-and-go-seek affair. • Axle shafts may suddenly collapse. **All models: 1995–99**—Chronic engine head gasket failures. • Engine camshaft seal leaks oil • Engine motor mount failures. **1995–2000**—NHTSA probe of seat belt latch. **1999**—Vehicle suddenly jumps out of gear. **2000**—Almost 400 safety complaints indicate that the 2000 model-year refinements haven't improved overall reliability or safety. Main problem areas: automatic transmission, power steering, tire, and brake failures; engine fires; premature brake rotor and pad wear; seat belts failing to retract; and an inoperative horn. • Snapping noises from the front suspension may be caused by loose front crossmember mounting bolts. • An upgraded right-side motor mount may reduce steering-wheel or chassis shaking. **2001**—Electrical shorts (lights and gauges), engine damage caused by water ingested through the air-intake system, and an annoying reflection in the front windshield. **2002**—Stalling because of water ingestion into engine when it rains. • Transmission slips between First and Second gear. • Vehicle pulls when cruising or on acceleration, and tends to wobble side to side at low speeds. • Excessive steering-wheel vibration makes it hard to maintain control. **2003**—Engine manifold failure. • Poor braking. **2004**—Seat belts failed to lock during a collision. • Unoccupied passenger seat flew off its track during a collision. • Electrical system suddenly shuts down. • Rusted, prematurely worn brake rotors. **2005**—Radio caught on fire. • Hard starting, followed by engine surging. • Manual transmission self-destructed. • CV joint failure. • Brake pedal goes to the floor without effect. • Faulty multifunction switch causes the battery to fail and fog lights to flicker. • Motor mounts often fail.

Secret Warranties/Internal Bulletins/Service Tips

All models/years: Paint delamination, peeling, or fading. • Tips on getting rid of an AC musty smell. **All models: 1998–2000**—Low-mileage AC lock-up. **2000**—Delayed automatic transmission engagement, likely caused by a faulty front pump. • Harsh AC engagement and clunk noise. • Front-door water leaks. • Rear-door glass won't roll down all the way. • High window-cranking effort or slow power-window operation. • Blower motor noise or vibration. • Deck-lid rattle, and water/dust intrusion past the deck-lid seal. • Difficulty moving front seats forward. • Water enters the horn assembly. **2000–01**—Poor performance of AC and engine. • Remedy for AC honking. • Rattling wheel covers. **2000–05**—Headlight water condensation. • TSB #M19-07-05 admits that a clicking noise heard when turning may be due to a misaligned or defective steering column. A similar clicking may emanate from the drivetrain. **2001**—Engine hesitation. • No-start problem in cold weather. • Rear window may not go all the way down. **2002**—Poor engine and AC performance caused by miscalibrated or faulty computer modules. **2002–03**—Delayed shifts may require the installation of a new automatic transmission front pump assembly:

A/T—DELAYED GEAR ENGAGEMENT/POSSIBLE DTCS

BULLETIN NO.: 21-004-05   DATE: JANUARY 22, 2005

OVERVIEW: This bulletin involves replacing the front pump assembly in the transmission and checking the Transmission Control Module (TCM) for the latest software revision level.
2004 Pacifica; 2002–04 Sebring/Stratus; 2003 Liberty; 2002–04 300M/Concorde/Intrepid; 2002–03 Neon; 2002–03 PT Cruiser; 2002–03 Town & Country/Caravan/Voyager; 2003 Wrangler
SYMPTOM/CONDITION: A delayed or temporary loss of transmission engagement after initial start up. The condition follows an extended soak (several hours) and may be accompanied by a harsh 4–3 downshift.

2003—Water leaks onto the right front-seat floor. • Hard starting requires the reflashing of the PCM. **2003–04**—TSB #09-007-04 says an engine snapping sound is Chrysler's fault and can be remedied by chamfering the bore radius on cam bearing caps through L5 and R2 through R5. • Misaligned exhaust tips. **2004**—Hard starts, acceleration stumble. • Intermittent loss of audio. • Poor idle. **2005**—Rough, shuddering 1–2 upshifts. • Engine runs poorly.

NEON, SX 2.0, SRT4 PROFILE

	1999	2000	2001	2002	2003	2004	2005
Cost Price ($)							
Base	15,215	17,995	18,375	18,505	—	—	—
Sport/SX 2.0	—	—	—	—	14,995	15,195	15,605
SRT4	—	—	—	—	—	26,950	27,380
Used Values ($)							
Base ▲	2,500	3,000	3,500	5,500	—	—	—
Base ▼	2,000	2,500	3,000	4,000	—	—	—
Sport/SX 2.0 ▲	—	—	—	—	3,500	4,500	5,500
Sport/SX 2.0 ▼	—	—	—	—	2,500	3,000	4,500
SRT4 ▲	—	—	—	—	—	10,000	12,000
SRT4 ▼	—	—	—	—	—	9,000	11,000
Reliability	1	1	2	2	3	3	3
Crash Safety (F)	3	—	4	4	4	4	4
Side	2	—	3	3	3	3	3
IIHS Side	—	1	1	1	1	1	1
Offset	1	2	2	2	2	2	2
Head Restraints (F)	2	1	1	1	1	1	1
Rollover Resistance	—	—	4	4	4	4	4

Daewoo

Not Recommended

South Korean automaker Daewoo marketed three cars in Canada from 2000 to 2002: the Lanos subcompact, the Nubira compact sedan and wagon, and the Leganza luxury sedan. All of these cars are rated Not Recommended because Daewoo sold its car division to GM and neither company will service these models, let alone respect their original warranties. By the way, Daewoo depreciation is mind-boggling: An entry-level, $13,395 2002 Lanos is now barely worth $1,200, and the top-of-the-line 2002 Leganza CDX that originally sold for $25,495 now sells for about $2,500.

Daewoo/General Motors

Daewoo skipped the 2003 model year in Canada and brought out three models under the GM banner as 2004 models. Chevrolet dealers sell the entry-level Aveo (a Lanos spin-off); the Optra, a compact based on the Daewoo Lacetti; and the Epica, a mid-sized vehicle based on Daewoo's Magnos. Suzuki sells the subcompact Swift+, based on the Kalos, and the Verona for GM.

AVEO, AVEO5, LANOS, WAVE ★★★

RATING: Average (2006–07); Below Average (2004–05). An economical small car that has improved marginally since General Motors bought Daewoo. Best used as a bare-bones urban runabout. Although the Pontiac Wave is identical to Chevy's Aveo and Suzuki's Swift+, it isn't sold in the U.S. Aveo5 is a similarly priced four-door hatchback base model. **"Real" city/highway fuel economy:** 8.8/6.1 L/100 km. Owners report fuel savings may undershoot this estimate by about 10 percent. **Maintenance/Repair costs:** Average. **Parts:** Easily found and relatively inexpensive. **Extended warranty:** Not needed, judging by the handful of complaints registered with NHTSA. **Best alternatives:** The Dodge Neon (post-'99); GM Firefly, Metro, Cavalier, or Sunfire (2000 or later); Honda Civic; Hyundai Accent; Mazda3 or Mazda Protegé; Suzuki Aerio, Esteem, or Swift+; and Toyota Corolla, Echo, Tercel, or Yaris.

Strengths and Weaknesses

First launched by Daewoo as the Lanos, this nondescript, cheaply made small South Korean car had practically no redeeming values, much like Kia's pre-2005 models. After a year's absence (2003), the car returned under GM's aegis as the Chevrolet Aveo and Pontiac Wave. Although they are nicely restyled and use better-quality components, both cars carry an underpowered 103 hp 1.6L 4-cylinder engine mated with a 5-speed manual or a 4-speed automatic. Overall, the powertrain and performance lack the refinement found with many other bantamweights anchoring the compact-car division. The engine is particularly noisy and strains going uphill with its maximum four-passenger load. Four *small* passengers. Around town, though, the car is peppy and nimble.

The 2004 Aveo's $3,000 price tag is very reasonable for a four-door that originally sold for $13,595. It saves buyers a couple of thousand over a $5,000 four-door Toyota Echo that's comparatively priced new but depreciates more slowly. Don't fret, however, if you pay a few thousand dollars extra for a better-performing and more reliable Honda, Mazda, or Toyota—the difference means nothing when spread out over a number of years, and it will likely be refunded through a higher resale price.

Lanos owners complain of an unending series of powertrain failures, serious fit and finish deficiencies, and electrical short circuits. These problems have moderated with the 2004 and later versions built under General Motors' supervision. Most Aveo glitches concern the automatic transmission shifting erratically, continuing electrical system shorts, infrequent stalling, brake malfunctions, excessive suspension noise, and premature tire wear. Fit and finish is about average, although owners report the occasional water leak and a plethora of squeaks, grunts, and rattles.

VEHICLE HISTORY: 2001—The SE hatchback and SX four-door sedan are dropped. A gussied-up sport hatchback is launched, and power steering is offered as an option on the entry-level S model. **2002**—Daewoo goes bankrupt. After Ford dithers for almost a year, GM buys Daewoo's assets and dumps the dealers, who finally get a few crumbs in an out-of-court settlement. **2003**—Skips a model year. **2004**—Aveo launches in early 2004 with a slightly longer sedan, the same puny engine, optional ABS, and no side airbags. **2006**—Standard front side airbags and larger optional wheels. Many GM-imposed quality improvements mirror Hyundai's successful efforts to address similar Kia deficiencies during that fateful 2005 model year.

 **Safety Summary**

All models: 2004—Stalling. • Brake failures. • Premature brake pad/rotor wearout. **2004–05**—Transmission won't go into Reverse. • Excessive on-road vibration felt in the front end and steering. • Early wiper replacement. **2005**—Sudden acceleration. • Airbags fail to deploy:

> The driver stated that in a front end collision the airbags did not deploy. Vehicle was travelling about 50 mph [80 km/h] and went under a truck. Most of the impact was to the hood, rooftop, and windshield. The steering wheel was completely damaged. There was no substantial damage to the bumper. The driver sustained the following injuries: the nose was fractured, left eyeball went out of orbit, and the cheekbone was crushed. The manufacturer stated all three sensors have to be hit simultaneously for the airbags to deploy.

• Repeated brake failure when car is put into Reverse. • Accelerator and brake pedal are mounted too close to each other. • Poor-quality windshield wipers. • Sudden acceleration; no brakes. • Transmission sticks in Park. • Clutch overheats and fails. • Snapped side shock bolt. • Plastic thermostat splits, allowing engine to overheat. • Windshield cracking. • Door lock falls into the door's interior. **2006**—Passenger-side airbag is disabled by an average-sized seated adult. • Sudden automatic transmission failures. • Chronic stalling in cold weather. • Early coil spring replacement. **2007**—More windshield cracks after chipping at the base. • A voltage spike burns out the headlights. • Automatic door locks won't open from the inside. • Tires provide poor traction.

Secret Warranties/Internal Bulletins/Service Tips

All models: 2004—Engine runs poorly when first started. **2004–06**—Can't shift out of Park or remove ignition key. **2004–07**—Engine front-end oil leaks. • Suspension squawk, rubbing noise on bumps.

AVEO, AVEO5, LANOS, WAVE PROFILE

	2000	2001	2002	2004	2005	2006	2007
Cost Price ($)							
Aveo	—	—	—	13,480	13,595	11,995	12,995
Aveo5	—	—	—	13,820	14,785	12,195	12,995
Lanos	12,750	12,900	13,395	—	—	—	—
Wave	—	—	—	—	13,595	11,795	12,950
Wave5	—	—	—	—	13,935	11,995	12,951
Used Values ($)							
Aveo ▲	—	—	—	3,000	4,000	5,500	6,500
Aveo ▼	—	—	—	2,500	3,500	5,000	6,000
Aveo5 ▲	—	—	—	3,000	4,000	5,500	6,500
Aveo5 ▼	—	—	—	2,500	3,500	5,000	6,000
Lanos ▲	800	900	1,000	—	—	—	—
Lanos ▼	750	850	950	—	—	—	—
Wave ▲	—	—	—	—	3,500	4,500	6,000
Wave ▼	—	—	—	—	3,000	4,000	5,500
Wave5 ▲	—	—	—	—	3,500	4,500	6,000
Wave5 ▼	—	—	—	—	3,000	4,000	5,500
Reliability	1	1	1	3	3	4	4
Crash Safety (F)	—	—	—	5	5	5	5
Side	—	—	—	3	3	4	4
IIHS Side	—	—	—	—	—	—	2
Offset	—	—	—	—	—	—	3
Rollover Resistance	—	—	—	4	4	4	4

OPTRA (FORENZA), OPTRA5 ★★★

RATING: Average (2006–07); Below Average (2004–05). A bit larger Daewoo *cum* Chevrolet, the Optra isn't versatile or reliable enough to compete against the Honda Civic, Mazda3, Hyundai Elantra, Kia Spectra, and Toyota Corolla, Echo, or Yaris. **"Real" city/highway fuel economy:** 11.0/7.1 L/100 km. Owners report fuel savings may undershoot this estimate by at least 15 percent. **Maintenance/ Repair costs:** Average. **Parts:** Often in short supply. **Extended warranty:** Not needed, due to the few complaints recorded. **Best alternatives:** The Honda Civic and Toyota Corolla, Echo, Tercel, or Yaris.

Strengths and Weaknesses

Depreciation has hit these models hard. Known in the U.S. as the Suzuki Forenza, the 2004 Optra was a uniquely Canadian car that sold for $16,190, or almost $3,000 more than the same model-year Aveo. Presently, a 2004 Optra or Optra5 hatchback is worth between $3,000 and $3,500, while a 2004 Aveo, originally priced at $13,480, now costs only a thousand dollars less ($2,000–$2,500).

The Optra/Forenza is a reasonably equipped compact sedan that carries a puny 119 hp 2.0L 4-cylinder engine that has only 16 more horses than the entry-level Aveo. Standard features include a four-wheel independent MacPherson strut suspension, an AM/FM/CD stereo and four speakers, front power windows, power door locks, variable intermittent wipers, folding rear seats, a tachometer, a tilt steering wheel, 15-inch tires and wheels, and a driver's seat that is height-adjustable and includes a lumbar adjustment. The car has a nicely finished interior, but seating is comfortable for up to four passengers only.

Safety Summary

All models: 2004—Airbag failed to deploy. • Passenger-side wheel sheared off. • Chronic stalling and hard starts. • Premature tire wear; vehicle easily hydroplanes. **2005**—Back wheel sheared off. • Sudden loss off power. • Erratic transmission shifting. • Passenger-side airbag is disabled when an average-sized passenger is seated. • Driver-side seat belt suddenly unlatches. • Wipers operate too slowly. **2006**—Sudden acceleration. • Jerky transmission shifts. • Hard starts.

Secret Warranties/Internal Bulletins/Service Tips

All models: 2004—Door frame paint peeling. **2004–05**—Rough idle and stalling. • Excessive rear brake noise. • Door lock falls into door. **2004–06**—Steering rubbing and growling. • Can't shift out of Park or remove ignition key.

OPTRA, OPTRA5 PROFILE

	2004	2005	2006	2007
Cost Price ($)				
Optra, Optra5	16,190	13,595	11,995	12,995
Used Values ($)				
Optra, Optra5 ▲	3,000	4,000	5,500	8,500
Optra, Optra5 ▼	2,500	3,500	5,000	7,000
Reliability	1	1	3	3
Crash Safety (F)	4	4	4	4
Side	3	3	3	3
Rollover Resistance	4	4	4	4

Ford

ESCORT, ZX2 ★★

RATING: Below Average (1999–2000). The Escort is a risky buy, mainly because of its many powertrain deficiencies and Ford's lack of parts and servicing support in Canada. **"Real" city/highway fuel economy:** *Manual:* An impressive 7.7/5.7 L/100 km. *Automatic:* Owners report fuel savings are about 10 percent less than that estimated by Natural Resources Canada: 9.4/6.9 L/100 km. **Maintenance/Repair costs:** Higher than average. Repairs can be done by independents or by Ford or Mazda dealers. **Parts:** Expensive, and getting harder to find. **Extended warranty:** You will need a bumper-to-bumper extended warranty, which will add at least $1,500 to the price—wiping out the attraction of a low price tag. **Best alternatives:** Consider the wagon version: It's easy to load, quite versatile, and offers a raised rear roof that augments rear-passenger headroom. Other choices include the GM Firefly or Metro; Honda Civic; Hyundai Accent; Mazda Protegé; Suzuki Esteem or Aerio; and Toyota Corolla, Echo, Tercel, or Yaris.

Strengths and Weaknesses

These front-drive small cars are usually reasonably priced and economical to operate, and they provide a comfortable, though jittery, ride and adequate front seating for two adults.

VEHICLE HISTORY: 1997—Improved over 1982–96 models. Better steering, ride, and handling, plus a bigger and more-powerful 2.0L engine. Fresh styling, dual airbags, a new 110 hp 2.0L 4-cylinder engine, a standard 5-speed manual transmission and optional 4-speed automatic, and optional ABS with rear discs. **1999**—Debut of a sporty Escort ZX2 coupe. **2000**—Wagons are axed, and the ZX2 coupe gets a firmer suspension and a 130 hp engine.

Owner complaints primarily concern annoying seat belts; airbag, fuel-tank, coil-spring, and tie-rod failures; automatic transmission and engine breakdowns (premature timing-belt replacement at around 90,000 km); and cooling system, brake, electrical, air conditioning, fuel-pump, and ignition system failures. Quality control and reliability improved a bit with the 1997 through 2000 models, but most of the earlier powertrain deficiencies remained.

Safety Summary

All models: 1995–2000—An incredibly high number of safety-related complaints were recorded for these years. • No airbag deployment. • Inadvertent airbag deployment. • Airbag-induced injuries. • Chronic surging and stalling. • Electrical and engine wiring fires. • Brake failures, and premature rotor and pad replacement. • Snapped front and rear coil springs damage tire. • Sudden tie-rod failure, leading to steering loss. • Automatic transmission slips, jumps out of gear, leaks, or fails early. • Seat belt malfunctions. • Horn blows inadvertently, won't blow, or is hard to access. • Faulty door locks. **1999**—Headlight socket melts. • Hood flies open. • Poor structural integrity (broken welds and distorted sheet metal). • Suspension and alignment problems. • Poor defrosting. **2000**—Vehicle suddenly jumps forward or rearward when the accelerator is only slightly depressed. • Transmission coolant line clamp comes apart. • Delayed transmission engagement. • Power-steering loss caused by snapped serpentine belt. • Brake pedal slowly creeps to the floor when applied. • Shock absorber rubbed against tire, causing a blowout. • Sunroof shattered while vehicle was parked. • Windshield suddenly shattered. • Blower runs when vehicle is shut down, rendering the radio and windshield wipers inoperative. • Key may no longer work in the ignition.

Secret Warranties/Internal Bulletins/Service Tips

All models/years: Radio whining or buzzing noise can be eliminated by following the service tips found in TSB #01-7-3. • Repeated heater core failures have also been a frequent problem, covered in TSB #01-15-6. • Paint delamination, peeling, or fading. **All models: 1997–99**—Positive crankcase ventilation (PCV) system may freeze, resulting in a serious oil leak through the dipstick tube. • A front brake grinding noise, pulling or drag, and uneven brake pad wear are all signs of corrosion affecting the caliper slide pins. • Tips on silencing a variety of squeaks and rattles. • No restart in cold weather, the cooling fan not shutting off, or the battery going dead all signal the need to change the integrated relay control module. **1999**—Tips on reducing noise, vibration, and harshness. **2000**—Delayed transmission engagement; MIL (malfunction indicator light) comes on. • Troubleshooting intake manifold air leaks. • Exhaust system buzzing or rattling (a problem for over a decade). • Fuel fill nozzle clicks off too soon when fuelling up. • Troubleshooting poor engine performance at idle and excessive gas consumption. • Vehicle may not start in freezing weather because of moisture freezing in the fuel-pump relay. • Diagnostic tips to eliminate wind noise around doors.

ESCORT, ZX2 PROFILE

	1999	2000
Cost Price ($)		
Base/LX	14,895	—
ZX2	15,895	17,995
Used Values ($)		
Base/LX ▲	1,800	—
Base/LX ▼	1,500	—
ZX2 ▲	2,000	2,500
ZX2 ▼	1,700	2,000
Reliability	3	3
Crash Safety (F)	3	3
Side	3	3
Offset	3	3
Head Restraints	1	—

RATING: Average (2005–07); Not Recommended (2000–04). The biggest lemon in the orchard? Consider this: Some models can't be driven through puddles because the low-mounted air-intake hose ingests water into the engine ($5,000 repair). And then Ford blames the owner for driving through puddles! Chronic stalling is also a major problem, and Ford's secret warranty for earlier models doesn't cover afflicted 2002–07s. **"Real" city/highway fuel economy:** *Manual:* 8.6/6.1 L/100 km. *Automatic:* 9.0/6.7 L/100 km. *SVT:* 11.3/7.8 L/100 km, but owners say the automatic transmission cuts fuel economy by over 20 percent. **Maintenance/ Repair costs:** Higher than average, once the warranty expires. **Parts:** Expensive and sometimes hard to find, especially if they're part of a recall campaign. **Extended warranty:** Having a bumper-to-bumper warranty, or a rich uncle, is a prerequisite to owning a 2000–04 Focus. **Best alternatives:** Asian small cars are your best bet. Try the Honda Civic (it's softer-riding, quieter, and has a smoother-running engine); Hyundai Accent; Mazda Protegé or Mazda3; Suzuki Esteem or Swift; and Toyota Corolla, Echo, Tercel, or Yaris.

Strengths and Weaknesses

Hailed as Europe's 1999 Car of the Year (a big mistake), Ford's 2000 Focus came to North America shortly thereafter as a premium small car. Its base engine, a 110 hp 2.0L 4-cylinder, was carried over to the Focus LX and SE, while the 130 hp twin-cam 2.0L (also used on the Escort ZX2 coupe) became the standard powerplant on the ZTS and ZX3. Both engines were given more power with the 2005 models and the beefed-up 151 hp 2.3L 4-cylinder.

VEHICLE HISTORY: 2002—Debut of a high-performance 170 hp SVT Focus with sport suspension and 17-inch wheels, and the ZX5, a four-door hatchback. **2004**—No more anti-skid system, and a 145 hp 2.3L 4-cylinder is added. **2005**—Totally revamped with a horsepower boost, new exterior and interior styling, and the use of more-reliable, durable components. ZX4 ST models offer standard ABS and traction control.

While early models are agile and fun to drive, the 130 hp 2.0L powerplant is barely sufficient for highway cruising, where passing and merging require a bit more power. The 2005–07 2.0L and 2.3L engines are the strongest and most reliable performers. The Focus isn't a quiet car, no matter what model year you choose. Constant engine buzz and some hard shifting with the automatic gearbox accompany any decent speed. Brakes add to the Focus's symphony of sound by emitting a grinding noise when applied, and the front suspension creaks when the car is put through its paces. Uneven terrain causes the car to bounce about.

This small car does handle well in city traffic, thanks to its tight turning radius and nimble steering. The small back-corner windows are also handy for keeping the rear visibility unobstructed. The car's unusually tall roofline gives ample headroom and allows for a higher, more upright riding position than you'll see with traditional small cars. Front and rear legroom is impressive as well, as long as the front passengers don't push their seats too far back.

After all these positives, keep in mind that from a reliability and performance standpoint, the Focus is a Dr. Jekyll/Mr. Hyde car with everything depending on the model year owned. 2004 and earlier models are mediocre highway performers and often sidelined for repairs. Later models have more power and handle a bit better on the highway, and are far more reliable. Nevertheless, powertrain, fuel, electrical, and brake system failures are commonplace for all model years. Service bulletins are replete with special instructions telling dealers how to practically rebuild the car to make it tolerably driveable. Expect chronic stalling (covered up to 10 years by a secret warranty); excessive vibration; poor engine and transmission performance; and 2003 SVT flywheel, pressure plate, and clutch assembly failures. Other problems: premature rotor and brake pad wear and squeaking; a failure-prone ignition switch that won't turn, locks up, and eats keys (unlocking costs $300); a seatback bar that digs into the driver's back; power-window failures; excessive engine, brake, steering-column, suspension, and wheel noise; a trunk latch that sticks or suddenly opens; trunk and AC leaks; a driver's door that won't open from the inside (help!); a fuel-door lid that breaks in half; hood latches that break off when the hood is closed; door mouldings that fall off; and interior panels that don't fit or align properly.

The Focus can be a threat to your wallet and your genitalia:

> The 2004 Focus cigarette lighter after being pushed in and getting hot popped out of the holder and landed either on the occupant's lap or on the carpeting. When this was shown to the rental company, and a demonstration was done, the lighter burned the representative's legs.

 **Safety Summary**

2000—Rear-door latch failures on wagons. **2000–01**—Ford admits to chronic stalling and extends engine computer warranty to 10 years (see "Secret Warranties/Internal Bulletins/Service Tips"). **2000–02**—Many complaints of chronic stalling with loss of brakes and steering. • Defective speed control causes sudden acceleration in spite of corrective recall. • Other sudden acceleration incidents ascribed to faulty power control module (PCM) and driver's shoe being caught under the plastic console. • Sudden acceleration in Reverse. • Collapse of tie rod and axle, leading to loss of control. • Defective axle wheel bearing. • Sudden pull to the left when turning left. • Clutch pedal spring pops out, injuring driver. • Pedal fell on floorboard. • Transmission slippage and failure. • Smoking electrical wiring in dash. • Under-hood fire ignited after AC engaged. • Driver-side seat belt won't deploy. • Emergency brake often fails to engage because button on handle stays depressed. • Vehicle was cruising at 110 km/h when gas pedal fell off its mounting. • Frayed accelerator throttle cable snapped; cable also kinks, causing hesitation, acceleration, and surging. • Stabilizer bar suddenly broke. • Car left in Park rolled downhill. • Rear end is very unstable in snow, feels wobbly under normal conditions, and throws rear passengers about. • Sudden, unintended acceleration, and then engine cuts out. • Engine shuts down while cruising on the highway. • New engine needed after rainwater ingested into engine because of low air-intake valve. • Transmission hard to shift into Second or Reverse in cold weather. • Fuel-tank leak due to cracked filler pipe. • No brakes. • No steering. • Steering wheel locks while driving. • Broken rack and pinion. • Tie rod suddenly broke off. • Front and rear wheels buckle. • Collapsed front wheel:

> My father owns this vehicle, but he bought it for me for safety reasons. I am a 16-year-old female. Travelling at normal highway speed on a dry, two-lane highway with no traffic at night, my 2002 Ford Focus lost control due to the front control arm fracturing. My right front tire ended up totally unattached to the control arm and only staying attached to the vehicle by the hold of the tie rod. My vehicle swerved into the median and into the oncoming traffic (thankfully no traffic was around).

• Rear hatch opens on its own. • Faulty rear wheel bearings cause wheel to wobble and wander. • Original Firestone tires wear out prematurely. • Dash lights flicker, then quit. **2002–03**—Airbags failed to deploy. • Sudden brake loss. • Windshield cracks or shatters for no reason. **2003**—Chronic stalling. • Reports of severe back trauma from seatback failure in rear-enders. • Transmission and axle failures. • Excessive vibration. • Trunk latch suddenly releases. • Sunlight washes out speedometer reading. **2004**—Car fire believed to be caused by faulty fuel-line connection. • Sudden acceleration. • Cruise control self-activates, causing vehicle to surge suddenly. • Hood flew up, shattering windshield while car was cruising on the highway. • Automatic transmission, bearings, and throttle body replaced during first year. • Total brake failure and frequent rotor, pad, and caliper replacements:

> Brakes failed on our 2004 Ford Focus ZX5 4-door hatchback as my wife went to stop at a stop sign leaving our development and was broadsided by a truck. This resulted in a total loss of vehicle and injuries sustained to my wife.

• Chronic stalling and surging continues to be a problem:

> Contact owns a 2004 Ford Focus. While driving on the highway the car shut down without warning. No particular speed or circumstance. This incident happened several times on interstate. While going 70 to 75 mph [110–120 km/h], the car shut down, no battery, no lights, and it was very hard to steer. It happened at stop signs or at speeds of 35 to 45 mph [56–72 km/h]. After putting vehicle in park then in neutral or park it will start back up.

• Bent steering tie rod makes vehicle wander all over the road. • Wheel bearing failure. • No-start because ignition cylinder seized:

> I drove and parked the 2004 Ford Focus about 40 mins from my home. About 2 hours later, I went to get in my car and the steering wheel was locked. I inserted

the key and it would not turn. Several people tried jiggling the steering wheel, stepping on the brake all to no avail.

• Water entry destroys the horn. • Snow kills the windshield wiper motor:

Windshield wiper motor goes if it gets clogged up with a small amount of snow. The way the car is designed when you brush the car off from snow, some of it lodges into an area that is hard to get the snow out of, when wipers are turned on the motor does not work. Had this replaced approx. 4 or 5 months ago, and now it has happened again.

Secret Warranties/Internal Bulletins/Service Tips

2000—Ford Campaign No. 03M02 allows for the free replacement of fractured front coil springs up to 10 years or 240,000 km (150,000 mi.). • Under Special Service Instruction 00204, Ford will reprogram the powertrain computer module to correct poor engine performance on vehicles equipped with a manual transmission. • ONP 99B21 will replace the fuel pulse damper free of charge, and ONP 99B22 will pay the costs associated with replacing the side engine mount. • Vehicles equipped with a manual transmission will have their clutch master cylinder and pedal return spring replaced, free of charge, under ONP 00B59. **2000–01**—Chronic stalling fix. Reuters News Service reported on November 20, 2003, that a faulty fuel delivery module linked to chronic engine stalling would be replaced free of charge by Ford up to 10 years, without any mileage limitation (Campaign No. 03N01). **2000–02**—Low power and stalling. • AC evaporator case/cowl leaks water into the interior. • Repeated heater core failure. **2000– 03**—Troubleshooting rear-end water leaks. **2000–04**—Remedy for front suspension creak, crunch, grinding, or rattle. **2000–05**—Getting a little wet, are you? The following bulletin looks at some of the reasons why:

WATER LEAKS TO VEHICLE INTERIOR	
BULLETIN NO.: 05-13-3	DATE: JULY 11, 2005

WATER LEAKS/A/C CONDENSATION LEAKS AT FRONT FLOOR AREA
2000–05 Focus
ISSUE: Some 2000–05 Focus vehicles may exhibit a difficult to diagnose or difficult to repair water leak or AC system condensation leak condition in the front floor area. This may be caused by sealer skips, loose grommets, mis-positioned seals or condensation leaking from the A/C evaporator case.
ACTION: Determine if the concern is an A/C condensation leak or a water leak and repair as necessary. Some common water leak locations and repair recommendations are listed in this article to help reduce repair time and increase repair effectiveness.

2001—Difficult to shift out of Park. • 2.0L Zetec engines may hesitate, surge, or idle roughly in cold weather. • Intermittent stalling, hesitation, or lack of power. • Troubleshooting the Check Engine light. • Ignition key may be difficult to turn in cylinder. **2003–05**—If the door locks lock or unlock when they shouldn't, try cleaning the door-latch connectors. **2004**—Loss of power, hesitation, or misfire after a cold start. • Runs rough in wet weather. • Harsh transmission engagement. • Premature clutch wear. • Transmission clunking or rattling. • Inoperative speed-control system. • Intermittent no-starts; odometer may show all dashes. • Customer Satisfaction Program #04B16 will pay for the correction of faulty front-seat heater element pads.

FOCUS PROFILE

	2000	2001	2002	2003	2004	2005	2006	2007
Cost Price ($)								
LX/S	14,995	16,015	15,970	16,275	16,475	—	—	14,799
ZX3S	16,697	16,690	17,390	17,550	17,775	17,555	17,599	—
ZX4 ST	—	—	—	—	—	22,995	23,001	—
Wagon SE	17,695	17,271	18,995	19,165	19,365	19,565	19,599	17,099
Used Values ($)								
LX/S ▲	3,000	3,500	4,000	4,500	5,000	7,000	8,500	9,500
LX/S ▼	2,500	3,000	3,500	4,500	4,500	6,000	7,500	8,500
ZX3S ▲	3,000	4,000	4,500	5,500	6,500	7,000	8,500	—
ZX3S ▼	2,500	3,500	4,000	5,000	5,500	6,500	7,500	—
ZX4 ST ▲	—	—	—	—	—	8,500	10,000	—
ZX4 ST ▼	—	—	—	—	—	7,500	9,500	—
Wagon SE ▲	2,500	3,000	4,000	5,000	6,500	8,000	9,000	10,000
Wagon SE ▼	2,000	2,500	3,500	4,500	6,000	7,500	8,000	9,000
Reliability	1	1	1	1	1	4	4	4
Crash Safety (F)	1	1	1	1	2	3	4	4
Side	—	3	—	—	5	5	3	3
IIHS Side	1	1	1	1	1	1	1	1
Offset	5	5	5	5	5	5	5	5
Head Restraints	—	2	2	2	2	2	3	3
Rollover Resistance	—	—	4	4	4	4	4	4

General Motors

CAVALIER, SUNFIRE ★★★

RATING: Average (2003–05); Below Average (1999–2002). GM's best small cars, which isn't saying much. Side crashworthiness is unacceptably poor. Engine, transmission, and brake repair bills will run you bankrupt if get a pre-1999 model. Try to get a 2003 or later version with a 4-speed automatic transmission, because it will be a bit more reliable, have reduced engine noise, and make for more responsive performance. The base Sunbird changed its name to Sunfire in 1995; it shares the Cavalier's basic design. **"Real" city/highway fuel economy:**

9.8/6.6 L/100 km, but owners say automatic-transmission-equipped cars use about 15 percent more fuel. **Maintenance/Repair costs:** Average. Repairs aren't dealer-dependent; however, ABS troubleshooting is a real head-scratcher, and ABS parts are rare and costly. **Parts:** Mostly reasonably priced and often available for much less from independent suppliers. **Extended warranty:** Not essential. You should balance the cost of an engine head gasket ($800–$1,000) with that of an extended warranty, which will likely cost twice as much. **Best alternatives:** Honda Civic; Hyundai Accent or Elantra; Mazda Protegé or Mazda3; Nissan Sentra; Suzuki Aerio, Esteem, or Swift; and Toyota Corolla, Echo, Tercel, or Yaris. Also take a look at the slightly more upscale Hyundai Elantra or Tiburon.

 ## Strengths and Weaknesses

These twins are two of the lowest-priced small cars to come equipped with standard ABS and dual airbags (1995–2003). In fact, GM claims it lost $1,000 on every one it sold. They are attractively styled (especially the Pontiac Sunfire), come with lots of interior room, and offer a nicely tuned suspension. The ride and handling have also improved markedly since 1999, with power rack-and-pinion steering, a longer wheelbase, and a wider track. The Sunfire is identical to the Cavalier, except for its more rakish look. The Z24s are performance versions, equipped with a more refined form of the less-than-reliable Quad 4 2.4L DOHC 16-valve, 4-cylinder powerplant.

VEHICLE HISTORY: 1999—2.4L twin-cam engine and front brake lining upgrades. **2000**—A slightly restyled front and rear end; an improved storage area; standard AC and PASSLOCK security system; upgraded standard ABS; and a smoother-shifting 5-speed manual transmission. **2003**—Restyled and lengthened; a new 140 hp 2.2L engine; a stiffer suspension; larger wheels and rear brakes; three-point centre seat belts; optional front side airbags; and ABS. **2004**—ABS is no longer standard on base models; CD player reads MP3-formatted discs.

Snappy road performance (with the correct engine and transmission hookup) has been marred by abysmally poor powertrain reliability. Since 1999, these vehicles have become a bit more reliable and durable. Nevertheless, owners are still plagued by troublesome engines (watch for blue exhaust smoke or excessive oil burning), faulty brakes, airbags that continue to malfunction and injure occupants, chronic stalling, and transmission and fuel-pump failures. The Getrag manual gearbox isn't very reliable, nor is it easily repaired, and faulty computer modules, fuel injections, and cooling systems cause stalling and a shaky idle. The power steering may lead or pull, and the steering rack tends to deteriorate quickly, usually requiring replacement sometime shortly after 80,000 km. The front MacPherson struts also wear out rapidly, as do the rear shock absorbers. Many owners complain of rapid front brake wear and warped brake discs after a year or so.

Fit and finish quality is quite variable, often leading to poor paint application, inside and outside body panel gaps, lots of exposed screw heads, and trunk and rear-window water leaks, giving the car a mildew smell. Paint delamination is chronic.

 ## Safety Summary

All models/years: Engine head gasket and intake manifold failures. • Transmission slippage or breakdown. • Owners report complete brake failure and lock-up, extended stopping distances, ABS that self-activates, premature rotor warpage and pad wear, and a grinding and knocking noise when braking. • Airbags fail to deploy, or deploy accidentally. • Sudden acceleration or stalling. • Weak door hinges. • Inoperative horn. **All models: 1999–2001**—Engine fires. • Leaking fuel tank. • Plastic fuel tank is easily punctured. • Right wheel axle twisted off vehicle. • Chronic hesitation, stalling, and surging. • Clutch will not disengage, causing sudden acceleration. • Brake failure caused by leaking master cylinder fluid. • ABS locked up, causing vehicle to go into a skid. • Seat belt failed to retract. • Transmission wouldn't go into Reverse, transmission failed to engage upon start-up, automatic transmission locks up in Second gear, and vehicle rolled away even though parked with parking brake engaged. • When vehicle is in Drive with foot on the brake, it lurches forward, stalls, and produces a crashing sound. • During highway driving, the vehicle suddenly accelerated without steering control. • Rear leaf spring U-bolts broke, causing entire rear end to drop. • Front right side of the vehicle collapsed because of wheel bolts shearing off, causing the wheel to detach completely. • Springs are too weak, causing poor stability and control. • Floor mat impedes clutch pedal travel. • Sudden brake cable breakage while driving. • When driving with door locked, door came ajar. • Hood flew up while driving. **2002**— Reverse tail light bulb exploded, causing light assembly to catch on fire. • Considerable fuel spillage when refuelling. • Left rear axle fell off. • Headlights often go out. **2003**—Tire jack collapsed. • Transmission allows vehicle to roll backward when parked. • Inoperative fuel gauge. • Stalling caused by defective fuel pump. • Burnt electrical wires and light sockets. • Excessive driver-side mirror vibration. **2004**—Fire ignited in engine compartment. • Strong fuel odour in the interior. • Stuck accelerator pedal. • Engine surging, sudden acceleration, and hard starts due to defective computer module. • Frequent transmission clutch assembly and flywheel failures. • Windshield wiper motor malfunctions. • Sun visor slips down while driving. • Trunk-lid bolts sheared off. **2005**—Automatic transmission failure. • Clutch cable cut, rendering clutch inoperative:

> The hydraulic clutch hose got a hole in it from rubbing on the wiring harness that is next to it. This is something that I would assume be re-routed or better put in an area where this would not happen.

• A faulty master cylinder may be the cause of sudden brake loss. • Steering column froze while vehicle was underway. • Driver's seat belt jams. • Driver's seat is not well anchored; it moves constantly. • To access the accelerator pedal, some drivers have to move their seat uncomfortably close to the steering wheel. • Premature rusting of the door hinges. • Horn goes off when vehicle is parked. • Rolled-down backdoor window shattered. • Power window and rear tail light failures. • All dash gauges suddenly go haywire (speedometer, especially); covered by GM's 5 year/100,000 km "goodwill" policies.

Secret Warranties/Internal Bulletins/Service Tips

All models/years: Paint delamination, peeling, or fading. **All models: 1985–2000**—Snow may intrude into the rear brake drum assembly and interfere with braking, says TSB #00-05-24-001, April 2000. Upgraded backing plates are a must-buy in certain regions. Bargain down the installation cost since it is GM's fault in the first place. **1995–2003**—Engine head gasket failures that include overheating, loss of coolant, coolant odour, coolant leaks around the cylinder head, and white smoke from the exhaust. Sometimes the heater won't work, or a film (from the coolant) will be deposited on the inside glass surfaces. If the coolant leaks inside the engine, it can cause severe engine damage from overheating. GM "goodwill" covers head gasket problems for 7 years/160,000 km (100,000 mi.). Remember, if you have an engine head gasket failure on a GM vehicle, or your engine isn't included in the above-noted programs, don't despair. Simply use the same benchmarks for your own vehicle to threaten small claims action on those grounds. Make sure to cite TSB #98054A, "Campaign: Cylinder Head Gasket Failure, Coolant Leakage," published September 1998. Incidentally, some *Lemon-Aid* readers say inexpensive sealers can plug minor head gasket leaks. • Automatic transmission delay and surging (flare). **1996–2002**—Coolant leakage from the water pump weep hole will be plugged by installing a free coolant collector, says TSB #01-06-02-012. **1997–2005**—A clunk noise from the front of the vehicle when turning may be fixed by simply lubricating the intermediate shaft, says TSB #01-02-32-001G. **1998–2004**—TSB #03-08-67-009A says a binding sunroof likely needs a new sunroof motor. **1999–2000**—No Third and Fourth gear may require a new direct clutch piston assembly. **1999–2002**—Problems opening the fuel-filler door can be fixed by installing a free fuel-filler pocket, says TSB #01-08-65-001. **2000–02**—Harsh transmission shifts accompanied by the Service Engine Soon light are caused by a short in the input speed sensor wiring, says TSB #00-06-04037A. • A wet road sizzle noise coming from the rear of the vehicle requires the installation of wheelhouse liners, says TSB #01-08-58-005. • Inaccurate fuel gauge readings can be corrected by installing a new fuel-tank sender sensor kit under Customer Satisfaction Campaign #00101. **2000–03**—Troubleshooting engine problems. **2000–05**—A damp trunk carpet means you may have to replace the pressure relief valve. **2001–02**—If the vehicle fails to crank or start, the battery cable connection may be at fault. **2001–05**—TSB #01-07-30-030A says there are four likely causes for harsh 1–2 upshifts. None of them are the owner's fault. **2002**—ABS light comes on when transmission is placed in Second or Fourth gear. • 4-speed automatic transmission fluid leakage. • Faulty automatic transmission converter pump. • Customer Satisfaction Campaign inspection for transaxle converter bearing failure is detailed in TSB #01031. **2002–04**—A slipping automatic transmission may need a new driven sprocket support assembly, says TSB #03-07-30-012A. • Stuck in Second or slipping in Fourth gear: Owner should repair conduit, splice/reposition conduit, or inspect/reinstall evaporation emission vent solenoid or replace, if necessary, per TSB #03-07-30-036. • Power steering may cut out in cold weather. **2002–05**—A suspension rattle, creak, or pop when turning could mean that the two front stabilizer bar brackets need replacing (TSB #02-03-08-008B). Dealers and GM will usually absorb half the repair cost up to 5 years/80,000 km. **2003**—Engine flares when shifting:

A/T—SHIFT FLARE/SES LAMP ON/DTCS

BULLETIN NO.: 03-07-30-021   DATE: MAY 2003

NEUTRAL FLARE AND/OR RPM FLARE WHILE IN DRIVE, NO 1–2 UPSHIFT, SERVICE ENGINE SOON (SES) LIGHT ILLUMINATED, DIAGNOSTIC TROUBLE CODES (DTCS) P1810, DTC P1815 SET (REPLACE TRANSMISSION FLUID PRESSURE (TFP) MANUAL VALVE POSITION SWITCH)

1995–2003 Chevrolet Cavalier; 1997–2003 Chevrolet Malibu; 1999–2003 Oldsmobile Alero; 1995–2003 Pontiac Sunfire; 1998–2003 Pontiac Grand Am with 4T40E Transmission (RPO MN4) or 4T45E Transmission (RPO MN5)

• Correcting transmissions that won't shift, or shift erratically (replace driven sprocket support assembly). **2003–04**—Troubleshooting AC problems, per TSB #03-01-38-005A. **2004**—Automatic transmission fluid leak caused by faulty reverse servo cover and seal. **2004–05**—Excessive oil consumption is corrected through the replacement of the engine intake manifold gasket or cam cover:

EXCESSIVE OIL CONSUMPTION/BLUE SMOKE ON ACCELERATION

BULLETIN NO.: 05-06-01-003A   DATE: MAY 25, 2005

EXCESSIVE OIL CONSUMPTION, BLUE SMOKE ON ACCELERATION (INSPECT INTAKE MANIFOLD AND/OR CAM COVER, REPLACE IF NECESSARY)

2004 Alero; 2004–05 Cavalier, Classic, Grand Am, Malibu, Saturn L-Series, ION, VUE, Sunfire; 2005 Cobalt and Pursuit (Canada Only)

ATTENTION: This bulletin covers any vehicle with the Ecotec 2.2L L61 engine built during calendar year 2004.

CONDITION: Some customers may comment on excessive oil consumption or blue smoke on acceleration. Excessive oil consumption, not due to leaks, is the use of 0.9L (1 qt) or more of engine oil within 3,200 km (2,000 mi).

CAUSE: Incorrect sizing of the PCV orifice and/or misalignment of the oil baffle in the cam cover may allow higher than desired amounts of oil into the combustion chamber.

2005—Water leaks onto driver-side floor.

CAVALIER, SUNFIRE PROFILE

	1999	2000	2001	2002	2003	2004	2005
Cost Price ($)							
Cavalier	15,365	15,765	14,260	15,100	15,785	16,125	16,230
Z24	20,035	20,515	21,165	22,475	21,550	22,125	22,230
Z24 Conv./LS	26,450	27,200	—	—	—	—	—
Sunfire GT	21,300	21,420	21,940	21,950	20,385	19,445	19,550

Used Values ($)

Cavalier ▲	1,500	2,000	2,500	3,000	3,000	3,500	4,500
Cavalier ▼	1,500	2,000	2,000	2,500	3,000	3,500	3,500
Z24 ▲	3,000	3,500	4,500	5,500	6,000	7,000	8,000
Z24 ▼	2,500	3,000	4,000	5,000	5,500	6,500	7,500
Z24 Conv./LS ▲	3,500	4,000	—	—	—	—	—
Z24 Conv./LS ▼	3,500	3,500	—	—	—	—	—
Sunfire GT ▲	1,500	2,000	2,500	3,000	3,500	4,000	4,500
Sunfire GT ▼	1,500	2,000	2,500	3,000	3,500	3,500	4,000

Reliability	3	3	3	3	3	3	3
Crash Safety (F)							
Cavalier 2d	3	3	3	3	4	4	4
Cavalier 4d	4	4	4	4	4	4	4
Side							
Cavalier 2d	1	1	1	1	1	1	1
Cavalier 4d	1	1	1	1	1	1	1
Offset	1	1	1	1	1	1	1
Rollover Resistance	—	—	4	4	4	4	4

Note: NHTSA says the Sunfire's safety ratings should be identical to the Cavalier's scores.

S-SERIES, L-SERIES, ION ★★

RATING: *S-Series:* Below Average (1999–2002). *L-Series:* Below Average (2000–05). *ION:* Below Average (2003–07). The Saturn division has lost billions of dollars because its early models were late to market, bland, and lacklustre performers. Quality control was the pits, especially as it related to powertrain dependability. Even GM's less-pretentious models, like the Cavalier and Sunfire, or the minuscule Metro and Firefly, offer better quality and value for your money. Saturn's latest entries, like the Aura, Sky, and Outlook SUV, are winners from a performance and styling perspective. It'll take a few years to find out if the company's poor-quality demons have been exorcized. **"Real" city/highway fuel economy:** *SL 1.9L:* 9.4/6.2 L/100 km. *ION 1.9L:* 10.2/6.8 L/100 km, though owners report that the automatic transmission burns almost 20 percent more fuel. **Maintenance/ Repair costs:** Average; repairs aren't dealer-dependent, unless you're seeking some Saturn "goodwill" refunds or have continuously variable transmission (CVT) glitches. **Parts:** Higher-than-average costs. CVT parts are often back ordered, and they're hellacious to troubleshoot. **Extended warranty:** Don't go anywhere near a used Saturn unless you're armed to the teeth with a comprehensive extended warranty. **Best alternatives:** The Honda Civic LX, Hyundai Elantra, and Toyota Corolla.

Strengths and Weaknesses

S-Series

This entry-level model is far from high-tech and remained virtually unchanged until it was replaced by the 2003 ION. The base model provides a comfortable driving position, adequate instrumentation and controls, unobstructed visibility, good braking, dent-resistant body panels, and better-than-average crashworthiness scores. But, balancing these advantages, buyers have to contend with excessive engine noise, limited rear seatroom, glitch-prone anti-lock brakes and traction control, the coupe's third-door window that doesn't roll down, and serious factory-related deficiencies.

L-Series

In an attempt to save money by adapting a European car to the American market, Saturn brought out the LS sedan and LW wagon, derivatives of GM's Opel Vectra. Some major differences, however, include a lengthened body, a standard ignition theft-deterrent system, a reengineered chassis to give a more comfortable ride, and the use of a homegrown 137 hp 2.2L 4-banger constructed with aluminum components (not a good idea). Other components lifted directly from the European parts bin are the Opel's 3.0L V6 engine, a manual transmission from Saab, and German-made braking systems.

The higher-priced L-Series models provide a more comfortable driving position and a roomy interior with a full range of convenience features and a good V6 power-train matchup that provides a firm ride and impressive high-speed stability and braking.

ION

A larger, more-comfortable, and more-powerful vehicle than its S-Series predecessor, the ION is powered by a 140 hp 2.2L 4-cylinder engine and gives buyers the choice of either a four-door coupe or sedan.

The ION's deficiencies mirror those of the S-Series coupe and its L-Series big brother. The only added wrinkle is the CVT transmission, which, despite an extended warranty following widespread quality complaints, is destined for the trash heap. In the meantime, ION and VUE SUV owners are likely to face long servicing waits and mind-boggling depreciation.

VEHICLE HISTORY: *Coupe:* **2003**—ION replaces the coupe. *L-Series:* **2002**—Standard side curtain airbags. **2003**—Four-wheel disc brakes. **2004**—Standard ABS and traction control; the 5-speed manual transmission is no more. *ION:* **2003**—ION arrives with a continuously variable transmission (CVT). After first extending the warranty in 2003, Saturn drops the CVT in its 2005 models because of quality problems. **2004**—Upgraded interior materials, and a high-performance Red Line model sporting a 205 hp 4-cylinder engine and sundry other performance features.

2005—The 5-speed automatic is replaced by a 4-speed automatic. Suspension and steering are also upgraded. Improved seating for the ION-1 and ION-2 versions. **2006**—The ION-1 sedan is dropped, and the ION-3 gets a 170 hp 4-cylinder engine.

TSBs and owner complaints indicate that a variety of major quality problems are likely to crop up throughout all model years. These include self-destructing engines; chronically malfunctioning automatic transmissions; failure-prone brake, ignition, fuel, and electrical systems (are flickering, dimming lights your cup of tea?); alternator and AC compressor failures; a host of body defects, led by paint delamination, rattles, and wind and water leaks; poorly welded exhaust systems; and failure-prone Firestone tires (mostly the Affinity brand).

 ## Safety Summary

All models/years: Reports of stuck accelerators. • Airbag failed to deploy. • Seat belt failed to restrain driver in collision. • Hard starts, surging and chronic stalling. • Gear lever slips out of gear and is hard to put into Reverse. • Manual transmission jumps out of Third and Fifth gears. • Frequent brake failures. • Brake rotor warpage and frequent pad replacement. • Sudden head gasket failure causes other engine components to self-destruct. • Loss of steering control. • Poor horn and radio performance. *SC1:* **2000–01**—Brake pedal makes a loud popping noise or drops to the floor without warning. *SC2:* **2000–01**—The small, recessed horn buttons are hard to find; can't activate the horn without looking down. **2002**—Ineffective, noisy brakes. *SL:* **2000–01**—Steering wheel came apart while driving. *SL1:* **2002**—Seat belt suddenly unlatched when vehicle was rear-ended. Engine makes a ticking noise and then suddenly stalls in traffic. • In a rear-ender, seat lever released, causing seatback to suddenly recline. • Unable to shift to a lower gear when going downhill. • Inaccurate fuel gauge. *SL2:* **2000–01**—Sudden acceleration. • When driving at night, one sees multiple lights when looking through the rear-view mirror at the vehicle in back, as well as the reflection of the defroster lights. • During rainy weather, rear windshield view is distorted or wavy. **2002**—Faulty throttle position sensor (TPS) causes vehicle to maintain speed when braking. *SW2:* **2000–01**—Automatic transmission slippage. *L-Series:* **2000–01**—Transmission can't be shifted into a Forward gear. • Location of power-seat button allows it to be accidentally activated, causing seat to suddenly recline. • Power door locks short out. **2000–02**—Inoperative rear-door glass confirmed by TSB #02-T27. • Electrical short causes all lights and gauges to suddenly come on. • Seat belt won't lock up at sudden stops. **2002**—Headlights and interior lights go out, flicker, or dim intermittently when foot is taken off accelerator or when clutch or cooling fan is engaged. *ION:* **2003**—Transmission gear slippage creates a highway hazard. • Steering knuckle sheared off. • Steering lock-up. • Chronic turn signal failures; turn signal won't work if cigarette lighter is being used. • Key sticks in ignition. • Seat belt anchor bolt broke. • Seat belt retractor fell apart. **2004**—Accelerator pedal fell off. • CVT transmission causes sudden deceleration. • Multiple transmission replacements. • Engine replacement. • Doors don't close fully. • Water leaking into the trunk caused serious electrical shorts (lights, etc.). • Electronic assisted steering almost caused fatalities. • Fuel-filler pipe spits back fuel when refuelling. • Saturn cell phone charger can short circuit lights, etc., until more robust resistors and capacitors are installed. • Firestone tire-tread separation. • Steering failures:

> Steering failure during static and very slow turning exercises. This is a consistent problem with the vehicle. We teach new drivers and re-train elderly drivers and this is a major issue for a training vehicle.

• Vehicle suddenly went out of control; airbags failed to deploy. • Headlights create a shadow on the road, and they flicker or go out. • Headlight glazing. • Constant dash light dimming. • Manual shifter knob falls off. • Brake failures. • Unsafe safety belts:

> While driving down the road the child in the rear left seat complained that the seat belt harnessing the child was too tight around his/her neck. The driver had to call 911 to have the seat belt cut away.

2005—Electrical fire ignited near the battery. • Transmission sticks in gear or suddenly pops out of gear. • Complete loss of braking:

> I was driving my 2005 Saturn ION-2 and the brakes totally failed when I depressed the clutch on my 5 speed transmission. After taking it in for service the mechanic told me that the slave cylinder was leaking and allowed air into the brake system because the brakes and clutch have a shared hydraulic fluid reservoir. I couldn't downshift because the clutch failed and I couldn't brake because the brakes failed. The warning system failed because there was still some fluid in the shared reservoir.

• Defective rear brake rotors and drums (drums will warp if car isn't driven for several weeks). • Shifter knob fell off; shifter shaft replaced. • Dash gauges fail suddenly. • Door panels crack. • Driver's window fell into the door. • Water leaks into headlights.

Secret Warranties/Internal Bulletins/Service Tips

All models/years: Reprogramming of the power control module (PCM) and engine control module (ECM) now have equal coverage under the emission warranty up to 8 years/130,000 km (80,000 mi.), per TSB #04-1-08, published June 2004. **All models: 1991–2001**—GM admits in TSB #01-T-07 that a cracked engine-coolant temperature sensor may be the culprit behind hard starts, poor engine performance, engine overheating, and leaking or low coolant. **1996–2001**—Water leaks into headliner are likely caused by a faulty sunroof or plugged drain hole grommets. **1996–2004**—A rotten-egg odour coming from the exhaust is likely the result of a malfunctioning catalytic converter. **1999**—Harsh shifting. • Troubleshooting chronic short circuits. • Water leak onto headliner and/or left footwell area and rear luggage compartment. **2000–01**—Delayed, harsh engagement into Reverse or Drive, erratic shifting between First and Second gears, or no

Second or Third gears. • Steering-wheel shake or vibration at highway speeds. • Inoperative power windows and sunroof. **2000–02**—If the engine produces a whistling noise, GM suggests you replace the engine intake manifold gasket in TSB #02-T-22. Of course, this should be a free repair, under #J025-1. • GM has a quick fix for headliner sagging at rear of sunroof opening. • Water leaks into the interior will be fixed under warranty, says TSB #00-T-41A. **2002**—Transmission fluid leakage is likely from a faulty transaxle temperature sensor. *L-Series, ION:* **2003–04**—Engine coolant leakage into oil:

LOSS OF COOLANT/NO EXTERNAL LEAKS EVIDENT

BULLETIN NO.: 03-06-123-001   DATE: NOVEMBER 2003

SLIGHT LOSS OF COOLANT OR LOW COOLANT LIGHT COMING ON WITH NO SIGNS OF EXTERNAL LEAKS

2003–04 Saturn VUE and ION; 2004 L300 Vehicles with 2.2L Engine (VINs D, F–RPO L61)

Some customers may comment that the low coolant light is coming on and/or the coolant level is low with no external leaks visible. Low coolant may be accompanied by one of the following when the engine is cold:

• Engine difficult to start; misfiring; or white smoke, or coolant odour from the tailpipe.

This condition may be caused by porosity in the aluminum of the cylinder head casting and require a new cylinder head or cylinder block.

L-Series: **2000–01**—Front doors relock after being unlocked with key. • Inoperative rear-door glass. **2000–02**—Troubleshooting the most common water leaks into the interior. • Headliner sagging. • Misaligned rear bumper. **2000–03**—Poor AC automatic temperature control performance. **2000–04**—Blue smoke at a V6 engine's start-up can mean you need to replace the engine valve guides or cylinder head, per TSB #04-06-01-010. This bulletin and implied warranty statutes mean GM has to assume the cost of this repair up to 7 years/160,000 km. • A defective or contaminated fuel sender is the likely cause of inaccurate fuel readings. (see TSB #03-08-49-022). *ION:* **2003–04**—Intermittent no-starts may be caused by solidified grease in the ignition switch; a new switch must be installed. • All Saturn ION and VUE vehicles produced since the summer of 2002 and equipped with a CVT have extended warranty coverage on the transmission up to 5 years/120,000 km (75,000 mi.). • Low-speed grinding noise or hesitation requires the installation of a new transaxle control module (TCM) or its recalibration, says TSB #03-07-30-051. • Automatic transmission delay and surging requires the replacement of the control-valve body and recalibration of the ECM (TSB #03-07-30-052). • Clutch chatters and won't release. • No movement in Drive may require a new VT25E transaxle assembly, per TSB #04-07-30-024. • If you're lucky, the TCM may only need to be reprogrammed to cure upshift delays, harsh downshifts, or erratic gear engagement. • Coolant leak from water-pump plug; upgraded water pump. • A squeak, rattle, pop, or clunk from the front of vehicle can be silenced by replacing the front stabilizer shaft insulators, says TSB #04-03-08-003A. • Water leaks into the interior. • Rear-door cracking. • Noisy sunroof. • Faulty blower motor. **2003–06**—Premature or irregular tire wear. **2003–07**—Saturn will replace the instrument-panel cluster lens if it is cloudy, scratched, cracked, or broken. • Remedy for incomplete rear-window defogging. • Your key ring can kill you:

ACCIDENTAL ENGINE SHUT-OFF

BULLETIN NO.: 05-02-35-007A   DATE: OCTOBER 25, 2006

INADVERTENT TURNING OF KEY CYLINDER, LOSS OF ELECTRICAL SYSTEM AND NO DTCS

2003–07 Saturn ION; 2005–06 Pontiac Pursuit (Canada Only); 2005–07 Chevrolet Cobalt; 2006–07 Chevrolet HHR and Pontiac Solstice; 2007 Pontiac G5 and Saturn Sky

There is potential for the driver to inadvertently turn off the ignition due to low ignition key cylinder torque/effort. The concern is more likely to occur if the driver is short and has a large and/or heavy key chain. In these cases, this condition was documented and the driver's knee would contact the key chain while the vehicle was turning and the steering column was adjusted all the way down. This is more likely to happen to a person who is short, as they will have the seat positioned closer to the steering column. In cases that fit this profile, question the customer thoroughly to determine if this may be the cause. The customer should be advised of this potential and should take steps to prevent it such as removing unessential items from their key chain.

Engineering has come up with an insert for the key ring so that it goes from a "slot" design to a hole design. In addition, the previous key ring has been replaced with a smaller, 13 mm (0.5 in) design. This will result in the keys not hanging as low as in the past.

Oh, I get it... It's the customer's fault

2004–05—Poor engine performance:

LOW ENGINE POWER/HESITATION/STUMBLE

BULLETIN NO.: 05-06-02-003   DATE: MARCH 21, 2005

ENGINE LACKS POWER, HESITATES, AND/OR STUMBLES ON HARD ACCELERATION AND/OR LOSES SOME POWER AFTER HIGH RPM CRUISING IN HIGH TEMPERATURES (INSPECT COOLANT CHARGE PUMP ELECTRICAL CONNECTOR TERMINAL LOCATION, ADJUST IF NEEDED)

2004–05 Saturn ION Red Line Vehicles with the 2.0L Engine

CONDITION: Some customers may comment that the engine lacks power, hesitates, and/or stumbles on hard acceleration and/or loses some power after extended high speed (high revolutions per minute [RPM]) cruising in high ambient temperatures.

CAUSE: The condition may be caused by a wiring variation in the coolant charge pump wire connector that may reduce coolant flow from the pump.

CORRECTION: Inspect the coolant pump/air cooler charger electrical connector for correct wire terminal location, and adjust if necessary.

• Free engine-position sensor housing seal replacement:

CPS HOUSING SEAL REPLACEMENT (CANADA)

05522 CAMSHAFT POSITION SENSOR HOUSING SEAL REPLACEMENT (CANADA)
2004–05 ION Red Line Vehicles with Supercharged 2.0L 4-Cylinder Engines
CONDITION: Saturn has learned that certain 2004 and 2005 model year Saturn ION Red Line vehicles equipped with supercharged 2.0L 4-cylinder (LSJ) engines have a condition where the camshaft position sensor housing seal may fail prematurely, resulting in an engine oil leak. Engine damage could occur if the oil level is significantly low.
CORRECTION: To correct this condition, Saturn retailers will install a new camshaft position sensor housing seal that has been re-designed to improve seal life.

S-SERIES, L-SERIES, ION PROFILE

	1999	2000	2001	2002	2003	2004	2005	2006	2007
Cost Price ($)									
SL	13,488	13,588	14,358	14,245	—	—	—	—	—
SC	16,618	16,743	16,763	16,765	—	—	—	—	—
LS/L100	—	19,255	20,065	21,125	—	—	—	—	—
LW/LW200	—	24,400	25,235	23,325	23,480	—	—	—	—
L300	—	—	—	—	—	23,030	24,995	—	—
ION	—	—	—	—	15,495	14,775	14,935	15,995	15,665
Red Line	—	—	—	—	—	—	—	23,995	24,075
Used Values ($)									
SL ▲	1,500	2,000	2,500	3,000	—	—	—	—	—
SL ▼	1,500	2,000	2,000	2,500	—	—	—	—	—
SC ▲	3,000	3,500	4,500	6,000	—	—	—	—	—
SC ▼	2,500	3,000	4,000	5,000	—	—	—	—	—
LS/L100 ▲	—	4,500	5,500	7,000	—	—	—	—	—
LS/L100 ▼	—	4,000	5,000	6,000	—	—	—	—	—
LW/LW200 ▲	—	2,500	3,000	3,500	5,500	—	—	—	—
LW/LW200 ▼	—	2,500	2,500	3,000	5,000	—	—	—	—
L300 ▲	—	—	—	—	—	7,000	10,500	—	—
L300 ▼	—	—	—	—	—	6,000	9,000	—	—
ION ▲	—	—	—	—	3,000	4,000	5,000	7,000	8,000
ION ▼	—	—	—	—	2,500	3,500	4,500	6,000	7,500
Red Line ▲	—	—	—	—	—	—	—	12,000	14,000
Red Line ▼	—	—	—	—	—	—	—	10,500	12,500
Reliability	1	1	2	2	2	2	2	3	3
Crash Safety (F)	5	—	—	—	—	—	—	—	—
L-Series	—	—	4	5	4	4	4	—	—
ION	—	—	—	—	5	5	5	5	5

All ratings on a numbered scale where 5 is good and 1 is bad. See pages 108–109 for a more detailed description.

	C1	C2	C3	C4	C5	C6	C7	C8	C9
Side	3	—	—	—	—	—	—	—	—
L-Series	—	—	2	3	3	3	3	—	—
ION	—	—	—	—	3	3	3	4	4
IIHS Side									
L-Series	—	—	1	1	1	1	1	—	—
ION	—	—	—	—	1	1	1	1	1
Offset	3	3	3	—	—	—	—	—	—
L-Series	—	3	3	3	3	3	3	—	—
ION	—	—	—	—	—	3	3	3	3
Head Restraints	1	1	1	1	—	—	—	—	—
L-Series	—	—	1	1	1	1	1	—	—
ION	—	—	—	—	1	1	2	2	2
Rollover Resistance	—	—	4	4	4	4	4	4	4

Honda

CIVIC, INSIGHT, CIVIC HYBRID ★★★★★ / ★

RATING: *Civic:* Recommended (1999–2007). *Insight:* Not Recommended (2001–06); 2006 was its last model year, though it may come back as a 2009 model. *Civic Hybrid:* Not Recommended (2003–07). **"Real" city/highway fuel economy:** *Civic manual:* 7.5/5.7 L/100 km. *Civic automatic:* 8.0/5.7 L/100 km, though owners report they burn about 10 percent more. *High-performance SiR versions:* 9.2/7.0 L/100 km. *Hybrids:* These models get nowhere near their estimated 4.9/4.6 L/100 km fuel consumption; expect to burn as much as 30 percent more. **Maintenance/Repair costs:** Average. Independent garages can carry out repairs, but the 16-valve engine's complexity means that more-expensive dealer servicing may be unavoidable. Owners should check the engine timing belt every 3 years/60,000 km and replace it every 100,000 km ($300). **Parts:** A bit more expensive than with most other cars in this class; airbag control modules and body panels may be back ordered for weeks. **Extended warranty:** A waste of money. **Best alternatives:** GM Firefly or Metro; Hyundai Accent or Elantra; Mazda Protegé; Nissan Sentra; Suzuki Aerio, Esteem, or Swift; and Toyota Echo, Corolla, or Yaris.

Strengths and Weaknesses

Civics have distinguished themselves by providing sports car acceleration and handling with excellent fuel economy and quality control that is far better than what American, European, and most other Asian automakers can deliver. Other advantages: a roomy, practical trunk; a smooth-shifting automatic transmission; a comfortable ride; good front and rear visibility; high-quality construction; bullet-proof reliability; and simple, inexpensive maintenance. Also, these cars can be easily and inexpensively customized for better driving performance, or to gain a racier allure.

Si models are Honda's factory hot rods (the Acura 1.6 EL is a Si clone), providing lots of high-performance thrills without the bills. Despite four-wheel disc brakes, the Si's mediocre braking and its lack of low-end torque are the car's main performance flaws. It's suspension may be too firm for some, and its spoiler may block rear visibility.

Some Civic disadvantages: It's hard to modulate the throttle without having the car surge or lurch. The base engine loses its pep when the Overdrive gear on the automatic transmission engages in city driving, and the VTEC variant is noisy. Seats lack sufficient padding, rear access is difficult, rear seatroom is limited to two adults, there's lots of engine and road noise, and an unusually large number of safety-related complaints include airbag malfunctions, sudden acceleration, and complete brake failure.

Civic underbodies are rust-prone and are often sold with severe structural damage that compromises safety. The fuel tank, front suspension, and steering components, along with body attachment points, should be examined carefully in any Civic more than a decade old.

A 1996 redesign improved overall reliability and handling and increased interior room over previous model years, but engine head gasket failures on non-VTEC engines continued to be a problem through the 2000 model year.

The 2001–04 models move from the subcompact to the compact class and increase interior volume while providing seats that are wider and higher. They are also marginally better performers, from a power and handling standpoint. Although steering feedback is a bit vague and over-assisted, the softly sprung suspension still gives the base car a floating feel, and there's excessive body lean when cornering under speed (EX and Si models have a firmer stance). Drivers will find that parking is more of a chore because the car's increased size makes it difficult to see its rear corners.

Quality control still needs improvement. Heading the list of owner complaints are engine crankshaft failures, transmission malfunctions, weak front springs and shocks, and early strut failure resulting in degraded handling. Owners also complain of frequent brake repairs (rotor warpage and pad replacement), AC failures, suspension knocks and squeaks, a subpar stereo system, erratic fuel gauge readings, delaminated paint, chronic water leaks, trunk hinges that steal storage room and damage cargo, a constantly lit Check Engine light, a faulty engine computer module and oxygen sensor, early replacement of the crankshaft pulley and timing belt, and fuel- and electrical system failures.

Other common problems include windshield air leaks and noise; warped windshield mouldings; hard-to-access horn buttons; windows that fall off their tracks; side mirrors that vibrate excessively; headlights that can't be focused properly and are prone to water leaks; gas-tank fumes that leak into the interior; and premature rusting, uneven paint application, chalky spots, and paint delamination. Here's what this owner of a 2001 Civic discovered:

> Paint is developing crow's feet in four separate places...body shop said it was due to bird droppings or sap. I believe this to be impossible and believe it to be a defect in the paint. Blemishes and loss of gloss continue to develop in the paint.

Insight and Civic Hybrid

Stay away from used hybrids, regardless of whether they're made by Ford, GM, Honda, or Toyota. Build quality is inconsistent, the electrical and braking systems can be quite hazardous, maintenance is highly dealer-dependent, depreciation is a bit faster than with comparable makes, and fuel economy is illusory. *Consumer Reports* says the Civic Hybrid's fuel economy may fall short by at least 25 percent. And says this owner of a 2003 Civic Hybrid:

> The Hybrid is supposed to get 48 mpg/city [4.9 L/100 km] and 47 mpg/highway [5.0 L/100 km]. Even the fine print states that the actual mileage should range between 40–56 [4.2–5.9 L/100 km] in the city and 39–55 [4.3–6.0 L/100 km] on the highway.
>
> I have been tracking/documenting my actual mpg. My mpg has never exceeded 35 [6.7 L/100 km]. Since fuel economy is the primary reason for purchasing the Hybrid, potential customers should be extremely skeptical of the claims.

Honda was the first automaker to introduce gas-electric hybrid technology to North American consumers when it launched the Honda Insight in the States in December 1999, followed by the Civic Hybrid in March 2002. Neither vehicle has sold as well as the Toyota Prius.

The Insight, a two-passenger hatchback coupe, uses a small electric motor to assist the 3-cylinder gasoline engine during hard acceleration. The engine recharges the battery pack when coasting or braking and returns to battery power when the car is stopped. The car has very little interior room and poor rear visibility, is slow to accelerate, has a harsh ride and little soundproofing, and is tossed about by moderate crosswinds. Toyota's Prius seats four and uses a more-versatile hybrid system, wherein the electric motor is dominant and gasoline and electric power vary, depending upon driving conditions.

The Civic Hybrid looks and feels just like a regular Civic, both inside and out. It carries a 3-year/60,000 km base warranty, a 5-year/100,000 km powertrain warranty, an 8-year/160,000 km battery pack warranty, and emissions-related equipment that's covered by a more extensive warranty. It does offer some fuel savings—plus it's smooth-shifting, gives a comfortable ride, and provides good front and rear visibility—but it comes in second to the Ford Escape and Toyota Prius, two more-refined hybrids. Good alternatives are the Honda Civic DX and base Toyota Echo or Yaris—three cars that sell for about half the price, get great gas mileage, and don't depreciate as much.

Cold weather performance isn't as fuel-efficient as advertised, and the AC increases gas consumption and shuts off at stoplights, encouraging drivers to sneak up on lights. *Car and Driver* magazine concluded in its September 2004 issue that one would have to drive a Toyota or Honda hybrid 265,500 km (165,000 mi.) to amortize its higher costs. Furthermore, the car's unique dual powerplants can make for risky driving, as this Hybrid owner warns:

> [With a] 2003 Honda Civic Hybrid on a snowy road, coming over a small rise while going around a moderate curve under 40 mph [64 km/h], the battery charging function, activated by driver taking foot off the gas before cresting the hill, produced progressively stronger engine braking effect on the front wheels, equivalent to an unwanted downshift and causing fishtailing and poor response to corrective steering, so that the car slid across the road and into a snow bank and concrete abutment, causing $6,000 (US) in damage. If there had been oncoming traffic, there could have been serious injuries or fatalities.

Repairs and servicing are very complicated to perform; rescuers are wary of cutting through the 500-volt electrical system to save occupants; and there's no long-term reliability data. Honda Hybrid performance and overall quality issues include rough shifting; a rotten-egg smell that intrudes into the cabin; premature brake and rear strut wear; a constantly lit Airbag light; poor-quality radio speakers; a rear bumper cover that may fall off, be misaligned, or come loose; and chipped paint.

VEHICLE HISTORY: 1999—The Si is upgraded with new front and rear styling. **2001**—More interior room, additional horsepower, and fresh styling; no more hatchback; Insight hybrid is launched in Canada a year after its American debut. **2002**—The 160 hp SiR sporty hatchback arrives. Improved fit and finish, a firmer suspension, and a rear stabilizer bar (except on the base model). Front suspension uses MacPherson struts, which increases interior space while watering down the car's sporty performance. Insight is given a continuously variable transmission (CVT). **2003**—New gauges, a CD player for the HX, and the Civic Hybrid arrives. **2006**—Redesigned with an emphasis on new styling, new safety equipment, and more power. The sedan is larger outside and somewhat smaller inside; the coupe is a bit smaller overall. Side curtain airbags and ABS are standard features. A sedan Si joins the Civic lineup.

 ## Safety Summary

All models: 1995–2005—Spoiler and head restraints restrict rear visibility, and large rear-view mirror restricts forward visibility for tall drivers. • Numerous safety defects, including sudden acceleration and stalling, a sticking accelerator pedal, engine and transmission malfunctions, and airbags that fail to deploy, deploy inadvertently, or deploy with such force they cause severe injuries:

My 2002 Honda Civic EX hit another vehicle squarely in the rear end while traveling approximately 15 mph [24 km/h]. Neither of the front airbags deployed! The collision repair centre could find nothing wrong with my airbags. The tow truck operator and the collision repair centre told me that there was some sort of alert out for 2001 and 2002 Honda Civics where the airbags didn't deploy after a front-end collision.

• Ball joints on these vehicles don't have a castellated nut to secure the ball in position; the nut can back off, and the ball pulls out of the steering arm. • Other safety-related complaints: dangerous instability on wet roads; faulty cruise control; ABS brake failures, and constant rotor and pad replacement; defective automatic transmissions; transmission may suddenly jump into Reverse; surging when brakes are applied; vehicle may roll away when parked on an incline; original-equipment tire failures; hood and trunk lids that come crashing down; inoperative door locks; cracked windshields; and headlights and interior lights that suddenly go out. **2000**—Accelerator cable got hung up in the cruise control, causing the vehicle to suddenly accelerate. • While driving, vehicle suddenly accelerated because of the throttle sticking open, and brakes couldn't stop the car. • Brakes locked up and vehicle pulled to the left when coming to an emergency stop. • Sudden steering loss while driving. • Transmission sometimes fails to change gear. • Vehicle suddenly went into Reverse even though shift lever was put into Drive. • Transmission was stuck in Reverse. • Faulty power-door lock makes it impossible to open door from the inside or outside. • Tail lights don't work when the headlights and dash lights are on. • Rear-view mirror is poorly located and is nonadjustable, creating a large forward blind spot for tall drivers. **2001**—Car caught on fire near where the oxygen sensor wires are located. • Child became entangled in rear-seat shoulder belt and had to be cut free. • Vehicle surged forward when put into Reverse, and engaged Reverse when put into Drive. • Transmission may suddenly pop out of Second gear while underway, or refuse to shift into Third or Fourth gear. • Sudden brake failure (master cylinder replaced). • When brakes are applied first thing in the morning, they don't "grab," resulting in extended stopping distances. • Leaking front strut causes poor handling and front-end noise. • Incorrect fuel gauge and speedometer readings. • Airbag warning light is constantly lit (heating coil or core is suspected). • Loose door latches. **2002**—Vehicle downshifts on its own. • Sudden failure of the front tie rod. • Complete loss of steering. • Seat belt doesn't fully retract. • Windshield cracked for no apparent reason. **2003**—Sudden steering lock-up. • Transmission jumps into Neutral; multiple transmission failures. • Power-window failure. • Faulty Firestone tires. • Loose driver's seat. • Seat belts ratchet up uncomfortably. • The head-high interior support handle may injure the driver in a collision. **2004**—Loss of brakes; hit a brick wall head-on, but front airbags didn't go off. • Problems with the main rear crankshaft seal. • Drivetrain bucks and jolts when descending a hill. • Loose tie-rod bolts. • Premature leakage, failure of the front struts. • Sudden front wheel bearing failure. • Weak trunk springs allowed lid to drop on owner's fingers. • Dunlop original-equipment tire's (SP20FE P185/70R14) side wall blew; these tires are also frequently blamed for causing excessive vibration/shimmy. • Weak seatbacks collapse when the vehicle is rear-ended at moderate speeds. • Rear seat belt unlatched on its own. • Defective door lock actuators. • Driver-side quarter window shatters from freezing temperatures. • Head restraints restrict driver's rearward visibility. **2005**—Fire ignited in the seat belt wiring under the passenger seat. • Sudden front wheel lock-up:

> Our new 2005 Honda Civic had both front wheels lock while my wife was going to work, driving down the freeway. The car was totalled, crashing into a guard rail, blowing the air bags, spinning around, starting a fire at the left front wheel and spreading to my wife's coat.

• Brake and accelerator pedals mounted too close together. *Insight:* **2001**—Random events of power loss cause significant reduction of engine power when it is most needed. • CVT transmission failure. • Steering becomes abnormally unstable when vehicle is driven above 50 km/h over uneven or grooved roadways. • Vehicle is prone to hydroplaning on wet roads. • Tire-tread separation. *Civic Hybrid:* **2003**—Vehicle lost all forward power while cruising on the highway. • Chronic stalling. • Excessive brake vibration; vigorous brake pumping needed to get adequate braking. • Hazardous braking system. • Seat belt locks up. • In cold weather, power windows won't roll back up until vehicle warms up. • Prematurely worn shock absorbers. • Driver seat's design can cause serious back pain. • Electromagnetic field may be a health hazard:

> With the use of a gaussmeter, an instrument used to measure electro magnetic fields, the consumer found that vehicle had a high electromagnetic field. The highest level occurred when the engine draws power from the battery via the integrated motor assist or when the battery was charging.

2004—Airbag suddenly deployed for no reason:

> The airbag deployed while driving at about 5–7 mph [8–11 km/h]. Consumer was attempting to park the vehicle and had not hit anything, no curve or debris in the road or no potholes. Consumer went to turn into the parking space and the air bags deployed and the consumer crashed into a wall. Driver sustained burns to the arm from the force of the air bag.

• Trunk caught fire while vehicle was parked. • Sudden, unintended acceleration when foot was taken off of the accelerator pedal, or when braking:

> All of a sudden the car lurched at a high speed three times, and I was trying to brake it to make it quit and it wouldn't quit or brake. My car bashed in the window of the 7/11 and my foot was not on the gas…it was a horrible experience. However, Honda dealer is saying they cannot find anything wrong with it. I was just on the forum and there are lurching problems.

• Front wheels locked up when brakes were tapped lightly. • Excessive vibration caused by prematurely worn brakes. • Vehicle wanders all over the road:

Civic drifts to the side while driving. All of the uneven, worn out tires were replaced as well as the rims. Even though the tires and rims were replaced, it still did not correct the problem.

Secret Warranties/Internal Bulletins/Service Tips

All models/years: Most Honda TSBs allow for special warranty consideration on a "goodwill" basis, even after the warranty has expired or the car has changed hands. Referring to the "goodwill" euphemism will increase your chances of getting some kind of refund for repairs that are obviously related to a factory defect. • Seat belts that are slow to retract will be replaced for free under Honda's seat belt lifetime warranty, says TSB #03-062, issued September 16, 2003. **All models: 1988–2000**—A rear suspension clunk can be silenced by replacing the rear trailing arm bushing. **1996–2000**—Poor AC performance. • Harsh shifts. **1998–2004**—Deformed windshield moulding. **2000**—Steering pull or drifting. • Whistling or howling noise comes from the top middle of the windshield at highway speeds. • Moonroof seal sticks up or leaks. • Key is difficult to remove from the ignition switch; rear-door lock tab is hard to open. **2001**—Delayed upshift after a cold start. • Stiff manual transmission shifter; pops out of gear. • Rear main seal leak troubleshooting tips. • Separation of the lower control-arm ball joints. • Noisy or stiff steering. • Front suspension noise. • Sticking speedometer and tachometer needles. • Windshield cracking at the lower corners. • Damaged or cracked foglight lens. • AC condensate drips onto passenger-side carpet. • Water leaks into trunk through tail lights or onto driver-side carpet through door or firewall, or wets front passenger-side carpet (AC condensate suspected). • Seat belt slow to retract. **2001–02**—Engine hesitation when accelerating is often caused by low oil pressure. • Troubleshooting front brake groan or squeal. **2001–04**—If vehicle won't move in Drive, it's likely caused by excessive Second clutch wear:

VEHICLE WON'T MOVE/MIL ON/DTC P0730

BULLETIN NO.: 04-036   DATE: JANUARY 7, 2005

WON'T MOVE IN DRIVE; MIL COMES ON OR D INDICATOR BLINKS WITH A/T DTC P0730

2001–04 Civic

SYMPTOM: The vehicle does not move when you select Drive. The MIL comes on ('01–03 models) or the D indicator blinks ('04 models) with "A" DTC P0730 (shift control system) set.

PROBABLE CAUSE: Excessive wear in the 2nd clutch.

CORRECTIVE ACTION: Replace the A/T. Use the Honda Interface Module (HIM) to update the PGM software ('01–03 models only).

2001–05—Starter grinds while engine cranks. • Inoperative or erratically operating power windows. • Driver's seat rocks back and forth (see first bulletin on following page). • Water leaks into the trunk (see second bulletin on following page). • Hard-to-close trunk lid. • A-pillar rattles. **2002**—Automatic transmission slippage. • Shift lever may be difficult to move. • Creaking or ticking from the dash or front strut; clean and install shims. • Front windows won't fully roll down.

DRIVER'S SEAT ROCKS BACK AND FORTH

BULLETIN NO.: 01-057   **DATE: FEBRUARY 22, 2005**

2001–05 Civic

SYMPTOM: The driver's seat rocks back and forth during normal driving.

PROBABLE CAUSE: Worn bushings in the height adjustment mechanism.

CORRECTIVE ACTION: Install new seat bushings, nuts, and spacers.

WATER LEAKING INTO TRUNK

BULLETIN NO.: 03-067   **DATE: FEBRUARY 18, 2005**

WATER LEAKS INTO THE TRUNK FROM A BODY SEAM

2001–05 Civic

SYMPTOM: Water in the trunk.

PROBABLE CAUSE: Lack of sealer at various seams.

FUEL GAUGE INACCURATE

BULLETIN NO.: 05-002   **DATE: MARCH 4, 2005**

2003–04 Civic 4-Door EX and LX

SYMPTOM: At any fuel level, the fuel gauge reading drops by 1/4 tank, or 3 to 4 graduation marks. In some cases, the fuel gauge indicates "E" and the low fuel warning light is on. After driving for several minutes, or cycling the ignition switch off/on, the fuel gauge returns to the correct reading. This problem is intermittent, and it affects only Civics with Visteon gauge assemblies.

PROBABLE CAUSE: The software specification for calculating the current fuel level is incorrect.

CORRECTIVE ACTION: Replace the gauge assembly. In warranty: The normal warranty applies: Defect Code: 03214. Out of warranty: Any repair performed after warranty expiration may be eligible for goodwill consideration by the District Parts and Service Manager or your Zone Office. You must request consideration, and get a decision, before starting work.

2003–04—Sticking door lock cylinder. • Inaccurate fuel gauge (see bulletin above). *Insight:* **2001–02**—Water leaks into the trunk. *Civic Hybrid:* **2003**—A CVT transmission update. • Sticking door lock cylinder. **2003–04**—Deformed windshield moulding. **2003–05**—Inoperative or erratically operating power windows. **2004**—Hard-to-close trunk lid. • A-pillar rattles. • Sticking door lock cylinder.

CIVIC, INSIGHT, CIVIC HYBRID PROFILE

	1999	2000	2001	2002	2003	2004	2005	2006	2007
Cost Price ($)									
Civic	14,200	14,200	15,800	15,900	16,000	16,150	16,200	17,180	17,180
Si	18,800	18,800	19,800	19,902	20,700	20,800	21,600	25,880	26,380
SiR	—	—	—	25,500	25,500	25,500	—	—	—
Insight	—	—	26,000	26,000	26,000	26,000	26,000	26,000	—
Hybrid	—	—	—	—	28,500	28,500	28,500	25,800	26,250
Used Values ($)									
Civic ▲	3,000	3,500	4,000	5,000	6,000	7,000	8,500	10,500	12,500
Civic ▼	3,000	3,500	3,500	4,500	5,500	6,500	8,000	10,000	11,000
Si ▲	5,500	6,000	6,500	7,500	8,500	10,000	12,000	15,500	18,000
Si ▼	4,500	5,500	6,000	6,500	8,000	9,000	10,500	14,500	17,000

SiR ▲	—	—	—	8,000	9,000	11,000	—	—	—
SiR ▼	—	—	—	7,000	8,000	10,500	—	—	—
Insight ▲	—	—	6,000	7,500	9,000	13,500	19,000	16,000	—
Insight ▼	—	—	5,000	6,500	8,000	12,500	17,000	14,500	—
Hybrid ▲	—	—	—	—	9,000	11,500	14,000	15,000	18,000
Hybrid ▼	—	—	—	—	8,500	10,500	13,000	14,000	17,000
Reliability	3	3	3	3	4	4	4	5	5
Insight	—	—	—	—	3	3	3	3	3
Hybrid	—	—	—	—	—	—	4	4	5
Crash Safety (F)	4	4	4	4	5	5	5	5	5
4d	4	4	4	4	5	5	5	5	5
Insight	—	—	—	4	4	4	4	4	4
Side	—	3	2	2	5	3	3	3	4
4d	3	3	3	3	4	4	4	4	4
Insight	—	—	—	—	4	4	4	4	4
IIHS Side	—	—	—	—	—	—	—	5	5
Offset	3	3	5	5	5	5	5	5	5
Head Restraints	2	—	2	—	2	3	1	5	5
4d	—	—	—	—	1	1	1	5	5
Rollover Resistance	—	—	—	—	4	4	4	4	4
Insight	—	—	—	—	—	—	4	4	4

FIT ★★★★★

RATING: Recommended (2007). **"Real" city/highway fuel economy:** 7.1/5.7 L/100 km. Very few complaints that actual fuel consumption doesn't match fuel economy claims. However, 2008 models were tweaked to get under Ottawa's "green" rebate benchmark. **Maintenance/Repair costs:** Predicted lower-than-average maintenance costs. **Parts:** Reasonably available; relatively inexpensive. **Extended warranty:** A waste of money. **Best alternatives:** Honda Civic; Hyundai Elantra or Tiburon; Mazda Protegé or Mazda3; Nissan Sentra or Versa; Suzuki Esteem or Swift; and Toyota Corolla, Echo, or Yaris.

Strengths and Weaknesses

The Fit, launched as a 2007 model, is Honda's newest entry-level four-door hatchback. Powered by a 109 hp 1.5L 4-cylinder engine and coupled to a 5-speed manual or automatic transmission, this small car provides better fuel economy than the Nissan Versa, is easily accessed, and has a surprisingly large interior for cargo, thanks to the clever seating arrangement (only a bit less room than in a Civic sedan). Highway performance is fairly good, with sufficient power and agile handling; city handling is better than with the larger Versa. Side curtain airbags and ABS brakes are standard, and the Fit's first-year reliability has been a few notches better than the Versa's.

A 2007 base Fit DX hatchback sold new for $14,980 and is now worth $9,500–$10,000; an LX sold for $17,180 and now fetches $10,500–$11,500. The all-dressed Sport version retailed for $19,480 and is now worth $12,000–$13,000. Depreciation for next year will vary between $1,000 and $2,000.

NHTSA awarded the 2007 Fit five stars for occupant protection in a frontal impact, five stars for a side collision, and four stars for rollover prevention—better-than-average scores for a small car. IIHS gave the 2007–08 Fit its top rating for occupant protection in both frontal offset and side collisions. Head-restraint protection was rated Poor.

A few complaints: Owners have endured gas-tank fuel sloshing underneath the driver's seat, automatic transmission gears that fail to engage smoothly, rear-bumper paint chipping, and the front side bumper falling from the vehicle. Many owners warn that the AC condenser is highly vulnerable to pebble damage:

> Rock damage to condenser caused AC failure due to aluminum grade condenser and lack of adequate protection. Aluminum condenser can be crushed by finger force, clearly not designed to hold up to road projectiles, such as pebbles or small rocks impacting at interstate speeds. First repair on vehicle less than 1 year old and under 14K miles [22,530 km]. No protection offered to prevent [the problem] from occurring again. Out $700 to repair condenser. Modifications to protect condenser will void warranty.

Safety Summary

2007—Airbags failed to deploy:

> After a tear down by the body shop it was determined that the [airbag] sensors were installed at the sides at the front end of the frame rail. This is a very low position

on this car since it's already low to the ground.... Had these sensors been placed at a higher elevation...the airbags would [likely] have gone off and the injuries would have been...minor. This design decision seems like it was developed to satisfy the frontal crash tests conducted by the Insurance Institute for Highway Safety. During those tests the cars are evaluated for crashes to a solid object anchored to the ground. The airbags would not deploy in a crash scenario with any vehicle that would not be a compact car.

• Engine raced and brakes failed after passing over a speed bump. • Turning the steering wheel right or left, or applying the brakes, may cause the engine to increase rpms. • After making a right turn, the automatic transmission failed to engage while the engine raced for five seconds. • Automatic transmission hesitates when gearing down from 10 to 5 km/h in rolling stops for yield signs. • Power-steering control unit often fails when turning, causing a sudden loss of steering. • While making a right-hand turn, the steering locked up because the ignition key was stuck in the steering-column orifice. • Significant forward and rearward blind spots. • Angle at which foot must depress accelerator pedal can be painful; driver's seat position blamed. • Headlights are aimed too low, reducing visibility. • Tires leak air.

Secret Warranties/Internal Bulletins/Service Tips

2007—Vehicle pulls or drifts to the right or left. • Windshield wiper chatter. • Passenger seat won't slide. • Wind noise at top of windshield. • Warranty extension for odometer inaccuracy (5 percent), following a U.S. class action settlement.

Hyundai

ACCENT	★★★★

RATING: Above Average (2006–07); Average (2004–05, 1999–2000); Below Average (2001–03). Having dumped and then abandoned its Pony, Stellar, and Excel junk on Canadian soil, it's about time Hyundai got a product right, even if it did take them almost a decade and involve them pirating away Toyota's quality-control engineers a few years ago. Just as Honda and Nissan have improved since bringing out their '70s rustbuckets, Hyundai has learned from its mistakes (with the help of quality-control documents purloined from Toyota). Hyundai now makes highly reliable cars with better warranties—at bargain prices. Think of the Accent as a refined GM Firefly/Metro/Sprint from South Korea, but with more standard features. The absence of ABS is no big loss and should lead to cheaper maintenance costs as the car ages. However, the skinny tires and small engine relegate the car to an urban environment. **"Real" city/highway fuel economy:** 8.9/6.2 L/100 km. Owners report fuel savings may undershoot this estimate by about 10 percent. **Maintenance/Repair costs:** Average. **Parts:** Reasonably priced and easily found. **Extended warranty:** Consider getting an optional powertrain warranty as protection from occasional engine head gasket and tranny failures. **Best alternatives:** GM Firefly or Metro; Honda Civic (getting an old Honda CRX in good condition would be a master stroke); Hyundai Elantra; Mazda Protegé; Nissan Sentra; Suzuki Esteem; and Toyota Echo, Corolla, or Yaris.

Strengths and Weaknesses

Launched as a '95 model, the early Accent was basically an Excel that had been substantially upgraded to provide decent performance and reliability at a phenomenally low price. Of course, with its small 4-cylinder engine, the Accent is no tire-burner, but it will do nicely for urban commuting and grocery shopping. Consider investing in larger wheels and tires that equip the GT for safer highway handling.

VEHICLE HISTORY: Until the redesigned 2000 models arrived, the Accent hadn't changed much over the years. **2000**—A smoother-shifting automatic transmission; a stiffer, better-performing suspension; a stronger and quieter-running engine; and a more-comfortable driving position with good visibility. **2001**—Engine gets 16 more horses. **2003**—A slightly larger engine; restyled front and rear ends. **2006**—Redesigned to be safer, larger, and more powerful (six more horses). Front side airbags, side curtain airbags, ABS, and four-wheel disc brakes are standard features. **2007**—ABS becomes an optional feature—no big deal.

Owner complaints are surprisingly rare; however, the following problem areas have been noted: faulty engine cooling system and cylinder head gaskets (engine overheating), engine sputtering, Check Engine light that constantly comes on, and chronic automatic transmission failures (an extended transmission warranty is suggested for models no longer under warranty). Owners also frequently complain of excessive front-end vibration; wheel bearing, fuel system, and electrical component failures; premature front brake wear; and excessive noise when braking, particularly an annoying clicking emanating from the rear brake drums.

Safety Summary

All years: Airbags fail to deploy, or deploy inadvertently. • Horn controls may be hard to find in an emergency. • Rear head restraints appear to be too low to protect occupants. • Rear seat belt configuration complicates the installation of a child safety seat (pre-2001 models). **1998–99**—Complete brake failure. • Sudden transmission failure. • Headlights flicker when turning, and high beam is inadequate. • Engine control monitor melted. • Fuel gauge failures. **2000**—Fire erupted in the dashboard area. • Accelerator sticks. • Hood flew up and smashed through the windshield. • Left and right axles broke while vehicle was underway. • Transmission sticks between First and Second gear and pops out of Fifth gear. **2000–04**—Automatic transmission–equipped cars lurch into Reverse (TSB #05-36-003-2). **2001**—Gas pooled underneath the rear seat. • Transmission jumps from Drive to Neutral. • Gearshift jumps out of Reverse. • Seat belts unlatch during impact; passenger seat belt tightens uncomfortably. • Windshield and rear window suddenly shattered. **2002**—Throttle body sensor failure causes car to accelerate on its own; intermittent high engine revs. • Chronic stalling. • Automatic transmission failures characterized by slippage, free-wheeling, jerky shifts, and a clunking noise. • When stopped, brake pedal sinks slowly to the floor and car rolls away (possibly faulty brake master cylinder). • Manual windows fall down. **2003**—Under-hood fire. **2004**—Sudden stalling and total loss of power while driving. • Airbag deployed when passing over railroad tracks. • Small original-equipment wheels and tires make the car unstable at high speeds or when cornering. • Automatic transmission downshifts abruptly or won't shift at all. **2005**—Fire ignited in the engine compartment. • Fuel sloshes out from the fuel-filler pipe. • Rear window shattered as car was warming up. **2006**—Windshield wiper bolt constantly works loose. **2007**—Passenger-side airbag is disabled even though seat occupant is an adult. • Car sped forward when parking in a garage.

Secret Warranties/Internal Bulletins/Service Tips

All years: Tips on troubleshooting excessive brake noise. • Apparent slow acceleration on cold starts is dismissed as normal. • A new AC "refresher" will control AC odours. **1995–2001**—TSB #03-40-018 says a defective kickdown servo switch could cause automatic transmission malfunctions. **1996–2004**—A defective pulse generator may cause harsh, delayed, and erratic shifting, says TSB #03-40-022. • A TSB published in March 2004 says many automatic transmission breakdowns can be traced to faulty transaxle solenoids. **2000–06**—Automatic transaxle oil leak behind the torque converter. **2002**—Harsh or delayed automatic transmission shifting. **2007**—Remedy for a cold rough start/idle. • Free replacement of the clutch pedal ignition lock switch (Service campaign T38).

ACCENT PROFILE

	1999	2000	2001	2002	2003	2004	2005	2006	2007
Cost Price ($)									
L/GS	11,565	11,565	11,995	12,395	12,395	12,895	12,995	12,995	13,495
GL 4d	13,245	13,595	13,595	13,795	13,795	14,195	13,995	13,495	14,295
Used Values ($)									
L/GS ▲	2,000	2,500	2,500	3,000	3,500	4,000	5,000	6,000	7,000
L/GS ▼	2,000	2,500	2,500	3,000	3,500	3,500	4,500	5,500	6,000
GL 4d ▲	2,500	3,500	4,000	4,500	5,500	5,500	6,000	7,000	8,000
GL 4d ▼	2,500	3,000	3,500	4,000	5,000	5,500	6,000	6,000	7,000
Reliability	1	1	1	1	4	4	4	4	4
Crash Safety (F)	—	—	—	—	—	5	5	5	5
4d	3	—	—	4	4	4	4	5	5
Offset	—	—	—	—	—	—	—	3	3
Side	—	—	—	3	—	4	4	4	4
4d	—	—	3	3	3	5	5		4
IIHS Side	—	—	—	—	—	—	—	1	1
Head Restraints	—	—	3	3	3	—	—	1	1
Rollover Resistance	—	—	4	4	4	4	4	4	4

RATING: Recommended (2001–07); Above Average (1999–2000). Shh! This is the car auto columnists laugh at and then buy themselves. They know that Hyundai's quality is the best of the South Korean automakers' and is generally much better than what Detroit offers. Another advantage is that the Accent, Elantra, and Tiburon fly under most buyers' radar, making them more available and much more reasonably priced than better-known brands. There's only a $1,000–$3,500 difference between the high-end and entry-level models. Try to find a 2004–07 model with an unexpired comprehensive 5-year/100,000 km base warranty, or buy any post-2001 version but give up some of your savings to buy an extended transmission warranty. **"Real" city/highway fuel economy:** *Manual:* 8.9/6.4 L/100 km. *Automatic:* 9.6/6.7 L/100 km. **Maintenance/Repair costs:** Average. Dealer servicing has improved considerably, and independent garages find the Elantra's simple mechanical layout quite easy to diagnose and service. **Parts:** Reasonably priced and easily found. **Extended warranty:** Yes, for the transmission, mainly. **Best alternatives:** Honda Civic; Hyundai Accent; Mazda Protegé; Nissan Sentra; Suzuki Aerio, Esteem, or Swift; and Toyota Echo, Corolla, Tercel, or Yaris.

 ## Strengths and Weaknesses

This conservatively styled, "high-end" front-drive sedan was first launched as a 1992 model. It's only marginally larger than the failure-prone Hyundai Excel, but its overall reliability is much better, making it a credible alternative to GM Saturns and the Mazda Protegé, Nissan Sentra, and Toyota Corolla. The redesigned 1996 and later versions actually narrow the handling and performance gap with the segment leader, Honda's Civic.

There is some excessive body lean when cornering, but overall handling is fairly good, mainly because of a relatively long wheelbase and sophisticated suspension. Brakes are adequate, though sometimes difficult to modulate. Conservative styling makes the Elantra look a bit like an underfed Accord, but there's plenty of room for four average-sized occupants.

VEHICLE HISTORY: 2001—A revision makes the wagon disappear, increases interior and engine size (now a 140 hp 2.0L 4-cylinder), and adds four-wheel disc brakes and ABS. **2002**—Debut of a GT hatchback, which is a bargain when one totes up the cost of its standard features. **2003**—The GT adds a four-door sedan. **2005**—A new base GLS hatchback comes online. **2006**—The sporty GT sedan is gone; front side airbags are standard, but no side curtain airbags.

Owners of 1996–2000 model Elantras are relatively happy campers; nevertheless, as with most Hyundai products, transmission failures are commonplace and have been the object of numerous service bulletins (see the Accent "Secret Warranties/ Internal Bulletins/Service Tips") and recalls. Airbag failures are another frequent complaint. Other problem areas include body deficiencies (fit, finish, and assembly), a leaking sunroof, paint cracking, engine misfire and oil leaks (some oil burning), hard starting, and warped brake rotors. Post-'95 models' passing power with the automatic gearbox is perpetually unimpressive, and the trunk's narrow opening makes for a relatively small storage space. The power problem is attenuated with the revamped 2001 versions.

This having been said, the above-noted problems are in no way as severe or as frequent as what you would find with the Detroit competition.

The 2001–07 Elantras are noted for chronic stalling; early manual transmission clutch burnout; prematurely worn-out rear brake drums, cylinders, and shoes; and excessive brake noise and chassis vibration.

Owners also complain of wind howling in the interior when encountering a crosswind, a humming noise emanating from the corners of the windshield, dash front-panel console squeaking and tire thumping, delayed window defrosting, rainwater seeping in under the door, paint/clearcoat cracking, and the steering wheel covering peeling away.

 Safety Summary

All years: Airbags failed to deploy, or deployed for no reason. • Chronic stalling. • Erratic transmission shifting and excessive noise. • Sudden brake loss. • Warped front brake rotors, and master cylinder failure. • Passenger seat belt retracts and locks so that passengers are unable to move. **1998–2000**—Poorly designed jack; too small and weak. **1999**—Defective heater fan and motor assembly. • Trunk lid doesn't close properly. • Loose driver seat. • Defective door handle. **2000**—Vehicle rolled forward even though emergency brake was applied. • Clutch slave cylinder failure. • Vehicle pulls left continually. • Sudden steering failure; loose steering. • Low beam doesn't light up driver's view; instead, the light reflects outward to the left or right. **2001**—Sudden, unintended acceleration. • Child had to be cut free from jammed rear centre seat belt. • Seat belt failed to lock up in a collision. • Brakes randomly engage by themselves and overheat/pulsate. • Rear doors freeze shut in cold weather. **2002**—Seatback failure when car was rear-ended. • Brake and gas pedals are set too close together. • While driving in a rainstorm, all interior and exterior lights shut off. **2003**—Engine surging while on the highway. • Vehicle suddenly lost all power. • Complete loss of brakes. • Headlights will read "dim" but will actually be on high. • Distracting windshield glare. • Seat belts fail to lock. **2004**—Under-hood fire:

> Vehicle caught on fire in the engine compartment while driving 40 mph [64 km/h]. The local fire department arrived to extinguish the fire. Dealer and the manufacturer were notified. The consumer stated that she smelled smoke coming through the vents while driving. The engine light came on, and the vehicle lost all power. Vehicle brakes went out. The consumer stopped the vehicle, and her and the passengers got out of the vehicle within seconds of flames.

• Airbag fails to deploy, or deploys for no reason. • Almost 100 complaints that the passenger-side front airbag is disabled when an average-sized adult is seated; recall doesn't correct the problem for all claimants:

> Repeated intermittent illumination of "passenger airbag off" beginning within days of purchase. Failures occur when anyone sits in passenger seat. Adults weighing 190, 170, and 140 have turned airbags off. Poodle weighing 9 lbs turned airbags on!

• Chronic stalling. • Sudden, unintended acceleration. • Back cover on passenger seat pops out. • Faulty crankshaft position sensor causes the engine to stall. • Engine surging. • Stabilizer bar snapped, causing vehicle to fishtail. • Warped brake rotors. • Defective batteries corrode cables and leak acid. • Passenger seat collapsed in a frontal collision at moderate speed. • Roof buckled while car was underway. • Seat belt extenders not available. **2005**—Sudden acceleration. • Rear brake wheel-cylinder fluid leaks. **2005–06**—Faulty sensor continues to disable airbag when the seat is occupied. It is designed to disable the system *only* when an underweight occupant is seated. **2006**—Seat belt failed to lock in a collision. • Gas and brake pedals are mounted too close together. • Automatic transmission slippage. • Snow builds up in the wheels, causing severe vibration above 50 km/h. • Excessive vibration reported for other reasons. • Sunroof exploded for no reason. • Frequent headlight failures. • Faulty speedometer. **2007**—Car suddenly accelerated while parking. • Chronic stalling due to a faulty fuel pump; stalling often occurs after a fill-up. • Vehicle swerved and went out of control while changing lanes. • Other complaints that the rear end sways, especially when carrying a full load. • Camber settings make the car oversteer. • Transmission shift lever locks in Drive or Park. • Seatback collapsed in a collision. • Passenger seat belt may not unlatch. • Brake light suddenly goes out. • Inaccurate speedometer registers 8km/h more than the actual speed.

Secret Warranties/Internal Bulletins/Service Tips

All years: Hyundai has a brake pad kit (part #58101-28A00) that the company says will eliminate squeaks and squeals during light brake application. • A harsh downshift when decelerating (TSB #98-40-001). • Poor shifting may be caused by an inhibitor switch short circuit. • Intermittent slippage in Fourth gear. • Troubleshooting vibration and ride harshness. **1996–2002**—Harsh or delayed Park–Reverse or Park–Drive engagement. **1999–2006**—A rear drum brake kit will reduce rear brake noise. **2001**—Troubleshooting harsh shifting with the automatic transmission (TSB #05-40-011). **2001–02**—Troubleshooting 2–3 shift flaring usually requires a simple updating of the TCM, says TSB #02-40-001. **2001–05**—Automatic transaxle oil leak behind the torque converter. **2001–06**—Automatic transmission delayed/harsh shifting into Park or Drive. **2002–03**—Excessive chassis vibration when cruising. **2002–04**—Poor engine performance when driving in high-altitude regions may require an upgraded fuel pump. **2003**—Automatic transmission sticks in Second gear. • Harsh shifts into Drive or Reverse. • Rough-running engine may require an upgraded fuel pump. • Corrosion in the front-door wiring connector. **2004**—To eliminate a driveline "bump" when accelerating, reprogram the PCM. **2006–07**—Remedy for harsh/delayed transmission shifts. **2007**—Automatic transmission cannot be shifted in or out of Park. • Hyundai confirms speedometer failures and recommends that the ECU be reprogrammed under an extended warranty. The company has added 3 percent to all of its warranties to compensate for the mileage errors. • Glove box damper replacement is covered by a secret warranty. • Windshield water leaks are covered by a secret warranty (see bulletin).

CAMPAIGN T39—POTENTIAL WINDSHIELD WATER LEAK

BULLETIN NO.: 07-01-004-2   DATE: FEBRUARY 2007

ELANTRA 2007
SUBJECT: Windshield glass water leak (Service Campaign T39).
IMPORTANT: Dealers must perform this campaign on all affected vehicles prior to customer retail delivery and whenever an affected vehicle is in the shop for any maintenance or repair.

ELANTRA PROFILE

	1999	2000	2001	2002	2003	2004	2005	2006	2007
Cost Price ($)									
GL	14,595	14,875	14,875	15,295	15,295	15,630	14,995	14,995	15,595
GLS/VE	17,695	17,475	17,075	16,995	16,995	17,525	17,365	17,365	23,095
GT	—	—	—	18,495	18,495	19,015	19,895	19,985	—
Used Values ($)									
GL ▲	2,500	3,000	3,500	4,000	4,500	5,500	6,500	7,500	9,500
GL ▼	2,000	2,500	3,000	3,500	4,000	5,000	6,000	7,000	8,000
GLS/VE ▲	3,500	4,500	5,000	5,500	6,000	7,000	8,500	9,500	14,000
GLS/VE ▼	3,000	4,000	4,500	5,000	5,500	6,000	8,000	9,000	13,000
GT ▲	—	—	—	6,000	6,500	7,500	9,500	11,000	—
GT ▼	—	—	—	5,500	6,000	7,000	9,000	10,000	—
Reliability	4	4	4	5	5	5	5	5	5
Crash Safety (F)	3	—	4	4	4	5	5	5	5
Side	—	—	5	5	5	5	5	5	4
IIHS Side	—	—	1	1	1	1	1	1	—
Offset	3	3	1	1	1	5	5	5	5
Head Restraints	3	—	1	1	1	1	1	1	3
Rollover Resistance	—	—	—	—	4	4	4	4	4

Kia

After going bankrupt in 1998, Kia was bought by Hyundai (and is also partly owned by Ford through Ford's Mazda affiliation) and now sells a full lineup of vehicles that includes small cars, mid-sized sedans, a minivan, and several sport-utility vehicles. With Hyundai's infusion of cash and better-quality components, 2006 and later Kias have been transformed into remarkably dependable performers.

Not so with earlier models: 2004 and earlier Kias are known for their poor quality control and below-average crashworthiness scores. Mediocre, erratic automatic transmission performance and durability (a Daewoo bugaboo, too) has also been a well-known Kia trait ever since these vehicles were first imported into Canada over a decade ago. The 2005 versions are more reliable, however, and the 2006 model redesign improved the cars' performance considerably.

RIO, RIO5, SPECTRA/SEPHIA, SPECTRA5 ★★★

RATING: Average (2006–07); Not Recommended (2000–05). The 2006 and later models give you better reliability and more safety and performance features. Why am I so hard on the early Rios? Simple: They don't offer even a modicum of the crashworthiness, safety features, performance, or reliability that other cars deliver for the same price or less. **"Real" city/highway fuel economy:** *Manual:* 8.9/6.6 L/100 km. *Automatic:* 9.3/6.7 L/100. **Maintenance/Repair costs:** Average. **Parts:** Average costs, and parts are easily found, despite the small dealer network. **Extended warranty:** A bumper-to-bumper warranty is a must-buy, which wipes out your low sales-price savings. **Best alternatives:** *Rio, Spectra/Sephia:* GM Firefly or Metro; Honda Civic; Hyundai Accent or Elantra; Mazda Protegé; Nissan Sentra; and Toyota Corolla, Echo, Tercel, or Yaris. *Spectra GS-X:* Hyundai Elantra GT, Mazda Protegé5, and VW Golf.

Strengths and Weaknesses

A bit smaller than the earlier Kia Sephia and Spectra, the Rio was originally a South Korean spin-off of the Aspire, marketed from 1995 to 1997 under the Ford nameplate. It's one of the cheapest cars on the market and offers both sedan and wagon versions, a limited number of standard safety and performance features, and cheap interior and exterior materials. 2005 and earlier versions put a low base price before safety, reliability, and performance.

Rios are equipped with a puny 104 hp 1.6L 4-cylinder engine that gives adequate power when teamed with a 5-speed manual transmission. Add an automatic transmission, and you'll need an hourglass to clock your speed. Options available include a 4-speed automatic transaxle; ABS; air conditioning; power steering, door locks, and windows; and foglights. Side airbags are offered on only the most recent models.

Rios are highly manoeuvrable in city traffic and quite fuel efficient, but early models equipped with the 1.5L 4-cylinder engine are poorly suited for highway cruising or driving situations that require quick merging with traffic. Kia's horsepower ratings may be just as suspect as Hyundai's, and reports of chronic stalling sap owner confidence even more. The car's Poor head-restraint rating from IIHS through 2007 and two-star side crashworthiness score from NHTSA on 2003–05 models are also worrisome (2006–07s manage to eke out a three-star rating).

Rio owners report problems with the automatic transmission, seat belts, and electrical and fuel systems; frequent front-end alignments; unreliable tires; and weak, prematurely worn, noisy brakes. Writes this owner of a 2002 Rio:

I had the front brakes replaced due to a clip that fell off and got between the brake pad and drum, and the rear brakes replaced due to brake dust and glazing of drums. Now less than two weeks later, I'm starting to have the same grinding noise in the rear brakes again.

Other areas of complaint involve weak and noisy engine performance; a busy, harsh ride; slow and imprecise highway handling; limited passenger room, with little rear headroom or legroom; problematic entry and exit; small door openings; tire thumping; small audio controls; a missing remote trunk release; low-budget interior materials; a small trunk opening that doesn't take bulky items and doesn't offer a pass-through for large objects; an optional tilt steering wheel that doesn't tilt much; poor body construction (stagnant water collects in the dash on the 2006 model); and a small dealer network that complicates servicing and warranty performance.

Spectra/Sephia

The 2000–01 Sephia is a four-door sedan that bears a passing resemblance to the Toyota Corolla. It's powered by a 125 hp 1.8L inline 4-cylinder engine and is fairly well-appointed. On the other hand, the car's engine is woefully weak, braking is barely adequate, and fit and finish is deplorable.

The Sephia became the Spectra in 2002. This four-door, five-passenger, South Korean–built car came with new styling, an upgraded interior, and a new hatch-back/four-door sedan body style based on the Mazda Protegé platform, housing Mazda's 4-cylinder powertrain.

In the spring of 2004, revamped Spectra models arrived with new styling, more power, and additional safety features, but they kept the 2004 designation—look at the car's features carefully to make sure you get an improved 2004. For example, the old 2004s came in Base, GS, LS, and GSX trim, while the newer 2004s were sold as LX or EX. Remember, mid-2004 Spectras use the Hyundai Elantra's platform and 130 hp 2.0L 4-cylinder engine. You will also find standard front side airbags, side curtain airbags, and four-wheel disc brakes.

The GSX hatchback is a well-equipped, sporty version of the Spectra, powered by a 125 hp 1.8L engine. It has more storage space and performs adequately on the highway. On the other hand, the engine is quite noisy, braking is subpar, and fit and finish that is unbelievably bad.

Spectra owners' litany of complaints is similar to Rio owners': Chronic stalling and surging, airbag failures, steering malfunctions, premature brake wear and brake failures, and fit and finish that is highlighted by poor-quality materials and slap-dash workmanship.

VEHICLE HISTORY: You may be wondering how such low-quality cars originally saw the light of day, so I will digress a bit. Vehicles like the Rio are built and propped up through import tariffs to prevent foreign automakers from capturing the home country's market and jobs. Quality isn't a consideration when you're one of the few players in the game. To keep the factories humming, these cars are exported to developing countries where a low purchase price gives them a huge advantage. When they arrive in Europe and North America, price takes a backseat to quality, reliability, and safety, and auto shoppers look elsewhere for their "bargains." This has been the story with Daewoo, Kia, Fiat, Lada, Dacia, and Yugo.

Kia's products, unlike Daewoo's, do have a track record—and it's not good. In fact, *Consumer Reports* reported on the cars' debut and said in its April 1999 New Car edition, "You'd have to search far and wide to find a car that's worse than this small Korean model." And the proportionally large number of safety-related complaints recorded by NHTSA through 2005 confirms *CR*'s early conclusion.

Rio: **2003**—Subtle styling changes, a slightly larger engine, and extra standard and optional features. Kia claims engineering updates reduce noise and vibrations, suspension alterations improve ride comfort, and larger front brakes increase stopping power. None of these pretensions are supported by driver feedback, however. **2006**—A complete redesign gives the car more room, power, and safety features. A four-door hatchback called the Rio5 joins the lineup. The sole engine is a 110 hp 4-cylinder mated with a standard 5-speed manual transmission; a 4-speed automatic is optional. Front side airbags and side curtain airbags are standard for 2006, though anti-lock four-wheel disc brakes are optional. *Spectra*: **Mid-2004**—Considerably upgraded. **2005**—The Spectra5 hatchback arrives. **2006**—Standard cruise control on the SX and Spectra5. **2007**—A revised interior and a plug-in for digital audio players.

 ## Safety Summary

All models/years: Airbag non-deployment. • Chronic stalling and engine surging. **All models: 2001–03**—Defective fuel line ignited an under-hood fire. • Hood flew up and broke front windshield. • Side airbag failed to deploy. • Vehicle disengages from Overdrive because of a missing transmission control modulator. • Transmission jumps out of gear when brakes are applied. • Brakes stick and pedal goes to the floor without vehicle stopping. • Brakes are noisy. • Excessive shaking and vibration; vehicle swerves all over the road. • Rear seat belt shreds or jams. • Steering binds and grinds when turned; on other occasions, it's too loose. • Premature tire wear. • Various mechanical and electrical problems, including clock spring failure. • Check Engine light, Airbag light, and Fuel light constantly stay lit. • Bent wheel rims. **2003**—Sudden steering loss. • No-starts, particularly in cold weather, due to faulty engine computer module. • Premature failure of the engine and transmission. • In damp weather, brakes grab abruptly and won't release, or they don't "catch" at all:

> The brake fell off the pad. In most normal cars the brakes are held on with a pop rivet. Not this car. They are held on with thin pieces of aluminum. Everyone knows how

easy aluminum bends and twists and that's exactly how mine were. And the brake is held onto the pad with glue!!!

• Steering-column bolt snapped. • Seat belt cuts across the driver's and passenger's throats. • Wheel lug nuts sheared off. • Windshield wiper nuts often come off. **2004**—Mass airflow sensor failures are the likely cause of chronic stalling. • Windshield wiper nut loosened and caused the wiper to fail:

> The retaining nut on the windshield-wiper arm loosens, causing the windshield wipers not to function. The dealership inspected and tightened the retaining nut, but the problem still exists.

2005—Airbag deployed for no reason. • Stalling complaints continue unabated. • Manual transmission clutch replaced at 9,000 km. • Child safety door lock failure; door could not be opened. **2006–07**—Passenger-side airbag is disabled when an average-sized adult is seated. **2007**—Airbags failed to deploy. • Sudden brake failure. *Spectra:* **2005**—Tremendous engine surging while stopped at a light. • Chronic stalling. • Steering locks up. • Defective tie rods, struts, and sway bar linkage cause the vehicle to constantly pull to one side. • Key sticks in the ignition. • Cigarette lighter popped out of its housing and started a fire in the cabin. • Front seat belt latches detach on their own. • Headlights frequently burn out. • Premature tire wearout. **2006**—Side airbag deployed as door was closing. • Airbag failed to deploy. • Engine surges when brakes are applied. • Stalling caused by faulty alternators or malfunctioning engine computer. • Rear brakes suddenly locked up while cruising on the highway. • Early tire failures. • Front windshield moulding blew out while cruising:

> While driving my 2006 Kia Spectra5 at high speed on the interstate, the front windshield molding blew out of the track on the drivers side. I came close to having an accident because it scared me beyond words. The dealership personnel stated that this was not the first car they had replaced this molding on. Last week, the windshield molding popped out again. This time on both sides of the windshield.

Secret Warranties/Internal Bulletins/Service Tips

All models: **2001**—Revised transmission shift lever and bushing spacer. • Reinforced fuse box–cover latch. • Troubleshooting automatic transmission concerns. **2001–02**—Special Service Campaign addresses premature transmission failures. **2001–04**—*KIA Technician Times* (Volume 7, Issue 6, 2004) says some vehicles may develop a vacuum leak that will cause the car to run rough. The main cause of this concern is a broken plastic vacuum-line Y-connector (part #0K30C13744A), located below the fuel rail. **2003–04**—TSB #013 addresses different remedies for curing hard starts in cold weather (reprogramming software is one field fix). *Rio:* **2006–07**—More remedies for poor cold starts or a rough idle. • Rear seatback may stick in the folded position. *Spectra:* **2006**—Key sticks in the ignition. **2006–07**—Troubleshooting tips for automatic transmission 2–3 gearshift shock, slip, or flare.

	2000	2001	2002	2003	2004	2005	2006	2007
Cost Price ($)								
S/EX	—	11,995	12,095	12,351	12,650	12,995	13,295	13,595
RS	—	12,995	13,095	13,251	13,550	13,995	—	—
Sephia	12,995	13,845	—	—	—	—	—	—
Spectra	—	—	14,595	14,795	14,995	15,995	15,595	15,995
GSX	—	—	17,595	17,795	17,995	—	—	—
Used Values ($)								
S/EX ▲	—	2,000	3,000	3,500	4,000	4,500	5,500	7,000
S/EX ▼	—	1,500	2,500	3,000	3,500	4,000	5,000	6,000
RS ▲	—	3,000	3,500	4,000	4,500	5,500	—	—
RS ▼	—	2,000	3,000	3,500	4,000	4,500	—	—
Sephia ▲	1,000	1,500	—	—	—	—	—	—
Sephia ▼	1,000	1,000	—	—	—	—	—	—
Spectra ▲	—	—	4,000	5,000	6,000	7,000	8,500	9,500
Spectra ▼	—	—	3,500	4,500	5,000	6,500	8,000	9,000
GSX ▲	—	—	5,000	5,500	6,500	—	—	—
GSX ▼	—	—	4,500	5,000	5.500	—	—	—
Reliability	1	2	2	2	3	3	3	3
Crash Safety (F)	—	—	4	4	4	4	4	5
Side	—	3	3	2	2	2	3	4
IIHS Side	—	—	—	—	—	—	1	1
Spectra	—	—	—	—	1	1	1	1
Offset	—	—	—	—	1	3	3	3
Head Restraints	—	1	1	1	1	1	1	1
Spectra	—	—	—	—	—	3	3	3
Rollover Resistance	—	—	4	4	4	4	4	4

Mazda

MAZDA3, MAZDA5, PROTEGÉ ★★★★★ / ★★★★★

RATING: *Mazda3:* Recommended (2006–07); Above Average (2004–05). Owner complaints continue to be remarkably few in number. Nevertheless, make sure the AC cools the car sufficiently and the brake calipers and rotors are sound. *Mazda5:* Above Average (2006–07). *Protegé:* Above Average (1999–2003). These cars are plentiful at bargain prices. **"Real" city/highway fuel economy:** There isn't a lot of variation in fuel economy among the different model years, except for the turbocharged engine that wastes gas at a rate of 10.0/7.3 L/100 km. Owners say they burn about 10 percent more fuel than the following estimates indicate.

Mazda3 2.0L manual: 8.5/6.2 L/100 km. *Mazda3 2.0L automatic:* 9.1/6.4 L/100 km. *Mazda3 2.3L manual:* 9.2/6.7 L/100 km. *Mazda3 2.3L automatic:* 9.8/7.5 L/100 km. *Mazda5 2.3L manual:* 10.6/8 L/100 km. *Mazda5 2.3L automatic:* 11.2/8.3 L/100 km. *Protegé manual 1.6L:* 8.5/6.7 L/100 km. *Protegé automatic 1.6L:* 9.3/6.9 L/100 km. *Protegé 2.0L manual:* 9.6/7.3 L/100 km. *Protegé 2.0L automatic:* 9.9/7.4 L/100 km. **Maintenance/Repair costs:** Average. **Parts:** Expensive, but easily found. **Extended warranty:** Not necessary. **Best alternatives:** Honda Civic; Hyundai Accent or Elantra; Nissan Sentra; Suzuki Aerio, Esteem, or Swift; and Toyota Corolla, Echo, or Yaris.

Strengths and Weaknesses

Protegé

First introduced in 1990, Protegés are peppy performers with a manual transmission hooked to the base engine. As with most small cars, the automatic gearbox produces lethargic acceleration that makes highway passing a bit chancy. Overall durability started improving with the 1991 and later Mazda 323 and Protegé, both of which were also sold as Ford Escorts. Nevertheless, pollution-control components and the electrical system have been troublesome. Watch out for automatic transmission malfunctions, air conditioning breakdowns, and engine oil leaks, as well.

Although 1996–2003 Protegés are far more reliable than most American-made small cars, automatic transmissions continue to be their weakest link (a problem also seen with Ford's Escort and Hyundai's lineup), characterized by erratic shifting and locking up in Fifth gear. Owners also endure fuel-system glitches, electrical problems, front brake vibration, rotor warping, and premature pad wear. Other generic deficiencies are weak rear defrosting, chronic engine stalling (a secret warranty applies, up to seven years), AC failures, and body defects, including wind and water leaks into the interior.

Mazda3

An econobox with flair, the front-drive 2004 Mazda3 is the entry-level small car that replaced the Protegé. With considerable engineering help from Ford and Volvo, these cars use a platform and 4-cylinder engines that will also serve future iterations of the Ford Focus and Volvo S40. Powered by a 148 hp 2.0L or a 160 hp 2.3L, coupled with either a 5-speed manual or a 4-speed Sport-mode automatic transmission, the car offers spirited acceleration and smooth, sporty shifting. Handling is enhanced with a highly rigid body structure, front and rear stabilizer bars, a multi-link rear suspension, and four-wheel disc brakes. Interior room is also quite ample with the car's relatively long 263.9 cm (103.9 in.) wheelbase, extra width, and straight sides, which maximize headroom, legroom, and shoulder room.

The Mazda3 is a breeze to break into. Bizarre, but true—all it takes is a blow to the door on either side of any 2004–07 model, and the lock is popped. The Internet is full of reports telling how easily the cars and their contents are stolen. This information first came to light in the fall of 2006 in Western Canada, and now the police and insurers like the Insurance Corporation of British Columbia (ICBC) are scrambling to answer complaints coming in from all over the country.

There aren't a lot of other owner complaints. However, some drivers say the car could use a bit more passing power with the standard engine; prematurely worn-out brake rotors and pads continue unabated; there are some electrical shorts and numerous minor fit and finish deficiencies; a high deck cuts rear visibility; there's limited rear footroom; and some Mazda dealers have been accused of overcharging for scheduled maintenance. Other reported problems: excessive fuel consumption, which is about 15 percent more than advertised; the 5-speed manual gearbox sometimes has trouble shifting from First to Second gear; the gas and brake pedal are too close together; drivers easily catch the side of their shoe against the brake when accelerating (consider getting customized racing pedals); drivers' right knees rub the console; a front-end clunk is felt on hard acceleration; a popping/creaking/rattling noise emanates from the rear end (hatch struts may be the culprit); the dash and driver's door rattle; a steering clicking/ticking sound; cracked dashboards; broken window regulators; excess brake dust on rear wheels; the Door Ajar light comes on for no reason; paint is unusually thin, and aluminum rims peel; the CD changer is failure-prone; wimpy AC performance; and the passenger-side wiper may not clean the windshield sufficiently. Original-equipment and Goodyear tires perform poorly in rain and slush (Kumho Ecsta, Michelin Pilot, and Hakkapeliitta winter tires are better performers; check with *www.tirerack.com* for the best tire combination).

Mazda5

The Mazda5 is mostly a compact miniwagon that's based broadly on the Mazda3 and carries six passengers in three rows of seats. Used mostly for urban errands and light commuting, the "5" employs a peppy, though fuel-frugal, 153 hp 2.3L 4-cylinder engine (the same engine that produces three more horses in the Mazda3 and Mazda6)

hooked to a standard 5-speed manual transmission or a 4-speed automatic.

So far, that engine has had few problems during the past three years the Mazda5 has run in Canada. In its favour, the vehicle has all the advantages of a small minivan without the handling or fuel penalties. Furthermore, it's reasonably priced used and provides a comfortable ride and relatively quiet interior (except for omnipresent road noise—a common trait with small wagons). There are a few minuses, however. The small 4-cylinder engine doesn't have much torque ("grunt," or pulling power) for heavy loads or hill climbing, and towing isn't recommended. There isn't much room for two passengers in the third-row seat. There's also a history of automatic transmission malfunctions (but much fewer than with Honda or Toyota), prematurely worn-out brake rotors and pads, and fit and finish deficiencies.

So far, only 13 complaints have been reported to NHTSA concerning transmission malfunctions, steering lock-up, the vehicle rolling downhill with the parking brake engaged, poor wet-road traction, and premature tire wear. In the past, some Mazda dealers have been caught overcharging for scheduled maintenance.

VEHICLE HISTORY: *Protegé:* **1999–2003**—Totally revamped with a restyled interior and exterior and a more-powerful engine lineup; handling, acceleration with the automatic tranny, and entry/exit are improved. Better-performing than earlier versions. **2000**—Premium models receive front-seat side airbags and an improved ABS system. **2001**—A restyled front end, optional disc brakes, and a 130 hp 2.0L engine is offered. **2002**—Introduction of the Protegé5 four-door hatchback sport wagon and the MP3, a higher-performing sedan variant. **2003**—A turbocharged 170 hp MazdaSpeed Protegé debuts and is sold in small quantities. **2004**—Protegé is replaced by the 2004 Mazda3. *Mazda3:* **2004–07**—Mazda3 launches with two 4-cylinder engines: a base 148 hp 2.0L and a 160 hp 2.3L. **2007**—A new performance model equipped with the highly recommended traction/anti-skid control feature. *Mazda5:* **2006**—Mazda5's first model year.

Safety Summary

All models/years: Airbags failed to deploy. • Chronic stalling. • Transmission failures and malfunctions. • If you stop or park on an incline, vehicle will likely roll away even with brakes applied. *Protegé:* **1995–99**—Cracked fuel line caused fire. • Metal rods in driver's seat could cause severe back injuries in a rear-end collision. • Driver's seat belt buckle wouldn't unlatch. • Brake pedal pad is too narrow. **2000–02**—Delayed braking. • Vehicle constantly pulls to the right. • Passenger unable to disengage seat belt. • Bucket-seat seatbacks contain metal support bars that are extremely uncomfortable. **2001**—Loss of brakes. • Gearshift lever jumped from Drive to Neutral while driving. • Defective steering-column coupling. • Broken rear axle causes severe pulling to one side. • Windows take a long time to defrost. • **2002**—Brake line split, leading to rear-ender. **2003**—Nauseating fumes entered the vehicle. • Brake pedal pushed almost to the floor before brakes work; they produce excessive noise. • Passenger seat belt won't disengage. • Passenger seat belt broke; seat belt case and release button broke while trying to release belt. *Mazda3:* **2004**—Premature wearout of brake pads and rotors. • The transmission can be hard to shift, especially from Third to Fourth gear. • Transmission replaced during the first year. • Huge accumulation of brake dust on the rear wheels. • Brake rotors are prematurely grooved. • Chronic hard starts, stalling, and poor idling. **2004–05**—AC is inadequate; it doesn't cool the car and compromises acceleration. **2005**—When car stalls on the highway, both steering and brakes fail. • Brake failures. • Windshield wiper flew off the car. • Vehicle stalled and then crashed:

> I was going about 35 mph [56 km/h] and all of a sudden the power went out. I had no brakes, no steering, nothing…and in front of me was an above ground cement manhole we have on the base and I knew I was going to hit it so I just held on tight. The next thing I remember is people screaming "Are you OK" and when I opened my eyes I was upside down. I flew in the air and landed on the car behind me and came within an inch of going into his windshield but that also saved my life.

• In a collision, some safety features perform poorly, or not at all:

> 1. The driver's seatback broke during impact. 2. The airbag did not deploy when she struck the vehicle in front of her. 3. The emergency switch that shuts down the fuel system did not activate. Our vehicle was totaled from all the damage.

2006—Airbag failed to deploy. • Frequent stalling. • Sudden acceleration when using the cruise control. • Engine failure due to defective lower engine rod. • Vehicle goes into Reverse when shifted into Fourth gear. • Brake and accelerator pedal mounted too close together. • Early rear brake pad and rotor replacement. • Driver's seatback collapsed in a rear collision. • Tire rims are easily damaged when passing over potholes. • Premature Toyo tire wearout at around 32,000 km; side wall failures; poor all-season tire traction in snow:

> The tires that are sold on this car are rated as all-season, so I should not have any problems. I was traveling about 20 mph [32 km/h], and [slid] sideways for about 50' [15 m] then hit another vehicle coming in the opposite direction, then I went off the road into a 5' [1.5 m] deep ditch. My car had about $1,400 [U.S.] in damage, which the insurance paid.

> •

> I am a mature driver living in this type of weather for many years. I have never driven a vehicle that handled so badly in the snow. This vehicle with the tire combination as sold is unsafe. After the accident, I searched the Internet and found numerous reviews claiming how poor the tires are in winter weather.

2007—Driver's airbag failed to deploy. • Car was rear-ended, and driver's seat slid all the way back, preventing driver from applying the brakes. • Gas tank puncture. • Warped front brake rotors. • Large rear blind spot. • Xenon headlights provide poor visibility. • Toyo tire side walls blew out. • Sudden failure of the MazdaSpeed3 engine:

Mazda Speed3 2007 has been having problems, with engine mounting failure it seems the engine mount is not bolted correctly or the bolt itself to the engine is defective, I believe Mazda is aware of these three incidents, but has not issued any recalls or recommendations.... Mazda3Forums [h]as some picture[s] provided by actual consumers who had this [happen] to their cars: *www.mazda3forums.com/index. php?topic=68463.0.*

Mazda5: **2006**—Driver's seat collapsed in a rear-end collision. • Chronic engine overheating (faulty AC compressor?). • Hesitation when shifting. • Stalling in traffic believed to be caused by a defective power control module (PCM). • Leaking casing requires a transmission replacement. • Brake failures. • Sudden power-steering failure. • Leaking front struts. • Shocks, front stabilizer bushing, and damper wear out early. • Prematurely worn original tires (cupping). • Weak side walls on Dunlop Signature Sport tires. • Very poor traction on wet roads. • AC compressor failure. • Doors freeze shut. **2007**—Car parked 3 m (10 ft.) from the house with the engine running suddenly accelerated, damaging the house. • Airbags did not deploy in a collision. • Third-row safety belt anchor is placed too far forward to secure the passenger. • Fob-controlled door locks don't work. • Engine runs poorly as the temperature drops, and there is an antifreeze smell in the car (engine head gasket?).

Secret Warranties/Internal Bulletins/Service Tips

All models: **1997–2007**—Troubleshooting tips for eliminating wind noise around windows. **1998–2003**—Dealing with musty, mildew-type AC odours. **2003**—Cold engine rattling. • Wind noise around doors. *Mazda3, Mazda5:* **2006–07**—Wind noise from windows. *Mazda3:* **2004**—Poor AC performance. • Mazda-upgraded shock absorbers will reduce suspension knocking when passing over bumps. • A splashing sound comes from the dash area. • Trunk lid difficult to open. • Power-window failures require a new window motor. • Fix for squeaking rear brakes. **2004–05**—Hard starts and poor idle are tackled in TSB #01-013/05, and the correction is covered by the warranty. • Engine stalls at low rpms. • Possible causes for a noisy, smelly engine coming from any Mazda3 equipped with a manual transmission. • Installing countermeasure washers can stop drivetrain clicking. • Excessive engine vibration fix. • Rear brake squeal and grinding has been remedied with upgraded brake pads, says TSB #04-003/05. • Modified pads and a mounting support for the front brake calipers to correct front brake squeaking. • Front-door rattle correction guidelines. • One-touch window stops halfway down. **2004–06**—Hard starts in cold weather require a software recalibration under warranty. • Rough idle and engine hesitation. • Troubleshooting a snap or clunk noise when operating the windows. **2004–07**—Body vibration at cruising speed. • High power-steering effort. • Corroded wiper arm hinges. • Inability to adjust driver-seat manual lift. **2006–07**—Idle dip when AC cycles on. • Engine stalls or hesitates after a hot start (reprogram the PCM). *Mazda5:* **2006–07**—High power-steering effort. • Intermittent engine stumble. • Engine stalls at low rpms. • Idle fluctuation and engine vibration. • Body vibration at cruising speeds. • Front suspension squeak, knock, or rattle. • Outer mirror wind noise.

	1999	2000	2001	2002	2003	2004	2005	2006	2007
Cost Price ($)									
Protegé	14,970	15,095	15,795	15,795	15,795	—	—	—	—
Mazda3	—	—	—	—	—	16,195	16,295	16,495	16,795
Mazda5	—	—	—	—	—	—	—	19,995	19,995
Used Values ($)									
Protegé ▲	2,500	3,000	3,500	4,500	5,000	—	—	—	—
Protegé ▼	2,000	2,500	3,000	3,500	4,500	—	—	—	—
Mazda3 ▲	—	—	—	—	—	7,500	9,000	10,500	11,000
Mazda3 ▼	—	—	—	—	—	6.500	8,000	9,000	10,500
Mazda5 ▲	—	—	—	—	—	—	—	11,500	13,000
Mazda5 ▼	—	—	—	—	—	—	—	10,500	12,000
Reliability	4	4	5	5	5	3	4	4	4
Crash Safety (F)	—	4	5	5	5	4	4	4	4
Side	—	3	3	3	3	3	3	3	3
IIHS Side	—	—	—	—	—	—	1	1	1
Offset	3	3	3	3	3	5	5	5	5
Head Restraints (F)	2	2	3	3	3	2	2	2	2
Rear	—	—	2	2	2	2	2	—	—
Rollover Resistance	—	—	—	—	4	4	4	4	4

Note: Neither IIHS nor NHTSA tested the 2006 or 2007 Mazda5; 2008s did get five-star ratings for front and side occupant protection, while rollover resistance was rated four stars.

Mercedes-Benz

SMART FORTWO ★

RATING: Not Recommended (2005–07). The Smart Fortwo Coupe and Cabriolet are Not Recommended because cheaper Asian microcars—like the Honda Fit, Nissan Versa, and Toyota Yaris—are almost as economical to drive, more refined, and easier to service and repair. **Parts:** Rare and expensive; few independent suppliers stock Smart parts. **Maintenance/Repair costs:** Extraordinarily high. **Extended warranty:** An expensive prerequisite for such a cheap car. **Best alternatives:** Honda Civic or Fit; Hyundai Accent; Mazda3, Mazda5, or Protegé; Nissan Sentra or Versa; and Suzuki Forsa, Swift, Esteem, or Aerio.

Strengths and Weaknesses

What was once a cutting-edge and cute econobox has turned into a rather primitive conveyance for saving fuel at all costs. Not a "smart" idea when competitors abound that are cheaper to buy and that perform much better on the highway and in city congestion. Daimler has lost billions on the Smart since its 1998 European debut, and the company is leery of expanding the brand into the States, especially after fuel prices fell almost 50 percent in the latter half of 2008. Without that American expansion, Canadian Smart owners may be limited to Canadian roads if they're at all worried about servicing. And even if they stay home, parts supply and servicing could become a larger problem than it is at present.

The Smart, sold in most of Canada's Mercedes-Benz dealerships, *is* fuel-frugal and distinctively styled. On the other hand, you will pay a maxi price for a minicar that has lethargic acceleration, highly dealer-dependent servicing (trips must be planned carefully for servicing accessibility), no long-term reliability figures, and no NHTSA crashworthiness data. It is not a "green" car, as many pretend, since diesel emissions contain particulates that exacerbate lung disorders. Furthermore, Asian microcars are cheaper by a few thousand dollars and are all-around better performers.

Smart depreciates much too quickly for a small car that one would imagine to be in high demand by fuel-frugal drivers. For example, sold new for $16,500, a used 2005 entry-level Smart Fortwo Coupe now goes for about $8,000; a new $19,500 2005 entry-level convertible now sells for about $10,000.

Smarts are powered by an 800 cubic centimetre 3-cylinder turbodiesel motor that produces 41 hp—nowhere near the 108 horses offered by Toyota's smallest car, the $13,165 2008 Yaris. Furthermore, the Smart is only 2.5 metres long and weighs in at only 730 kg, which is very light when compared to the Toyota Echo or Yaris. These factors combine to give the Smart an estimated 4.4 L/100 km rating, much better than the Toyota Echo's estimated city/highway fuel economy of 6.7/5.2 L/100 km, and much more frugal than the outrageously inaccurate fuel-savings claims bandied about by Honda and Toyota when they hype their hybrids.

Like Fiat, Lada, Peugeot, and Renault—four automakers that abandoned Canada after failing to expand into the States—Mercedes may leave Smart owners high and dry if it decides Smart cannot compete successfully against the existing and forthcoming Asian economy cars. Mercedes wouldn't hesitate to "flip the switch," as it did by dumping Chrysler in May 2007. In fact, you have to admit that Mercedes hasn't had a great record with small entry-level models. Remember the "Baby Benz" models, such as the 190 model that was introduced over a decade ago and then quickly abandoned, or the C-Class hatchback that was recently dropped? This wouldn't be much of a problem if Smarts were conventional small cars backed by an extensive dealer network and a large parts inventory. But that's not the case. Furthermore, unlike old MGs and Triumphs, there isn't a body of independent repairers and part suppliers who can step into the breach.

As for safety and reliability concerns, the 2008 Smart Fortwo has earned Good ratings for frontal and side occupant crash protection and Acceptable for head-restraint protection from IIHS. NHTSA hasn't tested the car yet. Second-generation models come with standard electronic stability control and side curtain airbags. For reliability and overall highway performance, all first-generation Fortwos (built through 2007) come up far short. The 40 hp turbodiesel that powers these vehicles (up to 2008, when a 71 hp 1.0L gasoline engine takes over) is clearly inadequate for merging in highway traffic; passengers will find the ride to be jiggly and unsettling and handling to be barely competent. Shifting also requires a great deal of patience and foresight because there can be considerable "lag and lurch."

SMART FORTWO PROFILE

	2005	2006	2007
Cost Price ($)			
Coupe	16,500	16,700	16,700
Convertible	19,500	19,700	19,700
Used Values ($)			
Coupe ▲	8,500	9,500	11,500
Coupe ▼	7,500	8,500	10,000
Convertible ▲	10,500	12,500	14,000
Convertible ▼	9,500	11,000	13,000

Note: Safety ratings may be found in the text above and pertain to the 2008 models only.

Nissan

SENTRA ★★★★

RATING: Above Average (2007); Average (2001–06); Not Recommended (1999–2000). Below-average crashworthiness scores for 1999–2006 models. **"Real" city/highway fuel economy:** *Manual 1.8L:* 8.5/6.1 L/100 km. *Automatic 1.8L:* 8.3/6.2 L/100 km. *Manual 2.5L:* 10.2/7.3 L/100 km. *Automatic 2.5L:* 10.2/7.7 L/100 km. Owners report fuel savings vary little from these estimates. **Maintenance/Repair costs:** Average costs and availability; anyone can repair these cars. **Parts:** Owners report waiting weeks for recall-related parts. **Extended warranty:** Not required. **Best alternatives:** Honda Civic; Hyundai Elantra or Tiburon; Mazda Protegé or Mazda3; Suzuki Esteem or Swift; and Toyota Corolla, Echo, or Yaris. High-performance enthusiasts will love Sentra's 2007 and later SE-R and Spec V models, although the Honda Civic Si and MazdaSpeed are still the benchmark for the most performance for your dollar.

Strengths and Weaknesses

Until the 1991 models arrived, early Sentras were fairly reliable, fuel-thrifty, mediocre performers that provided a rudimentary ride and handling. 1991–97 model year Sentras handle better, but have a number of quality problems, including faulty fuel tanks, leaking manual and automatic transmissions, and noisy engine timing chains and front brakes—problems that continue to afflict these cars. Fortunately, with the exception of computer failures and ABS malfunctions, repairs are relatively simple and cheap.

VEHICLE HISTORY: 2000—A major redesign produces more-powerful engines, a better ride, and enhanced handling. It's basically identical to the costlier 2001 version. **2002**—The 145 hp SE model was replaced at the top of the line by the SE-R and SE-R Spec V; the latter offers a 180 hp engine, a limited-slip differential, and a sport-tuned suspension to compete against the Honda Civic SiR and Mazda's high-performance spin-offs. Four-wheel disc brakes also become a standard feature. **2003**—Arrival of the GXE, equipped with a 165 hp 2.5L engine, ABS, and front side airbags. **2007**—Redesigned with fresh styling, more power, a longer wheelbase, and added standard features, like a 140 hp 2.0L that boosts horsepower by 14, a 6-speed manual transmission, an automatic CVT (2.0 SL), AC and side curtain airbags, ABS on higher-end models, four-wheel disc brakes (Spec V), and a sizzling 177 hp 2.5L 4-cylinder powerplant (SE-R) that's pumped up to 200 horses on the Spec V.

1995–2002 owner complaints concern stalling and hard starting; engine rattles; electrical glitches; premature brake wear and excessive brake noise; an automatic transmission whine; AC solenoid failures, and an AC that blows hot air or freezes up; and malfunctioning accessories. Owners have also had to contend with a recurrent steering clunk noise and clutch, clutch-switch, suspension-strut, wheel bearing, and catalytic converter failures. Crank position sensor malfunctions may prevent the vehicle from being started. Body assembly is also targeted, with some complaints of loose windshield mouldings, poor body fits, paint defects, and air and water leaks into the interior through the trunk and doors.

2003–06 models are just as problem-prone. One gets the impression Nissan held back many quality improvements for later inclusion in the 2007 model redesign. Owners of these versions are plagued by cylinder head gasket leaks; cracked #4 cylinder heads on the 1.8L engine; a misfiring #3 cylinder; early replacement of the engine serpentine belt; engine pinging and rattling; and automatic transmission, fuel-system, and electrical problems:

> My car had its serpentine belt going bad at 10,000 miles [16,000 km]. It makes a squeaky sound which can only be fixed by changing the belt. This seems to be a problem with many Sentra owners. Mine is a 2006 Nissan Nentra (Special Edition).

Front brake pads and rotors also wear out quickly; there's excessive noise, bouncing, and vibration caused by prematurely worn struts and control-arm bushings; the doors vibrate noisily; passenger-side windows leak; the hood allows water to leak onto the drivebelt; rear bumpers may fall off; many incidents of excessive wind noise around the windshield moulding; and a poor AC design that wastes fuel:

Above about 35 or 42F [about 2°C–7°C] the air cond. runs if the air selector is positioned on any selection that includes defrost, and the only way to turn this off is to turn the air selector to a position that does not contain defrost, pull over, stop the vehicle, turn the ignition off, then restart the vehicle.... This is not green, the air is often running all day wasting gas mileage [and] putting more pollution in the air. Heater must be turned on to compensate for the cooling effect of the air conditioner.

2007 Sentras were much improved, especially for crashworthiness, but some serious problems remain. The CVT is smooth and usually very responsive (though cold weather may adversely affect its performance), the ride is more comfortable, interior trim has gone upscale, there are handy flip-forward rear-seat cushions and flat-folding rear seatbacks, and more attention has been paid to fit and finish. On the minus side, get used to limited passing power on the highway with base models, excessive engine noise in the higher revs, numb steering, mediocre manual shifting, instrument gauges that wash out in sunlight, and tight rear seating.

Owners report having to frequently replace front brake calipers and warped brake rotors as well as fuel-delivery system glitches that cause loss of power, hard starting and stalling, and audio system malfunctions.

 ## Safety Summary

All years: Chronic stalling. • Sudden acceleration. • Brake failures. • Brake and accelerator pedals are set too close together. • Airbags fail to deploy, or deploy inadvertently. • Steering lock-up. • Premature tire wear. • Horn blows on its own. **1998–99**—Sticking throttle. • Ignition key breaks off in the ignition. • Faulty power-door locks. • Front seats jam when moved back. **1999**—Fuel-filler flap fell into fuel-filler tube. **2000**—Suspension attachment bolts broke off. **2001**—Brakes easily lock up at all speeds. • Warped brake rotors. **2002**—Fire ignited in the headlight assembly:

I am a professional fire investigator. This vehicle fire originated with the headlight assembly. The burn patterns clearly indicate this to be the area of origin and the supporting burn patterns indicate the fire originated in the headlight assembly. Even though this recall does not specifically address a possible fire hazard, I believe the fire is related to the recall problem.

• Fire erupted in the engine compartment. • Sudden acceleration and frequent stalling. **2003–04**—Windshield wipers, turn signals, headlights, horn, and hazard lights may suddenly fail. • Brakes lock up at low speed, particularly on wet roads. **2004**—Stalling; repeatedly loses all engine power; and high-speed bucking (surging). • Erratic, rough idling. • Early automatic transmission replacement. • Keyless remote doesn't work, and back door doesn't open from the inside, apparently due to a short in the electrical system. • Continental and Firestone tire tread peels off. **2005**—Rear wheel lock-up. • Warped rear brake drums. • Front seatback collapsed from a rear-end collision. • Frequent horn malfunctions. • Inoperative driver's door handle. **2006**—Engine serpentine belt failures. • Automatic transmission stays in Neutral, or slips out of gear. • Complete brake loss. • Door locks lock with the keys in the ignition. • Faulty front wheel bearings. • Defective window regulators. • Firestone Firehawk GTA 02 side wall failure. • Gas tank pressure forces fuel out of the tank:

> A new gas tank and fuel filter were needed. The vehicle is currently being repaired at the dealer. They covered half of the repair costs. The failure is identical to NHTSA Campaign ID Number 05v269000 (Fuel System, Gasoline: Storage) for an earlier model of the same vehicle; however, the VIN was not included in the recall.

2007—Vehicle caught fire while driving on the highway. • Broken motor mounts and steering-column bolts (steering wheel turns without effect). • Cracked engine block. • Complete loss of brakes. • Original tires are poor winter performers. • False illumination of the Low Tire Pressure light. • Poor crossmember design eats tires:

> A manufacturing defect of the rear cross member does not allow adjustment for toe alignment which resulted in excessive tire wear creating an incalculable risk of failure.

•

> Rear tires are worn out @ 11,000 miles [17,700 km]. Nissan replaced 2 rear axles and rear suspension assembly and 2 rear tires. They changed the alignment specs and said it was fine.

•

> We are experiencing severe rear tire wear. Dealership refused to acknowledge problem until the third visit when we went with handful of testimonials (printed from car review sites on Internet) from other people experiencing this same problem with their Nissan 2007–2008 Sentra.

Secret Warranties/Internal Bulletins/Service Tips

All years: Remedies for brake pedal judder and noise. • Faulty master cylinder causes brake pedal to slowly drop to the floor. **1995–99**—Harsh shifts and low power with the automatic transmission may be due to reduced movement of the A/T throttle wire cable inside the cable housing. • A self-activating horn can be fixed by replacing the horn springs and spring insulators. **1997–99**—Harsh shifts and low power with the automatic transmission. • More tips on silencing squeaks and rattles. • Diagnosing causes of brake judder and steering-wheel shimmy. • Slow retraction of the front seat belt. **1999–2001**—Hard starting in cold weather or at high altitudes. • Engine pings with light to moderate acceleration. • Exhaust manifold heat-shield rattle. • Automatic transmission won't upshift. • Tips to improve downshifting (modified downshift spring). • Brake pedal slowly drops to floor (master cylinder check). • Vehicle wanders or pulls to one side. • Water condensation from AC. • Anti-theft system prevents starting. **2000**—Vehicle lacks power; transmission sticks in Third gear. • Slow fuel fill; pump nozzle clicks off continually. • Erratic AC vent flow. • Front suspension squeak and rattling. • Windshield hum or whistle. **2000–04**—TSB #AT04-002, published March 10, 2004, says abnormal shifting of the automatic transmission is likely due to a defective control valve assembly. **2000–05**—Alternator chirping or squealing is caused by a defective alternator drivebelt; "goodwill" adjustment available. **2000–06**—Front-door windows may not work properly. **2001–02**—Low power or poor running. • Water leak in trunk area. • Rear brake caliper knock, clunk, or rattle. **2002–05**—A 2–3 shift chirping noise can be silenced by pouring in two bottles of Nissan's special ATF transmission treatment fluid. Do this first, before spending big bucks on unneeded repairs, inspections, etc. **2002–06**—Hard starts and long crank time. **2003**—Anti-theft system may make for hard starts or no-starts. • Troubleshooting tips for a lit MIL. • AC may operate erratically and have a sticking case door. **2003–05**—A harsh-shifting automatic transmission apparently afflicts a large part of Nissan's lineup. **2004–06**—Nissan's remedy for excessive brake squeaking. **2005**—Cold engine stumbling, stalling fix. **2007**—Doors are hard to open with the outside handle in cold weather. • Hard-to-close trunk lid. **2007–08**—AC compressor noise, poor cooling, and window fogging. • Inoperative power-window "Auto Up" function.

SENTRA PROFILE

	1999	2000	2001	2002	2003	2004	2005	2006	2007
Cost Price ($)									
Sentra	15,398	15,398	15,298	15,598	15,598	15,798	15,598	16,698	16,798
SE-R	—	—	—	19,998	20,498	21,498	21,498	21,698	—
Spec V	—	—	—	21,498	21,998	21,998	21,998	22,198	24,298
Used Values ($)									
Sentra ▲	1,500	2,500	3,500	4,500	5,500	6,500	7,500	8,500	10,000
Sentra ▼	1,500	2,000	3,000	4,000	5,000	6,000	6,500	7,500	9,000
SE-R ▲	—	—	—	5,500	6,000	7,500	9,500	11,000	—
SE-R ▼	—	—	—	4,500	5,500	7,000	8,500	10,500	—
Spec V ▲	—	—	—	6,500	7,500	9,000	10,000	12,000	15,000
Spec V ▼	—	—	—	5,500	7,000	8,500	9,500	11,500	14,000
Reliability	3	3	4	4	3	3	3	3	4
Crash Safety (F)	—	—	4	4	4	4	4	4	5
Side	—	—	—	—	2	2	2	2	5
IIHS Side	—	1	1	1	1	1	1	1	—
Offset	3	3	3	3	3	3	3	3	—
Head Restraints	2	2	2	1	1	1	1	1	5
Rollover Resistance	—	—	—	4	4	4	4	4	4

RATING: Recommended (2007). **"Real" city/highway fuel economy:** 7.9/6.1 L/100 km. **Maintenance/Repair costs:** Predicted lower-than-average maintenance costs. **Parts:** Several weeks' delay for some parts (fuel pump and airbag). **Extended warranty:** Not needed. **Best alternatives:** Honda Civic or Fit; Hyundai Elantra or Tiburon; Mazda Protegé or Mazda3; Suzuki Esteem or Swift; and Toyota Corolla, Echo, or Yaris.

Strengths and Weaknesses

Versa is Nissan's entry-level small hatchback and sedan, first launched as a 2007 model. Powered by a 122 hp 1.8L 4-banger and coupled to a 6-speed manual transmission or a 4-speed automatic CVT, this small car gives decent fuel economy and a comfortable ride, is easily accessed, and, like a jumbo shrimp, is one of the roomiest econocars on the market. Side curtain airbags are standard, and first-year reliability has been better than average. On the downside, the manual tranny isn't as smooth as the automatic CVT, and handling is only so-so.

A 2007 base Versa S Hatchback sold new for $14,498 and is now worth $8,500–$9,000; an all-dressed SL Hatchback sold for about $2,600 more, or $17,098, and is now worth $10,500–$11,000. A used 2007 Versa S Sedan costs only about $300 more than the used SL Hatchback, and the top-of-the-line SL Sedan goes for just $700 more. Expect additional depreciation of only $1,500–$2,000 over the next year.

NHTSA awarded the 2007 Versa four stars for occupant protection in a frontal impact, five stars in a side collision, and four stars for rollover prevention, which are better-than-average scores for a small car. IIHS gave the 2007–09 Versa its top rating for occupant protection in both frontal offset and side collisions and for head-restraint protection.

Owner complaints have been mostly over fuel economy claims. Drivers say that the Versa's fuel consumption is about 10 percent higher than what Canadian government figures show:

> This is a 2007 Nissan Versa and [it has] been getting only about 22 to 24 miles per gallon [9.8–10.7 L/100 km] in town. Sticker says the car gets 30 miles per gallon [7.8 L/100 km] in town. I have never gotten close to that. Took car to dealer and they said the air intake temp was 165 degrees [74°C] and they replaced the sensor. Gas mileage is still not what it should be.

Other areas of complaint concern rapid brake caliper/rotor wear; electrical shorts; a faulty fuel pump, leading to hard starts and stalling; front-end "popping" when turning; and body hardware deficiencies.

Safety Summary

2007—A fire ignited in the rear wheelwell. • Airbags failed to deploy during a collision. • Airbag cover came out of the dash. • No brakes. • Vehicle shut down while cruising, and airbag deployed, knocking the driver unconscious. • Steering column had to be replaced twice. • Car veers left and right while cruising. • Car suddenly swerved out of control for no apparent reason. • Tie rod suddenly snapped, pulling the vehicle sharply to the right. • Gasoline spurted out of the filler neck when refuelling. • Many complaints that the Tire Pressure warning light comes on even though the tires are properly inflated.

Secret Warranties/Internal Bulletins/Service Tips

2007—Front airbag cover not flush. • Inoperative driver-door mirror. **2007–08**—Tips on installing a child safety seat. • AC compressor noise and window fogging. • Inoperative "Auto Up" power-window feature.

Subaru

IMPREZA, FORESTER, WRX	★★★ / ★★★★ / ★★★

RATING: *Impreza:* Average (1999–2007). *Forester:* Above Average (2003–07); Average (1999–2002). *WRX:* Average (2007); Below Average (2002–06). The WRX has tricky handling and reliability issues (powertrain, brake, and steering). Except for the Forester, Subaru's model lineup is mostly the bland leading the bland. There's nothing remarkable about Subaru except for its early use of AWD for its entire lineup as a desperate move to stave off bankruptcy in the mid-'90s. Incidentally, the company isn't in great financial shape right now. Quality control has declined markedly over the past few years, and customer service has suffered equally. Smart shoppers will choose a cheaper Asian vehicle until Subaru lowers its prices and raises performance and quality-control levels. The 2006 Forester improvements are a good start. **"Real" city/highway fuel economy:** *Impreza 2.5L manual: 11.2/7.7 L/100 km. Impreza 2.5L automatic:10.6/7.6 L/100 km. Forester: 10.9/7.9 L/100 km. Forester turbocharged manual: 13.0/9.3 L/100 km. Forester turbocharged automatic: 12.5/9.3 L/100 km.* Generally, owners report the turbocharged Forester's actual gas consumption is often 20 percent higher than the above estimates. *WRX: 11.8/8.0 L/100 km.* **Maintenance/Repair costs:** Higher than average; changing any of the exterior lights can cost up to $50. Expensive servicing is hard to overcome because independent garages can't service key AWD components. **Parts:** Parts aren't easy to find and can be costly; delayed recall repairs. **Extended warranty:** Not needed. **Best alternatives:** If you don't need the AWD capability, you're wasting your money. Here are some front-drives worth considering: Honda Civic; Hyundai Elantra; Mazda3 or Protegé; Nissan Sentra; Suzuki Aerio, Esteem, or Swift; and Toyota Corolla, Echo, or Yaris. Some recommended small vehicles with 4×4 capability that are set on a car's frame, not a truck's (to provide more carlike handling and better fuel economy), include the GM Vibe, Honda CR-V, and Toyota Matrix or RAV4.

 ## Strengths and Weaknesses

These well-equipped small cars have one of the most refined AWD drivetrains you'll find (prior to 1996, they were mostly mediocre front-drive economy cars). With their four-wheel traction, Subarus provide lots of storage space with the wagons, good fuel economy, and good handling without any torque steer. On the other hand, Subaru makes you pay dearly for the AWD capability, overall mechanical reliability is so-so, body workmanship is barely average, and braking can get downright scary. Furthermore, small doors and entryways restrict rear access, the coupe's narrow rear window and large rear pillars hinder rear visibility, heat and air distribution is often inadequate, and front- and rear-seat legroom may be insufficient for tall drivers. Without their AWD capability, these cars would be back-of-the-pack used-car picks.

The full-time 4×4 Impreza is essentially a shorter Legacy with additional convenience features. It comes as a four-door sedan, a wagon, and an Outback Sport wagon, all powered by a 135 hp 2.2L or a 165 hp 2.5L 4-cylinder engine. The 2.5L performs much better with the Impreza and Forester than with the Legacy Outback. It is smooth and powerful, with lots of low-end torque for serious off-road use. The automatic transmission shifts smoothly. The manual transmission's "hill holder" clutch prevents the car from rolling backward when starting out. These Subarus hurtle through corners effortlessly, with a flat, solid stance and plenty of grip. Tight cornering at highway speeds is done with minimal body lean and no loss of control, and steering is precise and predictable.

An AWD car for the high-performance crowd, the WRX first showed up as a goofy-looking, squat little wagon/SUV with a large rear end, a 227 hp 2.0L 4-cylinder engine mated to a high-boost turbocharger, lots of standard performance features, a sport suspension, an aluminum hood with a functional scoop, and higher-quality instruments, controls, trim, and seats.

Another Subaru spin-off, the Forester is a cross between a tall wagon and a sport-utility. Based on the shorter Impreza, the Forester added eight horses to the Legacy Outback's 165 hp 2.5L engine and coupled it to a 5-speed manual transmission or an optional 4-speed automatic. Its road manners are more subdued, and its engine provides more power and torque for off-roading than do most vehicles its size. One minus: cramped rear seating.

VEHICLE HISTORY: 1999—Stronger engines, more torque, and upgraded transmissions. **2002**—2.2L 4-cylinder is dropped, along with Subaru's pretensions for making affordable entry-level cars. Totally redesigned models include the 2.5 TS Sport Wagon, 2.5 RS sedan, Outback Sport Wagon, the WRX sporty sedan, and the Sport Wagon. There is no longer a two-door version available. *Impreza:* **2004**—New front end with larger headlights and a restyled interior and exterior. **2006**—A small horsepower increase, enhanced front end, additional airbags, and a freshened interior. *Forester:* **1999**—A quieter, torquier engine; a smoother-shifting transmission; and a more-solid body. **2000**—Standard cruise control (L) and limited-slip differential (S). **2003**—Improved interior materials, an upgraded suspension, and enhanced handling and ride quality. You'll also find larger tires and fenders, and revised head restraints and side-impact airbags. **2004**—A turbocharged 210 hp 2.5L 4-banger and a racier appearance. **2006**—More power and a slightly restyled interior and exterior. The 2006 turbocharged XT adds 20 hp, now up to 230 hp via a redesigned engine intake manifold (this could be troublesome in the future); other models get eight more horses, for a total of 173 hp. A retuned suspension enhances ride smoothness and handling response, and there's improved braking feel on all models. Ground clearance is slightly increased, and an alarm system is now standard. **2007**—17-inch wheels replace the 16-inchers. *WRX:* **2004**—A 300 hp engine comes on the scene. **2006**—2.5L gets 20 extra horses (up to 230 hp).

Subarus are noted for only average quality control, spotty, expensive servicing, and serious automatic transmission and brake deficiencies. There's also a history of premature clutch failures and shuddering, particularly after a cold start-up. Owners report poor engine idling; frequent cold-weather stalling; manual transmission malfunctions; rear wheel bearing failures; excessive vibration caused by the alloy wheels; premature exhaust system rust-out and early brake caliper and rotor scoring and wear; minor electrical short circuits; catalytic converter failures; doors that don't latch properly; body panel and trim fit and finish deficiencies, characterized by water leaks and condensation problems from the top of the windshield or sunroof; the sunroof not closing properly; the windshield cracking and scratching too easily; and paint peeling. In addition to the paint peeling from delamination, owners report that Subaru paint chips much too easily:

> My Subaru Forester 2006 has paint chips all over. Dealer says they are rock chips. I took it to [an] auto body paint shop and one of the techs said it's very odd for there to be rock chips all over the car since we live in the city.

Safety Summary

All models/years: Sudden acceleration, stalling, transmission failures, steering loss, airbag and brake malfunctions, Brake and Engine lights continually on, front seats move fore and aft, and windshield is easily cracked, especially in freezing weather. **All models: 2000**—A mountain of complaints relative to loss of braking and premature wearout of key brake components. **2001**—ABS overreacts when braking over an irregular surface. • Rear wheel bearings fail repeatedly. • Factory-installed anti-theft device disables the starter. **2002**—Chronic brake failures. • Brake rotors are frequently scored after only a few kilometres. • Many reports of blown transmissions. **2003**—Very poor braking when passing over rough surfaces:

> On my 2003 Subaru Impreza Outback Sport, the anti-lock brakes are dangerous. If you hit a bump while braking, it will trigger the ABS—and result in an almost complete loss of braking ability. I notice a bulletin is listed for the WRX only, but this is a major problem in my car as well.

• Seat belt ratchets tighter; refuses to unlock. **2004**—Vehicle won't go into gear. • Complete loss of brakes. • Raw fuel smell in the cabin. • Car wanders all over the road because of defective suspension struts. **2004–05**—Windshield is easily cracked. **2005**—Chronic rear strut failure. • Fuel odour inside the cabin. • Side window shatters spontaneously. *Impreza, Forester:* **2000**—Driver burned from airbag deployment. • Sudden loss of transmission fluid. • Driver's seatback may suddenly recline because seat belt gets tangled up in the recliner lever. • Frequent wheel bearing failures. • Fuel-filler cap design is too complicated for gas station attendants to put on properly, which causes the Check Engine light to come on; driver, therefore, has to pay dealer to reset it. **2001**—Rear wheel bearings broke. • Brake and accelerator pedals are too close together. • In a collision, airbags failed to deploy and seat belt didn't restrain occupant. • In a similar incident, shoulder belt allowed driver's head to hit the windshield. • Headlights don't illuminate the edge of the road and are either too bright on High or too dim on Low. • Alarm system self-activated, trapping a baby inside the car until fire rescue arrived. **2002**—Dangerous delay, then surging, when accelerating forward or in Reverse. • Surging at highway speeds, and stalling at lower rpm. • Transmission failure; gears lock in Park intermittently. • Open wheel design allows snow and debris to pack in the area and throw wheel out of balance, creating dangerous vibration. • High hood allows water onto the engine. *Forester:* **2003**—When backing vehicle into a parking space, the hill-holder feature activates, forcing the driver to use excessive throttle in Reverse. • Brake pedal went to floor without braking. • Heater, defroster failure. • Five doors but only one keyhole makes for difficult access when the keyless entry fails. **2004**—Airbags failed to deploy. • Airbag warning light comes on whenever the driver's seat is moved; dealer wants $800 to fix it. • Automatic fuel pumps overfill the fuel tank. • Sudden acceleration. • Hard starting in cold weather. • Premature wheel bearing replacements. • Because Subaru does not make winter wiper blades for the rear wiper, the wiper blade ices up and rear visibility is impeded. • Hood latch released while Forester was underway. • Premature tire failure. **2005**—Side airbag failed to deploy. • Many reports of sudden, unintended acceleration. • Car was too flimsy to protect occupants in a rollover:

> The symmetrical all wheel drive system of my 2005 Subaru Forrester XT failed, the vehicle fishtailed and drifted, resulting in a rollover, and severe bodily injury. The vehicle was so flimsy, it was disgusting. Every door and window opening collapsed, glass flew everywhere. The ceiling collapsed on the passengers' heads.

• Car hesitates and bucks in cold weather. • Plugs and coil back are replaced frequently. • Cruise control fails to disengage. • ABS sticks. • Windshield wipers often won't work. **2006**—Driver's seatback collapsed when vehicle was rear-ended. • Engine surges and sags, especially after a cold start. • Sudden, unintended acceleration, and the brakes failed. • Oil leaks onto the exhaust system. • Rear tailgate hydraulic struts fail, and the tailgate falls. • Gas station pumps don't shut off automatically when the car is fuelled. • Low-beam headlights fail to provide adequate illumination. **2006–07**—Passenger-side airbag is disabled when an average-sized passenger is seated. • Several reports that original-equipment Yokohama tires' side walls blow out, plus they're poor winter performers and wear out quickly. **2007**—Side frontal airbag failed to deploy. • Cruise control failed to disengage. • Engine surges when vehicle goes downhill. • Vehicle surged forward as driver shifted the manual transmission from First to Second gear. • Transmission locked up. • Constant tire vibration at 110 km/h. *WRX:* **2001**—Brake rotors are easily grooved, degrading braking ability. **2002**—First gear is hard to engage. **2002–03**—Chronic ABS brake failures. • Fuel smell in the cabin caused by fuel pooling in the engine manifold recess. **2003**—Increased braking distance when brakes are applied on an uneven surface. **2004**—Turbocharger failure. • Loss of power on the highway. • Failure-prone, clunking struts will not rebound, causing the rear end to sag and degrading handling. **2004–05**—Difficulty shifting into Fifth gear:

> I discovered that this is a common problem in 2004 and 2005 STIs. Apparently, Subaru of America put an inferior synchro in 5th gear. 1st, 2nd, 3rd, 4th, and 6th all have upgraded synchros. Starting in 2006, Subaru began putting the upgraded synchros in all 6 gears.

2005—Tricky handling is still a problem. **2006**—Cracked oil pickup tube:

> Broken oil pickup tube, driving home from work the pickup tube broke causing the oil in the oilpan to not circulate through the system. This destroyed all internal bearings and likely fatigued many other engine internals. The dealership replaced all bearings under warranty but did not replace any other engine block.

• Fuel-system lines and hoses leak fuel and emit fuel odour. • Premature manual transmission clutch failure.

Secret Warranties/Internal Bulletins/Service Tips

All models/years: Automatic transmission pops out of gear. • At least three bulletins deal with manual transmission malfunctions. • Diagnostic and repair tips for transfer clutch binding and/or bucking on turns. • Troubleshooting a sticking anti-lock brake relay; this problem is characterized by a lit ABS light or the ABS motor continuing to run and buzz when the ignition is turned off. • Premature brake pad, caliper, and rotor wear. • A rotten-egg smell could be caused by a defective catalytic converter. It will be replaced, after a bit of arguing, free of charge up to five years under the emissions warranty. **All models: 2000–01**—Front oxygen air/fuel sensor cracking. **2002–03**—Insufficient AC cooling. **2002–07**—Tips on eliminating radio speaker vibration. **2003**—Defective 4EAT transmission parking pawl rod. • Clutch pedal sticking. **2006**—Poor washer nozzle operation. *WRX:* **2004–05**—Tips on silencing a noisy rear differential. **2007**—Remedy for hard acceleration surge.

IMPREZA, FORESTER, WRX PROFILE

	1999	2000	2001	2002	2003	2004	2005	2006	2007
Cost Price ($)									
Impreza 4×4	21,995	21,995	22,196	21,995	22,995	22,995	22,995	23,495	22,695
Forester	26,695	26,895	28,395	28,395	28,395	27,995	27,995	27,995	26,995
Base/Brighton	17,795	—	—	—	—	—	—	—	—
WRX	—	—	—	34,995	34,995	35,495	35,495	35,495	35,495
Used Values ($)									
Impreza 4×4 ▲	3,000	3,500	5,000	6,500	8,000	9,000	11,500	13,000	14,000
Impreza 4×4 ▼	2,500	3,000	4,000	5,500	7,000	8,000	10,500	12,000	13,000
Forester ▲	4,500	5,500	7,000	8,500	10,000	11,000	14,500	17,000	18,000
Forester ▼	4,000	5,000	6,000	7,500	9,000	10,000	13,000	15,500	17,000
Base/Brighton ▲	2,500	—	—	—	—	—	—	—	—
Base/Brighton ▼	2,000	—	—	—	—	—	—	—	—
WRX ▲	—	—	—	8,500	10,000	11,500	14,500	18,500	21,000
WRX ▼	—	—	—	8,000	9,000	10,500	13,000	17,000	19,000
Reliability	3	3	3	3	3	3	3	4	4
Crash Safety (F)									
Forester	4	4	4	4	5	5	5	5	5
Impreza	—	—	—	4	4	—	—	4	4
Side (Forester)	—	—	5	5	5	5	5	5	5
Impreza	—	—	—	4	4	—	—	4	4
IIHS Side	—	—	—	—	5	5	5	5	5
Offset	—	—	—	5	5	5	5	5	5
Forester	5	5	5	5	5	5	5	5	5
Head Restraints	—	—	2	3	3	—	5	5	5
Forester	3	3	3	—	—	—	—	5	5
WRX	—	—	—	—	—	2	2	2	2
Rollover Resistance									
Forester	—	—	3	3	3	4	4	4	4
Impreza	—	—	—	4	4	—	—	4	4

RATING: Average (1999–2007). A competent full-time 4×4 performer for drivers who want to move up in size, comfort, and features. Available as a four-door sedan or five-door wagon, the Legacy is cleanly and conventionally styled, with a hint of the Acura Legend in its rear end. The AWD is what this car is all about. It handles difficult terrain without the fuel penalty or clumsiness of many truck-based SUVs. The Outback is a marketing coup that stretches the definition of "sport-utility" by simply customizing the all-wheel-drive Legacy to give it more of an outdoorsy flair. Interestingly, what was a $10,000 gap between the high-end and entry-level model narrows to a couple thousand dollars after a few years. **"Real" city/highway fuel economy:** *Manual:* 11.0/7.8 L/100 km. *Automatic:* 10.9/7.9 L/100 km. *3.0L 6-cylinder:* 12.4/8.4 L/100 km. Owners say their fuel consumption is about 15 percent more than these estimates. **Maintenance/Repair costs:** Higher than average. Repairs are dealer-dependent. **Parts:** Parts aren't easily found and can be costly. **Extended warranty:** Get an extended warranty to cover likely powertrain deficiencies after the base warranty has expired. **Best alternatives:** Honda CR-V, Hyundai Tucson or Santa Fe, and Toyota RAV4.

 ## Strengths and Weaknesses

Costing a bit more than the smaller Impreza, these Subaru models are well-appointed, provide a comfortable ride and acceptable handling with the right options, and have lots of cargo room. On the downside, owners report problematic automatic transmission performance when it's hooked to the base engine; sluggish performance from the 2.5L, undoubtedly because of the car's heft; excessive engine noise; sloppy handling on base models; excessive 4-cylinder engine noise; cramped back seats, with a tight fit for the middle rear-seat passenger; limited rear head-room for tall passengers; trunk hinges that can damage cargo and cut into storage space; seat belts that may be too short for large occupants; and very dealer-dependent servicing.

First launched in 1989 as front-drives, these compacts are a bit slow off the mark. The 5-speed is a bit "notchy," and the automatic gearbox is slow to downshift, has difficulty staying in Overdrive, and is failure-prone. Early Legacy models are noisy, fuel-thirsty cars with bland styling that masks their solid, dependable AWD performance. Actually, the availability of a proven 4×4 powertrain in a compact family sedan or wagon makes these cars appealing for special use.

VEHICLE HISTORY: 1999—Debut of an upgraded 2.2L engine. **2000**—Longer, carrying a new 2.5L engine. **2001**—Two new Outback wagons, featuring a more-powerful 3.0L engine, join the lineup. **2002**—The H6-3.0 VDC Outback sedan, equipped with a standard 3.0L engine, joins the lineup. **2003**—New front-end styling; GT gets an upgraded engine and a semi-manual Sport Shift; Outback suspension is upgraded to improve cornering and reduce front-end plow. **2005**—Subaru's mid-sized cars are restyled and have larger dimensions, additional features, and more power. In fact, 2.5i models use a 168 hp 4-cylinder with a manual transmission or optional 4-speed automatic. However, a new 250 hp turbocharged version of that engine powers the Legacy 2.5 GT/GT Limited and Outback 2.5 XT models, and it's mated with a manual or an optional 5-speed automatic. The Outback 3.0 R sedan, L.L. Bean Edition wagon, and VDC Limited wagon come only with the 5-speed automatic and a 250 hp 3.0L 6-cylinder engine (up from 212 hp). The automatic transmissions include a manual-shift feature. On the safety front, all these Subarus have anti-lock brakes, front side airbags, and side curtain airbags. An anti-skid system is standard on the Outback 3.0 R VDC wagon but is otherwise unavailable. **2006**—A new sporty version of the GT, called the spec.B. **2007**—A 60/40 split-folding rear seatback.

The 6-cylinder engine is adequate but doesn't feel as if it has much in reserve. The automatic transmission shifts into too high a gear to adequately exploit the engine's power, and it's reluctant to downshift into the proper gear. On pre-2005 models, the 2.5L engine is a better performer with the manual gearbox, although its shift linkage isn't suitable for rapid gear changes. The 4-cylinder has several drawbacks as well: It's noisy and rough-running, and it's tuned more for low-end torque than speedy acceleration.

Base models don't handle well. They bounce around on uneven pavement, the rear end tends to swing out during high-speed cornering, and there's too much body lean in turns at lesser speeds. Higher-end models handle well, though there's some excessive lean when cornering. The GT's firmer suspension exhibits above-average handling.

The Legacy and Outback have had more than their share of reliability problems over the years. Powertrain defects can sideline the car for days. Engine and transmission problems keep showing up. Servicing can be awkward because of the crowded engine compartment, particularly on turbocharged versions.

Automatic transmission front seals and clutch breakdowns are most common through 2004; the transmission sometimes downshifts abruptly while descending a long grade or travelling on snow-packed highways; and the front brakes require frequent attention. Check Engine and ABS warning lights come on constantly, for no reason. Shock absorbers, constant velocity joints, and catalytic converters also often wear out prematurely. Other problems that appear over most model years include chronic electrical and fuel-system malfunctions; hard starting, surging, and stalling in cold weather; starter and ignition relay failures; and snow packing inside the wheelwells, binding steering. Misadjusted door strikers make for hard closing/opening.

 Safety Summary

All models/years: Many reports of sudden acceleration in Drive and in Reverse, constant stalling followed by engine surging, severe pulling to one side, ABS brake failures, and the premature wearout of brake components. • Small horn buttons may be hard to find in an emergency. **All models: 1999**—When accelerating or decelerating, vehicle will begin to jerk because of excessive play in the front axle. • Front bumper skirt catches on parking blocks, resulting in the bumper twisting and ripping off. **1999–2001**—A cracked #2 piston may cause major engine failure. • The centre rear seat belt's poor design prohibits the installation of many types of child safety seats. **2000–01**—Vehicle suddenly veers to the right when accelerating or braking. • Cruise control failed to disengage when brake pedal was depressed. • During a collision, airbags deployed but failed to inflate. • Excessive steering and vehicle vibration when passing over uneven pavement. • Steering lock-up while driving. • Vehicle's rear end bounces about when passing over bumps. • Frequent surging from a stop. • Cracked seat belt buckle. • Seat belts are too short for large occupants. **2002**—While idling in Park, vehicle suddenly jumped into Drive. **2004**—Automatic transmission failure. • Seat belt came undone during a collision. **2004–06**—Owners still complain of engine hesitation when accelerating from a coastdown or a stop, then sudden surging as the transmission hunts for a lower gear. This has been a generic problem with many Subarus for almost a decade. **2005**—Cruise-control failure. **2006**—No airbag deployment. • Sudden acceleration while underway, especially when the cruise control is engaged. • Oil pickup tube sheared off, causing major engine damage. • Fuel-pump fuse burns out repeatedly. • Early wearout of the rear brakes (front and rear rotors warped). • Coolant cap doesn't hold pressure. • Low-beam headlight illumination is inadequate. • Noxious smell emanates from the clutch. • Windshield wipers come on and go off on their own, as if possessed. **2007**—No airbag deployment. • Oil return line cracked and ignited a fire in the engine compartment:

> Two weeks later same problem same oil line and its cracked again. This is obviously a manufacturing defect among these parts and a design flaw as well.

> •

> The contact owns a 2007 Subaru Legacy. While driving 15 mph [24 km/h], oil leaked on the exhaust and caused a small engine fire. The dealer replaced the oil line.

Secret Warranties/Internal Bulletins/Service Tips

All models/years: Troubleshooting tips on a sticking anti-lock brake relay; this problem is characterized by a lit ABS light or the ABS motor continuing to run/buzz when the ignition is turned off. • Diagnostic and repair tips for transfer clutch binding and/or bucking on turns. • A rotten-egg smell is likely caused by a defective catalytic converter. It will be replaced, after a bit of arguing, free of charge under the emissions warranty. **All models: 2000–01**—Loose bolts on the front seat belt retractor. • Inlet heater hose leaks engine coolant. • Probable causes for the automatic transmission Temperature light flashing. • Measures that will eliminate brake squeal. • Mirror makes wind noise. **2002**—Excessive blower motor noise. • More countermeasures to reduce brake squeal. **2003**—Defective engine water pump. • Improved Sport Shift cold-weather operation. • Defective transmission parking pawl rod. • Roof-rack wind noise. • Premature suspension corrosion:

Certain rear suspension subframe components were produced with poor paint quality, which, after continued exposure to corrosive road salts for a period of several years, could result in rust-out of the component and possible breakage of the subframe. If such breakage occurs while the vehicle is being operated, control of the vehicle could be affected, increasing the risk of a crash. Remedy: Dealers will clean and rustproof the rear suspension subframe.

2004—Possible causes of transfer clutch binding when cornering. 2005—Seat belt warning chimes when seat is unoccupied. 2005–06—Free radiator cooling fan relay #2 replacement. • Troubleshooting instrument panel squeaks. 2005–07—How to fix front-door rattles. 2005–08—Sunroof sunshade rattles. 2006—Fixing rattles from the liftgate area. 2007—Rubbing noise when turning steering wheel. • Transmission Temperature light flashing. 2007–08—Transmission shift-lever boot cracking.

LEGACY, OUTBACK PROFILE

	1999	2000	2001	2002	2003	2004	2005	2006	2007
Cost Price ($)									
Legacy 4×4	20,495	23,595	24,295	27,395	27,295	27,295	27,995	28,495	26,996
Outback	30,895	34,695	35,195	31,995	37,995	26,995	32,995	32,995	30,995
Used Values ($)									
Legacy 4×4 ▲	4,000	4,500	6,500	7,500	9,500	10,500	14,000	15,000	17,000
Legacy 4×4 ▼	3,000	4,000	5,500	7,000	8,500	9,500	13,000	14,500	15,500
Outback ▲	5,500	6,500	8,000	9,500	10,500	11,500	14,500	17,000	19,500
Outback ▼	5,000	6,000	7,500	8,500	9,500	10,500	13,000	15,000	18,000
Reliability	3	3	3	3	3	3	3	3	3
Crash Safety (F)									
Legacy 4d	4	—	4	4	4	4	5	5	5
Side	3	—	4	4	3	4	—	—	5
Wagon	—	—	—	—	4	4	—	—	5
IIHS Side	—	—	—	—	—	—	2	5	5
Offset	3	5	5	5	5	5	5	5	5
Head Restraints	2	2	3	3	3	4	3	5	5
Rollover Resistance	—	—	—	4	4	4	—	—	4

Suzuki

RATING: *Aerio:* Recommended (2003–07). *Swift, Swift+:* Recommended (2002–07); Above Average (1999–2001). *SX4:* Recommended (2007). *Esteem:* Above Average (1999–2002). *Verona:* Average (2004–06). Getting the most horsepower bang for your buck means shopping for a sport model or looking at the upgraded 2000+ model years. Wagons are especially versatile and reasonably priced for the equipment provided. Both the base GL and upscale GLX come loaded with standard features that cost extra on other models. **"Real" city/highway fuel economy:** *Aerio manual:* 9.4/7.0 L/100 km. *Aerio automatic:* 9.3/7.0 L/100 km. *Aerio AWD automatic:* 9.9/7.6 L/100 km. *Swift manual:* 8.9/5.9 L/100 km. *Swift automatic:* 9.1/6.3 L/100 km. *SX4 AWD manual:* 10.1/7.6 L/100 km. *SX4 AWD automatic:* 9.9/7.1 L/100 km. *Esteem manual:* 8.3/6.0 L/100 km. *Esteem automatic:* 9.0/6.3 L/100 km. *Verona automatic:* 12.0/7.9 L/100 km. **Maintenance/Repair costs:** Cheap to keep up and repair. **Parts:** Average costs, and parts are easily found. **Extended warranty:** A toss-up. Some long-term powertrain protection would be helpful; buy your brakes from independents who give long warranties. **Best alternatives:** GM Firefly or Metro; Honda Civic; Hyundai Accent or Elantra/Tiburon; Mazda3 or Protegé; Nissan Sentra; and Toyota Corolla, Echo, Tercel, or Yaris.

Strengths and Weaknesses

The Esteem is a small four-door sedan that is a step up from the Swift. Smaller than the Honda Civic and Chrysler Neon, it has a fairly spacious interior, offering rear accommodation (for two adults) that is comparable to or better than most cars in its class. It stands out with its European-styled body and large array of such standard features as AC, a fold-down back seat, and remote trunk and fuel-door releases. The roomy cabin has lots of front and rear headroom and legroom. Cargo space is fairly good with the sedan and exceptional with the wagon's rear seats folded.

The small 95 hp engine delivers respectable acceleration, and overall performance is acceptable, thanks to the Esteem's four-wheel independent suspension, which gives just the right balance between a comfortable ride and no-surprise handling. For a bit more power, look for a '96 or later sport variant that carries a 125 hp powerplant.

Suzuki's Aerio entry-level front-drive sedan and wagon replaced the Esteem for the 2003 model year. Equipped with optional all-wheel drive, it is one of the lowest-priced AWD vehicles available in Canada. Both models come with a 145 hp 4-cylinder engine that's among the most powerful standard engines in this class. Every Aerio comes with AC, power windows and mirrors, a tilt steering wheel, a CD player, and split-folding rear seats.

Suzuki's Swift is built at CAMI Automotive in Ingersoll, Ontario, and was first launched in 1995 for the American and Canadian markets. It was dropped in the States in 2001 but continues to be sold in Canada as the Swift and the Swift+. The Swift+, essentially a GM/Daewoo Aveo knock-off, was first launched as a 2004 model. It has posted good reliability scores, though crashworthiness info is quite sparse.

VEHICLE HISTORY: 1999—New front-end styling, 14-inch wheels, and an upgraded sound system. **2000**—More power provided by a 122 hp 1.8L engine. **2003**—Aerio makes its debut. **2004**—The 145 hp 2.0L is replaced by a 155 hp 2.3L engine. Swift+ debuts. **2005**—Standard front side airbags and a host of new exterior styling touches. **2006**—ABS becomes a standard item.

Here are some of the drawbacks to owning one of these econoboxes: Small tires compromise handling, and power steering doesn't transmit much road feedback. The automatic transmission may shift harshly and vibrate excessively between gear changes. Braking is mediocre for a car this light.

During the relatively short time the Esteem was around, it proved to be a high-quality, reliable small car. In this respect, it competes well with its Detroit-built rivals such as the Chevrolet Cavalier, Dodge Neon, and Ford Escort, while being outclassed by the Honda Civic, Mazda3 and Protegé, and Toyota Corolla, Echo, and Yaris. Problems reported by Esteem and Aerio owners include premature transmission, clutch, tire, and brake wear; noisy front brakes, and the early wearout of brake pads and rotors; occasional electrical short circuits; wind and water intrusion into the passenger compartment and engine through the Aerio's air-intake breather; fragile body panels and trim items; and paint peeling.

 ## Safety Summary

Aerio: **2000**—Sudden acceleration from a stop. • Automatic transmission bangs into gear. • Gearshift lever fell from Drive to Neutral and is hard to move. • Windshield seal vibrates and cracks in cold weather. **2001**—Automatic transmission stuck in lower gear. • Brake failure. • Complete electrical failure fixed temporarily by lifting the hood and jiggling the master control fuse. **2002**—Brake caliper may leak fluid, and early rotor wear. • Faulty wheel bearings. • Ball joints may fall out. • Lower control arm snapped. • Loose heat shield bolts. • Premature tire wear. **2003**—Many complaints of broken, cracked, or bent aluminum wheel rims and wheel bearing failures. • Delayed shifts. • Vehicle refuses to go into Reverse gear. • CV axle joint separation. • Misaligned power-steering bracket. • Trunk pops up while driving. **2004**—Sudden, unintended acceleration. • Original-equipment tires wear out prematurely. **2005**—Passenger-side airbag deployed for no reason. • Front brake failure; faulty brake pads. • Excessive body shake caused by defective stabilizer bushing, bracket, and mount. • Engine was damaged after Aerio was driven through a puddle of water. • Prematurely worn brakes and Yokohama and Michelin tires continue to top the list of owner complaints. **2006**—Driver-side airbag deployed for no reason while the car was underway. •

Brake pads often need changing. • Emergency Brake light comes on for no reason.
• Premature engine failures. • Serpentine belt failures (early symptom is excessive squealing). • Air intake sucks up water on flooded streets and causes serious engine damage, stalling:

> While driving 25 mph [40 km/h] on a rainy day, the vehicle shut off when it drove over a puddle. The vehicle was towed to the dealer and they stated that the failure was caused by water intrusion. They further stated that the rod failed and went through the aluminum motor. Both times the rod went through the motor, the water intrusion was caused by the air [breather] positioned under the motor.

• Yokohama Geolandar tires wear out early.

Secret Warranties/Internal Bulletins/Service Tips

All models: 2000–04—Battery discharge can be avoided by installing an upgraded alternator, says TSB #TS-03-06304. **2002–03**—Popping noise when turning. **2002–04**—Loose door mirrors. • Left driveshaft pops out of final drive. • Instruments don't display. **2004–05**—Changed alignment specifications. **2004–06**—Suzuki admits that its own faulty suspension may cause abnormal tire wear (TSB #TS 05-11225). **2005**—The stabilizer-bar mount bushing may cause a clunking sound coming from underneath the vehicle.

AERIO, SWIFT, SWIFT+, SX4, ESTEEM, VERONA PROFILE

	1999	2000	2001	2002	2003	2004	2005	2006	2007
Cost Price ($)									
Aerio sedan	—	—	—	—	15,785	15,995	17,995	18,595	18,995
Aerio SX (AWD)	—	—	—	—	—	20,495	23,995	22,995	—
Swift	11,495	11,595	11,595	—	—	—	—	—	—
Swift+	—	—	—	—	—	13,495	13,595	13,745	13,895
SX4	—	—	—	—	—	—	—	—	15,996
Esteem GL	13,995	15,495	15,695	16,195	—	—	—	—	—
Esteem GLX	17,195	18,491	18,795	19,795	—	—	—	—	—
Verona	—	—	—	—	—	22,995	22,995	22,995	—
Used Values ($)									
Aerio sedan ▲	—	—	—	—	4,500	6,000	9,500	11,000	12,500
Aerio sedan ▼	—	—	—	—	3,500	4,500	8,500	10,000	11,500
Aerio SX (AWD) ▲	—	—	—	—	—	8,000	11,000	13,000	—
Aerio SX (AWD) ▼	—	—	—	—	—	7,000	10,000	12,000	—
Swift ▲	1,500	2,000	2,500	—	—	—	—	—	—
Swift ▼	1,500	1,500	2,000	—	—	—	—	—	—
Swift+ ▲	1,000	1,500	2,500	—	—	—	—	—	—
Swift+ ▼	1,000	1,500	1,700	—	—	—	—	—	—
SX4 ▲	—	—	—	—	—	—	—	—	10,500
SX4 ▼	—	—	—	—	—	—	—	—	9,000

Esteem GL ▲	2,500	3,000	4,000	4,500	—	—	—	—	—
Esteem GL ▼	2,500	3,000	3,000	4,000	—	—	—	—	—
Esteem GLX ▲	3,500	4,000	4,500	5,500	—	—	—	—	—
Esteem GLX ▼	3,500	3,500	4,000	4,500	—	—	—	—	—
Verona ▼	—	—	—	—	—	8,000	10,000	11,000	—
Verona ▲	—	—	—	—	—	7,000	9,000	10,000	—
Reliability	4	4	4	4	5	5	5	5	5
Crash Safety (F)	—	—	—	—	—	4	—	—	—
Side	—	—	—	—	—	5	—	—	—
IIHS Side	—	—	—	—	—	—	1	1	1
Offset	—	—	—	5	5	5	5	5	5
Head Restraints	—	—	—	2	2	2	2	2	2

Toyota/General Motors

COROLLA, MATRIX/VIBE ★★★

RATING: *Corolla:* Average (1999–2007). This model is no longer a paragon of high quality, so be wary of serious safety deficiencies that include airbag malfunctions, airbag-induced injuries, sudden acceleration, hesitation and then surging, brake failures, seat belt failures, windshield reflections, dash gauge "wash out," poorly designed headlights that misdirect the light beam, and hard starting. Since the 1997 model was "de-contented" through the use of lower-quality materials, less soundproofing, and fewer standard features, there has been a noticeable reduction in quality control—though their horsepower-enhanced engines make them better performers than earlier versions. Be sure to ditch the poor-performing or failure-prone Bridgestone, Firestone, and Goodyear Integrity tires. *Matrix/Vibe:* Average (2003–07). Aimed at the youth market, these versatile spin-offs don't provide enough horsepower to justify their sporty pretensions, and they aren't suitable for any place more rugged than Ontario's Highway 401. Higher Vibe prices quickly fall near the Matrix level after a few years. **"Real" city/highway fuel economy:** *Corolla manual:* 7.1/5.3 L/100 km. *Corolla automatic:* 8.1/5.8 L/100 km. *Matrix manual:* 7.7/6.0 L/100. Matrix automatic: 8.3/6.4 L/100 km. *Matrix 6-speed manual:* 9.5/6.8 L/100 km. *Vibe manual:* 7.7/6.0 L/100 km. *Vibe automatic:* 8.3/6.4 L/100 km. *Matrix/Vibe AWD:* 9.1/6.9 L/100 km. Owners report that their fuel consumption is about 10 percent higher than these estimates. **Maintenance/ Repair costs:** *Corolla:* Lower than average, and repairs can be done anywhere. *Matrix/Vibe:* Powertrain and body part supply is a bit problematic, plus owners complain that they cost more than similar parts used on the other models. **Parts:** Electronic and powertrain parts can be expensive at the dealership, but they are easily found at reduced prices from independent suppliers. **Extended warranty:** Not needed. **Best alternatives:** Matrix/Vibe third-year depreciation is brutal—a bargain for buyers, but a disappointment come trade-in time. Instead of the Matrix/Vibe or Corolla, consider the Hyundai Accent or Elantra; Mazda3, Mazda5, or Protegé; Nissan Sentra; and Suzuki Aerio, Esteem, Forsa, Swift, or Verona. For extra cabin storage space and all-wheel drive, check out the Suzuki Aerio AWD and Subaru Forester.

 ## Strengths and Weaknesses

A step up from the Tercel, Echo, and Yaris, the Corolla has long been Toyota's standard-bearer in the compact-sedan class—many late '80s Corollas are still on our roads after 20+ years. Over the years, however, the car has grown in size, price, and refinement to the point where it can now be considered a small family sedan. All Corollas ride on a front-drive platform with independent suspension on all wheels.

The 1995–99 models have chronic seat belt retractor glitches and airbag malfunctions. Additionally, owners report powertrain, brake, and electrical problems; poor rear windshield defrosting; vibrations, squeaks, and rattles afflicting the brakes, steering, and suspension; and body trim imperfections that include water leaking through the doors.

The 2000–02 models continue to have relatively serious quality problems that include engine hesitation and surging; oil leaks; stalling out after a refuel; tire failures; transmissions that pop out of Drive into Neutral, or refuse to shift at all; a suspension that easily bottoms out; the vehicle wandering all over the road; faulty strut assemblies; warped brake rotors; fenders that are easily dented; a windshield that's easily cracked; and seat belt shoulder straps mounted too high, cutting across the driver's neck.

2003–07 Corolla, Matrix, and Vibe owners report many more mechanical and body problems. In fact, *Consumer Reports* warned Toyota in 2007 that the automaker's ratings could be downgraded due to an overall decline in quality affecting Toyota's entire lineup. Problems include hard starts; engine hesitation and surging; engine sludge buildup, requiring expensive repairs; excessive steering wander; transmission/clutch failures and thumping; the vehicle rolling away with the transmission in Park; loss of braking; defective crankshafts; power-steering-pump and fuel-pump failures (a new fuel pump can cost $771 U.S.); electrical short circuits; dash and tail lights that don't come on right away; an AC condenser that's vulnerable to road debris damage; a loose driver's seat; seat belts that lock up when in use; front dash noise; hubcaps that continually fall off; sunroof and door rattles; paint that chips off the hood; and a rotten-egg smell that comes from the exhaust or through the vents. Owners also say the Corolla is hard to control in inclement weather, and it surges whenever the AC is enabled:

> The 2005 Toyota Corolla has a defective temperature control system in that whenever the vehicle's air conditioning activates or while...the two defrost settings are on, at idle speeds the vehicle surges or accelerates forward to the extent it overrides the braking action at a stopped position.

VEHICLE HISTORY: 1999—A front stabilizer bar is added to improve handling. **2000**—Five additional horses and tilt steering on the CE and LE. **2001**—A slight facelift, and a new sport-oriented variant called the Corolla S is added. The VE is dropped, and the formerly mid-level CE replaces it, carrying fewer standard features. The LE is dropped to the CE's former level and is also "de-contented," losing its standard AC and power windows, locks, and mirrors. **2003**—Corolla is redesigned to be taller, wider, and longer; adds a new 4-speed automatic transmission; and gets five more horses. Matrix/Vibe launches. **2004**—Matrix XRS loses 10 horses (to 170 hp). **2005**—A light restyling, and side curtain airbags are optional for all models. Toyota also launches its new high-performance Corolla XRS sedan. **2007**—Matrix/Vibe loses all-wheel-drive. All sporty models are dropped.

Matrix/Vibe

Redesigned for 2009 with a new look and more performance, these small front-drive or all-wheel-drive sporty wagons are crosses between mini SUVs and station wagons, but they're packaged like small minivans. Vibe is built in Fremont, California, at GM's NUMMI factory. The nearly identical Toyota Matrix is manufactured in Toyota's Cambridge, Ontario, plant alongside the Corolla, whose platform it shares, though it provides a larger interior volume. Unlike the similar Matrix XRS, Vibe GTs are not available with an automatic transmission.

The front-drive Matrix/Vibe is equipped with a 1.8L 130 hp engine, a 5-speed manual overdrive transmission, and lots of standard features; however, the weak, buzzy base engine can be felt throughout the car. The 4×4 models are about 10 percent heavier and get seven fewer horses (123 hp) than the already power-challenged 130 hp front-drive. Says *Forbes* magazine:

> [B]oth all-wheel-drive cars are saddled with a really wretched 4-speed automatic that almost has to be shifted manually to get the car moving. To put it bluntly, the AWD Vibe and Matrix are so pokey, they feel like they're towing Winnebagos. To boot, the 1.8L engine doesn't hit its paltry torque peak...until a screaming 4200 rpm, at which point the vibration—did somebody say Vibe?—in the cabin is worse than a little off-putting.

The Matrix XRS and Vibe GT are the top-of-the-line performance leaders, with a 170 hp 4-cylinder engine and a high-performance 6-speed manual gearbox, plus ABS, a premium six-speaker stereo, an anti-theft system, 17-inch alloy wheels, and unique exterior cladding.

If you really need additional horsepower, get either the XRS or GT. But keep in mind that there are better-quality high-performance choices out there, such as the Honda Civic Si, Mazda5, or a base Acura RSX. Other front-drives worth considering are the Chrysler PT Cruiser, Hyundai Elantra or Tiburon, Honda Civic, Nissan Sentra, and Toyota Corolla. The Subaru Impreza or Forester are other good choices for the 4×4 variant.

New-car buyers can save $4,000 and get the same platform and 2.4L engine offered with the 2009 revamped Matrix/Vibe by buying a 2009 Scion xB for less than $18,000.

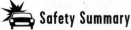

Safety Summary

All models/years: Chronic airbag malfunctions; they deploy when they shouldn't, or don't deploy when they should. • Sudden, unintended acceleration. • Engine hesitation and surging. • Poor headlight illumination. • Engine compartment fires, gas fumes in the interior, and brake and power-steering failures. • Excessive drifting and high-speed instability because of the lack of a stabilizer bar. • Premature control arm failure. • Seat belt released in accident. • Rear wheel broke at the axle. • Windshields crack easily. **All models: 1998–2000**—Brakes lock up. • Side winds increase the vehicle's instability. • Gearshift dropped from Drive to Neutral while driving. • Floor mat jams the accelerator. • Engine stalls after refuelling. • Front strut assembly failure. **1999**—Engine compartment fire. • Loss of braking ability. • Cruise control self-activates. • Automatic transmission locked up while driving. • Vehicle went out of control after rear control arm failure. • Defective engine camshaft gets inadequate oil lubrication and loses compression. • Rear seat belts aren't compatible with many child safety seats. **2001**—Stuck accelerator pedal. • Rear driver-side axle sheared in half; vehicle rolled over. • Excessive front brake pad wear; premature failure of the brake proportioning valve and rear brake shoes. • Hole in the oil pan. **2002**—Fuel leakage:

> On 04/29/02 consumer discovered that vehicle was leaking fuel. Vehicle was repaired by dealer who advised consumer that the fuel lines had come loose. On 07/29/02 while driving, engine compartment caught on fire as a result of fuel leaking.

• Airbag deployed and injured a child. • While using cruise control, gas pedal suddenly went to the floor. • Weak climate-control system. **2002–03**—Left rear tire falls off, sometimes while driving. • Unable to shift out of Park. **2003**—Fire ignited because of loose fuel line. • Vehicle suddenly shut down while underway at 100 km/h; in another case, vehicle suddenly accelerated while cruise control was engaged. • Several owners report that a hole in the oil pan caused vehicle to stall. • When the vehicle was parked, the parking brake was released and both airbags deployed; both airbags deployed right after driver turned on the ignition switch; airbags deployed after car passed over a bump in the road; in a rear-end collision, front airbag came out but failed to deploy; side airbag failed to deploy in a side impact; both airbags failed to deploy in a frontal collision:

> [Our] [t]hirteen-year-old daughter sustained [a] severe traumatic brain injury after [a] head-on collision. Her airbag deployed, [but the] top of passenger-side airbag was completely blown apart from one side to the other, allowing her head to strike [the] dash. We both had seat belts on. I sustained bruising of [my] hips and right rib. She was in [a] coma and [is] just now beginning to move [her] left side. She still cannot sit up, stand, walk, talk coherently, eat, or do anything for herself.

• Faulty seat belt wiring could cause a fire. • Floormat catches accelerator pedal. • Brake failure when decelerating. • Pedal goes soft when brakes are applied, and brakes lock up when coming to a gradual stop, resulting in extended stopping distances. • Rear welding broke away from the frame, resulting in complete loss of control. • Sudden collapse of the rear axle. • Rear control arm broke while driving at 110 km/h. • Shifter refused to go into gear while driving; transmission sometimes goes from Drive to Neutral while driving. • In windy conditions, vehicle becomes hard to steer, veering left or right. • Glow-in-the-dark inside trunk release doesn't glow in the dark because it is rarely exposed to light (owner actually crawled inside trunk to test it out!). • Sunlight washes out dash readings. **2004**—Hand brake doesn't hold very well. • Vehicle crashed after suddenly accelerating on the freeway. • Engine surges when stopped at a traffic light and AC compressor is engaged. • Brake and gas pedals are mounted too close together. • Front passenger-side windshield frame obstructs visibility. • Sun visor interferes with the rear-view mirror. • Sunroof came unglued from the metal frame; glass from the sunroof flew off. **2005**—Sudden brake lock-up. • Power-steering failure. • Passenger-seat sensor is too sensitive and rings an alarm when there is the slightest pressure on the seat. • Water pools in the ventilation system:

> [S]evere mildew growth has occurred in ventilation system. This mildew creates an awful sewage smell, and is extremely irritating to my allergies. Dealer sprayed Lysol disinfectant in ventilation intake. The problem came back a week later. To this day, I continually must spray Lysol in the ventilation system. Many types of mildew can be toxic to any human (not just allergy sufferers), and are *known* to cause cancer, which is very concerning to me…. I personally know other 2005 Corolla owners, and their Corollas suffer from the same problem.

• Car will not slow down when foot is taken off the accelerator pedal. • Low engine intake ingests water when going through puddles, causing severe engine damage. • Steering-wheel lock-up. • Excessive play in rear hub bearings. *Matrix:* **2003**—Engine surges when braking with AC engaged. • Excessive steering wander; feels a bit vague, with too much play; some torque steer (twisting) evident, especially on wet roads. • The manual shift lever's upward and forward position is counterintuitive and feels a bit ragged. • Instrument panel lights are dimmed by automatic sensor to the point where they can't be read in twilight hours, and the automatic headlights come on and go off for no apparent reason. **2004**—Hand brake doesn't hold very well. • Clutch failures with the manual transmission. • Car drifts out of control and crashes; steering is non-responsive:

> Matrix drifted to the left while driving, resulting in the consumer losing control and the vehicle flipping over. As the consumer attempted once more to gain control of the steering, the vehicle veered off to the left, hit a ditch, went airborne, and flipped. Toyota determined that there were steering problems.

Dealers have blamed a defective steering yoke and poor-quality original-equipment tires as the causes for this instability and steering loss. • Sudden, unintended acceleration:

While at a stop sign, the sudden acceleration happened again, and I was unable to immediately stop my car from lurching forward. It moved several inches into oncoming (perpendicular) traffic before I finally threw it into Park and pulled the emergency brake to stop it.

• Warped front brake rotors. • Dashboard reflected onto the windshield. • Front bumper/spoiler drags on the ground over any uneven surface. • Ice collects in wheel rims, throwing tires out of balance. **2005**—Hard starting and chronic stalling. • Engine began racing while vehicle was stopped. • Alloy wheel split in half. • Complete brake loss. **2006**—Sudden acceleration when rolling to a stop or accelerating. • Frequent replacement of the engine control module, throttle body assembly, transmission, and clutch. **2006–07**—Original-equipment tires are notorious for premature wearout; faulty shocks, poor differential alignment, and a too-light rear end are blamed:

> Had to replace the tires at 15K miles [24,000 km] due to cupping caused by camber/ toe in way out of spec. Toyota said that tire alignment was well within design specs. Drove for 15K miles on second set, was told by tire specialist that 2nd set of tires (not same as original) was also cupping, and that the problem was definitely in the alignment of the rear end. Had to threaten Toyota with a lawsuit before they admitted there was a problem. They added shims to car (I had to pay for parts), but flat out refused to reimburse for ruined tires.

2007—Gasoline fumes in the cabin caused by the failure of the fuel-pressure regulator and fuel-injector seals. *Vibe:* **2003**—The Vibe has generated a few more safety-related complaints than the Matrix, and they are in response to different failures, for the most part. • Vehicle surges when foot is taken off the accelerator; several accidents caused by sudden acceleration. • Vehicle will roll while in Park. • Faulty ABS. • Dash gauges can't be read when wearing sunglasses. • Automatic headlight sensor turns the headlights on and off, about 20 times per day, depending on sun and shade variations. • When the lights go on, dash lights become unreadable. • Transmission indicator isn't lit at night. • When driving away after start-up, 15–20 seconds elapse before headlights and tail lights are automatically turned on. • Sunroof suddenly exploded. • Excessive condensation on interior glass. • Wet windows aren't wiped clean when rolled back up. • Refuelling cannot be done without a large amount of fuel being spit out. • Rear outboard seat belts constantly tighten. **2004**—Too much steering play, making the Vibe, like its Toyota counterpart, highly unstable on the highway. • Rear-passenger seat belt may be hazardous to children:

> The rear-passenger seat belt twisted around the child's abdomen and would not release. Every time the child moved, it clicked tighter. The child had to be cut out of the seat belt.

• Loose driver's seat. • Automatic door locks don't secure the door shut. • Instrument-cluster chrome finish reflects into windshield. • Power side window cracked as it was being raised. • Speedometer needle can't be seen on sunny days. • Headlights are too dim for night driving. • Wheel lug nuts may fail:

> We took our 2004 Pontiac Vibe all-wheel drive in to Discount Tire to buy four new tires. Discount Tire called us later to inform us that four lugs snapped off while torquing the lugs to 80 ft. lbs. They checked their torque stick and used two other sticks, which continued to snap off the lugs. They sent the car over to Midas to have [it] repaired, and days later when we went to pick it up, I had them check all the lugs again…at 80 ft. lbs. one more lug snapped. So, again, we waited for a new lug to arrive. A total of five lugs snapped off the back end of the car, well before 80 ft. lbs. of torque was applied. I work at a steel plant, and had our lab check a broken lug, and their results were that the lugs were [so] brittle that there was no longation of the bolt before it broke…. I am concerned with how many more lugs out on the roads are too brittle and may snap.

• Many electrical shorts. • Loose firewall shield screws. **2005**—Engine surging when braking. • Poor rear visibility. • Hard starts. • Power steering malfunctions. • Severe pulling to one side when accelerating or braking. • Premature tire wear. • Mice can crawl into the dash/air vents. **2006**—Engine accelerates when the brakes are applied. • Sudden loss of power due to a malfunctioning powertrain control module. • Complete loss of braking ability. • Driver-side window doesn't roll down completely; when it is lowered, it interferes with the door's operation. • Annoying dash reflection onto the windshield. **2007**—Stalling, hard starting caused by a defective throttle body. • Accelerator pedal is too sensitive, leading to jerky acceleration. • Vehicle pulls to the left when underway, due to a misaligned rear end. • Windshield distortion.

Secret Warranties/Internal Bulletins/Service Tips

All models/years: Steering-column noise may require the replacement of the steering-column assembly. • Toyota has developed special procedures for eliminating AC odours and excessive wind noise. These problems are covered in TSBs #AC00297 and #BO00397, respectively. *Corolla:* **1990–2001**—Toyota has developed a special grease to eliminate clicking when the vehicle goes into Drive or Reverse. **1999–2002**—Accessory drivebelt/belt tensioner assembly noise is addressed in TSB #EG015-01. • Vibration troubleshooting tips. • Countermeasures for vehicle pulling to one side. **2002–04**—Troubleshooting tips for fixing a poorly performing AC. **2002–07**—Repair tips for correcting a severe pull to one side when underway (TSB #ST005-01). **2003–04**—Deformed roof mouldings. **2003–05**—Ways to silence front- and rear-door wind noise and a rear hub axle bearing humming. **2003–06**—Excessive transmission noise. **2003–07**—Remedy for a windshield ticking noise and a front brake squeak when in Reverse. • Engine compartment squeaks and rattles. • Rear hatch is slow to open. **2004–06**—Front-seat movement correction. **2004–07**—Fixing front-seat squeaking. **2005–06**—Engine vibration/drone when accelerating. • Toyota's correction for hard starts (see bulletin). • A grill mesh is available to protect the AC condenser

EXTENDED CRANK TIME/HARD START

BULLETIN NO.: EG053-06   DATE: SEPTEMBER 4, 2006

2005–06 Corolla & Matrix

Some 2005 and 2006 model year Corolla and Matrix vehicles equipped with a 1ZZ-FE engine may exhibit a "no start" or "extended crank" condition. This may be caused by insufficient fuel pressure after the vehicle has been parked for a period of time. The fuel pump assembly manufacturing process has been improved to correct this condition.

from damage from road debris (TSB #AC002-06). **2005–07**—Troubleshooting tips to fix a harsh-shifting automatic transmission and hard starts. *Matrix:* **2003**—Upper suspension tapping noise. • No airflow from centre vents. • Loose or deformed front or rear glass door run. • AC doesn't put out sufficient cool air. • Headlights come on when turned off. **2003–06**—Correction for a rear-end whining, humming, or growling. **2005–06**—Troubleshooting no-starts. *Vibe:* **2003**—Poor engine performance after 7000 rpm. • Transmission shifts too early when accelerating at full throttle and the engine is cold. • Harsh shifting. • Water leak from the A-pillar or headliner area. • Upper suspension tapping noise. • Low voltage display or dim lights. **2003–04**—Harsh 1–2 upshifts. • Slipping transmission. **2003–08**—Silencing a hoot or whistle heard on light acceleration (replace the automatic transaxle cooler hoses). **2004**—Reverse servo cover leak.

COROLLA, MATRIX/VIBE PROFILE

	1999	2000	2001	2002	2003	2004	2005	2006	2007
Cost Price ($)									
Base Corolla	15,090	15,625	15,625	15,765	15,290	15,410	15,490	15,715	15,785
Matrix	—	—	—	—	16,745	16,745	16,925	17,200	17,200
XR AWD	—	—	—	—	24,115	24,210	24,550	24,825	—
XRS AWD	—	—	—	—	24,540	24,640	25,560	25,835	—
Vibe	—	—	—	—	20,995	21,150	19,900	19,900	19,950
GT AWD	—	—	—	—	27,000	27,140	25,670	25,670	—
Used Values ($)									
Base Corolla ▲	2,500	3,000	3,500	4,500	5,500	6,000	7,500	8,500	10,000
Base Corolla ▼	2,500	3,000	3,000	4,000	5,000	5,500	6,500	7,500	9,000
Matrix ▲	—	—	—	—	6,500	7,500	9,000	10,500	12,000
Matrix ▼	—	—	—	—	5,000	6,000	7,500	9,000	10,500
XR AWD ▲	—	—	—	—	9,000	10,500	13,000	14,500	—
XR AWD ▼	—	—	—	—	8,000	9,500	11,500	13,000	—
XRS AWD ▲	—	—	—	—	8,500	10,500	13,500	15,500	—
XRS AWD ▼	—	—	—	—	7,500	9,500	12,500	14,000	—
Vibe ▲	—	—	—	—	9,000	11,000	13,000	9,500	12,500
Vibe ▼	—	—	—	—	7,500	9,500	11,500	8,000	11,000
GT AWD ▲	—	—	—	—	11,000	14,000	16,500	12,500	—
GT AWD ▼	—	—	—	—	9,000	12,500	15,000	11,000	—
Reliability	3	3	3	3	3	3	3	3	3
Crash Safety (F)	—	4	4	4	5	5	5	5	5
Side	—	4	4	4	4	4	4	3	3

All ratings on a numbered scale where 5 is good and 1 is bad. See pages 108–109 for a more detailed description.

IIHS Side	—	—	—	—	1	1	3	—	—
Offset	3	3	3	3	5	5	5	—	—
Head Restraints	3	—	2	2	3	3	1	—	—
Matrix	—	—	—	—	5	5	—	—	—
Rollover Resistance	3	3	3	3	4	4	4	4	4

Toyota

ECHO, YARIS ★★★★★ / ★★★★

RATING: *Echo:* Recommended (2000–05). *Yaris:* Above Average (2006–07). Both cars are practical and cheap, if you can get past the tall, function-over-form styling of the newer Yaris. They are excellent alternatives to the similarly styled, glitch-ridden early Ford Focus models and the discontinued Chrysler Neon. Now that the Echo has been replaced by the larger and slightly better-performing Yaris, Echo resale values have declined a bit faster than usual. **"Real" city/highway fuel economy:** *Echo manual:* 6.7/5.2 L/100 km. *Echo automatic:* 7.1/5.5 L/100 km. *Yaris manual:* 7.0/5.5 L/100 km. *Yaris automatic:* 7.0/5.6 L/100 km. Owners say fuel economy can sometimes be almost 30 percent less than advertised. **Parts:** Easily found and cheap. **Maintenance/Repair costs:** Extraordinarily low. **Extended warranty:** A waste of money. **Best alternatives:** Honda Civic; Hyundai Accent; Mazda3, Mazda5, or Protegé; Nissan Sentra; and Suzuki Forsa, Swift, Esteem, or Aerio.

Strengths and Weaknesses

Toyota scrapped its highly recommended Tercel in favour of the 2000 Echo for a six-year run, before it was replaced by the Yaris. Echo is an entry-level, five-passenger econocar that usually gives good fuel economy without sacrificing performance. Both two- and four-door models are available, and the car costs substantially less than the Corolla. The Echo also offers about the same amount of passenger space as the Corolla, thanks to a high roof and low floor height.

Cockpit controls and instrumentation are particularly user-friendly, located high on the dash and more toward the centre of the vehicle rather than directly in front of the driver, where the steering column would hide many gauges and controls. A 108 hp 1.5L DOHC 4-cylinder engine, featuring variable valve timing (VVT) cylinder-head technology, powers the Echo. Normally, an engine this small would provide wimpy acceleration, but thanks to the Echo's light weight, acceleration is more than adequate with the manual gearbox and acceptable with the automatic.

Standard safety features include five three-point seat belts (front seat belts have pretensioners and force limiters), two front airbags (sadly, side airbags are not available), four height-adjustable head restraints, rear child-seat tether anchors, and rear door locks.

The Echo has more usable power than the Tercel and provides excellent fuel economy and lots of interior space. There's plenty of passenger room, along with an incredible array of storage areas, including a huge trunk and standard 60/40 split-folding rear seats. All models are reasonably well equipped with good-quality materials, well-designed instruments and controls, comfortable seating, easy rear access, and excellent fore and aft visibility. It's quite nimble when cornering, very stable on the highway, and surprisingly quiet for an economy car. The car didn't change much after its 2000 model debut and has generated almost no complaints—an amazing feat when compared with the quality decline in Corollas, Camrys, and Siennas since 1997.

A tall profile and light weight make the Echo vulnerable to side-wind buffeting, base tires provide poor wet traction, excessive torque steer makes for sudden pulling to one side when accelerating, and the narrow body limits rear bench seating to two adults. There have also been a few complaints about rough idling, engine ticking and rattling, hard transmission shifts, some interior and brake squeaks, a high-pitched whine and pulling to the right when underway, leaking shock absorbers, and broken door latches.

Yaris

You can't beat a Yaris for giving good fuel economy and offering top-drawer reliability, but it lags in other important areas better dealt with by the competition. Although the Yaris *does* provide a comfortable ride, handling is surprisingly sloppy and the car can be hard to control when buffeted about by side winds, or when it gathers speed (hatchbacks, especially). Another drawback is braking. Stops seem to take forever without the optional anti-lock brakes. Acceleration with the 106 hp 1.5L 4-cylinder engine is acceptable, but you will have to contend with lots of engine and road noise entering into the cabin area as the car picks up speed. The positioning of the steering wheel and centre-mounted dash gauges may be hard for some drivers to accept, as well. Yaris models are selling at discounts, now that the Honda Fit and Nissan Versa are eating into the small-car market, which Toyota once practically owned.

VEHICLE HISTORY: *Echo:* **2003**—A major restyling adds 4 cm to overall length, via new front and rear sheet metal, as well as revised bumpers, hood, front fenders, headlights, tail lights, trunk lid, and grille. *Yaris:* **2006**—Replaces Echo.

 **Safety Summary**

Echo: **All years:** Airbag malfunctions. • Several incidents of sudden, unintended acceleration:

> While driving, the Echo will accelerate to 60 mph [100 km/h] without [my] hitting the gas pedal. I have to put the vehicle in Neutral to stop it. I contacted [the] dealer, but

he cannot locate the cause. The sudden acceleration incident occurred three times. The dealer was unable to duplicate the problem in test-driving, but removed the cruise control. The problem was not corrected by removing the cruise control.

2000—Vehicle blown out of control by side winds. • Inoperative horn. • Brake loss said to be caused by a faulty master cylinder. • Warped brake rotors. • Broken steering-wheel tilt mechanism. **2000–01**—Brake pedal is mounted too close to the accelerator pedal. **2001**—Partial brake loss. • Fuel line came undone; fuel line cracked. • Driver's seat belt failed to lock in a collision. **2002**—Sudden steering loss led to crash. • Vehicle often jumps out of Drive into Neutral. **2003**—Engine hesitates when shifting gears. • Chronic stalling when decelerating. • Dash lights are not bright enough. **2005**—Airbags failed to deploy. • Brake failure caused by a warped brake rotor. • Vehicle won't remain in Overdrive. • A gasoline smell permeates the cabin. • Leaking shock absorbers. • Broken door latches.

Secret Warranties/Internal Bulletins/ Service Tips

Echo: **All years:** Brake vibration caused by rotor rust requires the installation of new pads and rotors as a set. **2000**—Probable causes for interior squeaks and rattles. • Wheel covers may click or squeak. • Excessive wind noise. • Fuel gauge and speedometer malfunctions. • Brake-clicking

---

WATER IN PASSENGER FOOTWELL AREA

BULLETIN NO.: AC005-05   DATE: SEPTEMBER 13, 2005

FRONT PASSENGER FOOT AREA WET

2003–05 Echo and 2004–06 Scion xA & xB. A condition may exist that allows the evaporator drain hose to become detached, causing the passenger foot well to become wet.

---

countermeasures. • Defective airflow rotary control knob. **2001**—Roof moulding may come loose or become deformed. **2002–05**—Fixes for a vehicle that pulls to one side. **2003–05**—AC evaporator leaks water into the cabin (see bulletin). **2003–05**—Windshield ticking noise. **2004–05**—Front seat squeaks. *Yaris:* **2006–07**—Front windshield ticking noise. **2007**—Trunk lid full-open improvement. • Drivebelt squealing. • Engine compartment rattle heard when car is put into Reverse. • Intermittent odour in the cabin. • Paint staining along horizontal surfaces. **2007–08**—Water on front and rear carpets. • Noise, vibration with the blower motor on. • ABS light stays on.

ECHO, YARIS PROFILE

	2000	2001	2002	2003	2004	2005	2006	2007
Cost Price ($)								
Echo	13,835	13,980	14,084	13,690	12,995	12,995	—	—
Yaris	—	—	—	—	—	—	13,580	13,725
Used Values ($)								
Echo ▲	2,500	3,500	4,500	5,500	5,500	6,500	—	—
Echo ▼	2,500	3,000	3,500	5,000	5,500	5,500	—	—
Yaris ▲	—	—	—	—	—	—	8,000	9,500
Yaris ▼	—	—	—	—	—	—	7,000	8,000

Reliability	4	5	5	5	5	5	5	5
Crash Safety (F)	—	4	4	4	4	4	—	4
Side	—	3	3	3	3	3	—	3
IIHS Side								
Yaris	—	—	—	—	—	—	—	5
Offset								
Yaris	—	—	—	—	—	—	—	5
Head Restraints								
Yaris	—	—	—	—	—	—	—	2
Rollover Resistance	—	4	4	4	4	4	—	4

Volkswagen

GOLF, JETTA, CABRIO, EOS / DIESEL MODELS ★★★

RATING: Average (2007); Below Average (1999–2006). In addition to aging badly, these small cars are much more expensive than their competition, despite VW's efforts to bring down actual transaction prices over the past few years. Golfs are entry-level models that are the cheapest of the lot and depreciate fairly rapidly. A Jetta is a Golf with a trunk, the most popular configuration, which fetches fair resale prices. A Cabrio is a Golf without a roof; it depreciates steeply after its first five years of use. An Eos is an overpriced 2007 and later Cabrio; it's a car for big wallets and small minds—$10,000 depreciation after its first year on the market. *Diesel models:* Average (2005–07); Below Average (1999–2004). Old-technology, pre-2007 diesel resale prices are average and will likely ratchet upwards as buyers shy away from the newer 2007 and later versions. **"Real" city/highway fuel economy:** *City Golf manual:* 9.8/7.1 L/100 km. *City Golf automatic:* 9.6/7.2 L/100 km. *Golf manual:* 9.8/7.2 L/100 km. *Golf automatic:* 9.6/7.2 L/100. *Golf TDI manual:* 6.2/4.6 L/100 km. *Golf TDI automatic:* 7.1/4.2 L/100 km. *GTI manual:* 9.8/6.9 L/100 km, or 11.1/7.3 L/100 km with the 6-speed. *Jetta 1.8 manual:* 9.9/6.9 L/100 km. *Jetta 1.8 automatic:* 10.8/7.4 L/100 km. *Jetta 2.0 manual:* 9.8/7.0 L/100 km. *Jetta 2.0 automatic:* 9.6/7.2 L/100 km. *Jetta 2.8 manual:* 11.1/7.3 L/100 km. *Jetta TDI manual:* 6.2/4.6 L/100 km. *Jetta TDI automatic:* 7.1/4.9 L/100 km. *Eos 2.0L manual:* 10.1/6.8 L/100 km. *Eos 2.0L automatic:* 10.3/6.9 L/100 km. *Eos 3.2L V6 automatic:* 10.8/7.5 L/100 km. *Diesel versions:* Although owners report that their consumption is about 15 percent higher than these estimates, the TDI engine still burns about 30 percent less fuel than an equivalent 4-cylinder gasoline engine and has an impressive 1,000 km (600 mi.) or more range. You'll need that range, however, since only one fuel station out of three or four sells diesel fuel. Plus, diesel fuel is usually much more expensive than gasoline. **Maintenance/Repair costs:** Maintenance costs are unreasonably high; for example, TDIClub (*www.tdiclub.com*) warns that the power-steering fluid, the brake fluid, and the special automatic transmission fluid should be purchased only from the dealer for optimal performance, even though the VW power-steering fluid is many times more expensive than fluid sold by independents. Repairs have always been dealer-dependent, and even more so since VW changed its diesel technology in 2007. **Parts:** Expensive, and not generally available from independent suppliers. Recall campaign parts may be back ordered for months. **Extended warranty:** A smart idea. "Goodwill" warranty repairs are practically nonexistent in Canada. **Best alternatives:** Any small car that doesn't punish backseat passengers as much as this VW trio does. Try the Honda Civic; Hyundai Elantra or Tiburon; Mazda3, Mazda5, or Protegé; Nissan Sentra; and Toyota Corolla, Matrix, or Vibe. The only viable diesel alternative is a Jeep Liberty—a small SUV that has performed quite well. If a convertible tickles your fancy, buy a Mazda Miata.

Strengths and Weaknesses

Like most European imports, these small cars give a comfortable ride, are fun to drive, and provide good fuel economy. Both engines are easily started in cold weather. But here's the rub: Golfs and Jettas, like the failure-prone Rabbit they replaced, aren't reliable once the warranty expires. What you save with less fuel consumption, you lose in the car's high retail price and higher diesel fuel costs. Also, the ever-mounting maintenance costs as the vehicle gains years and mileage will easily wear you down. Finding a qualified independent repairer can offset the high maintenance charges, but qualified independents are rarer than hens' teeth. And 2007 and later models use a new diesel technology that has a steep learning curve.

VEHICLE HISTORY: 1999—Updated interior and exterior styling, and a more-powerful engine; Cabrios are given new European styling. **2001**—A 150 hp 1.8L turbo-four becomes available for the GLS and is standard in the base GTI; a Jetta wagon is added, along with steering-mounted audio controls (on some models). **2002**—Debut of a more-powerful 1.8L 4-cylinder engine, a 5-speed automatic transmission, and an optional 6-speed manual transmission; 2.8L V6 horsepower is boosted (200 hp). **2003**—An anti-skid system becomes standard with the V6 engine; GL gets power windows, heated power mirrors, and cruise control; GLS versions come with alloy wheels and a sunroof. **2004**—An all-wheel-drive Golf arrives. **2005**—Jetta's GLI VR6 sedan and the limited-edition all-wheel-drive V6 Golf R32 are ditched. Mid-year, revamped Jettas with a larger platform, 150 hp 5-cylinder engine, four-wheel ABS disc brakes, and head-protecting side airbags arrive. **2006**—A turbocharged gasoline engine and rear side airbags. The Jetta 2.0T and GLI get the 200 hp turbocharged 4-cylinder and 6-speed manual transmission. Frequently stolen Xenon headlights are standard on the GLI and optional for the 2.0T. **2007**—Jetta GL's suspension is lowered by 2 cm (0.8 in). A few leftover 2006 diesel-engine Jettas are sold for the 2007 model year in the States. A Wolfsburg Edition joins the lineup, with its 5-cylinder engine, heated front seats, and sunroof.

Jettas and Golfs rust prematurely, usually around areas where panels join or chrome strips have been placed. Undercarriages suffer from deterioration and increasingly frequent mechanical/electrical failures after their fourth year in service. For example, starters often burn out because they are vulnerable to engine heat; as well, sunroofs leak, door locks jam, window cranks break, and windows bind. Owners also report engine head gasket leaks as well as water-pump and heater-core breakdowns. It's axiomatic that all diesels are slow to accelerate, but VW's Fourth gear often can't handle highway speeds above 90 km/h. Engine noise can be deafening when shifting down from Fourth gear.

VW reliability is about average—for the first few years. Then your wallet gets lighter as the brake components and fuel and electrical systems start to self-destruct, requiring expensive repairs that are often ineffective. Exhaust system components aren't very durable, body hardware and dashboard controls are fragile, the paint often discolours and is easily chipped, and window regulators constantly fail.

Volkswagens, Audis, and Porsches are undoubtedly top-performing vehicles, but they're bedevilled by serious quality problems that can't be diagnosed or repaired at the corner garage. Owners have to endure chronic electrical short circuits; heater/defroster resistor and motor failures; leaking transmission and stub-axle seals; and defective valve-pan gaskets, head gaskets, timing belts, steering assemblies, suspension components, and alternator pulleys. Body problems are legion, with air and water leaks, faulty catalytic converters, inoperative locks and latches, poor-quality body construction and paint, and cheap, easily broken accessories and trim items.

Owners also complain of chronic automatic transmission/clutch and diesel-engine turbocharger problems; noisy brakes and wheel bearings; leaky sunroofs and assorted water leaks from other areas (when it rains, both the front and rear floors are soaked); malfunctioning gauges and accessories; fragile bumpers that become brittle and crack as the temperature falls; defective security systems; and disagreeable AC-induced interior odours.

Eos

A four-seater Jetta with a folding metal hardtop, the Eos is a convertible that offers a sunroof when the metal top is closed. Powered by a peppy 200 hp 2.0L turbocharged 4-cylinder or a torquier 250 hp 3.2L V6 coupled to either a standard 6-speed manual or an automated manual DSG transmission, the Eos provides the same superb handling and ride comfort as the Jetta—without the wind buffeting, wind and water leaks, and chassis flexing found with many convertibles. Occupant crash protection is assured with door-mounted head-protecting side-impact airbags.

The Diesel Dilemma

People who buy a diesel-powered vehicle such as VW's TDI usually cite at least one of these three reasons for their decision: lower fuel costs, lower maintenance costs, and the popular notion that diesel engines are more durable. Unfortunately, none of these reasons stands up to close scrutiny.

Higher operating costs

Diesel-fuelled vehicles *do* provide 20–30 percent better fuel economy than gasoline-burners. But that savings is being progressively wiped out by higher diesel fuel prices and maintenance costs. Diesel fuel usually sells for 81.1–99.9 cents per litre, while a litre of regular gasoline goes for an average price of 80.4 cents. Here is how much diesel fuel cost across Canada as of January 23, 2009. *Ontario:* 81.9 cents/L; *BC:* 79.9 cents/L; *Alberta:* 73.7 cents/L; *Nova Scotia:* 81.1 cents/L; *Quebec:* 76.1 cents/L. And diesel fuel costs are expected to go even higher as North American refiners are forced to produce cleaner, more-expensive fuel.

Servicing price-gouging

Diesel owners decry the high cost of regular maintenance and claim that parts and fluids can cost many times what a non-diesel engine would require. Furthermore, dealerships' service personnel are in a monopolist "take it or leave it" position because few independent mechanics will be available to service diesel cars—good diesel mechanics are rare in most dealerships, and diesel engine diagnostic tools and parts inventories are often wanting.

Reliability: The dark side of diesels

Diesel engines are promoted by automakers for their fuel-efficient and dependable performance; however, recent studies and owner complaints indicate diesels burn more fuel than advertised, are more likely to break down than gasoline-powered engines, and produce emissions that exacerbate lung diseases like emphysema and may be responsible for 125,000 cases of pulmonary cancer in the States.

J.D. Power's 2004 Vehicle Dependability Study found that the most fuel-efficient vehicles—diesels and gas-electric hybrids—have more engine problems than similar gasoline-powered vehicles. And this conclusion is backed by automaker service bulletins and owner complaints sent to NHTSA. The discrepancies are an eye-opener:

- Ford and Chevrolet diesel pickups had more engine problems than similar gas-powered models, while Dodge and GMC trucks were better overall.
- Owners of Volkswagen diesels reported up to twice as many engine problems than did owners of VWs that burn gas.

VW diesel owner clubs have published long lists of failure-prone components found in the TDI over the years. The table on the following page is a catalogue of the problems that the TDIClub found.

Intercooler leaking oil @ 16K miles [25,750 km] on a 2006 VW Golf TDI. Failure is due to chaffing of the aluminum intercooler pipes by the perpendicular piece of plastic that extends to it from the front passenger side grill and touches the intercooler. During normal driving, over time, the plastic moves and rubs against the intercooler and eventually creates holes where oil leaks out and puddles on the front side of the passenger wheel well.

TOP TDICLUB VW DIESEL PROBLEMS

1. Hard starts or no-starts.
2. Engine stalls and may not restart.
3. Engine lacks power.
4. High fuel consumption.
5. Oil leaks onto ground.
6. Smokes on cold start-up, when accelerating, or at any time.
7. Bucks and jerks at low speeds when cold.
8. Noisy exhaust system.
9. Shuddering, misfiring, and stumbling once underway.
10. Surging, hesitation during acceleration; turbo-boost pressure varies.

 Safety Summary

All models/years: Golfs and Jettas, as well as many Audis, are easily stolen due to a flawed door lock mechanism design, reports *Lemon-Aid* reader and British Columbia resident Susan O.:

> Basically, it is a factory-installed flaw in the design that if you pop the silver cylinder off the only keyed door, you can remove the lock mechanism, which allows anyone to get into the vehicle. Further to that, you are also able to deactivate the alarm, so the VW/Audi consumer would not hear anyone gaining entry.

• NHTSA's database shows that the following problems are reported repeatedly: fires; airbags that fail to deploy or cause severe injuries when they go off; inadvertent deployment; Airbag light stays on for no apparent reason; transmission and wheel bearing failures; transmission pops out of gear; electrical malfunctions leading to chronic stalling; self-activating alarms; lights going out; erratic cruise-control operation; brake, tire, and AC failures; early replacement of brake pads; inadequate defrosting; AC mould and mildew smell; poor-quality body components; window regulator failure; and inoperable power windows. Also, doors may open suddenly; locks jam shut, fall out, or freeze; power-window motors and regulators self-destruct; hoods suddenly fly up; cigarette lighters pop out of their holders while lit; the seat heater may burn a hole in the driver's seat; and battery acid can leak onto the power-steering reservoir and cause sudden steering loss. **All models: 2000–03**—Airbag cover pops off while driving. • Cracked oil pan. • Engine burns oil. • Chronic stalling in traffic. • Hard starting. • Noisy, prematurely worn brakes. • Sudden headlight failure; poor headlight illumination. • Faulty power-window regulators cause windows to fall down into door panels. **2001**—Timing chain exploded. • Frequent stalling because of defective airflow sensor. • Premature constant velocity joint replacement. **2001–03**—Stalling, no-starts because of faulty ignition coils. **2002**—Fires under the bumper and in the engine compartment. • Sudden, unintended acceleration. • Many reports that the front/side airbags deployed for no reason; driver burned:

> Driving on the turnpike, the driver-side airbag deployed without any sort of impact. There is no visible damage to the vehicle, which was only two months old at the time. Fortunately, the only injury was a burn from the airbag on the side of my arm.

• Brake failure. • Vehicle hesitates on acceleration. • Engine warning light is constantly lit. • Broken window regulator; window falls into the door panel:

> On three separate occasions the driver-side front window (twice) and the passenger-side front window (once) has fallen down into the door. On the first occasion, the window shattered inside the door and had to be replaced.

2003—Driver's seat burst into flames. • Vehicle will suddenly veer to the left or right. • Clutch pedal slips; vehicle won't change gears. • Early replacement of the rear axle. 2004—Golf totally destroyed by a fire of unknown origin. • Jetta fire ignited in the seat-heater control, which was shut off at the time. • Brake failures. • Chronic engine stalling and no-starts, often due to defective ignition coils. • VW says engines need a special oil to prevent engine sludge. • Transmission clutch slipping:

> This is the second time we have had issues with our 2004 VW Jetta wagon. Both times, the car has suddenly, with no warning, had a clutch failure. The first time this happened was [at] 16,000 miles [26,000 km], now a second occurrence [at] just 29,000 miles [47,000 km]. VW tries to pass blame as driver error, but since I drive tractor/trailers for a living and in my 15 years of driving have never had a clutch failure prior to this car, I do not think that my driving is to blame. It is apparent from the numerous experiences I have read about that there is a serious defect in the quality or build of the VW clutch system in newer models.

• There is such a long delay when shifting the automatic transmission in Reverse or Drive, the vehicle is free to roll as if it were in Neutral. • Harsh downshifts. • Transmission locks up between Third and Fourth gears. • Tread separating from the front-passenger tire. • Frequent electrical shorts (windows, lights, gauges, alarm system, etc.). • Dash gauges cannot be read in sunlight. • There is a distracting reflection from the chrome shifter panel. 2005—Engine surges when shifted into Reverse. • Faulty fuel gauges. • Driver's seat became unattached. *TDI:* 2004—Many reports of engine overheating, chronic stalling, and EGR/turbocharger failures:

> TDI engine will stall at times due to coolant leaking internally into [the] intake manifold through [a] faulty EGR cooler, causing vehicle to lose steering and brake assist. I have looked on VW web forums, and many owners have had a similar incident.

•

> TDI engine and manual transmission: While driving, vehicle lost power intermittently. Pressed accelerator; no change in rpm—just idled. [The] "glow plug" flashed and [the] Engine Warning light...lit after [the] first two occasions, not on [the] third. Re-start solves problem for 30 seconds. Dealership was notified, but did not resolve the problem in two attempts. Vehicle is in for third attempt.

The EGR problem is so rampant and expensive to correct that VW owners are pleading for relief, so enterprising independent repair shops are seizing the opportunity to make a profit by offering cheaper fixes for the well-known turbocharger problems. • Stripped manifold bolts are another cause of the turbo's demise. **2005**—The clutch disengages from the flywheel. • TDI's fuel-filler pipe is too small for most truck stop gas stations. • Chronic surging and stalling. • Sunroof's drains clog, causing serious electrical problems and mould growth:

> Sunroof drains clog causing backup of water to settle on floors ruining carpet, causing mold. Water gets into door frames causing buckling of doors during winter months. Water damage also caused an electrical wiring short which caused an airbag failure as well as ruined two batteries. I have not used or opened the sunroof since for fear of more problems. I was informed that the cost to replace the carpeting again would be charged to me if the car had another water problem again due to the clogged drains.

2006—In a rear-ender, the driver's seatback collapsed and the airbag failed to deploy. • The vehicle stalls out when the accelerator pedal is depressed. **2007**—Water pump may fail, causing the engine to suddenly overheat; replace the pump with an upgraded one that uses a metallic impeller.

Secret Warranties/Internal Bulletins/Service Tips

All models/years: It's surprising that, despite the many owner complaints, VW has issued few service bulletins. This means these problems don't exist in Volkswagen's opinion, or the automaker doesn't have corrective fixes to apply and will simply carry on as if all systems are "normal." **All models: 1995–2008**—Repair tips on fixing heated rear windshield lines that are inoperative. **1998–2006**—Possible reasons why the car won't start or is hard to start. **1999–2008**—Inoperative window regulator. **1999–2008**—Noisy, binding sunroof. **2001**—Leaking intake hoses. • Inoperative secondary air pump (blown fuse). • Troubleshooting "defective control module" indication. • Leaking transmission pan gasket. **2000–03**—Faulty ignition coils (chronic stalling, no restart) once covered reluctantly by a warranty extension after VW first denied the problem existed. **2003–10**—Causes for excessive vibration when braking (a warranty item, admits VW). **2004–06**—Shift delay upon acceleration. **2005**—Humming noise when turning at low speeds. • Rattling noise from the AC front centre air outlets. • Fuel-tank lid won't close. • Musty odours from vents. **2005–06**—Inoperative rear window defogger. **2005–07**—Engine knocking noise. • Rattle from front passenger-side floor area. **2005–08**—How to silence front and rear suspension and front-seat creaks. • Troubleshooting sound system malfunctions. • Fix for an inoperative seat heater. • Detached door seals. • Seized AC compressor. **2006**—Faulty door lock cylinders. **2006–08**—Remedy for inoperative sun/visor light. • Fuel door won't close. • AC isn't cold enough.

GOLF, JETTA, CABRIO, EOS PROFILE

	1999	2000	2001	2002	2003	2004	2005	2006	2007
Cost Price ($)									
Cabrio/Eos	25,300	25,300	28,530	28,530	—	—	—	—	36,900
Golf/City	15,610	18,950	19,040	19,230	17,950	18,300	18,530	18,530	14,900
Jetta/City	18,620	21,170	21,280	21,490	24,260	24,520	24,750	24,975	16,700
Jetta TDI	19,945	23,100	23,220	23,450	25,860	26,080	26,310	26,650	—
Jetta TDI wagon	—	—	—	—	25,860	27, 550	27,780	27,780	—
Used Values ($)									
Cabrio/Eos ▲	5,000	6,500	8,000	10,000	—	—	—	—	26,000
Cabrio/Eos ▼	4,500	5,500	6,500	8,000	—	—	—	—	24,000
Golf/City ▲	3,500	4,000	4,500	5,000	5,500	7,000	8,500	9,000	10,000
Golf/City ▼	3,000	3,500	4,000	4,500	5,000	6,000	7,000	8,500	9,000
Jetta/City ▲	4,000	4,500	5,000	6,000	8,500	9,500	11,500	14,000	10,500
Jetta/City ▼	3,500	4,000	4,500	5,000	7,000	8,500	10,000	13,000	9,500
Jetta TDI ▲	5,000	5,500	6,000	7,000	8,500	10,500	12,000	16,500	—
Jetta TDI ▼	4,500	5,000	5,500	6,000	7,500	9,000	11,000	15,000	—
Jetta TDI wagon ▲	—	—	—	—	9,000	10,500	13,000	17,000	—
Jetta TDI wagon ▼	—	—	—	—	8,000	9,000	11,500	14,500	—
Reliability	3	3	3	3	3	3	3	3	3
Crash Safety (F)									
Golf	3	5	5	5	5	5	5	5	—
Jetta	—	5	5	5	5	5	5	4	4
Side									
Golf	—	—	—	—	4	4	4	4	—
Jetta	3	4	4	—	4	4	5	5	5
IIHS Side	—	—	—	—	—	—	5	5	5
Offset	2	5	5	5	5	5	5	5	—
Jetta	5	5	5	5	5	5	5	5	5
Head Restraints (F)									
Golf 2d	2	—	5	5	5	5	—	—	—
Golf 4d	3	—	3	3	3	3	—	—	—
Jetta	—	—	3	3	3	3	3	3	2
Eos	—	—	—	—	—	—	—	—	2
Rollover Resistance	—	—	4	4	4	4	—	4	4

Note: NHTSA didn't test the Eos.

MEDIUM CARS

Honda's Accord is an Above Average family sedan.

Medium-sized cars, often referred to as family cars, are trade-offs between size and fuel economy, offering more room and convenience features but a bit less fuel economy than small cars. They're popular because they combine the advantages of smaller cars with those of larger vehicles. As a result of their versatility, as well as both upsizing and downsizing throughout the years, these vehicles overlap both the small and large car niches. Their trunks are usually large enough to meet average baggage requirements, and their interiors are spacious enough to meet the needs of the average family (seating four people in comfort and five in a pinch). These cars are best for combined city and highway driving, with the top choices traditionally dominated by Japanese automakers: the Honda Accord; the Mazda5, 626, and Mazda6; and the Toyota Camry. South Korean automakers, however, are catching up fast, with Hyundai's Elantra, Tiburon, and Sonata leading the pack.

But there are lots of bad cars in this group too, and they belong mostly to the Detroit automakers. Take the Ford Taurus and Sable, for example. Bestsellers for many years and easily found used at incredibly low prices, these two models don't cost much because they are no longer built and are generally unreliable. Engine, transmission, brake, electrical, and body problems are legion, and repair costs for the automatic transmission alone can easily run about $3,500. GM's mid-sized lineup is only marginally better (its minivans comprise the worst of a bad lot). Chrysler is the Detroit automaker with the worst quality-control record. The Sebring, Breeze, Cirrus, and Stratus have declined dramatically in quality during the past several years and are mediocre highway performers. Chrysler cars, SUVs, trucks, and minivans are much cheaper than competing makes mainly because their reputation is so bad.

Bottom line? Stick with the Asian models, not only for their dependability and solid highway performance but also for the odds that their manufacturers won't go bankrupt in 2009.

MEDIUM CAR RATINGS

Recommended

Acura 1.6 EL, 1.7L EL (1999–2005)

Acura CSX (2006–07)

Acura Integra (1999–2001)

Honda Accord (2000–02)

Above Average

Acura RSX (2002–06)
Honda Accord (2003–07; 1999)
Hyundai Sonata (2006–07)

Mazda6 (2004–07)
Toyota Camry, Solara (2006–07)

Average

Chrysler Avenger, Sebring (2005–07)
Honda Accord Hybrid (2005–07)
Hyundai Sonata (2004–05)
Mazda6 (2003)
Mazda 626 (1999–2002)

Nissan Altima (1999–2001)
Toyota Camry, Solara (1999–2005)
Volkswagen New Beetle (2000–07)
Volkswagen Passat (2006–07)

Below Average

Chrysler Avenger, Sebring (1999–2004)
General Motors Alero, Grand Am
    (1999–2005)
General Motors Bonneville, Cutlass,
    Delta 88, Grand Prix, Impala, Intrigue,
    LeSabre, Lumina, Malibu, Monte Carlo,
    Regal (1999–2007)

Hyundai Sonata (1999–2003)
Nissan Altima (2002–07)
Volkswagen New Beetle (1999)
Volkswagen Passat (1999–2005)

Not Recommended

Ford Sable, Taurus (1999–2006)

Acura

1.6 EL, 1.7 EL, CSX ★★★★★

RATING: *1.6 EL, 1.7 EL:* Recommended (1999–2005). *CSX:* Recommended (2006–07). Basically a gussied-up Honda Civic (EL signifying "entry-level"), the redesigned 2001 EL and later models offer the most reliability and performance for the least amount of money. They are the cheapest Acuras available and are closely based on the Honda Civic EX sedan, albeit they offer more features and a slightly more powerful, torquier engine. As the Civic grew in size from a subcompact to a compact during the past decade, so did the EL. The 2006–07 CSX is a twin of the 2006 Civic. **"Real" city/highway fuel economy:** *1.6L manual:* 7.8/6.1 L/100 km. *1.6L automatic:* 7.9/6.0 L/100 km. *1.7L manual:* 8.1/6.3 L/100 km. *1.7L automatic:* 7.9/6.0 L/100 km. **Maintenance/Repair costs:** Average. Repairs aren't dealer-dependent. **Parts:** Average costs, thanks to the use of generic Civic parts sold through more price-competitive independent suppliers. **Extended warranty:** Not needed. **Best alternatives:** Honda Civic EX or Si; Hyundai

Elantra wagon, Sonata, or Tiburon; Mazda3 or Protegé; Mitsubishi Lancer; Pontiac Sunfire; and Toyota Camry, 2006 or later, or Corolla.

Strengths and Weaknesses

The first Japanese automobile built exclusively in and for the Canadian market, the EL is essentially an all-dressed Civic sedan, built in Alliston, Ontario, and sold under the Acura moniker.

VEHICLE HISTORY: 2001—Roomier, more fuel-efficient, and better equipped. Buyers get standard side airbags, four-wheel disc brakes, and front seat belt pretensioners. The standard 5-speed manual transmission is revised for smoother shifts and quieter operation, and the 4-speed automatic transmission boosts fuel economy. Even though horsepower remains the same, torque increases by almost 8 percent. **2003**—A retuned suspension and steering system for better handling and enhanced ride comfort reduce engine vibration through improved engine mounts and upgraded brakes. New features: adjustable head restraints and upgraded instrument clusters, armrests, and front seats. **2006**—CSX is launched.

First generation ELs come with a peppy 127 hp VTEC 1.6L 4-banger that's both reliable and economical to run. Add the Civic's chassis and upgraded suspension components, and you have competent performance that's as good as or better than the Civic Si's. Weak points: a narrow interior, with seats and seatbacks that are not to everyone's liking; emergency braking that's only average; head restraints rated Poor by IIHS; an overly soft suspension; and excessive engine noise intruding into the passenger compartment.

The 1.6 and 1.7 EL have done quite well over the years they've been on the market. The cabin is quieter than the Civic's, the steering is quick and responsive, handling is quite nimble with 15-inch tires versus the Civic's 14-inchers, and the suspension is firmer. Braking and acceleration have also improved; however, the engine's maximum torque is reached at only about 5000 rpm, which means lots of downshifting with a full load of passengers and cargo. Interestingly, Honda recommends premium gasoline, yet the equivalent Civic gets by with regular fuel. One major safety complaint targets premature strut failures that degrade handling (see the "Honda Civic" section). Otherwise, the few owner complaints recorded have typically concerned premature suspension wear (mostly springs and bushings), merely adequate engine power, wind noise, easily dented body panels, malfunctioning accessories (AC, audio system, electrical components, etc.), and fragile trim items. Some minor turn-offs with the 2001 model include the car losing power when the AC is activated, the lack of stereo controls on the steering wheel, and the driver-seat armrest interfering with the gearshift lever.

CSX

The CSX went on sale in November 2005 as a 2006 model replacement for the 1.7 EL and a template for the JDM Civic. Still a Civic spin-off, the CSX is a luxury compact for penny-pinchers who can't afford the high prices and servicing costs of competitive German luxe performers. Acura differentiates the car from the Civic through exterior upgrades that include chrome wheels and door handles, Acura rims, a double exhaust, and a restyled front fascia. Other differences: The manumatic comes with cheap-feeling thin paddles mounted on the steering column, plus there are Lilliputian instrument controls and heated leather seats.

A 155 hp 2.0L 4-cylinder engine, also used in the RSX, delivers power smoothly; however, acceleration times are merely middle of the pack. The BMW MINI Cooper and 128i, Volvo C30, Audi A3 2.0T, and similarly priced Civic Si all give faster takeoffs.

Secret Warranties/Internal Bulletins/Service Tips

All models/years: Most Honda/Acura TSBs allow for special warranty consideration on a "goodwill" basis even after the warranty has expired or the car has changed hands. Referring to this euphemism will increase your chances of getting some kind of refund for repairs that are obviously related to a factory defect. Keep in mind that many Honda bulletins often apply to Acuras, as well. So check out the Civic's and Accord's TSBs and safety complaints before assuming that a particular Acura problem doesn't exist or is your responsibility. • Acura will replace any seat belt's tongue stopper button for the life of the vehicle. • Interestingly, the automatic transmission failures afflicting 2000–03 Acuras and Hondas don't seem to be much of a problem with this entry-level Acura. Still, should you have a tranny breakdown within 7 years/160,000 km, don't hesitate to cite Honda's latest transmission extended warranty, applicable to the Civic and Accord, to back up your claim. • Seat belts that are slow to retract will also be replaced for free, says TSB #91-050.
All models: 2003–04—A soft brake pedal feel or any noise from the brake assembly when braking may indicate there's a problem with the brake-booster master cylinder.

1.6 EL, 1.7 EL, CSX PROFILE

	1999	2000	2001	2002	2003	2004	2005	2006	2007
Cost Price ($)									
1.6/1.7 EL	19,800	20,005	21,500	21,700	22,000	22,200	23,000	—	—
CSX	—	—	—	—	—	—	—	25,400	25,900
Used Values ($)									
1.6/1.7 EL ▲	3,500	4,500	5,500	7,000	9,000	10,500	11,500	—	—
1.6/1.7 EL ▼	3,000	4,000	4,500	6,000	8,000	9,500	10,500	—	—
CSX ▲	—	—	—	—	—	—	—	15,500	18,000
CSX ▼	—	—	—	—	—	—	—	14,000	16,000
Reliability	5	5	5	5	5	5	5	5	5

Note: These vehicles have not been crash tested, but should perform as well as the Civic.

RATING: *RSX:* Above Average (2002–06). *Integra:* Recommended (1999–2001). The Integra's rating is unusually high because of the few owner complaints recorded, the car's all-around competent performance, and the ease with which it can be customized through inexpensive ground effects and other options. Interestingly, there's little price difference between used entry-level and high-end models. **"Real" city/highway fuel economy:** *Integra 1.8L manual:* 9.3/7.0 L/100 km. *Integra 1.8L automatic:* 10.0/7.1 L/100 km. *RSX 2.0L 5-speed manual:* 8.8/6.6 L/100 km. *RSX 2.0L 6-speed manual:* 9.7/6.9 L/100 km. *RSX 2.0L automatic:* 9.7/6.6 L/100 km. Owners report fuel savings may undershoot these estimates by at least 15 percent. **Maintenance/Repair costs:** Average. Repairs can be done practically anywhere. **Parts:** Costs are a bit higher than average, but most parts can be bought from cheaper, independent Honda suppliers. Integra body parts can be expensive. **Extended warranty:** Not necessary; save your money for performance tires (see *www.tirerack.com*). **Best alternatives:** *Integra:* Honda Accord; Hyundai Elantra wagon, Sonata, or Tiburon; Mazda6; and Toyota Camry, 2006 or later. *RSX:* Mazda Miata and Toyota Celica GT or GT-S.

Strengths and Weaknesses

Integra

Based on the Honda Civic, the Integra evolved into more of a sports car than an econocar. Dramatically redesigned for 1994, the compact Integra two-door hatchback coupe and four-door notchback were built on a front-drive platform. Little changed in dimensions or weight. The 1994 through 2001 models provided a smoother ride than previous versions, and crash protection was augmented by the use of front airbags. The powerful VTEC engine, however, requires lots of shifting, and interior room is problematic. Nevertheless, these are the benchmark cars for optimum savings, performance, and quality.

What Integras give you in mechanical reliability and performance, they take away in poor quality control on body components and accessories. Water leaks, excessive wind noise, low-quality trim items, and plastic panels that deform easily are all commonplace. Owners also report severe steering shimmy, excessive brake noise, and premature front brake-pad wearout. Squeaks and rattles frequently crop up in the door panels and hatches, and the sedan's frameless windows often have sealing problems.

RSX

The RSX was built on the Civic platform and is powered by a base 170 hp 2.0L twin-cam iVTEC 4-banger or a torquier 200 hp variant used by the high-performance Type S. Three transmissions are available: a 5-speed manual and a 4-speed automatic offered with base models, and a 6-speed manual found on the Type S. Both engines are torquier than the powerplants they replaced; however, the base engine has more useful commuting low-end torque than the so-called sportier Type S engine.

The RSX appeals to drivers who want to shift fast and often, and who don't mind a firm ride. The car is well appointed; has good acceleration and handling above 3000 rpm; provides user-friendly gauges and controls; brakes well, especially with the Type S; gives good fuel economy (first tune-up at 160,000 km); depreciates slowly; has garnered a five-star frontal crash rating for both the driver and front-seat passenger and a four-star front side-impact rating; and has head restraints that IIHS rates Good up front and Average in the rear. The car has high-quality construction, except for transmission components and electronic glitches.

On the downside, the car exhibits so-so acceleration in lower gears; overall acceleration that's compromised by the automatic transmission; heavy steering that's a bit vague; limited front and rear headroom; cramped rear seating, with barely adequate knee and foot space; difficult rear access; a high rear-hatch liftover that complicates loading; excessive road and engine noise; and rearward visibility that's obstructed by small side windows, thick roof pillars, and a tall rear deck. There have also been many manual and automatic transmission complaints (see *forums. clubrsx.com*).

All components are of above-average quality except the airbag sensors and the manual and automatic transmissions, which are quite problematic on Acura's entire vehicle lineup. Owner reports target defective airbag sensors that disable the passenger-side airbag; engine hesitation on acceleration, with excessive exhaust noise; Second to Third gear shifting glitches and grinding; automatic transmission leaks; a faulty half-shaft shield that causes a buzzy exhaust, and a plastic cover over the cylinder head/valve cover that buzzes a bit, too; heater blower motor overheating; rough shifting; premature brake and rear strut wear; an Airbag light that remains lit; a rear bumper cover that may fall off, is often misaligned, or comes loose; and chipped paint. Original-equipment tires are poor performers in snow; however, reducing front-tire pressure to 31 psi (approximately 214 kPa) improves performance. In very cold weather, flip-up wipers freeze at the joint.

VEHICLE HISTORY: *Integra:* **1994**—A major restyling, addition of two airbags. ABS only on the LS and GS-R. **1999**—The high-performance Type R and RS are dropped. **2000**—The Type R returns with standard AC and a 195 hp engine. *RSX:* **2004**—Heated mirrors. **2005**—Restyled, upgraded suspension, steering, brakes, and seat bolstering, and 10 more horses for the Type S.

 ## Safety Summary

Integra: **All years:** No airbag deployment, or inadvertent deployment. • Sudden acceleration; automatic transmission defects; poor headlight illumination; and chronic brake failures are common in every model year. • Steering wheel may lock when making a left turn. • Prematurely warped rotors are the cause of excessive vibration and pulling. *RSX:* **All years:** Airbags fail to deploy. • Prematurely worn suspension struts; first indication is a popping or clicking sound produced during slow-speed turns. • Manual transmission often jumps out of gear or grinds (*www.*

petitiononline.com/RSXgrind/petition.html). **2002**—Fire started in the engine area. • Sudden loss of steering as vehicle suddenly veered to the right. • Headlights often burn out. **2002–03**—Airbag light stays lit. **2003**—Sudden, unintended acceleration. • Early engine valve and camshaft replacement. • Transmission failures. • Premature brake pad and rotor replacement. • Power-steering fluid leaks. • Defective window regulators. • Foglights crack often. **2004**—Airbags failed to deploy. • The Supplemental Restraint System (airbags) computer is failure-prone. Also, plugging a cell phone into the cigarette lighter may cause the SRS to fail. • Poor traction on icy surfaces. **2005**—Headlights are aimed directly at oncoming traffic when the vehicle is loaded in the rear. • AC produces a toxic mildew odour. **2006**—Parking brake failed, and vehicle crashed into a tree.

Secret Warranties/Internal Bulletins/Service Tips

Integra: **All years:** Vehicle cranks but won't start. • Severe and persistent steering-wheel shimmy is likely due to an imbalanced wheel/tire/hub/rotor assembly. • Headlight fogging. • Window guide channel comes loose. • Front brake squeal countermeasures. • Reducing rattles from the rear shelf area. • Seat belts that are slow to retract will be replaced for free, says TSB #91-050. **1990–2001**—Remedy for a rear suspension clunk or squeak. **1992–99**—A defective seat belt tongue stopper will be replaced free of charge with no ownership, time, or mileage limitations. *RSX:* **All years:** Drivetrain rattling, pinging, or squealing on light acceleration. • Moonroof squeaking. • Inoperative, noisy rear windshield wiper. **2002–03**—Excessive exhaust noise during hard acceleration. **2002–04**—Engine hesitation when accelerating from a stop. • A notchy feel when shifting gears. • A squeaking clutch pedal. **2002–05**—Wind noise from the top of the windshield. **2005–06**—Front suspension clunking on turns. • Dash creaks.

INTEGRA, RSX PROFILE

	1999	2000	2001	2002	2003	2004	2005	2006
Cost Price ($)								
Integra RS	19,500	21,000	—	—	—	—	—	—
Integra LS/SE	23,800	23,800	21,800	—	—	—	—	—
RSX	—	—	—	24,000	24,300	24,400	24,900	27,200
RSX Type S	—	—	—	31,000	31,300	31,400	33,000	33,400
Used Values ($)								
Integra RS ▲	3,500	4,000	—	—	—	—	—	—
Integra RS ▼	3,000	3,500	—	—	—	—	—	—
Integra LS/SE ▲	4,500	5,000	6,000	—	—	—	—	—
Integra LS/SE ▼	4,000	4500	5,000	—	—	—	—	—
RSX ▲	—	—	—	8,000	9,000	11,000	13,000	18,000
RSX ▼	—	—	—	6,500	8,000	9,500	11,500	16,500
RSX Type S ▲	—	—	—	10,500	10,500	12,000	14,000	20,000
RSX Type S ▼	—	—	—	9,500	9,000	10,500	12,500	18,000

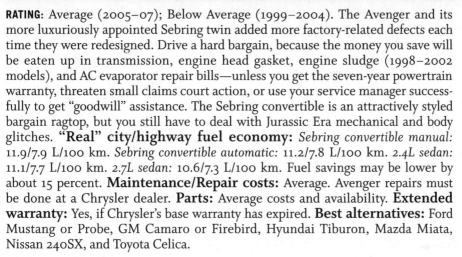

Reliability	4	4	5	3	3	3	3	3
Crash Safety (F)	—	—	—	5	5	5	5	5
Side	—	—	—	4	4	4	4	4
Head Restraints (F)	3	—	3	—	—	—	—	—
Rollover Resistance	—	—	—	4	4	4	4	4

Chrysler

AVENGER, SEBRING ★★★

RATING: Average (2005–07); Below Average (1999–2004). The Avenger and its more luxuriously appointed Sebring twin added more factory-related defects each time they were redesigned. Drive a hard bargain, because the money you save will be eaten up in transmission, engine head gasket, engine sludge (1998–2002 models), and AC evaporator repair bills—unless you get the seven-year powertrain warranty, threaten small claims court action, or use your service manager successfully to get "goodwill" assistance. The Sebring convertible is an attractively styled bargain ragtop, but you still have to deal with Jurassic Era mechanical and body glitches. **"Real" city/highway fuel economy:** *Sebring convertible manual:* 11.9/7.9 L/100 km. *Sebring convertible automatic:* 11.2/7.8 L/100 km. *2.4L sedan:* 11.1/7.7 L/100 km. *2.7L sedan:* 10.6/7.3 L/100 km. Fuel savings may be lower by about 15 percent. **Maintenance/Repair costs:** Average. Avenger repairs must be done at a Chrysler dealer. **Parts:** Average costs and availability. **Extended warranty:** Yes, if Chrysler's base warranty has expired. **Best alternatives:** Ford Mustang or Probe, GM Camaro or Firebird, Hyundai Tiburon, Mazda Miata, Nissan 240SX, and Toyota Celica.

Strengths and Weaknesses

These coupes, sedans, and convertibles are mediocre buys mainly because they're so poorly made. Defects affect body and mechanical components equally, and lead to serious long-term reliability and durability problems. On the positive side, these vehicles are dirt cheap as new or used models because the public has little confidence in the reliability of Chrysler products or in the solvency of the automaker itself. As Chrysler drifts toward bankruptcy, however, servicing won't be affected much due to the length of time these cars have been on the market with the same design. For example, powertrains, platforms, safety features, and other mechanical components are shared among the entire lineup and can be bought easily from independent suppliers for much less than dealers charge.

VEHICLE HISTORY: 1995–99—Minor restyling touches, and the 4-cylinder engine is dropped in mid-1999. **2000**—Avenger ES is given a standard 2.5L V6 and an automatic transmission. **2001**—The redesigned Sebring adds a sedan, a more-powerful V6, and a premium sound system. The Avenger is dropped. **2002**—Sebrings are joined by a 200 hp 2.7L V6 R/T sedan equipped with a manual 5-speed gearbox. **2003**—Four-wheel disc brakes. **2005**—Coupes are dropped.

The 3.0L and 3.5L V6 are the engines of choice to overcome the power-hungry automatic transmission and to avoid a persistent 4-cylinder engine head gasket defect affecting all model years through 1999. Handling is better than average, and the ride is generally comfortable, except for a bit of choppiness because of the firm suspension.

The 2.7L V6 would normally be a good alternative to the small 4-cylinder; however, it is subject to early engine primary timing-chain tensioner and tensioner O-ring failures and oil sludging on 1998–2002 models—a problem covered by a secret "goodwill" warranty. Owners also report automatic transmission failures, grinding when shifting, shuddering from a stop, and defaulting to Second gear; engine oil leaks; loss of steering and a clanking or rattling heard when turning over rough pavement; premature suspension replacement, brake wear, and brake failures; ignition, electrical system, and PCM glitches; sunroof malfunctions; and sloppy body construction (water leaks and lots of wind noise) as the areas most needing attention. Would you believe that the driver-seat motor burns out because it doesn't have a fuse? Replacement cost: $2,000!

As with 2005–06 Corvettes, the convertible tops can fly off on early models, plus they leak water and air and operate erratically. A faulty window regulator allows the window to run off its track. Poor design and sloppy construction allow water into the vehicle when the window is partly opened; rear windshield sealant lets water leak into the vehicle; wheel rims are easily bent and leak air from normal driving; there's excessive brake dust; a black goo oozes from body panels and the undercarriage; side door mouldings melt; and the chrome wheels and airbag coating peels.

Safety Summary

All models/years: Brake and gas pedals are too close together. **All models: 2001**—Brake failure accompanied by sudden, unintended acceleration. • Brake caliper bolt falls off. • Brake and accelerator pedals are too close together. • Window shatters when convertible top is lowered. **2002**—When putting vehicle into Reverse, it sometimes surges forward. • Engine stalls out after fill-ups. • Sudden brake failure. • Suspension feels loose at high speeds when passing over bumps or potholes. • Steering wheel catches and pulls right when turning. • Back windows suddenly explode. **2003**—Sudden loss of steering. • Driver's airbag deploys for no reason. • Tapping brakes locks them up. • ABS brake failure. • Rodents can get into the heater blower area. • Headlights dim and shut off intermittently. **2004**—Electrical wiring in the rear defroster ignites a fire. • Airbags fail to deploy. • Tall front occupants may suffer considerable trauma despite airbag deployment. • Sudden, unintended acceleration when stopped or accelerating. • Sticking accelerator pedal. • Firewall fuel line leakage. • Engine overheating and stalling. • Transmission slippage—not engaging the gear selected and shifting to a higher and then a lower gear, making the car surge. • Transmission sticks in Park. • Steering failure. • Seat heater overheats. • Dash lights flicker, and headlights may suddenly go off. • Key sticks in the ignition. • Warped driver-side airbag cover. • Chrome door handles can cut a finger. • Bumper falls off. **2005**—Airbags deploy and start a fire. • Delayed shifts. • Steering failure caused by broken steering knuckle. • Left front wheel breaks away from vehicle. • Filler pipe collapses while vehicle is refuelling. • Inaccurate fuel gauge readings. • Passenger-side window spontaneously explodes. • Horn sounds on its own.

Secret Warranties/Internal Bulletins/Service Tips

All models: 1998–2002—The 2.7L V6 engine sludging "goodwill" warranty was never confirmed by any service bulletin. Nonetheless, Chrysler spokesman Sam Locricchio told *AutoWeek* on September 3, 2004, that the automaker was working hard to "find a reasonable and appropriate resolution" for individual complaints. Chrysler hasn't shown any production changes that guarantee engines will not sludge up in the estimated 10 percent of its 2005 lineup that are sold with the same V6 (mounted front-to-back rather than sideways). **2001**—Rough 2.7L engine idle. • Automatic transmission bump, sag, and surge. • Rear suspension squawk. **2001–02**—Moderate to severe highway engine surge. • Exhaust rattle, vibration. • Low or no cabin heat. • Loose, warped front door trim panel. **2001–06**—Musty AC smell. • Wind noise from the dash area. **2002**—Hard-to-remove fuel cap. **2002–04**—Delayed gear engagement:

DELAYED GEAR ENGAGEMENT

BULLETIN NO.: 21-004-05   DATE: JANUARY 22, 2005

TRANSMISSION DELAYED ENGAGEMENT

2004 Pacifica; 2002–04 Sebring Convertible/Sebring Sedan/Stratus Sedan; 2003 Liberty; 2002–04 300M/ Concorde/Intrepid; 2002–03; Neon 2002–03 PT Cruiser; 2002–03 Town & Country/Caravan/Voyager; 2003 Wrangler

This bulletin involves replacing the front pump assembly in the automatic transmission and checking the Transmission Control Module (TCM) for the latest software revision level.

2003—Horn blows on its own. • Rear brake clunk. **2003–04**—Harsh downshifts. **2003–05**—Automatic transmission whine at 100 km/h. **2004**—Driveability improvements to fix engine stumbling and rough running, idle fluctuations, and surging when at idle or coming to a stop. • Harsh 4–3 downshifts. • Low-speed transmission bumps. • Pop/clunk sound from front of vehicle; engine snapping noise. • Steering-column click. • Revised suspension lateral-control links. • Door clunk noise. • Power seat won't adjust; front seat movement. • Intermittent loss of accessories. • Customer Satisfaction No. C30, relative to the PCM connector seal. • Window fogging. **2004–05**—Inoperative AC. **2004–06**—AC leaks water onto passenger floor.

AVENGER, SEBRING PROFILE

	1999	2000	2001	2002	2003	2004	2005	2006	2007
Cost Price ($)									
Avenger	20,360	—	—	—	—	—	—	—	—
Avenger V6	23,545	—	—	—	—	—	—	—	—
Sebring	23,380	27,685	23,240	23,320	23,610	24,115	24,560	24,880	22,995
Sebring V6	28,675	26,525	30,095	27,380	27,795	28,415	28,855	—	—
Convertible	32,100	32,585	33,595	33,580	34,305	35,195	35,795	36,115	—
Used Values ($)									
Avenger ▲	2,500	—	—	—	—	—	—	—	—
Avenger ▼	2,000	—	—	—	—	—	—	—	—
Avenger V6 ▲	4,000	—	—	—	—	—	—	—	—
Avenger V6 ▼	3,500	—	—	—	—	—	—	—	—
Sebring ▲	2,500	3,000	3,500	4,000	4,500	5,500	7,500	9,500	12,000
Sebring ▼	2,500	3,000	3,500	3,500	4,000	4,500	6,000	8,000	10,500
Sebring V6 ▲	3,000	3,500	4,000	4,500	5,000	6,500	8,500	—	—
Sebring V6 ▼	3,000	3,500	3,500	4,000	4,500	5,500	7,500	—	—
Convertible ▲	4,000	4,500	5,000	6,000	6,500	8,000	10,000	12,500	—
Convertible ▼	3,500	4,000	4,500	5,500	6,000	6,500	8,500	11,000	—
Reliability	2	2	2	2	2	2	3	3	3
Crash Safety (F)									
Sebring 2d	—	—	4	4	4	4	4	—	—
Sebring 4d	—	—	5	5	5	5	5	5	5
Sebring cvt.	—	—	3	3	3	3	3	3	—
Side (Sebring)	—	—	3	3	3	3	3	—	—
Sebring 4d	—	—	3	3	3	3	3	3	5
Sebring cvt.	—	—	3	3	3	3	3	5	—
IIHS Side	—	—	1	1	1	1	1	1	5
Offset	—	—	3	3	3	3	3	3	5
Head Restraints									
Avenger	2	—	—	—	—	—	—	—	—
Sebring	3	—	2	3	1	1	1	1	3
Rollover Resistance	—	—	5	5	5	5	5	5	4
Sebring 2d	—	—	—	4	4	4	—	—	—
Sebring cvt.	—	—	—	—	5	5	5	5	—

Ford

RATING: Not Recommended (1999–2006). Wow! A 2002 Taurus for less than $3,500? What a bargain—NOT! These quintessential lemons make the Ford "You Light Up My Life" Pinto and Vauxhall Firenza look good. They are easy to find and dirt cheap because their owners can't wait to get rid of them before they pay another $3,000 in powertrain repairs (if they're lucky). And the extra engine and transmission warranty protection you must buy will wipe out any savings realized from a low selling price. The high-performance Taurus SHO (Super High Output) is worse. It's a double-whammy wallet buster with major engine deficiencies that can cost up to $15,000 to remedy; plus it shares most of the other generic safety- and performance-related defects that have long plagued the Taurus and Sable. The last model year for the Sable and the Mercury brand in Canada was 1999; Taurus managed to hold on through the 2006 model year. The restyled and slightly upgraded 2008 Ford Five Hundred and Ford Freestyle have been renamed the Taurus and Taurus X, respectively. **"Real" city/highway fuel economy:** 3.0L *automatic:* 12.4/8.2 L/100 km. These Fords are real gas hogs; owners report fuel savings may undershoot this estimate by at least 20 percent. **Maintenance/ Repair costs:** Much higher than average, but repairs aren't dealer-dependent. Shopping at engine, transmission, brake, and muffler shops offering lifetime warranties can prevent some repeat repair costs. **Parts:** Average costs (independent suppliers sell for much less), and parts are very easy to find, except for the discontinued SHO engine and Taurus parts such as the fuel pumps and electrical components needed to correct chronic stalling and electrical shorts. **Extended warranty:** Nothing less than a bumper-to-bumper extended warranty will do. Even with additional protection, you're taking a huge risk with your wallet. **Best alternatives:** Honda Accord; Hyundai Elantra wagon or Sonata; Mazda6; and Toyota Camry, 2006 or later. A good alternative to the SHO and its failure-prone engine is the Ford Mustang GT.

Strengths and Weaknesses

Although they lack pickup with the standard 4-cylinder engine, these mid-sized sedans and wagons are competent family cars, offering lots of interior room, nice handling, a good crash rating, and many convenience features. From a performance standpoint, the best powertrain combination for all driving conditions is the 3.0L V6 hooked to a 4-speed on the family sedan. The Yamaha powerplant harnessed to a manual gearbox on the high-performance SHO is a recipe for disaster. Total engine rebuilds are the norm, not the exception.

Yet the first generation Taurus LX was *Motor Trend* magazine's Car of the Year for 1986 and placed on *Car and Driver*'s annual Ten Best list from 1986 to 1991. Two examples of why most automobile journalists can't be trusted.

These cars are extremely risky buys, and they are getting worse as they age. To see just how badly time is taking its toll, look up Sable or Taurus on NHTSA's website (*www.nhtsa.dot.gov*). Chronic engine head gasket/intake manifold and automatic transmission failures; a plethora of hazardous airbag, fuel-system, brake, suspension, and steering defects; and chronic paint/rust problems are the main reasons these cars' rating is so low. Owners also report that engine and transmission repairs don't last: Some owners are routinely putting in new engines or transmissions every few years.

Up until 2001, Ford's "goodwill" programs usually compensated owners for most of the above-noted failures (except for self-destructing SHO engines) once the warranty had expired. Unfortunately, these refund programs have dried up. Owners are routinely faced with $3,000 engine or automatic transmission repair bills in addition to thousands of dollars in repairs for defective fuel systems, brakes, and suspension and steering assemblies. Ford rejects many owner complaints on the grounds that repairs were done by independent agencies, or the vehicle was bought used, or it is no longer under the original warranty—three reasons that are often rejected by small claims court judges.

The 4-cylinder engine is a dog that no amount of servicing can change. It's slow, noisy, prone to stalling and surging, and actually consumes more gas than the V6. The 3.0L 6-cylinder is noted for engine head bolt failures and piston scuffing and is characterized by hard starting, stalling, excessive engine noise, and poor fuel economy. Transmission cooler lines leak and often lead to the unnecessary repair or replacement of the transmission.

Other things to look out for are blown heater hoses, malfunctioning fuel gauge sending units, and brakes that need constant attention—they're noisy, pulsate excessively, tend to wear out prematurely, require a great deal of pedal effort, and are hard to modulate. Master cylinders need replacing at around 100,000 km.

SHO

The Taurus SHO high-performance sedan debuted in 1989 and sold through the 1999 model year. It carried a Yamaha 24-valve 3.0L V6 with 220 hp; a stiff, performance-oriented suspension; and a 5-speed manual transmission. In 1993, a 4-speed automatic transmission became available. In mid-1996, a redesigned SHO debuted with a standard Yamaha 32-valve V8 and 15 additional horses (235). Ford dropped the manual transmission at that time, a move that turned off most diehard performance enthusiasts. The SHO is an impressive high-performance car that, unfortunately, has its own unique Yamaha-sourced engine problems in addition to carrying Ford's failure-prone automatic transmission and sharing a host of other deficiencies with the Taurus and Sable.

VEHICLE HISTORY: 1995—A watershed year for engine head gasket failures and cooked engines. **1996**—A third-generation redesign highlighted by an ugly ovoid restyling where windows look like portholes, headroom is reduced, and entry/exit becomes problematic. **2000**—Redesigned and restyled to provide a more comfortable ride, a more-powerful and quieter powertrain, upgraded airbags, adjustable pedals, seat belt pretensioners, and improved child safety seat anchors. Ford drops the oval design. **2005**—LX and SES versions are dropped. **2006**—The wagon and 201 hp V6 engine are ditched.

Each Taurus and Sable provides a symphony of rattles, buzzes, whines, and moans to keep you company on long drives. The most annoying? The incessant snapping and creaking of the plastic in the centre console and dash caused by the plastic sections binding against each other when the body flexes, especially if the sun has been shining on it. The reliability of 2000 model year vehicles continues to go downhill. Fuel-system failures result in surging, stalling, and a gasoline smell that invades the interior; electrical shorts cause the vehicle to suddenly shut down and not start again; the ABS and airbag malfunction; powertrain and body components have a short lifespan; and owners have found that the restyled head restraints block rear and side visibility.

Fourth-generation 2000–06 models use an adequate, though dated, base 155 hp 3.0L Vulcan V6. Other nice standard features include heated outside mirrors, a 60/40 split-fold rear seatback for additional cargo space, a driver's footrest, and reserve power to operate the power windows and moonroof after the engine is shut off. The suspension is softened, and four-wheel disc brakes are eliminated.

These cars are generally quiet running, provide good handling and road holding, and offer a comfortable ride along with better-than-average crash protection. Some of the minuses include insufficient storage space, limited rear headroom and access, and a history of serious transmission and engine failures. Engine intake manifold defects top the list, accompanied by sudden engine shutdown. Furthermore, Flex-Fuel models may be difficult to start.

The automatic transmission often shifts out of First gear too soon, shifts slowly, constantly bangs through the gears, and frequently chooses the wrong gear. Also expect chronic warped brake rotors; AC failures; electrical system shorts (lots of blown fuses); steering, front suspension, fuel (faulty fuel pumps), and brake system deficiencies; and extremely poor fit and finish, highlighted by numerous water leaks into the interior.

 ## Safety Summary

All models/years: Tie rod may collapse suddenly. Although the 1992 models were recalled to fix this defect, many other model years are affected and haven't been recalled. • Front coil springs may fracture because of excessive corrosion. Ford has replaced many coils for free under a secret warranty. Interestingly, Ford's Windstars have the same problem and benefit from the same 10-year extended warranty. Use that as your Taurus coil benchmark. • Strong fuel odour seeps into the interior. • Power steering suddenly fails. • These vehicles eat brake rotors, calipers, and pads every 8,000 km (5,000 mi.). • Warped rotors. • Transmission slips out of Park. • Frequent complaints of sudden acceleration or high idle when taking the foot off the gas pedal at a standstill, shifting into Reverse, slowly accelerating, or applying the brakes. • Chronic stalling and brake failures. • Airbag fails to deploy, or is accidentally deployed. • Dash reflects onto windshield. **All models: 2001**—Car accelerates while backing up. • Driver-side seat belt tightens by itself while driving. • Left rear wheel came off in transit; driver lost control of car. **2001–02**—Interior rear-view mirror location obstructs visibility. • Adjustable brake and accelerator pedals are set too close together and are often too loose; when coming to a stop, vehicle continued to accelerate because foot pressed brake and gas pedal at the same time. **2002**—Engine compartment fire. • Sudden acceleration; vehicle surges and then shuts off when fuel tank is filled. • Frequent stalling, hard starts, and poor idle caused by chronic fuel-pump failures or a contaminated fuel-pressure sensor. • Strong fuel smell comes from the air vents. • Fuel gauge stuck on Full. • Fuel tank is easily punctured • Seat belts may not reel out or retract. • Seat belt continually tightened around child and had to be cut. • Rear brake lines rub together. • High beam lights are too dim. • Cigarette lighter pops out and falls under passenger seat. **2003**—Airbag warning light stays lit. • Rear left wheel and rim fly off because of defective lug nuts. • Engine belt tensioner shatters. • Right rear wheel almost fell off because of faulty stabilizer bolt. **2003–06**—Inoperative AC compressor; low Freon shaft seal leaks. • Cowl water leaks short out the heater/AC and other climate-control items:

> I have a 03 Taurus which leaked water onto the passenger floor board also causing my AC blower motor to short out. I could not get Ford to act even though a related recall existed under 03v087000. I have found many others with this problem.

2004—Replacing the original radio will render the airbag inoperative since the controls run through the original-equipment radio supplied by Ford. • Several reports of coil spring breakage causing loss of steering control (a problem for over a decade). • Driver's seat catches on fire. • Chronic stalling. • Automatic transmission shifts erratically and slips. • Seat belt choked passenger in a collision. • Brake failure and engine surging occur simultaneously along with lit ABS and Traction Control warning lights. • Only driver-side door has a key-operated lock. • Sunroof opens and closes on its own. **2004–06**—Spark knock and hesitation. **2005**—Engine compartment fire. • Transmission shifts erratically:

> The transmission started slipping around 38,500 miles [62,000 km]. It has been repaired 3 times. I was almost hit twice because the transmission slipped from 50 mph to 25 mph [80 to 40 km/h] in a matter of seconds. The vehicles behind me had to slam on brakes and jump lanes to keep from hitting me.

• Vehicle wanders all over the road. • Side windows implode while driving. • Inaccurate fuel gauge. • Static electricity shocks driver exiting vehicle. • Ventilation system allows polluted air to enter the cabin. • Driver's seat belt fails to latch. • Child safety seat tips to the side when car corners at 15–20 km/h. **2006**—Airbags fail to deploy, or deploy while vehicle is parked. • Sudden acceleration while stopped at a stop sign. • Car accelerates on its own when cruise control is engaged.

• Transmission failure. • Defective power-steering pump replaced via a "goodwill" warranty extension. • Head restraints force occupants' heads down into their chins. • Water leaks into the driver-side floor area, causing mould buildup. • More water leaks from the cowl area into the front-passenger area, where it short-circuits the climate controls and blower. • Rear brake lights work intermittently. • Headlights are too bright for oncoming drivers. • Sudden failure of all the instrument panel gauges • Hard starts; no-starts. • Tread peeled off of tire. • Poorly performing Goodyear tires.

Secret Warranties/Internal Bulletins/Service Tips

All models/years: Many reports of sudden coil spring breakage puncturing tires and throwing vehicles out of control; there are no confirming TSBs, however. Writes the owner of a 1999 Taurus SE in 2004:

> Driver side coil spring failed, cutting the tire in half. Not too bad at 60 km/h but would have been a disaster at 100 km/h. Seems there were "not enough failures" to require recall earlier, but ANOTHER investigation has been opened by [the] government. Dealer said it was a "common" failure!!! I would not drive a Taurus/Windstar until I put something other than Ford springs on them. There are also reports of similar failures in Contours, Escorts, Focus, and F-150s. Problems with Ford coil springs and corrosion date from at least 1993. So, 11 years later, they clearly have done NOTHING to fix the problem. The corrosion where my spring broke was NOT visible externally, but was clearly rusted internally at the point where it broke.

• Repeated heater core leaks. • A buzz or rattle from the exhaust system may be caused by a loose heat shield catalyst. • A sloshing noise from the fuel tank when accelerating or stopping requires the installation of an upgraded tank. • Paint delamination, fading, and peeling. **All models: 1995–2000**—A harsh 3–2 down-shift/shudder when accelerating or turning may have a simple cause: air entering the fluid filter pickup area because of a slightly low ATF fluid level. **1996–2003**—Repair tips for when the torque converter clutch doesn't engage. **1997–2006**—Remedy for chronic heater core leaks. **2000–03**—Power window "grunting." **2000–06**—An inaccurate fuel gauge will be repaired under the emissions warranty. • Aluminum body panels may be afflicted with early corrosion. • Loose leather steering-wheel wrapping. • Erratic fluid level readings on the transaxle dipstick; transmission fluid leaks. **2000–06**—Vibration or booming at idle. • Seat belt is slow to retract. **2001–05**—Tips on eliminating an engine ticking noise. **2002–05**—Troubleshooting transmission malfunctions. • Engine-cooling-fan-induced body boom. • Rough engine idle sensation; unusual engine noise at idle. • Incorrectly installed gear-driven camshaft-position-sensor synchronizer assemblies may cause engine surge, loss of power, or MIL to light. • Rattling, clunking front suspension. **2003**—Transmission may not go into Reverse. **2003–06**—Inoperative AC compressor. **2004**—3.0L engine oil leaks; cold hard start, no-start, and surging. • Hesitation when accelerating. • Wipers won't shut off. • Inoperative rear window defroster. • Accelerator pedal vibration. • Speedometer malfunctions. • Wheel cover and front suspension noise. **2005–06**—Troubleshooting a misfiring engine.

SABLE, TAURUS PROFILE

	1999	2000	2001	2002	2003	2004	2005	2006
Cost Price ($)								
Sable GS	24,595	—	—	—	—	—	—	—
LS Wagon	25,795	—	—	—	—	—	—	—
Taurus LX	23,495	24,495	24,250	24,550	24,750	24,995		—
GL/SE Wagon	24,695	26,495	26,555	27,285	27,630	28,355	26,345	25,099
SHO	37,995	—	—	—	—	—	—	—
Used Values ($)								
Sable GS ▲	2,500	—	—	—	—	—	—	—
Sable GS ▼	2,000	—	—	—	—	—	—	—
LS Wagon ▲	3,000	—	—	—	—	—	—	—
LS Wagon ▼	2,500	—	—	—	—	—	—	—
Taurus LX ▲	2,500	2,500	3,000	3,500	4,500	5,500	—	—
Taurus LX ▼	2,000	2,500	3,000	3,500	4,000	4,500	—	—
GL/SE Wagon ▲	3,000	3,500	4,000	4,500	5,500	6,000	7,500	8,500
GL/SE Wagon ▼	3,000	3,000	3,500	4,000	5,000	5,500	6,500	7,500
SHO ▲	4,000	—	—	—	—	—	—	—
SHO ▼	3,500	—	—	—	—	—	—	—
Reliability	1	1	2	2	2	2	2	—
Crash Safety (F)	—	5	5	5	4	4	4	—
Side	—	3	3	3	3	3	3	—
Offset	5	5	5	5	5	5	5	—
Head Restraints (F)	1	3	5	2	3	2	2	—
Rear	—	3	3	3	—	—	—	—
Rollover Resistance	—	—	4	4	4	4	4	—

General Motors

ALERO, GRAND AM ★★

RATING: Below Average (1999–2005). Keep in mind that the 4-cylinder engines are noisy and rough-running. **"Real" city/highway fuel economy:** *2.2L manual: 9.4/6.0 L/100 km. 2.2L automatic: 9.8/6.6 L/100 km. 3.4L V6 automatic: 11.7/6.7 L/100 km.* Owners report fuel savings may undershoot these estimates by at least 20 percent. **Maintenance/Repair costs:** Higher than average. Repairs aren't dealer-dependent. **Parts:** Higher-than-average costs, but parts can be bought from independent suppliers for much less than from the dealership. **Extended warranty:** Extended powertrain coverage is a must. **Best alternatives:** Acura Integra; Honda Accord; Hyundai Elantra wagon, Sonata, or Tiburon; Mazda6; and Toyota Camry, 2006 or later.

Strengths and Weaknesses

Redesigned in 1999, these cars aren't very impressive. The best engine choice for power, smoothness, and value retention is the 207 hp 3.4L V6; it gives you much-needed power and is quite fuel-efficient. The 2.2L engine is quieter, but its lack of power is noticeable, particularly when coupled with an automatic transmission. Stay away from the Computer Command Ride option; true, it allows you to choose your own suspension settings, but the settings aren't quite what they pretend to be.

Taking their styling cues from GM's Grand Prix, the Grand Am and its Alero twin offer a roomy, comfortable interior in two- and four-door body styles, and they share the same platform and mechanical components. The base Grand Am SE uses a 140 hp 2.2L powerplant, while other trim levels use a 150 hp 2.4L Quad DOHC engine. A 170 hp 3.4L V6 engine is standard on the SE2. The upscale Alero, Oldsmobile's entry-level model, debuted in 1999 as the replacement for the slow-selling Achieva—often referred to as the "under-Achieva." The Alero shares the Grand Am's chassis and powertrains, although only the 2.2L 4-cylinder and 3.4L V6 are offered. The V6 may be teamed with either a 5-speed manual or a 4-speed automatic transmission.

VEHICLE HISTORY: 1999—Given better engines, a new platform, more standard equipment, and a restyled, more-comfortable interior. **2002**—A quieter, more-efficient 140 hp 2.2L base engine with 10 fewer horses than the engine it replaced; a revised console storage area. **2004**—An MP3 speaker upgrade. Alero's last model year. **2005**—Grand Am's last model year.

Grand Ams from 1999 to 2005 are well-appointed with many more standard features, like traction control, than previous versions. They have a competent V6, good steering and handling, and average quality control. Some of their disadvantages include a mediocre ride over rough terrain, excessive 4-cylinder noise, and a noisy interior. Also, expect difficult rear-seat access (coupe), awkward radio controls, rear visibility that's obstructed by the spoiler, problematic trunk access, annoying body creaks and rattles, and doubtful long-term powertrain reliability.

Equally well equipped, Aleros give impressive V6 acceleration (even though it's the same engine found in the Grand Am, it performs better in the Alero). You'll find logical, user-friendly gauges and controls, a fairly spacious interior for cargo and passengers, standard traction control, and a quiet-running V6 powertrain. Here's the Alero's downside: excessive 4-cylinder engine noise and torque steer, steering that's not as crisp as the Grand Am's, difficult rear-seat access (coupe), and questionable long-term durability. The Alero was dropped during the 2004 model year after GM's phase-out of its Oldsmobile division.

Overall quality control is poor. Owners warn of powertrain malfunctions, including sudden transmission failure and poor shifting; engine overheating; and premature brake pad and rotor wear. Also mentioned are electrical problems; suspension squeaks; and substandard body assembly that produces squeaks and rattles, water leaks, and poor paint adhesion. There are reports that the sunroof may leak water into the electrical panel, causing short circuits. The spoiler may obstruct rear visibility.

Safety Summary

All models/years: Airbag fails to deploy. • Inadvertent airbag deployment. • Sudden acceleration and stalling. • Frequent brake failures and extended stopping distances; brake caliper seizure damages pads and rotors. • Power-steering failures and fluid leakage. • Transmission jumps out of gear. • Shoulder belt rides across driver's neck. • Erratic fuel gauge operation. • Headlights suddenly shut off or don't provide enough illumination. • Head restraints block rear vision. • Dash is reflected onto the windshield. • Water leaks everywhere. **All models: 2001—** Stalling, brake rotor warpage, and sunroof leaks. Other problems include fires igniting at the right rear of vehicle; fuel tanks being easily punctured; and rear axles bending or breaking, leading to a loss of control. **2002–05—**Frequency of safety complaints increased substantially. • Transmission suddenly fails while cruising at speeds over 100 km/h. • Chronic stalling. • Vehicle continues accelerating after passing another car on the highway. • Car constantly surges and hesitates. • Vehicle tends to wander all over the road; pulls to one side when accelerating. • Steering shudders on braking or acceleration; faulty power-steering pump; steering feels too loose. • ABS light comes on, followed by brake failure; brake pedal set too low; parking brake failure. • Fuel-pump failure. • Shoulder belts twist in their housing; in the GT two-door, they ride abnormally high on the shoulder/neck area. • Power doors lock on their own. • Headlights blink on and off. • Middle rear lap seat belt is too short to secure a child safety seat. • Loose driver's seat. • Windshield wipers shut off intermittently. • Rear windshield shatters when defogger is activated; side door glass shatters behind mirror for no reason. • Inside door edge is razor sharp. • Slight front impact causes the battery tray to break off, or results in the battery sliding off the tray. *Alero:* **All years:** Engine compartment fire. • Right front wheel separates because the lug nuts and bolts shear off. • Tapped brakes to turn cruise control off, and vehicle accelerated. • Rear main oil seal leak blows oil onto exhaust pipe. • Fuel-tank leakage. • Water leakage onto the back of the instrument panel causes the instruments and gauges to malfunction; other electrical shorts cause instrument panel gauges and controls to fail. • Windshield water leaks cause electrical shorts. • Hard to find horn "sweet spot" in an emergency.

Secret Warranties/Internal Bulletins/Service Tips

All models/years: GM has a special kit to keep AC odours at bay. • Paint delamination, peeling, or fading. • Reverse servo cover leaks. **All models: 1998–2003—**Automatic transmission flaring. **1999—**Hesitation or lack of power when accelerating on vehicles equipped with the 3.4L engine may simply require reprogramming the PCM. **1999–2000—**No Third or Fourth gear may signal a defective direct clutch piston. • A wet front or rear carpet may mean the front-door water deflectors need to be replaced. • Simply changing the radiator cap may cure your hot-running engine. **1999–2001**—A front-end clunk or rattle can be silenced by replacing the brake pedal assembly. • Water leak troubleshooting. • Wind rush from the front windshield. **1999–2002**—Excessive pedal or steering-wheel pulsation when braking can be eliminated by using GM's Front Pad Kit #18044437, says TSB #00-05-23-002A. **1999–2004**—Faulty rear lights cost up to $300 to repair, but GM will cover the cost through a secret warranty, a recall, and its implied warranty obligations. • Poor automatic transmission performance and slipping. • Faulty front-door window glass and power-window motor. **1999–2005**—Side windows won't roll up. **2000**—If the vehicle stalls, hesitates, or won't start, you may need to replace the modular fuel-sender strainer. **2000–01**—If the Check Engine light comes on, it may mean the fuel-sender-to-tank O-ring is defective. • Install a fuel-tank sender kit if the fuel gauge gives inaccurate readings. **2000–03**—Firm transmission shifts and shudders, or transmission slips or fails to shift. • Loss of power steering. • Inaccurate fuel gauge readings. • Front-door window glass comes out of run channel. **2001–04**—Silencing a creaky door. **2001–05**—Harsh upshifts. **2002**—No-starts; harsh transmission shifts. • Transmission fluid leakage. • Premature failure of the transaxle converter pump. • A Customer Service Campaign will pay for the inspection and correction of a transaxle converter bearing failure, detailed in TSB #01031. • Remedy for suspension noise or malfunctions. **2002–04**—Poor transmission performance can be caused by a defective driven sprocket support assembly. **2002–05**—Water leaking on the floor requires a clean drain hose to correct. **2003**—Poor shifting and inaccurate gauges. **2004**—No-starts, stalling. • Transmission growl or howl when accelerating from a stop. • Trunk water leaks. *Grand Am:* **1999**—Paint chipping from the Grand Am SE's rocker panel and lower quarter panel can be prevented by installing upgraded driver- and passenger-side rocker mouldings.

ALERO, GRAND AM PROFILE

	1999	2000	2001	2002	2003	2004	2005
Cost Price ($)							
Alero	20,995	20,445	21,335	21,745	22,285	22,335	—
Grand Am/Coupe GT	21,795	20,625	20,915	21,405	21,640	21,885	27,000
Used Values ($)							
Alero ▲	2,500	3,000	3,500	4,000	5,000	6,000	—
Alero ▼	2,500	3,000	3,500	3,500	4,500	5,000	—
Grand Am/Coupe GT ▲	3,000	3,500	4,000	5,000	6,000	7,000	8,500
Grand Am/Coupe GT ▼	2,500	3,500	4,000	4,500	5,500	6,000	7,500
Reliability	2	2	2	2	2	2	3
Crash Safety (F)							
Grand Am 2d	—	—	4	4	4	4	4
Grand Am 4d	4	4	4	4	4	4	4
Side							
Grand Am 2d	2	1	3	1	3	1	1
Grand Am 4d	1	3	3	3	3	3	3

Offset	**1**	**1**	**1**	**1**	**1**	**1**	**1**
Head Restraints							
Grand Am 2d	—	**2**	**1**	**1**	**1**	**1**	**1**
Grand Am 4d	—	**2**	**1**	**1**	**1**	**1**	**1**
Alero	—	—	—	—	**2**	—	—
Rollover Resistance							
Grand Am 2d	—	—	—	—	4	4	4
Grand Am 4d	—	—	—	4	4	4	4

BONNEVILLE, DELTA 88, GRAND PRIX, IMPALA, INTRIGUE, LESABRE, LUMINA, MALIBU, MONTE CARLO, REGAL ★★

RATING: Below Average (1999–2007). Many model years are "hot," not because they are popular, but because they have a propensity to catch fire. **"Real" city/ highway fuel economy:** *Malibu 2.2L automatic: 9.9/6.6 L/100 km. Malibu 3.5L 6-cylinder automatic: 10.4/6.8 L/100 km. LeSabre, Bonneville 3.8L 6-cylinder automatic: 11.9/7.3 L/100 km. Monte Carlo 3.4L 6-cylinder automatic: 11.8/7.1 L/100 km.* Owners report fuel savings may undershoot these estimates by about 20 percent. **Maintenance/Repair costs:** Higher than average, but repairs aren't dealer-dependent. **Parts:** Higher-than-average costs (independent suppliers sell for much less), but parts aren't hard to find. Nevertheless, don't even think about buying one of the front-drives without a supplementary 3- to 5-year powertrain warranty. **Extended warranty:** Yes, mainly for the engine and automatic transmission. **Best alternatives:** Acura Integra; Honda Accord; Hyundai Elantra Wagon, Sonata, or Tiburon; Mazda6; and Toyota Camry, 2006 or later.

Strengths and Weaknesses

The following problems are common to all models: no-start or no-crank conditions caused by a defective ignition and start switch assembly; engine oil pan leaks; harsh shifting, with harsh 1–2 upshifts; poor engine performance and transmission slipping; delayed shifts, slips, flares, or extended shifts in cold weather; poor braking, and frequent replacement of the brake rotor pads; moaning, leaking steering assembly (bad spool and input seals are the likely culprits); and the sudden loss of power steering.

Body assembly on all models is notoriously poor, evidenced by premature paint peeling and rusting, squeaks and rattles, wind and road noise, and water leaks:

> Water leaks into the vehicle on the passenger side through the fuse box panel. The failure creates a puddle of water on the passenger floor and also affects the electrical system, especially the window motors.

Accessories are also plagued by problems, with defective radios, power antennas, door locks, cruise control, and alarm systems leading the pack. Premature automatic transmission failures and excessive noise when shifting have been endemic. Engine intake manifold gaskets have a high failure rate and are covered by a 7-year/ 120,000 km out-of-court settlement in Canada (see *gmcanadianclassaction.ca*).

GM front-drives

The rear-drive versions of these cars have been off the market for over a decade (but if you can get your hands on an early "classic" one, they're highly recommended (1984–87)). The rear-drives were competent and comfortable cars, but they definitely came from a time when handling wasn't a priority and fuel economy was unimportant. Front-drive technology is not GM's proudest achievement, so it's not surprising to see the company embrace rear-drives in its post-2004 models.

Its front-drives, phased into the lineup in the '80s, are a different breed of car: less reliable and more expensive to repair than rear-drives, with a considerable number of mechanical (e.g., brake, steering, and suspension components) deficiencies directly related to their front-drive configuration. Nevertheless, acceleration is adequate, fuel economy is good, and handling is better than with their rear-drive cousins—except in emergencies, when their brakes frequently lock up or fail, not-withstanding ABS technology. The Detroit automakers' front-drive designs and manufacturing weaknesses make for unimpressive high-speed performance, a poor reliability record, and expensive maintenance costs. That's why most fleets and police agencies use rear-drives when they can get them. They've seen the rear-drives' safety and operating cost advantages.

GM's medium-sized front-drives aren't particularly driver-friendly. Many models have a dash that's replete with confusing push buttons and gauges that are washed out in sunlight or reflect annoyingly upon the windshield. At other times, there are retro touches, like the Intrigue's dash-mounted ignition, that simply seem out of place. The keyless entry system often fails, the radio's memory is frequently forgetful, and the fuel light comes on when the tank is just below the one-half fuel-level mark. The electronic climate control frequently malfunctions, and owners report that warm air doesn't reach the driver-side heating vents. Servicing, especially for the electronic engine controls, is complicated and expensive, forcing many owners to drive around with their Service Engine, Airbag, and ABS warning lights constantly lit.

Other major problem areas include automatic transmission failures and clunking; leaking and malfunctioning AC systems (due mainly to defective AC modules); faulty electronic modules; rack-and-pinion steering failures; weak shocks; excessive front brake pad wear; warping rotors; seizure of the rear brake calipers; rear brake/wheel lock-ups; myriad electrical failures, requiring replacement of the computer module; leaking oil pans; and early replacement of the suspension struts.

The high-performance 3.4L V6, available since 1991, gives out plenty of power, but only at high engine speeds. Overall, the 3.8L V6 is a more suitable compromise. One major powertrain problem found in 1995–2004 models carrying 3.1L, 3.4L, and 3.8L V6 engines is head gasket leaks and plastic intake manifold cracking. These engine defects affect almost all GM and Saturn models.

Other deficiencies: Lots of road and wind noise comes through the side windows, thanks to the inadequately soundproofed chassis. Seating isn't very comfortable because of the lack of support caused by low-density foam and knees-in-your-face low seats combined with the ramrod-straight rear backrest. The ride is acceptable with a light load, but when fully loaded, the car's back end sags and the ride deteriorates.

On one hand, 2002–05 models do have a nice array of standard features, a good choice of powertrains that includes a supercharged 3.8L engine, a comfortable ride, and an easily accessed, roomy interior. On the other hand, they continue to have noisy engines at high speeds, rear seating that's uncomfortable for three, bland styling, and obstructed rear visibility because of a high-tail rear end.

Except for the automatic transmission upgrade, owners report that newer versions still have many of the same shortcomings seen on earlier front-drive models. Body construction is still below par, with loose door panel mouldings, poorly fitted door fabric, misaligned panels, and water accumulation in the backup lights. Other common problems are fuel-pump whistling, frequent stalling, vague steering, premature paint peeling on the hood and trunk, heavy accumulation of hard-to-remove brake dust inside the honeycomb-design wheels, scraped fenders from contact with the front tires when the wheel is turned, and hard starts due to delayed cranking.

The 3.1L engine is still problematic. Engine controls, faulty intake manifold gaskets (a chronic problem affecting the entire model lineup; see "Secret Warranties/Internal Bulletins/Service Tips"), and electronic fuel-injection systems have created many problems for GM owners. The 4-speed automatic transmission shifts erratically and sometimes slams into gear. The front brakes wear quickly, as do the MacPherson struts, shock absorbers, and tie-rod ends. Steering assemblies tend to fail prematurely. The electrical system is temperamental. The sunroof motor is failure-prone. Owners report water leaks from the front windshield. Front-end squeaks may require the replacement of the exhaust manifold pipe springs with dampers.

VEHICLE HISTORY: *Bonneville:* **2000**—Restyled similarly to the Buick LeSabre, with a larger wheelbase and longer platform but less headroom. Also new this year: standard front seat side-impact airbags, four-wheel disc ABS brakes, a tire-inflation monitor, and an anti-skid system (SSEi). **2001**—SLE is given standard traction control. **2004**—A 275 hp V8 arrives; the 240 hp V6 is dropped. *Lumina:* **2000**—Lumina's standard 3.1L engine gets a bit more torque and a small horsepower boost, in addition to the model getting more standard equipment. This is the Lumina's last year before the Impala replaces it. Monte Carlo carries on; it's reworked and brought out on the Impala platform for 2000. *Malibu:* **2000**—A restyled front end, and no more 4-cylinder engine. **2004**—Completely redesigned.

The sedan uses Saab's 9-3 platform and a base 145 hp 4-cylinder engine (a 200 hp V6 comes with the LS and LT) hooked to a 4-speed automatic transmission. A Maxx hatchback uses the same powertrain but adds a sliding rear seat with a reclining seatback, a cargo cover that transforms into a tailgate table, a glass skylight, four-wheel disc brakes, and head-protecting side curtain airbags. *Impala:* **2004**—An SS model equipped with a 240 hp supercharged V6. **2007**—A 3.9L V6 with GM's Active Fuel Management, which deactivated some cylinders to save fuel; a tire-pressure monitor becomes a standard feature. *Monte Carlo:* **2001**— Standard driver-side airbag, traction control, OnStar, and emergency inside trunk release. **2004**—A supercharged 3.8L SS. *Impala, Monte Carlo:* **2006**—Chevrolet updates its largest sedan and Monte Carlo coupe with new engines, upgraded suspensions, and revised exterior styling. The 3.5 models come with a 211 hp 3.5L V6 (an increase of 30 hp); LTZ sedans carry a 242 hp 3.9L V6; and Chevrolet SS models are equipped with a potent 303 hp V8 with Displacement on Demand, which cuts off four cylinders under light throttle conditions to save fuel. Supercharged models are dropped. All come with a 4-speed automatic transmission. Except for the SS, all models use bench seats for six-passenger capacity. The SS comes with front bucket seats only. Head-protecting side curtain airbags are standard in Impalas but unavailable in the Monte Carlo.

1995–2005 Impala, Lumina, and Monte Carlo

These models are popular two- and four-door versions of Chevy's "large" mid-sized cars, featuring standard dual airbags, ABS, and 160 hp V6 power. The Monte Carlo was formerly sold as the Lumina Z34. Powertrain enhancements have increased horsepower and fuel efficiency. Each car has been given a slightly different appearance and a distinct personality. A 3.1L V6 is the base engine, a standard 3.4L 210 hp V6 powers the coupe and is optional with the LS Lumina, and a 3.8L V6 equips the more upscale versions. The 2004 SS comes with a supercharged 3.8L engine.

1997–2004 Cutlass and Malibu

These two front-drive medium-sized sedans are slotted in between the Cavalier and Lumina in both size and price. They are boringly styled cars that use a rigid body structure to cut down on noise and improve handling. Standard mechanicals include a 2.4L twin-cam 4-cylinder engine or an optional 3.1L V6. These cars offer plenty of passenger and luggage space. Although headroom is tight, the Malibu can carry three rear passengers and gives much more legroom than either the Cavalier or Lumina. The 1998 model year was Cutlass' last, while its Malibu twin continued on.

Here are other points to consider: The base 4-cylinder is loud, handling isn't on par with the Japanese competition, there's lots of body lean in turns, outside mirrors are too small, there's no traction control, and the ignition switch is mounted on the dash (a throwback to your dad's Oldsmobile).

1998–2002 Intrigue

Strikingly similar to the Alero, the Oldsmobile Intrigue was GM's replacement for the Cutlass Supreme and represents the most refined iteration of the front-drive platform shared by the Century, Grand Prix, Lumina, and Regal. It's more luxurious than the Lumina and performs as well as the Accord, Camry, or Maxima. Its rigid chassis has fewer shakes and rattles than are found on GM's other models, and its 3.8L engine provides lots of low-end grunt but lacks the top-end power that makes the Japanese competition so much fun to toss around. The '99 versions got a torquier 3.5L V6 coupled with standard traction control. This engine's a bit more refined, but it's still not smooth, and the automatic transmission still struggles to get past its first two gears. Year 2001 models dropped standard traction control and added automatic headlights.

2004–07 Impala and Malibu

In the 2004 model year, there were two vehicles sold as Malibus: the "old" Malibu (N-body) that was renamed the Classic, and the redesigned (Z-body) Malibu. The latter Malibu's engine feels underpowered for highway cruising, with constant shifting with the 4-cylinder hooked to the 4-speed automatic transmission (which is the only set-up available). It handles well, but the ride is a bit firm and the original-equipment tires don't inspire confidence. Interior seating is okay up front but knees-to-chin in the rear. The Maxx version excels at providing rear-seat comfort.

In addition to the generic front-drive problems listed previously, owners also report the following: early failures of the exhaust and intake manifold gaskets; fuel-injector deposits that cause chronic stalling, poor idling, or hard starts; excessive vibration at any speed; failure-prone transmissions; unpredictable steering; sensors failing throughout the vehicle; premature suspension strut failures (vehicle bottoms out with four or more passengers aboard); annoyingly loud brake squeal; early wearout of the brakes, steering assembly alternator, and tire-pressure sensor; poor headlight illumination; and an intermittently failing high beam light switch.

 ## Safety Summary

All models/years: Airbag fails to deploy. • Sudden engine failure or overheating (faulty intake manifold). • Vehicle suddenly accelerates or stalls in traffic. • Frequent loss of braking, and premature rotor warpage and pad wearout. • Vehicle rolls downhill when parked on an incline. • Many incidents of total loss of steering or power steering. • Dash reflection in the windshield obstructs view. • Automatic trunk lid flies up and falls down on one's head. • Improper headlight illumination. • Horn is difficult to activate because of the hand pressure required. *Bonneville:* **2000–01**—Battery located in the back of the rear seat goes bad, causing sulfuric acid fumes to escape into the passenger compartment, making passengers ill. **2003**—Defogger was activated, and fire ignited. • Fire erupted in the rear deck speaker. • Shifter can be moved without key in the ignition or brakes applied. *Impala:* **2003**—Frequent complaints of dash area and engine compartment fires. •

Front harness wires overheat; excessive current load from fuel pump may burn the ignition block wire terminal; inhalation injuries caused by the melting of the wiring harness plastic. • Electrically heated seat burns the driver's back. • The connection that goes to the brake pedal piston collapses, causing total brake failure. • Chronic stalling; engine sputters, hesitates; Service Engine and battery lights come on (dealer unable to correct problem). • When traction control is activated, wheel slip computer is also activated, and security system kills the engine and prevents it from being restarted. • Driver-side wheel falls off. • Left and right control arm, lower control arm, ball joint, and steering failures. • AC refrigerant leaks into car interior. • Driver-seat adjuster failed, and seat suddenly moved backward, causing loss of vehicle control. • The rubber seal on the windows, which sometimes acts as a squeegee when lowering and raising the window, has been replaced with a new design that allows road salt to enter and short-circuit the window mechanism. • Front driver-side windshield wiper doesn't clean the windshield completely; poor design allows dirty windshield washer fluid to be deflected off the windshield and cuts the view from the side windows. **2004**—Crankshaft position sensor failures cause vehicle to stall and not restart. • Vehicle can be shifted out of Park without applying the brakes. • Vehicle hydroplanes easily, wanders all over the road, and jerks to one side when braking. • Steering wheel suddenly jerks to one side and resists driver's pull in the other direction. • Unreliable steering assembly. • Lights dim when power windows are raised or lowered. • Poorly designed daytime running lights blind oncoming drivers. • Fuel-tank failures. **2005**—Inadvertent airbag deployment:

> A 2005 Chevy Impala police car was traveling on a gravel road in rural Ogle County, Illinois when both front air bags deployed, the car never made contact with anything, there are at least 30 pictures of the car and the roadway. Since the 30th I personally have called General Motors about my concerns involving the rest of my 2005 squad cars, I've called every day since the 30th, with no response.

• Fuel-pressure regulator may leak fuel. • Intermediate steering shaft is a sealed unit, yet requires frequent lubrication. • Steering-pump failure. • Parking brakes won't hold on an incline, and the transmission fails to hold the vehicle in Park or in Reverse. • Car can be shifted into any gear without depressing the brake pedal. • ABS failure. • Frequent traction-control system failures. • Automatic window could easily kill a child:

> The way that the window switch is designed it can easily shut on a child's body or body part. There was something about this six months ago on TV. This was a rental vehicle for a trip for vacation.... When the consumer's son leaned his head out the window, his elbow hit the switch, and the window began to go up. The consumer suggested that a different type of switch be installed, the type that one would have to pull in order to close the window.

• Inadequate headlight illumination. • AC blower seizes, causing an electrical fire. *Impala, Malibu:* **2006**—Seat belts fray and tear under normal use. • Frequent water-pump and power-steering-hose failures. • Steering froze while cruising:

The power steering mechanism was replaced with a newly designed system. The mechanic informed me that this was the 6th replacement of such a device for the Impala.

• Early tie-rod replacements. • Doors unlock, or lock on their own. • Car cannot be shut off. • Melted wiring harness. • Tire side walls blow out. **2007**—Driver's seatback collapsed twice. • Brake rotors and pads wear out prematurely, and vehicle shakes excessively when braking. • Broken exterior door handle. • Faulty tire-pressure sensors ($600). • Original-equipment tire failures, and early wear on the inner sides of the rear tires (covered by a secret warranty). *LeSabre:* **2000– 01**—Under-hood fire ignited as driver was parking car. • When the fuel tank is full, fuel leaks from the top. • Cruise-control cable disconnects from cruise-control module, jamming the accelerator cable to full throttle. • Accelerator cable pops out of its bracket, causing vehicle to go to full throttle. • When applying brakes, pedal becomes very hard, resulting in extended stopping distances. • Sudden steering loss. • Shoulder belt crosses at driver's neck. • Difficulty seeing dashboard controls because of dash-top design. **2003**—Brake pedal goes almost to the floor without stopping the vehicle. **2004**—Dash panel lights dim constantly. *Monte Carlo:* **1995–2001**—Under-hood fires. • Airbag deployment caused driver's shirt to catch on fire. • Side airbag falls out of its mounting. • Dash gauges go haywire from chronic electrical shorts. • Shoulder belt crosses at neck, and seat belts don't retract properly. **2002**—Fire ignites from overheated seat heater. • Sudden steering loss; excessive steering effort required. • Vehicle rolls back on an incline. **2003**—Fire ignited in the trunk area. • Engine cradle mounting welds come apart from the steering gear. • Automatic transmission slips in First gear because of faulty pressure valve. • Sudden loss of braking. • Because brake pedal sits a bit higher than it would on other makes, foot can easily slip under the pedal. • Bent stabilizer bar. • Driver and passenger seat belts tighten up progressively to the point where they are extremely uncomfortable. • Tail light failures. **2004**—Mushy brakes; pedal goes to the floor when brakes are applied. **2005**—Crack in the right rear hub assembly caused the Traction Control light to come on. • Vehicle shut down while cruising, lost all electrics, and would not restart. • Entire instrument panel shuts off and headlights go out. • Previously noted electrical malfunctions are likely caused by a defective multifunction switch ($550). • Water accumulates in the tail lights, causing them to fail. • Speedometer failures.

Secret Warranties/Internal Bulletins/Service Tips

All models/years: Keep in mind that some of the following service bulletins may apply to subsequent model years. • Reverse servo cover seal leak (transmission). **All models: 1993–2004**—TSB #01-08-42-001A covers the causes and remedies for moisture in the headlights. **1995–2001**—Troubleshooting engine oil pan leaks. **1995–2004**—Five GM service bulletins confirm a pattern of engine intake manifold gasket defects, which are covered by a 7-year/120,000 km out-of-court settlement (see *gmcanadianclassaction.ca*) **2001–02**—Poor engine performance and erratic shifting. • Intermittent no-starts. **2001–04**—Erratic shifting, slipping transmission. • Troubleshooting a noisy blower motor. **2001–05**—Harsh 1–2 upshifts. **2001–07**—Correcting a shift shudder during light acceleration. **2003–05**—Remedy for side window binding. **2004–05**—Troubleshooting an inoperative horn. **2004–06**—Assorted steering noises. **2005**—AC compressor noise. **2005–06**—Engine knocking, ticking requires the replacement of the flexplate and torque converter. **2006–07**—Troubleshooting tips to stop coolant loss and leaks from the 3.5L engine. **2006–08**—Correcting engine coolant loss and leaks, and a rear brake rattle. *Cutlass, Malibu:* **1997–2003**—Inoperative tail lights due to water intrusion. • Automatic transmission flaring. *Malibu:* **1999–2002**—Troubleshooting tips for plugging water leaks into the trunk and interior. **2003**—Firm shifts, no downshifts, or shudder. **2004**—Noisy steering column, and lack of steering assist. • Ignition key hard to remove in cold weather. • Instrument panel rattle or buzz. **2004–05**—Correcting increased steering effort on start-up. • Steering pop or snap noise when turning. • Hood won't latch in the primary position. • A special lube must be applied to prevent door latches from freezing. **2004–06**—Poor instrument panel backlighting. • Inoperative tail/turn lights. **2004–08**—Front-end clunk or rattle when passing over small bumps at low speeds. **2005–07**—Rear brake creak or squeak. *Grand Prix:* **2004–06**—Correcting AC compressor growl/whine. **2006–07**—Correcting a shift shudder during light acceleration. *Impala:* **2007**—Troubleshooting wind/road noise.

BONNEVILLE, DELTA 88, GRAND PRIX, IMPALA, INTRIGUE, LESABRE, LUMINA, MALIBU, MONTE CARLO, REGAL PROFILE

	1999	2000	2001	2002	2003	2004	2005	2006	2007
Cost Price ($)									
Bonneville	29,000	30,740	32,065	32,365	33,430	34,345	35,310	—	—
Delta 88 LSS	32,515	—	—	—	—	—	—	—	—
Grand Prix	27,489	28,050	28,110	28,050	28,277	28,125	27,865	25,885	25,595
Impala	—	24,595	24,490	24,875	26,020	26,810	26,405	24,685	25,230
Intrigue	27,994	28,365	28,450	28,365	—	—	—	—	—
LeSabre	28,845	30,465	32,120	32,960	33,720	33,935	34,550	—	—
Lumina	23,074	—	—	—	—	—	—	—	—
Malibu	20,895	22,050	22,495	22,760	22,980	22,370	22,375	21,995	20,230
Malibu Maxx	—	—	—	—	—	26,320	26,495	25,595	25,930
Monte Carlo	24,715	26,090	26,165	26,525	27,620	28,200	27,840	24,685	25,231
Regal	27,695	29,120	28,895	29,080	29,980	29,975	—	—	—
Used Values ($)									
Bonneville ▲	3,500	4,000	4,500	5,000	6,000	8,000	9,000	—	—
Bonneville ▼	3,000	3,500	4,000	4,500	5,500	7,000	8,000	—	—
Delta 88 LSS ▲	3,000	—	—	—	—	—	—	—	—
Delta 88 LSS ▼	2,500	—	—	—	—	—	—	—	—
Grand Prix ▲	3,500	4,500	5,500	6,000	7,500	9,000	10,500	12,000	13,500
Grand Prix ▼	3,000	4,000	5,000	5,500	6,500	8,000	9,000	11,000	12,000
Impala ▲	—	3,500	4,500	5,500	6,500	7,500	9,500	12,000	14,000
Impala ▼	—	3,500	4,000	5,000	5,500	6,500	8,500	11,000	13,000
Intrigue ▲	2,500	3,000	3,500	4,500	—	—	—	—	—
Intrigue ▼	2,500	2,500	3,000	3,500	—	—	—	—	—

LeSabre ▲	4,500	6,000	8,000	11,000	14,000	17,000	20,000	—	—
LeSabre ▼	4,000	5,000	6,000	8,500	11,500	15,000	18,000	—	—
Lumina ▲	3,500	—	—	—	—	—	—	—	—
Lumina ▼	3,000	—	—	—	—	—	—	—	—
Malibu ▲	2,500	3,000	3,500	4,500	5,000	6,000	8,000	9,500	11,000
Malibu ▼	2,500	2,500	3,000	4,000	4,500	5,000	7,000	9,000	9,500
Malibu Maxx ▲	—	—	—	—	—	7,500	10,000	11,500	13,500
Malibu Maxx ▼	—	—	—	—	—	6,000	8,500	10,500	12,000
Monte Carlo ▲	3,000	3,500	4,500	5,000	6,500	7,500	9,000	10,000	11,500
Monte Carlo ▼	3,000	3,500	4,000	4,500	5,500	6,500	8,000	9,000	10,000
Regal ▲	4,000	5,000	5,500	5,500	6,000	7,500	—	—	—
Regal ▼	3,500	4,500	5,000	5,500	5,500	6,000	—	—	—
Reliability	3	3	3	3	3	3	3	3	3
Crash Safety (F)									
Bonneville 4d	—	—	4	4	4	4	4	—	—
Grand Prix 4d	—	—	4	4	4	3	3	5	4
Impala	—	5	5	5	5	5	5	5	5
Intrigue	4	4	—	—	—	—	—	—	—
LeSabre 4d	4	—	—	4	4	4	4	—	—
Lumina 4d	4	4	4	—	—	—	—	—	—
Malibu	4	4	4	4	4	4	5	5	5
Monte Carlo	—	—	5	5	—	5	5	5	5
Regal 4d	4	4	4	4	4	4	—	—	—
Side									
Bonneville 4d	—	—	4	4	4	4	4	—	—
Grand Prix	—	—	—	2	2	3	3	3	3
Impala	—	4	4	4	4	4	4	5	5
Intrigue	—	—	3	3	—	—	—	—	—
LeSabre 4d	3	4	4	4	4	5	4	—	—
Lumina	4	4	4	—	—	—	—	—	—
Malibu	1	2	2	3	3	4	4	5	5
Monte Carlo	—	—	3	3	—	3	3	3	3
Regal 4d	3	3	3	3	3	3	—	—	—
IIHS Side									
Grand Prix	—	—	—	—	—	2	2	2	2
Impala	—	—	—	—	—	—	—	5	5
Malibu 4d	—	—	—	—	—	5	5	5	5
Offset									
Bonneville 4d	—	5	5	5	5	5	5	—	—
Grand Prix 4d	3	3	3	3	3	5	5	5	5
Impala	—	5	5	5	5	5	5	3	3
Intrigue	3	3	3	3	—	—	—	—	—
LeSabre	3	5	5	5	5	5	5	—	—
Malibu	—	—	—	—	—	5	5	5	5
Regal	3	3	3	3	3	3	—	—	—

All ratings on a numbered scale where 5 is good and 1 is bad. See pages 108–109 for a more detailed description.

Head Restraints									
Bonneville	1	—	—	—	1	1	1	—	—
Grand Prix	3	—	2	2	2	1	1	—	—
Intrigue	1	—	1	1	—	—	—	—	—
Impala	—	—	1	1	1	1	1	2	2
LeSabre 4d	1	—	—	—	1	1	1	—	—
Lumina	1	—	—	—	—	—	—	—	—
Malibu	2	—	2	2	1	3	3	3	3
Malibu Classic	—	—	—	—	1	1	1	—	—
Monte Carlo	1	—	2	2	2	2	—	—	—
Regal 4d	1	—	1	1	1	1	—	—	—
Rollover Resistance									
Bonneville	—	—	—	—	5	5	5	—	—
Grand Prix	—	—	—	—	4	4	4	4	4
Impala	—	—	4	4	4	4	4	4	4
LeSabre	—	—	—	—	—	—	5	—	—
Malibu	—	—	—	4	4	4	4	4	4
Monte Carlo	—	—	—	—	—	4	4	4	4

Note: 2004–06 Malibus without side airbags received a Poor side-impact injury rating.

Honda

ACCORD, ACCORD HYBRID ★★★★ / ★★★

RATING: Above Average (2003–07, 1999); Recommended (2000–02). Most knee-jerk "anything Japanese is good" car guides give the Honda Accord and Toyota Camry equally positive ratings. Not *Lemon-Aid*. For the past decade, Toyota has been asleep at the switch and allowed the Camry's quality to decline. That's why the Accord has higher scores with both the 16-valve 4-cylinder and the V6 engine. In a nutshell, the Accord is one of the most versatile compacts you can find. Think of it as a better-performing Toyota Camry with better-quality components and fewer powertrain defects, especially Toyota's dreaded delay/surge problem acceleration. Nevertheless, the 2003 through 2007 models don't get top scores because of redesign glitches that are still being addressed by Honda. These deficiencies include powertrain defects, sudden acceleration and stalling, brake failures, and airbag malfunctions. *Accord Hybrid:* Average (2005–07). The Hybrid has been off the market for almost two years, which seriously compromises servicing and parts availability. **"Real" city/highway fuel economy:** *2.4L manual:* 9.1/6.4 L/100 km. *2.4L automatic:* 10.0/6.4 L/100 km. *3.0L 6-cylinder manual:* 9.1/6.4 L/100 km. *3.0L 6-speed manual:* 11.5/6.3 L/100 km. *3.0L automatic:* 11.4/7.3 L/100 km. Owners report actual fuel economy doesn't vary much from these estimated figures. **Maintenance/ Repair costs:** Lower than average. Repairs aren't dealer-dependent. Recall repairs may be delayed. **Parts:** Higher-than-average costs, but parts can be easily found for much less from independent suppliers. **Extended warranty:** Not needed. **Best alternatives:** Acura Integra; Hyundai Elantra wagon, Sonata, or Tiburon; Mazda6; and Toyota Camry, 2006 or later.

Strengths and Weaknesses

Fast and nimble even without a V6, this is the mid-sized sedan of choice for drivers who want maximum fuel economy and comfort along with lots of space for grocery hauling and occasional highway cruising. With the optional V6, the Accord is one of the most versatile mid-sized cars you can find. It offers something for everyone, and its top-drawer quality and high resale value mean there's no way you can lose money buying one.

Whether hybrid or gasoline-powered, the Accord doesn't really excel in any particular area; it's just very, very good at everything. It's smooth, quiet, mannerly, and competent, with outstanding fit and finish inside and out. Other strong points are comfort, ergonomics, reliability, driveability, and impressive assembly quality. Unlike Toyota's lineup, there's no acceleration delay and surge. Nevertheless, Accords do have some problems: insufficient torque with the base engine on early models makes for constant highway downshifting; the automatic transmission tends to shift harshly and slowly (covered by a "goodwill" warranty); rear passenger room is tight; and in recent years there have been a number of serious safety-related complaints reported to NHTSA.

Accord Hybrid

After successfully launching its 2003 Civic Hybrid, Honda introduced the 2005 Accord Hybrid. Equipped with a 255 hp V6 engine, the Hybrid is assisted as needed by an electric motor and a 5-speed automatic transmission. An innovative Variable Cylinder Management System automatically deactivates three cylinders when cruising or on deceleration. Like the Civic Hybrid, the Accord Hybrid can't be driven on electricity alone.

The primary complaint of Hybrid owners is that the vehicle gets nowhere near the advertised gas mileage; owners say it's about 30 percent worse than promised. Other Hybrid-specific complaints involve electrical short circuits and premature brake wear. Overall, though, there are proportionately fewer complaints from Accord Hybrid owners than from Toyota Prius owners, and the complaints are less serious in nature. Due to slow Hybrid sales, 2007 was the car's last model year.

VEHICLE HISTORY: 1998—Substantially reworked, with more-powerful engines (150–200 hp), including a new 200 hp 3.0L V6; a more-refined suspension and automatic transaxle; upgraded ABS; additional interior space; and more glass. Wagon version dropped. **1999**—ABS on the LX. **2000**—Side airbags with all V6-equipped models. **2001**—A restyled exterior, dual side airbags, V6 traction control, and improved soundproofing. **2003**—This larger, totally restyled model offers a V6 and 6-speed manual tranny combo, and increased 4-cylinder and V6 horsepower (160 and 240 hp, respectively) and fuel economy. **2004**—V6 models add traction control. Head-protecting side curtain airbags are standard on EX V6 models. **2005**—Introduction of the Hybrid sedan, standard side curtain-type airbags along with front torso airbags, and better interior soundproofing.

Bulletins and owner complaints relating to the reworked 1998–2000 models show a surprisingly large number of factory-related powertrain and body defects, undoubtedly a result of the Accord's redesign. Some of those deficiencies, which affect both safety and performance, are chronic lurching, hesitation, and stalling while on the highway, accompanied by the Check Engine light coming on; hard starting; frequent transmission failures; poor tracking that allows the vehicle to wander; defective rear computerized motor mounts; electrical shorts; coolant and brake master cylinder leakage; ABS and AC failures; and poor radio reception.

Body and accessory problems for these same model years include a plethora of squeaks, creaks, groans, and rattles; wind noise; water leaks; fuel gauge defects; paint chipping, bubbling, and peeling on the hood, trunk, and roof (Honda blames it on bird droppings); leaky sunroofs; windshields with vertical lines of distortion; driver-side mirrors that shake excessively; faulty fuel-sending units that make for inaccurate fuel readings (when full, they indicate three-fourths full); and speedometers that are off by 10 percent.

Owners of 2001 and 2002 models report that sudden, unintended acceleration remains a serious problem and can occur at any time, as the owner of this 2001 Accord relates:

> While taking the car through a car wash, vehicle accelerated and ran into two other cars and through a fence.

Other performance-related problems include automatic transmission breakdowns, expensive and frequent servicing of the brake rotors and pads, and electrical glitches.

The 2003 redesign has contributed to a continued decline in quality through the 2007 model year, resulting in the Accord losing its Recommended rating for those model years. Up to 268 safety-related complaints were registered by NHTSA, when merely one-quarter of this number is considered normal. Sadder still, Honda promised us better-performing, more-durable transmissions in its redesigned 2003 models. The company lied, and then later reluctantly extended the warranty up to eight years. Furthermore, some 2003–06 model year Accord owners say their cars have similar problems but haven't been included in the new warranty program; others complain that the corrective repairs haven't fixed the tranny problems and that they were forced to pay a deductible, which should be Honda's responsibility. So far, the 2007 models appear to be much improved, but we'll need more owner feedback before restoring a Recommended rating to earlier Accords.

And here are other problems related to the 2003 model's redesign: coolant in the engine oil pan; frequent hard starts; erratic transmission shifts; engine oil leaks onto the manual transmission clutch, causing shifting slippage (the problem is caused by a low vent valve on the 6-speed tranny); brake shuddering, grinding, and squealing; warped brake rotors; a popping noise heard when accelerating; a steering-column ticking; an AC condenser that's easily punctured by road debris; defective CD changer; stereo speaker hum or popping and frequent speaker blowouts; passenger-side seat heater coming on by itself and overheating; windshield creaks in cold, dry weather; moonroof that doesn't close all the way; non-stop rattles, squeaks, and vibrations in door panels, tops of windows, and rear shelves, and in the B-pillars around the top seat belt anchor; wrinkled, bubbling door window moulding; doors closing on occupants as they leave the vehicle; the rear headliner becoming unglued and sagging, causing water to leak into the cabin and trunk (the carpeting and rear seat are saturated after moderate rainstorms); defective paint; and roof buckling:

> 2005 Honda Accord EXL experienced a buckling roof. The consumer's wife was driving and had run over a pot hole when she heard a loud noise. The consumer found the roof severely buckled. The consumer had taken the vehicle to the dealer when they found other 4 door Honda Accords with the same problem.

The increase in engine, transmission, and brake failures is worrisome. Nevertheless, CAA surveys have shown that customer satisfaction is at an impressive 88 percent, compared to 85 percent for both the Toyota Camry and Mazda 626. Also, to its credit, Honda puts a "goodwill" clause in almost all of its service bulletins, allowing service managers to submit any claim to the company long after the original warranty period has elapsed.

 ## Safety Summary

All models/years: Sudden acceleration, stalling. • Airbags fail to deploy, or deploy for no reason. • Check Engine light is always on. • Excessive windshield glare. • AC failure. • Premature front/rear brake wear. • Gas and brake pedals are too close together and often get pressed at the same time. • Faulty power windows. • Seat belt continually ratchets tighter. **All models: 2001**—Excessive front-end vibration and wandering over the highway. • Automatic transmission leaks and jerks into gear. • Rear stabilizer bar links break. • Vehicle rolls back when stopped on an incline. • Complete brake loss. • Incorrect fuel gauge readings. • The front windshield has a UV-protective coating that gives the windshield a wavy appearance. **2002**—Car suddenly shuts down in traffic because of a defective immobilizer system. • Automatic transmission failures. • Seat belt won't retract, or continually tightens; in one incident, child had to be cut free. • Child safety seat can't be installed because buckle latch is located too far into the seat. • Partial brake failure; brakes fail to catch at first, then suddenly grab. • Vehicle pulls sharply when braking. • Trunk lid may suddenly fall. **2003**—Sudden, unintended acceleration while car is in motion or when put into Reverse. • Axle suddenly snaps. • Severe pulling to the right. • Power-steering groan believed to be caused by the steering pump. • Console overheats and smells burnt. • Keys overheat in the ignition. • Complete brake failure. • ABS and Traction-Control lights stay lit, and corrective parts aren't easily found. • Rear vision is obstructed by head restraints, high rear deck, and roof pillar. **2004**—Several reports of fires igniting in the insulation material:

> While driving vehicle caught fire. Dealership found that the sound deadening material came too close to the heat of the engine.

Also, one report of fire igniting behind the right front tire while vehicle was underway. • Brake light bulb drops down into the trunk area and burns through luggage. • Axle collapses while vehicle is underway. • Vehicle accelerates when brakes are applied. • Engine surges when shifting gears. • Complete brake failure; Brake Alert is constantly lit. • In one incident, brakes applied, car jerked to the side, total loss of braking (other complainants say the brakes lock up), and Accord hit guardrail. • Steering suddenly locks up. • Seat belt failed to retract in a rear-end collision; several complaints allege the front seat belts failed to restrain occupants in frontal collisions. • Passenger-side mirror slipped off; another one "exploded." • Steering pulls to one side while driving. • Side window shatters after morning moisture is wiped off. • Side-airbag sensor won't warn you if passengers are improperly seated. • If you put your purse on the front passenger-side seat, the airbag is disabled. The same thing occurred when a driver's 90-pound daughter sat in the same seat. • Driver's seat moves forward on its own. • Carbon monoxide fumes invade the passenger compartment. • Defogger causes condensation on inside windshield, which then freezes. **2004–05**—Key sticks in the ignition. • Distorted windshields. **2005**—Sudden acceleration after a cold start. • Intermittent stalling. • Cell phone interference can affect airbag sensors. • Right front wheel comes apart. • Cracks in the steering wheel just above the airbag. • Intermittent power-steering failure. • Honda's jack is a knuckle-buster that won't hold the car. • Shifter slips by Drive mode into D3, or sticks in Second gear. • Michelin MXV4 tire side wall blowout. • Poorly lit heating and cooling control panels. **2006–07**—Airbags still fail to deploy when needed, or deploy when not needed. **2007**—Driver-side seat caught fire. • When accelerating, engine hesitates and then surges. • Manual transmission pops out of Third gear, or grinds when going into Third gear. • Vehicle vibrates so badly that hands on the steering wheel go numb. • The dash lights are illuminated and the daytime running lights are lit, but the headlights aren't automatically activated, as with most cars. • Dash lights and headlights flicker when the AC compressor cycles; compressor is also easily damaged by pebbles on the highway, due to Honda's poor design. Honda says it's an insurance issue, but no, it's Honda's responsibility. • Intermittent failure of the power door locks, especially when it rains. • Serious blind spots due to the design of the front windshield pillars. • Horn may not sound in cold weather. • Michelin tires bubble on the side wall (a frequent complaint over many model years). • Check Gas Cap warning will light if cap isn't tightened with three clicks. • LED tail lights are nausea-inducing. *Hybrid:* **2005**—Instead of a spare tire, owners are given a can of sealant that won't work if the puncture is located outside the tread. **2006–07**—Long hesitation when accelerating invites a rear-end accident.

⌕ Secret Warranties/Internal Bulletins/Service Tips

All models/years: Troubleshooting tips for vehicles that pull sharply to one side. Accord service bulletins may also apply to the Hybrid. **All models: 1998–2004**—V6 engine oil leaks (an extension of a problem first noticed on 1994–97 models). **1998–2006**—Vehicles with broken rear stabilizer links are eligible for a free replacement under a Honda "goodwill" program. **1999–2000**—Coolant leaks from the water passage near the EGR valve. **1999–2003**—Automatic transmission malfunctions and failures will be fixed or replaced under a more recent and comprehensive "goodwill" extended warranty program (see Part Two, "Psst... 'Secret' Warranties Are Everywhere"). **1999–2006**—Repair tips applicable to vehicles that pull/drift to one side. **2001**—Windshield hum or whine. • Cracked, damaged foglight lens. **2002–06**—Honda has offered American owners a warranty extension of 5 percent off the indicated mileage because its vehicles' odometers were found to over-register mileage. **2003**—"Goodwill" campaigns to replace automatic transmissions and multiplex integrated control units (MICUs) that regulate door locks, trunk alarm, etc. • Corrective action for coolant leakage into the engine oil pan; oil leaks at the cylinder head cover. • A faulty air-intake air-breather pipe hose may cause the Engine warning light to remain lit. Its replacement is covered by a special Honda Product Update Campaign. • An automatic transmission that won't go into Reverse is eligible for a free correction under another Honda "goodwill" campaign (TSB #03-042). • Automatic transmission leaks on the cooler lines. • Hard starts. • Troubleshooting calipers, rotors, and pads, following complaints of excessive brake vibration (wait a minute, weren't these the same chronic problems present before Honda's much-vaunted 2003 brake upgrade?). • Troubleshooting ABS brake light illumination. • Inaccurate gauges and odometer. • Vehicle pulls to the right. • Excessive steering vibration. • Noisy power steering countermeasures. • Investigating owner reports of cracked windshields. • Doors don't unlock in cold weather. • Poor AC cooling. • Rear shelf rattling. • Dash or pillar creaking or clicking. • Roof moulding channel leaks water; roof water leak fix. • Wrinkled door window moulding. • Remedies for front brake noise or judder when braking. **2003–04**—If the brake pedal is stiff, a new booster vacuum hose may be required. • Loose steering or clunky steering response:

LOOSENESS FELT/CLUNKING NOISE WHEN TURNING

BULLETIN NO.: 05-013　　　　　　　　　　　　　　　　**DATE: MARCH 25, 2005**

2003–04 ACCORD V6—CLUNKING OR LOOSENESS IN THE TIE ROD INNER JOINT

While turning, clunking is heard from the steering or looseness is felt in the steering wheel.

PROBABLE CAUSE: Water entered the tie-rod inner ball joint, causing rust that wore the plastic liner inside of the socket.

CORRECTIVE ACTION: Inspect the tie-rod ball joints, and replace the boots and tie-rod ball joints as required.

• Troubleshooting dim headlights. **2003–05**—Low Fuel warning is activated even though fuel tank is a quarter full. **2003–06**—Guidelines for fixing dashboard/A-pillar creaks and clicks. **2003–07**—Drivetrain ping, rattle, squeal when accelerating. • Brake pedal feels low and soft. • Power-steering moan/whine. • Headlights give inadequate low-beam illumination (faulty Sylvania bulb). **2004**—Excessive engine vibration in idle. • Noisy steering. • No-starts and faulty power windows. • Door rattles. • Wheel bearing humming or growling. • Heater blower overheats or blows a fuse. **2007**—A fix for the manual transmission grinding or popping out of Third gear (TSB #08-020, dated 07/18/08). • Inadequate AC cooling. • Noisy rear window regulator.

ACCORD, ACCORD HYBRID PROFILE

	1999	2000	2001	2002	2003	2004	2005	2006	2007
Cost Price ($)									
LX/SE sedan	23,800	23,000	22,800	23,000	25,000	25,100	25,500	26,301	26,501
EXi/EX V6	26,801	31,300	30,800	31,100	32,500	32,900	33,600	34,100	34,900
Hybrid	—	—	—	—	—	—	36,990	38,900	38,100
Used Values ($)									
LX/SE sedan ▲	5,000	6,000	7,000	8,000	10,500	11,500	14,000	16,000	17,500
LX/SE sedan ▼	4,000	5,000	6,000	7,000	9,000	10,000	12,500	14,500	16,000
EXi/EX V6 ▲	6,000	7,000	8,000	9,500	11,000	13,500	17,000	20,000	23,500
EXi/EX V6 ▼	5,000	6,000	7,000	8,000	9,500	12,000	16,000	18,500	22,000
Hybrid ▲	—	—	—	—	—	—	17,500	21,000	24,500
Hybrid ▼	—	—	—	—	—	—	16,000	19,500	23,000
Reliability	4	5	5	5	4	4	4	4	4
Crash Safety (F)	4	—	5	5	5	5	5	5	5
4d	4	4	5	5	5	5	5	5	4
Side (2d)	3	3	4	4	5	4	4	4	4
4d	4	4	4	4	5	5	4	4	4
IIHS Side	—	—	—	—	1	1	5	5	5
Offset	3	3	3	3	5	5	5	5	5
Head Restraints (2d)	3	—	—	—	3	3	1	—	—
4d	2	—	3	3	1	1	1	1	1
Rear	—	2	2	2	1	1	1	1	1
Rollover Resistance	—	5	5	5	4	4	4	4	4

Note: The Accord Hybrid's rate of depreciation is similar to that of the Civic Hybrid and Toyota Prius: not impressive.

Hyundai

SONATA ★★★★

RATING: Above Average (2006–07); Average (2004–05); Below Average (1999–2003). Recent iterations of the Sonata haven't registered one-tenth the number of safety complaints of the highly rated Honda Accord or Toyota Camry. On the other hand, Sonata's crashworthiness ratings aren't impressive. For maximum savings, I suggest you buy a 1999–2004 version, keep it at least five years to amortize the depreciation, and put some of the savings on the purchase price into a comprehensive supplementary warranty to protect yourself when the warranty ends. **"Real" city/highway fuel economy:** *2.4L automatic: 10.9/7.2 L/100 km. 2.7L 6-cylinder automatic: 12.3/7.9 L/100 km. 3.5L 6-cylinder automatic: 13.9/8.4 L/100 km.* Owners report fuel savings may undershoot these estimates by at least 10 percent, or up to 20 percent with the 3.5L engine. **Maintenance/Repair costs:** Higher than average. Repairs aren't dealer-dependent. **Parts:** Higher-than-average costs, and parts are often back ordered. **Extended warranty:** An extended powertrain warranty is a smart buy. **Best alternatives:** Acura Integra, GM Cavalier or Sunfire, Honda Accord, Hyundai Elantra wagon or Tiburon, Mazda 626, and Toyota Camry, 2006 or later.

Strengths and Weaknesses

This mid-sized front-drive sedan went from bad to good in an incredibly short period of time. Could it be just a coincidence that major improvements were made several years ago, once Hyundai hired Toyota's top quality-control engineer, who brought with him a bushel basket of internal quality reports? It's a moot question now. The papers were returned to Toyota's lawyers several years ago, following threats of legal action. Hyundai assured Toyota the documents went unread (wink, wink; nudge, nudge).

Corporate intrigue aside, the Sonata is a decent performer in most areas, with some notable exceptions. Acceleration is impressive with the manual gearbox and passable with the automatic. Handling and performance are also fairly good, although emergency handling isn't confidence-inspiring, particularly because of the imprecise steering and excessive lean when cornering. As with other early Hyundai models, the automatic transmission continues to shift erratically up through the 2006 model, and the engine is noisy.

VEHICLE HISTORY: 1999—A redesigned body and suspension, side airbags, two new engines, and a huge price increase that isn't reflected in the vehicle's low resale value. **2000**—Side airbags and larger wheels. **2001**—A new grille and additional standard features of minor importance. **2002**—GL is given four-wheel disc brakes. **2003**—Standard front side airbags. **2006**—A major redesign gives the Sonata new looks, more passenger room (especially rear-seat legroom), additional trunk space, and more power. The new 162 hp 2.4L 4-cylinder adds 24 more horses, while the 235 hp 2.7L V6 puts out 65 more horses. Traction and stability control, anti-lock four-wheel disc brakes, front side airbags, and head-protecting side curtain airbags are standard features. **2007**—GL and LX sedans are dropped.

Throughout the Sonata's history, Hyundai's technical service bulletins have been replete with references to automatic transmissions that exhibit what Hyundai describes as "shift shock" as well as delayed shifting.

2006 and 2007 Sonatas have elicited very few quality-control and safety complaints, and represent the best buys. Nevertheless, automatic transmissions, brakes (rotors and pads), airbags, steering, suspension struts, power door locks, and fuel- and electrical-system components still top the list of parts most vulnerable to premature failure or malfunctioning. Fit and finish continue to be problematic. For example, dashboard cracks near the airbag panel are common.

Safety Summary

All years: Airbags don't deploy when they should, or deploy when they shouldn't. • Frequent automatic transmission failures. **2001**—Hood flies up and shatters windshield. • Engine sleeves can come loose, causing pistons to smash spark plugs. • Engine bucks and hesitates before rpm suddenly increase and car takes off. • Faulty crankshaft position sensor is blamed for the poor engine performance. • Automatic transmission may suddenly shift into Neutral, or the shift lever sometimes pops out of gear. **2002**—Axle (U-bolt) fails while car is underway. • Seat belt latch releases when jostled by passenger's elbow. **2003**—Driver-side seat belt buckle suddenly releases. • Large rear-view mirror obstructs the view. • Tire valve stem failure (cut) on both front tires. **2004**—Gas fumes enter the cabin. • Stalling because of a faulty throttle sensor. • Early clutch failure. • Automatic transmission slippage and seizure. • Complete brake loss. • Rear wheel bearing seizure. • Seat belt came loose during a collision. • Side mirrors are no longer clear. **2004–06**—Sudden, unintended acceleration. **2005**—Failure of the passenger-side front suspension. • No brakes. • Loose front passenger seat. • Vibration caused by loose engine mount bolts. • Excessive heat generated under the driver-side dash. • Windshield is easily scratched. **2006**—Sunroof glass exploded. **2006–07**—After recall repairs, front passenger-side airbag is still disabled even though an adult is seated. • Driver-side sun visor continually drops down. **2007**—Vehicle rolls back on an incline while shifter is in Drive.

Secret Warranties/Internal Bulletins/Service Tips

All years: Troubleshooting tips for delayed engagement of the automatic transmission. • Harsh shifting when coming to a stop or upon initial acceleration is likely caused by an improperly adjusted accelerator pedal switch transmission control unit (TCU). • Troubleshooting hard, delayed shifts. • A faulty air exhaust plug could cause harsh shifting into Second and Fourth gears on vehicles with automatic transmissions. • Brake pedal pulsation can be corrected by installing upgraded front discs and pads. • Troubleshooting tips for reducing brake noise. **1999–2001**—Correcting erratic shifts. • Key sticks in ignition cylinder. • Silencing gear whine. **1999–2002**—Harsh, delayed shifts. **1999–2006**—Troubleshooting tips relative to differential seal oil leaks. **2000–01**—Correcting droning or rumbling brake noise at freeway speeds. **2001–02**—Hyundai will fix a noisy rear suspension by replacing the rear stabilizer bar bushing. **2002**—Troubleshooting poor shifting and torque converter clutch malfunctions. • 2–3 shift flare. • Erratic operation of the automatic climate control. **2003**—Harsh shifts into Drive or Reverse. • Sticks in Second gear. **2003–04**—Low-speed drive-line "bump." **2004**—Engine hesitation requires a reprogrammed PCM. **2005**—Oil leak from the bell housing/torque converter area. **2006**—Front drive axle snapping noise. **2006–07**—Front windshield creak or squeak. **2006–08**—Engine hesitation and misfire repair tips.

SONATA PROFILE

	1999	2000	2001	2002	2003	2004	2005	2006	2007
Cost Price ($)									
Base	19,495	19,995	20,495	21,195	21,595	22,395	22,395	21,900	23,595
Used Values ($)									
Base ▲	2,500	3,500	4,000	4,500	5,000	7,500	9,000	11,500	13,000
Base ▼	2,500	3,000	3,500	4,000	4,500	6,500	8,000	10,000	12,000
Reliability	2	2	2	2	2	3	3	4	4
Crash Safety (F)	—	—	—	4	4	4	4	5	5
Side	—	4	4	4	4	4	4	5	5
IIHS Side	1	1	1	1	1	1	1	3	3
Offset	3	3	3	3	3	3	3	5	5
Head Restraints (F)	3	—	1	1	1	1	1	5	5
Rear	1	—	—	—	—	—	—	—	—
Rollover Resistance	—	—	—	5	5	5	5	4	4

Mazda

MAZDA6, 626 ★★★★

RATING: *Mazda6:* Above Average (2004–07); Average (2003). *626:* Average (1999–2002). Tall drivers should be wary of the low headrests, which can be hazardous in a collision, and short drivers will want to ensure they can see adequately without getting dangerously close to the airbag housing. **"Real" city/highway fuel economy:** *Mazda6 2.3L:* 9.6/6.7 L/100 km with a manual transmission or 10.4/7.5 L/100 km with an automatic. *Mazda6 3.0L:* 12.1/8.1 L/100 km with a manual or 12.3/8.1 L/100 km with an automatic. *Mazda 626 2.0L:* 9.4/6.8 L/100 km with a manual or 11.3/7.9 L/100 km with an automatic. *Mazda 626 2.5L:* The 6-cylinder gets 11.8/8.5 L/100 km with a manual or 12.2/8.5 L/100 km with an automatic. There isn't a lot of difference in fuel consumption rates between these models. Although the newer versions like the Mazda6 are a bit more fuel frugal, their higher price tag means any savings are illusory. Gas mileage may be 15 percent lower than advertised. **Maintenance/Repair costs:** Average. Repairs aren't dealer dependent, however, so save bagfuls of loonies by frequenting independent repair shops. **Parts:** Easily found, but sometimes costly; compare prices with independent suppliers. **Extended warranty:** An extended powertrain warranty is recommended as protection against automatic transmission breakdowns and other factory-related defects. **Best alternatives:** Acura Integra; GM Cavalier or Sunfire; Honda Accord; Hyundai Elantra wagon, Sonata, or Tiburon; and Toyota Camry, 2006 or later.

Strengths and Weaknesses

626

Although far from being high-performance vehicles, these cars ride and handle fairly well and still manage to accommodate four people in comfort. These cars changed little over the years and are still easy-riding, fairly responsive, and not hard on gas. On the downside, the automatic transmission downshifts roughly, the power steering is imprecise, and the car leans a lot in turns. The manual transmission is a better choice because the automatic robs the engine of much-needed horsepower, as is the case with most cars this size.

Owners of 1998–2002 models report malfunctioning automatic transmissions, engine head gasket failures, fuel system glitches that cause sudden acceleration and stalling, faulty airbags, and electrical shorts that result in the Check Engine light staying lit and engine stalling or shutdown.

Other complaints point out that shifting isn't all that smooth, nor is the automatic gearbox very reliable; the car is hard-riding over uneven pavement; there's too much body lean in turns; excessive torque steer (pulling) to the right often occurs when accelerating; road noise intrudes into the cabin; the rear spoiler blocks rear visibility; and the trunk opening isn't conducive to loading large objects. As if that wasn't enough, Mazda has a history of automatic transmission and fit and finish deficiencies and scheduled maintenance overcharges.

Mazda6

The 2003 through 2007 Mazda6 offers one of two powerplants: a 156 hp inline 4-cylinder and a 212 hp V6 that are adequate for most tasks but come up short for fuel economy and power when compared with the 240 horses unleashed by the Accord V6 and the 268 hp Camry V6. Either Mazda engine can be hooked to a 5-speed manual or automatic transmission that also offers a semi-manual "Sport Shift" feature.

Don't get the idea that this is a warmed-over 626. It's set on an entirely new platform and carries safety and convenience features never seen by its predecessor, such as two-stage airbags and a chassis engineered to deflect crash forces away from occupants. The Mazda6's interior allows for a comfortable ride and carries an unusually large trunk.

During its first year on the market, there was a wide range of owner complaints that have become fewer with more-recent models. Owners mention various water leaks, omnipresent interior and exterior clunks (suspension), and a number of driveability concerns that include poor engine and transmission performance (clutch failures, predominantly).

Also, the 5-speed transmission is difficult to shift in its lower gears, hesitates when accelerating or decelerating, and gets stuck in gear. Many owners report chronic stalling and hard starts, defective engine knock sensors, noisy brakes and steering, electrical shorts everywhere, window motor failures, excessive condensation on the inside bottom of the front windshield, paint bubbling, dash rattles, the separation of the radiator's bottom seam, and waits of a month or more for replacement parts.

VEHICLE HISTORY: *626:* **2000**—Restyled and substantially improved with a small horsepower boost (5 hp) and enhanced handling, steering, and interior appointments. **2001**—Improved sound system, an emergency trunk release, and user-friendly child safety seat anchors. *Mazda6:* **2003**—Mazda6 arrives. **2004**—A four-door hatchback and wagon are added, along with passenger-side airbags. **2005**—Standard anti-lock braking and traction control; a 6-speed automatic transmission replaces the 5-speed unit for S models. **2007**—Side curtain airbags.

 ## Safety Summary

All models/years: The 626's different iterations have registered far fewer complaints than their Asian, European, or American counterparts. • Inadvertent airbag deployments, or airbags that fail to deploy in a collision. • Sudden, unintended acceleration. • Frequent automatic transmission malfunctions and failures. *626:* **2000**—Cylinder head failures at the #2 cylinder. • 4-cylinder engine stumbles badly in cold weather. • Automatic transmission jerks during 2–1 shifts, lurches into gear because of sudden high revs, and sometimes won't go into gear. • Cracked passenger-side rear axle. **2001**—Automatic transmission jerks into gear. • Seat belts fail to retract. **2002**—Driver-side seat belt unlatched during an accident. • Excessive right-side vibration when vehicle is underway. *Mazda6:* **2003**—Hard starts. • Steering failures. • Centre defroster vent doesn't close completely, allowing condensation to form and impair visibility. • Child injured hand in door handle. **2004**—Injury from airbag:

> Driving in stop and go traffic. Speed of about 15 mph [24 km/h] when a car 3 cars ahead of me quick[ly] stopped. I hit the car in front of me, and both airbags deployed. Fumes and powder or dust of some sort came out of airbag, landed on my hand and gave me a 2nd degree burn.

• Fuel line detached from engine on two occasions:

> I have a 2004 Mazda6 S. I have had two incidents where the fuel line has detached from inside the engine and the car has stalled and gasoline has poured out from underneath the car. The first time, the dealership told me that there was a recall and I should receive [notification] in the mail. I later found out there was no recall. They then fixed the car supposedly, and three months later it happened again.

• Dangerous automatic transmission design cuts engine power when passing another vehicle. • Total brake failure. • Brakes suddenly disengage and then reengage with a severe jolt. • Early severe brake rotor warpage. • Airbag light comes on due to cracked front sensors that short out from water ingress. • Rear windshield shatters because the defroster shorts out. • AC fogs up the windshield. • Passenger-assist handle above the rear seat breaks off. • Electronic door lock often will not allow occupant to open car door from the inside (help!). **2005—** Slow to accelerate from low speeds. • Harsh shifts, automatic transmission slippage, getting stuck in gear (has to be put into manual mode), and dropping into the next lower gear for no reason. • Manual transmission seizure. **2006—** Sudden, unintended acceleration. • Side airbag failed to deploy. • Automatic transmission failure; took a month to be repaired. • Chronic stalling. • Car loses power when accelerating in cold weather (see *forum.mazda6club.com/index.php? showtopic=65171&st=0*). • Frequent replacement of brake pads and rotor. • Low-quality original-equipment battery located where it can spew acid onto critical engine components and corrode wiring. • Vehicle shifts from Sixth gear down to Third gear. **2007—**Hesitation when shifting gears. • Engine rear main seal oil leak; complete transmission failure due to a leaking seal at the torque converter. • Automatic windows will not reverse if they are closing on an object.

Secret Warranties/Internal Bulletins/Service Tips

626: **2002—**Rough idle, hesitation, and stumble. • Grinding, rubbing noise at front of vehicle. • Tips to silence wind noise around doors. *Mazda6:* **2003—**Seat fails to heat. • Doors hard to close in cold weather. • Sticking traction-control system switch. • Trunk lid staining. • Wind noise around doors. **2003–04—** Inoperative turn signals. **2003–05—**Procedures to cure an engine camshaft ticking noise. • 1–2 gear shift shock with automatic transmission. • Engine speed fluctuation when shifting. • Manual transmission clutch noise, vibration upon warm-up. • Front brake squeaks and moans. • Erratic seat heater operation. • Driver-side kick panel falls off. • Lower windshield fogging. **2003–06—**Rough idle and hesitation. • Excessive body vibration. • AC won't go into recirculation mode. **2003–07—**Pull or drift to the side when driving. **2003–08—**3.0L engine ticking. • Headlight lens condensation or water entry. • Steering shaft clunk. **2004—**Engine surging at 80 km/h. • Hesitation or rough idle at high altitudes. • Remedies for brake judder and moan. • Special Service Program #60 to replace the fan control module. • Special Service Program for evaporative emission-system leak monitoring failures. • Special Service Program for O_2 sensor failure. • Front suspension popping, clunking. **2005—**Surging at 60–90 km/h with the 2.3L 4-cylinder engine. **2005–08—**3.0L engine surging. • AC is inoperative when brakes are applied. **2006–07—**Front axle knocking noises in extreme cold. • Low-speed engine stalling.

MAZDA6, 626 PROFILE

	1999	2000	2001	2002	2003	2004	2005	2006	2007
Cost Price ($)									
626	20,140	20,140	23,175	23,470	—	—	—	—	—
Mazda6	—	—	—	—	24,295	24,395	23,795	23,795	24,395

Used Values ($)

626 ▲	3,000	3,500	5,000	6,000	—	—	—	—	—
626 ▼	2,500	3,000	4,000	5,000	—	—	—	—	—
Mazda6 ▲	—	—	—	—	9,000	11,000	13,000	14,500	17,500
Mazda6 ▼	—	—	—	—	7,500	9,500	12,000	13,000	16,000
Reliability	3	3	3	3	3	4	4	4	4
Crash Safety (F)	4	4	4	4	5	5	5	5	5
Side (626 4d)	3	3	3	3	—	—	—	—	—
Mazda6	—	—	—	—	3	3	3	4	4
IIHS Side	—	—	—	—	1	1	1	1	—
Offset	3	5	5	5	5	5	5	5	5
Head Restraints	1	—	1	1	1	1	1	1	—
Rollover Resistance	—	—	—	—	5	5	5	5	5

Note: The 2003–05 Mazda6 earns a higher, Marginal score for head-restraint protection if the vehicle doesn't have optional lumbar adjustment on the seats.

Nissan

ALTIMA ★★

RATING: Below Average (2002–07); Average (1999–2001). Here's the Altima dilemma: Until 2001, these cars were bland-looking but fairly reliable, though so-so, performers. Thereafter, performance was improved incrementally as the list price jumped by thousands of dollars. Safety- and performance-related defects flourished, and word quickly got around that these redesigned models were troublesome, overpriced toys. Resale values nosedived. Although the SE gives the sportiest performance, the less-expensive GXE is the better deal from a price and quality standpoint. **"Real" city/highway fuel economy:** *2.5L manual: 10.3/7.3 L/100 km. 2.5L automatic: 10.3/7.4 L/100 km. 3.5L manual: 11.3/8.3 L/100 km. 3.5L 6-speed manual: 11.5/7.3 L/100 km. 3.5L automatic: 12.3/8.3 L/100 km. 1.8L manual: 8.8/6.2 L/100 km. 1.8L automatic: 9.0/6.5 L/100 km. 2.0L manual: 9.9/7.0 L/100 km. 2.0L automatic: 9.8/7.2 L/100 km. 2.4L automatic: 10.9/7.6 L/100 km.* Although the upgraded 2002–07 versions are peppier, owners say fuel savings are much less than estimates show—sometimes they are off by as much as 20 percent. **Maintenance/Repair costs:** Higher than average. Repairs are dealer-dependent. **Parts:** Owners complain of frequent parts shortages. Parts on earlier models are relatively inexpensive. **Extended warranty:** Get an extended warranty to protect you from automatic transmission failures and a host of other problems. **Best alternatives:** Acura Integra; later model GM Cavalier or Sunfire; Honda Accord; Hyundai Elantra wagon, Sonata, or Tiburon; Mazda6; and Toyota Camry, 2006 or later.

Strengths and Weaknesses

Expect only average acceleration and fuel economy with the pre-2002 4-cylinder engine. It has insufficient top-end torque and gets buzzier the more it's pushed. In order to get the automatic to downshift for passing, for example, you have to practically stomp on the accelerator. Manoeuvrability is good around town but twitchy on the highway. There are few reliability problems reported with the 16-valve powerplant; however, the 5-speed manual transmission is sloppy and the automatic transmission's performance has been problematic. Late '90s through 2001 models are better choices than previous model years from reliability and fuel economy standpoints. The uncluttered under-hood layout makes servicing easy. Body assembly is only so-so, with more than the average number of squeaks and rattles.

The 2002–07 redesigned models are shaped like Passats with Maxima hearts, and provide scintillating V6 acceleration, flawless automatic transmission operation, good braking, well laid-out instruments and controls, and better-than-average interior room and craftsmanship. Too bad their exceptional performance is hobbled by chronic stalling, unreliable brakes, and suspension glitches.

Highway handling isn't impressive. The 4-cylinder engine isn't as refined as the competition and is noisy when pushed, and the V6's acceleration overpowers this car and causes excessive rear-end instability and steering pull to one side. Brakes tend to lock up on wet roads; interior appointments lack panache; there's limited rear headroom; rear seating for three adults is snug, and rear visibility is obstructed; the dashboard reflects onto the windshield; dash gauges wash out in sunlight; and parts are often back ordered. Quality problems multiply as these cars age.

The car's 180 hp 2.5L 4-cylinder engine is almost as powerful as the competition's V6 powerplants, and the optional 245 hp 3.5L V6 has few equals among cars in this price and size class. And when you consider that the Altima is much lighter than most of its competitors, it's obvious why this car produces sizzling (and sometimes uncontrollable) acceleration.

VEHICLE HISTORY: 2000—Slightly restyled to look longer and wider; the engine gets five more horses (155 hp); and suspension/chassis enhancements improve handling somewhat and make for a quieter ride. **2002**—Completely revised with two high-performance engines (a 180 hp 2.5L 4-cylinder or an optional 245 hp 3.5L V6), a larger interior, and a more-supple ride combined with sportier handling. Quality declines. **2005**—The sporty new SE-R model arrives with a 260 hp V6. Other V6 models now use a 5-speed automatic. Interior trim is upgraded throughout the lineup.

Problem areas with early, 1993–97 models are prematurely worn, noisy front brakes, fuel system malfunctions, transmission and electrical system failures, and body glitches. The 1998–2001 models have generated fewer complaints, but owners still report sudden acceleration and stalling; front brakes locking up or failing completely; failure of the airbags to deploy; transmission breakdowns; and poor body fit and finish, notably causing water leaks (mainly in the trunk) and body squeaks and rattles.

2002–07 models improved marginally, but engine, automatic transmission, brake (squeaking and premature wearout of pads and rotors), fuel and electrical systems, and fit and finish continue to be troublesome. Owners report engine surging, stalling, and hard starting, possibly because of a defective engine crank sensor or throttle switch; an annoying and hazardous dash reflection onto the windshield; electrical glitches; and excessive brake wear, noise, and pulsations. Snow builds up in the small wheelwells, making steering difficult and causing excessive shimmy; the clutch pressure plate throw-out bearing and flywheel may fail when downshifting into Fourth gear; rear shocks are noisy and failure-prone; the ABS warning light stays lit; and there's lots of ignition noise in the radio speakers.

Safety Summary

2000—Dashboard bursts into flames while vehicle is underway. • Vehicle continues to accelerate when slowing down to a stop or when put into Reverse. • Chronic stalling. • Automatic transmission won't stay in gear. • The rear wheelwell's inner fender has sharp, jagged edges. **2001**—Sudden, unintended acceleration. • Engine will suddenly shut down. • Engine motor mount failure. • Automatic transmission makes a grinding or clunking noise when shifting. • Defective sway-bar bushing. • In one incident, wheel fell off, causing vehicle to slam into a wall. **2001–03**—Airbags fail to deploy. **2002–03**—Safety defects become more common as these cars age. • Dealerships said to be aware of redesigned Altima's tendency to catch fire. Fire erupted after collision; fire ignited because of a faulty fuel-injection system; fire ignited while vehicle was cruising on the highway. • Vehicle was idling and then suddenly went into Reverse and accelerated as groceries were being unloaded from the trunk (dash indicator showed car in Park). • Driver run over by his own car when it slipped into Reverse. • Sudden acceleration when brakes are applied. • Transmission slips and engine hesitates when accelerating. • Chronic stalling. • Windshield distortion. • Exhaust-pipe hanger pin catches debris that may ignite. • Crankshaft position sensor failure. • Tail lights constantly fail. • Seat belt fails to retract. • Instrument panel gauges wash out in sunlight. **2004**—Sudden stalling and hard starts. • Vehicle starts, but won't move forward. • Brake rotors completely wear out during first year. • Rear windshield shatters as door is closed. • Rear seat belt will not slacken when pulled gently. • Right front tire falls off vehicle. • Car is a "hostage-taker":

> The problem that I face now is that I cannot get out of my car!!!!!! I arrived home one day and found that the driver's side door would not open from the inside. I am 7 months pregnant and was very scared when I found this problem. What if there is ever a car fire or an accident and I cannot get out? You can open the door from the outside but not the inside. Hyannis Nissan claims it's a door latch problem and it had to be replaced. So since my warranty just ran out I have to pay $192.00 to get this repaired. Are you kidding me?

2005—Sudden, unintended acceleration while parking. • Seat belts fail to lock when Altima is rear-ended. • Rear control bar breaks (see also TSB #NTB05-114b in "Secret Warranties/Internal Bulletins/Service Tips," below):

> Rear passenger control bar (2 rods) broke at the weld while driving and caused my car to spin out of control, causing damage to the tire, and the rear housing. I was told it would not be covered under either warranty that I carry. I was told to turn it over to my insurance company. This same part has a recall in other states, just not Florida?

• Transmission hesitates and then slams into gear. • Excessive steering vibration resolved:

> I have a 2005 Nissan Altima 3.5 SL. Last summer I was having problems with the car's handling at highway speeds. I had the car aligned, replaced all 4 tires, one by one and was still having [problems] with the car—which was shaking at speeds over 60 mph [97 km/h]. I took it to the dealer again and they determined that the shaking was like a turbulence effect. The spoiler under the car was not allowing the wind to flow through properly.

2006—Many complaints that the 2.5L engine stops running without warning, due to an overheated crankshaft position sensor (not included in an earlier recall). • Engine surges after vehicle comes to a complete stop. • Early strut and tie-rod failures. • DOT 3 brake fluid breaks down too easily, and clutch pedal goes to the floor and stays there. • Dry-rotted tire valve stems. • Side wall splits on Bridgestone Turanza EL-42 tires. **2007**—Snapped stabilizer bar. • Passenger-side airbag is disabled when an average-sized adult is seated. • Defective tire-pressure sensor. • Unstable driver's seat moves back and forth as the car accelerates or slows down.

Secret Warranties/Internal Bulletins/Service Tips

All years: Diagnostic and correction tips for brake vibration and steering-wheel shimmy. • TSB #NTB99-028 outlines the procedures necessary to fix slow-to-retract seat belts. • TSB #NTB00-037a covers possible causes of the vehicle's pulling to the side. **2002–03**—Hard starting. • Excessive engine, fuel-sloshing, and suspension noise. • Low power, poor running, and MIL stays lit. • Inoperative AC; warm air flows from vents. • Poor heater performance. • AC temperature isn't adjustable. • AC drain hose may leak into interior. • Sunroof wind noise and water leaks. • Water leakage on front floor area. • Wind noise from doors. • Sunroof won't close at highway speeds. • Automatic transmission slips in Reverse and won't brake when in Drive 1 range. **2002–04**—The control valve assembly may be the culprit responsible for erratic shifting. • Grease streaks on front-door glass. **2002–05**—Secret 13-year extended warranty on the rear subframe (see following page). • If the automatic shifter is hard to move or the sliding plate is deformed, replace both. • Replacing the seal and insulation can eliminate front-door wind noise. **2002–06**—Hard, no starts in cold weather. • Ticking noise from the engine area. • Oil cooler oil leaks do *not* require the replacement of the complete engine oil cooler assembly, says TSB #NTB06-029. • Pop, thump noise when operating front-door

CAMPAIGN—REAR SUSPENSION MEMBER, BUSHING REPLACEMENT

BULLETIN NO.: NTB05-114B

DATE: MARCH 24, 2006

VOLUNTARY SERVICE CAMPAIGN REAR SUSPENSION REPLACEMENT/BUSHING REPLACEMENT AND SEALING

On some model year 2002–05 Nissan Altima and 2004–05 Nissan Maxima vehicles, there is a possibility that corrosion of the rear sub-frame may occur. Corrosion is most likely in cold climates where heavy salting of roads is common practice in freezing conditions.... In severe cases, cracking of the rear sub-frame may occur, which may result in a knocking noise coming from the rear of the vehicle.... On most vehicles, Nissan will replace the rear sub-frame assembly. On some 2005 Model Year vehicles, where sub-frame replacement is not necessary, Nissan will replace and seal the front bushings and seal the rear bushings.

WARRANTY EXTENSION: To ensure the highest levels of customer satisfaction, Nissan is also extending the warranty for cracking of the rear sub-frame due to corrosion to a total of 13 years with unlimited mileage on all model year 2002–05 Nissan Altima and 2004–05 Nissan Maxima vehicles. Vehicles included in the Service Campaign (as described above) are also covered by the Warranty Extension.

window. **2003–05**—Nissan's bulletin admits that a harsh-shifting condition is factory-related. **2004**—Hard starts or no-starts may signal the need for a new fuel-pump assembly. • Engine won't crank in low temperatures. • Alternator noise after engine shutoff. **2004–05**—Measures that will silence a rattling, buzzing exhaust system. **2004–06**—V6 engine emits a buzzing, whining noise from the timing-chain area. **2004–08**—Tire-pressure-monitor sensor leak. **2007**—Excessive brake squeal. **2007–08**—Erratic speedometer readings; ABS and Brake lights lit. • Sunroof seals poorly. • Front suspension rattling. • Inoperative "power up" window.

ALTIMA PROFILE

	1999	2000	2001	2002	2003	2004	2005	2006	2007
Cost Price ($)									
XE/S	19,898	19,998	19,998	23,498	23,798	23,798	23,798	24,698	24,398
GXE/SE	22,698	22,698	22,698	27,698	24,675	24,298	29,098	29,698	30,198
Used Values ($)									
XE/S ▲	2,000	3,000	4,500	5,500	7,000	8,500	12,500	14,500	15,500
XE/S ▼	1,500	2,000	3,000	4,500	5,500	7,000	11,000	13,000	14,000
GXE/SE ▲	3,500	4,000	5,500	7,000	8,500	10,000	13,500	16,500	18,500
GXE/SE ▼	3,000	3,500	4,500	6,000	7,000	8,500	12,000	15,000	17,000
Reliability	2	2	2	3	3	3	3	4	4
Crash Safety (F)	3	—	4	4	4	4	5	5	5
Side	3	3	3	3	3	3	3	3	5
IIHS Side	—	—	—	1	1	1	1	1	5
Offset	—	2	2	5	5	5	5	5	5
Head Restraints (F)	2	1	1	3	3	3	3	3	2
Rear	—	—	—	2	2	2	—	3	2
Rollover Resistance	—	—	—	4	4	4	4	4	4

All ratings on a numbered scale where 5 is good and 1 is bad. See pages 108–109 for a more detailed description.

Toyota

CAMRY, SOLARA ★★★★

RATING: Above Average (2006–07); Average (1999–2005). Interestingly, many pre-1997 models offer more quality than some later versions. The Solara, a two-door Camry clone, is outrageously overpriced when bought new; however, the 2005–07 models are good buys because they are more reasonably priced as used cars and are likely to have some of the original factory warranty coverage left. Of all the model years, I'd go for the 2006 Solara to get the maximum depreciation discount and low mileage. Just a word of caution: 1997–2004 model Camrys and Solaras have elicited an unusually high number of safety complaints that are carried over from one model year to the next. The complaints include hesitation followed by sudden acceleration; engine compartment fires; V6 engine failures from sludge buildup; automatic transmission breakdowns; transmission interlock failures, which allow a parked vehicle to roll away; severe wandering at highway speeds; loss of braking; and poor headlight illumination. There's nothing you can do to prevent these failures, and you may have to force Toyota to pay for their correction through CAMVAP arbitration or small claims court. **"Real" city/highway fuel economy:** *Camry, Solara 2.4L automatic: 10.1/6.7 L/100 km. Camry, Solara 3.3L 6-cylinder: 11.7/7.4 L/100 km. Camry 2.2L manual: 10.0/6.8 L/100 km. Camry 2.2L automatic: 9.0/6.5 L/100 km. Camry 2.4L automatic: 10.4/7.3 L/100 km. Camry 3.0L automatic: 11.9/7.3 L/100 km.* These estimates may be off by as much as 20 percent. **Maintenance/Repair costs:** Higher than average, but repairs aren't dealer-dependent. **Parts:** Parts can be more expensive than for most other cars in this class, making it worth your while to shop at independent suppliers. Parts availability is excellent. **Extended warranty:** Not needed for 1996 and earlier models, but essential for 1997 and later vehicles. **Best alternatives:** The Acura Integra; Honda Accord; Hyundai Elantra wagon, Sonata, or Tiburon; and Mazda6.

Strengths and Weaknesses

The Camry is basically a Japanese Oldsmobile (the old rear-drive kind); it drives and coddles you. Safety complaints aside, it's an excellent small family hauler because of its spacious, comfortable interior, good fuel economy, and impressive reliability and durability. Just make sure you change the oil more frequently than Toyota (or Lexus, for that matter) suggests for its V6 engine, if you want to prevent engine sludge.

The 1995–96 Camrys are fairly reliable and reasonably priced, but they exhibit the first evidence of what will become a decade-old safety defect: surging and shuddering when decelerating, and an automatic transmission that slips out of gear when parked. Still, the number of chronic breakdowns is nowhere near that seen with 1997–2004 Camrys.

"De-contenting" hit Toyota's 1997–2004 lineup hard, resulting in many changes that cheapened the Camry and precipitated a huge increase in owner complaints over problems that had never appeared on Toyota vehicles before. Many of these defects continue to reappear to this day. One of the worst problems, first showing up in 1997 and continuing through the 2000 models, is engine sludge buildup, leading to engine failures that may cost as much as $7,000 to correct (see the "Sienna" section). Toyota has also admitted to engine head gasket leaks for the first time.

Quality problems continue to plague these early models, giving the impression that Toyota has been riding on a reputation it no longer deserves. Specifically, owners have endured failure-prone engine head gaskets and automatic transmissions (to Toyota's credit, both problems are covered by an extended "goodwill" warranty, but this is little solace for the hazardous predicaments, inconveniences, and out-of-pocket expenses they cause); frequent hesitation or stalling out when accelerating or braking; front power windows that often run off their channels; excessive steering-wheel vibrations; constantly irritating brake pulsations, plus brake components (calipers, rotors, pads, master cylinder, and the ABS valve) that wear out early; self-destructing AC; warning lights that constantly come on; charcoal canisters that need early replacement (covered by the emissions warranty, if you insist on it); a suspension that bottoms out when carrying four adults; leaky, noisy struts; water leaking into the car on the driver's side after a hard rain; and moonroofs that are prone to water leaks and annoyingly loud wind noise. Side pillar rattling is also a chronic annoyance.

2006 and 2007 models are particularly failure-prone, with the 2007 leading the pack in sheer number of complaints reported to NHTSA. Engine stalling and surging and transmission failures lead the list. Other problems relate to poor-quality fit and finish, evidenced by loose headliners and moulding; chronic water and air leaks; brake problems; and electrical shorts.

VEHICLE HISTORY: 1999—Debut of the Solara; adjustable front headrests; new upholstery. **2000**—Slightly restyled with larger tires and a small horsepower boost for 4-cylinder engines. **2002**—Car gets larger and now carries a 157 hp 2.4L 4-cylinder engine. **2004**—SE version gets a 225 hp 3.3L V6 hooked to a revised 5-speed automatic, improved fuel injection, and additional soundproofing. The 3.0L V6 available in the LE and XLE also gets the new 5-speed automatic and gains 18 hp, giving it 210 hp. **2005**—Standard ABS, and an upgraded automatic transmission for models equipped with a 4-cylinder engine. Less effective rear drum brakes are kept on the entry-level models, while other Camrys have four-wheel discs.

Solara

Introduced in the summer of 1998 as a '99 model, the Solara is essentially a longer, lower, bare-bones, two-door coupe or convertible Camry with a sportier power-train and suspension and a more-stylish exterior. But don't let this put you off.

Most new Toyota model offerings, such as the Sienna, Avalon, and RAV4, are Camry derivatives. Year 2000 models returned unchanged, except for the addition of a convertible version and three additional horses; 2001 models were carried over without any significant improvements.

The Solara was redesigned for 2004 and adopted the latest Camry sedan platform and upgrades. Convertibles arrived with seating for four instead of five, and resemble the two-seat Lexus SC 430 hardtop convertible. 2007 Solaras were given standard side curtain airbags.

Relatively rare on the used-car market, a base model Solara will cost you $3,000–$4,000 more than an entry-level Camry sedan. And if you get one with the Sienna and Lexus ES 300's V6 powerplant, you're looking at a few thousand dollars more. You have a choice of either four or six cylinders. Unfortunately, vehicles equipped with a V6 also came with a gimmicky rear spoiler and a headroom-robbing moonroof. The stiff body structure and suspension, as well as tight steering, make for easy, sports-car-like handling with lots of road feel and few surprises.

 ## Safety Summary

All models/years: Airbag fails to deploy, or is accidentally deployed. • Sudden acceleration when braking, shifting, or parking. • Stalling, then surging when accelerating or braking. • Car rolls away when parked on an incline. • Owners report that Firestone original-equipment tires fail prematurely. • Vehicle wanders all over the road or drifts into oncoming traffic. **All models: 2001**—Under-hood fire (left side) while vehicle is parked overnight. • Fire ignites from underneath vehicle while driving. • Excessive grinding noise and long stopping distances associated with ABS braking. • Brake pedal pushed to floor, but no braking effect. • ABS brakes suddenly lock up when coming to a gradual stop. • Defective rear brake drum. • Vehicle tends to drift to the right at highway speeds. • Excessive steering-wheel vibrations at speeds over 100 km/h. • Vehicle's weight is poorly distributed, causing the front end to lift up when the vehicle's speed exceeds 90 km/h. • Suspension bottoms out too easily, damaging the undercarriage. • Too-compliant shock absorbers make for a rough ride over uneven terrain. • Automatic transmission slippage. • In once incident, with engine running and transmission in Park position, car rolled down a hill. Two small girls inside of car jumped out, but one was then run over. • Car rolls backward after it is put into Park and ignition key is removed. • Vehicle parked overnight had its rear window suddenly blow out. • Windshield distortion is a strain on the eyes. • Floor-mounted gearshift indicator is hard to read. • Seat belts are too tight on either side and tighten up uncomfortably with the slightest movement. • Shoulder belt twists and won't lie straight. • Leaking suspension struts and strut-rod failure. • Trunk lid may suddenly collapse. • Faulty driver's window track. • Driver-side door latch sticks. • Tire jack collapses during change of tire. **2002**—An astounding 620 owner complaints up to May 2007 puts the Camry in Ford Focus territory for safety-related failures. • Starter caught on fire in the parking lot; under-hood fire (left side) while vehicle was parked overnight; fire ignited from underneath vehicle while driving. • Faulty cruise control causes vehicle to suddenly accelerate. • Sudden acceleration without braking effect. • Brake pedal goes to floor with no braking effect. • ABS brakes suddenly lock up when coming to a gradual stop. • Defective rear brake drum. • Many owners complain of poor brake pedal design:

> Arm that holds up brake pedal is interfering with the driver's foot. Driver stated if consumer had a large size foot, it could easily get wedged and stuck on brake pedal. Foot gets caught between the floormat and the brake arm, needs to be redesigned.

• Front right axle broke six months after car was purchased. • High rear end cuts rear visibility. • Turn signal volume is too low. **2003**—376 safety-related complaints were registered by NHTSA, mostly identical to the 2002 model's incidents already detailed. **2004**—263 safety-related complaints were logged into NHTSA's database, almost double what one would expect for a so-called top-quality car. • Fire ignites in the side wheelwell. • Airbags fail to deploy. • Sudden, unintended acceleration when using the cruise control, braking, shifting from Park to Reverse, or pulling into a parking space:

> Difficulty shifting from Park to Reverse, then upon shifting into Drive the car accelerated uncontrollably, would not stop, collided with a mobile home, airbags did not deploy, resulting in the death of one passenger and injury of driver.

•

> While parking the car, the steering locked turning the car to the right. The car accelerated and surged despite depressing the brake (same as ODI PE04021), the car broke a metal flag pole, damaged a retaining wall, and fell seven feet [2 m] into a major street. The airbags did not deploy.

•

> Caller's mother-in-law just got her car washed and when she pulled out of the car wash, the vehicle accelerated without warning. She pumped the brakes and tried to stop the car, and it would not stop. The car went into an 8-lane highway and was hit by an 18-wheeler and a pickup truck. Driver sustained injuries and so did the driver of the pickup truck.

• Steering U-joint bearing fell out. • Steering knuckle defective:

> Problem has been going on for two weeks. Now after taking it to an official Toyota dealer repair shop, problem still not fixed. Now at least two weeks to a month wait on part. Was told we were number 536 on waiting list, and was told it was not a safety issue in short term, but do not believe that. Steering is loose, and a catch occurs in steering. Passenger can even feel when this occurs. Dealer has reported three exact same problems with other Camrys in the same week.

• Brake and gas pedal are mounted too close together. • Sudden brake failure. • Brake pedal goes all the way to the floor, and braking distance is increased. • Many complaints that the car drifts to the left into oncoming traffic. • When in Drive on a hill, the vehicle rolls backward. • When shifted into Reverse, vehicle goes forward. • When accelerating, engine and transmission will hesitate for up to four seconds, then will surge forward. This problem extends over several model years and also includes the Lexus ES 300/330. • Poorly designed, misadjusted headlights cause a blinding glare. • Backup lights are too dim. • Repeat failures of the cruise-control, odometer, and speedometer control modules. • Airbags are disabled even when a heavy adult sits in the seat. • Inside cabin hood release latch not attached to release mechanism. • The bumpers are easily dented. • Premature wearout of Firestone tires. • Original-equipment Goodyear Integrity "all-season" tires perform poorly in snow, and Bridgestones don't have much traction on wet roads:

> I have a new 2004 Camry 4 cyl. LE sedan with 5,500 miles [8,800 km] on the original Bridgestone tires. These tires have very poor traction on rainy roads, and with even light snow you can slide easily at 3 mph [5 km/h] as we did. These tires are dangerous and should not be allowed on the market.

• Unstable tire jack. • Odometer over-registers by 3 percent (affects warranty, etc.). • Electronic gas mileage calculator is off by 2 km/L (4.7 mpg). Dealer says they are all off and no repair is being contemplated. • Are 2004 Camrys "rat-prone"? Read the following owner's complaint, and decide for yourself:

> O_2 sensors failed due to rodents or rabbits chewing the plastic wiring housing the internal electrical wires. O_2 sensors had to be replaced at a cost of about $600. The outside coatings, or sheaths, for the wiring is made of a soy-based plastic and possibly contains a "fish oil" in the sheath, which attracts rodents and rabbits, and they chew on the plastic wire coverings, thereby destroying the O_2 sensor's wiring mechanism. This problem is prevalent in the Denver and mountain state areas and should be corrected as the problem could lead to engine fires or engine failures. The wiring housing should be changed to a "retardant" type of wiring to prevent other incidents of this problem, and not just for Toyota but for all manufacturers.

2005—Vehicle hesitates and then surges. • Sometimes, the Camry will suddenly lurch forward when easing into a parking space:

> I was slowly turning right to park in front of a store with my foot on the brakes preparing to stop when my 2005 Camry accelerated, jumped the curb and crashed into a storefront window.

• V6 has chronic hesitation problems at lower speeds. • Engine surges when slowing for a traffic light, or when applying moderate brake pressure. • Car constantly veers left. • Transmission shifts with a jolt when car slows down and then accelerates. • Brake pedal will sink to the floor intermittently. • Windshield has hash marks that obstruct vision when sun shines through. • Continental tire suddenly separates from the rim. **2006**—Sudden brake failure. • Too much steering play, knocking noise. • Side windows fall down. • Drivers often neglect to turn on the headlights, thinking they are on when the instrument lights are lit. •

Odometer reads 10 percent higher than actual mileage. **2007**—Almost 500 safety-related complaints reported to NHTSA; 100 complaints would be normal. • Sudden, unintended acceleration. • Many complaints that the car hesitates on takeoff; transmission slips. • Steering wheel binds. • Premature wearout of Bridgestone original-equipment tires.

Secret Warranties/Internal Bulletins/Service Tips

All models/years: To reduce front brake squeaks on ABS-equipped vehicles, ask the dealer to install new, upgraded rotors (#43517-32020). • Owner feedback over the last decade as well as dealer service managers who wish to remain anonymous tell me that Toyota has a secret warranty that will pay for replacing front disc brake components that wear out before 2 years/40,000 km. If you're denied this coverage, threaten small claims court action. • Toyota has a special kit to reduce AC odours. **All models: 2002**—Special Service Campaign to replace the driver-side front airbag. • Automatic transmission shift quality improvements. • Catalytic converter heat-shield rattle. • Campaigns to repair the washer reservoir tank; remove coil-spring spacers. **2002–05**—No more tips on removing odours. Toyota finally "comes clean" and authorizes the free replacement of the catalytic converter on almost its entire lineup. **2002–06**—Plugging a front-door water leak. • Sunroof binds or squeaks. **2003–06**—Tips for silencing intermediate steering shaft noise. • Remedy for a windshield ticking noise. **2004–05**—Correction for drifting or pulling into oncoming traffic involves installing new springs and struts. **2004–06**—Rear suspension thumping. • Front seat squeaking. **2007**—Engine oil leaks from the timing cover. • Rough idle, stalling. • Shift flare. • Water leaks at headliner and floor areas. • Noisy rear suspension. **2007–08**—Premature brake pad wear; squeaking rear brakes. • Excessive steering-wheel vibration, flutter, and noise. • Instrument panel rattle. **2007–09**—Torque converter shudder. • Moonroof knocking when underway. *Solara:* **All years:** Water leaking into the trunk area. • Poor durability of rear-view mirrors. **2002–03**—Harsh automatic transmission shifts. • Excessive brake vibration. • Sliding-roof repair tips (TSB #BO002-03). • Power front seat feels loose (TSB #BO004-03). Poor AC/heating. **2002–05**—Fuel door hard to open. • Remedy for rotten-egg-smelling exhaust. **2004–06**—Convertible top hard to close. **2004–07**—Water leaks at headliner and floor areas.

CAMRY, SOLARA PROFILE

	1999	2000	2001	2002	2003	2004	2005	2006	2007
Cost Price ($)									
Base Sedan CE	21,680	22,180	24,565	—	—	—	—	—	—
LE	26,508	27,070	27,695	23,755	24,800	24,800	24,990	24,990	25,800
LE V6	—	—	—	27,585	27,070	27,070	27,475	27,475	29,400
Base Solara	26,245	26,665	27,580	28,175	28,175	28,800	26,850	27,545	29,200
V6	29,815	30,270	33,075	33,990	34,290	27,777	30,950	32,850	33,400

Used Values ($)

Base Sedan CE ▲	4,000	5,000	7,000	—	—	—	—	—	—
Base Sedan CE ▼	3,500	4,500	6,000	—	—	—	—	—	—
LE ▲	5,500	6,500	7,500	8,000	9,000	10,500	12,500	14,500	17,500
LE ▼	5,000	6,000	7,000	7,500	8,500	9,500	11,000	13,000	16,000
LE V6 ▲	—	—	—	8,500	10,000	13,500	15,500	17,500	20,500
LE V6 ▼	—	—	—	7,000	9,000	12,000	14,000	16,000	19,000
Base Solara ▲	4,500	5,500	6,500	8,000	10,000	11,500	14,500	16,500	20,000
Base Solara ▼	4,000	5,000	6,000	7,000	8,500	10,000	13,000	15,500	18,500
V6 ▲	5,500	7,000	8,000	9,000	11,000	14,500	17,000	19,000	22,000
V6 ▼	5,000	6,000	7,000	8,000	9,500	13,000	15,500	17,500	21,000

Reliability	3	3	3	3	3	3	4	4	4
Crash Safety (F)	4	4	4	5	5	4	5	5	5
Side	3	3	3	2	3	4	4	4	5
Solara	—	—	3	3	3	3	3	5	5
IIHS Side	—	—	—	—	—	1	1	1	1
Offset	5	5	5	5	5	5	5	5	5
Head Restraints	—	3	3	—	4	2	2	5	5
Solara	—	—	3	—	3	3	3	3	—
Rollover Resistance	—	—	5	4	4	4	4	4	4

Note: Without head- and torso-protecting side airbags, 2002–06 Camrys receive a side crashworthiness rating of Poor from IIHS.

Volkswagen

NEW BEETLE ★★★

RATING: Average (2000–07); Below Average (1999). The New Beetle's cute styling is no longer a sufficient enticement to draw buyers. Beetle sales are suffering because hard-nosed shoppers want reliability and fuel economy, and they are finding that VW's products are not making the grade. Safety-related complaints registered by NHTSA include electrical fires, chronic stalling, and transmission failures. **"Real" city/highway fuel economy:** *1.8L manual: 9.6/7.2 L/100 km. 1.8L automatic: 10.3/7.3 L/100 km. 2.0L manual: 9.8/7.0 L/100 km. 2.0L automatic: 9.6/7.2L/100 km. 1.9L diesel manual: 6.2/4.6 L/100 km. 1.9L diesel automatic: 6.5/5.2 L/100 km.* Owners report gasoline fuel savings may undershoot these estimates by at least 10 percent, or 15 percent for diesel fuel. **Maintenance/Repair costs:** Average, but only a VW dealer can repair these cars. **Parts:** Usually easily found, since they're taken mostly from the Golf parts bin, but body parts are harder to find. **Extended warranty:** A good idea. **Best alternatives:** Acura Integra; GM

Cavalier or Sunfire; Honda Accord; Hyundai Elantra wagon, Sonata, or Tiburon; Mazda6; Nissan Sentra; and Toyota Camry, 2006 or later.

Strengths and Weaknesses

I lost my virginity in a Beetle. (Apparently, many of my friends did too.) Nevertheless, I moved on—and VW should as well.

Why so much emotion for an ugly German import that never had a functioning heater, was declared "Small on Safety" by Ralph Nader and his Center for Auto Safety, and carried a puny 48 hp engine (about one-third the horsepower of a Hyundai Elantra)? The simple answer is that it was cheap—it was the first car many of us could afford as we went through school, got our first jobs, and dreamed of…getting a better car. Time has taken the edge off the memories of the hardships the Beetle made us endure—such as having to scrape the inside windshield with our nails as our breath froze—and left us with the cozy feeling that the car wasn't that bad after all.

But it was.

VW resurrected the Beetle as a 2000 model and produced a competent front-engine, front-drive compact car set on the chassis and running gear of the Golf hatchback. It's much safer than its predecessor, but, oddly enough, it's still afflicted with many of the same deficiencies that we learned to hate with the original. Without the turbocharger, the 115 hp 2.0L engine is underwhelming when you get it up to cruising speed (the 90 hp turbodiesel isn't much better), plus there's still not much room for rear passengers, engine noise is disconcerting, front visibility is hindered by the car's quirky design, and storage capacity is at a premium.

On the other hand, the powerful optional 1.8L turbocharged engine makes this Beetle an impressive performer; the heater works fine; steering, handling, and braking are quite good; and the interior is not as spartan or as tacky as it once was.

VEHICLE HISTORY: 2000—Addition of a 150 hp turbocharged 4-cylinder engine, firmer suspension, and improved theft protection. **2001**—Larger exterior mirrors, and a trunk safety release. **2002**—Introduction of the 180 hp Turbo S and a new Electronic Stabilization Program. **2003**—Convertible and turbodiesel arrive. **2004**—Upgraded head-protecting airbags and front head restraints, improved spoiler, and new wheels. The GLX model is axed. **2006**—The 115 hp 2.0L and 150 hp turbocharged 1.8L are replaced by a 150 hp 2.5L 5-cylinder engine. A hatchback TDI model with a 100 hp 1.9L turbodiesel is the only diesel model available. Standard anti-lock four-wheel disc brakes and front side airbags with head and torso protection, and an anti-skid system and traction control. **2007**—No more diesel-engine Beetles; all models come with a 150 hp 5-cylinder gasoline engine.

In a nutshell, here are the New Beetle's strong points: standard side airbags; easy handling; sure-footed and comfortable, though firm, ride; impressive braking;

comfy and supportive front seats with plenty of front headroom and legroom; and a cargo area that can be expanded by folding down the rear seats.

On the minus side, owners have reported serious safety defects (see "Safety Summary"), powertrain performance is unimpressive, and body construction is second-rate. Here are specific owner gripes: The 2.0L engine runs out of steam around 100 km/h and may overheat; diesel engines lack pep and produce lots of noise and vibration; faulty O_2 sensors cause the Check Engine light to come on; coolant leaks onto the wiring harness also cause the Check Engine light to come on; frequent ECM failures; axle oil pan and oil pump failures; delayed shifts from Park to Drive, or failure to shift into Fourth gear; car is easily buffeted by cross-winds; optional high-mounted side mirrors, large head restraints, and large front roof pillars obstruct front and rear visibility; limited rear legroom and headroom; difficult rear entry/exit; excessive engine and brake noise; early brake component replacement; malfunctioning dash gauges; awkward-to-access radio buttons and door-panel-mounted power switches; faulty window regulators; skimpy interior storage and trunk space; interior vent louvre loosens and breaks; hatchback rattles and sometimes fails to open; AC disengages when decelerating; AC fan motor howls and engine makes a loud humming noise when the AC is turned on; front lights retain water and short out; and the low-slung chassis causes extensive undercarriage damage when going over a curb.

Safety Summary

2000–01—Airbags fail to deploy. • Airbag warning light stays lit constantly. • Many complaints of prolonged hesitation when accelerating. • Steering suddenly locks up. • Low-mounted fuel tank is easily punctured. • Mass airflow sensor and secondary air-injection-pump motor failures. • Windows fall into door channel because of defective regulators. • Hard to keep rear window free of rain, snow, or dew. • Windshield distortions impede vision. • Rear seat-belted passengers hit their heads on the unpadded side pillars. **2000–03**—Back glass suddenly shatters. **2002**—ABS failure. • Window goes up and down on its own. • Brake fluid leakage. • Harsh downshifts; vehicle loses power (mass airflow sensor is the suspected cause). **2003**—Sudden acceleration, stalling. • Side airbag deploys for no reason. • Driver-side airbag fails to deploy. • Punctured fuel tank leaks fuel. • Steering-wheel lock-up; excessive shake; constant pulling to the right (torque steer). • Rear windshield is hard to see through. • Dash warning lights come on constantly for no apparent reason. • Head restraints still sit too high to be comfortable, and obstruct rear visibility. • Open sunroof sucks exhaust into the cabin. • Left front strut slips down through the spindle, causing the spindle to hit the wheelwell. **2004**—Complete transmission failure; replaced transmission also shifts poorly. • Delayed shifting and long hesitation when accelerating. • Sudden stalling and loss of electrical power while underway. • Complete loss of steering. • Electrical shorts cause the odometer and other accessories to malfunction. • Wiper suddenly quits working. • Airbag warning light comes on constantly. • Annoying beep when seat belt isn't buckled. • Driver-side window lowers on its own. • On convertible models, the windows catch on the top when the doors are opened.

2004–05—Airbags fail to deploy. **2005**—Owners report the worst of both worlds when describing engine performance. For example, there are reports of the car suddenly accelerating when coming to a stop, or, conversely, losing power when accelerating. • Driver's window exploded. **2006**—Rear seat belt unlatched in a rear-end collision. • Sudden stalling in traffic. • All electrical systems failed, leading to an immediate stall-out. • Megatronic automatic transmission shifts roughly and binds; long wait for parts. • Rear engine mount failure. • Dual-mass flywheel blew apart in the manual transmission clutch assembly. • Brake pedal went to the floor with no braking effect. • Right side of the windshield distorts the driver's view. **2007**—Hard starting due to electrical failures. • Trunk is hard to open. • Dashboard feels hot.

Secret Warranties/Internal Bulletins/Service Tips

All years: Sudden, unintended acceleration. • Airbags fail to deploy when they should. • Door windows separate from regulators. • Lousy radio reception. • Heated rear window; one or more lines are inoperative. **2000–01**—Prematurely worn rear brake pads (TSB #00-01, November 27, 2000). **2000–08**—Removing a musty smell emanating from the air vents. **2001**—Inoperative secondary oil pump. **2001–08**—Inoperative or malfunctioning sunroof. **2002**—Transmission appears to leak fluid. • Inoperative fresh-air blower motor. **2003–05**—Corroded rotors may be the cause of excessive brake vibration. • Convertible top may not operate correctly. **2003–10**—Brake vibration troubleshooting tips. **2004**—Hard starting, no-starts, rough running when wet; may emit light gray smoke. • Front-seat passenger airbag disabled when a full-sized passenger is seated. • Inoperative rear window heating element. **2004–07**—Transmission fluid leakage between case halves. **2006–07**—6-speed automatic transmission won't shift out of Park. **2006–08**—AC doesn't get cold enough. **2007**—Insufficient heater output at idle. **2007–08**—Cluster lights flicker with wipers on.

NEW BEETLE PROFILE

	1999	2000	2001	2002	2003	2004	2005	2006	2007
Cost Price ($)									
Base	21,500	21,950	21,950	21,950	23,210	23,690	23,910	24,490	22,780
Cabrio	27,200	27,500	27,900	28,530	29,250	29,610	30,160	29,880	27,790
Used Values ($)									
Base ▲	3,500	4,000	5,000	6,000	7,500	9,500	11,500	15,000	15,000
Base ▼	3,000	3,500	4,500	5,000	6,500	8,000	10,500	13,500	14,000
Cabrio ▲	5,500	6,500	8,000	10,000	11,000	13,000	15,500	17,500	21,000
Cabrio ▼	5,000	6,000	6,500	8,500	9,500	11,500	13,500	16,000	19,500
Reliability	2	3	3	3	3	3	3	4	4
Crash Safety (F)	4	4	4	4	4	4	4	4	4
Cabrio	—	—	—	—	5	4	—	—	4
Side	5	5	5	5	5	5	5	5	5
IIHS Side	—	—	—	—	—	1	1	1	1

Offset	5	5	5	5	5	5	5	5	5
Head Restraints (F)	5	—	5	5	5	3	3	3	3
Rear	3	—	—	3	3	3	—	—	—
Rollover Resistance	—	—	—	—	4	4	4	4	4
Cabrio	—	—	—	—	4	4	—	—	4

Note: Used diesel models will cost from $500 to $1,000 more than the gasoline-powered versions.

PASSAT ★★★

RATING: Average (2006–07); Below Average (1999–2005). Don't listen to the car journalists who love European cars like the Passat. They don't pay for service visits. Read owner opinions, and you'll see that the Passat is a big disappointment. Word has gotten out that these cars are over-hyped for their performance prowess, that they aren't very dependable, and that they cost a lot to maintain. Consequently, Passats have lost their lustre to Japanese luxury cars, and they now depreciate quickly. But beware; their low price won't cover the extraordinarily high repair bills you'll get from Otto, Hans, and Ingrid. **"Real" city/highway fuel economy:** *1.8L manual: 9.8/6.9 L/100 km. 1.8L automatic: 11.7/7.3 L/100 km. 2.8L 6-cylinder automatic: 12.7/8.3 L/100 km. 4.0L 8-cylinder 6-speed manual: 14.0/8.9 L/100 km. 4.0L 8-cylinder 6-speed automatic: 13.4/8.8 L/100 km.* Owners say the 8-cylinder engines burn at least 20 percent more fuel than the above figures show. **Maintenance/Repair costs:** Higher-than-average costs; dealer-dependent. **Parts:** Parts and service are more expensive than average; long waits for parts are commonplace. **Extended warranty:** Yes, principally for the powertrain. **Best alternatives:** Acura Integra, Audi A4 or A6, and Honda Accord.

Strengths and Weaknesses

These front-drive compact sedans and wagons use mechanical parts borrowed from the Golf, Jetta, and Corrado. A 2.8L V6 became the standard powerplant beginning with the '99 wagon. Its long wheelbase and squat appearance give the Passat a massive, solid feeling, while its styling makes it look sleek and clean. As with most European imports, it comes fairly well-appointed.

As far as overall performance goes, the Passat is no slouch. The multi-valve 4-cylinder engine is adequate, and its handling is superior to that of most of the competition. The 2.8L V6 provides lots of power when revved and is the engine that works best with an automatic transmission.

VEHICLE HISTORY: 1998—Based on the Audi A4 and A6, this model offers more usable interior space, better handling, and better engine performance with its 150 hp turbocharged 1.8L engine and 190 hp 2.8L V6. **2000**—An AWD model, heated front seats, a brake wear indicator, and an improved anti-theft ignition. **2001**—Mid-year changes include a new nose, upgraded tail lights and dash gauges, chassis improvements, and the debut of a 170 hp engine alongside a new W8

270 hp AWD luxury car. **2002**—Given a 134 hp 2.0L turbocharged diesel coupled to either a front-drive or an all-wheel-drive powertrain. Also new is a 5-speed automatic transmission with manual capability. **2003**—W8 is given a 6-speed manual transmission. **2004**—A diesel powerplant joins the lineup, and AWD is offered on more models. **2005**—No more W8 series, GL models come with a turbodiesel only, and the GLX gets 17-inch wheels. **2006**—Redesigned with fresh styling, a larger interior, and more power. The turbocharged 2.0L picks up 30 more horses, while the 280 hp 3.6L V6 added 90 more horses. V6 models come with an automatic transmission only.

Passats are infamous for automatic transmission failures, engine ignition coil/fuel-system stalling and no-starts, and engines gummed up by oil sludge—all costly-to-repair items. Even when they're operating as they should, the Passat's manual and automatic gearboxes leave a lot to be desired; for example, the 5-speed manual transmission's gear ranges are too far apart (there's an enormous gap between Third and Fourth gear), and the 4-speed automatic shifts poorly with the 4-banger. Also, owners report that the transmission won't shift from lower gears, and there are problems with clutch slave cylinder leaks, front brakes (master cylinder replacements, brake booster failures, rotor warpage, premature wear, and excessive noise), MacPherson struts, and fuel and electrical systems as the car ages. Additionally, defective tie-rod and constant velocity joint seals allow debris to enter into the vehicle's system, effectively causing the premature wearout of internal components; engines often leak oil; early replacement of the power-steering assembly is often needed; and fuel and computer module problems lead to hard starts and chronic stalling.

On the body side, there's a helicopter-type wind noise when cruising with the windows or sunroof open; the sunroof rattles; the front spoiler and rear trim fall off; water leaks persistently from the pollen filter; interior trim and controls are fragile; heated seats are a pain in the...well, you know; the driver-seat memory feature fails; door speakers need frequent replacing; rear door mouldings warp easily; the fuel gauge malfunctions, indicating fuel in the tank when it's empty; windshields may be optically distorted; and the rear-view passenger-side mirrors are too small and cause several blind spots.

Owners report that VW dealer servicing is the pits. Cars have to be brought in constantly to fix the same problems, recall campaign repairs are often slow because parts aren't available, and warranty coverage is spotty because VW headquarters doesn't empower or pay dealers sufficiently to take the initiative. Competent servicing and parts are particularly hard to find away from large cities, and many of the above-mentioned deficiencies can cost you an arm and a leg to repair.

 ## Safety Summary

All models/years: Sudden, unintended acceleration. • An incredible number of automatic transmission malfunctions, breakdowns, and early replacements. • Airbags fail to deploy, or deploy for no reason. One VW employee told U.S. federal investigators he was fired shortly after complaining about the airbag hazard:

> The driver-side head airbag (air curtain) of a 2003 Volkswagen Passat W8 sedan deployed spontaneously while I was driving the car…a few minutes later, when the car was stopped, the steering wheel airbag deployed spontaneously…I suffered a permanent wrist injury and am suffering from post-traumatic stress syndrome…the incident, which happened during a test drive, was reported to the management of the VW dealership for which I was working and to the VW of America by the management.

• Airbag light comes on for no reason. **All models: 2000–03**—Many reports of fire igniting in the engine compartment. • Excess raw fuel flows out of the exhaust system. • Hard starts and chronic stalling. • Check Engine light comes on intermittently, and then engine shuts down. • While cruising, vehicle speeds up; when brakes are applied, it slows down until foot is taken off the brake, then surges again. • Braking doesn't disengage cruise control. • Hesitation and long delays when accelerating. • Automatic transmission suddenly drops out of gear. • Many complaints of windshield distortion (there's an accordion effect where letters and objects expand and contract as they pass by). • Passenger window suddenly explodes just after being rolled up. • Windshield wipers cut out. • Plastic engine nose shield falls off. • Rear tire failure damages the fuel-filler neck, causing a fuel leak. **2002**—Premature CV joint failure. • Oil pan is easily punctured because of low ground clearance. • Some electrical and fuel-system glitches cause chronic stalling, loss of engine power. • Gas pedal remains stuck to the floor. • Brakes don't grab as well when vehicle is cold; premature brake wear. **2003**—Vehicle runs out of fuel despite the fuel gauge showing one-quarter tank of gas. • Super-heated seats. **2004**—Vehicle lurches forward when braking or accelerating. • Transmission control module and clutch failure, hard shifting, and gears slam into place with a clunking sound. • Automatic transmission tends to hesitate and then jumps forward. • Loss of power steering; grinding noise. • Prematurely worn rear brake pads. • Electrical short circuits shut off lights. • Seat heater burns through seat:

> The heated drivers seat in my 2004 VW Passat caught on fire and burned through my wife's jeans. This occurred after driving only 1/4 mile [0.4 km]. She felt something on her leg, and when she looked down there was smoke coming out of the seat. She stopped and got the fire out, but it had burned her (left a red mark on her leg), her jeans, and put a hole in the seat.

• Insufficient space between the footrest and clutch pedal; foot gets trapped. • Windshield wiper collects snow and ice in wiper groove. • Water leaking into interior causes serious electrical shorts, primarily affecting the drivetrain:

> Water coming into front passenger seat resulting in damages to the TCM (transmission control module), wet carpeting, and rust under the passenger seat.

• Low-mounted oil pan is easily damaged when passing over uneven terrain. **2005**—Chronic stalling may cause engine failure. • Seat belts fail to retract. **2006**—More safety incidents reported than is normal for a three-year-old vehicle. • Several under-hood fires. • Sudden loss of power while cruising on the highway. • Engine over-revs when the AC is turned on; foot has to be kept on the brake pedal. • The bolt that holds the oil pump in place backs out and shears off, requiring an engine replacement:

> Sheared oil pump bolt at 16,000 miles [25,750 km]. [Engine] lost all power. Dealer replaced oil pump, timing chain and all related hardware. Asked manufacturer (Volkswagen) and dealership for new engine due to [likely] oil starvation after oil pump was inoperative. Request denied.

• Steering-column lock failure (lock control module: $2,400 (U.S.)). • Catalytic converter busted at a flange seam, damaging the brake vacuum tube with hot gases. • Tires wear out prematurely. • Trunk will not latch. • Airbag light is always lit. **2007**—Under-hood electrical harness fire. • Vehicle was recalled for sudden acceleration, and problem reappeared after the fix. • Engine over-revs when decelerating. • Chronic loss of power and misfiring diagnosed as a bad coil. • Brakes slip and then grab when applied. • Subframe bolt failure. • Dash gauge cluster behaves erratically. • Original-equipment Pirelli tires develop side wall bulges.

Secret Warranties/Internal Bulletins/Service Tips

All models/years: Failure-prone, malfunctioning automatic transmissions. **All models: 1995–99**—An erratically shifting automatic transmission may be caused by an improper throttle angle setting. **1995–2008**—Inoperative heated rear glass lines. **1996–2006**—Condensation inside exterior lights. **2003–06**—Excessive vibration when braking may be caused by corroded brake rotors. **2006–07**—Airbag light constantly lit. • Insufficient heater output. • Front suspension creak. **2006–08**—Front-seat creaking, cracking. • Inoperative AC and seat heater. *Diesels:* **2004–05**—Engine hesitation on acceleration.

PASSAT PROFILE

	1999	2000	2001	2002	2003	2004	2005	2006	2007
Cost Price ($)									
Sedan	29,100	29,100	29,500	29,550	29,550	29,550	30,190	29,950	29,970
Used Values ($)									
Sedan ▲	3,500	5,000	6,000	8,000	9,000	10,000	12,500	18,000	20,000
Sedan ▼	3,000	4,000	5,000	7,000	8,500	9,000	11,000	16,500	18,500
Reliability	2	2	2	2	3	3	3	3	3
Crash Safety (F)	—	5	5	5	5	5	5	4	4
Side	—	4	4	4	4	4	4	5	5
IIHS Side	—	—	—	—	—	—	—	5	5
Offset	5	5	5	5	5	5	5	5	5
Head Restraints (F)	2	—	1	1	1	1	1	3	2
Rear	1	—	—	—	—	—	—	—	—
Rollover Resistance	—	—	—	—	4	4	4	4	4

LARGE CARS

Honest, officer, I wasn't going that fast... Hey, does that patrol car have a Hemi?

Quintessential highway cruisers for law enforcement agencies, travelling sales-people, large families, or retirees, full-sized American cars are icons of a time long passed. No longer able to compete due to unpredictable fuel costs and the avail-ability of more-versatile crossover minivans and small sport-utilities, most of these "land yachts" have been axed or are being phased out, as is the case with Ford's Crown Victoria and Grand Marquis. Chrysler's possible bankruptcy would make their high-tech, low-volume large cars almost impossible to service.

Chrysler has stayed in the game longest with its spacious and attractively styled Concorde, Intrepid, and 300M sedans. Unfortunately, these family sedans were several notches below Ford's and GM's when it came to dependability and highway performance. Chrysler hoped to climb back up the performance and quality ladder with its 2005 rear-drive Magnum wagon and 300 Series fully featured cars equipped with Hemi engines, but higher fuel prices, poor quality control, and a shortened powertrain warranty made for dismal sales and angry owners who vowed to never buy a Chrysler again. Ironically, lower fuel prices haven't raised the retail value of large cars.

Owners once had to pay a premium for these large-car behemoths, which usually came fully loaded with performance and convenience features, but they were happy to do so because these vehicles offer considerable comfort and stability at high speeds. They also depreciate quickly and can be reasonably reliable (making used Fords better bargains than Chrysler's used-car offerings), they can seat six adults comfortably, and they're ideal for motoring vacations. Ford and GM repairs are a snap and can be done almost anywhere, and there's a large reservoir of reasonably priced replacement parts sold through independent agencies. Chrysler owners will have to scrounge around more.

The downside? Terrible fuel economy, mediocre highway performance, and handling that's neither precise nor exciting. The interior is comfortable but not as versatile as in a minivan or SUV, seniors find entry and exit physically challenging, and you don't get as commanding a view of the road as in taller vehicles.

Station Wagons (Full-Sized)

Once-popular full-sized rear-drive wagons—such as the GM Caprice and Roadmaster (both axed in 1996)—lost out to sport-utilities and minivans over a decade ago, and have now been reincarnated as crossover front-drives. If passenger and cargo space and carlike handling are what you want, a large station wagon may not be the answer. A used minivan, van, light truck, downsized SUV, or compact wagon can meet your needs and be just as cheap, and it will probably still be around a decade from now.

Some disadvantages of large station wagons include difficulty in keeping the interior heated in winter, atrocious gas consumption, sloppy handling, and poor rear visibility. Also, rear hatches and rear brake supporting plates tend to be rust-prone, and the bodies become rattletraps.

LARGE CAR RATINGS

Average

Chrysler Charger, SRT8 (2006–07)   Ford Crown Victoria, Grand Marquis (1999–2007)

Below Average

Ford Cougar, Thunderbird (2003–05)

Not Recommended

Chrysler 300, 300C, 300M, Concorde,   Ford Cougar, Thunderbird (1999–2002)
Intrepid, LHS, Magnum
(1999–2007)

Chrysler

RATING: *300, 300C, 300M, Concorde, Intrepid, LHS, Magnum:* Not Recommended (1999–2007). *Charger, SRT8:* Average (2006–07). Styling trumps practicality with this disappointing lineup of front- and rear-drives. One would have thought the Mercedes connection would have seen the sharing of top-quality front- and rear-drive components by Daimler. No such luck. Chrysler has gone from subpar front-drive vehicles to rear-drive 300 and Magnum models that are just as unreliable. Sure, they look good, but that's about all the 2005–07 gas hogs offer. Although all of these cars are cheap as dirt, factory glitches can steal away most of your savings—and endanger your life, too. Be especially wary of the discontinued Intrepid, LHS, New Yorker, and Vision. Parts are rare, and mechanics cringe when these hard-to-service cars arrive in their service bays. **"Real" city/highway fuel economy:** *Concorde 2.7L:* 12.6/8.0 L/100 km. *Concorde 3.5L:* 12.5/7.9 L/100 km. *Intrepid 2.7L:* 11.0/7.4 L/100 km. *Intrepid 3.5L:* 12.5/7.9 L/100 km. Owners report fuel savings may undershoot these estimates by at least 20 percent. **Maintenance/Repair costs:** Higher than average, but most repairs aren't dealer-dependent. **Parts:** Higher-than-average costs; Hemi engine parts are hard to find and cost an arm and a leg. If Chrysler *does* go bankrupt soon, as many expect, these cars may not be repairable, due to a lack of parts. **Extended warranty:** If you can't get a powertrain warranty, don't give these cars a second glance. In fact, what you really need is bumper-to-bumper protection—a $2,000–$3,000 extra expense. **Best alternatives:** GM Bonneville, Caprice, LeSabre, or Roadmaster; and Ford's early Cougar, T-Bird, Crown Victoria, or Mercury Grand Marquis.

Strengths and Weaknesses

All the cars in Chrysler's full-sized lineup share the same chassis and offer most of the same standard and optional features. They provide loads of passenger space and many standard features, such as four-wheel disc brakes and an independent rear suspension. Since their 1998 redesign, base models are equipped with a failure-prone 2.7L V6 aluminum engine that delivers 200 hp. Higher-line variants get a more-powerful 3.2L V6 225 hp powerplant or a 242 hp 3.5L V6. (Earlier models also carried a 3.3L 153 hp 6-banger, but 70 percent of buyers chose the 3.5L for its extra horses.) Both variant engines provide plenty of low-end torque and acceleration, but this advantage is lost somewhat when traversing hilly terrain—the smaller V6 powerplant strains to keep up.

The early cars have better handling and steering response than the Ford Sable and Taurus or GM mid-sized front-drives, but the difference is marginal when you tote up the $3,000–$10,000 cost of powertrain, brake, and AC repairs.

Furthermore, these cars can be as unsafe as they are unreliable. Read the following owners' experiences, which are both scary and typical:

> Travelling on the freeway at 100 km/h, my 1999 Chrysler 300M's rear windshield was sucked out and flew to the side of the road. I had no prior problems with the windshield. Entire rear windshield and casing flew off.

> •

> My 2000 Concorde accelerated on its own. I had to hit a tree to stop the car. The airbags did not deploy upon impact. Tires continued spinning after impact, until I turned off the ignition.

Owner reports confirm that there are chronic problems with leaking 3.3L engine head gaskets, engine sludge gums up the works of the 2.7L engine (change your oil more often than recommended), and noisy lifters wear out prematurely around 60,000 km. Water pumps often self-destruct and take the engine timing chain along with them (a $1,200 repair). Complaints of engine surging and unintended acceleration are also frequent refrains regarding all model years. However, the one recurring safety problem affecting almost all model years concerns the steering system. As you can read at *www.daimlerchryslervehicleproblems.com* (The Truth Behind Chrysler):

> Chrysler has been under investigation by NHTSA for more than 55,000 warranty claims for steering problems with these vehicles and 1,450 reports of steering control problems, some including complete loss of steering control....

> Many consumers have also paid over $1,200 (U.S.) for replacement steering assemblies.... Common symptoms of steering problems with these vehicles are typically loose steering, excessive play in the steering, vibration, wandering, steering out of alignment, clunks, rattle, rubbing, or binding.

The 4-speed LE42 automatic transmission is a spin-off of Chrysler's failure-prone A604 version, and owner reports show it to be just as unreliable. Owners tell of chronic glitches in the computerized transmission's shift timing and other computer malfunctions, which result in early replacement and driveability problems (stalling, hard starts, and surging). AC failures are commonplace and costly to repair.

Body problems abound, with lots of interior noise; uneven fit and finish with misaligned doors and jagged trunk edges; poor-quality trim items that break or fall off easily; exposed screw heads; faulty door hinges that make the doors rattle-prone and hard to open; distorted, poorly mounted windshields; windows that come off their tracks or are misaligned and poorly sealed; power-window motor failures; and steering-wheel noise when the car is turning.

VEHICLE HISTORY: 1998—Concorde and Intrepid are completely redesigned and given two new V6s (a 200 hp 2.7L and a 225 hp 3.2L), ABS, traction control (on the LXi), and dual front airbags. **2002**—The 300M Special performance model comes with a new grille, upgraded ABS, and more user-friendly child safety seat anchors. Concorde gets the LHS's styling and most of the other LHS amenities, including a 250 hp 3.5L V6, leather trim, high-tech gauges, ABS, traction control, and 17-inch alloy wheels. The LXi acquires the 3.2L V6 with a 234 hp variant of the 3.5L V6. **2003**—Intrepid gets a 244 hp 3.5L V6, Concorde horsepower goes to 250, and the 300M's power is boosted to 255 hp. **2005**—Debut of the rear-drive 300, 300C, and Magnum.

300M and LHS

More show than go, these cars are near-luxury and sport clones of the Chrysler Concorde. Although they use the same front-drive platform as the Concorde, their bodies are shorter and they're styled differently. Both cars are powered by a 253 hp 3.5L V6 mated to Chrysler's AutoStick semi-automatic transmission. Mechanical and body deficiencies generally mirror those of the Concorde and Intrepid.

300, 300C, and Magnum

These rear-drive, full-sized, and feature-laden (standard traction control, electronic stability control, and ABS) sedans and wagons were first launched as 2005 models. Their first year on the market was accompanied by a plethora of factory-related problems, as well as limited parts supply and problematic servicing due to the cars' new design and relatively small sales volume. The residual value for these cars is in freefall as more buyers flock to fuel-efficient front-drives.

The top-of-the-line Chrysler 300 shares its platform with the sportier Dodge Magnum wagon and comes in three packages: the base model with a 190 hp V6; a Touring version with a 250 hp V6; and the high-performance 300C with a 340 hp V8 Hemi engine. The V8 employs Chrysler's Multi-Displacement System, which uses eight cylinders under load and then switches to 4-cylinder mode when cruising. AWD is available on Touring and 300C models. V6-equipped models have a 4-speed automatic transmission. AWD and V8 versions use a 5-speed automatic with a manual shiftgate.

 Safety Summary

All models/years: No airbag deployment in a collision. • 2.7L engine suddenly self-destructs because of excess oil sludge and overheating. Owners describe the failure this way:

> The primary symptom is that the car heater, for no reason, does not blow hot air. If this has been happening it is likely that your car engine has been overheating and causing sludge to build up in the top half of the engine. Ultimately your engine will fail with very little warning. Some symptoms are: car starts to burn oil, very light traces of white smoke from exhaust, and the engine may seem to run a little rough at idle.

Cost for repairs averages $6,500 (U.S.). Two excellent websites that cover this problem from both a Canadian and an American perspective are *www.intrepid horrorstories.blogspot.com/2003_11_01_archive.html* (Dodge Intrepid Owner? Read This!) and *www.autosafety.org/article.php?did=961&scid=122*. Interestingly, Mercedes-Benz settled a class action lawsuit for $32 million (U.S.) over engine sludge breakdowns affecting its 1998–2001 lineup of luxury cars. See *www.legal newswatch.com/news_182.html*. • Engine rod bearing failure. • Chronic stalling, engine surging, and sudden, unintended acceleration. • Many reports of sudden transmission failures, often because of cracked transmission casings. • Transmission fluid leakage caused by defective transmission casing bolt. • Gas fumes enter the interior. • Windshields are often distorted and may fall out while vehicle is underway. • A high rear windowsill obstructs rear visibility. • Headlights may be too dim for safe motoring, may cut out completely, or may come on by themselves. • Both ABS and non-ABS brakes perform poorly, resulting in excessively long stopping distances or the complete loss of braking ability. • Brake rotors rust prematurely and warp easily, and pads have to be changed every 15,000 km. • Overhead digital panel is distracting and forces you to take your eyes from the road. • Emergency brake pedal catches pant cuffs and shoelaces as you enter and exit the vehicle. **All models: 2000–01**—Transmission won't shift to Reverse, and engine stalls. • Side seat belts don't retract. • Front and rear windshields distort view; there may be an annoying reflection on the inside of the windshield, particularly evident on vehicles with beige interiors. **2002**—Yikes! Transmission malfunctions continue unabated. • Steering drifts; sometimes takes undue effort or squeaks and clunks. • Seat belt button is too sensitive; belt is easily unlatched inadvertently. **2005**—Safety-related complaints archived by NHTSA are far more numerous than one can accept. Owner complaints for 2005 model year vehicles include burns from the seat heater; premature tire wear; chronic stalling and hard starting (especially in vehicles with the Hemi engine); automatic transmission failures; a transmission that hesitates, then slams into gear; steering that freezes or breaks in low temperatures; stabilizer bar separation; persistent electrical shorts; lights that suddenly shut off; a horn that doesn't work; pulling to the right while driving (the camber bolt service bulletin fix doesn't help); and a rear hatch that seizes shut so that the owner has to crawl through the back of the vehicle to open it. Sudden acceleration with the Hemi engine is particularly common among these more recently reported incidents:

> I have a new 2005 Dodge Magnum. The car has the 5.7L Hemi motor. My wife cranked the car and put it in reverse. She then depressed the accelerator and the engine did not respond with any rpm change until the accelerator pedal was depressed in excess of 50%. When the engine did respond, it was violent, causing the car to spin tires and accelerate backward at a high rate of speed, hitting another car in our driveway. This has happened about 6 times and actually happened while the insurance appraiser was in the car.... I have posted this problem on a Dodge talk forum and am finding additional people with very similar problems.

2006—Fire ignited in the wiring harness and in the trunk. • Seat warmer burned driver's back. • Sudden acceleration when taking off from a stop. • Constant stalling. • Shifter replaced because it wouldn't go into Drive (a "goodwill" repair). • Automatic transmission slams into gear. • Faulty tie rod caused excessive front-end shake. • Vehicle rolled away when parked with emergency brake applied. • Brake rotors warped. • Original-equipment Goodyear tires wore out after only two years of use; Vogue tires have side wall cracks. **2007**—Many drivers report their vehicle suddenly stalls or surges while cruising on the highway. • Hard downshifts. • Air intake is poorly designed and will suck water into the engine. • Excessive torque converter shudder. • Continental tire-tread separation. • Water leaks from the rear windshield area. • Tail light, fuse failures:

> I am a master technician in the state of Calif. I have worked on Chrysler for 16 years. What burns me is this particular manufacturer uses a system called Star to hide defects from becoming full recalls to avoid cost. I am complaining about all Dodge, Chrysler 300, Magnum, Charger 3.5L models. The rear license plate harness retainer clip above the oversize 3.5L muffler comes loose and the two wire harness melts to the muffler and causes parklight/taillamp failure. The consumer will attempt in desperation to install fuses of a larger amp causing a major meltdown of the fusebox (wire domino of one wire in the fusebox melts to other sources). Well, I complained and was told to shut up by Chrysler!!! I've seen six [other] cases.

• Doors close without warning. • Limo conversions may be unsafe:

> When is NHTSA going to look into the extra long limousine conversions being completed on the Chrysler 300 and Dodge Charger cars? Chrysler does not offer a limo conversion chassis like Lincoln and Cadillac. The axles, wheels, tires and brakes are seriously overloaded based on the federal door labels.... Operators are experiencing premature front end component failures and excessive tire wear. Does someone have to die before this industry practice is reviewed?

300M: **1999**—Airbags suddenly deploy for no reason. • Transmission jumps from Park to Reverse with engine running. • One driver's son took shifter out of Park without key in ignition, and vehicle rolled down a hill. **2001**—Unstable driver's seat. • Fuel tank easily overflows. **2002**—Brake failure, then engine surges. • Sunroof explodes. • Right front wheel disconnects from vehicle. **2003**—Sudden brake and automatic transmission failures. • Surging when stopped. • Rear visibility compromised by narrow rear windows. **2004**—Automatic rear-view mirror operates erratically. • Trunk collects water, interferes with spare-tire access. • Premature wearout of Continental and Goodyear tires. • Transmission failure; the car suddenly downshifts to First gear while the vehicle is underway. • Bolts fall from the driveshaft. • Many complaints that the car always pulls to the right. • Seat belts do not restrain a child safety seat sufficiently. • Passenger-side airbag is disabled when an average-sized passenger sits in the seat. • Rear windows won't go down.

All models/years: A rotten-egg odour coming from the exhaust is probably caused by a malfunctioning catalytic converter; this problem is covered by Chrysler's original warranty and by the emissions warranty. Don't take no for an answer. The same advice goes for all the squeaks and rattles and the water and air leaks that afflict these vehicles: Don't let Chrysler or the dealer pawn these problems off as maintenance issues. They're all due to factory-related defects and should be covered for at least five to seven years. • Paint delamination, peeling, or fading. **All models: 1993–2000**—If the vehicle leads or pulls at highway speeds, TSB #02-16-99 suggests a whole series of countermeasures, including replacing the engine mounts, if necessary. • Loose or noisy steering may be corrected by servicing the inner tie-rod bushings or by simply replacing the tie rod. • Harsh, erratic, or delayed transmission shifts can be corrected by replacing the throttle position sensor (TPS) with a revised part. **1998–2004**—Remedy for a 3.5L engine that stumbles or misfires (TSB #09-002-03). • Rear headliner sags or rattles. • Erratic AC operation. **2000–04**—Fuel tank slow to fill; this has been a chronic problem affecting five model years. **2001**—Troubleshooting automatic transmission surge and sag and shift bump complaints (TSB #18-007-01). **2002**—Transaxle limp-in; engine misfire; engine no-start. **2002–04**—Vehicles equipped with a 3.5L engine that has a rough idle when cold may need the PCM recalibrated or replaced, a free service under the emissions warranty (TSB #18-042-03). **2003**—Engine stumbling or misfire. • Defective PCM. • Delayed or temporary loss of transmission engagement after initial start-up. • Transmission goes into "limp home" mode. • Harsh 4–3 downshift. • Headliner sag or rattle. • Front brake noise or pulsation. • Poor AC performance. • Rear strut squeaks. • Wind noise from sunroof or B-pillar when driving. **2003–04**—Harsh downshifts. • Poor transmission shifting:

AUTOMATIC TRANSMISSION DELAYED ENGAGEMENT	
BULLETIN NO.: 21-007-04	DATE: MAY 11, 2004

OVERVIEW: This bulletin involves replacing the front pump assembly in the transmission and checking the Transmission Control Module (TCM) for the latest software revision level.

2004 Pacifica; 2003–04 Sebring Convertible/Sebring Sedan/Stratus Sedan; 2003 Liberty; 2003–04 300M/Concorde/Intrepid; 2003 Neon/SX2.0; 2003 PT Cruiser; 2003 Town & Country/Caravan/Voyager; 2003 Wrangler

2005–06—Hard starts with the V6. • Automatic transmission 1–2 upshift shudder or rough shift. • Transfer case shudder on slow-speed turns. • Transmission shudder or buzz due to water contamination; torque converter may require replacement. • Inoperative power-steering tilt. • Sunroof glass not flush with roof; will not close. • Sunroof rattles. • Upper windshield buzz, hum. • Headliner sags. • Gap between rear fascia and body side tail light. • Loose body cladding. • Poor radio reception with the defroster on. **2005–07**—Dash squeak, rubbing sound. • Sunroof rattles. • Inoperative window "express up" feature. **2005–08**—Steering pulls to one side. **2006–07**—Drivetrain ping noise when shifting. • Water leaks from the A-pillar area. **2006–08**—Horizontal paint surface etching. • Exterior light lens fogging. **2007**—Torque converter shudder. • Oil Pressure light on intermittently. **2007–08**—AC won't come on when engine is started.

300, 300C, 300M, CHARGER, CONCORDE, INTREPID, LHS, MAGNUM, SRT8 PROFILE

	1999	2000	2001	2002	2003	2004	2005	2006	2007
Cost Price ($)									
300	—	—	—	—	—	—	29,995	30,225	30,785
300C	—	—	—	—	—	—	43,095	43,595	44,190
300M	39,150	39,675	40,900	39,900	40,335	40,910	—	—	—
Charger	—	—	—	—	—	—	—	27,635	28,370
Concorde	27,635	28,115	28,485	29,690	30,240	30,775	—	—	—
Intrepid	25,060	25,520	25,910	25,765	25,095	25,615	—	—	—
LHS	41,150	41,370	41,655	—	—	—	—	—	—
Magnum	—	—	—	—	—	—	27,995	28,135	28,800
SRT8	—	—	—	—	—	—	—	44,790	45,690
Used Values ($)									
300 ▲	—	—	—	—	—	—	8,500	11,000	13,000
300 ▼	—	—	—	—	—	—	7,500	9,500	11,500
300C ▲	—	—	—	—	—	—	14,500	18,000	21,000
300C ▼	—	—	—	—	—	—	13,000	16,500	19,000
300M ▲	3,500	4,000	4,500	5,000	6,000	7,500	—	—	—
300M ▼	3,000	3,500	4,000	4,500	5,500	6,000	—	—	—
Charger ▲	—	—	—	—	—	—	—	11,000	12,000
Charger ▼	—	—	—	—	—	—	—	9,500	11,000
Concorde ▲	3,000	3,500	4,000	4,500	5,500	6,500	—	—	—
Concorde ▼	2,500	3,000	3,500	4,000	5,000	5,500	—	—	—
Intrepid ▲	3,000	3,500	4,000	5,000	5,500	6,500	—	—	—
Intrepid ▼	3,000	3,000	3,500	4,500	5,000	6,000	—	—	—
LHS ▲	3,000	3,500	4,000	—	—	—	—	—	—
LHS ▼	2,500	3,000	3,500	—	—	—	—	—	—
Magnum ▲	—	—	—	—	—	—	8,000	9,500	10,500
Magnum ▼	—	—	—	—	—	—	7,000	8,000	9,000
SRT8 ▲	—	—	—	—	—	—	—	19,500	24,500
SRT8 ▼	—	—	—	—	—	—	—	18,000	22,000
Reliability	1	1	2	2	2	2	2	2	2
Crash Safety (F)	4	4	4	4	4	4	5	5	5
300M	—	—	3	3	3	4	—	—	—
Side	4	4	4	4	4	4	4	4	4
IIHS Side	—	—	—	—	—	—	1	1	1
Offset	—	3	3	3	3	3	5	5	5
LHS/300M	1	1	3	3	3	3	—	—	—
Head Restraints									
300/Magnum	—	—	—	—	—	—	1	1	1

300M (F)	2	—	2	1	1	1	—	—	—
300M (R)	1	—	—	—	—	—	—	—	—
Intrepid (F)	—	2	4	4	4	4	—	—	—
Intrepid (R)	—	—	—	3	3	3	—	—	—
LHS	2	—	3	—	—	—	—	—	—
Rollover Resistance									
300/Magnum	—	—	—	4	4	4	4	4	4
300M	—	—	—	4	4	4	—	—	—
Concorde	—	—	—	—	5	5	—	—	—
Intrepid	—	—	—	—	5	5	—	—	—

Note: All these vehicles are practically identical and should have similar crashworthiness scores, even though not every model was tested in each year.

Ford

COUGAR, THUNDERBIRD ★★

RATING: Below Average (2003–05); Not Recommended (1999–2002). Flashy, but not one of Ford's better ideas from a reliability and performance perspective. The early rear-drives (1985–97) improved over the years; however, the 1999–2002 front-drive iterations carry the deficiencies of all of Ford's front-drives. As a first-year vehicle, the 1999 Cougar saw quality control decline even more. As for the resurrected 2003–05 Thunderbird's low rating, it has little to show for its high price tag in the performance department. **"Real" city/highway fuel economy:** *3.8L:* 12.7/8.4 L/100 km. *4.6L 8-cylinder:* 13.6/8.6 L/100 km. *2004 Thunderbird 3.9L:* 14.0/9.4 L/100 km. Owners report fuel savings may undershoot these estimates by at least 15 percent, or by 20 percent for the 2004 model. **Maintenance/Repair costs:** About average, and most repairs aren't dealer-dependent. **Parts:** Moderately priced (independent suppliers sell for much less) but getting hard to find. **Extended warranty:** Yes, for the front drives. **Best alternatives:** GM Caprice, LeSabre, or Roadmaster; and Ford's early Cougar, T-Bird, or Crown Victoria or more-recent Mercury Grand Marquis.

 ## Strengths and Weaknesses

These are no-surprise, average-performing, two-door rear-drive luxury cars that have changed little over the years. Handling and ride are far from perfect, with considerable body lean and rear-end instability when taking curves at moderate speeds or on wet roadways.

Overall reliability of these models has been average, as long as you stay away from the turbocharged 4-cylinder engine and watch out for 3.8L V6 engine head gasket failures and automatic transmission glitches.

True, these cars offer lots of power, but excessive noise and expensive repairs are the price you pay when they're pushed too hard. Front suspension components wear out quickly, as do power-steering rack seals. Owners of recent models have complained of ignition module defects, electrical system bugs, premature front brake repairs, steering-pump hoses that burst repeatedly, erratic transmission performance, early AC failures, defective engine intake manifolds, numerous squeaks and rattles, faulty heater fans, and failure-prone power-window regulators.

VEHICLE HISTORY: *Thunderbird:* **2002**—A new Thunderbird debuts. **2003**—28 more horses for the 3.9L V8 (280 hp); the 5-speed automatic is offered with optional manual-shift capability; and the instrument cluster is upgraded. **2004**—Revised interior trim, restyled wheels, and a new garage-door opener. *Cougar:* **1999**—First year on the market. **2000**—Interior trunk release handle. No more driver-door map pockets. **2001**—Interior and exterior styling revisions.

1999–2002 Cougar

A Not Recommended vehicle, the Cougar's best attributes are its attractive styling and pleasant handling. However, owners have to accept mediocre acceleration with the base models; problematic transmission performance; a narrow, claustrophobic interior for a four-seater; limited rear seatroom; obstructed rear visibility; an ugly and superfluous trunk-lid spoiler; and excessive interior noise.

The front-drive Cougar, restyled as a hatchback, is equipped with a 16-valve, 125 hp 2.0L inline-four or a 24-valve, 170 hp 2.5L V6, later replaced with an upgraded 200 hp powerplant, and optional ABS and side airbags. It shares the Contour's chassis (with 2.5 cm added), base 4-banger, and V6, but its suspension and steering are much tighter. Emergency handling is acceptable, but it's not in the same league as Japanese sedans. The firm suspension and quick, responsive steering make the Cougar both nimble and stable when cornering under speed, especially with the optional Sport Group's rear disc brakes and larger wheels (you'll have to put up with a harder, noisier ride, though). The car is also quite peppy around town, with a good amount of low-end torque. Braking is also good, with little fading after successive stops.

Owner-reported problems include chronic engine stalling; automatic transmission failures accompanied by slipping or hunting during the 1–2 shift; humming and clanking noises; a manual transmission that's hard to shift from one gear to another; electrical glitches; an engine that increases rpm when shifting; chronic stalling, rough running, and hard starts; premature front and rear brake wear with a low grinding noise or squeak when the brakes are applied; a misaligned trunk lid; sunroof, door, and side-window jamming; door latch failures; doors that lock and unlock themselves; faulty driver-side door weather stripping that produces excessive wind noise; and water leakage into the interior (be wary of car washes).

2002–05 Thunderbird

After a brief hiatus, the Thunderbird name returned for the 2002 model year, affixed to a $51,550 retro-styled two-seater rear-drive convertible that looks nothing like its 1955–57 namesake or the $25,095 '97 model it replaced (now worth $3,500–$4,000). This T-Bird shares variations of the engine and chassis used by the Lincoln LS and Jaguar S-Type as well as their 5-speed automatic transmission. Power is supplied by a retuned 280 hp 3.9L V8.

The car is way overpriced. Sure, owners got lots of bells and whistles for their $50,000, but other cars offer just as much for far less money. Second, this is one dull-looking luxury roadster with few features that distinguish it from half a dozen cheaper imports in the same genre. Other minuses: a tiny, shallow trunk; a cheap-looking, boring instrument panel; limited headroom; an unwieldy folding top cover; and excessive air turbulence when driven with the top down. Ford wants you to believe that the new Thunderbird iteration is true to the heritage of its classic forebears and represents good value for your money. Unfortunately, this Thunderbird proves just the opposite. Head restraints are rated Poor by IIHS, the official launch and delivery was delayed several times because of factory-related problems, the base manufacturer's suggested retail price was double what the original Thunderbird cost, and the car was discontinued in 2005.

 ## Safety Summary

All models/years: Airbags fail to deploy. • Inadvertent airbag deployment. • Transmissions are noisy, won't shift properly, and often won't shift at all. • Frequent reports of sudden brake failures, front brake rotor warpage, and noisy brakes. • Brake pedal sinks below the accelerator pedal level, causing driver to depress the accelerator. • Power-window regulator failures. • Electric door locks are failure-prone. • Speedometer and fuel gauge work erratically. • Horn is hard to activate. *Cougar:* **1999–2000**—Faulty sunroofs. **2000–01**—Broken stabilizer-bar bracket allows wheel to drop under car. • Intermittent brake failure. • Automatic transmission hesitates as it hunts for the correct gear and then shifts with a jerk. • Faulty seal causes fuel-tank leakage. • Fuel smell in the interior comes in through the vents; fuel also leaks onto the ground. • Engine hangs in higher rpm when foot is taken off the gas pedal and clutch is depressed. • Lights flicker; loss of all electrical power. • Headlight failures. • Key won't work in the ignition. • Hard to find a child safety seat that fits in the rear. • The silly, nonfunctional rear spoiler is distracting and cuts rearward vision. **2001**—Engine compartment fire ignites while in traffic. • Brake lights often fail. **2002**—Gas fumes seep into the cabin. • Chronic stalling. • Transmission fails. • Frequent failure of the sway bar bushing. • When brakes are applied, vehicle hesitates, then car surges forward. • Fuel-pump failures; incorrect fuel gauge reading. *Thunderbird:* **2002**—Water leaks onto the airbag housing. • Frequent stalling, especially when making a left turn. • Driver's seat belt fails to release. • Sun visor can't be tilted toward the driver or passenger. • Convertible top flies up while car is underway. **2003**—Erratic shifting. • Transmission failure. • ABS failure; vehicle hops all over the road. • Front brake caliper comes off and locks wheel up. • Vehicle accelerates when brakes are applied. **2004**—Several reports of sudden acceleration accompanied by loss of brakes. • Passenger-side rear airbag deploys for no reason, burning passenger. • Brake and accelerator pedals are mounted too close together. **2005**—Airbag deploys for no reason.

Ꞩecret Warranties/Internal Bulletins/Service Tips

All models/years: Ford's "goodwill" warranty extensions cover engine and transmission breakdowns up to about seven years. There's nothing like a small claims court action to focus Ford's attention. The same advice applies if you notice a rotten-egg odour coming from the exhaust. **All models: 1993–2000**—Brake vibration diagnosis and correction. **1993–2002**—Paint delamination, peeling, or fading. **1999–2002**—Harsh, delayed upshifts. • Repeated failure of the heater core. • There's a 10-year secret warranty on fuel pumps. **2000–07**—Aluminum body panels may be afflicted by early corrosion. **2002–05**—Engine misfire may be caused by water in the coil on plug (COP) or the coil wells. • Hard starting or low battery. • Water leaks from convertible top. • Cracked brake lever boot. • Heater core leakage. *Cougar:* **1999**—Three bulletins target automatic transmission failures, suggesting that either the Overdrive/Reverse ring gear be replaced or an upgraded transaxle assembly be installed. **1999–2000**—Engine knock. • An exhaust sulfur odour evident just after highway cruising may signal the need to replace the catalytic converter. • Automatic transmission fluid leaks. • Water leaks and wind noise troubleshooting tips. **1999–2001**—No forward gear. **2000**—Low Engine Coolant light on for no apparent reason. • Automatic transmission fluid leakage. • Water leak or wind noise at the upper corner of the B-pillar. *Thunderbird:* **2003**—No-starts; discharged battery. • Harsh shifting. **2003–05**—Steering noise, vibration. **2004**—Rough-running, misfiring engine. • Harsh shifts. • Driveline vibration. • Rear brake squealing. **2004–05**—Harsh, delayed shifts continue to plague these cars. **2005**—Engine knock, ticking.

COUGAR, THUNDERBIRD PROFILE

	1999	2000	2001	2002	2003	2004	2005
Cost Price ($)							
Cougar	19,995	20,595	23,655	26,995	—	—	—
T-Bird	—	—	—	51,550	56,615	56,775	56,775
Used Values ($)							
Cougar ▲	3,500	4,000	4,500	6,000	—	—	—
Cougar ▼	3,500	3,500	4,000	4,500	—	—	—
T-Bird ▲	—	—	—	15,000	17,000	19,000	21,500
T-Bird ▼	—	—	—	14,000	15,500	18,000	19,500
Reliability	2	2	2	2	2	3	3
Crash Safety (F)	—	—	—	4	—	4	4
Side	—	—	3	5	—	5	5
Cougar	—	—	3	3	—	—	—
Rollover Resistance	—	—	—	—	—	5	5

RATING: Average (1999–2007). Downgraded from Recommended to Average during the past decade because powertrain failures and other safety-related deficiencies are on the rise. Yet, dollar for dollar, these are good choices, particularly now that high gas prices are stampeding owners into selling their large cars at rock-bottom prices. **"Real" city/highway fuel economy:** 13.9/8.7 L/100 km. Owners report fuel savings may undershoot this estimate by about 20 percent. **Maintenance/ Repair costs:** Average, but some electronic repairs can be carried out only by Ford dealers. **Parts:** Average parts costs (independent suppliers sell for much less), but they're not hard to find. **Extended warranty:** Yes, invest in an extended powertrain warranty. **Best alternatives:** Think seriously about getting a down-sized SUV, like the Honda CR-V, Hyundai Tucson, and Toyota RAV4.

Strengths and Weaknesses

These rear-drive cars are especially well suited to seniors, who will appreciate the roomy interiors and convenience features (although entry and exit may require some acrobatics). The high crash protection scores and ease of servicing are also major advantages. Handling, though, is mediocre and can be downright scary on wet roads, where the car can quickly lose traction and fishtail out of control.

Both the 4.6L and 5.0L V8s provide adequate, though sometimes sluggish, power, with most of their torque found in the lower gear ranges. The Lincoln Town Car shares the same components and afflictions as the Crown Vic and Grand Marquis.

As is the case with most full-sized sedans, high insurance premiums and fuel costs have walloped the resale value of both models, making these cars incredibly good used buys. The only caveat is to make sure the undercarriage, powertrain, electronics, and brakes are in good shape before you ink a deal.

VEHICLE HISTORY: 2000—An emergency trunk release, user-friendly child safety seat anchorages, and an improved handling package for quicker acceleration. Last model year for the Crown Victoria in Canada (except for police or commercial fleets), as the Grand Marquis continues alone. *Grand Marquis:* **2001**—A small horsepower boost, minor interior improvements, adjustable pedals, seat belt pre-tensioners, and improved airbag systems. **2002**—Traction control to offset the car's notoriously poor wet-weather traction. **2003**—A revised frame and upgraded suspension, plus the debut of a high-performance Marauder equipped with a 302 hp V8, sport suspension, and exclusive trim. **2006**—Not much new, except for a restyled grille, front fascia, headlights, and different interior trim.

A number of factory-related problems appear year after year. These include failure-prone fuel-pump, sender, fuel-filter, and fuel-hose assemblies; ignition module and fuel cut-off switch malfunctions that cause hard starting and frequent stalling; brakes (rotors, calipers, and pads), shock absorbers, and springs that wear out more quickly than they should; and chronic front suspension noise when passing over small bumps. Inadequate inner fender protection allows road salt to completely cover engine wiring, brake master cylinder, and suspension components; therefore, frequent inspection and cleaning is required. Hubcaps frequently fall off. Finally, there is such a high number of safety-related complaints concerning brake and fuel lines, the suspension, and steering components that an undercarriage inspection is a prerequisite to buying models three years old or older. Other annoying body defects include poor fit and finish, trunk leaks, subpar interior materials, and flimsy plastic trim.

Safety Summary

All models/years: From 1991 to the present, Ford has known that the fuel tanks on these cars are easily punctured in a rear-end accident. Unfortunately, the company has not seen fit to recall the vehicles, even after losing a $43 million lawsuit for the death of the owner of a Lincoln Town Car that burst into flames after being rear-ended. • Fuel line and electrical fires. • Sudden, unintended acceleration. • Cracked intake manifolds cause loss of coolant. • Airbags fail to deploy, or deploy for no reason. • ABS brake failures. • Premature brake rotor warpage and pad wearout cause excessive brake noise (grinding), vibration, and extended stopping distances:

> Fleet of 15 police cars, Crown Victoria had the front brake, rotors, and pads replaced every 20,000 miles [32,000 km].

• Brake and accelerator pedals mounted too close together. **All models: 2001—** When the car is driven in rainy weather, water gets into the engine compartment, causing the water pump to throw the fan belt and leading to loss of control of the vehicle. • Frequent complaints of little traction on wet roads. • ABS failure leading to brake lock-up or loss of braking ability. • Spongy brakes sink to floor with little braking effect. • Vehicle moves forward when shifted into Reverse. • Vehicle rolls back when stopped on an incline. • Windshield wipers fail intermittently and easily freeze up in sleet. **2002—**There continue to be many Crown Victoria complaints concerning the powertrain, fuel-tank fire fears, cracked wheel rims, and poor rainy weather performance. • There are also many Grand Marquis complaints concerning sudden acceleration and the cruise control not disengaging. **2003—**Vehicle struck from behind exploded into flames. • Tire-tread separation. • Missing upper control arm bolt. • Brake booster fails. • Fan belt comes off in rainy weather, causing overheating and loss of power steering, water pump, and other accessories. • Horn "sweet spot" too small; horn takes too much effort to sound. • Sunlight causes a reflection of the defrost vents onto the windshield and poor dash panel illumination. **2004—**Transmission slips; shifts into Reverse on its own. • Excessive steering vibration may be caused by original-equipment wheels and faulty tires. • Turn signal fails intermittently. **2005—**Sudden, unintended acceleration. • Stuck accelerator. • Fuel tank punctured by road debris. • Brake pedal travel is excessive before brakes are applied. • Horn does not blow. **2006—**Airbags failed to deploy. • Sudden acceleration when coming off the highway. • Engine surges when vehicle is stopped in gear. • Foot can get caught under the brake pedal. • Floormat can get trapped under the accelerator pedal. • Faulty AC blower motor. • Digital speedometer is unreadable in daylight. **2007—**Many complaints of faulty TR414 tire valve stems that leak air. • Accelerator pedal is easily depressed when braking. • Inaccurate fuel gauge.

Secret Warranties/Internal Bulletins/Service Tips

All models: 2000–07—Aluminum body panels may be afflicted with early corrosion. • Loose leather steering-wheel wrapping. **2001—**Correcting a 3–4 shift flare. **2001–02—**Front-end accessory drivebelt slips off water-pump pulley when splashed with water (TSB #02-5-4). **2001–04—**Tips on silencing engine ticking (includes replacing the cylinder head). **2003—**Ford says rear axles "may be noisy or exhibit rear axle shaft and/or axle bearing premature wear. This is caused by excessive load, temperature, and inadequate lubrication." Ford will replace the axle bearings under dealer operation code 030505A. • Water in the headlights and erratic headlight operation. • Inaccurate fuel gauge. • Excessive power-steering pump noise. • Front wheel area click or rattle. • Anti-theft system may cause the transmission to stick in Park or the steering wheel to lock. • Defective front coil springs may cause the vehicle to have a harsh ride or the suspension to sit low in the front. Install revised front coil springs: #3W1Z-5310-EA and #3W1Z-5310-HA. • Cracked wheel rims. **2003–04—**Countermeasures for suspension squeaking or rubbing. • Excessive engine vibration at idle. • An engine knock after a cold start can be silenced by installing an exhaust shield kit, says TSB #04-2-1. • Ignition-lock cylinder binding. • AC rattling. **2003–06—**Noisy suspension air compressor. **2004—**Vehicle won't shift into Overdrive. **2004–05—**Delayed shifting into Reverse:

DELAYED REVERSE ENGAGEMENT

BULLETIN NO.: 05-2-3   DATE: FEBRUARY 7, 2005

2004–05 Crown Victoria, Town Car, and Grand Marquis
Some 2004–05 Crown Victoria/Grand Marquis/Town Car vehicles may exhibit a delayed reverse engagement, greater than 2 seconds, after shifting the gear selector lever into reverse.
ACTION: It may be necessary to replace the detent spring and adjust the shifter linkage.

• Catalytic converter buzzing or rattling. **2005–06—**Sagging driver's seat cushion. • Steering too light at highway speeds. **2006–07—**Engine overheating; inoperative cooling fan.

CROWN VICTORIA, GRAND MARQUIS PROFILE

	1999	2000	2001	2002	2003	2004	2005	2006	2007
Cost Price ($)									
Crown S/LTD	31,895	32,095	—	—	—	—	—	—	—
Grand Marquis GS	33,695	31,195	34,125	35,120	35,800	36,720	36,735	37,099	43,099

Used Values ($)

Crown S/LTD ▲	3,000	3,500	—	—	—	—	—	—	—
Crown S/LTD ▼	3,000	3,500	—	—	—	—	—	—	—
Grand Marquis GS ▲	3,500	4,000	4,500	5,500	7,500	8,500	10,500	11,000	15,000
Grand Marquis GS ▼	3,500	3,500	4,500	5,000	6,500	7,500	8,500	10,500	13,500

Reliability	3	3	3	3	3	3	4	4	4
Crash Safety (F)	5	5	5	5	5	5	5	5	5
Side	4	4	5	4	4	4	5	4	4
IIHS Side	—	—	—	—	1	1	1	1	1
Offset	—	—	—	—	5	5	5	5	5
Head Restraints	1	—	1	1	2	2	2	2	2
Rollover Resistance	—	—	5	5	5	5	5	5	5

LUXURY CARS

Cheap Luxury

Used luxury cars can be great buys if you ignore most of the hype and remember that many high-end models don't give you much more than the lower-priced, entry-level versions. For example, the Lexus ES 300 is a Toyota Camry with a higher sticker price; the Audi A4 isn't much different from the Volkswagen Passat; Lincoln's front-drive Continental uses mostly junky Ford Taurus and Sable power-trains; and the Acura 3.2 TL, Infiniti I35 (formerly called the I30), and Jaguar X-Type are fully loaded, high-tuned versions of the Honda Accord, the Nissan Maxima, and the European Ford Mondeo, respectively.

Both high- and low-end models project a flashy cachet, come loaded with high-tech safety, performance, and comfort features, and can be bought, after three years or so, for half of what they sold for as new. Furthermore, if you can get servicing and parts from independent garages, you'll save even more. On the downside, there are overpriced luxury lemons out there (such as the front-drive Lincoln Continental and the Cadillac Allanté and Catera) that aren't sold anymore and are unreliable, with hard-to-service engines and transmissions and servicing costs that rival Neiman Marcus prices.

Mercedes-Benz owners, for example, can't say they weren't warned. Almost two decades ago, a $5 million study conducted over five years by the Massachusetts Institute of Technology said that the German automaker had begun making lousy cars by committing the same assembly-line mistakes as American automakers: allowing workers to build poor-quality vehicles and then fixing the mistakes at the end. As one reviewer of *The Machine That Changed the World*, by James P. Womack, Daniel T. Jones, and Daniel Roos (HarperCollins, November 1991), wrote:

> This study of the world automotive industry by a group of MIT academics reaches the radical conclusion that the much vaunted Mercedes technicians are actually a throwback to the pre-industrial age, while Toyota is far ahead in costs and quality by building the automobiles correctly the first time.

Readers of *Lemon-Aid* know from the internal service bulletins I quote extensively that Mercedes' C-Class compacts and M-Class sport-utilities have been plagued by serious factory defects, running the gamut from powertrain failures to fit and finish deficiencies. However, a confidential January 2002 quality survey leaked to the press confirms that Mercedes' quality problems continue to affect its entire vehicle lineup.

The survey, commissioned by European automakers from TÜV Rheinland, a German auto-inspection and research association, ranked Mercedes 12th in quality control, just behind GM's much maligned Opel. You have to be European to appreciate what a slap in the face this represents to Mercedes-Benz. A few weeks earlier, J.D. Power and Associates had released an American-based study of 156,000 car owners that showed that five-year-old Mercedes vehicles had a higher-than-average number of problems (engine oil sludge being foremost on 1998–2001 models). J.D. Power subsequently lowered the company's rating for quality control to "Fair" from "Good."

Several years later, German drivers reached the same conclusion as J.D. Power and Associates. The 38,454 members of ADAC, Germany's largest automotive club, who responded to a December 2003 survey rated Volkswagen as number 31, Mercedes as number 32, and Land Rover as number 33 among the 33 brands polled regarding overall customer satisfaction.

European automakers were understandably shocked by their low quality rankings, yet they still haven't taken the quality-control steps needed to produce vehicles that can compete with Asian automakers. Industry insiders believe Mercedes' quality problems are symptomatic of a malaise affecting many luxury-car manufacturers: rushing too many new models into production and building cheaper, smaller, bare-bones knock-offs of popular models.

Traditionally, the luxury-car niche has been dominated by American and German automakers. During the past decade, however, buyers have gravitated toward Japanese models. This shift in buyer preference has forced Chrysler out of the market, has made Ford drop its problem-plagued Lincoln Continental, and has GM returning to rear-drive Cadillacs. BMW, Audi, MINI, and Porsche are the only European automakers with respectable sales.

Depreciation is your friend

Okay, so you're well advised to choose a Japanese model, but doesn't that mean you'll have to dig deep in your wallet, wiping out most of your expected savings from buying used? Not necessarily. Smart buyers can pick up a fully equipped 2003 Toyota Camry V6 for $9,000 to $10,000, or two-thirds less than what it originally cost. A 2003 luxury-class Avalon that originally sold for $47,000 now sells for $11,000. Similar savings are realized by purchasing a Honda Accord, Nissan Maxima, or Mazda6, all of which offer similar equipment, reliability, and performance to their higher-end brethren sold by Acura, Infiniti, and Lexus, but for much, much less.

Some winners

I am not a big fan of luxury cars. If I was, however, I would limit my choice to several vehicles that look good, are reliable, and can be relatively easy to maintain. For me, that would be the BMW 3 Series and the Lexus SC 430. The quality of these cars, the durability of their powertrains, and their overall performance cannot be faulted.

Older BMWs are almost all good buys, but the 3 Series stands out because it comes as a two-door, a four-door, a wagon, and a convertible, and has gradually evolved over the years. Unlike Mercedes and Audi, BMW models are consistently well built. A 2005 320i in good condition can be found for less than $16,000, and 2001 models cost less than half that. Therefore, buy a three-year-old Bimmer, drive it for four years, and then sell it for close to $10,000—you will pay a little more than $1,500 a year to own a BMW that others paid $35,000 to buy new.

The same savings can be realized in buying a Lexus 2003 SC 430 convertible, a popular luxe toy that gives you gobs of smooth V8 power, first-class build quality, and classic styling. It sold new for $85,000 and can now be picked up for a third of that price, while an equivalent model today would cost more than $80,000, including tax.

The Future of Luxury Cars

Let's face it: There aren't any American luxury cars that can match an equivalent Japanese model for overall reliability, durability, and value. And this isn't because Japanese products are that well made; far from it, as anyone who's purchased an engine-sludged Lexus will attest. No, it's simply because GM, Ford, and Chrysler vehicles are so poorly made that they make everyone else's look better. This fact has been reflected in the head-spinningly high depreciation rates and plummeting market share seen with most large-*cum*-luxury cars put out by the Detroit automakers. GM's rear-drive Cadillac DeVille and Lincoln's Town Car come closest to meeting the imports in overall reliability and durability, yet they still come nowhere near the quality level of many entry-level imports.

What does this foretell for the future of used luxury cars? Prices for American entries will plummet as the economy falters and automakers consolidate, dumping new and off-lease inventory. And Cerberus, Chrysler's majority owners, will certainly flood the market with heavily rebated new cars, trucks, and minivans. A flood of cheap off-lease cars will further cut into prices and give buyers a wider choice among imports and the American models. Finally, we'll likely see the renaissance of rear-drives, with Cadillac and Ford leading the parade, while the equity investors who own Chrysler start selling off its Jeep and Caravan divisions, and grab Fiat as a partner.

LUXURY CAR RATINGS

Recommended

Infiniti I30 (2000–03)

Lexus ES 300/330/350, GS 300/350/430, IS 300/350, LS 400/430, SC 300 (1999–2001)

Above Average

Acura RL (1999–2004)
Acura TL (1999–2007)

BMW 5 Series (1999–2003)
Ford/Lincoln Zephyr/MKZ (2006–07)

Infiniti I30 (1999)
Infiniti I35 (2002–04)
Infiniti M35, M45 (2006–07)
Infiniti Q45 (2001–05)
Kia Magentis (2007)

Lexus ES 300/330/350, GS
  300/350/430/450h, IS 250/300/350,
  LS 400/430/460, SC 400/430 (2002–07)
Toyota Avalon (1999–2004)
Volvo S60, XC70 (2004–07)

Average

Acura RL (2005–07)
Acura TL (2000–03)
Audi A3, A4 S-Line, A6, A8, S4,
  TT Coupe (2006–07)
BMW 3 Series (1999–2007)
BMW 5 Series (2004–05)
BMW M Series (1999–2007)
BMW Z3 (1999–2002)
BMW Z4 (2003–07)
Ford/Lincoln LS (2005–06)
Ford/Lincoln Town Car (1999–2007)
General Motors Aurora (1999–2003)

General Motors Park Avenue
  (1999–2005)
Infiniti G35 (2007)
Infiniti M35, M45 (2003–05)
Infiniti Q45 (1999–2000)
Kia Amanti (2007)
Kia Magentis (2005–06)
Mercedes-Benz B-Class (2006–07)
Nissan Maxima (2007; 1999–2001)
Toyota Avalon (2005–07)
Volvo S60, XC70 (2002–03)

Below Average

Audi A3, A4, A4 S-Line, A6, A8,
  S4, S6, TT Coupe (2000–05)
BMW 5 Series (2006–07)
Ford/Lincoln Continental
  (1999–2002)
Ford/Lincoln LS (2000–04)
General Motors Concours,
  DeVille, DTS, STS (1999–2007)

Infiniti G35 (2003–06)
Kia Amanti (2004–06)
Kia Magentis (2001–04)
Mercedes-Benz 300 Series, 400 Series,
  500 Series, E-Class (1999–2007)
Nissan Maxima (2002–06)

Not Recommended

Audi A4, A6, A8 (1999)
General Motors Catera, CTS, Eldorado,
  Seville (1999–2007)
General Motors Riviera (1999)
Infiniti G20 (1999–2002)

Mercedes-Benz C-Class (1999–2007)
Volvo C30, C70, S40, S70, S80, V40, V50, V70
  XC90 (1999–2007)

Acura

RL ★★★

RATING: Average (2005–07); Above Average (1999–2004). The RL's price-gouging is almost a felony. Basically, it's a fully loaded, longer, wider, and heavier TL, equipped with a larger engine that produces less horsepower than its smaller brother. Watch out for the failure-prone, notchy 6-speed manual transmission. There is no justification for pricing the redesigned 2005 version almost $15,000 higher than the 2004. Interestingly, a $54,000 2002 can be had for around $11,000. The retail price was cut almost $6,000 on the 2007s. **"Real" city/ highway fuel economy:** There's not much difference in gas consumption between the old and new V6 engines. *2004 and earlier V6 models:* 13.0/9.1 L/100 km. *2005 and 2006 V6 models:* 12.9/8.4 L/100 km. These estimates are fairly accurate, according to owners' actual experiences. **Maintenance/Repair costs:** Average; most repairs are dealer-dependent. **Parts:** Most mechanical and electronic components are easily found and moderately priced. Body parts may be hard to come by and can be expensive. **Extended warranty:** No, save your $2,000. **Best alternatives:** Consider the departed Acura Legend, BMW's 5 Series, Infiniti's I30 or I35, and Lexus' GS 300/400. Also, you may want to take a look at the TL sedan: It's not as expensive, and it's a better performer, though passenger room is more limited.

Strengths and Weaknesses

RL has good (though not impressive) acceleration that's smooth and quiet in all gear ranges, exceptional steering and handling, a comfortable ride, and top-quality body and mechanical components, and it's loaded with goodies. The steering can be numb, however, and manual and automatic transmissions are sometimes problematic.

The 3.5 RL is Honda's—oh, I mean Acura's—flagship sedan. It's loaded with the innovative high-tech safety and convenience features one would expect to find in a luxury car. These include heated front seats, front and rear climate controls, a rear-seat trunk pass-through, xenon headlights (get used to oncoming drivers flashing you with their headlights), "smart" side airbags, ABS, traction control, and an anti-skid system. The 3.5L 210–225 hp V6 mated with a 4-speed automatic transmission provides good acceleration that's a bit slower and more fuel-thirsty than the TL, partly because of the RL's extra pounds. The 2005's 300 hp V6 coupled to a 5-speed automatic (a manual shifter wasn't offered) resolves this problem. The car handles nicely, with a less firm ride than the TL, although steering response doesn't feel as crisp. Interior accommodations, which fit four occupants, are excellent up front and in the rear because of the RL's use of a larger platform than the TL's. Headroom is a bit tight, though, and the 2005's smaller dimensions may irk some buyers who don't mind sacrificing performance for extra room. Be wary of the poorly performing Collision Mitigation System and run-flat tires on the 2006 and 2007 models.

VEHICLE HISTORY: 1996—RL replaces the Legend. **1999**—Side airbags, high-intensity discharge headlights, larger brakes, and a retuned suspension. **2000**—A Vehicle Stability Assist system and upgraded side airbags. **2001**—An in-trunk emergency opener. **2002**—A small horsepower boost (15 hp), OnStar assistance, wider tires, larger brakes, and more sound deadening. **2003**—Improved child safety seat anchors, wheels, and tail lights. **2005**—A major redesign reduces the car's size but makes it more feature-laden, with standard all-wheel drive, a 300 hp V6 hooked to a 5-speed automatic, more safety and convenience features, and refreshed styling. Safety features include standard front side airbags and side curtain airbags, anti-lock four-wheel disc brakes, anti-skid control, steering-linked xenon headlights, and a navigation system. **2006**—Horsepower is cut by 10 to total 290 hp. Run-flat tires and a Collision Mitigation System.

Owner-reported problems include frequent stalling; a failure-prone, misshifting manual transmission; noisy transmission engagement and steering; malfunctioning accessories; electrical shorts; premature brake wear, and a loud, metallic-sounding squeal when braking; and front-wheel liner cracking (see *www.cbel.com/acura_cars* and *www.acurasucks.com*).

Safety Summary

All years: Early automatic transmission replacements. • Chronic stalling when accelerating. • Premature wearout of the front and rear brake pads at around 24,000 km (15,000 mi.). • Dash display is unreadable in daylight. **2001**—Transmission shifts poorly when accelerating or decelerating; vehicle stalls at slower speeds. • 6-speed manual transmission misshifts when going from Third to Fourth gear; it engages Second gear instead, causing extensive engine damage. • In cold weather, Second gear is hard to engage and produces a grinding noise. • Sometimes transmission pops out of Second gear. **2002**—Extensive engine damage caused by downshifting into Second gear, grinding. • Seat belt does not restrain driver. **2004**—Xenon headlights are blinding. **2005**—Inadequate headlight illumination:

> The vertical self adjusting headlights pose serious safety concerns on unlit roadways.... On hilly terrain, the headlights will adjust down as the vehicle starts uphill, illuminating [only] approximately 40 feet [12 m] in front of the vehicle. This also occurs when the vehicle travels over bumps and any minor changes in vehicle attitude. It is very easy to overdrive the headlights, often at speeds less than 20 mph [32 km/h]. You simply cannot see road hazards or pedestrians.

• Suspension bottoms out with a full load and damages the undercarriage. • Loose steering high-pressure hose may detach. • Faulty AC compressor. **2006**—Vehicle accelerates when the cruise control is engaged. **2007**—Sudden stall-out on the freeway (fuel pump is suspected). • Collision Mitigation System does not perform as advertised.

Secret Warranties/Internal Bulletins/Service Tips

All years: Like Honda's, most of Acura's TSBs allow for special warranty consideration on a "goodwill" basis, even after the warranty has expired or the car has changed hands. Referring to this euphemism will increase your chances of getting some kind of refund for repairs that are obviously factory defects. • Seat belts that fail to function properly during normal use will be replaced for free under the company's lifetime seat belt warranty. • Diagnostic procedures and correction for off-centre steering wheels. **1996–2002**—A guide to diagnosing and fixing intermittent electrical shorts. **1997–2001**—Master cylinder clutch fluid leakage. **1999**—A navigation system that locks up or resets can be corrected by rewriting the unit's software; a remanufactured unit may also be considered. **1999–2000**—A squeaking, creaking driver's seat is addressed in TSB #00-010. **1999–2006**—Diagnosis and correction of drift/pull problem. **2000**—Troubleshooting noisy automatic transmissions. • Moonroof rattles. • Driver-seat noise. • Steering-wheel clunk. **2000–01**—Stability Assist may activate too soon. • Engine starts and dies when ignition is released. **2000–02**—Low-speed stalling. **2002–06**—Mileage warranty extended by 5 percent. **2003**—Airbag light comes on for no reason. • Troubleshooting automatic transmission malfunctions. **2004**—Sticking fuel-filler cap. **2005**—Hot weather may cause stalling, hard starts caused by vapour lock. **2005–06**—Front brake rattle, squeal. • Defective automatic door locks.

RL PROFILE

	1999	2000	2001	2002	2003	2004	2005	2006	2007
Cost Price ($)									
Base	52,000	52,000	53,000	54,000	55,000	55,800	69,500	69,500	63,900
Used Values ($)									
Base ▲	6,500	8,000	9,500	11,500	15,000	16,500	27,000	31,000	40,000
Base ▼	5,500	7,000	8,500	10,000	13,500	15,000	25,000	29,000	37,000
Reliability	5	5	5	5	5	5	5	4	4
Crash Safety (F)	4	4	4	4	4	4	5	5	5
Side	—	—	—	—	—	4	5	5	5
IIHS Side	—	—	—	—	—	—	5	5	5
Offset	3	3	3	3	3	3	5	5	5
Head Restraints	2	—	1	1	1	1	2	2	2
Rollover Resistance	—	—	—	—	4	4	5	5	5

TL ★★★★

RATING: Above Average (1999–2007). Every year that these Acuras are redesigned, their purchase price becomes even more out of reach. **"Real" city/highway fuel economy:** 11.7/7.7 L/100 km. Owners report fuel savings may undershoot this estimate by about 10 percent. **Maintenance/Repair costs:** Average costs for the most part, but many repairs are dealer-dependent, which drives up servicing costs. **Parts:** Higher-than-average costs, but parts aren't hard to find. **Extended warranty:** Not needed. **Best alternatives:** Consider the Acura Integra, BMW 3 Series, redesigned Infiniti I30 or I35, Mazda Millenia, and Lexus ES 300, ES 330, or ES 350. Also, take a look at Acura's CL coupe: It isn't as expensive, and it's as close as you can get to the Accord, with lots of standard bells and whistles thrown in.

Strengths and Weaknesses

The TL has impressive acceleration, handles well, rides comfortably, and is well put together, with quality mechanical and body components. However, the suspension may be too firm for some, and the vehicle creates excessive road noise and has uncomfortable rear seating and problematic navigation system controls (see *www.vtec.net* (The Temple of VTEC), *www.acuraworld.com/forums, www.cbel.com/ acura_cars*, and *www.autosafety.org/autodefects.html*).

Filling the void left by the discontinued Vigor, the TL combines luxury and performance in a nicely styled front-drive, five-passenger sedan that uses the same chassis as the Accord and CL coupe. A 235 hp 3.2L V6 engine came on board with the 1999 models. A 5-speed automatic transmission replaced the 4-speed unit for 2000. The 2002 Type-S carried a 260 hp version of the same V6. From 2004 to the present, the sole engine remained the 3.2L V6, putting out 270 horses, versus 225 or 260 hp on previous TLs.

Performance enthusiasts will opt for versions equipped with the more-refined 3.2L 225/270 hp V6 mated to a 6-speed manual transmission and a firmer suspension introduced with the 2004 model. It provides impressive acceleration (0–100 km/h in just over eight seconds) in a smooth and quiet manner, without any fuel penalty. Handling is exceptional with the firm suspension but can be a bit tricky when pushed. Bumps are a bit jarring, and the ride is somewhat busier than with other cars in this class.

VEHICLE HISTORY: 1999—The 2.5L engine is dropped, and practically everything else is upgraded. **2000**—A better-performing 5-speed transmission, a free-flowing intake manifold, side airbags, and depowered front airbags. **2002**—A new performance version based on the CL Type S, a minor facelift, new wheels and headlights, and more-comfortable seat belts. **2004**—New styling, 10 more horses, and more standard safety features like head-protecting side curtain airbags. Other improvements include a 6-speed manual tranny, a sportier suspension, high-performance tires, Brembo front brakes, and a limited-slip differential (LSD).

Interior accommodations are better than average up front, but rear occupants may discover that legroom is a bit tight and the seat cushions lack sufficient thigh support. The cockpit layout is very user-friendly, due in part to the easy-to-read gauges and accessible controls (far-away climate controls are the only exception).

Common complaints involve chronic automatic and manual transmission failures (covered by a "goodwill" warranty up to eight years), the 6-speed manual transmission shifting roughly into Third gear and sometimes popping out of gear, engine surging and stalling, malfunctioning airbags and accessories, electrical shorts, premature brake and tire wear, and poor body fits. Owners point out that the window regulator may need replacing, the ignition switch buzzes, the trunk lock jams, and the rear bumper is often loose.

Safety Summary

All years: Horn is difficult to locate in emergency situations. • Airbags fail to deploy in a collision. • Sudden, unintended acceleration. • Automatic transmission failures at high speeds; grinds when shifting from First to Second gear; and sometimes fails to downshift or upshift. • Front brake rotors warp early. • Door locks operate erratically. Frequent tire failures. • Instrument panel is washed out in daylight. • It's easy for drivers to confuse the brake and gas pedals. **2004—** Erratic automatic transmission shifting. • Stability control activated right front brake, causing the vehicle to swerve suddenly. • Excessive steering-wheel shake and chassis vibration often blamed on tires, but it can be caused by a defective transmission torque converter. • Cracked alloy wheel rim caused tire failure. • Headlight low beam creates a dark/blind spot. • Multiple malfunctions with the hands-free phone system. • Windshield is easily broken. • Many complaints of hydroplaning and excessive vibration from the Bridgestone Turanza EL42 tires. • Windshield wiper washer, power-seat position memory, power mirrors, and auto-dimming mirror often malfunction due to the system's fuse constantly blowing. **2005—**Car pulls to either side when it is underway. • Severe rear brake corrosion and grooving extends stopping distances. • Premature failure of Bridgestone and Michelin tires. • Early replacement of the side window motor and regulator. **2006—**Sudden brake and steering failures. • Vehicle stabilization system and ABS fail to work in icy conditions. • Vehicle stopped, and keys couldn't be taken out of the ignition; doors wouldn't unlock. **2007—**Under-hood fire. • Clutch failure ($1,000) at 20,000 km. • Manual transmission frequently pops out of Third gear. • False alerts from the Fuel System light.

Secret Warranties/Internal Bulletins/Service Tips

All years: Seat belts that fail to function properly during normal use will be replaced for free under the company's lifetime seat belt warranty. • Diagnostic procedures and correction for off-centre steering wheels. **1999–2002—**Front, middle, or rear engine oil leaks likely caused by a too-porous cast aluminum engine block (TSB #01-041). **1999–2006—**Diagnosing and fixing a drift/pull to one side. **2000–03—**Honda extended its warranties to 7 years/160,000 km (100,000 mi.) on automatic transmissions. **2004—**A Fifth-gear vibration or drone may require the installation of a dynamic damper (Part #50207-SEP-305). • A lit ABS light may indicate that there's moisture in the sensor. **2004–05—**TSB #05-033 says you should install a #10A fuse if the windshield wiper washer, power-seat position memory, power mirrors, and auto-dimming mirror don't work. • A faulty outside temperature gauge probably needs a new gauge control module. • A clicking or popping brake pedal may have a misaligned brake-pedal position switch plunger. Turn it around so the connector lock faces the 5 o'clock position. **2004–06**—Tips on silencing front brake squeal. • Inoperative, noisy side window regulators.

TL PROFILE

	1999	2000	2001	2002	2003	2004	2005	2006	2007
Cost Price ($)									
Base	35,000	35,000	36,000	37,000	37,800	40,800	41,000	42,000	42,500
Used Values ($)									
Base ▲	6,000	7,000	8,000	10,500	12,000	15,500	20,000	26,000	29,000
Base ▼	5,500	6,500	7,000	9,500	10,500	14,000	18,500	24,000	27,000
Reliability	3	3	3	3	3	4	5	5	4
Crash Safety (F)	—	—	4	4	4	5	5	5	5
Side	—	—	4	4	4	4	4	5	4
IIHS Side	—	—	—	—	—	5	5	5	5
Offset	5	5	5	5	5	5	5	5	5
Head Restraints	1	—	1	1	1	2	2	2	2
Rollover Resistance	—	—	—	5	4	4	4	5	4

Audi

A3, A4, A4 S-LINE, A6, A8, S4, S6, TT COUPE   ★★★

RATING: Average (2006–07); Below Average (2000–05); Not Recommended (1999). *Lemon-Aid* has dropped this rating repeatedly because of these vehicles' poor wet-weather braking performance, serious transmission and engine failures, and chronic electrical shorts. **"Real" city/highway fuel economy:** *A3 2.0L 6-speed manual:* 10.2/7.1 L/100 km. *A4 1.8L manual:* 11.2/7.2 L/100 km. *Quattro 3.0L manual:* 13.5/8.7 L/100 km (this version burns a lot more fuel than the A4!). *S4 manual:* 15.8/10.2 L/100 km. *A6 3.0L:* 11.5/8.1 L/100 km. *TT Coupe 1.8L Selectronic:* 11.3/7.5 L/100 km. *TT Coupe 3.2L:* 10.9/8.1 L/100 km. Owners report fuel savings are fairly accurate for those models equipped with a manual transmission. Estimates for vehicles with an automatic tranny may be off by about 10 percent. **Maintenance/Repair costs:** Higher than average, and almost all repairs have to be done by an Audi dealer. Expect long delays for routine repairs. **Parts:** Very expensive, and independent suppliers have a hard time finding parts. **Extended warranty:** A good idea, considering how badly past engine, coil pack, and sludge problems were handled by Audi in Canada. **Best alternatives:** Acura Integra, TL, or RL; BMW 3 Series; Infiniti I30 or I35; and Lexus ES300. TT Coupe shoppers may also want to look at the BMW Z3 or Z4, Honda S2000, and Mazda Miata.

Strengths and Weaknesses

A3

Launched as a 2006 model, the A3 is Audi's entry-level ($33,800 in 2007) small car. The A3 is a conservatively styled compact hatchback with a small interior, too-light steering (be prepared to make lots of steering corrections at highway speeds), and average reliability. The base model is quite manoeuvrable and quick, thanks to the turbocharged 200 hp 2.0L 4-cylinder engine hooked to a 6-speed manumatic transmission. The AWD variant comes with a powerful 250 hp 3.2L V6, borrowed from Volkswagen, that quiets the ride and improves handling a touch while sucking up premium fuel.

Sales of the 2006 model ($32,950) were quite good, prompting Audi to boost 2007 prices almost $1,000. Fortunately, resale prices between the two model years haven't been that different. Nevertheless, 2007 models are favoured over the 2006 versions because of the fewer factory-related defects evidenced after the cars got through their first-year teething period, when product quality is at its lowest.

A4

Audi's best-selling line, these cars are attractively styled and comfortable to drive, handle well, and provide a fairly comfortable interior. But you'd better know how to separate the wheat from the chaff, since some model years can be wallet-busters due to their rapid depreciation, poor quality, and high servicing costs.

Replacements for the Audi 90 for the 1996 model year, these alphabetically named cars are conservatively styled, often slow off the mark (in spite of the V6 addition when hooked to an automatic), and plagued by electrical glitches, mechanical breakdowns, and outrageously expensive servicing and repair costs—when you can find a competent Audi mechanic. The 4-speed automatic shifts erratically (delayed and abrupt engagement), and the 2.8L V6 engine needs full throttle for adequate performance. Handling is acceptable, on a par with the BMW 3 Series, but the ride is a bit firm and the car still exhibits considerable body roll, brake dive, and acceleration squat when pushed, although acceleration times beat out those of Mercedes.

Overall quality control has improved very little over the last two decades. To this day, there continues to be an inordinate number of safety- and performance-related defects reported by owners. The automatic transmission and electrical system are the cars' weakest links and have plagued Audi's entire lineup. Normally this wouldn't be catastrophic; however, as the cars become more electronically complex, with more functions handled by computer modules, you're looking at some annoying glitches, to say the least (failure to go into gear, false obstacle warnings, etc.). Here are some other "annoyances": the transmission suddenly downshifts or jerks into Forward gear, brakes fail in rainy weather, premature brake wear and then loud grinding when in Reverse, fuel-system malfunctions that lead to surging and stalling, early lower control arm replacement, steering grinds, defective mirror memory settings, distorted windshields, and body glitches that would shame Lada. Furthermore, servicing is still spotty because of the small number of dealers in Canada and the fact that these cars are extremely dealer-dependent (see *www.audiworld.com*, *www.vwvortex.com*, *MyAudiTTsucks.com*, and *www.thetruthaboutcars.com*).

TT Coupe

The best of the Audi lineup, but still plagued by failure-prone electrical and mechanical components, the TT Coupe is a sporty front-drive hatchback with 2+2 seating set on the same platform used by the A4, Golf, Jetta, and New Beetle. A two-seat convertible version, the Roadster, was launched in the spring of 2000. The base 180 hp 1.8L engine (lifted from the A4) is coupled with a manual 5-speed, while the optional engine uses a 6-speed manual transaxle. Shorter and more firmly sprung than the A4, the TT's engines are turbocharged.

More beautifully styled and with better handling than the discontinued Chrysler Prowler, the TT comes with lots of high-tech standard features that include four-wheel disc brakes, airbags everywhere, traction control (front-drive models), a power top (Quattro), a heated-glass rear window, and a power-retractable glass windbreak between the roll bars (convertible). An alarm system employs a pulse radar system to catch prying hands invading the cockpit area.

Problem areas reported by owners include premature transmission failures and grinding of the Second gear synchronizers, early tie-rod wearout, excessive brake noise, electrical shorts causing dash gauges and instruments to fail, premature wheel bearing failures, poorly performing window regulators, steering-wheel clunks, and loose bolts that cause the subframe to move while driving over bumps and while braking.

VEHICLE HISTORY: *A4:* **1998**—Addition of the A4 2.8L V6 wagon, equipped with a 5-speed Triptronic transmission. **1999**—Addition of the A4 1.8L wagon. **2000**—A high-performance S4 joins the A4 lineup. The S4 is a limited-production, high-performance spin-off that carries a 227 hp turbocharged rendition of the old 5-cylinder powerplant. **2001**—The base 1.8L engine gets 20 extra horses; an all-new 2001 S4 sedan and Avant, featuring a 250 hp 2.7L twin-turbocharged V6, also join the lineup. Standard side curtain airbags. **2002**—A4 is totally revamped, getting a roomier interior, a 10 hp boost to the base engine, and a 3.0L all-aluminum, 5-valve-per-cylinder, 220 hp V6 engine hooked to a new 6-speed manual transmission. Other features: a more-rigid body, an upgraded independent rear suspension, and brake assist. **2003**—Addition of a convertible. **2004**—S4 returns using the A4's new design. More high-performance models and greater all-wheel-drive availability. Quattro models drop the old 5-speed for a 6-speed manual transmission. **2005**—A mid-year redesign. **2007**—S4 is restyled. *A6:* **2000**—Addition of two performance sedans and side curtain airbags (standard on the 4.2). **2001**—2.7T and the 4.2 A6 models get Audi's electronic stabilization program, which prevents fishtailing and enhances traction control. **2002**—Debut of all-wheel drive, a 2.7L engine, and adjustable air suspension. **2003**—The new RS6 debuts, equipped with a 450 hp 4.2L V8; the sporty S6 Avant adds a more-powerful V8 and sport suspension. On the downside, front-passenger seat memory is no more, and steering-wheel shift buttons are gone. **2004**—A V8 for the allroad Quattro, and a new sports model, the 2.7T S-Line sedan. **2005**—Refreshed styling and additional room and power. Wheelbase is increased and models are equipped with either a 255 hp V6 or a 335 hp V8, coupled to a 6-speed automatic transmission with manual-shift capability and all-wheel drive. Audi's MMI operating system, like BMW's iDrive, uses a centre console knob to control many of the car's accessories. All A6s now have front side airbags, side curtain airbags, and optional rear side airbags. Anti-lock four-wheel disc brakes and an anti-skid system are both standard. **2006**—A new Avant wagon and front-drive sedan spin-off. **2007**—Debut of the 435 hp V10 S6 Quattro sedan. *TT:* **2001**—A two-passenger softtop Roadster debuts; addition of Electronic Stability Program (ESP), a rear spoiler, and a 225 hp turbocharged 4-cylinder engine. **2003**—All-wheel drive now found only on uplevel models; a revised grille. **2004**—A 250 hp V6, a manumatic transmission, and standard xenon headlights (thieves will love you).

Other 1996 and later Audi models are just as poorly designed and built as the A4 and its many spin-offs. For example, the A6, a reincarnation of the 100 Series, is packed with standard convenience and safety features and is a comfortable, spacious front-drive or all-wheel-drive luxury sedan. It uses the same V6 powerplant as the A4, its smaller sibling, but has 47 additional horses. Unfortunately, the engine is no match for the car's size (0–100 km/h in 13 seconds), and steering and handling are decidedly trucklike.

The A8 competes with the BMW 7 Series and the Mercedes S-Class and loses. Equipped with a WHO 174 hp 2.8L V6 or a 300 hp V8, the A8 is a decently performing—though equally defect-ridden—buy. Its drawbacks: a high price, subpar reliability, imprecise steering, and an aluminum body that can be repaired only by an Audi dealer.

Launched in 1994 and powered by a turbocharged 227 hp 2.2L 5-cylinder engine, the S6 is a high-performance spin-off of the A6. Its reliability is mediocre at best, though its sporty performance leaves the A6 in the dust.

 ## Safety Summary

All models/years: Airbag failures. • Chronic stalling. • Sudden acceleration. • Extremely poor wet braking on later models, caused by water contaminating the brake rotor and disc; braking delay is almost two seconds. • Many cases of distorted windshields. **All models: 1999**—Vehicle will roll away even though parking brake is engaged. • Brakes suddenly lock up. • Headlights burn out prematurely and don't provide sufficient illumination. • Booming noise heard if the sunroof or any window is open when the car is underway. **2001**—Brakes fail to stop vehicle. • Headlights blind oncoming drivers. • Hood latch breaks, allowing hood to smash into windshield. **2002–03**—Frequent coil pack failures forced

Audi to pay for their replacement. **2003**—Stuck accelerator pedal. • No-starts believed to be caused by instrument cluster or steering lock/ignition cylinder failures. • Stalling believed to be caused by a defective fuel pump. • CVT hesitates before engaging. • Parking brake fails to hold. • Outside mirrors don't automatically readjust. • Ice glazes the brake rotors. • Frequent failure of the windshield wiper motor and washer. • Doors fill with water when it rains. **2004**—Stuck accelerator causes sudden acceleration. • Tire jack stand collapsed. • Convertible top failures. **2005**—Car constantly drifts to the right side of the roadway. • Car is a rodent magnet:

> At 2,200 miles [3,540 km], a headlight warning light came on, and I took my car to the dealership. I was told that a mouse had climbed into my engine, built a nest out of the hood insulation, and chewed through wires. Audi refused to cover any damages. This incident cost me $1,400.

• Vehicle hesitates for two to three seconds when accelerating from a complete stop:

> I have almost been T-boned while trying to make a left hand turn, 3 times. The car is dangerous!! I took it in to the dealer on July the 1st. They told me then that that is the way the car is designed to operate.

A3: **2006**—Engine coolant line flange failure allows coolant to drain out:

> Engine coolant line flange failure causes engine coolant to drain from vehicle. The dealer indicates that this is common on the 2.0 engines. Part unavailable in the US (on back order). The car was parked, luckily. Could have been a major expense if on the highway. Drained within several hours while parked. If this is an issue, why isn't Audi replacing this with a metal flange instead of a plastic one?

• Premature automatic transmission failure. • Wheels passed over a manhole cover, and the airbags deployed. • In warm weather, the car's fuel pump will shut off, causing the vehicle to stall in traffic. • Weak sun shade latch. • Horn may not work. **2007**—Faulty Pirelli tires howl and hum; uneven, premature wear. *A6 Sedan:* **1998–99**—During refuelling, gasoline spits back violently from the filler pipe. **2003**—Car fails to start (not coil-related, they say). • Sudden acceleration. • Airbags fail to deploy. • Numerous complaints of delayed braking; no brakes in rainy weather; parking brake failure; and premature replacement of the front brake rotors. • Sudden headlight failure. • Blue-white headlights blind oncoming drivers. **2004**—More Pirelli tire failures. **2005**—Acceleration is still plagued by engine hesitation. • Right outside mirror tilts down in Reverse gear for parking but does not go back to normal until the vehicle is up to speed in Second gear. Result: No mirror while entering traffic. *TT Coupe:* **2000**—Engine compartment howling or moaning heard when accelerating. • Periodic grinding of the Second gear synchronizers. • Parking brake failure. • Engine explodes following a computer malfunction. • Electrical short causes vehicle to lose power. • Fuel gauge shows full, even though fuel is low. **2001**—Defective fuel gauge gives false reading

(A6 models recalled for the same defect). • All windshields have some kind of visual distortion (anything viewed, especially straight lines, is distorted). • Central computer failure causes door locks to jam, trapping occupants. **2002**—Serious drivetrain failures. • Owners report a multitude of electrical shorts affect the radio, horn, lights, dash gauges, and controls. • Ignition coil failures. • Xenon headlights don't adequately light the roadway. **2003**—Dash panel continues to operate erratically, and gauges show false readings. **2004**—Fuel gauge failures. • Original tires may have weak side walls. **2006**—Brake failure caused a collision.

Secret Warranties/Internal Bulletins/Service Tips

All models: 2000–08—Hesitation on acceleration. *A3:* **2006–07**—Xenon headlights flicker and fail. • Inoperative daytime running lights and window One Touch feature. • Tips on eliminating brake squeal. • Dash ticking noises. **2007**—Multiple electrical failures. *A4, A6, S6:* **1997–2007**—Tips on eliminating brake squeal. **2002–03**—Automatic transmission jerks going into Reverse. **2002–05**—Bucking when accelerating with vehicles equipped with the Multitronic automatic transmission. **2002–08**—Noisy power steering. • Inoperative daytime running lights. **2004–07**—AC compressor rattling. **2005**—Cold engine stumble; warm engine stall. **2005–06**—Oil leak from oil filter housing. **2005–08**—Eliminating brake moan on low-speed turns. • Front window reverses when closing. • Inoperative sunroof switch. • Inoperative window One Touch feature. **2007–08**—Eliminating paint spots or stains on upper surfaces. *A4:* **2002–04**—Oil leak at camshaft adjuster. **2002–06**—Faulty glove compartment door. • Noisy power steering. **2003–04**—Service campaign to replace the engine wire harness. **2005–06**—Remote won't lock/unlock doors. **2005–07**—Xenon headlights flicker and fail. **2005–08**—Remedy for a vehicle that pulls to one side. • Dash clicking noises. • Headlights vibrate. **2007**—Multiple electrical failures. *A6:* **1998–2004**—Noisy power steering. **2000**—Automatic transmission goes into "limp home" mode and won't shift. **2001**—Inoperative self-levelling system. **2005**—AC whining, howling. • Fuel gauge reads empty with a full tank. **2005–06**—Rough-running cold engine. • Inoperative sunroof. **2005–07**—Cooling fan runs continuously. **2007**—AC doesn't cool. • Loose, broken control knobs. *TT Coupe:* **2004**—Front stabilizer bar upgrade to reduce noise. **2004–05**—Xenon headlight failure. **2004–06**—Momentary delay when accelerating. • Vehicle won't go into gear. **2007–08**—Inoperative window One Touch feature.

A3, A4, A6, A8, S4, S6, TT COUPE PROFILE

	1999	2000	2001	2002	2003	2004	2005	2006	2007
Cost Price ($)									
A3	—	—	—	—	—	—	—	32,950	33,800
A4	32,700	32,990	33,785	37,225	37,310	34,435	34,985	35,270	35,310
A6	48,880	49,170	49,835	54,235	51,740	51,950	59,500	62,500	62,700
A8	90,540	86,250	86,500	86,500	86,500	97,750	93,90	96,250	97,190
S4	—	56,000	57,200	57,200	—	67,950	68,250	68,950	70,390
S6	—	—	—	88,500	88,500	—	—	—	—

TT	—	49,500	50,400	50,400	48,650	49,975	55,475	55,980	—
Used Values ($)									
A3 ▲	—	—	—	—	—	—	—	18,000	21,000
A3 ▼	—	—	—	—	—	—	—	16,500	19,500
A4 ▲	5,500	7,000	8,500	11,000	12,500	13,000	16,000	20,000	24,000
A4 ▼	4,500	6,000	7,500	10,000	11,500	11,500	14,500	18,000	22,000
A6 ▲	8,500	9,500	11,000	13,500	17,500	21,500	28,000	37,000	42,000
A6 ▼	7,500	9,000	10,000	12,500	15,500	20,000	26,000	35,000	41,000
A8 ▲	9,000	11,000	13,000	18,000	23,500	31,000	37,000	50,000	61,000
A8 ▼	8,500	10,000	11,500	16,500	21,500	29,000	35,000	48,000	58,000
S4 ▲	—	10,000	13,500	17,500	—	27,000	32,000	41,000	49,500
S4 ▼	—	8,500	12,000	16,000	—	25,000	30,000	39,000	46,000
S6 ▲	—	—	—	19,000	25,000	—	—	—	—
S6 ▼	—	—	—	17,500	23,500	—	—	—	—
TT ▲	—	10,500	13,000	14,500	17,000	19,000	23,000	31,000	—
TT ▼	—	9,000	11,500	13,500	15,500	17,000	21,000	29,000	—
Reliability	2	2	3	3	3	3	3	3	3
Crash Safety (F)									
A4/S4	—	—	—	4	4	4	4	4	4
A6	—	—	—	—	—	—	5	—	—
A8	5	5	5	5	5	—	—	—	—
Side (TT)	—	—	—	5	5	5	5	5	—
A4/S4	—	—	—	5	5	5	5	5	5
IIHS Side									
A3	—	—	—	—	—	—	—	5	5
Offset (A6)	3	3	3	3	3	3	5	5	5
A3	—	—	—	—	—	—	—	5	5
A4/S4	—	—	—	5	5	5	5	5	5
Head Restraints									
A3	—	—	—	—	—	—	—	3	3
A4/S4 (F)	3	—	5	5	5	1	1	2	3
A6	3	—	5	5	5	3	3	3	3
A8	3	—	3	2	2	5	—	—	—
TT Coupe	—	—	—	3	3	3	—	—	—
TT Roadster	—	—	5	5	5	5	5	—	—
Rollover Resistance									
A4/S4	—	—	—	4	4	4	4	4	4
TT	—	—	—	—	5	5	5	5	—

Note: A convertible TT Coupe AWD will cost between $3,000 and $6,000 more than the hardtop front-drive Coupe listed above. The A3 has not yet been crash tested by NHTSA.

BMW

RATING: *3 Series:* Average (1999–2007). *5 Series:* Below Average (2006–07); Average (2004–05); Above Average (1999–2003). *M Series:* Average (1999–2007). *Z3:* Average (1999–2002). *Z4:* Average (2003–07). Sorry, but *Lemon-Aid* can't jump on the "BMW is always best" bandwagon. Sure, these models are the best performing and most reliable vehicles Europe has to offer, but that's faint praise when one considers the overall poor quality, dangerous safety-related malfunctions, needlessly complex engineering, and exorbitant retail prices. There's no reason why Bimmers should be so overpriced. Owner feedback and internal service bulletins show these cars come with a performance and quality reputation that far exceeds what they actually deliver. Safety defects that are carried over year after year confirm BMW's arrogant, "What, me worry?" attitude. Some notable examples: hesitating, surging gear changes, jammed door latches that "kidnap" occupants, and Turanza tires that self-destruct. **"Real" city/highway fuel economy:** *2.2L manual: 11.3/7.2 L/100 km. 2.2L automatic: 11.6/7.4 L/100 km. 2.5L manual: 11.7/7.4 L/100 km. 2.5L automatic: 12.3/8.0 L/100 km. 3.0L manual: 11.7/7.2 L/100 km. 3.0L automatic: 12.2/8.0 L/100 km. 5 Series 2.5L manual: 11.7/7.4 L/100 km. 5 Series 2.5L automatic: 12.5/7.6 L/100 km. 3.0L manual: 11.7/7.2 L/100 km. 3.0L automatic: 12.9/7.8 L/100 km. 4.4L manual: 14.4/8.6 L/100 km. 4.4L automatic: 13.0/8.2 L/100 km.* BMW owners report fuel savings estimates are relatively accurate for vehicles equipped with manual transmissions. Other models burn about 10 percent more fuel than estimated. **Maintenance/Repair costs:** Higher than average, but many repairs can be done by independent garages who specialize in BMWs. Unfortunately, these experts are usually concentrated only around large urban areas. **Parts:** Higher-than-average costs, and parts are often back ordered. **Extended warranty:** A good idea. **Best alternatives:** There are a number of credible alternatives to the Z Series, such as the AWD 3 Series and the Mazda6. Also look at the Acura Integra, TL, or RL; Infiniti I30 or I35; Mazda Millenia; and Toyota Avalon.

Strengths and Weaknesses

3 Series

The 3 Series vehicles exhibit great 6-cylinder performance with the manual gearbox, and ride and handling are commendable. The 318's small engine is seriously compromised, however, by an automatic transmission.

Although the 1997 models come with traction control, it is not very effective in giving these vehicles acceptable wet pavement traction. A problem since the early '90s, the rear end tends to slip sideways when the roadway is wet (much like Ford's rear-drive Mustang). The 325e is more pleasant to drive and delivers lots of low-end torque. Through 1998, rear passenger and cargo room is limited. After a redesign of the '99 models, passenger and cargo space was increased. Smart shoppers who opt for the improved 2000 models will keep in mind that rear interior room is still a joke—unless you happen to be sitting there. Various upgrades make the 2001 and later models the better choices, although safety- and performance-related failures are legion.

VEHICLE HISTORY: 1998—Given a 2.5L inline 6-cylinder and side airbags. **1999**—Improved base engines, and a more-refined transmission and chassis. **2000**—A redesigned lineup of coupes, convertibles, and wagons; the hatchback is gone. **2001**—An engine upgrade, larger brakes and wheels, and optional 4×4 capability. High-performance M3 Coupe returns with a 330 hp engine. **2002**—Entire lineup gets recalibrated steering, reshaped headrests, and an in-dash CD player. **2003**—Coupes and convertibles are restyled, along with a transmission upgrade. **2004**—Expanded availability of the sequential manual transmission. **2005**—Coupes get a sunroof (except the M3) and run-flat tires along with a tire-pressure monitor (all three items are of doubtful value). **2006**—New styling (vehicles are longer and wider than before) and more power; the much-hated, complicated iDrive is offered as an option. Debut of a premium sedan and wagon. 325i and 325xi models are powered by 215 hp engines, up from 184 hp produced by the previous model's 2.5L 6-cylinder. Wagons get a 30 hp boost. All cars come with a 6-speed manual transmission. Coupes and convertibles are carried over unchanged. **2007**—Coupes are revamped with more power (45 more horses with the turbocharged 6-cylinder), a standard 6-speed manual tranny, a larger platform, steering-linked xenon headlights that bring joy to thieves and parts suppliers, and 90 kg (200 lb.) of extra weight. Rear-drive coupes get a firmer suspension and more-comfortable seats. The new convertible has a retractable hardtop that uses a complex electronic mechanical system to open and close the roof.

Handling with all model years is still tricky on wet roads, despite the ASC+T traction control; rear-seat access is problematic; rear passenger space continues to be disappointing; and styling is the essence of bland. The engine, transmission, suspension, brakes, electrical system, tires, and some body trim and accessories are the most failure-prone components. Engine overheating is a serious and common failure (see *www.straight-six.com*, *www.mwerks.com*, *www.bmwnation.com*, *www.roadfly.com*, *yoy.com/yoy/auto/m3_failure_index.html* (2002 BMW M3 Engine Failures Page), *www.bmwboard.com*, and *www.bmwlemon.com*).

5 Series

Essentially a larger, more-powerful 3 Series, the 5 Series has made its reputation by delivering more performance in a larger, more-versatile interior. The 6-cylinder and V8 engines are somewhat fuel-thirsty and occasionally a bit noisy, but they are quite remarkable, durable performers. There is no problem with rear seatroom or cargo room with the 5 Series Bimmer. Handling and ride are superb, although these weighty upscale models do strain when going over hilly terrain if they have the automatic gearbox.

5 Series owners report numerous electrical and fuel glitches, faulty turn signal indicators, starter failures, and excessive steering-wheel or brake vibrations.

Overall reliability has been very poor with Bimmers during the past decade; engine, transmission, brake, and electrical failures lead the list of problems. Also, whenever a problem arises, repair costs are particularly high because of the small number of dealers, the relative scarcity of parts, and the difficulty of getting a correct diagnosis. Door seams, rocker panels, rear-wheel openings, and fender seams are particularly prone to rust. Check the muffler bracket for premature wear and the weather seals and door adjustments for leaks.

Owners say that premature brake wear causes excessive vibration, noise, and severe pulling to one side when the brakes are applied. The 4.0L engines are known to sometimes click, rattle, and knock due to faulty crankshaft main bearing shells or poor oil viscosity. The 3.0L 6-cylinder engines were also noted for producing an irregular clicking noise. There are some reports of water leaks through the doors.

Year 2000–07 models are plagued by cooling fan malfunctions, leading to engine overheating and fires; airbag malfunctions; a manual transmission that's hard to shift into Second gear, pops out of gear, and grinds when shifting; automatic transmission failures; steering degradation when braking at slow speeds; and front-door water leaks.

The 5 Series 2004 and later models seem to have hit a quality plateau, and the addition of parts of the 7 Series' iDrive feature is an accident waiting to happen. iDrive uses a console "joystick" knob to control entertainment, navigation, communication, and climate functions, which annoys and distracts drivers who aren't so techno-savvy.

VEHICLE HISTORY: 1997—The redesigned model is longer and comes with an enlarged V6 or V8 engine, dual front and side airbags, anti-lock brakes, and traction control. **1998**—Head-protection system introduced. **1999**—Station wagons get both 6-cylinder and V8 power, xenon headlights, memory for power seats and mirrors, a Park Distance Control that warns of obstacles when backing up, and a self-levelling rear suspension. Standard on V8 models is BMW's Dynamic Stability Control. **2000**—528i versions get a standard anti-skid system. **2001**—525i Sedan and Wagon debut. **2002**—540i's V8 gets an extra 8 hp. **2003**—A sunroof for all 6-cylinders, and a new Sport Package with the manual 540i Sedan. **2004**—Redesigned with new styling, new features, and a more-powerful V8. The 545i 6-speed is given a sport suspension teamed with run-flat tires, plus Active Steering and Active Roll Stabilization to counteract body lean. All models still come with BMW's controversial iDrive console joystick. Critics say that the iDrive takes a University of Waterloo degree in engineering to operate, plus it's a safety hazard. The 545i and 545i 6-speed models use a 4.4L V8 with 325 hp, up from 290 hp in last year's 540i. The wagon is gone. **2005**—Coupes get a sunroof, and coupes and convertibles join the M3 in getting a standard tire-pressure monitor. **2006**—Return of wagons, a redesigned M5, and an overall power increase.

M Series

Launched in 1996 as a four-door model, the M3 is a high-performance vehicle originally equipped with a potent 240 hp 3.0L engine (later bumped up to 3.2L), a manual shifter, a firm suspension, and 17-inch tires.

VEHICLE HISTORY: 2000—Return of the high-performance M5 Sedan, with rear side airbags. **2001**—Arrival of a new 315 hp inline-six, Dynamic Stability Control, and a tighter suspension (watch those kidneys), while the M3 returns in convertible and coupe formats, equipped with a high-performance 333 hp engine. **2002**—M3 gets a new 6-speed sequential manual transmission. All models are given a modified aluminum suspension, wider 18-inch tires and wheels, a new limited-slip differential, and a refreshed interior. **2007–08**—The new M3 is now available as a coupe, sedan, and convertible and is powered by a 414 hp 4.0-L V8.

Owning any M3-powered BMW is a breathtaking driving experience, but at too high a cost. Servicing must be done by the book, and it's expensive, as is maintenance on all BMWs (use dealers only as a last resort). Insurance premiums are way beyond what would normally be reasonable. Another serious problem is that M-car and Z-car reliability isn't very good; owners say most of the failures that have become legendary during the past decade are related to the fuel system (frequent stalling when decelerating), electrical and climate control systems, accessories (sound system, AC, etc.), premature brake and tire wear, and poor-quality fit and finish characterized by paint delamination and poor paint application. And don't forget that the 2001s and 2002s have a serious wallet-busting, life-endangering flaw: Their engine self-destructs and has been dubbed by owners as "The Engine of Damocles."

Z Series

BMW's first sports car, the two-seater Z3 debuted in early 1996 and was based on the 3 Series platform. Its 138 hp 1.9L 4-banger is outclassed by the competition (such as the Porsche non-S Boxster, the Mercedes-Benz 3.2L V6 SLK, and the Honda S2000), and you have to get the revs up past 3000 rpm to get adequate passing torque. The 2001 model, with its 2.5L 184 hp 6-cylinder engine, is an all-around better performer and offers more features at a fairly depreciated price.

Dynamic Stability Control, large 17-inch wheels, and Dunlop SP Sport performance tires don't enhance handling as much as BMW pretends they do: Get used to lots of steering corrections.

The Z4 is a more feature-laden convertible, equipped with an inline 6-cylinder engine and a standard manual softtop. It still carries a base 184 hp 2.5L engine coupled with a 5-speed manual transmission; the higher-end Z4 3.0i has a 225 hp

3.0L mated to a 6-speed manual gearbox. Run-flat tires, ABS, and an anti-skid system are standard features.

In 2000, BMW launched its $190,000 super-luxury Z8: a limited-production, fully equipped model with a power softtop, a removable hardtop, a body made largely of aluminum, and a 4.9L V8 hooked to a mandatory 6-speed manual transmission. The car lasted four model years; a 2000 Z8 is now worth about $50,000 in Canada.

VEHICLE HISTORY: 1996—BMW's Z3 1.9L roadster arrives on the scene. **1997**—An optional 2.8L engine is added, along with standard traction control. **1998**—Standard rollover bars and upgraded sport seats. **1999**—Standard side airbags (318Ti excepted), and a new 2.8L coupe. A 2.5L inline-six replaces the 1.9L 4-cylinder engine. **2000**—A slight restyling, and standard Dynamic Stability Control. **2001**—Debut of the Z8. Roadsters and coupes adopt a 3.0L powerplant (instead of the 2.8L), and bigger brakes and wheels are added. Also, the 2.5L engine is tweaked to unleash 14 additional horses. **2003**—Launch of the Z4, a longer, wider variant of the Z3. The Z8's last model year. **2005**—The Sequential Manual Gearbox is dropped from the 2.5i. **2006**—More power, restyled, and the addition of a new hatchback coupe. The new 215 hp 3.0i boosts horses by 31 on the base convertible. Debut of the 255 hp 3.0si convertible and coupe.

 Safety Summary

All models/years: Sudden acceleration. • Airbag malfunctions include the bag deploying inadvertently or failing to go off in an accident. • Seat belt doesn't retract properly. • Premature failure of the magnesium alloy control arms and steering damper. • Severe suspension hop when passing over small bumps. • Transmission pops out of gear. • Multiple electrical failures. • Inoperative door latches that will make you exit through the window (if you're lucky). • Poorly performing Turanza tires. **2001–02**—Cooling fan failure causes engine to overheat or a fire to ignite (see *www.roadfly.com/bmw*). *318:* **1999**—Automatic transmission failures. • Several incidents of fire igniting when high beams are activated. • Heated seats get too hot. **2001**—Defective gas pedal assembly causes jerky acceleration. *320:* **2002**—Distorted windshield. *323:* **2002**—Poor steering when braking at slow speeds. • In rainy weather, brakes stiffen as they are applied, leading to extended stopping distances. • Faulty sunroof. *325i:* **All years:** Transmission failure within five days of purchase. • Electrical system fire. • Steering column is kinked to the left. • In one case, right-door airbag deployed even though vehicle was hit on the left. • Sunroof glass suddenly explodes (several incidents reported). • Doors lock without prior warning. **2005**—Three of four Continental ContiSport tires blew out within a year. **2005–06**—When parking in an indoor garage, vehicle suddenly accelerated as the brakes failed. **2006**—When accelerating, car delays, then surges. • Fire ignited under the hood while vehicle was underway. • More Turanza tire failures. • Jammed door latch forces you to open the lock with the key from the outside:

> I was at the store when the car locks jammed. The only way to get into the car was by manually using the key. The key fob would not unlock the door. The real issue was that the only door that could be opened was the drivers side all the others were jammed shut.... This is a very common problem with this make. It['s] attributed to a faulty design. See thread...www.e90post.com/forums/showthread.php?p=3080752.... [T]he consequences are that if there is an accident, there is no way to get to passengers, also, fire situations would be deadly, submerging in water could also prove to be... disastrous. The only repair is replacement with the same actuator, but the problem is only a temporary fix. Over time it will reoccur. It is a design flaw. Employee: Kennedy Space Center Space Shuttle Program (United Space Alliance) safety, quality, and mission assurance engineer.

328: **2002**—Sudden acceleration; when accelerating, engine cuts out, then surges forward (suspected failure of the throttle assembly). • If driver wears a size 12 shoe or larger and their foot is flush against the accelerator pedal, the top of the shoe rubs up against the panel above the pedal, preventing full pedal access. • Rear-quarter blind spot with the convertibles. **2007**—Sudden acceleration as the car was turning into a garage. • When accelerating to merge with freeway traffic, vehicle hesitates and then surges. • Steering wheel locked when vehicle was underway. • Cracked tie rod. • Chronic electrical short circuits make most gauges and controls go haywire. • Key sticks in the ignition. • A blown fuse could deactivate the electronic door latches and force occupants to exit through a broken window; automatic locks operate erratically. • Convertible roof tries to put itself in the trunk when the trunk is closed. • Windshield cracks easily. • Excessive road noise and premature wear of the Bridgestone Turanza tires. Tires will be replaced free of charge on a case-by-case basis.

> I found out that these tires are not wearing properly. In my searches on the Internet, I have found that this problem has been ongoing for at least 2 years. BMW refuses to pay for replacing all the tires if you are over 10K miles [32,190 km]. My tires are wearing horribly and causing a safety risk. BMW knew of this problem in January 2007 when they issued a service info bulletin to all the dealers.

330i, 330Ci: **2002**—Side airbag deploys when vehicle hits a pothole. • Vehicle overheats in low gear; tires lose air. • Vehicle slips out of Second gear when accelerating. **2003**—Chronic stalling, rough idle. • Transmission slipping. **2004**—Airbags fail to deploy. • Constant stalling • Engine bearing failures:

> The issue is the dual VANOS unit they put into the M54 engine using [D]elrin bushings and they are failing. There is a company called Dr. Vanos that fixes this issue by rebuilding the OEM VANOS with upgraded bushings. This unit cost $500.

• Automatic transmission failure. • Transmission delays going into gear up to 30 seconds, after a cold start. • Distorted windshields. • Door locks operate erratically. **2005**—More delayed gear shifts. **2006**—Water enters through the door sills and causes the doors to freeze shut. • Turanza tire blowouts. *M3:* **1998**—Brake failure. • Chronic horn failures. • Rear-view mirror blocks a substantial portion of the field of vision. **1999**—ABS failure. **2001**—Rear-end clunking, leading to failure of the driveshaft attachment at the differential (confirmed by other complaints on *www.roadfly.com/bmw*). *Z3:* **1998**—Defective rear stabilizer bar. • Automatic transmission jumps out of gear. • Intermittent headlight and instrument cluster failures. • Rear-view mirror creates a huge blind spot. **2000**—Computer keeps engine at high revs when throttle is released. **2001**—Engine stalls when decelerating. • Exterior and interior lights dim and engine loses power when AC is engaged. • Driver's seat rocks to and fro.

Secret Warranties/Internal Bulletins/Service Tips

All models: **2001–04**—Engine cylinder head oil leaks. *3 Series:* **2000**—Erratic automatic transmission shifting. **2002**—Incorrect fuel gauge readings. • Rattling, tapping engine noise. • Troubleshooting navigation system malfunctions. • No 1–2 upshifts. **2003**—Harsh 3–2 and 2–1 downshifts. **2004**—Delayed Park to Drive shift. • Numerous malfunctions of telematics components. *5 Series:* **All years:** Water inside of headlight. • Erratic performance of the navigation system. *525i:* **2000**—No 1–2 upshifts. *M Series:* **2001–03**—After a plague of self-destructing engines, BMW put out SIB #11-04-02 in June 2003, which extended the warranty to 6 years/161,000 km (100,000 mi.) on all 6-cylinder engines, initiated a Service Action to replace key components free of charge, and recalibrated software for easier cold starts. Owner repair bills were also paid retroactively, including demands for consequential damages. **2004**—Door locks lock and unlock on their own. • Convertible-top creaking. • Inoperative xenon headlights.

3 SERIES, M SERIES, Z SERIES PROFILE

	1999	2000	2001	2002	2003	2004	2005	2006	2007
Cost Price ($)									
318ti	27,800	—	—	—	—	—	—	—	—
Convertible	45,900	—	—	—	—	—	—	—	—
320i 4d	—	—	33,900	34,500	34,900	34,950	34,950	—	—
323i 4d	—	—	—	—	—	—	—	35,200	35,600
325i, 328i	50,902	44,900	37,950	41,200	39,300	39,450	39,900	40,300	41,000
Convertible	58,900	—	52,500	52,800	53,400	53,950	54,400	55,800	56,300
330Ci Convertible	58,900	—	62,800	62,900	63,500	63,950	64,400	71,700	—
335Ci Convertible	—	—	—	—	—	—	—	—	66,300
M/M3 2d	62,900	62,900	69,800	73,500	73,800	73,950	73,950	68,900	68,900
M Performance	—	—	—	—	—	—	54,300	—	—
M5 4d	—	102,650	104,250	105,500	105,500	—	—	115,500	113,300
Z3 1.9L/2.3L	43,900	45,901	46,900	47,200	—	—	—	—	—
Z3 2.8L	52,900	54,900	55,900	56,200	—	—	—	—	—
Z4 2.5L	—	—	—	—	51,500	51,800	51,900	—	—
Z4 3.0L	—	—	—	—	59,500	59,900	59,900	53,900	53,900
Z8	—	190,000	190,000	195,000	195,000	—	—	—	—
Used Values ($)									
318ti ▲	6,000	—	—	—	—	—	—	—	—
318ti ▼	5,000	—	—	—	—	—	—	—	—

Convertible ▲	10,000	—	—	—	—	—	—	—	—
Convertible ▼	8,500	—	—	—	—	—	—	—	—
320i 4d ▲	—	—	7,000	9,000	10,500	13,000	17,000	—	—
320i 4d ▼	—	—	6,000	7,500	9,000	11,500	15,500	—	—
323i 4d ▲	—	—	—	—	—	—	—	21,000	25,000
323i 4d ▼	—	—	—	—	—	—	—	19,000	23,000
325i, 328i ▲	5,500	7,000	9,000	11,000	12,500	15,000	19,000	24,000	29,000
325i, 328i ▼	4,500	6,000	8,000	10,500	11,000	13,500	17,500	22,000	27,000
Convertible ▲	12,500	—	16,000	18,000	20,000	22,000	26,000	36,000	42,000
Convertible ▼	11,000	—	14,500	17,000	18,000	20,000	24,000	34,000	40,000
330Ci Convertible ▲	13,500	—	17,000	20,000	23,000	25,000	28,000	36,000	—
330Ci Convertible ▼	12,500	—	15,500	18,500	21,000	23,000	26,500	34,000	—
335Ci Convertible ▲	—	—	—	—	—	—	—	—	45,000
335Ci Convertible ▼	—	—	—	—	—	—	—	—	43,000
M/M3 2d ▲	13,000	15,000	17,000	19,500	22,000	27,000	33,000	39,000	42,000
M/M3 2d ▼	11,500	13,500	15,500	18,000	20,000	25,000	31,000	37,000	40,000
M Performance ▲	—	—	—	—	—	—	26,000	32,000	—
M Performance ▼	—	—	—	—	—	—	24,000	30,000	—
M5 4d ▲	—	20,000	23,000	27,000	31,000	—	—	60,000	72,000
M5 4d ▼	—	18,000	21,000	25,000	29,000	—	—	57,000	70,000
Z3 1.9L/2.3L ▲	12,000	14,000	16,500	17,000	—				
Z3 1.9L/2.3L ▼	10,500	12,500	15,000	15,000	—				
Z3 2.8L ▲	16,000	19,000	22,500	26,000	—				
Z3 2.8L ▼	14,000	18,000	20,000	24,000	—				
Z4 2.5L ▲	—	—	—	—	20,000	23,000	27,000	—	—
Z4 2.5L ▼	—	—	—	—	18,000	21,000	25,000	—	—
Z4 3.0L ▲	—	—	—	—	23,000	27,000	31,000	35,000	40,000
Z4 3.0L ▼	—	—	—	—	21,000	25,000	29,000	33,000	37,000
Z8 ▲	—	43,000	52,000	63,000	75,000	—	—	—	—
Z8 ▼	—	39,000	47,000	58,000	71,000	—	—	—	—
Reliability	3	3	3	4	4	4	4	4	4
Crash Safety (F)	—	—	—	4	4	4	4	4	4
Side	—	—	3	3	3				
IIHS Side	—	—	—	—	—	—	—	5	5
Offset	—	5	5	5	5	5	5	5	5
Head Restraints	1	3	3	1	1	1	1	3	3
M3	—	—	2	2	2	2	2	—	—
Convertible	1	—	—	—	—	—	—	—	1
Z3	3	—	3	3					
Z4	—	—	—	—	5	5			
Rollover Resistance	—	—	—	4	4	4	4	4	4

Note: The huge price difference between entry-level models and their top-of-the-line variations narrows to almost nothing after seven years. Additionally, when friends point out how little Bimmers depreciate, point to the above price chart, singling out the Z8's freefall—from $190,000 for a new 2000 or 2001 to a shocking $47,000–$52,000 as of November 2008.

5 SERIES PROFILE

	1999	2000	2001	2002	2003	2004	2005	2006	2007
Cost Price ($)									
525i, 528i, 530i	57,200	55,500	54,700	55,200	55,500	66,500	66,500	58,600	58,600
Used Values ($)									
525i, 528i, 530i ▲	9,000	11,000	13,000	15,000	18,500	25,000	29,000	33,000	39,000
525i, 528i, 530i ▼	7,500	9,500	11,500	13,500	16,500	23,000	27,000	31,000	37,000
Reliability	5	5	5	5	5	4	4	4	4
Crash Safety (F)									
Offset	5	5	5	5	5	5	5	5	5
Head Restraints (F)	3	—	3	—	5	1	1	1	1

Note: NHTSA hasn't crash tested the 5 Series; however, European crash tests have rated the 1994–2007 models Good to Excellent, and the U.S.-based IIHS has rated it Good since 1997.

Ford/Lincoln

CONTINENTAL, LS, TOWN CAR, ZEPHYR/MKZ ★★★ / ★★★★

RATING: *Continental:* Below Average (1999–2002). *LS:* Average (2005–06); Below Average (2000–04). *Town Car:* Average (1999–2007). *Zephyr/MKZ:* Above Average (2006–07). In a nutshell: Rear-drives are generally more reliable buys than front-drive versions. For example, the discontinued 1988–2002 front-drive Continentals are dirt-cheap, mediocre performers. Servicing will likely become more problematic as parts dry up and knowledgeable mechanics die off, leaving you with a garaged car that's more of a sculpture than a conveyance. The rear-drive Town Car and LS are the best choices for quality and performance. The MKZ and its Zephyr twin are competent performers that haven't yet been bedevilled by first-year production snafus. A really smart move would be to buy a fully equipped Grand Marquis or Crown Victoria, thereby escaping the luxury price penalty altogether. Then, after a few years, consider buying a used Zephyr/MKZ, or the less-expensive Fusion/Milan, if they have held up fairly well. **"Real" city/highway fuel economy:** *Town Car:* 13.9/8.7 L/100 km. *LS 3.9L:* 14.0/9.4 L/100 km. *Zephyr 3.0L:* 11.9/7.8 L/100 km. *MKZ 3.5L:* 12.6/8.0 L/100 km. *MKZ 3.5L AWD:* 13.2/8.4 L/100 km. Owners report fuel savings may undershoot these estimates by at least 20 percent. **Maintenance/Repair costs:** Higher than average, if done by a Ford or Lincoln dealer. **Parts:** Higher-than-average costs, but parts aren't hard to find (except electronic components and body panels). **Extended warranty:** Yes, for the front-drive Continental; no, for any of the rear-drives. **Best alternatives:** Acura Integra or RL, Cadillac DeVille, and Infiniti I30 or I35.

Strengths and Weaknesses

These large luxury cruisers are proof that quality isn't always proportional to the money you spend. Several designer series offer all the luxury options anyone could wish for, but the two ingredients most owners would expect to find—high quality and consistent reliability—are sadly lacking, especially with the front-drive versions. All models have poor-quality automatic transmissions, electrical systems, brakes, body hardware, and fit and finish. NHTSA-recorded safety complaints also target more front-drive than rear-drive Lincolns, with engine, transmission, airbag, and brake failures cropping up repeatedly over the years.

Continental (front-drive)

When the Continental converted to front-drive in 1988, what was merely a mediocre luxury car became a luxury lemon with serious safety-related deficiencies. The frequency and cost of repairs increased considerably, and parts became more complex, complicating easy diagnosis and repair. The automatic transmission tends to self-destruct; engine head gaskets blow; electrical components are unreliable, with intermittent loss of all electrical power; stopping performance is compromised by premature brake wear and wheel lock-up; and body hardware is an embarrassment. The redesigned 1995 Continental featured a new V8 powerplant, more-aerodynamic styling, and fibreglass panels. That redesign engendered an upsurge in complaints relative to engine, transmission, electrical system, and brake deficiencies until the Continental was finally ditched after the 2002 model-year run.

VEHICLE HISTORY: 1999—Front side airbags and a 15 hp boost (to 275 hp). **2000**—Rear child seat anchors and an emergency trunk release.

These cars don't offer the kind of trouble-free driving one would normally expect in a luxury vehicle. The failure-prone and expensive-to-repair automatic levelling air-spring suspension system makes for a stiff ride (especially on early models) while still allowing the Continental to "porpoise" because of its heavy front end. The Continental's anemic V6 powertrain is poorly suited to a car of this heft. The engine hesitates in cold weather, and the automatic transmission shifts roughly.

Mechanical defects include frequent engine flywheel and transmission forward clutch piston replacements; failure-prone ABS, electrical, suspension, and steering systems; and glitch-ridden electronic modules, causing hard starts and sudden stalling. The mass of electrical gadgets increases the likelihood of problems as the cars age. For example, automatic headlight doors fail frequently, and the electronic antenna and power windows often won't go up or down. The computerized dashboard is particularly glitch-ridden.

Other reliability complaints concern transmission fluid leakage, rough upshifting caused by a defective valve body, and inadequate air conditioning and heating.

Town Car

The rear-drive Town Car shares most of its parts with the Crown Victoria and Grand Marquis, and is easily found with little mileage and at bargain prices. Cheaper high-mileage units are frequently sold by airport limousine companies and taxi services that run the airport shuttle service. Transport authorities force the companies to update their fleet every few years, creating a flow of perfectly suitable luxury cars sold at next-to-nothing prices. The car's rear-drive configuration is relatively inexpensive to repair, and parts aren't hard to find. Nevertheless, the Town Car is still afflicted with many generic problems that appear year after year. Some of the more common problems are engine head gaskets that warp because a plastic part in the intake manifold has failed; transmission, AC, and electrical system failures; disintegrating tie-rod ends; and body hardware fit and finish deficiencies.

VEHICLE HISTORY: 1999—Side airbags. **2000**—Improved child seat anchorages, and a trunk emergency escape release. **2001**—25 horses are added to the engine; adjustable pedals; and seat belt pretensioners. **2003**—Restyled; a revised frame, suspension, and steering system; and 17-inch tires. Also new are four-wheel, fully assisted ABS disc brakes, front side airbags, an upgraded navigation system, and a 14 hp boost. **2004**—Standard rear obstacle detection system, and additional rear legroom. Executive model is dropped. **2008**—Standard navigation system is dropped.

Incidentally, Ford Canada announced on December 19, 2005, that it would pay all engine intake manifold gasket repair claims going back seven years (enter "Ford intake manifold extended warranty" into an Internet search engine such as Google). Nevertheless, this warranty extension leaves some customers in the lurch.

LS

The LS rear-drive sedan comes with a high-performance 200 hp variant of the Taurus 3.0L V6, mated with an optional manual or standard automatic gearbox. Also available is a 250 hp 3.9L V8, based on the Jaguar XK8 coupe's engine, coupled with a semi-automatic transmission. Both engines are identical, but the Lincoln produces 30 fewer horses than the Jag equivalent. There is very little difference between the 2000 and 2001 models, except that the 2001 carries standard traction control. The 2002 models came back unchanged.

The LS offers a lot for a reasonable base price. The V6 version is priced in the range of the BMW 3 Series, Lexus ES 300, and Mercedes C-Class while delivering standard equipment and interior space that rivals the 5 Series, GS, and E-Class.

Lincoln's return to rear-drive opened up a Pandora's box of powertrain, AC, electrical system, and body glitches. Owners report jerky transmission shifting, excessive drivetrain and body noise and vibrations, inconsistent braking response, and erratic AC performance. The 2005–06 models have generated few complaints. The LS was dropped in mid 2006.

VEHICLE HISTORY: 2001—Standard traction control. **2002**—The V6 got 10 more horses. Debut of an LSE version with a rear spoiler, special wheels, and new lower-body trim. **2003**—More-powerful engines; restyled; quieter running. The manual transmission is dropped. **2004**—Suspension tweaked to reduce vibration, harshness, and noise.

Zephyr/MKZ

Ford's smallest Lincoln ever, the mid-size, entry-level 2006 Zephyr was sized and priced below the rear-drive Lincoln LS that it replaced. It's essentially a luxury-equipped spin-off of the front-drive Ford Fusion and Mercury Milan mid-size sedans, vehicles that are quite similar to the Mazda6. Zephyr carries a 221 hp V6 engine hooked to a 6-speed automatic transmission, plus all of the most important safety features. Lincoln says the car can tow more than 1,600 kg (3,500 lb.). Zephyr and MKZ's competitors are the Acura TL, Cadillac CTS, Infiniti G35, and Lexus ES 330 or ES 350.

Both Zephyr and MKZ are decent performers with above-average reliability scores. Crash tests have been very good, although IIHS-sponsored side-crash results are rated as only Acceptable.

VEHICLE HISTORY: 2007—Zephyr's name is changed to MKZ—no one knows why. All-wheel drive is added, styling is revamped, and a larger V6 engine corrals 42 more horses, for a total of 263 hp (the Ford Fusion and Mercury Milan keep their anemic 221 hp V6).

Safety Summary

All models/years: Sudden, unintended acceleration; gas pedal sticks. • Sudden forward acceleration when shifter is placed into Reverse—a common theme that has affected the entire model lineup, including the 2005 Town Car. It is believed to be a software or pedal position problem and isn't confined to front- or rear-drives only. • Loss of braking. • Airbags deploy inadvertently, or don't deploy when they should. • Gas and brake pedal are mounted too close together. • Sudden loss of electrical power. • Severe pull and vibration when braking. • Brake failures caused by premature wear of rear drums and rotor warpage. • Steering control degrades or locks up when car passes through puddles. • Annoying reflections onto the front windshield. • Horn is hard to activate. • Mirrors vibrate excessively and don't adjust easily. *Continental:* **1999**—Brake line ruptured. • Headlights fail to adequately light side of the road. **2000**—Warning lights come on constantly, and car's central computer module often malfunctions. • Brakes don't work well; require extended stopping distance. • Side-view mirror can't be adjusted properly because of a design defect. **2001**—Car suddenly accelerated while in Reverse; brake/transmission interlock not connected. • Driver's foot can be snared by two console cables when going from the gas pedal to the brakes. • Instrument panel washes out in bright sunlight. **2002**—Car speeds up while going downhill with cruise control engaged. • In one incident, while in Park with the brakes applied, vehicle rolled back into another car. • Sticking, binding shoulder belt. • Plastic front air dam is easily broken:

> Damage to the engine could occur if it is not replaced, because it directs the air through the engine compartment. We have personally inspected other Lincoln vehicles and numerous have...either completely missing or damage[d] air dams. It appears this is a quick $80.00 profit for the company that could be easily fixed using softer material.

LS: **2000–01**—Lurching, hesitating automatic transmission shifting. • Brakes fail during the first five minutes after a cold start. • Brake pedal becomes hard and resists application, or turns mushy and goes to the floor. • Warning lights come on for no reason. • Defective steering causes violent swerving from side to side. • Automatic door locks engage by themselves, locking out driver. **2002**—Sudden shutdown while on the highway. **2003**—Transmission suddenly seizes. • Loss of steering due to computer malfunction. • Head restraints obstruct visibility. **2004**—Airbag deploys for no reason. • Stalling continues to be a chronic problem. • Hard starts. • Brake failure. • Harsh upshifts and gear hunting. • When accelerating, vehicle hesitates and then surges. **2005**—Fuel leak from a cracked fuel tank. • Side airbag deploys for no reason. • Sudden loss of power. • Broken wheel lug nuts. • Defective side wall (Continental tires). *Town Car:* **2000**—Vehicle suddenly accelerates when cruise control is engaged and brakes are applied. The following NHTSA report is rather typical of other, similar complaints:

> Driver was going 75 mph [120 km/h] with cruise control set. When approaching a curve, driver applied the brakes to slow down, and as brake pedal was pressed, vehicle [sped] up. Driver was coached from limousine service on a two-way radio how to control vehicle. Driver turned off cruise control switch and vehicle returned to normal.

• Inadvertent airbag deployment. • Frequent brake failures (brake pedal will fade and not hold). • Horn is hard to activate. • Vehicle pulls hard to one side when braking. • Faulty trunk light bulb ignited clothing in trunk. • Power windows fail intermittently. **2001**—Sudden acceleration when brakes are applied. • NHTSA has been looking into side-impact airbags deploying for no reason. • Frequent brake failures. • Wheel lug studs break off at the hub. • Ignition locks up when key is inserted. • Brake and accelerator pedal set too close together. • Dash reflects onto windshield. **2002**—Repeated brake master cylinder failures. • Head restraints set too low. • While driving, sunroof blew off. **2003**—Sudden, unintended acceleration. • Complete brake failure. • Brake light causes an annoying reflection onto the rear windshield. • Hood latch snapped while driving. **2004**—When key was turned in the ignition, fire ignited immediately. • No airbag deployment. • Sudden, unintended acceleration; many reports that the vehicle accelerates when brakes are tapped. • Cruise control doesn't hold the car's speed when descending a hill. • Poor braking. • Sunshine reflects on dashboard metal strip, creating an annoying glare. • Tires leak air due to faulty chrome wheels. **2005**—Engine surges as brakes are applied. • Vehicle suddenly accelerated when put into Reverse. Dealer saw no computer error code present, so ignored the problem. • Vehicle hesitates a few seconds before going into passing gear. • Due to the front seat belt's location, the buckle cuts off circulation, causing right leg numbness. • It can take up to 15 minutes to put in a few gallons of gas due to a faulty fuel-tank valve. • Trunk slams shut due to a dislodged torque rod in the closure assembly. **2006**—Car was in Park when it rolled backward down an incline. *Zephyr/MKZ:* **2006**—Windows and sunroof can be opened by the remote fob, without the vehicle being started. • Inadequate heater output. • Michelin tires lose air. **2007**—Seat belt and airbag failure during a collision. • The accelerator pedal can be inadvertently depressed when braking. • Michelin tire valve stem failures.

Secret Warranties/Internal Bulletins/Service Tips

All models: 1985–2002—Repeated heater core leaks. **1993–2006**—Paint delamination, peeling, or fading. *Continental:* **1994–99**—Tips on plugging door, window, and moonroof wind noise. **1998–2002**—Hard-to-turn ignition switch. **1999**—No Reverse engagement with the automatic transmission may be caused by torn reverse clutch lip seals. **1999–2002**—Engine hesitation, surging, and bucking can be fixed by reprogramming the PCM. *LS:* **2000–01**—Hard starts or no-starts. • Frequent bulletin references to automatic transmission defects producing delayed engagement (PCM module seen as likely culprit), driveline vibration and buzz/clunk/drone, and fluid leakage. • Trunk may suddenly open. • Inoperative AC dual zone heater. • ABS, Airbag, and Service Engine lights come on for no apparent reason. • 3.9L oil leak from the bell housing area. • Poor braking on V6-equipped models. • V6 engine noise on acceleration; highway drone noise. • Instrument panel squeaks and rattles. **2000–02**—Inoperative power windows. • Oil pan drain plug leaks. • Correction for a noisy suspension. **2000–05**—Troubleshooting engine misfires. • Inoperative defroster. **2000–06**—AC heater core leakage or electrolysis. **2001–02**—A faulty cooling fan is the likely cause of engine overheating. **2003–04**—Harsh upshifts require the reprogramming of the PCM. • An engine stumble or backfire may also be corrected in the same way. • Moisture in the Reverse tail light. • Steering gear noise, vibration. **2004**—Harsh upshifts. • The water pump hose is prone to bursting on 3.0L-equipped models. Ford extended the warranty. *Town Car:* **1995–2006**—Ford will install for free a fuel-tank fire shield on all limos. **1997–2006**—AC heater core leakage or electrolysis. **1998–2005**—Troubleshooting tips for engine misfiring. **2000–06**—Aluminum body panel corrosion "goodwill" warranty (see bulletin on following page). **2001–04**—Engine ticking countermeasures. **2002–05**—Rear axle shudder or chatter. **2003**—Premature wear of the axle shaft or axle bearing. • Erratic AC blower motor operation. • Blower motor whistling. • Inaccurate fuel gauge. • Power-steering-assist calibration; excessive power-steering pump noise. • Front wheel area click or rattle. • Anti-theft system may cause the transmission to stick in Park or the steering wheel to lock. • Rear parking-brake clicking. **2003–04**—Cold-start engine knocking. • Suspension squeaking and rubbing. • Erratic operation of the AC blower. **2003–05**—Inoperative parking assist. **2004**—Exhaust manifold to converter leak. **2004–05**—Delayed Reverse engagement. **2005–06**—Hesitation, lack of power during the 1–2 shift. *Zephyr/MKZ:* **2006–**

ALUMINUM BODY PANELS—CORROSION

BULLETIN NO.: 06-25-15   DATE: DECEMBER 11, 2006

FORD: 2000–07 CROWN VICTORIA, TAURUS; 2005–06 FORD GT; 2005–07 MUSTANG; 2000–03 RANGER; 2000–07 EXPEDITION; 2002–07 EXPLORER; 2004–07 F-150; 2007 EXPLORER SPORT TRAC
LINCOLN: 2000–06 LINCOLN LS; 2000–07 TOWN CAR, NAVIGATOR
MERCURY: 2000–07 GRAND MARQUIS AND SABLE

ISSUE: Some vehicles may exhibit a bubbling or blistering under the paint on aluminum body parts. This is due to iron contamination of the aluminum panel.

ACTION: This TSB provides service tips and procedures, outlining methods to properly prepare and protect aluminum body parts from cross contamination.

BACKGROUND: Ford's Scientific Research Laboratory has performed a number of tests on vehicle body parts returned for corrosion related concerns. Testing has revealed that the aluminum corrosion was caused by iron particles working their way into the aluminum body part, prior to it being painted.

07—Front axle clicking, ratcheting noise. • Water leak from the roof-opening panel area. • Front-seat squeak, rattle. • Underbody rattle, vibration from the heat shield. • Wind noise from the B-pillar. • Erratic AC blower motor operation. • Poor AM/FM reception with the rear defroster on. **2006–08**—Power-steering fluid leaks. • Slow glass movement. **2007**—Hesitation on acceleration. • Poor heater output at idle.

CONTINENTAL, LS, TOWN CAR, ZEPHYR/MKZ PROFILE

	1999	2000	2001	2002	2003	2004	2005	2006	2007
Cost Price ($)									
Continental Ex.	52,795	52,895	51,920	52,900	—	—	—	—	—
LS	—	40,595	40,870	42,300	42,500	43,750	43,865	50,599	—
Town Car	52,195	51,495	53,970	53,445	55,205	57,645	58,865	58,199	58,499
Zephyr	—	—	—	—	—	—	—	36,999	—
MKZ	—	—	—	—	—	—	—	—	37,499
Used Values ($)									
Continental Ex. ▲	4,000	4,500	5,500	7,500	—	—	—	—	—
Continental Ex. ▼	4,000	4,000	4,500	6,000	—	—	—	—	—
LS ▲	—	5,500	6,500	7,500	9,000	10,500	12,000	15,500	—
LS ▼	—	4,500	6,000	7,000	8,000	9,500	10,500	14,000	—
Town Car ▲	4,500	6,000	7,500	8,500	10,500	13,000	15,500	17,000	22,000
Town Car ▼	4,000	5,000	6,500	7,500	9,000	11,500	14,000	15,500	20,000
Zephyr ▲	—	—	—	—	—	—	—	15,000	—
Zephyr ▼	—	—	—	—	—	—	—	13,500	—
MKZ ▲	—	—	—	—	—	—	—	—	23,000
MKZ ▼	—	—	—	—	—	—	—	—	21,000

Reliability

Continental Ex.	2	3	3	3	—	—	—	—
LS, Zephyr/MKZ	—	3	3	3	3	4	4	4	—
Town Car	3	4	4	4	4	5	5	5	5

Crash Safety (F)

LS	—	5	5	5	—	5	5	5	—
Town Car	—	4	5	5	5	5	5	5	5
Zephyr/MKZ	—	—	—	—	—	—	—	4	4

Side

LS	—	—	4	4	4	4	4	4	—
Town Car	4	4	4	4	5	5	5	5	5
Zephyr/MKZ	—	—	—	—	—	—	—	5	5

IIHS Side

Zephyr/MKZ	—	—	—	—	—	—	—	3	3

Offset

Continental Ex.	3	3	3	3	—	—	—	—	—
LS	—	5	5	5	5	5	5	—	—
Town Car	—	—	—	—	3	5	5	5	5
Zephyr/MKZ	—	—	—	—	—	—	—	3	5

Head Restraints

Continental Ex.	1	—	2	2	—	—	—	—	—
LS	—	1	2	2	3	3	3	3	—
Town Car	1	—	1	1	2	2	2	2	2
Zephyr/MKZ	—	—	—	—	—	—	—	2	2

Rollover Resistance

LS	—	—	5	5	5	5	5	5	5
Town Car	—	—	—	—	5	5	5	5	5
Zephyr/MKZ	—	—	—	—	—	—	—	4	5

General Motors

PARK AVENUE ★★★

RATING: Average (1999–2005). **"Real" city/highway fuel economy:** 11.9/7.3 L/100 km. Owners report fuel savings may undershoot this estimate by at least 20 percent. **Maintenance/Repair costs:** Higher than average, but repairs aren't dealer-dependent. **Parts:** Higher-than-average costs (independent suppliers sell for much less), but not hard to find. Nevertheless, don't even think about buying one of these front-drives without a three- to five-year extended warranty backed by the automaker. **Extended warranty:** A must-have. **Best alternatives:** Acura Integra or RL, Cadillac DeVille, Infiniti I30 or I35, Nissan Maxima, and Toyota Avalon.

Strengths and Weaknesses

Full-sized luxury sedan aficionados love the flush glass, wrap-around windshield and bumpers, and clean body lines that make for an aerodynamic, pleasing appearance. But these front-drive cars are more than a pretty package: They provide lots of room (but not for six), luxury, style, and—dare I say—performance. On one hand, plenty of power is available with the 205 hp 3.8L V6 engine and the 240 hp supercharged version of the same powerplant. On the other hand, owners decry the car's ponderous handling, caused partly by a mediocre suspension and over-assisted steering with the base model; obstructed rear visibility; hard braking accompanied by a severe nosedive; interior gauges and controls that aren't easily deciphered or accessed; and surprisingly high fuel consumption.

Although the 1991–96 Park Avenue models improved over the years, they compiled one of the worst repair histories among large cars. Main problem areas are the engine, automatic transmission, fuel system, steering, brakes, electrical system (including defective PROM and MEMCAL modules), starter, and alternator, plus the badly assembled, poor-quality body hardware. The 3.0L V6 engine is inadequate for a car this heavy, and the 3.8L has been a big quality disappointment.

Under-hood servicing is complicated. Other problems: Automatic transmission and engine computer malfunctions are common, the fuel-injection system is temperamental, window mechanisms are poorly designed, the power-steering assembly is failure-prone, there are frequent electrical failures, front brake pads and rotors require frequent replacement, and shock absorbers leak or go soft very quickly. Extensive surface corrosion has been a problem because of poor, and often incomplete, paint application at the factory.

VEHICLE HISTORY: 1997—Park Avenue and Ultra are redesigned to include a reworked powertrain, a stiffer body, improved interior amenities, upgraded four-wheel disc brakes, and an upgraded ventilation system. **2000**—StabiliTrak stability control is added. **2003**—Ultra gets side VentriPorts, a new grille, and chrome exhaust tips.

Plenty of power is available with the 205 hp 3.8L V6 engine and the Aurora's 240 hp supercharged powerplant, if you don't mind burning the extra fuel and confronting never-ending reliability issues. The revised 1998–2005 models continue to have serious engine intake manifold and transmission problems in addition to airbag, AC, fuel, and electrical system failures. Poor fit and finish is characterized by leaks, squeaks, rattles, moans, and whines.

 Safety Summary

All years: Airbags don't deploy, or deploy when they shouldn't. • Chronic stalling and loss of electrical power, particularly when braking. • With cruise control engaged, vehicle picks up speed when going downhill. • Faulty fuel gauges. • Cracked engine head gasket. • Transmission failures. • Premature failure of brake rotors, pads, and calipers. • Windshield dash glare. **2000**—Steering may suddenly lock up. • Horn is hard to activate, especially in cold weather. • Front-seat lap belts may be too short; GM will give owners a free extension if they sign a waiver of liability. **2001**—Sudden, unintended acceleration. • Delayed and extended shifts, slippage in cold weather. • Trunk lid fell on driver's head. • Excessive dash reflection onto windshield. **2003**—Multiple brake failures. **2004**—Headlight high and low beams are a fixed unit, not allowing mechanic to aim them for better illumination.

Secret Warranties/Internal Bulletins/Service Tips

All years: Automatic transaxles on front-drive models equipped with V6 engines are particularly failure-prone. • Reverse servo cover leak. • Intermittent horn and windshield wiper failures. **1993–2005**—AC odours can be reduced by applying a cooling-coil coating or by installing a special kit. • Paint delamination, peeling, or fading. **1993–2005**—No Reverse, Second, or Fourth gear. **1995–2001**—Engine oil pan leaks. **1996–2004**—GM Canada will pay $200–$800 to cover engine intake manifold repairs. **1997–2001**—Troubleshooting steering vibration, shudder, or moan. **1997–2005**—Oil leaks from transmission vent. **2001**—Delayed and extended shifts, slippage in cold weather. **2001–02**—Poor engine performance and erratic shifting (TSB #02-07-30-013). **2001–04**—Transmission slippage, and harsh 1–2 shifts. **2002–03**—Door lock falls into door panel. **2003**—Transmission grind/growl when vehicle is parked on an incline. • Defective front outer tie-rod ends.

PARK AVENUE PROFILE

	1999	2000	2001	2002	2003	2004	2005
Cost Price ($)							
Park Avenue	41,060	42,075	43,000	43,700	45,790	47,550	47,610
Used Values ($)							
Park Avenue ▲	4,000	4,500	5,500	7,500	8,500	10,500	11,500
Park Avenue ▼	4,000	4,000	4,500	6,000	7,500	9,000	10,500
Reliability	3	3	3	4	4	4	4
Crash Safety (F)	—	—	4	4	4	4	4
Side	—	—	4	4	4	4	4
Offset	5	5	5	5	5	5	5
Head Restraints	1	—	1	1	1	1	1
Rollover Resistance	—	—	—	—	4	4	4

AURORA, RIVIERA ★★★

RATING: *Aurora:* Average (1999–2003). There was no year 2000 model. Aurora resale values have nosedived, making the 2001–03 models good buys only for owners who do their own repairs and are handy in finding parts. *Riviera:* Not Recommended (1999). **"Real" city/highway fuel economy:** The Aurora gets

13.5/8.3 L/100 km, but, interestingly, a 1999 Buick Riviera gets slightly better fuel economy, at 13.2/7.7 L/100 km. Owners report fuel savings may undershoot these two estimates by about 20 percent. **Maintenance/Repair costs:** Higher than average, but repairs aren't dealer-dependent. **Parts:** Higher-than-average costs, and some body panels and electronic modules are hard to find. **Extended warranty:** Yes; powertrain repairs alone can cost double what you will pay for an extra warranty. **Best alternatives:** Acura Integra, TL, or RL; Cadillac DeVille, Fleetwood, or Brougham; Ford Crown Victoria or Mercury Grand Marquis; Nissan Maxima; and Toyota Avalon.

Strengths and Weaknesses

Riviera

GM skipped the 1994 model year and introduced an all-new 1995 version. Overall, 1995–99 models offer many more luxury features but continue their checkered repair history (the redesigned 1988–93 cars kept the same low level of quality control as previous versions, with multiple design and manufacturing defects that haven't been solved to this day). There are still many generic deficiencies affecting the automatic transmission (torque converter constantly engages and disengages); engine, fuel, and electrical systems; computer modules; AC compressor; brakes (rotor warpage and premature pad replacement); steering; suspension; and fit and finish (surface rust and poor paint quality are the most common body complaints for all model years). Because of their problematic brakes, these cars usually have a pronounced low-speed shudder/vibration and severe pull that intensifies when passing over uneven terrain or when braking.

VEHICLE HISTORY: 1995—Totally redesigned with standard dual airbags, ABS, a 3.8L V6, and a supercharged variant. **1997**—Additional standard features and a smoother-shifting automatic transmission. **1998**—A supercharged engine. **1999**—Traction control.

Aurora

This front-drive Olds luxury sedan uses the same basic design as the Riviera but doesn't share the same major mechanical features or popular styling. Because it was a relatively late entry into the Oldsmobile line, GM took more care in the selection of mechanical, electronic, and body components. Too bad that this progress was all for naught, as Aurora folded along with the entire Oldsmobile line.

VEHICLE HISTORY: 2001—A new platform; equipped with a 3.5 V6 or 4.0L V8 engine. **2002**—GM changes to a V8.

The Aurora's main advantages are its sporty handling and unusual aero styling. In contrast to the Riviera, the Aurora seats only five and offers a 4.0L V8 derived from the failure-prone, hard-to-repair Cadillac 4.6L V8 Northstar engine. Acceleration is underwhelming (this is a heavy car) but adequate for highway touring. Road and wind noise are omnipresent, and the trunk's small opening compromises its ability to handle odd-sized objects.

1995–2000 Auroras have similar quality failings to those of the Riviera, but they're not as extensive and they generally become less common with the 2001–03 models. Nevertheless, owners of these recent models complain of engine coolant leaks, chronic electrical and fuel supply glitches, harsh shifting, drivetrain vibrations, brake failures, water leaks through the front corner moulding, and overall high maintenance costs.

Safety Summary

Aurora: **1995–2001**—Chronic stalling. • Horn is hard to access and operates erratically. • Headlights short out or come on inadvertently. **1999**—Water is sucked up into the engine when the car passes over puddles. • Power steering loses power at low speeds. • Loss of all electrical power, including interior and exterior lights. • Exhaust fumes enter interior. **2001**—Total brake failure. • Electrical shorts cause complete electrical shutdown or erratically operating interior and exterior lights and gauges. • Head restraints block rear vision. • Windshield wipers fail intermittently. **2001–03**—Loss of engine coolant. • Will not go into First gear when cupholder is extended. • Reflection of the defrost grate is very distracting to short drivers. **2003**—Vehicle suddenly accelerated when started up and put in Reverse. • Sudden loss of steering. • High headrest obstructs rear visibility. • Interior and exterior lights go out periodically.

Secret Warranties/Internal Bulletins/Service Tips

All models: 1993–2005—Paint delamination, peeling, or fading. **1995–99**—Floor pan corrosion perforation in the battery compartment can be corrected by installing a GM repair kit. *Aurora:* **1997–2005**—Fluid leak from transmission vent. **1999–2003**—Harsh shifts, chuggle (slipping), and no downshifts when decelerating. **2000–01**—If there's a sudden loss of power when accelerating, the transmission fluid pressure switch may be defective. **2000–02**—Poor shifting. **2001**—Coolant leaks. • Delayed Reverse engagement. **2001–03**—Premature hood blistering and corrosion. • Inoperative seat heater. **2003**—Intermittent no-start, no-crank condition. • Engine overheating in cold weather. • Sudden engine shutdown. • Harsh shifting remedy. • Automatic transmission grind/growl when vehicle is parked on an incline. • Poor transmission and engine performance may be caused by debris in the transaxle valve body and case oil passages, says TSB #02-07-30-013. • Incorrect First gear ratio; delayed Reverse engagement; harsh shifting upon start-up; transmission whining noise and cooling line leaks; leakage from the quick-connect fitting at the case cover; no Fourth gear, or slipping in Fourth gear; oil leakage from the oil level sensor; and intermediate shaft clunk. • Water contamination of the ABS sensor. • Broken sunroof deflectors.

	1999	2001	2002	2003
Cost Price ($)				
Aurora	46,190	39,590	40,030	46,590
Riviera	44,125	—	—	—
Used Values ($)				
Aurora ▲	5,500	6,500	7,500	9,000
Aurora ▼	5,000	6,000	7,000	7,500
Riviera ▲	5,000	—	—	—
Riviera ▼	4,500	—	—	—
Reliability				
Aurora	3	3	3	4
Riviera	3	—	—	—
Crash Safety (F)				
Aurora	3	4	4	4
Side				
Aurora	—	3	3	3
Offset				
Aurora	—	5	5	5
Head Restraints				
Aurora	1	5	5	5
Riviera	1	—	—	—

CATERA, CTS, ELDORADO, SEVILLE ★

RATING: Not Recommended (1999–2007). A defective axle/differential may make CTS a "killer" car. **"Real" city/highway fuel economy:** *Catera:* 13.8/9.2 L/100 km. *CTS 3.2L V6 manual:* 12.6/8.2 L/100 km. *CTS 3.6L V6 automatic:* 13.4/7.8 L/100 km. *2001 Eldorado, Seville 4.6L:* 14.0/7.9 L/100 km. *2004 Seville 4.6L:* 13.3/8.2 L/100 km. Owners report fuel savings may undershoot these estimates by at least 20 percent. **Maintenance/Repair costs:** Higher than average. Catera repairs are more expensive because they are dealer-dependent and parts can't be found. **Parts:** Higher-than-average costs. Rear axle/differential seals are constantly on several months' back order due to their high failure rate. **Extended warranty:** Don't buy any of these cars without a three- to five-year supplementary warranty. **Best alternatives:** Acura Integra or RL; Cadillac DeVille, Brougham, or Fleetwood; Ford Crown Victoria; and Mercury Grand Marquis.

Strengths and Weaknesses

Front-drive Cadillacs are unreliable, cobbled-together embarrassments. The biggest tip-off that GM was conning us with these front-drives was in 1987 when GM sold gussied-up V6-equipped Cavaliers as Cadillac Cimarrons. They flopped, and Infiniti and Lexus carved out a huge chunk of the American luxury car market that they have never given up. Even though later Cadillacs used many of the same mechanical components as the Riviera and Toronado, they continued to be no match for the Asian competition because of their poor quality and complexity.

In recent years, Cadillac has realized its mistake, and now most models are marginally more reliable rear-drives (CTS, Escalade, SRX, and STS); only the 2005 DTS remained a front-drive.

Catera

Assembled in Germany and based on the Opel Omega, the rear-drive, mid-sized Catera comes with a 200 hp V6 engine, 4-speed automatic transmission, 16-inch alloy wheels, four-wheel disc brakes, a limited-slip differential, traction control, and standard dual front airbags. This conservatively styled car (the uninspired styling has Lumina written all over it) was designed to compete with the BMW 328i, Lexus ES 300, and Mercedes-Benz C280. It was also a flop.

VEHICLE HISTORY: 1999—More-complex electronics and emissions systems to meet federal standards. **2000**—Slight styling changes, side airbags, improved throttle control, and a retuned suspension.

Cateras have a quiet, spacious, and comfortable interior; responsive handling; fine-tuned suspension; and almost nonexistent lean or body roll when cornering. On the downside, the steering system lacks balance and allows the vehicle to wander, the controls aren't easy to figure out, some gauges are hard to read, and the driver's rear view is hindered by the large rear head restraints and narrow back windshield. Furthermore, owners report chronic stalling and hard starts, possibly because of a malfunctioning idle control valve; the transmission hunts for the right gear; and dash warning lights are constantly lit. Body fit and finish is subpar.

Another point you may wish to consider: GM dealers are notoriously bad when it comes to understanding and repairing European-transplanted cars (just ask any Saab owner). As well, low-volume cars that have been taken off the market generally don't have an adequate supply of replacement parts.

CTS

Cadillac's entry-level CTS replaced the Catera in 2003 and has quickly distinguished itself as a particularly unreliable, heavy rear-drive luxury car that performs like a European sports sedan. Its extra weight destroys any pretense for fuel economy, with an estimated city/highway rating of only 13.4/7.8 L/100 km. Suggested alternatives are the Acura TL, Infiniti G35, and Lincoln Town Car.

The CTS's problematic powertrain has been constantly evolving during its few years on the market because it was never made right in the first place. First-year models offered only a puny 220 hp 3.2L V6 coupled to a standard 5-speed manual gearbox or an optional 5-speed automatic transmission. The smoother and more-powerful 255 hp 3.6L V6 engine and automatic transmission powers the 2004 models. That same year, the 2004 CTS-V was launched, carrying a Corvette-derived, 400 hp 5.7L V8 that is even *more* unreliable than the V6. The 2005 CTS changed over to a 2.8L V6 with 10 fewer horses and a better-performing 6-speed manual gearbox. 2006 models were given revised sport/performances packages.

Nevertheless, the above-noted powertrain changes haven't improved differential reliability, which has been a chronic problem since the CTS was launched:

> The Cadillac CTS-V rear differential is weak and may break causing this car to skid or suddenly stop, causing an accident, injury, or death. Cadillac knows of the problem and has provided some customers with warranty repair, offered 100,000 mile [160,000 km] extended warranties for others and yet denied repair for customers with similar problems. This rear differential is under rated for this car's horse power and was designed for use in the standard CTS version of this car the rear tires have also been a problem showing early signs of wear. I had to replace my first set [of] front and rear [tires] at 8,500 miles [13,500 km] these tires are worst rated tire by consumers at *www.tirerack.com* and *www.cadillacfaq.com*.

Other problems include constant rear-end whine (a warning that total failure is just around the corner); stability control and ABS failures; early replacement of the fuel/water pump, radiator, and power windows; electrical system shorts causing lights, gauges, instruments, and power seats to malfunction; and poor fit and finish, highlighted by loud wind noise from the windshield, clunks and rattles, paint blistering and premature corrosion, and door handle, dash, and radio button plastic peeling.

Eldorado and Seville

Sitting on the same platform as the front-drive Eldorado, the Seville has European-style allure with a more-rounded body than the Eldorado. Apart from that, since its redesign in 1992, Seville's engine, handling, and braking upgrades have followed the Eldorado's improvements in lockstep fashion.

Although the base 4.9L V8 provides brisk acceleration, the 32-valve Northstar V8, first found on the 1993 Touring Coupe, gives you almost 100 more horses with great handling and a comfortable ride. Overall, the Touring Coupe or Sport Coupe will give you the best powertrain, handling, and braking features. Of course, you'll have to contend with poor fuel economy, rear visibility that's obstructed by the huge side pillars (a Seville problem, as well), confusing and inconvenient climate controls, and a particularly complex engine that's failure-prone and a nightmare to troubleshoot.

VEHICLE HISTORY: 1998–2001—The only real change is the Eldorado's Northstar engine tweaking for year 2000 models. *Seville:* **2002**—An upgraded suspension. **2004**—300 hp engine is dropped; Seville is replaced by the STS.

These cars have generic deficiencies that fall into common categories: poorly calibrated and failure-prone engines, transmissions, and fuel and ignition systems;

a multiplicity of electrical short circuits; and sloppy body assembly using poor-quality components. Specifically, engines and fuel systems often produce intermittent stalling, rough idling, hesitation, and no-starts; the Overdrive automatic is prone to premature failure; oil pumps fail frequently; front brakes and shock absorbers wear out quickly; paint is often poorly applied, and it fades or peels away prematurely; fragile body hardware breaks easily (front-bumper cracks are commonplace); and there are large gaps between sheet metal panels and doors that are poorly hung and not entirely square. Other body problems include the cracking of front outside door handles, door rattles (Eldorado), poor bumper fit, loose sun visor mounting, rear tail light condensation, fading and discolouring appliqué mouldings (Seville), interior window fogging, creaking body mounts, water leaking into the trunk from the licence plate holder (Eldorado), noisy roof panels and seatback lumbar motors, and a creaking noise at the front-door upper hinge area.

 ## Safety Summary

Catera: **1997–2001**—Chronic stalling. • Frequent wheel alignments. • Defective brake rotors cause excessive vibration and pull. • Vehicle wanders and pulls to one side. • Door locks don't work, and key sticks in the ignition. **1999**—Accelerator can be floored, and vehicle will only creep forward. • Head restraints block vision. • Loss of steering. • Door latch sticks in the closed position. **2000**—Hesitant shifting. • Defective ignition switch. **2001**—Airbags fail to deploy. • Gas pedal sticks. • Fuel line is exposed to road debris. • Windshield orange-peel pattern. *CTS:* **2003**—Airbags fail to deploy. • Unintended acceleration. • Many complaints of rear differential/casing failures and excessive hum or whine; insiders say the differential is overwhelmed by the powerful engine, causing excessive wheel hop. • Electrical shorts. • PCV valve may burst, spewing oil and causing engine to catch fire. • Car suddenly runs out of fuel. **2003–07**—Front or rear axle pinion seal leak. **2004**—Airbags fail to deploy. • In one incident, key was put into the ignition and the airbag deployed, breaking driver's nose. • Surging when brakes are applied. • CTS-V manual transmission often fails to shift properly. • Rear differential fractures and separates into half shafts:

> There needs to be an in-depth investigation regarding the number of CTS and CTS-V rear differentials that have been replaced. I have now been through 2 personally, and an online poll of 65 CTS-V owners showed this: 26% have had 1 replacement, 5% have had 2 or more replaced, and 8% have had 3 or more replaced. The link for this poll is: *cadillacforums.com/forums/showthread.php?p=305662&posted=1 #post305662.*

• Rear child safety seat latches don't latch properly. • Stability tracking system engages when it shouldn't, suddenly pulling the car into oncoming traffic. **2004–07**—Torque converter clutch surge, shudder, exhaust moan, and chuggle. • Inaccurate fuel gauge. **2005**—Headlights are too bright and sometimes flicker. • Faulty run-flat tires. • Dash reflects onto the front windshield, obstructing visibility. **2006**—Many more axle/differential failures. • Sudden acceleration after vehicle was parked. • Total electrical shutdown. • Sunroof shattered while car was parked overnight in an indoor garage. • Defective Goodrich Touring tires. • Trunk leak; trunk spring failure. **2007**—Under-hood fire. • Another fire ignited near the rear of the transmission (catalytic converter suspected), and one more occurred near the brake master cylinder. • In car wash, vehicle surged and brakes didn't work, except for the emergency brake. • Post-recall multiple axle/differential failures:

> Rear differential broke. Was driving on the highway and suddenly lost control of the car. The back wheels locked completely. No apparent trigger. Put on brakes (I was scared I was close to the edge of the overpass), shut off the car and the smoke dissipated. No warning at all.

• Rear end slips, growls. • Cruise control cut out. • Early replacement of the rear brake rotors. • Trunk opens on its own. • Water leaks. • Distracting noise emanating from the front windshield. *Eldorado, Seville:* **1986–2001**—A plethora of electrical short circuits and front axle, ABS brake, and steering failures. • Sudden, unintended acceleration. • Airbag malfunctions (deploying for no reason and injuring occupants). • Brake rotors and pads always need changing. • Poor headlight illumination. *Eldorado:* **2002**—No airbag deployment. *Seville:* **1999**—Front control arm snaps. • Tie-rod end comes apart. • Loss of power steering when driving in the rain. • Front and rear lights collect water. **2000**—Seat belt retractors don't work properly. • Excessive drifting at any speed. • Brake caliper locks up. **2001**—While driving, passenger-side wheel collapsed because of a missing suspension bolt. • Steering-column rubbing noise is heard when making a right turn. **2002**—Chronic stalling in traffic. • Noisy, erratic transmission shifting. **2003**—Display panel can be hard to see. • Excessive oil burning.

Secret Warranties/Internal Bulletins/Service Tips

All models/years: Reverse servo cover leak. **All models: 1993–2005**—Paint delamination, peeling, or fading. **1996–2003**—Excessive oil consumption may be caused by dirty piston rings, says GM TSB #02-06-01-009B. **1998–2003**—Water and musty smell in rear compartment. • Inoperative seat heater. **1999–2004**—Repair tips for a slipping automatic transmission. **2000–01**—If there's a sudden loss of power when accelerating, the transmission fluid pressure switch may be defective. **2000–02**—No power when accelerating; 1–2 shift concerns. **2001**—Delayed Reverse engagement. **2001–03**—Loss of engine coolant. • Steering clunk remedy is to replace the intermediate shaft. **2001–08**—Transmission slips in gear; axle seal leaks. **2003**—Erratic transmission performance. **2004**—Troubleshooting tips for hard starts. *Catera:* **1997–2001**—Coolant loss; engine overheating. • Key can't be removed from the ignition lock cylinder. *CTS:* **2003**—Transmission shudder upon hard acceleration (replace the transmission output shaft flange). • Windshield stress cracking. • An underbody thump noise can be silenced by replacing the engine mounts. **2003–04**—Automatic transmission has no Reverse gear or slips in gear. • Automatic transmission Reverse servo cover leak. • Oil leaks from cam valve cover seal (3.2L V6). **2003–05**—Harsh upshifts. **2003–06**—Aluminum hood blistering. • Noisy suspension when turning (install front lower control arm rear bushing spacer). **2003–07**—Front or rear axle pinion seal leak. **2004**—Transmission won't stay in Sport mode. **2004–05**—In TSB #05-04-114-001A, Cadillac admits its CTS models have rear-wheel hop and offers to replace the rear subframe bushings to correct the problem. • Remedy for frozen door locks. • Harsh upshifts. **2004–07**—Inaccurate fuel gauge readings. **2006–08**—Shifter binding, key stuck in ignition, and battery dead. *Eldorado, Seville:* **1996–2003**—Excessive oil consumption can be corrected with new piston rings if a new ring-cleaning process doesn't work (TSB #02-06-01-009C).

CATERA, CTS, CTS-V, ELDORADO, SEVILLE PROFILE

	1999	2000	2001	2002	2003	2004	2005	2006	2007
Cost Price ($)									
Catera	42,310	42,635	42,485	—	—	—	—	—	—
CTS	—	—	—	—	39,900	39,200	37,800	35,555	35,780
CTS-V	—	—	—	—	—	70,000	70,700	68,755	70,670
Eldorado	52,660	53,455	56,600	57,450	—	—	—	—	—
Seville	59,195	60,195	58,710	59,450	62,045	63,400	—	—	—
Used Values ($)									
Catera ▲	3,000	3,500	5,500	—	—	—	—	—	—
Catera ▼	2,500	3,000	4,000	—	—	—	—	—	—
CTS ▲	—	—	—	—	10,500	13,000	15,000	18,500	22,000
CTS ▼	—	—	—	—	9,000	11,500	14,000	17,000	20,000
CTS-V ▲	—	—	—	—	—	16,000	17,500	27,500	36,000
CTS-V ▼	—	—	—	—	—	15,000	16,000	26,000	34,000
Eldorado ▲	5,000	5,500	7,500	9,500	—	—	—	—	—
Eldorado ▼	4,500	5,500	6,000	8,000	—	—	—	—	—
Seville ▲	4,500	5,500	7,000	9,000	11,000	13,000	—	—	—
Seville ▼	4,000	5,000	6,000	7,500	9,500	12,000	—	—	—
Reliability	1	2	2	2	2	2	3	3	3
Crash Safety (F)	—	—	—	—	4	4	4	4	4
Side	—	—	—	—	4	4	4	4	4
Offset									
Catera	5	5	5	—	—	—	—	—	—
CTS	—	—	—	—	5	5	5	5	5
Seville	—	5	5	5	5	5	—	—	—
Head Restraints									
Catera	2	—	3	—	—	—	—	—	—
CTS	—	—	—	—	1	1	1	1	1
Eldorado	1	—	1	1	—	—	—	—	—
Seville	1	1	1	1	1	1	—	—	—
Rollover Resistance									
CTS	—	—	—	—	4	4	4	4	4

Note: A 2007 CTS-V sold originally for about $70,670, almost double the price of the 35,780 CTS. However, two model years later, there is only a few thousand dollars' difference between the two vehicles.

RATING: Below Average (1999–2007). Interestingly, new Concours models were sold at a premium over the DeVille, but the difference narrows considerably after a few years. There are two major safety problems affecting these models: inadvertent side and front airbag deployment and chronic stalling in traffic. **"Real" city/highway fuel economy:** 13.3/8.2 L/100 km. Owners report fuel savings may undershoot this estimate by at least 20 percent. **Maintenance/Repair costs:** Higher than average; repairs are very dealer-dependent. **Parts:** Higher-than-average costs, and parts are hard to find. **Extended warranty:** A good idea. **Best alternatives:** Acura Integra, RL, or TL; Infiniti I30 or I35; and Toyota Avalon.

Strengths and Weaknesses

Although they have better handling and are almost as comfortable as older, traditional Caddies, these front-drive luxury coupes and sedans aren't worth considering because of their dismal reliability, overly complex servicing, and dependence on parts that are impossible to find and not very durable. Poor reliability remains a problem, and the term "Cadillac fuel economy" is an oxymoron. Also, the dash controls and gauges are confusing and not easily accessible, and the high trunk lid and large side pillars obstruct the rear view.

The 4.3L V6, 4.1L V8, and 4.5L V8 engines and 4-speed automatic transmission suffer from a variety of terminal maladies, including oil leaks, premature wear, poor fuel economy, and excessive noise. The electrical system and related components are temperamental. Steering is noisy, the suspension goes soft quickly, and the front brakes often wear out after only 18 months/20,000 km. Problems with the digital fuel injection and engine control systems are very difficult to diagnose and repair. Premature paint peeling and rusting, excessive wind noise in the interior, and fragile trim items characterize poor body assembly.

VEHICLE HISTORY: 1996—DeVilles are given the problematic Northstar V8 and an upgraded automatic transmission and suspension. The Concours receive 25 additional horses along with improved steering and suspension. **1997**—Substantially reworked and given new styling, side airbags, and an upgraded interior. **1998**—Depowered airbags. **2000**—A number of high-tech improvements, including refinements to the V8 engine, Night Vision, Rear Parking Assist, and StabiliTrak traction control. **2005**—Redesigned and sold as the 2006 DTS.

DTS

About the same size as the DeVille it replaced, Cadillac's front-drive 2006 DTS carries a 4.6L V8, 4-speed automatic transmission, and self-levelling rear suspension. A 275 hp Northstar V8 with optional performance packages targets premium full-size sedans like the Buick Lucerne, Lexus LS 430, and Lincoln Town Car (Lexus and Lincoln are the better choices). Every DTS includes anti-lock braking, traction control, front torso side airbags, and head-protecting side curtain airbags. Also standard are Magnetic Ride Control, a tire-pressure monitor, a remote engine start feature, and xenon headlights. The vehicle has changed little since it was introduced.

Cadillac continued its not-so-proud history of making luxury lemons with the advent of the DTS. Owners decry the failure of the Collision Avoidance feature's sensors; a knocking, clicking sound that comes from the steering assembly; excessive Continental Tire noise; a driver-side mirror that fails to correct for a blind spot; hard starts and no-starts; a key that sticks in the ignition; a gas tank cap that's difficult to open; a Stability-Control Service light that remains lit; a plastic undercarriage cover that drags on the ground; and distracting (to other drivers) "strobe" LED tail lights.

STS

Whopping depreciation aside, this rear-drive/AWD Seville replacement has plenty of power and versatility. The V6 engine is more powerful than the BMW 5 Series' and Mercedes E-Class's 6-cylinders, while the V8 produces slightly less horsepower than the comparable BMW but more than the Mercedes or Lexus. Without question, Cadillac's switch to rear-drive or all-wheel drive improves the STS's balance, handling, and overall performance considerably. Shoppers will have to decide if the car's elegant interior and vastly superior performance make up for the loss of a little rear seatroom (it still has at least a couple centimetres more than its closest competitors, and it's close to 7.5 cm larger than the problematic Mercedes E-Class) and for its unproven mechanical components, mediocre fit and finish, and untested crashworthiness.

Although complaints relative to STS reliability have been fewer than average, owners do report a number of serious safety-related failures. For example, the passenger-side airbag sensor fails to detect the seat is occupied and leaves the system disabled:

> The dealership tried for over a week to solve the problem, but would only say that the procedure to activate the sensor requires the passenger to enter and sit in the vehicle in a certain convoluted way that is basically unnatural and impossible for certain passengers to achieve.

Acceleration is erratic, the car suddenly loses power when passing another vehicle, the rear differential may suddenly lock up, and the car has poor traction in snow:

> The contact stated that the 2006 STS fails to operate properly while driving in snow. The vehicle slides and causes crashes because there is no traction. The contact was involved in a crash, but no police report was filed. The manufacturer stated that nothing could be done and suggested the contact purchase new tires to accommodate the weather conditions.

Owners report that eye-watering, throat-burning emissions emanate from the interior, principally the trunk area; the sunroof may blow out from excessive interior air pressure; the voice recognition feature executes different commands than what it is given, and prior commands can't be countermanded; the wiring harness and module under the front seat may melt; and electrical shorts play havoc with lights, gauges, and accessory systems. There have also been some complaints that the differential leaks fluid, brake pads quickly wear out and brake rotors warp prematurely, the air dam shield falls down and drags on the pavement, windshields shatter for no reason, headlights have stress cracks, and the battery dies if the car isn't started for several days.

And if all of the above-listed failures aren't embarrassing enough, owners also report that their front seat makes a "noxious" noise:

> Front car seats are making a farting noise. I have had [the] car in the dealership three times and each time they said they fixed the problem. They have not.

 ## Safety Summary

DeVille: **All years**—Inadvertent airbag deployment. • In one incident, vehicle suddenly accelerated, killing one person and injuring others. • Accelerator sticking. • Chronic stalling while underway. • Leaking engine oil coolant. • Wheels fall off. • Many complaints of front and rear brake rotor warpage and premature pad and caliper failure. • Sudden loss of power steering. • Vehicle tends to wander all over the road. • Can't read speedometer in daylight. • Sun visor obstructs visibility. • Gas-tank sensor failure causes inaccurate fuel readings. • Interior lights frequently malfunction. **1999**—Engine overheating, loose head bolts, and excessive oil consumption. • Vehicle rolls backward when in gear. • Factory-equipped jack inadequate to support vehicle. • Power door locks operate erratically. **2001**—Transmission doesn't shift all the way into Drive; it pops out of gear and allows vehicle to roll down an incline. • Brake pedal goes to the floor without braking. • Side mirror creates a huge blind spot. **2002**—Seat belts are too short for some occupants. • Shoulder belt fits short drivers poorly. • Distorted windshield. **2003**—Total brake failure. • Instrument panel shuts down. **2004**—Vehicle caught fire while parked. • Transmission fluid leakage is a fire hazard. • Hesitation when accelerating. • Airbag fails to deploy. • Chronic stalling caused by electrical failure. • Sudden brake failure. • Early tie rod replacement. • Hood latch isn't secured tightly. **2005**—Headlights shut off when turning signals are enabled. • Tail lights have a "strobe effect" that blurs drivers' vision in following cars. • Door won't stay open when the car is parked on an incline. • Lengthy delay when transmission is shifted into Reverse. *DTS:* **2006**—Airbags failed to deploy. • Sudden, unintended acceleration when vehicle was underway. • Adaptive cruise control operates abnormally. • Cruise control fails to maintain speed when going downhill. • Steering suddenly pulls the vehicle to one side. • Total failure of the lower control arm sent the car careening out of control. • A fleet manager reports that all of their vehicles' high-intensity headlights go out due to defective ballast assemblies. • Sun reflects off of the clock into driver's eyes. • The front windshield has lines flowing across it. • Goodyear Vogue blowouts. **2007**—Airbags failed to deploy. • Car stalled in traffic and then proceeded at a snail's pace. • Stepped on gas to avoid hitting a truck, and the car failed to respond. • Wind can blow doors shut on occupants' legs. • Many reports that the driver's right foot gets stuck between the gas pedal and the centre console. • Twilight sensors come on too early and go off too late (see *www.cadillacforums.com/forums/cadillac-forum/t-92975.html*). • Centre door post and driver-seat head restraint block the driver's view when turning or looking rearward. • Sun visor falls down on its own; fails to block the sunlight. *STS:* **2006**—Sudden, unintended acceleration when parking. • Long wait for recall parts for the axle shaft seal repair. • Passenger-side airbag is disabled even though a 100 lb. adult is seated. • Seat bezel breaks constantly. • Michelin tires wear out early.

Secret Warranties/Internal Bulletins/Service Tips

All models/years: Reverse servo cover seal leak. • Paint delamination, peeling, or fading. **All models: 1996–2003**—Excessive oil consumption can be corrected with new piston rings if a ring-cleaning process doesn't work (TSB #02-06-01-009C). *DeVille:* **2000–02**—Loss of power when accelerating. • 1–2 shift concerns. **2000–04**—Remedies for excessive vibration, shaking while cruising. • Troubleshooting rear suspension noise. **2000–05**—Silencing a front-end clunk. • Hood blistering, premature corrosion. **2001**—Intermittent inoperative instrument panel (requires replacement of the I/P cluster assembly). • Delayed Reverse engagement. **2001–03**—Loss of engine coolant. **2001–05**—Harsh upshifts. **2003**—Intermittent no-starts; no electrical power (align engine wiring junction block, says TSB #06-03-009). • Erratic transmission shifting. **2003–04**—Right rear-door air leak. **2005**—Difficult to move shifter out of Park. • Moan, squawk during low-speed turns. *DTS:* **2006–07**—Automatic transmission slips, overheats, or won't shift. • Inoperative power seats. • Brake pulsation when travelling down steep grades (get improved brake pads). *STS:* **2005–07**—Front or rear axle pinion seal leak. • Torque converter clutch surge, shudder, exhaust moan, and chuggle. • Inaccurate fuel gauge. **2007–08**—Sunroof rattling.

CONCOURS, DEVILLE, DTS, STS, STS-V PROFILE

	1999	2000	2001	2002	2003	2004	2005	2006	2007
Cost Price ($)									
Concours	57,490	—	—	—	—	—	—	—	—
DeVille	49,710	51,995	51,895	52,555	54,925	56,235	57,050	—	—
DTS	—	—	—	—	—	—	—	52,680	52,935
STS V6	—	—	—	—	—	—	—	56,600	57,750
STS V8	—	—	—	—	—	—	—	69,470	71,275
STS-V	—	—	—	—	—	—	—	97,995	98,265
Used Values ($)									
Concours ▲	4,000	—	—	—	—	—	—	—	—
Concours ▼	4,000	—	—	—	—	—	—	—	—

DeVille ▲	3,500	4,500	5,500	8,500	10,000	13,500	16,000	—	—
DeVille ▼	3,000	3,500	4,500	6,000	9,000	12,000	14,000	—	—
DTS ▲	—	—	—	—	—	—	—	20,000	24,000
DTS ▼	—	—	—	—	—	—	—	18,000	22,000
STS V6 ▲	—	—	—	—	—	—	—	22,000	29,000
STS V6 ▼	—	—	—	—	—	—	—	20,000	27,000
STS V8 ▲	—	—	—	—	—	—	—	27,000	36,000
STS V8 ▼	—	—	—	—	—	—	—	25,000	34,000
STS-V ▲	—	—	—	—	—	—	—	34,000	45,000
STS-V ▼	—	—	—	—	—	—	—	31,000	41,000
Reliability	1	1	1	1	1	1	1	1	1
Crash Safety (F)									
DeVille	4	3	3	1	1	4	4	—	—
DTS	—	—	—	—	—	—	—	5	5
Side									
DeVille	4	4	4	4	4	4	4	—	—
DTS	—	—	—	—	—	—	—	4	4
IIHS Side									
DTS	—	—	—	—	—	—	—	3	3
STS	—	—	—	—	—	—	—	—	3
Offset									
DTS	—	—	—	—	—	—	—	5	5
STS	—	—	—	—	—	—	5	5	5
Head Restraints									
DTS	—	—	—	—	—	—	—	1	1
STS	—	—	—	—	—	—	1	1	—
Rollover Resistance									
DeVille	—	—	—	5	5	5	5	—	—
DTS	—	—	—	—	—	—	—	4	5

Infiniti

G20, G35, I30, I35, M35, M45, Q45 ★★★ / ★★★★★

RATING: *G20:* Not Recommended (1999–2002). *G35:* Average (2007); Below Average (2003–06); *I30:* Recommended (2000–03); Above Average (1999). *I35:* Above Average (2002–04). *M35, M45:* Above Average (2006–07); Average (2003–05). *Q45:* Above Average (2001–05); Average (1999–2000). **"Real" city/highway fuel economy:** *G20:* 10.0/6.9 L/100 km. *I30 3.0L:* 12.1/8.1 L/100 km. *I35:* 12.1/8.3 L/100 km. *Q45 4.1L:* 13.4/9.2 L/100 km. *Q45 4.5L:* 13.6/8.8 L/100 km. Owners report fuel savings may undershoot these estimates by about 10 percent. **Maintenance/**

Repair costs: Higher-than-average costs, and repairs must be done by either an Infiniti or a Nissan dealer. **Parts:** Higher-than-average costs, and hard to find:

> They found the problem...but told me that it couldn't be repaired and that the part wasn't sold separately. Instead the entire headlight assembly needed to be replaced with the light assembly costing $1,500.00 and with taxes and labour the cost would exceed $1,800.00.

Extended warranty: Not necessary. **Best alternatives:** The fully equipped Honda Accord and Toyota Camry are better buys from a price and quality standpoint, but they don't have the same luxury cachet. Also consider the Acura Integra, Legend, RL, or TL.

Strengths and Weaknesses

With its emphasis on sporty handling (diluted somewhat with the '97 and later model years), the Infiniti series takes the opposite tack from the Lexus, which focuses on comfort and luxury. Infiniti models do come fully equipped and offer owners the prestige of driving a comfortable and nicely styled luxury car, but the lineup isn't as refined or as reliable as the Toyota competition.

G20

The least expensive Infiniti, 1999 and later G20s aren't as refined as their entry-level Lexus counterparts in interior space, drivetrain, or convenience features. The 140 hp engine's lack of low-speed torque means that it has to work hard above 4000 rpm—while protesting noisily. The automatic transmission shifts roughly, particularly when passing; the power steering needs more assist during parking manoeuvres; and the dealer-installed foglights cost an exorbitant $500 to replace. Tall drivers will find the legroom insufficient, and rear passengers will feel cramped. Trunk space is limited by the angle of the rear window.

VEHICLE HISTORY: 1999—Returning after a three-year hiatus, the '99 G20 wasn't worth the wait. It's basically a package of unfulfilled expectations with its wimpy 2.0L 140 hp engine, firm and jiggly ride, and bland styling. **2000**—A bit more horsepower, and an upgraded transmission.

Owner complaints target automatic transmission failures, engine coolant leaks, prematurely worn brake rotors and brake pads, excessive noise when braking, malfunctioning power seats, and clunky springs and shock absorbers.

G35

Infiniti's rear-drive, sporty luxury car was introduced in the spring of 2002. The sedan is equipped with a 260 hp engine, versus 280 hp for the coupe. Coupes are feature-laden, stretched versions of Nissan's problem-prone 2003 350Z sports car, with less power and a small fold-down back seat added. Sedans are quite long and provide sportier performance than Infiniti's front-drive I35 does. Initially, both G35s offered a 5-speed automatic transmission with manual shiftgate, but a

6-speed manual was phased in within a year. Both body styles offer four-wheel ABS disc brakes, front side airbags, and side curtain airbags (only for the front seats in the coupe). Manual transmission coupes come with more performance-oriented upgraded brakes. Alternative choices would be the Acura TL, Audi A4, BMW 3 Series, and Cadillac CTS.

Owner complaints primarily concern excessive engine oil consumption requiring a rebuilt engine, chronic engine noise, automatic transmission failures and erratic shifting, a noisy manual 6-speed transmission, excessive brake squealing, metal flakes in the paint (bird droppings will eat through the finish), very poor fuel economy, and early replacement of brake pads and rotors ($600). Low-tire-pressure monitoring system must be reprogrammed by the dealer if wheels are rotated or a full-size spare tire is installed.

VEHICLE HISTORY: 2004—Debut of an all-wheel-drive sedan with Snow Mode that provides a 50/50 front/rear torque split. The base sedan gets larger, 17-inch wheels; manual-shift coupes receive upgraded brakes and 18-inch wheels; the sedan variant gets a limited-slip differential. **2005**—Automatic transmission–equipped sedans share the coupe's 280 hp V6, while manual-equipped models have 18 more horses (298 hp). The all-wheel-drive G35x comes only with an automatic transmission. Models using a manual tranny use a standard limited-slip differential and sport suspension.

I30/I35

Introduced as an early '96 model, the I30 is a sport sedan spin-off of the Nissan Maxima with additional sound-deadening material and a plushier interior. The car's interior is also roomier, but its ride is unimpressive and handling is compromised by excessive body lean when cornering. Engine and road noises are omnipresent. The redesigned 2000 model adds rear seatroom and reduces body lean considerably. I35s have a quieter and better-performing engine, a much improved ride, and more responsive handling.

VEHICLE HISTORY: 1996–99—Front side airbags, and new headlights and tail lights are added to the '98s. **2000**—Revamped with more-conservative styling, 37 more horses, and a larger cabin. Head restraints are also upgraded, suspension is improved, larger wheels are added, and high-intensity headlights are adopted. **2002**—Renamed the I35 and given a larger V6 engine, new styling, and more standard features.

Incredibly, the more-recently minted I35 models have elicited more performance-related complaints than the earlier I30, which was no paragon of quality control. This same phenomenon has been noted with Nissan's reworked Altima models, which continue to have serious factory-related glitches almost a decade after the model's launch.

I30 owners report chronic suspension failures, drivetrain vibration and clunking, faulty steering, and defective transverse links, springs, and struts. I35s are known for hesitation and surging when accelerating, electrical shorts, excessive front-end play, loose steering, vibration, drivetrain noise, rattling noises, incorrect fuel gauge readings, and inoperative seat memory buttons.

Q45

Faster and glitzier than other cars in its category, this luxury sedan provides performance, while its chief rival, the Lexus LS 400, provides luxury and quiet. Up to the '96 model, the Q45 used a 32-valve 278 hp 4.5L V8 tire-burner not frequently found on a Japanese luxury compact. It accelerates faster than the Lexus, going 0–100 km/h in 7.1 seconds without a hint of noise or abrupt shifting. Unlike the base engine of the G20, though, the Q45's engine supplies plenty of upper-range torque as well. That potent powerhouse was dropped with the less-than-dazzling 1997–2001 models' 266 hp 4.1L V8. High-performance power was rediscovered, however, when the 2002–06 models returned to a more-powerful 340 hp 4.5L V8. The suspension was softened in 1994, but the car still rides much more firmly than its Lexus counterpart. The four-wheel steering is precise, but the standard limited-slip differential is no help in preventing the car's rear end from sliding out on slippery roads, mainly because of the original-equipment "sport" tires, which were designed for 190 km/h autobahn cruising. ABS is standard. There's not much foot-room for passengers, and cargo room is disappointing. Fuel economy is nonexistent.

VEHICLE HISTORY: 1997—A downsized 4.1L V8 is set on a smaller platform, effectively changing the character of the car from a sporty performer to a highway cruiser. **2002**—A new 4.5L V8 produces 340 hp (up from 266 hp). The transmission is a 5-speed automatic with a manual shift mode. High-end electronics are standard, including traction control (TCS), Vehicle Dynamic Control (VDC), Electronic Brake Force Distribution (EBD), tire-pressure monitors, and high-intensity xenon headlights. **2003**—A rear-axle upgrade for faster and smoother acceleration. **2004**—A rear-view camera. **2005**—A minor facelift and a recalibrated transmission for smoother shifts.

The Q45 has been exceptionally reliable throughout its model run, despite some reports of premature AC failures, power-steering problems, excessive wind noise around the A-pillars, sunroof wind leaks, and tire thumping. Paint is easily scratched and flakes off.

M35, M45

The 2003 M45 replaced the I30/I35 as Infiniti's mid-size, rear-drive luxury car. Powered by a 340 hp V8 engine and coupled to a 5-speed automatic transmission, the first three model years sold poorly primarily due to the car's bland design and cramped interior. The redesigned 2006 and 2007 models offer more interior room and high-tech features, like a peppier V8 despite 15 fewer horses, four-wheel steering, a performance-tuned suspension/transmission, and upgraded brakes. M35 sedans use a 275 hp V6 that's available with rear-drive or all-wheel drive.

Owners complain of excessive oil consumption, poor tire performance with the Michelin Pilots, and a host of other problems:

> ...(perforated leather seats had mesh coming out, CD changer jammed, AC compressor busted, belts on the motor had to be replaced, glove box had to be readjusted, hood had to be readjusted to stop the squeaking when closing the doors, front window guides and stabilizer-inner door had to be replaced to stop all the squealing when letting the windows up/down) and schedule another visit to see if the engine/exhaust problem could be repaired. The dealership had my car for 3 weeks...and cleaned out the combustion chamber at their cost and the day I got it back, it was still smoking out the pipes. The dealership says they know nothing else to do but to replace the motor if it's consuming oil.

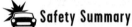 **Safety Summary**

G20: **2001**—Brake failure. • Brake rotors glaze over and need turning. • Airbags fail to deploy. *G35:* **2003**—Vehicle accelerates when coming to a stop with the AC engaged and a foot on the brake pedal. • Early automatic transmission replacement. • Poor upshifting from First gear. • Loss of front braking capability. • Premature wearout of brake pads and rotors. • Rear window shatters suddenly. • Seat belt cuts across the neck of small-statured drivers. • Driver's seat rocks back and forth. • Rear defroster takes forever to work. **2004**—Sudden acceleration due to pedal sticking, or when the speed control is engaged. • Transmission failures and premature brake replacement still dominate owner complaints. • Parking brake won't secure vehicle on an incline. • In one incident, ABS system locked up, flipping the car and killing the driver and two passengers. • Michelin Pilot tires perform poorly in winter conditions. • Heated air is constantly drawn in from the engine compartment. **2005**—Speed control causes the car to suddenly accelerate. Car also accelerates when brakes are applied. • Brake failure. • Car pulls to the right (service bulletins were issued for this problem, affecting 2003 and 2004 models). **2006**—Fire believed to have been caused by a defective seat heater. • Cruise control causes car to suddenly accelerate. • Stuck fuel-filler door. • Tail/brake lights are too bright; blind following drivers. **2007**—Passenger-side airbag is disabled when average-sized adult is seated. • Vehicle often hesitates when accelerating. • Dynamic Control system suddenly engaged, causing the car to speed up and veer to the right. • Car seems to be constantly braking when going downhill with the cruise control engaged. • Manual transmission clutch sticks to the floor due to insufficient pressure in the line. • Sunroof suddenly exploded. • Defective Goodyear Eagle RS-A tires. • Driver-side automatic window won't go up, or operates very slowly. • Intelligent Key failures. *I30/I35:* **1999**—When using the turn signal, it's easy to turn off the headlights. • Airbag warning light stays on. • Water seeps inside the vehicle from beneath. **2000**—Transmission jerks when shifting. • Premature wear of brake rotors. • Sunlight washes out gauges. • Headlight aimed too low. **2000–01**—Sudden, unintended acceleration. **2001**—Rear suspension fails. • Cruise control won't disengage when brakes are applied. **2002**—Airbags fail to deploy. • Steering wheel pulls sharply to one side when accelerating. • Poor braking. • Stalling. *M35:* **2006**—Brake failure. • Steering is hard to control; car wanders all over the road. • Emergency spare tire makes the car not drivable. *M45:* **2003**—Hesitation when accelerating:

> The vehicle has an unsafe operating characteristic. When calling for immediate acceleration, you get nothing for several seconds. It has a significant lag in throttle response, up to 4 seconds, which when lane changing or merging causes a significant safety problem. We have been nearly rear-ended on several occasions.

2006—Steering is unpredictable; vehicle wanders. • Driver seat frame stress crack. • Tire tread separates. • Leaky sunroof. *Q45:* **2001**—Sudden acceleration when vehicle is shifted into Reverse gear. **2002**—Excessive vibration caused by bent original-equipment wheels. **2004**—Laser-controlled cruise control abruptly cuts power when passing another vehicle and doesn't work in rain or when driving into the sun at sunset.

Secret Warranties/Internal Bulletins/Service Tips

All models/years: Troubleshooting tips to correct brake pedal judder and hard starts. • Windshield cracking. • Sunroof wind noise. • Erratic operation of the power antenna. *G20:* **1999–2000**—Countermeasures for front-end clunks when turning or braking. **1999–2001**—Power seat won't move, or makes a grinding noise. **2000**—Engine lacks power; stuck in Third gear. • Low idle, or engine dies when put into gear. • Cloudy, scratched instrument cluster lens. **2001–02**—Rear brake caliper clunk, rattle, or knock. *G35:* **2003–06**—No-starts in cold weather. **2005**—Dash squeak and rattle repair. **2005–06**—Gap between glove compartment and dash. *I30/I35:* **2000–01**—No-starts may be caused by a faulty engine wire harness. • Transmission slippage. • Troubleshooting tips to correct self-locking doors. **2000–04**—Poor transmission performance. **2001–02**—Rear brake caliper clunk, rattle, or knock. **2002**—Faulty sunroof. **2002–03**—Upgraded brake pads to reduce brake judder or other anomalies. *M45:* **2003–04**—A ticking or thumping noise coming from the engine area may signal the need to replace the fuel damper assembly. • Diagnosing and correcting an engine knocking or tapping noise. *Q45:* **1997–2000**—TSB #ITB00-010 gives a detailed list of brake judder countermeasures. **1998–99**—An automatic transmission that produces a "double thump" noise when coming to a stop likely needs a new transmission control module (TCM). **2002**—Engine hesitation. • Steering pull to the right; excessive vibration. • Difficult to move shift lever. • Front suspension noise. • Trunk lid hard to close. • Poor AC performance. **2002–03**—Incorrect shifting. **2002–04**—Remedy for engine knocking after a cold start. **2002–06**—Ticking, thumping noise at idle. **2004–06**—Tire-pressure monitoring system (TPMS) sensor seal leaks.

G20/G35, I30/I35, M35/M45, Q45 PROFILE

	1999	2000	2001	2002	2003	2004	2005	2006	2007
Cost Price ($)									
G20	29,950	29,950	29,900	29,900	—	—	—	—	—
G35 Sedan	—	—	—	—	38,900	39,600	39,900	39,990	39,990
G35 Coupe	—	—	—	—	45,000	45,200	46,100	47,000	47,200
I30/I35	41,350	41,950	39,900	39,500	39,700	41,200	—	—	—
M35	—	—	—	—	—	—	54,800	56,100	56,400
M45	—	—	—	—	62,000	62,000	64,400	65,700	66,000
Q45	71,000	71,000	70,000	73,000	74,900	75,500	88,000		
Used Values ($)									
G20 ▲	3,000	3,500	4,500	6,000	—	—	—	—	—
G20 ▼	2,500	3,000	4,000	5,000	—	—	—	—	—
G35 Sedan ▲	—	—	—	—	12,000	14,000	17,000	23,000	25,000
G35 Sedan ▼	—	—	—	—	10,500	12,500	16,000	21,000	23,000
G35 Coupe ▲	—	—	—	—	12,500	16,500	20,000	26,000	29,000
G35 Coupe ▼	—	—	—	—	11,000	15,000	18,500	24,000	27,000
I30/I35 ▲	4,000	5,000	6,000	8,000	10,000	12,500	—	—	—
I30/I35 ▼	3,500	4,000	5,000	6,500	8,500	11,000	—	—	—
M35 ▲	—	—	—	—	—	—	23,000	28,000	30,000
M35 ▼	—	—	—	—	—	—	21,000	26,000	28,000
M45 ▲	—	—	—	—	15,000	21,000	28,000	34,000	38,000
M45 ▼	—	—	—	—	13,000	19,000	26,000	32,000	35,000
Q45 ▲	5,500	7,000	9,000	11,500	17,000	23,000	32,000	—	—
Q45 ▼	5,000	6,000	7,500	10,000	15,500	21,000	29,000	—	—
Reliability	2	2	2	2	2	2	3	3	3
Crash Safety (F)									
I30/I35	—	4	—	4	4	4	—	—	—
Side									
I30/I35	—	4	4	4	4	4	—	—	—
IIHS Side									
G35	—	—	—	—	—	—		3	5
Offset									
G35	—	—	—	—	5	5	5	5	5
I30/I35	3	3	3	3	3	3	—	—	—
Q45	2	2	2	—	5	5	5	—	—
Head Restraints									
G20	2	—	1	1	—	—	—	—	—
G35	—	—	—	—	—	—	1	1	2
I30/I35	2	—	—	—	—	—	—	—	—
Q45	1	—	—	—	—	—	2	—	—
Rollover Resistance									
I35	—	—	—	4	4	4	—	—	—

Kia

RATING: *Amanti:* Average (2007); Below Average (2004–06). *Magentis:* Above Average (2007); Average (2005–06); Below Average (2001–04). With these two vehicles, you want to avoid the early models and go for a V6-powered Magentis; the 4-cylinder version is a dog. **"Real" city/highway fuel economy:** *2.4L:* 10.9/7.2 L/100 km. *V6:* 11.7/7.9 L/100 km. Owners say they get about 10 percent less fuel economy than these estimates indicate. **Maintenance/Repair costs:** Average. **Parts:** Average costs, but parts aren't widely available yet. **Extended warranty:** A good idea only if you plan to keep the car more than five years. **Best alternatives:** A loaded Honda Accord, Nissan Maxima, and Toyota Camry.

Strengths and Weaknesses

Amanti

Carrying the Hyundai XG350's 3.5L V6 and 5-speed manumatic transmission, the 2004 Amanti is Kia's first large sedan. Amanti's styling is different from the XG350's, though, and it sits on a 5 cm longer wheelbase and a 10 cm longer body, giving it about 180 additional kilograms that erode overall handling, on-road performance, and fuel economy. The car comes with a modicum of safety and convenience features, like anti-lock four-wheel disc brakes, front and rear side airbags, side curtain airbags, dual-zone climate control, keyless entry, and power front seats. Unfortunately, the much-recommended traction/anti-skid control is offered only as an option.

2006 models got additional standard features that included power front seats, leather upholstery, heated front seats, and a sunroof. The following year, the car's 200 hp V6 was replaced by a more-powerful 264 hp 3.8L V6, the suspension was made firmer, and the interior and exterior styling were updated. On the downside, Kia dropped the standard leather upholstery, heated front seats, and sunroof.

Amanti reliability has been worse than average, characterized by rapid brake and tire wear, electrical short circuits (Airbag light is constantly lit), chronic front-end noise, and fuel problems that cause the engine to start poorly, suddenly shut down, jerk when accelerating, or hesitate and then surge. Fit and finish is also problematic, with owners complaining of multiple water and air leaks.

Amanti highway performance is very disappointing. Engine power is unreliable, steering is imprecise, handling is clumsy, and body roll is excessive.

Magentis

Sold in the States as the Optima, this front-drive, five-passenger sedan is basically a Hyundai Sonata without traction control. The Magentis comes with a twin-cam 138 hp 2.4L 4-cylinder or an optional 170 hp 2.7L V6 hooked to a 4-speed automatic transmission (V6s have the Sonata's separate gate for manual shifting and four-wheel ABS). Other standard features include front seat belt pretensioners, a tilt steering column, independent double wishbone front suspension and independent multi-link rear suspension, a 60/40 split-folding rear seat, and tinted glass.

The Magentis is nicely appointed, provides good V6 performance with the 5-speed automatic, handles competently, and rides comfortably. There's also plenty of front headroom and better-than-average fuel economy with regular fuel. The car is a bit better built than Kia's other models, but fit and finish is still inferior to other Asian makes.

Unfortunately, this car has some major weaknesses that include a wimpy 2.4L 162 hp 4-cylinder engine; a poorly performing 4-speed automatic transmission; mediocre braking; limited rear headroom; considerable body lean when turning; faulty door locks that trap occupants; excessive wind, suspension, and tire noise; a small trunk opening; and a weak dealer network. Owner complaints deal primarily with poor servicing, sudden acceleration (maybe wimpy is good), harsh shifts, stalling, brake failures, premature brake pad and rotor wear, electrical shorts, AC overheating, faulty door locks, and subpar fit and finish.

VEHICLE HISTORY: *Magentis:* **2002**—A larger V6 engine with a gain of 8 horses and 15-inch wheels; SE sedans adopt standard automatic headlights. **2003**—Refreshed interior and exterior styling that includes new audio and climate controls, a new grille and hood, larger body mouldings, and restyled tail lights. Both engines return with slightly reduced horsepower ratings after Kia and its owner, Hyundai, pleaded guilty to fudging horsepower figures on earlier models. **2004**—Larger wheels and a newly designed grille.

 ## Safety Summary

All models/years: Airbags fail to deploy; warning light stays lit. • Poor fuel system, engine, and transmission performance. • Hesitation and surging. • Sudden acceleration. *Amanti:* **2004**—Fuel leaks when fuelling gas tank. • Engine hesitates and then surges when foot is taken off the gas pedal. • Car tends to surge just after a fill-up. • Car jerks when accelerating. • Engine sludge leads to chronic stalling. • Hard starts. • Accelerator and brake pedals are mounted too close together. • Power steering goes from insensitive to oversensitive. • Headlights blow out frequently. • Driver-side mirror wobbles in the wind. **2005**—Many complaints that the car still "lags and lurches." • Premature rear tire wear. **2006**—Repeated failure of the front suspension control arm. • Driver's power seat moves forward by itself. **2007**—Driver-side floormat was sucked into the engine. • Bright dashboard trim reflects onto driver-side mirror. • Sunroof suddenly shattered. *Magentis:* **2001**—

Chronic hesitation, stalling, and surging. • Transmission failures. • Excessive AC condensation in the interior. • Inaccurate fuel gauge. • Faulty door locks. **2002**—Delayed acceleration. • Sudden stalling while cruising on the highway. • Complete brake failure. • Windows won't go down. • Faulty door locks. **2003**—Accelerator sticks. • Sudden loss of power. • Brake failures. • Vehicle starts on its own. • Rainy weather causes the car to run roughly. • Large rear-view mirror blocks visibility. • Inoperative headlight high beams. • Doors lock and unlock on their own. • Sticking door locks trap occupants. **2004**—Fire ignites in the dashboard area. • Suspension pulls vehicle into oncoming traffic. • Engine surges when manual transmission is shifted from Second to Third gear. • Vehicle suddenly loses power. • Power-steering leaks. • Delayed acceleration. • Leaking fuel regulator. • Mud compromises EGR valve performance. • Inoperative cruise control. **2005**—Defective steering assembly causes the vehicle to suddenly veer right. • Faulty high-beam headlights. **2006**—Passenger-side airbag won't work if a small adult occupies the seat. • Headlights frequently burn out, and Airbag warning light is constantly lit. • Sometimes the transmission won't downshift.

Secret Warranties/Internal Bulletins/Service Tips

Amanti: **2004**—Suspension noise when passing over uneven surfaces. **2005–06**—Computer module upgrade to correct engine's poor performance. **2006–07**—Reducing suspension noise, especially when braking. **2007**—Engine hesitation and surging fix. • Measures to reduce engine and exhaust noise. *Magentis:* **2001–06**—Correcting engine hesitation by changing the throttle position sensor values. **2003–04**—Hesitation when accelerating can be corrected by recalibrating the engine control module (ECM).

AMANTI, MAGENTIS PROFILE

	2001	2002	2003	2004	2005	2006	2007
Cost Price ($)							
Amanti	—	—	—	34,995	35,995	30,995	31,995
Magentis Base	20,995	21,295	22,250	22,250	22,450	22,450	21,895
LX V6	23,995	24,295	25,750	25,750	25,850	25,850	23,995
SE/EX V6	27,995	29,095	28,750	28,750	28,850	28,850	—
Used Values ($)							
Amanti ▲	—	—	—	8,000	11,000	14,500	18,500
Amanti ▼	—	—	—	6,500	9,500	13,000	17,000
Magentis Base ▲	5,000	7,000	9,000	10,500	13,000	10,500	13,000
Magentis Base ▼	4,000	5,500	7,500	9,500	11,500	9,000	11,500
LX V6 ▲	6,000	7,500	9,000	11,500	14,000	11,000	13,500
LX V6 ▼	5,000	6,500	7,500	10,000	12,500	9,500	12,000
SE/EX V6 ▲	7,000	8,500	10,500	13,000	15,500	12,000	—
SE/EX V6 ▼	6,000	7,000	9,000	11,500	14,000	10,500	—

Reliability	2	2	2	2	2	3	3
Crash Safety (F)	—	—	4	4	4	5	4
Amanti	—	—	—	—	—	5	5
Side	—	—	—	4	4	5	4
Amanti	—	—	—	—	—	4	5
IIHS Side	1	1	1	1	1	3	3
Offset	3	3	3	3	3	5	5
Amanti	—	—	—	—	—	—	5
Head Restraints	1	1	1	1	1	5	5
Rollover Resistance	—	—	5	5	5	4	4

Lexus

ES 300/330/350, GS 300/350/430/450H, IS 250/300/350, LS 400/430/460, SC 300, SC 400/430 ★★★★

RATING: Above Average (2002–07); Recommended (1999–2001). A bit more refined than the Infinitis, Lexus' lineup offers first-class performance and better-than-average reliability, with the exception of a powertrain that is prone to dangerous stalling and surging. The latest model years have been downgraded because of serious design deficiencies relating to sudden acceleration; chronic engine/transmission stumble, shudder, and surge; and dash gauges that are unreadable during daylight hours. **"Real" city/highway fuel economy:** *ES 300: 12.3/8.2 L/100 km. ES 330: 11.6/7.5 L/100 km. GS 300: 13.1/8.6 L/100 km. GS 400: 13.4/9.4 L/100 km. GS 430: 13.3/9.3 L/100 km. IS 300 manual: 13.2/8.8 L/100 km. IS 300 automatic: 13.1/8.9 L/100 km. LS 430: 13.2/8.6 L/100 km. LX 470: 17.9/12.9 L/100 km.* Real-world fuel savings may be lower by about 10–15 percent. The ES 330 burns less fuel than its ES 300 predecessor, even though the ES 300 is equipped with a smaller, 3.0L engine. **Maintenance/Repair costs:** Higher-than-average costs, and repairs are highly dealer-dependent. **Parts:** Higher-than-average costs, but parts aren't hard to find (except body panels). **Extended warranty:** Not necessary. **Best alternatives:** Look at the fully equipped Acura Legend, Honda Accord, early Nissan Maxima, and Toyota Camry to provide airbags, comparable highway performance, and reliability at far less initial cost—but without the Lexus cachet. Nevertheless, if you do pay top dollar for a used Lexus, its slow rate of depreciation virtually guarantees a high trade-in value.

Strengths and Weaknesses

These are benchmark cars known for their impressive reliability and performance. Sports cars, they're not. But if you're looking for your father's Oldsmobile from a Japanese automaker, these luxury cars fit the bill. Like Acuras and Infinitis, Lexus models all suffer from some automatic transmission failures; engine sludge buildup (see *www.autooninfo.info/VCC200310ToyotaEngineReliability.htm*); early rear main engine seal and front strut replacements (front struts are often replaced under a "goodwill" warranty); and front brake, electrical, body, trim, and accessory deficiencies.

ES 300/330/350

Resembling an LS 400 dressed in sporty attire, the entry-level ES 300 was launched in 1992 to fill the gap between the discontinued ES 250 and the LS 400. In fact, the ES 300 has many of the attributes of the LS 400 sedan but sells for much less money. A five-passenger sedan based on the Camry, but 90 kg (200 lb.) heavier and with a different suspension and tires, it comes equipped with a standard 3.0L 24-valve engine that produces 181–210 horses coupled to either a 5-speed manual or a 4-speed electronically controlled automatic transmission. Like some Infiniti models, however, the ES 300 hesitates and surges when accelerating. Headroom is also surprisingly limited for a car this expensive.

ES 330s came on the scene as 2004 models and offered buyers a more-powerful 3.3L V6 that produced more horses and a bit more torque. 2005 models got very little that was new, except for power front seats with a memory feature and power door mirrors that tilt down when in Reverse.

The 2007 ES 350 arrived with new styling, more power, and additional features, but it remained an upscale Toyota Camry. It has a slightly larger wheelbase and a new 6-speed transmission, and is powered by a 272 hp 3.5L V6 instead of the ES 330's 218 hp 3.3L V6. Standard features include anti-lock braking, traction/anti-skid control, front side airbags, side curtain airbags, and front knee airbags. ES 350 competes against the Acura TL, BMW 3 Series, Cadillac CTS, and Infiniti G35.

VEHICLE HISTORY: *ES 300/330/350:* **1999**—Horsepower is increased to 210; upgraded automatic transmission; traction control. **2000**—Restyled front ends and tail lights, and improved child safety seat anchors. **2002**—A longer, taller body; new 5-speed automatic transmission; improved brakes, steering, and suspension; and more standard luxury features. No more standard traction control. **2004**—ES 330 (designating a 3.3L engine) debuts with 15 extra horses and larger head-protecting side airbags. **2007**—ES 350 debuts.

For a vehicle this well made, government-reported safety-related defects are surprisingly omnipresent. These reports include airbag-induced injuries; sudden acceleration; an unreliable powertrain that surges, stumbles, stalls, and shifts erratically; ABS and Goodyear tire failures; excessive vibration when underway; interior window fogging; unreadable dash gauges; poor AC performance; and a frequently disconnecting Bluetooth.

GS 300/350/430/450h

The rear-drive GS 300 is a step up from the front-drive ES 300 and just a rung below Lexus' top-of-the-line LS 400. It carries the same V6 engine as the ES 300, except that it has 20 more horses. This produces sparkling performance at higher speeds, though the car is disappointingly sluggish from a start. Fuel economy is sacrificed for performance, however, and the base suspension and tires pass noisily over small bumps and ruts. Visibility is also less than impressive, with large rear pillars and a narrow rear window restricting the view. There's not much usable trunk space, and the liftover is unreasonably high.

VEHICLE HISTORY: 2001—Substantially upgraded with a 300 hp 4.3L V8, upgraded transmission controls, standard side curtain airbags, smart airbags, an emergency trunk release, and a host of other convenience features. **2006**—More power, fresh styling, a larger interior, and all-wheel drive. The rear-drive and all-wheel-drive GS 300s get a 245 hp V6 engine. The rear-drive GS 430 keeps its 300 hp V8. All models use a 6-speed automatic manumatic transmission, anti-skid/traction control, and anti-lock brakes. The GS 430 adds driver-adjustable shock absorbers and 18-inch wheels. Run-flat tires (more a boondoggle than a boon) are standard with AWD. All models have front knee airbags, front torso side airbags, and head-protecting side curtain airbags. **2007**—Entry-level models get a new 3.5L V6 that produces 303 hp, up from 245 hp with the prior 3.0L. In fact, the added horsepower beats the V8 by 13 horses, though the V8 is torquier. The lineup now: a GS 350, GS 430, and GS 450h hybrid.

Owner complaints have centred on brake failures, electrical shutdowns, prematurely worn wheel bearings, excessive front-end vibrations, fragile wheel rims, run-flat tire problems (cost, availability, performance, and durability), and electrical and fuel system malfunctions resulting in hesitation followed by sudden, unintended acceleration ("lag and lurch").

IS 250/300/350

Targeting BMW's 3 Series, this rear-drive sports-compact sedan comes with similar power and features to the BMW 325i—for a few thousand dollars less. Moreover, there is practically no difference in fuel economy between the manual and automatic transmission modes. The only engine is a 215 hp 3.0L inline-six (borrowed from the GS 300) mated to a 5-speed automatic transmission and incorporating Lexus's E-shift feature for manual shifting. Other important features are four-wheel ABS-equipped disc brakes, 17-inch wheels, performance tires, front seat belt pretensioners, and traction control. Just a bit narrower than the BMW 3 Series, the IS 300 is a competent performer both for routine tasks and in emergency situations. Fortunately, it hasn't been afflicted by the ES 300's and Camry's chronic powertrain defects that cause a dangerous shift delay and surging when accelerating. Look for models equipped with a limited-slip differential, but don't pay more for models featuring a sunroof, heated seats, or leather upholstery.

VEHICLE HISTORY: 2002—A SportCross wagon is added, and it comes only with an automatic transmission. Manual-shift sedans have a firmer suspension; ABS is upgraded; side curtain/front side airbags and traction control are standard. **2006**—After dropping the slow-selling wagon, Lexus revampes its sporty small sedan along the lines of the larger GS sedans, creating two rear-drive models and an all-wheel-drive version: the IS 250 and IS 250 AWD, equipped with a 204 hp V6, and the IS 350, powered by a 306 hp V6. All IS models come loaded with the latest high-tech safety and performance features to compete primarily against the Acura TSX, BMW 3 Series, and Infiniti G35.

In a nutshell, these cars stand out with a nice array of standard features; quality-looking gauges; good acceleration, handling, and braking; a comfortable ride; a low beltline for a great view; and first-class workmanship. On the other hand, the automatic transmission's manual E-shifter is awkward to use and isn't as sporty as a BMW's; owners report excessive road noise and tire thump; the instrument panel reflects in the windshield; the interior doesn't feel as plush as the competition's; seat cushions don't provide adequate thigh support; rear seating is a bit cramped; trunk hinges eat up trunk space and may damage luggage; no crashworthiness data is available; and premium fuel is required. Other cars worth considering are the Acura TL and BMW's 3 Series.

LS 400/430/460

The Lexus flagship, the LS 400 rear-drive arrived in 1990 with a 250 hp 4.0L V8. It outclasses all other luxury sedans in reliability, styling, and function. Its powerful engine provides smooth, impressive acceleration and a superior highway passing ability at all speeds. Its transmission is smooth and efficient. The suspension gives an easy ride without body roll or front-end plow during emergency stops, delivering a major comfort advantage over other luxury compacts. Other amenities include anti-lock brakes, a driver-side airbag, and automatic temperature control.

VEHICLE HISTORY: 2001—Totally redesigned with a sleeker body, a 4.3L V8, an upgraded suspension, and a more-spacious, reworked interior. Additional safety and comfort features are also added. **2003**—A firmer suspension and 17-inch wheels. **2004**—A 6-speed manumatic transmission, driver's knee-protecting airbags, steering-linked headlights, a power rear sunshade, and a tire-pressure monitor are added. Suspension, steering, and ABS systems are also upgraded. **2007**—A redesigned LS 460 gains a long-wheelbase body style, more power, and the industry's first 8-speed automatic transmission, plus a basketful of high-tech safety, performance, and convenience features. Two models are offered: the regular-sized LS 460, which is slightly longer and wider than the 2001–06 models, and the LS 460 L, which is even larger. The 278 hp 4.3L V8 is replaced by a 380 hp 4.6L V8, hence the name change from the LS 430 to the LS 460. The additional power and larger dimensions clearly target the car's main rivals: the Audi A8, BMW 7 Series, and Mercedes-Benz S-Class.

The brakes don't inspire confidence, owing to their mushy feel and average performance. Furthermore, there's limited rear footroom under the front seats, and the rear middle passenger has to sit on the transmission hump. This car is a gas-guzzler that thirsts for premium fuel.

Owner complaints over the years deal mainly with sudden, unintended acceleration; stalling caused by a faulty throttle sensor; traction control that causes the vehicle to swerve (usually to the left) unexpectedly; failure of the Vehicle Stability Control (VSC) to activate; main computer failures; spongy brakes; electrical glitches; and door locks that stick shut, trapping occupants.

SC 300, SC 400/430

These two coupes are practically identical, except for their engines and luxury features. The cheaper SC 300 gives you the same high-performance 6-cylinder engine used by the GS 300 and Toyota Supra, while the SC 400 uses the 4.0L V8 engine found in the LS 400. You're likely to find fewer luxury features with the SC 300 because they were sold as options. Nevertheless, look for an SC with traction control for additional safety during poor driving conditions. On the downside, V8 fuel consumption is horrendous, rear seating is cramped, and trunk space is unimpressive. Also, invest in a good anti-theft device, or your Lexus relationship will be over almost before it begins.

VEHICLE HISTORY: 1998—SC 400 gets the 4.0L V8 engine, while the SC 300 continues to use the previous year's inline-six but ditches its 5-speed manual transmission. Other upgrades are variable valve timing, a more-refined 5-speed automatic transmission, a new anti-theft system, and depowered airbags. **1999**—American-sold models get larger brakes. **2005**—Upgraded shock absorbers and navigation system.

Safety Summary

All models: 1997–2002—Engine warranty extended to eight years to cover engine oil sludge claims (see *www.autosafety.org*). *ES 300/330/350:* **All years:** Sudden, unintended acceleration. **1999**—Rear seat belts don't hold a child safety seat firmly. **2000**—Sudden, unintended acceleration when in Reverse. • Engine stalls or won't accelerate in traffic. • Vehicle suddenly downshifts from Fourth to First in heavy traffic; jerky shifting. • Rolls backward when transmission is in Drive. • Swerves left on a straight road. • Rear-view mirror doesn't move, resulting in poor visibility. **2001**—In one incident, engine fire ignited from what investigator said was fuel leaking from a rubber hose that had disconnected from the fuel filter. • Car suddenly accelerates as driver slows coming to a stop sign or when pulling into a parking space. • Traction control engages much too easily when merging into traffic. • One vehicle started up and began moving down the street in Reverse, despite the fact that there was no key in the ignition cylinder and the vehicle was left in Park. • Vehicle hesitates when applying accelerator after decelerating. **2002**—Airbags fail to deploy. • Impossible to read speedometer and other gauges in sunlight. • Won't go into gear properly. • Warped brake rotors. **2002–03**—Chronic engine/transmission surging and stalling not fixed by computer module recalibration, switching to premium fuel, etc. **2004**—Sudden acceleration; brake failure. • Stuck accelerator. • Delayed shift and surging when accelerating still occurs frequently, despite Toyota's special campaign "fix" that involves changing the electronic module:

This car is extremely dangerous. It's either a defective transmission or bad drive-by-wire design. The car hesitates extremely badly on acceleration. For example, when you are entering a limited access highway, if you slow down and then step on the gas, there is a long lag before the car begins to pick up speed. This lag is often a second or more. I have nearly been hit numerous times while the car makes up its mind whether it wants to move or not. The dealer has refused to fix the problem.

• Transmission goes into Reverse when shifted into Drive. • Vehicle lunges forward when transmission is shifted into Reverse. • Steering pulls vehicle into oncoming traffic. • Passenger-side airbag is disabled when adult of any weight sits in the front passenger seat. • Serious blind spots caused by left and right side rear-view mirrors. **2005**—Hesitation and then surging continues to be a major complaint category. • Sudden loss of braking capability. **2006**—Car suddenly accelerated and killed a pedestrian. • Vehicle lags and lurches. • Headlight range is too short; HID lights may ignite on impact. **2007**—Airbag on passenger side is disabled when a small adult occupies the seat. • Sudden acceleration when cruise control is engaged. • Automatic transmission flares even though foot is taken off the accelerator (car suddenly accelerates). • Accelerator can get stuck under the floor mat. *GS 300:* **1999**—Sudden, unintended acceleration and unexpected delayed acceleration. • Airbags fail to deploy. • Wheels break under normal driving conditions. • Complete brake failure. • Excessive vibration at highway speeds. **2002**—Fire ignites from fuel filter leak. • Sticking accelerator. • Vehicle starts without key. • Traction control engages too easily. • Inadequate headlight illumination. • Digital dash indicator washes out in sunlight. **2003**—Again, reports of sudden, unintended acceleration and hesitation when accelerating. *GS 350:* **2007**—Vehicle crashed into a brick wall after suddenly accelerating. • Floormat caused accelerator pedal to stick. *GS 450h:* **2007**—Vehicle emits high levels of electromagnetic radiation emanating from the motor and/or generator (causes tingling in the hands and feet, numbness in the face, and dull headaches).

Secret Warranties/Internal Bulletins/Service Tips

All models: 2002—Harsh 2–3 shift. • Troubleshooting steering pull and interior squeaks and rattles. **2002–03**—TSB #TC004-03, issued August 4, 2003, gives recalibration instructions for correcting erratic shifting. This free repair is in effect for 96 months/128,000 km (80,000 mi.). • Unreadable dash gauges. • Body creak or snap from top of front windshield. **2002–04**—Inoperative AC. **2002–05**—Countermeasures for poor shift quality. **2002–06**—Troubleshooting tips for vehicles that pull to one side when underway. • Inoperative rear power window. **2003–05**—Steering clunk, pop. **2003–06**—Windshield ticking noise. **2004**—Troubleshooting tips for a malfunctioning front-seat occupant seat belt sensor. • Vehicle pulls into oncoming traffic. *GS 300:* **2000–02**—Front stabilizer bar noise. **2002**—Steering pull troubleshooting. *LS 400/430:* **1999–2000**—Countermeasures to reduce steering noise and improve smoothness. **2000**—Moonroof water leaks. **2001**—Moonroof rattle, and rear-corner air leak. • Instrument panel rattling. • Rear seat and luggage compartment creaking.

2002–06—Steering-pull troubleshooting. 2004—Ignition switch difficult to turn. • No picture displayed by backup camera. • Rear window water leaks.

ES 300/330/350, GS 300/350/430/450H, IS 250/300/350, LS 400/430/460, SC 400/430 PROFILE

354

	1999	2000	2001	2002	2003	2004	2005	2006	2007
Cost Price ($)									
ES 300/330/350	44,235	43,995	44,000	43,400	43,800	43,800	43,900	42,900	42,900
GS 300/350	59,220	59,420	60,700	60,700	61,700	61,700	61,700	64,300	59,750
GS 430	—	—	71,300	68,800	69,500	69,500	69,500	74,700	71,300
GS 450h	—	—	—	—	—	—	—	—	76,900
IS 250	—	—	—	—	—	—	—	36,300	36,400
IS 300/350	—	—	40,830	37,820	37,775	37,775	37,990	48,900	49,000
LS 400/430/460	78,690	78,950	80,000	81,900	82,800	83,200	84,900	85,700	86,440
SC 400/430	—	—	—	84,000	85,500	86,800	89,770	86,800	93,250
Used Values ($)									
ES 300/330/350 ▲	5,500	7,000	9,000	11,000	12,500	14,500	19,000	24,000	27,500
ES 300/330/350 ▼	5,000	6,000	7,500	9,500	11,000	13,000	17,500	22,000	26,000
GS 300/350 ▲	8,000	9,000	11,000	13,000	15,000	18,000	23,000	29,000	37,000
GS 300/350 ▼	7,500	8,000	9,500	11,500	13,500	16,500	21,000	27,000	34,000
GS 430 ▲	—	—	11,000	13,000	16,000	20,000	25,000	35,000	44,000
GS 430 ▼	—	—	8,500	11,500	14,500	18,500	23,000	32,000	41,000
GS 450h ▲	—	—	—	—	—	—	—	—	46,000
GS 450h ▼	—	—	—	—	—	—	—	—	43,000
IS 250 ▲	—	—	—	—	—	—	—	19,000	22,000
IS 250 ▼	—	—	—	—	—	—	—	17,000	20,000
IS 300/350 ▲	—	—	8,000	10,000	11,000	12,000	15,000	28,000	32,000
IS 300/350 ▼	—	—	6,500	8,500	10,000	11,000	12,500	6,000	30,000
LS 400/430/460 ▲	12,000	14,000	16,000	18,500	22,000	25,000	32,000	43,000	53,000
LS 400/430/460 ▼	10,500	12,500	14,500	17,000	20,000	23,000	29,000	40,000	49,000
SC 400/430 ▲	—	—	—	23,000	27,000	32,000	46,000	51,000	61,000
SC 400/430 ▼	—	—	—	21,000	25,000	30,000	43,000	47,000	57,000
Reliability	4	4	4	4	4	4	4	4	4
Crash Safety (F)									
ES 300/330/350	—	4	4	—	—	—	5	5	—
GS 300	3	—	—	—	—	—	—	—	—
Side									
ES 300/330/350	—	5	5	—	5	—	5	5	5
IS 300	—	—	—	—	—	—	—	—	5
IIHS Side									
ES 330	—	—	—	—	—	—	—	5	5
Offset									
ES 300/330/350	—	—	—	—	—	5	5	5	5
GS 300	—	—	5	5	5	5	5	5	5
LS 400/430	5	5	5	5	5	5	5	5	5

All ratings on a numbered scale where 5 is good and 1 is bad. See pages 108–109 for a more detailed description.

Head Restraints									
ES 300/350	3	—	3	—	3	3	3	1	1
GS 300	—	—	—	—	—	—	2	2	2
IS 300	—	—	—	—	2	2	2	2	2
LS 430	—	—	—	—	2	2	2	2	2
Rollover Resistance									
ES 300/330/350	—	—	—	—	—	—	4	4	4
IS 300	—	—	—	—	—	—	—	—	5

Mercedes-Benz

B-CLASS, C-CLASS ★★★ / ★

RATING: *B-Class:* Average (2006–07). *C-Class:* Not Recommended (1999–2007). These luxury lemons are outclassed by most Asian luxury models, which offer more safety, reliability, and comfort for much less money. **"Real" city/highway fuel economy:** *B200 manual:* 9.2/6.7 L/100 km. *B200 automatic:* 9.2/7.2 L/100 km. *B200 Turbo manual:* 10.3/6.9 L/100 km. *B200 Turbo automatic:* 9.5/7.4 L/100 km. *C230 manual:* 9.5/7.2 L/100 km. *C230 automatic:* 10.2/7.1 L/100 km. *C240 manual:* 12.9/8.4 L/100 km. *C240 automatic:* 12.4/8.9 L/100 km. *C32 AMG:* 14.6/10.3 L/100 km. *C320 manual:* 12.7/8.3 L/100 km. *C320 automatic:* 11.8/8.2 L/100 km. *CL500:* 14.7/9.1 L/100 km. *CL600:* 18.4/11.6 L/100 km. *CL55 AMG:* 16.6/10.3 L/100 km. Owners report fuel savings are lower than these estimates by about 15 percent. **Maintenance/Repair costs:** Higher-than-average costs, and most repairs must be done by a Mercedes dealer. Look out for electronic glitches, engine oil sludging (see page 60), and fuel-system malfunctions. **Parts:** Highly dealer-dependent and expensive. **Extended warranty:** A smart idea. **Best alternatives:** Acura Integra or RL, BMW 3 Series, Infiniti I30, and Toyota Avalon.

Strengths and Weaknesses

B-Class

Mercedes' B-Class, launched as a 2006 model spun off of the yet smaller A-Class, answers a question that few serious-minded motorists have asked: "Can Mercedes make a classy compact car?" The B-Class answers the question with a yes and a no. Can they make it small? Yes. Can they make it classy? No.

The car looks like a mini-minivan, without any of the stylistic lines that would identify the B200 as a Mercedes product. But it does have a roomy interior and smooth-running drivetrain. A 136 hp 2.0L engine is standard, and a torquier, turbocharged 193 hp variant is optional. Although the car is quite vulnerable to crosswinds due to its extra height, overall highway performance is above average. Nevertheless, there are half a dozen other cars that perform as well or better, with classier lines, more-extensive dealership networks, proven reliability, and good resale values.

C-Class

Replacing the low-quality, unreliable, power-challenged, and bland 190 series, the 1994 C-Class gained interior room and two new engines: a base 147 hp 2.2L and a 194 hp 2.8L 6-cylinder—a real powerhouse in this small car when coupled to the manual 5-speed transmission. The 4-speed automatic is a big disappointment—it requires a lot of throttle effort to downshift and prefers to start out in Second gear. Although this series got small, incremental power increases and additional features over the years, you don't see a major redesign until 2001. Unfortunately, the new engines and other features added at that time only add to the car's poor reliability, engine and road noise are still bothersome, and interior space is still inadequate. Since then, these cars have coasted on the Mercedes name and been touted mainly as fuel-sippers with a high-end cachet. That's poor recompense for what little the car actually offers. See *www.benzworld.org/forums, www.mercedes-benz-usa.com* (Mercedes-Benz Lemon Problem Vehicles), and *www.carsurvey.org/reviews/ mercedes-benz/c-class.*

VEHICLE HISTORY: 1999—Models get the SLK's 2.3L supercharged engine, replacing the C230's normally aspirated powerplant; a better-performing drivetrain; and standard leather upholstery. **2000**—A Touch Shift auto-manual transmission; stability control; and Tele-Aid, a communications system for calling for assistance. **2001**—Completely revamped, gaining two new engines, additional safety features, and more-aerodynamic styling. **2002**—Additional rear room and storage space, more high-performance features, a wagon, and an AWD sedan and wagon. **2003**—All-wheel drive and another wagon (C240) are added, and the C230 hatchback coupe gets a new supercharged 4-cylinder engine, losing 3 horses in the process. **2004**—Sports coupes adopt a standard three-spoke steering wheel, enlarged chrome exhaust tip, and other pseudo-sporty paraphernalia. **2005**—Restyled and joined by a high-performance 362 hp V8-equipped C55 AMG sedan. The C320 gets a 3.5L V6. **2006**—New engines and model designations, fewer body styles, and the wagons and coupes are gone. Sedans come with rear-drive and all-wheel drive. The C230 Sport gets a 201 hp V6 in place of a 189 hp supercharged 4-cylinder. The C280 Luxury has a 228 hp V6 instead of its predecessor's 168 hp engine. The C350 Sport and Luxury have a 268 hp V6 that replaces the 215 hp powerplant used by the C320. The C55 returns for its last year.

Owner surveys give the entry-level C-Class cars a worse-than-average rating. C-Class owners report frequent problems with sudden, unintended acceleration; slipping, or soft then hard, shifts; drivetrain noise and vibration; and windshield squeaks. Engines (oil sludge), brakes, the AC electrical system, and computer-controlled electronic components (telematics) are glitch-prone, hell to diagnose, and expensive to repair:

Check valve on my 2005 C230 has a defect allowing the supercharged air to enter into the crankcase of the engine pushing oil into it. It caused a misfire reading, loss of power and the Check Engine light to go on. The campaign I found identical to my problem is number...2008020002. However it[s] repair coverage is only associated with a range of VIN #'s throughout 2003–2005. My car is a 2005, but the campaign is not listed under my VIN#.

Fit and finish is also subpar (gearshift "chrome" shreds easily, for example), and original-equipment tires may have weak side walls.

Safety Summary

All models/years: Airbags fail to deploy. • Sudden, unintended acceleration and brake failure. • Faulty gas gauge sensor. • Rear suspension bouncing makes it difficult to maintain directional control. • Car is very vulnerable to side-wind buffeting. • Window failures. • Brakes fail on incline. • When the vehicle is cold, the automatic transmission slips, sticks in gear, and shifts abruptly. • Many reports of a sudden loss of power and stalling. • Multiple electrical short circuits. • Differential failure. • Vehicle wanders over highway. **All models: 2004**—Fire ignites in the electrical wires housed in the dashboard. • Transmission fails to shift into Reverse. • Loose driver's seat. • Front windshield is easily cracked by road debris. • Auto-dimming rear-view mirror sometimes turns pitch-black. • AC corrosion produces a noxious odour in the cabin. **2005**—Engine compartment fire. • No airbag deployment when needed. • Airbag suddenly deployed when it was *not* needed. • Vehicle hesitates and then slams into gear. • Instrument panel is hard to read in daylight. • Tire side wall failures. **2006**—Airbags failed to deploy in a collision. **2007**—Several incidents reported that the airbag deployed for no reason. • Sudden brake failure. • No-starts due to faulty fuel pump. *C240:* **All years:** Wide rear quarter panel blind spot.

Secret Warranties/Internal Bulletins/Service Tips

All models/years: Seat noises can be eliminated by installing a seat-noise kit. **All models: 1997–2004**—Engine oil sludge refund guidelines. **1999**—Hesitation after a cold start, and rough 1–2 and 2–3 shifts during warm-up. **2001**—Troubleshooting hard starts and poor engine performance. **2002**—Lack of power, engine hesitation. • Inoperative cruise control. • Power-window motor locks up when closing. • Inoperative central locking system. • Tail/brake lights stay on. **2002–04**—Engine rattling. • Inoperative cruise control. • Harsh transmission shifts. • Transmission fluid leaks at the electrical connection. • Scraping noise comes from the transmission tunnel area. • Inoperative trunk/cargo light. • Free corrosion repairs along the door bottoms. **2003–04**—Troubleshooting tips for fixing a rough-running engine. • Windshield blistering near rain/light sensor. **2004**—Engine oil leaks through the cylinder head bolt threads. • Steering leaks. • Suspension rumbling. • Exhaust rattling, hissing, and humming. **2004–05**—Campaign to check and replace, if necessary, the automatic transmission pilot bushing. **2005**—The following items may also apply to previous model years. If you have identical problems, ask your dealer service manager to check the files. • Engine won't start. • Engine oil leaks from the oil-level sensor. • Rough idle. • Harsh shifts with the automatic transmission. • Transmission fluid leaks at the electrical connector. • Inoperative central locking system and AC heater blower motor. • Steering assembly leaks fluid. • Sliding roof water leaks, rattling. • Moisture in the turn signal lights and mirrors. • Tail lights won't turn off; trunk light won't turn on. • Door frames will get free rustproofing under a special Service Campaign (read: "secret warranty"). • Another Service Campaign calls for the free modification of the lower door seal. **2006–07**—Countermeasures to rid the interior of an oily, vinegary smell. **2007**—Rough shifting. • Automatic transmission upshift, downshift chatter. • Steering rack leaks. • Inoperative AC blower motor. • Remedy for front and rear brake squealing. • Front-end/dash noise. • Front axle knocking when parking. • Torsion bar front-end creaking. • Inoperative turn signals. • Rear seatback rattle. • Loose head restraint. • Horn may not work due to premature corrosion of the assembly. • Front centre armrest may fall off.

B-CLASS, C-CLASS PROFILE

	1999	2000	2001	2002	2003	2004	2005	2006	2007
Cost Price ($)									
B200	—	—	—	—	—	—	—	30,950	31,400
C230	37,950	38,450	—	33,950	34,450	35,290	36,450	36,950	38,400
C240	—	—	37,450	37,950	38,450	41,290	42,250	—	—
C280	—	—	—	—	—	—	—	42,850	42,800
C320/C350	—	—	49,950	50,600	49,750	40,700	40,600	54,950	51,000
Used Values ($)									
B200 ▲	—	—	—	—	—	—	—	16,500	19,000
B200 ▼	—	—	—	—	—	—	—	15,000	17,500
C230 ▲	4,500	6,000	—	7,500	9,000	11,000	14,000	20,000	24,000
C230 ▼	4,000	5,000	—	7,000	7,500	9,500	12,500	18,000	22,000
C240 ▲	—	—	7,000	8,500	10,000	13,000	16,000	—	—
C240 ▼	—	—	6,000	8,000	8,500	11,500	14,500	—	—
C280 ▲	—	—	—	—	—	—	—	22,500	27,000
C280 ▼	—	—	—	—	—	—	—	21,000	25,500
C320/C350 ▲	—	—	9,500	11,000	12,000	13,000	16,000	29,000	34,000
C320/C350 ▼	—	—	10,000	10,000	11,000	11,500	14,500	26,500	31,000
Reliability	1	1	1	1	1	1	2	2	3
B200	—	—	—	—	—	—	—	3	3
Crash Safety (F)	—	—	—	—	4	4	4	4	4
Side	3	3	—	—	5	5	5	5	5
IIHS Side	—	—	—	—	—	—	3	3	3
Offset	—	—	5	5	5	5	5	5	5
Head Restraints (F)	3	—	5	5	5	2	2	3	3
Rollover Resistance	—	—	—	—	4	4	4	4	4

RATING: Below Average (1999–2007). Mercedes' quality has deteriorated over the past decade because of the increased complexity of mechanical, emissions, and electronic components. Beware of engine oil sludge. **"Real" city/highway fuel economy:** *E320:* 13.2/8.1 L/100 km. *E500:* 14.4/9.1 L/100 km. *E55 AMG:* 16.6/10.3 L/100 km. Owners report fuel savings are less than these estimates by about 20 percent. **Maintenance/Repair costs:** Higher-than-average costs, but many repairs can now be done by independent garages. **Parts:** Higher-than-average costs, and limited availability. **Extended warranty:** A good idea. **Best alternatives:** The natural inclination is to seriously consider one of the BMW variants. Don't. They are just as poorly made and unreliable. Equivalent 2001 and later 5 Series, 6 Series, 7 Series, and X5 models come with standard iDrive—a complicated cockpit electronic controller that will drive you batty. Says Electronic Design Magazine (*www.elecdesign.com/Articles/Index.cfm?AD=1&AD=1&ArticleID=8246*):

> BMW's 2001 introduction of iDrive, its pioneering driver information/entertainment system, was arguably the biggest corporate disaster since Coca-Cola Co. decided to tinker with the formula for its eponymous beverage.

Granted, by the time the 5 Series adopted iDrive a few years later, the system was redesigned so the driver could use it without looking at the small LCD panel. The 2007 X5 incorporates iDrive's third redesign in seven years. All this effort does make for a more user-friendly operation, but the learning curve is still rather steep. Instead, consider the Acura Integra, RL, or TL; Ford Crown Victoria or Mercury Grand Marquis; Infiniti I30 series; and Toyota Avalon.

Strengths and Weaknesses

These cars were once ideal mid-sized family sedans, until Mercedes started churning out feeble downsized models and installing failure-prone electronic components and sludge-prone engines. Nevertheless, the E-Class sedans are lemons that are a bit less sour because they have been around so long, depreciate slowly, and provide all the interior space that the early 190 Series and present-day C-Class leave out. Their major shortcoming is a weak dealer network that limits parts distribution and drives up parts and servicing costs.

VEHICLE HISTORY: *E-Class:* **2000**—Diesel dropped; a new all-wheel-drive E430 with standard side airbags is added. All models get new wheels, Touch Shift (an auto-manual device), and Electronic Stability. **2004**—Increased availability of all-wheel drive, a revamped wagon body style, and a new 7-speed automatic transmission. **2005**—A turbocharged diesel, the E320 CDI, debuts as an early 2005 model. **2006**—The E350 gets a more-powerful 268 hp 3.5L engine (47 additional horses). **2007**—New styling, more power, and additional safety features.

Quality control has traditionally been below average with the E-Class cars. Owners of pre-2002 models point out recurring problems with the fuel and electrical systems, causing lights, instruments, and gauges to shut off and the trunk lid to open when the engine is shut down. Other common problems include premature rusting and paint delamination; stalling and engine surging; engine oil leaks; engine problems caused by a stretched timing chain; oil sludging in 1998–2001 models (see "Secret Warranties/Internal Bulletins/Service Tips"); computer module failures (in both the engine and transmission); and erratically performing, leaky, and noisy transmissions (see *www.benzworld.org*, *www.mercedes-benz-usa.com* (Mercedes-Benz Lemon Problem Vehicles), *www.troublebenz.com*, *www.carsurvey. org/reviews/mercedes-benz*, and *www.oil-tech.com/32million.htm*).

The 2002–07 models haven't improved. Problem areas are similar to what's been reported with Mercedes' entire lineup, including the C-Class, CLK, M-Class, R-Class, S-Class, and SLK models. Foremost are transmission malfunctions, electrical short circuits, suspension problems, brake failures and the premature wearout of key brake components, unreliable climate and audio systems, and pathetically substandard fit and finish, best exemplified by complaints that the paint peels away on the lower doors.

 ## Safety Summary

All models/years: Frequent transmission breakdowns. • Serious, often total, electrical failures. • Chronic stalling. • Sudden, unintended acceleration. • Vehicle lags and lurches when accelerating. • Steering locks up. • No child safety locks for the rear doors. • Airbag warning light stays lit or doesn't light, and airbag deploys inadvertently:

> While driving down the highway, my passenger side curtain and rear side door airbags deployed for no reason at all…. It scared the hell out of me and nearly caused me to crash the car.

• Water enters the automatic transmission control module, preventing the transmission from changing gears. • Vehicle hesitates when accelerating with gas pedal halfway depressed, then it lurches forward. • Steering locks up while turning. • Total electrical failure in traffic, leading to vehicle shutdown. • Windows don't stay up. **All models: 2003**—Faulty gateway module and software cause failure in the braking system and tire-pressure feedback. • Electrical failures can leave the vehicle with no rear brakes and limited use of the front brakes. **2004**—Sudden loss of power while underway or merging. • Total brake failure. • Intermittent failure of the radar-controlled cruise control. • Mirrors tilt down when backing up but don't tilt up until car goes forward at 14 km/h. **2005**—Seat belt chime goes off when the seat is unoccupied. • Distracting reflections on the driver-side mirror; dash reflects onto the front windshield. • Diesel engine is unacceptably slow to accelerate. • Excessive black soot and a tar-like residue generated by the diesel engine. • Faulty AC/defrost blower motor. • Erroneous navigation/GPS directions will get you into serious trouble:

The problem, as I see it, is that a fair percentage of drivers will blindly follow the verbal instructions with serious consequences. Incidentally, talking with the salesman about this problem, he told me that they already had a woman drive into a lake.

320: 2006—Failure of many brake components, some of which cannot be easily repaired. • HID headlight glare angers and blinds oncoming cars. *320 Blue:* Diesel engine surges when shifting gears, causing car to lurch forward and skid on ice. • Sudden brake failure when parking. • Electrical short circuits caused by a dried-up, cracked wiring harness. *350: 2006*—7-speed automatic transmission failures disable steering and brake boost, ABS, and EPS system. • Other incidents where the tranny suddenly locks up in high gear and requires that the car be restarted to return to normal. • Automatic transmission behaves like the clutch is slipping, slowing car to a snail's pace. • Vehicle will often not start because electrical shorts have disabled the electronics. • Electronic key fob doesn't work. • Sunroof exploded while vehicle was underway. • All four original-equipment tires blew during their first year of use. • If the back seats are lowered to carry more cargo, the front seats cannot be pushed back. **2007**—Vehicle will suddenly stall while on the highway. • Child opened the rear door while car was idling at a red light. • All four wheels replaced because they were bent at the rim. • Rubber ring inside the fuel tank failed, allowing fuel to leak out of the tank.

Secret Warranties/Internal Bulletins/Service Tips

All models: 1998–2004—Free engine repairs or replacement if afflicted by engine oil sludge, following the O'Keefe class action settlement in April 2003. Order No. S-B-18.00/16a, published December 2003, gives all the details on the problem and Mercedes' payout rules. **2000**—A Special Service Campaign will replace, free of charge, side airbags that may deploy if the vehicle is left in the sun. **2002–05**—Free replacement of the alternator voltage regulator. **2003**—Piston-slap engine noise. **2004**—No-starts. • Harsh transmission shifts. • Steering leaks. • Sliding roof-rack cover cracks. • Wheelhouse water drain modification. • Rear axle rumbling. **2005**—Oil leaks from the oil-level sensor. • Rough automatic transmission engagement, droning, buzzing noises. • Transmission leaks fluid at the electrical connector. • Campaign to check and repair possible automatic transmission pilot bushing leakage; another campaign concerns the free cleaning of the front axle carrier sleeve and bolt replacement; a third campaign will reprogram the battery control module; and a fourth campaign will inspect or replace the alternator/regulator. • Foul interior odours. • Steering fluid leaks and steering squeal when turning. • Front-seat noise. • Sliding roof water leaks, rattling. • Moisture in the turn signal lights and mirrors. • Rear seatback rattle. • Loose passenger head restraints. • Fanfare horns may not work due to premature wiring corrosion. *350:* **2006–07**—Rough transmission shifts. • Upshift/downshift chatter or shudder. • Front axle creaking, grinding, knocking noise when parking, and other front-end noises. • Brake squeal. • Steering-rack leaks. • Rivet replacement to prevent water leakage. • Inoperative AC, faulty blower motor, or compressor failure. • False oil readings. • Inoperative turn signals. • Loose front centre armrest falls off. • Noisy seats.

	1999	2000	2001	2002	2003	2004	2005	2006	2007
Cost Price ($)									
280 AWD	—	—	—	—	—	—	—	—	45,400
300ED	59,950	—	—	—	—	—	—	—	—
320 Blue	66,750	67,150	67,900	68,350	69,950	72,050	73,000	75,450	67,801
350 AWD	—	—	—	—	—	—	—	57,200	53,600
420E, 430	74,250	74,750	75,750	76,150	—	—	—	—	—
500E/S/AWD	122,900	112,851	114,650	116,950	81,500	83,500	84,600	84,600	—
550 AWD	—	—	—	—	—	—	—	—	85,000
55/63 AMG	—	98,900	100,550	101,600	113,000	101,150	115,650	117,745	118,900
Used Values ($)									
280 AWD ▲	—	—	—	—	—	—	—	—	29,000
280 AWD ▼	—	—	—	—	—	—	—	—	27,000
300ED ▲	7,500	—	—	—	—	—	—	—	—
300ED ▼	6,500	—	—	—	—	—	—	—	—
320 Blue ▲	8,500	11,000	13,000	15,500	19,000	23,000	27,000	37,000	42,000
320 Blue ▼	7,500	10,000	11,500	14,000	17,000	21,000	25,000	34,000	39,000
350 AWD ▲	—	—	—	—	—	—	—	34,000	37,000
350 AWD ▼	—	—	—	—	—	—	—	31,000	34,000
420E, 430 ▲	9,500	11,500	14,000	17,000	—	—	—	—	—
420E, 430 ▼	8,000	10,500	12,500	15,500	—	—	—	—	—
500E/S/AWD ▲	11,000	13,500	16,000	18,000	20,000	25,000	30,000	41,000	—
500E/S/AWD ▼	10,000	12,000	14,000	16,500	18,500	23,000	27,000	38,000	—
550 AWD ▲	—	—	—	—	—	—	—	—	57,000
550 AWD ▼	—	—	—	—	—	—	—	—	54,000
55/63 AMG ▲	—	13,000	16,000	19,000	24,000	31,000	38,000	52,000	72,000
55/63 AMG ▼	—	11,000	14,000	17,000	22,000	29,000	35,000	48,000	67,000
Reliability	1	1	1	1	2	2	2	2	2
Crash Safety (F)	—	—	—	—	4	4	4	4	4
Side	—	—	—	—	5	5	5	5	5
IIHS Side	—	—	—	—	—	—	—	—	3
Offset	3	3	5	5	5	5	5	5	5
Head Restraints (4d)	3	—	5	5	5	3	3	5	5
Wagon	—	—	3	3	—	—	—	5	5
Rollover Resistance	—	—	—	—	5	5	5	5	5

All ratings on a numbered scale where 5 is good and 1 is bad. See pages 108–109 for a more detailed description.

Nissan

MAXIMA ★★★

RATING: Average (2007); Below Average (2002–06); Average (1999–2001). The 2002 and 2004 model redesigns led to an overall decline in quality. Redesigned 1995–2001 versions offer a peppier engine, more-rounded styling, and a slightly longer wheelbase. **"Real" city/highway fuel economy:** *3.0L manual:* 10.8/7.9 L/100 km. *3.0L automatic:* 12.1/8.1 L/100 km. *3.5L manual:* 11.5/7.3 L/100 km. *3.5L automatic:* 11.6/7.9 L/100 km. Owners report fuel savings are less than these estimates by about 10 percent. **Maintenance/Repair costs:** Higher than average. **Parts:** Higher-than-average costs, but parts are easy to find. Xenon headlights are frequently stolen from the car because they are easily accessed, and can cost $800 each to replace. **Extended warranty:** A must-have. **Best alternatives:** Acura Integra or RL, Infiniti I30 series, and Toyota Avalon.

 Strengths and Weaknesses

Early models (2001 and earlier)

These front-drive sedans are very well equipped and nicely finished, but they're cramped for their size. Although the trunk is spacious, only five passengers can travel in a pinch (in the literal sense). The 6-cylinder 190 hp engine, borrowed from the 300ZX in 1992, offers sparkling performance; the fuel injectors, however, are problematic. The '93 models got standard driver-side airbags, and the Maxima remained unchanged until the 1995 model's redesign. There was a second redesign for the year 2000 version.

Electrical and front suspension problems afflict early Maximas. Brakes and engine timing belts need frequent attention in all model years as well. Weak automatic transmissions and ignition systems fail frequently. There have also been many reports of cooked transmissions caused by the poorly designed transmission cooler. The cruise control unit is problematic: When it's engaged at moderate speeds, it hesitates or drifts to a lower speed, acting as if the fuel line was clogged.

Nissan has had problems with weak window regulators for some time. If the window is frozen, don't open it. Also, the rubber weather stripping around the window cuts easily and causes the window to go off track, which in turn causes stress on the weak regulators. Driver-side window breakage is common and can cost up to $300 to repair. Costly aluminum wheels corrode quickly and are easily damaged by road hazards. Maximas usually suffer from rust perforation on the sunroof, door bottoms, rear wheelwells, front hood edges, and bumper supports. The underbody should also be checked carefully for corrosion damage.

Recent models (2002 to present)

Each Maxima redesign has been followed by an increase in owner complaints, a normal occurrence with most revamped vehicles, but unusually severe with Nissan. Usually, after a couple of years, quality rebounds and complaints diminish.

Recent redesigns have hobbled the powertrain. Owners have difficulty controlling the engine speed with the gas pedal. There's engine popping and knocking when accelerating, surging or stalling when braking or decelerating, and transmission malfunctions galore. Premature front brake pad wear and rotor warpage; a choppy, jarring suspension; excessive front-end shaking and shimmy; faulty ignition coils; and inadequate headlight illumination continue to be major problems.

The 2004–06 revamped Maximas continue to have the following major quality problems: brake shimmy or judder (dealers lean toward all the usual suspects before they resort to the steering-rack friction adjustment that has cured the shimmy for some of the most persistent cases); broken struts; harsh automatic shifting; a gear grind from First to Second; windows that are slow to roll down; side mirrors that won't reposition; seat shifting; a screeching sound that's caused by a loose heat shield; transmission failures; HID lights with high beams that won't return to low and bulbs that burn out prematurely; no-starts caused by a loose fuel-pump connector or ignition switch failure; water leaks by right floorboard and through sunroof; inoperative steering-wheel stereo buttons; and paint that's easily chipped or scratched.

VEHICLE HISTORY: 1995—A longer wheelbase (adding to interior room), a new 3.0L engine, and more-rounded styling. Nevertheless, tall passengers will find the interior a bit cramped, and the automatic transmission is often slow to downshift and isn't always smooth. **2000**—Redesigned to offer more power, interior space (particularly for rear-seat passengers), and safety/convenience features. **2002**—Completely revamped, featuring a 260 hp 3.5L V6 coupled to a 6-speed manual or 4-speed automatic transmission; revised interior trim; larger front brakes; new front-end styling; and xenon headlights (a thief's Holy Grail). **2003**—GLE gets standard front side airbags. **2004**—Another redesign adds to the size and weight, along with 5 more horses. Once again, quality takes a big hit. **2005**—Improved 6-speed manual transmission. **2007**—Revised interior and exterior styling, keyless starting, and a new transmission. Sporty 3.5 SE and 3.5 SL models are offered with a 255 hp V6 coupled to a new, fuel-saving CVT automatic transmission with a manual shiftgate and six preselected gears.

Safety Summary

All years: Airbag failed to deploy. • Sudden loss of power, resulting in inoperative brakes and steering. • Chronic stalling. • Erratic transmission performance. • ABS failures. **2001**—Engine compartment fire. • Steering lock-ups and loss of brakes. **2002**—Vehicle suddenly swings to the right. • Steering wheel overheats. • Sudden acceleration in Reverse with gearshift lever indicating Drive. • ABS and traction control malfunction every time car is washed. • Front wheels lock up or get no power; ABS light remains lit. • Hesitation on acceleration. • Vehicle accelerates when foot is taken off accelerator. • Defective mass air sensor or crank sensor causes sudden loss of power and transmission bucking and jerking. • Vehicle rolls backward when parked on an incline. • Right front wheel buckles when brakes are applied. • In one incident, vehicle surged when brakes were applied while parking, and car hit a brick wall. • Faulty air control valve causes sudden acceleration. • Suspension transverse link failed, causing loss of control; owners report that cars not in the recall have the same defect. • Lower control-arm failure as in recall notice, but car isn't among those recalled. • Chronic brake failures. • Back window suddenly shatters. • Rear quarter window air leaks. • Trunk water leaks. **2002–03**—Xenon headlights are easily stolen and expensive to replace:

> Headlights easily stolen on Nissan Maxima 2002, 2003. I have a 2002 Maxima SE and the other day, my headlights were stolen while the car was parked outside my mother-in-law's house. I found out this has been an ongoing problem with this vehicle and Nissan isn't telling anyone about this problem when purchasing this vehicle…the way the lights are connected they are easily stolen and will be an ongoing problem…. Nissan will retrofit new lights at the owner's expense, about $300.00.

2003—Passenger-side airbag deploys on its own. • O_2 sensor failure. • Hard-to-read instrument panel lights. • Xenon headlight thefts. **2004**—Vehicle was underway at 100 km/h when the steering wheel suddenly locked up and the brakes failed. • In another instance, the front wheels locked up while the vehicle was in motion, causing extensive undercarriage damage. • Vehicle suddenly swerves out of control. • Vehicle suddenly accelerates in Reverse when put into Drive. • Sudden acceleration upon start-up (a faulty air control valve is suspected). • Unable to control engine speed with the accelerator pedal. • Vehicle stalls without warning in cold weather (suspect the computer module). • Many complaints that the headlights are poorly designed, placing the high beams too high for adequate visibility; drivers complain they can't see between the high and low beams. • Trunk lid and latch are hazardous when raised. • Several incidents where the SkyView roof shattered. • Sunroof opens and closes on its own. • Steering wheel overheats in direct sunlight. • The driver-side windshield washer may not work in cold weather. **2005**—Stalling and hard starts. • Engine surges when downshifting. • There is a one-second delay from when the accelerator pedal is released to when the car begins to slow down. • Engine threw a rod and had to be replaced. • Erratic transmission shifts. • Strong vibration and shimmy, probably related to faulty suspension strut assemblies that often wear out within a year. • Sudden total brake loss. • Accelerator and brake pedals are mounted too close together. • Rack-and-pinion steering assembly wears out early. • Broken axle. • Headlights don't work properly and are a thief magnet. **2006**—Airbag deployed for no reason; airbag deployed inadvertently. • Sudden, unintended acceleration. • Automatic transmission jerks and jumps. • Goodyear Eagle RS-A tire flew apart; the side wall caved in. • Corroded ABS sensors produce a brake grinding sound. • Car shakes, jerks, and veers to the right or left when brakes are applied. • Car is very difficult to steer. • Excessive steering-wheel vibration. • Crack in the rear suspension subframe. • Doors lock and unlock on their own. • Battery exploded when ignition was turned on. • Excessive windshield reflection impairs visibility. **2007**—Goodyear Eagle RS-A tires cause the car to shake violently. • Frequent stalling on the highway. • With the remote start package installed, one can use the lock/unlock buttons to start the vehicle.

Secret Warranties/Internal Bulletins/Service Tips

1999—Guidelines for correcting rocker panel creaking or popping. **2000**—Low idle or stalling in gear. • Excessive brake vibration countermeasures. • Right front strut noise. • Rear bumper scratched by trunk lid. • Tips on silencing interior squeaks and rattles and front brake groan. **2000–01**—Automatic transmission gear slippage. **2000–02**—Doors may intermittently lock by themselves. **2000–03**—Driver's seat won't go forward or backward. • Abnormal shifting (the control valve assembly is the likely culprit, says TSB #NTB04-035). **2000–06**—Oil leaks from oil-cooler oil seal. **2001–02**—Rear brake caliper clunk, rattle, or knock. • Rear suspension bottoms out (also an Infiniti problem). **2002**—Erratic sunroof operation. • Driver's power seat won't move forward or backward. **2002–03**—Hesitation on acceleration. • Lack of engine power. • Sunroof operates on its own. **2002–06**—How to silence an engine ticking noise. **2003**—Troubleshooting brake noise and judder. **2003–04**—Harsh 1–2 shifts. **2004**—Cold upshift shock; abnormal shifting. • Fuel system misfires. • Hard start after a cold soak. • Engine won't crank in cold weather. • Front brake noise. • Water leaks from roof. • Headlight fogging. • Loose headliner. **2004–05**—Exhaust rattle/buzz when accelerating. • Voluntary service campaign entails the free replacement of the rear suspension and bushing sealing for 13 years (see bulletin on page 260). **2004–06**—No-cranks in cold weather. • Erratic gauge, AC operation. • Front power-seat malfunction. • Hard-to-move shifter. **2004–07**—Engine noise coming from the timing chain area. • ABS activates when it shouldn't. • Noisy driver's power seat. **2004–08**—Tire-pressure-monitor sensor may leak fluid. • Inoperative power-door mirrors. **2007–08**—Front suspension rattling. • Inoperative lumbar support.

MAXIMA PROFILE

	1999	2000	2001	2002	2003	2004	2005	2006	2007
Cost Price ($)									
Base	28,598	28,598	29,000	32,900	32,900	34,500	34,600	35,098	36,998
Used Values ($)									
Base ▲	4,500	5,000	5,500	7,000	8,500	10,500	13,500	17,500	21,000
Base ▼	4,000	4,500	5,000	6,000	7,500	9,000	12,000	16,000	18,500
Reliability	4	4	3	2	2	2	3	3	4
Crash Safety (F)	4	—	4	4	4	5	5	5	5
Side	4	—	4	4	4	4	4	4	4
IIHS Side	—	—	—	—	—	2	2	2	2
Offset	3	3	3	3	3	5	5	5	5

Head Restraints (F)	3	3	5	5	5	1	1	1	2
Rear	2	—	—	—	—	—	—	—	—
Rollover Resistance	—	—	—	4	4	4	4	4	4

Toyota

AVALON ★★★

RATING: Average (2005–07); Above Average (1999–2004). The Avalon suffers from the same "less for more" philosophy we have seen since 1997 with most of Toyota's lineup (with a few exceptions such as the Echo and Celica). Surprisingly, post '97 Avalons fare better than most other Toyotas, but during the 2005–06 period, following the car's last major redesign, quality declined markedly. Hopefully, the 2007 model Avalon has fixed those glitches. **"Real" city/highway fuel economy:** 11.0/7.4 L/100 km. Owners report fuel savings match this estimate. **Maintenance/repair costs:** Average. **Parts:** Higher-than-average costs, and limited availability. **Extended warranty:** Not needed. **Best alternatives:** A fully loaded Camry, but if you want a more driver-involved experience in a Toyota, consider a Lexus ES 300 series or something in the GS 300 lineup. Other good choices are the Acura Integra, RL, or TL and the Infiniti I30 series.

Strengths and Weaknesses

This near-luxury four-door offers more interior space and performance than do other cars in its class that cost thousands of dollars more. Basically a front-engine, front-drive, mid-sized sedan based on a stretched Camry platform, the six-passenger (up to the 2004 model) Avalon is similar in size to the Ford Taurus. Sure, there's a fair amount of Camry in the Avalon, but it's quicker on its feet, better attuned to abrupt manoeuvres, and 5 cm longer.

VEHICLE HISTORY: 2000—Restyled and considerably improved. It's more powerful, roomier, and full of more high-tech safety and convenience features. **2005**—The third-generation Avalon is restyled and is larger and more powerful. It seats five instead of six, due to new front bucket seats, and offers 2.5 cm more legroom. Toyota's 280 hp 3.5L V6 coupled to a 5-speed automatic, instead of the previous year's 4-speed, replaces the 210 hp 3.0L V6 transmission. All models come with four-wheel ABS disc brakes, front side airbags, side curtain airbags, and a driver's knee airbag. Traction/anti-skid control is available for most models, except the Touring. Other features added to the 2005 models: reclining backrests for a split-folding rear seat, a steering wheel with telescopic as well as tilt adjustment, heated/cooled front seats, keyless starting, and xenon headlights (Touring and Limited).

Quality control up through 2004 is better than average, though steering, suspension, and fuel-system components are failure-prone, and many owners have complained of engine sludge forcing them to spend thousands of dollars on engine repairs.

Owners of 2005–07 Avalons report their cars continue to have serious safety, performance, and reliability problems. And word is getting around. Says *LemonLawClaims.com* (*www.lemonlawclaims.com/toyota_avalon__problems_lemon.htm*):

> For the [2005] Avalon, [Toyota] has provided service bulletins, which alerts dealers to problems [that include] bad U-joint welds, faulty catalytic converters and a leak in the oil supply line for variable valve timing…. Transmission hesitation problems, which have plagued the automaker in the past, also have resurfaced with the five-speed automatic transmission installed in the Avalon. While the earlier transmission problems were experienced by consumers in a variety of situations, this round of trouble surfaces particularly when the driver presses the acceleration pedal for greater speed.

Other performance gripes posted by *Lemon-Aid* readers include major engine oil leaks, poor transmission performance, faulty navigation systems, numerous electrical system glitches, a rotten-egg smell in the cabin, a malfunctioning laser-guided cruise control, clunky steering that vibrates and pulls to either side, highway wandering, under-steering when cornering, premature front brake repairs, suspension strut failures, hydroplaning, excessive body lean, and a problematic Vehicle Stability Control (VSC) and Traction Control system (TRAC):

> The problem with the 2005 Avalon is that there is no way of disengaging the Vehicle Stability Control (VSC) and the traction control (TRAC) feature to allow you to spin the tires if you become stuck in snow or mud…. So, what happens is when you get in snow, the tires refuse to spin and the vehicle just sits there and won't move…. Both the less costly Toyota Camry and 4Runner models have buttons to disengage the Vehicle Stability Control (VSC) and the traction control (TRAC) feature for this purpose or other emergency.

Body construction and assembly are no longer first class, with poor fit and finish, rattles, and water/air leaks the most common complaints. Trunk leaks have been reported on late '90s models, and paint spotting/flaking has afflicted all models. Except for some engine sludge complaints, premature brake wear, and body and accessory glitches (wind noise, AC, and audio system malfunctions), the 2002 and 2003 models have had fewer problems.

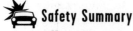 **Safety Summary**

All years: Airbags failed to deploy in an accident. • Sudden, unintended acceleration. • Excessive highway wandering. • Automatic transmission slippage. • Brake pedal goes to the floor with no braking effect. • Driver's seat rocks back and forth.

• Steering wheel is off-centre. • Dash lights and gauges reflect onto windshield. • Bridgestone/Firestone, Dunlop, and Michelin tire failures. **2001**—Engine surging at idle. • Front and rear suspension bottoms out when carrying four adults. • Insufficient steering feedback. • Jerky acceleration. • Sudden failure of the instrument and information panel lighting and headlights. • Driver's side-view mirror has a small viewing area. **2002**—Cruise control doesn't slow car when going downhill. • Vehicle veers to the left at high speeds. **2003**—Extended braking distances. • Front brakes appear to apply themselves. **2004**—Rear wheel seizes while vehicle is underway. • Stalling when AC is activated. • Key won't turn in the ignition. **2005**—Throttle stuck to the floor. • Hesitation and surging when accelerating. • Engine surges and then shuts off and can't be restarted. • Cruise control speed drop is hazardous:

> When my car slows down suddenly because of the car in front, there is no warning for the car behind me. Toyota was notified of this problem and told me not to use the sonar in heavy travelled roads. That is no solution. There should be a fix to make the brake lights go on when the car is slowed down by the sonar.

• Brakes suddenly fail due to a faulty master cylinder. • Loose motor mounts cause noise and instability when accelerating from a stop. • Wheel bearing axle grease leaks onto front disc pad, causing poor braking. • Rear windshield distortion causes road to appear wavy and cars to appear to be swerving. • Electrical shorts:

> Three different electrical shorts in a 2005 Toyota Avalon Limited with less [than] 5000 miles [8,000 km]. The shorts were in the brake light switch, the engine control unit, and the fuse box. The first and third short prevented the car from starting. The second short caused the engine to stall while traveling at 55 mph [90 km/h] on a major highway. It is a miracle that there was not an accident. The switch, engine control unit, and fuse box have all been replaced.

2006—Fire ignited in the rear middle seat from the seat heater overheating. • Sudden acceleration while cruising. • Engine hesitates on acceleration to merge with traffic. • WTI oil line corroded and ruptured, resulting in all of the oil leaking out of the engine. • Transmission hunts for the proper gear, lurches, and slips, and it shifts erratically at low speeds. • Navigation system doesn't function as intended. • Leaking brake master cylinder and booster may lead to loss of braking. • A sudden application of the brakes may cause the telescopic steering wheel to collapse inward. • Faulty "intermediate steering shaft" results in clunks when turning. • Laser cruise control fails intermittently. • Rough-riding Cooper Lifeliner tires. **2007**—Sudden acceleration when cruising. • Airbags failed to deploy. • Knee airbag deployment is alleged to have caused massive leg injuries to the driver. • When the laser cruise control is activated, rear brake lights don't come on to warn following drivers that the car is braking. • Excessive steering vibrations and pulling to the left and right. • Automatic transmission "bumps" into gear. • Inoperative push-button starter. • Smart Key ignition system can cause heart pacemakers and defibrillators to malfunction:

The owner's manual of my 2007 Toyota Avalon warns that persons with implanted pacemakers or defibrillator[s] should not go near the antennae on the Smart Key system. My 91-year-old dad has an implanted defibrillator. Is there any way to get in, start the car, and disable the Smart Key so he can then approach the car and get in? What is the radio frequency and effective radiated power of the system so I can pass the information along to his cardiologist? What is the liability if I have the car parked on a public street and someone with an implanted defibrillator or pacemaker should happen to walk past the car without knowing the danger? Please help, as the dealer has not been able to find anything out about this. Also, the owner's manual warns about getting the Smart Key too close to electromagnetic devices such as credit cards and cell phones, cordless phone rechargers, fluorescent lights, etc. How can my wife carry the Smart Key in her purse with credit cards and cell phone?... Do I have to rearrange my life to avoid problems with the Smart Key? Also, the owner's manual warns the Smart Key might not work near broadcast operations. Several times a week, I have to go to a cable television head end.... I haven't taken the car there yet for fear of what might happen. Will I have to have it towed some distance away before the Smart Key technology will work?

• Poor headlight performance when going uphill.

Secret Warranties/Internal Bulletins/Service Tips

1990–2000—Brake-pad clicking may be corrected by use of special, Toyota-recommended grease; however, some owners say it's not very effective. **1995–2000**—A power-steering squeak can be silenced by installing a new rack end shaft. **1997–99**—Front suspension noise can be eliminated by changing the suspension support. **1997–2002**—Extended warranty will pay for engine sludge damage up to eight years, without any mileage limitation. **2000**—Roof leaks water. • Sliding roof and door mirror noise. **2000–01**—Measures to reduce instrument panel luminosity. • Wheel bearing ticking noise. • Door popping and creaking. **2000–04**—Fuel door hard to open. **2003–07**—Windshield ticking noise. **2004**—Correction for vehicle tendency to pull to the left. • Front suspension knocking. **2004–07**—Front-seat squeak. **2005–06**—Engine oil leaks. • Water leaks onto the front floor area. • Pull/drift to one side while driving. • Diagnosis and correction of steering-column noise. • Creaking and ticking noise heard from base of rear windshield. • Rear suspension thump, clunk. • Inoperative horn. **2005–07**—Rear vents blow warm air with AC on. • Front-door window won't roll up. • Windshield wiper fluid leaks. • Water leaks at headliner and floor areas. **2005–08**—Knocking noise from front of sunroof. **2006–07**—Harsh shifting. **2006–08**—Excessive dust from vents. **2007**—Rough idle, stalling. **2007–08**—Steering-wheel flutter; body vibration.

	1999	2000	2001	2002	2003	2004	2005	2006	2007
Cost Price ($)									
XL	35,605	36,595	36,370	38,365	—	—	—	—	—
XLS	42,515	43,800	44,710	45,135	45,560	45,830	39,900	39,900	41,135
Used Values ($)									
XL ▲	6,500	8,000	8,500	9,000	—	—	—	—	—
XL ▼	5,500	6,500	8,000	8,500	—	—	—	—	—
XLS ▲	8,500	9,000	9,500	10,500	12,000	14,000	19,000	22,000	28,000
XLS ▼	8,000	8,500	9,000	9,500	11,000	12,500	17,500	20,000	26,000
Reliability	5	5	5	5	5	5	3	4	4
Crash Safety (F)	—	3	3	4	4	5	5	5	5
Side	—	4	4	4	4	4	5	5	5
IIHS Side	—	—	—	—	—	—	5	5	5
Offset	3	5	5	5	5	2	2	2	2
Head Restraints (F)	3	3	1	1	1	1	1	1	1
Rear	1	—	—	—	—	—	—	—	—
Rollover Resistance	—	—	—	4	4	4	4	4	4

Volvo

C30, C70, S40, S60, S70, S80, V40, V50, V70, XC70, XC90 ★ / ★★★★

RATING: *C30, C70, S40, S70, S80, V40, V50, V70, XC90:* Not Recommended (1999–2007). *C70, S70,* and *V70* are recent high-tech Volvos that are particularly dealer-dependent and will suffer most in servicing and value when and if Volvo is sold later this year. *S60, XC70:* Above Average (2004–07); Average (2002–03). Surprisingly, for a car company that emphasizes its commitment to safe cars and quality components, Volvo's entire lineup during the past decade has deteriorated from both quality and safety perspectives. There are two reasons for this decline: the use of more-complex, failure-prone electronics and Ford's poor stewardship of Volvo, which has led both firms to the point of bankruptcy. As a result, good dealers and technicians have left Volvo in droves, to sell used cars or to work in independent garages, parts suppliers are in hiding, afraid of their own suppliers who haven't been paid, and customers are reluctant to buy a car from a company soon to be on the skids. Horrendous reports of safety- and performance-related problems abound, including engine and seat fires, loss of steering, sudden acceleration, transmission failures, electrical shorts, light failures, and tire blowouts. As if this weren't bad enough, Ford's Marquis de Sade–trained customer relations staff has left many new- and used-Volvo buyers so angry they could spit nails. **"Real" city/highway fuel economy:** *Turbo manual: 12.8/8.4 L/100 km. Turbo automatic: 12.3/8.4 L/100 km. C70 manual: 11.7/8.0 L/100 km. C70 automatic:*

11.4/7.6 L/100 km. *XC70 2.5L:* 12.6/8.8 L/100 km. *XC90 2.5L:* 13.3/9.1 L/100 km. *XC90 T6 2.9L:* 15.6/10.6 L/100 km. *S40, V40 manual:* 10.8/7.3 L/100 km. *S40, V40 automatic:* 10.7/7.0 L/100 km. *S60 manual:* 10.8/7.3 L/100 km. *S60 automatic:* 10.7/7.0 L/100 km. *S60 2.4T AWD:* 11.7/7.9 L/100 km. *S60 R manual:* 13.1/8.6 L/100 km. *S60 R automatic:* 13.2/8.6 L/100 km. *S60 T5:* 11.5/8.0 L/100 km. *S70 manual:* 11.2/7.6 L/100 km. *S70 automatic:* 10.6/7.7 L/100 km. *S80 2.9L:* 11.9/7.8 L/100 km. *S80 2.5L AWD:* 11.7/7.9 L/100 km. *S80 T6:* 12.6/8.3 L/100 km. *V70 2.4L manual:* 10.8/7.3 L/100 km. *V70 2.4L automatic:* 10.9/7.1 L/100 km. *V70 2.5LT AWD:* 11.7/7.9 L/100 km. *V70 2.5LT R AWD manual:* 13.1/8.6 L/100 km. *V70 2.5LT R AWD automatic:* 13.2/8.6 L/100 km. Fuel savings may be lower than these figures by 10–20 percent. **Maintenance/Repair costs:** Higher-than-average costs, and repairs must be done by a Volvo dealer. **Parts:** Higher-than-average costs, and limited availability. **Extended warranty:** A good idea, considering that even some of the most mundane repairs can be costly to perform. **Best alternatives:** Acura Integra, RL, or TL; Infiniti I30 series; early Nissan Maxima; and early Toyota Avalon.

 ## Strengths and Weaknesses

70 Series

Bland and failure-prone but practical to the extreme, the 1998 model 850s were renamed the C70, S70, and V70; they all have a disappointingly high number of safety- and performance-related deficiencies reported by owners taken in by Volvo's safety and quality hype. The letters S, V, and C preceding the numerical designation stand for sedans, wagons, and coupes.

With the front-drive 70 Series, all-wheel drive is offered with the wagons, and the base 2.4L 5-cylinder engine comes with three horsepower ratings: 168, 190, and 236 hp. Only two transmissions are available: a manual 5-speed (relatively rare) and an automatic 4-speed. Handling is superb, with the suspension dampened somewhat for a more-comfortable ride than what many European imports offer. AWD performs flawlessly, road and body noise are muted, and the cars are well appointed with a full array of standard safety features, with the exception of traction control, which is optional.

VEHICLE HISTORY: 1999—An AWD GLT sedan debuts; the R wagon's engine gets 11 more horses (247 hp); automatic transmission shifts and braking performance are improved. A standard engine immobilizer is added, as are "smart" airbags. **2000**—No more base AWD V70 wagon nor T5. Side airbags are upgraded to protect occupants' heads, and the front seatbacks and headrests are redesigned to minimize whiplash. **2001**—Station wagons get more interior room. The S70 sedans, base and GLT wagons, and the high-performance R-type are gone, but the C70 coupe and convertible remain. Traction control is standard on the T5 only; all models have anti-lock all-disc brakes, front head/chest side-impact airbags, curtain window airbags, and more-protective head restraints. **2002**—An all-wheel-drive 2.4T AWD comes on board, Volvo's anti-skid system is standard on the T5, and traction control is standard on all front-drives. **2003**—The V70 2.5T AWD and XC70 get a power boost of 11 extra horses, and the T5's power is cranked up to 247 horses. **2004**—Debut of the high-performance 300 hp V70R, equipped with AWD and a 6-speed manual or 5-speed automatic transmission. **2005**—Refreshed styling, optional run-flat tires (a bad idea), and a firmer suspension for the T5. The AWD V70 2.5T is gone.

On the downside, rear seating is cramped for three adults, and the instrument panel appears overly busy, with a confusing array of gauges, instruments, and controls on the centre console. Plus, the three rear head restraints induce claustrophobia while severely restricting rear visibility.

As far as quality control and dealer servicing are concerned, Volvo technical service bulletins and owner complaints indicate that factory defects on all models have been on the rise over the past 10 years. For example, the car's electrical system may go berserk or shut down entirely in rainy weather or when the car is passing over puddles; headlights, turn signal lights, and other bulbs burn out monthly; power window switches and locks fail constantly; wheels are easily bent; the turn signal lever doesn't return; airbags deploy for no reason; and springs are noisy.

The above defects clearly show that quality control is less stringent at the factory level since Ford acquired the company almost a decade ago. Volvo blames Ford for its poor-quality cars, while Ford targets Volvo factories and dealers' service personnel for failing to prevent and repair factory mistakes. They both are arguing a moot point: Volvo sales have fallen so far that Ford has secretly put Volvo on the auction block (no takers, so far), and many dealers are shutting their doors before Ford's mismanagement bankrupts them.

C70

The C70's strong points: good acceleration with lots of torque, exceptional steering and handling, first-class body construction and finish, and predicted better-than-average reliability. Its weak points: difficult rear-seat entry/exit, some engine turbo lag, excessive engine noise, a jarring suspension, and an uncertain future.

Seating four comfortably, this luxury coupe and convertible are based on the 850 (pardon, S70) platform and marketed as high-performance Volvos. C70 comes with two turbocharged engines: a base 190 hp 2.4L inline 5-cylinder and a 236 hp 2.3L variant. Either engine can be hooked to a 5-speed manual or 4-speed automatic transmission. Of the two engines, the 2.4L appears to offer the best response and smoothest performance, although servicing and durability remain problematic. Acceleration is impressive, despite the fact that the car feels underpowered until the turbo kicks in at around 1500 rpm—a feature that drivers will find more frustrating with a manual shifter than with an automatic. Steering and handling are first class; build quality leaves much to desire.

Other things not to like are turbo lag, tire thumping caused by the high-performance tires, excessive engine and wind noise, and power-sliding rear seats that require lots of skill and patience to operate.

C30

The C30 two-door hatchback is Volvo's smallest car, and a mini version of the S40 sedan and V50 wagon. This $27,500 (new in 2007) midget performer is powered by a 227 hp 2.5L turbocharged 5-cylinder engine coupled to a 6-speed manual transmission (a 5-speed automatic is optional). Available safety features include ABS, traction control, anti-skid system, front side airbags, and side curtain airbags. All models have four bucket-style seats.

Drivers looking for a small car they can throw into corners and quickly merge with fast traffic will love this peppy, nice-handling, sporty luxury car. On the other hand, interior room in the rear is quite limited, and there's not much trunk space either. Quality is a crapshoot, if you use the poor ratings garnered by the V50 (fuel, electrical, audio, and climate systems as well as fit and finish) as your guide. Of more immediate concern is the imminent sale of Volvo by Ford to another auto-maker. This move will guarantee a low resale value, decimate the dealer network, and make parts and servicing a nightmare for this relatively new model.

S40 and V40

Volvo's small sedan and wagon come with a 150 hp 1.9L turbocharged 4-cylinder engine coupled with an automatic transmission. Two side airbags, anti-lock brakes, air conditioning, cruise control, and power windows are also standard. The 2001 model got a minor facelift, an upgraded engine and 5-speed automatic transmission, side curtain airbags, and some handling improvements.

These models have also generated an unacceptably high number of complaints concerning chronic brake repairs, automatic transmission failures, fuel-system malfunctions leading to poor driveability, and myriad electrical shorts and body defects.

S60

This sporty, mid-range sedan uses the same large-car platform as the V70 and S80 but has proven to be more reliable, beginning with the 2004 models. A 197 hp 5-cylinder engine teamed with an all-wheel-drive powertrain has been added to the lineup. Drivers will have the choice of three inline 5-cylinder engines: a 168 hp naturally aspirated version, a 197 hp low-pressure turbo, and a 247 hp high-pressure turbo.

Some of the S60's pluses are fair acceleration; exceptional handling and braking; a good array of user-friendly instruments and controls; comfortable front seating; and very good head-restraint, offset, front, and side crashworthiness scores. Some of the car's deficiencies include lots of turbo throttle hesitation and torque steer pulling when accelerating; an imprecise manual shifter; a jarring ride with some tire thump (worse with the T5) when passing over uneven pavement; rear visibility that's obstructed by a high parcel shelf, obtrusive head restraints, and a descending roofline; cramped rear seating, made worse by rear legroom that disappears when the front seats are pushed back only halfway; a narrow trunk with a small opening; and turbo engines that require premium fuel. Other cars worth considering are the Acura TL and Infiniti I35.

S80

The S80 is a redesign of the S90 (dropped after the 1998 model year) and offers several interesting new features, such as a powerful 268 hp transverse inline 6-cylinder engine and a sophisticated automatic transmission called the "Geartronic"—a 4-speed automatic with a feature for manually changing gears if one so desires. Additionally, the car is chock full of safety features, has the largest interior of any Volvo, gives impressive performance and handling, and is attractively styled.

VEHICLE HISTORY: 2001—Dual-stage airbags and 16-inch wheels. **2002**—Engine tweaks give more power at a lower rpm, and the base engine drops a few horses. Also an in-trunk emergency release and new alloy wheels. **2004**—Refreshed styling, new gauges, and the addition of all-wheel drive. **2005**—Wood interior trim, optional run-flat tires, and larger wheels on the high-performance models.

Unfortunately, the S80's numerous defects closely resemble the problems reported in prior years' models and seriously undermine Volvo's much-touted safety claims.

XC70, XC90

Essentially a renamed V70 station wagon, the XC70 is an SUV wannabe that offers five-passenger seating, high ground clearance, sleek styling, and AWD versatility. Its mechanical components are practically identical to those of Volvo's other sedans. The base engine is a 168 hp (non-turbo) 2.4L 5-cylinder. The turbo version has been replaced by a 208 hp 2.5L turbocharged 5-cylinder hooked to a 5-speed automatic gearbox. It is followed by the 247 hp 2.5L turbocharged T5 and a 300 hp variant found on the V70R.

XC90 models are based on Volvo's S80 car platform and aren't intended for off-road use. They offer seven-passenger seating along with a base turbocharged 208 hp 2.5L 5-cylinder and an optional 268 hp 2.9L V6 on the T6 version. All transmissions have a manual shiftgate. However, the AWD system lacks low-range gearing. Anti-lock four-wheel disc brakes, anti-skid/traction control, and Roll Stability Control are standard. Also included are front torso side airbags and head-protecting side curtain airbags that cover all seating rows.

Problem areas are limited to frequent brake maintenance (rotors and pads), chronic stalling, and electrical system and body faults (inoperative moonroof, door locks, and gauges), notably excessive windshield/dash glare and side windows that won't close until the control button is pressed three times. Poor fuel economy is also a recurring complaint.

Safety Summary

All models/years: Sudden acceleration when applying brakes. • Vehicle shuts down when making a left turn. • Airbags fail to deploy. • While underway, driver seat suddenly moved backward. • Fuel fumes leak into interior. • Brake pedal locks up. • Chronic light failures. • Automatic door locked, and trunk lock failed to open. • Automatic gas-tank door jams shut. • Tailpipe extends beyond bumper, burning occupant. • Inside door handles pinch fingers. *C70:* **2006**—Many complaints that tires lose air due to cracked rims. • Airbag light is always on. **2007**—Xenon headlights fail to illuminate the road sufficiently; they produce a black "curtain" extending halfway down the windshield. • Window rattling and various air and water leaks. • Defective driver-side seat heater, and the AC blows super-heated air from the driver-side air vent. *S40, S70, V70:* **2000**—Airbags fail to deploy. • Vehicle suddenly pulls to one side while cruising. • Unexpected total loss of power. • Engine sputters and then shuts off. • Prematurely worn front stabilizer-link rod. • Driver's window sticks in the down position. • AC allows exhaust fumes into the vehicle. • Chronic light failures. *S40:* **2006**—Sudden stall-out in traffic; doors automatically locked, wipers self-activated, lights went off, and vehicle would not restart. • Many complaints that the heater blower won't defrost the front windshield or side mirrors. • AC blows hot air. • Many owners report serious electrical malfunctions when it rains (2004 models were recalled for the same problem). • Brake and gas pedals are mounted too close together. • Michelin Energy tire side wall blowout. **2007**—Fire ignited in the rear brakes while vehicle was underway. • Manual 5-speed clutch pedal operation is compromised by a protruding panel. *V70:* **2001**—Excessive reflection of beige dash onto windshield. • Engine mounts break. • Vehicle can roll away when parked on an incline. • Brake pedal is too close to gas pedal. • Front door indent doesn't hold door open. • Sunroof blew in while going through a car wash. • Rear tailgate door won't lock. • Coffee spilled from cupholder shorted airbag computer. • Frequent bulb failures. **2002**—Shoulder belt crosses at neck. • Sunroof broke and fell into roof liner. **2003**—Emergency brake bracket comes apart. **2004**—Car easily damaged when going over a bump at low speed:

> Car was damaged going over a speed bump (on public road) at about 5 mph [8 km/h]. There is a recall in Europe to fix this problem (by removing a bracket that...can be forced upwards, damaging the exhaust and driveshaft).

• Fuel gushes out when refuelling. • Vehicle pulls to the right. • Loose steering caused by a prematurely worn-out tie rod. • Concussion suffered in an accident when head hit the interior handholds, which are often bumped into. • Poor headlight illumination. **2005**—Car frequently stalls out. • Unexpected and intermittent brake failure (see *forums.swedespeed.com/zerothread?id=32551*). • Passenger-side airbag is disabled if the occupant moves. *S80:* **2001–02**—Lights continually burn out. **2003**—Sudden, unintended acceleration. • Front wheel fell off when the ball joint separated. **2004**—Excessive steering shake caused car to go out of control. **2005**—Cracked oil pump. *V40:* **All years:** The brake pedal won't depress, causing total brake loss or extended stopping distances and premature wearout of the front brake pads (around 20,000 km). **2001**—Under-hood electrical fire. • Cracked fuel regulator pump spilled fuel onto hot engine, and fumes spread into the interior. • Sudden, unintended acceleration when vehicle put into Drive. • Chronic stalling attributed to faulty idle control valve and air mass meter. • Complete loss of braking. • Brakes don't stop vehicle within a reasonable distance. • Brake pedal is too close to the gas pedal. • Brake pedal snapped, went to the floor while going downhill. • When applying the brakes in cold weather, pedal won't depress, causing extended stopping distances. • Premature replacement of the front and rear rotors and pads. • Vehicle pulls to the left when accelerating or coming to a stop. • Repeated automatic transmission failures. **2002**—Sudden, unintended acceleration. • Airbags fail to deploy. • Annoying reflection of the dash onto the windshield. • ABS failure. • Rear brake pads wear out prematurely and ruin the rotors. • Horn is hard to activate. **2003**—Transmission slips from Second to Third and shifts harshly:

> This transmission slipping usually lasts for 2 to 3 seconds and this loss of power can easily put me into a major accident.

• Faulty engine fuel line. **2004**—Sudden, unintended acceleration. • Total loss of braking capability. • Brake and accelerator are mounted too close to each other. • Sun glare washes out dashboard instrument readings. • Gas gauge gives inaccurate readings. • Power windows and doors malfunction. • Tail lights, parking lights, and side marker lights won't come on, and sometimes all of the dash gauges go out. • Radio and climate controls turn off by themselves. **2005**—Parking brake won't hold the car on an incline. • Original-equipment scissor jack won't hold up the car. *XC70:* **2003**—Loose fuel lines. **2004**—While cruising on the highway, engine suddenly started racing, steering wheel and brakes locked, and all gauges went dead. • Rear-view mirror auto-dim feature doesn't work. *XC90:* **2003**—Unable to turn key in the ignition. **2004**—Airbags failed to deploy when car was hit from the side. • Vehicle's all-wheel-drive feature causes the car to handle erratically and go out of control. • When shifting into Park, shifter inadvertently goes into Reverse. • Engine seizure due to a buildup of engine sludge. • Transmission interlock becomes disengaged when remote door-lock key fob is activated; one incident caused the car to roll down a hill. • Transmission replacement during car's second year on the road. • Gearshift indicator either goes blank or shows the wrong gear. • Doors suddenly unlock themselves and open while vehicle is underway.

Secret Warranties/Internal Bulletins/Service Tips

All models/years: Check the valve-cover nuts at every servicing interval to prevent oil leakage. • Free front seat belt extenders available. • Rear suspension popping or "boing" noise. **All models: 1999–2004**—Knocking noise when turning. **1999–2005**—Manual transmission may not shift easily into First or Reverse gear. **2002–04**—Engine knock, rattle, and low power. **2003–04**—Xenon headlights may be inoperative due to a faulty ballast. **2003–06**—Eliminating musty odours from the air vents. **2004**—Reasons why engine may run roughly. •

Electrically powered seats rock back and forth. • Rear suspension noise. **2004–05**—Wheel bolt corrosion. **2005**—Engine may have a rough idle, misfire, run roughly, or lack power. • AC stops working intermittently. **2005–06**—Seat backrest play/noise. • Vent air temperatures cycle from hot to cold. *C70, V70, S60, S70, S80:* **1999–2001**—Defective throttles cause the vehicles to stall and fail air emissions tests, sticking owners with costly repairs. Volvo has "quietly" agreed with U.S. EPA and California authorities to extend the warranty up to 10 years/320,000 km (200,000 mi.). As part of the agreement, Volvo will also reimburse owners who have already had the defective throttles replaced. The cost to replace the throttle can reach up to $1,000. The faulty throttles are also the subject of a class action lawsuit charging that Volvo violated California law by issuing a "secret warranty" to assist some, but not all, owners of vehicles with defective throttles. *850, S70, V70:* **1998–2004**—Manual transmission doesn't easily shift into Reverse or First gear. *S60, S80, V70:* **1999–2004**—Brake, exhaust system resonance, vibration. *S60, V70:* **2001**—Uneven idle. • Front-seat noise, rocking. **2002–04**—Engine knock and rattle with reduced power. *C70:* **1997–99**—There are at least half a dozen bulletins addressing water leaks. **1998–2002**—Uneven idle. **2003–05**—Wheel bolt corrosion. *S80:* **1999–2001**—Defective electronic throttle module covered by a secret 10-year warranty. **1999–2003**—Suspension resonance, vibration. **2000**—Free engine oil grate inspection. **2001**—Body squeak or crunch noise brought on by wet or cold weather. **2002–04**—Engine knock and rattle with low power. **2003–06**—Eliminating musty odours coming from the air vents. **2004–05**—Park assist relay free replacement campaign. **2005–06**—Vent temperature cycles from hot to cold.

C30, C70, S40, S60, S70, S80, V40, V50, V70, XC70, XC90 PROFILE

	1999	2000	2001	2002	2003	2004	2005	2006	2007
Cost Price ($)									
C30	—	—	—	—	—	—	—	—	27,495
C70	49,995	50,595	52,995	49,995	59,595	59,595	—	55,995	56,495
S40	—	—	31,400	31,495	31,495	31,495	29,995	31,120	31,495
S60	—	—	35,995	36,495	36,495	36,495	36,995	40,620	40,995
S70	35,195	—	—	—	—	—	—	—	—
S80	49,995	55,995	54,395	54,395	54,895	54,895	54,995	54,995	54,995
V40/50	—	—	32,400	32,495	32,495	32,495	31,495	32,620	32,995
V70	36,295	36,495	37,495	37,995	37,995	37,995	38,495	39,120	39,495
XC70 AWD	—	—	—	—	49,495	49,495	46,495	47,121	47,496
XC90 AWD	—	—	—	—	54,995	49,995	49,995	49,995	50,995
Used Values ($)									
C30 ▲	—	—	—	—	—	—	—	—	18,500
C30 ▼	—	—	—	—	—	—	—	—	17,000
C70 ▲	5,500	6,000	8,000	10,000	19,000	22,000	—	31,000	38,000
C70 ▼	4,500	5,500	6,500	9,000	17,500	20,000	—	29,000	36,000
S40 ▲	—	—	6,000	8,000	8,500	9,500	11,500	15,500	19,000
S40 ▼	—	—	5,000	6,500	7,500	8,500	10,000	14,000	17,000

S60 ▲	—	—	6,500	8,500	9,500	11,000	15,000	22,000	26,000
S60 ▼	—	—	6,000	7,000	8,500	10,000	13,500	20,000	24,000
S70 ▲	5,000	—	—	—	—	—	—	—	—
S70 ▼	4,000	—	—	—	—	—	—	—	—
S80 ▲	4,500	6,000	7,500	9.000	12,500	14,000	20,000	26,000	33,000
S80 ▼	4,000	5,000	6,500	7,500	11,000	12,500	18,000	24,000	30,000
V40/50 ▲	—	—	6,000	8,000	9,000	10,500	12,500	16,500	20,000
V40/50 ▼	—	—	5,000	6,500	8,000	9,000	11,000	15,000	18,000
V70 ▲	4,000	5,000	7,000	8,500	10,000	11,500	16,000	22,000	26,000
V70 ▼	3,500	4,500	6,000	7,500	9,000	10,000	14,500	20,000	24,000
XC70 AWD ▲	—	—	—	—	11,000	14,500	19,000	25,000	30,000
XC70 AWD ▼	—	—	—	—	10,000	13,000	18,000	23,000	28,000
XC90 AWD ▲	—	—	—	—	14,000	17,000	21,000	27,000	32,000
XC90 AWD ▼	—	—	—	—	12,500	16,000	19,500	25,000	30,000

Reliability	3	2	2	2	2	2	2	2	2
S60	—	—	2	3	4	4	4	4	4

Crash Safety (F)

C70	—	—	—	—	—	—	—	5	5
S40	—	—	—	—	—	4	4	4	4
S60	—	—	4	4	4	4	4	4	4
S70	5	5	—	—	—	—	—	—	—
S80	—	—	—	—	—	—	—	5	—
V70	—	—	—	—	—	—	5	5	5
XC70 AWD	—	—	—	—	—	—	5	5	5
XC90 AWD	—	—	—	—	4	4	—	—	—

Side

S40	—	—	—	—	—	5	5	5	5
S60	—	—	5	5	5	5	5	5	5
S70	5	5	—	—	—	—	—	—	—
S80	—	—	—	—	—	—	—	5	—
V70	—	—	—	—	—	—	5	5	5
XC70 AWD	—	—	—	—	—	—	5	5	5
XC90 AWD	—	—	—	—	5	5	5	—	—

IIHS Side

C70	—	—	—	—	—	—	—	5	5
S40	—	—	—	—	—	—	—	3	3
S60	—	—	—	—	—	—	—	3	3
XC90 AWD	—	—	—	—	—	—	5	5	5

Offset

S70	5	5	—	—	—	—	—	—	—
S40	—	—	—	5	5	5	5	5	5
S60	—	—	5	5	5	5	5	5	5
S80	—	5	5	5	5	5	5	5	5
XC90 AWD	—	—	—	—	5	5	5	5	5

Head Restraints

C70	5	—	5	—	5	5	—	5	5
S40/V40	—	—	—	—	—	5	5	5	5
S60	—	—	—	—	5	5	5	5	5
S70	5	—	—	—	—	—	—	—	—
S80	—	—	—	5	5	5	5	5	5
V70	5	—	5	5	5	5	—	—	—
XC90 AWD	—	—	—	—	—	—	5	5	5

Rollover Resistance

S40	—	—	—	—	—	—	—	4	4
S60	—	—	—	—	—	—	—	5	5
S80	—	—	—	—	—	—	—	5	—
V70	—	—	—	—	—	—	—	—	4
XC70 AWD	—	—	—	—	—	—	—	4	4
XC90 AWD	—	—	—	—	—	4	4	—	—

SPORTS CARS

The Mazda Miata is the only sports car *Lemon-Aid* has rated Recommended every year since its first model year.

Big Isn't Always Better

Traditionally, a "sports" car was a roadster/open car. Once upon a time, Porsche asked if they could race a little car with a roof and a little air[-]cooled engine hanging off the back against the big boys. Jaguar, Ferrari, Mercedes, Corvette, etc. all laughed. They all got their asses kicked over decades. If Colin Chapman were alive today, I guarantee that he would have a ****-eating grin on his face driving a Miata.

www.sportscarforums.com

I Don't Care—I Want One!

Yes, we all know that these small, low cars with high-powered, fuel-thirsty engines and seating for only two are a dangerous choice for young drivers, and scream out "Mid-life crisis!" when driven by pony-tailed, open-shirted middle-aged men. They're also usually way overpriced and astronomically expensive to insure, most lose their value quickly, and they beg to be driven too fast.

But they're so much fun to drive, especially for those of us who missed our chance to own one in our youth because we were too poor, practical, or preoccupied with our Cavaliers, Corollas, or Beetles to give in to our primal instincts.

If real driving performance is important to you, though, remember that big isn't always better. Consider getting an agile, fun-to-drive small car, such as a used

Acura Integra, Honda Civic Si, Mazda Miata, or Nissan Sentra SE-R. If you want to be a little more "in your face," however, it's hard to lose money with a Detroit muscle-car sportster built through 1974.

There are three kinds of sports cars to consider: traditional two-seater roadsters, styled much like the MGB of the early '70s or Mazda's Miata; sporty coupes and hatchbacks, such as the Japanese Acura Integra, Honda Civic Si, Mazda MX-3, and Toyota Celica, which offer sportier styling, performance, and handling than their entry-level versions and are cheaper and more versatile to maintain than traditional sports cars; and muscle cars, which feature large engines and a few more creature comforts. The best deals in the latter category are the V8-equipped Ford Mustang and the GM Camaro or Firebird.

Other notable sports models are the BMW Z3 (a looker that lacks the precise steering of a Miata), the BMW Z4 (better steering and an upgraded suspension that equals the Porsche Boxster's), the Mazda6 (plenty of horsepower, and with a stick shift not found on the Accord and the Camry), and the Mazda3.

There's a comprehensive forum at *www.sportscarforums.com* that goes into mind-numbing detail as to what makes a good sports car. Different cars are rated, service tips are given, and the age-old feud between Camaro/Firebird or Corvette and Mustang owners is omnipresent and unresolved:

> Even [most die-hard GM fans] will admit that [for] bang for the buck, Mustangs are hard to beat.... The Mustang is coined as a pony car. The Corvette is a [sports car]. As is the Dodge Viper. Now for significantly less amounts of cash, you can make a Mustang hammer both those cars in any venue you like. Whether it be road-racing, street, or strip.... Remember though...a [M]ustang has rear seats, no transaxle, and no IRS. It[']s also a fraction of cost.... A lot of people will claim to hate [M]ustangs, usually based on a lot of people having [underpowered versions], or on their appearance. However you will never hear anyone involved in any venue of racing call a Mustang overrated. They simply know better. It[']s the same way I would never say a Corvette is overrated. The [C]orvette pulls off the same type of good stuff the [M]ustang does. Just at a higher level. They're both tremendous values for what they compete against, and can do. Mustang is the poor boy[']s extremely effective racer. Corvette is a full step up. Ask how many [']V]ette owners have been pounded hard by a...much less expensive Mustang and you'll know why they aren[']t overrated.

There are also fewer contemptuous references to Asian "rice-burners" now that Toyota and other Asian automakers are successfully racing their cars at NASCAR-sanctioned tracks and building solid full-sized pickups.

Nevertheless, there is some agreement among owners' Internet postings, *Consumer Reports* articles, and *Lemon-Aid* readers' opinions as to which sports cars give you the most performance, reliability, and cachet for your cash.

Most sports cars—or "high-performance vehicles," as they're euphemistically named—don't offer the comfort or reliability of a Honda Civic, a Toyota Celica, or even a Hyundai Tiburon. Instead, they sacrifice reliability, interior space, and a comfortable suspension for speed, superior road handling, and attractive styling. They also need a whole slew of expensive high-performance packages, because many entry-level sports cars aren't very sporty in their basic form. Remember, too, that used sports cars often have serious accident damage that may not have been repaired properly, resulting in serious tracking problems if the chassis is bent.

Fully loaded used sports cars usually sell at a fraction of their original cost, and very few end up as collectibles. Most models that have been taken off the market— such as the Toyota Supra, Nissan 300ZX, and Chevrolet Corvette ZR1—aren't likely to become collectors' cars with soaring resale values. Even discontinued Japanese sports cars like the Nissan 1600, which are usually in high demand, haven't done nearly as well as some of the British roadsters that were taken off the market at about the same time.

Like early Mustangs, 2002 and earlier GM Camaros and Firebirds can be fun cars to drive and can make you a tidy profit as well, once they've been tricked out with some relatively inexpensive options. Not only are they reasonably reliable and cheap to maintain, but their resale prices are fairly stable and there's plenty of used stock to choose from. But don't expect them to appreciate in value any time soon (although the early muscle versions are now breaking away from the pack).

When buying a sports car, keep in mind that the more features you add, the less reliable the car becomes, and that there are some modifications that are more important than others. For example, good-quality high-performance tires are the first investment you should make (check the owner-polled recommendations at *www.tirerack.com/tires/reviews/MenuServlet?search=surveyComments*). Other improvements that should have a high priority are an upgraded set of brakes and suspension. And, if you have a few dollars left, consider getting a more-responsive rear end and a high-performance transmission.

SPORTS CAR RATINGS

Recommended

General Motors Camaro, Firebird, Trans Am (1999–2002)

Mazda MX-5 (Miata) (1999–2007)

Above Average

Ford Mustang (2006–07)

Toyota Celica (1999–2005)

Average

Ford Mustang (2001–04)   General Motors Corvette (1999–2007)

Below Average

Ford Mustang (2005; 1999–2000)

Not Recommended

Ford Cobra (1999–2004)

Ford

MUSTANG, COBRA	★★★★

RATING: *Mustang:* Above Average (2006–07)—the 2006 version worked out many of the 2005 redesign glitches, and incremental improvements reduced factory-related defects found on the pre-2005 models; Average (2001–04); Below Average (2005, 1999–2000). *Cobra:* Not Recommended (1999–2004). Here's the problem: Ford has alienated its parts suppliers and reduced reliability through unrealistic price-cutting and last-minute, poorly thought-out component changes. Mustangs that aren't equipped with traction control are treacherous on wet roads, and they have had a frighteningly high number of safety-related mechanical failures (especially chronic stalling). Additionally, new crash data indicates the vehicles may be fire-prone following collisions at moderate speeds. GM's Camaro and Firebird are the Mustang's traditional competition as far as performance is concerned, and they're good buys even though they haven't been built since 2002. Ford has the pricing and servicing advantage, with a base Mustang costing a bit less than the cheapest Camaro, but it lags from a performance standpoint. In that area, the equivalent model-year Camaro and Firebird offer more sure-footed acceleration, crisper handling, standard ABS, a 6-speed transmission, and more-comfortable rear seats. Fuel-savers beware: All 4-cylinder Mustangs should be shunned because they provide insufficient power, they aren't very durable, and the fuel savings are much less than you'd think. **"Real" city/highway fuel economy:** *Mustang 3.8L manual: 11.8/7.4 L/100 km. Mustang 3.8L automatic: 12.0/8.0 L/100 km. Mustang 3.9L manual: 11.7/7.4 L/100 km. Mustang 3.9L automatic: 12.3/8.2 L/100 km. Mustang 4.6L manual: 14.0/8.7 L/100 km. Mustang 4.6L automatic: 13.2/9.4 L/100 km. Mustang Mach 1 manual: 13.9/8.5 L/100 km. Mustang Mach 1 automatic: 13.8/9.5 L/100 km. Cobra: 14.1/9.1 L/100 km.* Fuel savings may be lower by about 20 percent on 4-cylinder models, 15 percent with 6-cylinders, and almost 25 percent with 8-cylinders. **Maintenance/Repair costs:** Average, particularly because repairs can be done anywhere. **Parts:** Average costs, and parts are often sold for much less through independent suppliers. Some parts are continually back ordered, particularly if involved in recall repairs. **Extended warranty:** A good idea for the powertrain. **Best alternatives:** GM Camaro or Firebird, Honda Civic Si, Hyundai Tiburon, Mazda Miata or Mazda3, and Toyota Celica.

Strengths and Weaknesses

This is definitely not a family car. A light rear end makes the car dangerously unstable on wet roads or when cornering at high speeds, unless equipped with traction control (optional on most models). But for those who want a sturdy and stylish second car, or who don't need room in the back or standard ABS, 2001–04 and 2006–07 Mustangs are reasonably good sports car buys, thanks to their maxed-out depreciation, powertrain improvements, and fewer factory defects. Base models come equipped with a host of luxury and convenience items, which can make them real bargains once the base price has sufficiently depreciated—say, after the first three or four years.

1994–2004 Mustang

Through the years, these models got more-powerful engines, manumatic gearboxes with more gears, four-wheel disc brakes, additional airbags, and a more-rigid chassis meant to reduce rattles and water leaks (which didn't work). Unfortunately, Ford's performance- and safety-related problems are carried over year after year (see "Safety Summary"). Engines and transmissions continue to be glitch-prone: Both the V6 and V8 have a propensity for chronic surging and stalling, and they experience blown engine intake manifold and head gaskets; failed motor mounts; ticking and rattling at 3000 rpm until the car shifts into Second gear; poorly shifting automatic transmissions, especially from First to Second gear; differential howling or whining (ring and pinion failures); dying on deceleration; fuel-system malfunctions, highlighted by frequent fuel-injector replacement; faulty differential carrier bearings; and prematurely worn clutch pressure plates. Owners also frequently complain of electrical short circuits causing instrument panel shutdown; the early replacement of brake rotors, pads, and calipers; and unbelievably poor fit and finish highlighted by paint delamination and peeling, an easily pitted windshield, premature rusting, wind noise, water leaks, and various clunks and rattles. Other noises include engine ticking caused by bad lifters, steering creaks when turning, a clunking front suspension, tie-rod ends that "pop," and rear-end pinion gear whine. The Shaker 1000 stereo system constantly malfunctions, and fuel gauge readings are erratic, especially when the tank is less than half full. (See *forums.mustangworks.com*, *www.flamingfords.info*, *www.autosafety.org/autodefects. html*, *www.blueovalnews.com*, *www.tgrigsby.com/views/ford.htm* (The Anti-Ford Page), and *www.flatratetech.com* for more info.)

2005–07 Mustang

The redesigned 2005s gain about 15 cm in wheelbase and overall length over their 1999–2004 predecessors, plus about 45 kg on coupes and 125 kg on convertibles. A 210 hp 4.0L V6 replaces the previous 193 hp 3.8L. GTs carry a 4.6L V8, but with

300 hp instead of the 2004's 260 hp. The optional automatic is a 5-speed, versus the previous 4-speed. All 2005 Mustangs come with AC and four-wheel disc brakes, but ABS and traction control are standard only on the GT version. No anti-skid system is available, and full-body front side airbags are optional. All Mustangs come with air conditioning and a CD player.

Ford's reworking of the 2005 gives the Mustang a bit more muscle and slightly better performance, but the absence of ABS, an anti-skid system, independent rear suspension, and side airbags are four notable deficiencies when compared with the competition. Reliability actually went downhill during the first year of the redesign, only to improve with the 2006–07 models. Nevertheless, a new subset of failures appeared with the 2006–07 models, including tire-air leakage, lag-and-lurch acceleration, difficult refuelling, transmission clutch slippage, sudden control-arm breakage, and electrical, fuel delivery, and fit and finish deficiencies.

Cobra

Launched as a limited-production, high-performance 1993 sports car, the Cobra has garnered a reputation for mind-spinning depreciation, wallet-busting powertrain defects, and mediocre performance and handling. The first models came with a 240 hp V8, a firm suspension, all-disc ABS, and unique styling. In subsequent years (there were no 2000 or 2002 models), Cobras got more-powerful (yet unreliable) engines, a fully independent suspension, and hood and side scoops. The car's road performance remained seriously compromised by its loose rear end, which swings out when cornering under speed or on wet highways.

VEHICLE HISTORY: 1999—Fresh styling and a horsepower boost. The V6 models also get suspension and steering gear upgrades. Ford admits that its 1999 SVT Cobra delivers up to 50 hp less than the 320 hp advertised. **2000**—Ford is forced to cancel the Cobra's 2000 model year because no one believes in the horsepower claims; it takes a year to fix the problem and get the Cobra back to dealer showrooms for 2001. Improved child safety seat anchoring. **2001**—GT models receive hood and side scoops and larger wheels. All models get an upgraded centre console, blacked-out headlights, and spoilers. **2002**—New 16-inch alloy wheels; sporty Cobra stays home again this year. **2003**—Three 4.6L V8 models: the 260 hp GT, the new 305 hp Mach 1, and the 390 hp supercharged SVT Cobra. **2005**—Restyled, with more power, more features, and a 15 cm larger wheelbase. **2007**—Debut of the high-performance Shelby GT and GT500. All models get a digital audio jack.

 ## Safety Summary

All models/years: Get high-performance tires, and "feather" the accelerator. Regularly equipped Mustangs, like most rear-drive Fords, don't handle sharp curves or wet pavement very well. The rear end swings out suddenly, and the car tends to spin uncontrollably. Traction is easily lost, and braking is hardly reassuring. • Serious concerns have been raised about the Mustang's fuel system failing safety integrity standards and about the tendency of the convertible's doors to jam shut in a 57 km/h frontal collision. • Sudden acceleration because of a stuck throttle. • Transmission allows vehicle to roll away when parked on an incline; emergency brake disengages. • Airbag fails to deploy; inadvertent airbag deployment. • Seat belt becomes twisted, continually tightens up when worn, or fails to retract. • Brake failure, and premature replacement of the brake master cylinder. • Side windows fall off their tracks. **All models: 2000**—Almost 400 safety complaints recorded by NHTSA for this model year. • Fumes from airbag deployment make passengers ill and temporarily blind them. • Fuel leak caused by a rusted-out fuel-filler neck (cost: $500 to repair). • Alternator melted battery wires; car caught fire. • Convertible top unlatches and flips up while vehicle is underway. • Hood flies up. • Head restraints sit too low. • Many reports of rear axle failures. • Multiple function switch failure causes headlights to suddenly go out. **2001**—Safety-related complaints have trended downward dramatically; less than half the previous year's tally. • Lower control arm comes off. • Sudden brake lock-up. • ABS control module failures. • Foot hits fuse box when engaging clutch pedal. **2002**—Fire ignites in the wiring harness under dash area. • Chronic stalling when coasting or braking, or when clutch is depressed. • Serpentine belt comes off, causing loss of power steering and brakes. • Wheel lug nuts fall off. • Sudden acceleration. • Sudden loss of steering when making a left-hand turn. • In one incident, a car left on an incline with transmission in Park and motor shut off rolled down after 10 minutes and hit a tree. • Emergency brake ratchet assembly breaks, making mechanism inoperable. • Gas spills out of fuel tank because clamps not sufficiently tightened. • Left front wheel falls off when the lower control arm and ball joint become loose. **2003**—Gas pedal can be caught by the carpet. • Sudden acceleration tied to the cruise-control mechanism. • Chronic stalling when decelerating; computer reflash doesn't fix the problem. • Automatic transmission failures. • Loss of brakes. • Spark plug blows out of the passenger-side cylinder head:

> This left me with a $4,463 repair cost to fix my car that I only owned for three months. While doing research on the Internet and asking questions in mechanic shops, it has been apparent that Ford engines have defective cylinder heads.

• Serpentine belt often shreds, causing the brakes to fail and engine to overheat and stall. • Water leaks through side windows. • AC condensation drips onto the exhaust pipe, rusting it out prematurely. **2004**—Throttle sticks under the carpet. • Faulty rear differential; it whines and is wobbly when making turns. • Seatback collapsed from a rear-ender; seatback bolt broke while driving. • Head restraints don't adjust enough. • Steering locks up:

> Power steering unit was excessively noisy and distracting... Locks up on hard turn. Dealer says nature of the beast, won't replace it. Complained 3 times, car just went out of warranty... Several hundred local police cruisers have had their power steering replaced by dealer after "negative publicity on TV...." Dealers attempt to make you out as stupid, and keep obfuscating [until] you just go away.

• Sharp tailpipe sticks out and can severely cut anyone brushing against it. • Rear window explodes for no reason:

> When driver notified his insurance carrier, he was informed that their glass installer was aware of the spontaneous rear window explosions occurring in the 2002–2004 model year of Mustangs.

2005—Following Ford's redesign, almost 200 safety-related incidents were reported to NHTSA—about a third more complaints than normal and equal to what the 2001 models have registered over seven model years. • Stuck accelerator pedal. • When slowing for a stop, engine hesitates then surges, and the automatic transmission slams into gear. • When parking, car suddenly accelerates in Drive or in Reverse. • Faulty fuel pumps blamed for frequent stalling. • The manual transmission clutch engages abruptly. • Brake fluid leaks from the master cylinder. • Brakes suddenly lock up, and in some cases, catch fire:

> The parking brake calipers and pads freeze and will not release when temperature drops below 32 degrees [Fahrenheit] [0°C]—while the handle is fully released inside the vehicle. When in neutral and pushed, car will not roll, and when in gear and given gas car barely budges. Taken twice to dealership—by tow truck—but when arrived temperature had risen above 32 degrees and pads etc. had released.

• Parking brake cable seizes or breaks. • The powertrain "tunnel" located down the centre of the car gets extremely hot while driving. • Steering locks while turning left. • Rear strut/shock absorber support brackets rust out. • Fuel spews out the filler pipe, and gas station pumps shut off before the fuel tank is full—a problem that's carried over to the 2006 models:

> Intermittently, will not allow a full fill-up on gas. Several different gas stations tested. Only allows for half tank fill-up. Seems to worsen when the weather is cold.

• Fuses may not be seated properly, resulting in dash gauges going dark. • When underway, flimsy hood vibrates and twists violently. • Dash panel cannot be read on a sunny day while wearing sunglasses. • Airbag warning light remains lit. • Newly designed tail lights look lit in daylight, confusing following drivers. • Complete lighting failure; reprogrammed computer fixed the problem. • Convertible-top lifting mechanism froze halfway up; will cost $6,000 to fix. • Original-equipment tires pit and bulge. **2006**—So far, only 66 safety-related complaints have been posted; about half of what one would expect. • When accelerating, vehicle hesitates then surges. • Car continues to be hard to refuel (nozzle shuts off when tank is a quarter to half full). • Faulty fuel pumps. • Dim headlights due to interior condensation. • Manual transmission clutch slippage. • Manual transmission failure. • Side window shattered for no reason. • Windshield distortion causes wavy white lines to appear, or following car headlights "flash" in the mirror. • Broken seatback levers and side mirrors. **2007**—Mustang GT throttle stuck. • Car hesitates and then surges when accelerating. • Frequent complaints that the right control arm broke at the weld. • Fuel tank takes a long time to fill. • Clutch slippage. • Erratic shifting with the automatic transmission. • A faulty Second-gear clutch causes a whining noise and then transmission failure. • Parking brakes seize in cold weather. • Convertible top leaks and floods vehicle. • Many complaints of tires failing due to loss of tire pressure (cracked valve stems); have to be inflated three times weekly to maintain the proper pressure. • Saleen model rear visibility obstructed by the spoiler. • Some rear windshield defroster/defogger embedded wires don't work.

Secret Warranties/Internal Bulletins/Service Tips

All models/years: Paint delamination, peeling, or fading. • Ford's seven-year "goodwill" warranty extensions usually cover engine and transmission components. • Cold hesitation when accelerating, rough idle, long crank times, and stalling may all signal the need to clean out excessive intake valve deposits. • Excessive oil consumption is likely caused by leaking gaskets, poor sealing of the lower intake manifold, defective intake and exhaust valve stem seals, or worn piston rings; install new guide-mounted valve-stem seals for a better fit as well as new piston rings with improved oil control. • A thumping or clacking heard from the front brakes signals the need to machine the front disc brake rotors. **All models: 1996–2001**—Manual transmission may stick in Reverse or pop out of Reverse. **1997–99**—Delayed or no 2–3 upshifts may be caused by a leaking accumulator seal. • Road noise or dust/water leaks in the luggage compartment can be fixed by sealing the wheelhouse flange. **1997–2000**—Automatic transmission fluid leaks at the radiator can be stopped by installing an O-ring on the transmission oil cooler fitting. **1998–2002**—Guidelines for replacing defective ignition lock cylinders. **1998–2006**—Troubleshooting tips for correcting a rough-running engine. **1999–2004**—Manual transmission is hard to shift into Reverse or First. **2001–03**—Wind noise from the A-pillar area. **2001–04**—4.6L engine rattle. **2002**—Air leaks in the intake manifold or engine. • In 4.6L engines, oil leaks from the head gasket area. • Manual transmission clashes or grinds. • Rear whine heard during coastdown from 100 km/h. • Vehicles equipped with a 5-speed manual transmission may stumble or hesitate when cold. • Electrical problems include erratic operation of turn signals, hard starting, and illuminated ABS warning light. • Inoperative door window because of faulty window regulator. • Defective ignition-switch lock cylinder. **2003–04**—Hard to shift, rattling manual transmission. • Ford will install four revised hood scoop insulators (#2L7Z-9P686-AA) to eliminate a hood rattle. **2003–06**—Leaking, inoperative AC compressor. **2005–06**—Hesitation on acceleration. • AC compressor clutch failure. • Erratic fuel gauge. • Parking brake cable freezes; rear brakes drag. • Rattling from the gearshift, dash area. • Rear axle hum, whine. **2005–07**—Fourth gear rattle with the 4.0L engine. • Front-end noise on bumps. • Ford finally admits it has a fuel-tank fill-up problem and offers to change the tank under warranty, according to TSB #07-21-12. • Power window malfunctions. • Paint blistering and early corrosion on aluminum body panels. • Abnormal convertible-top wear; malfunction. • Premature convertible-top wear. **2005–08**—Water leaks onto front floor. • Exhaust system buzz, rattle. • Manual transmission ticking. • Door handle not flush, rattles. *Cobra:* **2001–05**—Rear axle shudder, chatter. **2003**—Defective engine cylinder heads or valve guides (replacement cylinder head Part #3R2Z-6049-GA). **2004**—Intermittent loss of power, no-starts. • Engine overheating. • Manual transmission gear whine and grind, and loss of Second gear. • Driveline clunk during gear changes or quick acceleration. • Squealing noise from the steering assembly. • Front suspension squeaking noise when vehicle passes over bumps. • Inoperative rear window defroster. • Thump noise when AC clutch engages. **2005–06**—Paint blistering and early corrosion on aluminum body panels.

MUSTANG, COBRA PROFILE

	1999	2000	2001	2002	2003	2004	2005	2006	2007
Cost Price ($)									
LX/Coupe	20,995	21,195	22,275	22,795	22,990	23,495	23,795	23,999	23,999
Cobra	36,995	—	38,495	—	41,995	50,650	—	—	—
Convertible	24,995	25,195	26,945	27,465	27,760	28,095	27,995	27,999	27,999
Used Values ($)									
LX/Coupe ▲	3,500	4,500	5,000	5,500	6,500	8,500	11,500	13,500	15,500
LX/Coupe ▼	3,000	4,000	4,500	5,000	6,000	7,000	10,000	12,000	14,500
Cobra ▲	5,500	—	9,500	—	12,000	13,000	—	—	—
Cobra ▼	4,500	—	8,000	—	11,000	12,000	—	—	—
Convertible ▲	5,500	6,000	6,500	7,500	9,500	11,000	14,500	16,500	19,500
Convertible ▼	5,000	5,500	6,000	6,500	8,000	9,500	13,000	15,500	18,000
Reliability	2	2	2	2	3	3	3	4	4
Crash Safety (F)	4	4	5	5	5	5	5	5	5
Side	3	3	3	3	3	3	4	4	4
Convertible	—	—	2	2	2	2	—	—	—
IIHS Side	—	—	—	—	—	—	—	—	5
Offset (Convertible)	—	—	—	—	—	—	3	3	3
Head Restraints (F)	1	—	1	1	3	3	—	—	—
Rear	—	—	—	—	—	1	1	—	—
Convertible	—	—	—	—	—	—	1	1	1
Rollover Resistance	—	—	—	5	5	5	5	5	5

General Motors

CAMARO, FIREBIRD, TRANS AM   ★★★★★

RATING: Recommended (1999–2002). Camaro and Firebird were dropped for the 2003 model year. GM should have axed its money-losing Saturn and Saab divisions, instead, and kept Oldsmobile and the Camaro and Firebird. Fun to drive and easily repaired, these cars are more reliable than the Mustang, despite having elicited similar safety-related complaints such as airbag deployment injuries, sudden acceleration, brake failures, and steering loss. Be especially wary of brake rotor warpage, requiring rotor replacement every two years (about a $300 job). Bargain-hunter alert: A V8-equipped Camaro convertible is the best choice for retained value a few years down the road. But you can do quite well with a used base coupe equipped with a high-performance handling package. **"Real" city/highway fuel economy:** *Camaro V6 manual:* 11.3/6.9 L/100 km. *Camaro V6 automatic:* 12.2/7.0 L/100 km. *Camaro V8 manual:* 12.5/8.0 L/100 km. *Camaro V8 automatic:* 13.1/8.8 L/100 km. Fuel savings will likely be lower by about 20 percent. **Maintenance/ Repair costs:** Average, and repairs can be done by any independent garage. **Parts:** Reasonably priced and easy to find. **Extended warranty:** A waste of money; instead, spend an extra $100 getting the car checked out thoroughly before you buy it. **Best alternatives:** Ford Mustang or Probe, Hyundai Tiburon, Mazda Miata, and Toyota Celica.

Strengths and Weaknesses

Camaros and Firebirds are reasonably priced rear-drive muscle cars that cost more but perform better than the Mustang and produce excellent crash protection scores and reasonable resale values. They also take the lead over the Mustang with their slightly better reliability record. Overall performance, however, varies a great deal depending on the engine, transmission, and suspension combination in each particular car. Base models equipped with the V6 powerplant accelerate reasonably well, but high-performance enthusiasts will find them slow for sporty cars. Like all rear-drive Detroit iron, handling is compromised by poor traction on wet roads, minimal comfort, and a suspension that's too soft for high-speed cornering and too bone-jarring for smooth cruising. The Z28, IROC-Z, and Trans Am provide smart acceleration and handling but at the expense of fuel economy—a small drawback, however, when you save thousands buying used. How many thousands? For example, a potent, head-turning 2002 Firebird Trans Am can be had for less than $11,000. A same-year Camaro will cost a few thousand less, and a 2002 convertible won't cost much over $12,000.

VEHICLE HISTORY: 1997—GM offers a 30th birthday styling package for the Camaro and some interior upgrades, V6 engine dampening for smoother running at high speeds, optional Ram Air induction, and racier-looking, ground-effects body trim for the Firebird. **1998**—A minor facelift, and the Z28 and SS both receive a slight horsepower boost. **1999**—Electronic throttle control on V6-equipped versions, and a new Zexel Torsion differential is used in the limited-slip rear axle. **2000**—Camaros and Firebirds get alloy wheels; improved throttle response for manual transmission–equipped cars. **2001**—Z28 and SS models are given 5 more horses and restyled chrome wheels. **2002**—Improved ride quality and dashboard layout.

Stick with the 1996–2002 models for the best performance and price. They are much better overall performers than previous models, and additional standard safety features are a plus. These sporty convertibles and coupes are almost identical in their pricing and in the features they offer (the Firebird has pop-up headlights, a more-pointed front end, a narrower middle, and a rear spoiler). All models got a complete makeover in 1995, making them more powerful and aerodynamic with less spine-jarring performance.

As one moves up the scale, overall performance improves considerably. The V8 engine gives these cars lots of sparkle and tire-spinning torque, but there's a fuel penalty to pay. A 4-speed automatic transmission is standard on the 5.7L-equipped Z28; other versions come with a standard 5-speed manual gearbox or an optional 6-speed. Many of these cars are likely to have been ordered with lots of extra performance and luxury options, including an attractive T-roof package guaranteed to include a full assortment of creaks and groans.

Owners report premature automatic transmission failures, a noisy base engine, and excessive oil consumption with the larger engine. Fuel economy is unimpressive, the AC malfunctions, front brakes (rotors and pads, mostly) and MacPherson struts wear out quickly, servicing the fuel-injection system is an exercise in frustration, electrical problems are common, and gauges operate erratically. Body problems are frequent. These include door rattles, misaligned doors and hatches, T-roof water and air leaks, a sticking hatch power release, and poor fit and finish. Owners also complain that the steering wheel is positioned too close to the driver's chest, the low seats create a feeling of claustrophobia, visibility is limited by wide side pillars, and trunk space is sparse with a high liftover. (See *www. autosafety.org/autodefects.html* and *www.sportscarforums.com*.)

 ## Safety Summary

All models/years: Early brake rotor warpage and pad replacement. One dealer mechanic explains the problem this way:

> The rotors are not thick enough and have insufficient air to cool them. ASE-certified independent mechanics and dealership employees (unofficially) buy slotted "racing" rotors or use ceramic non-metal pads from other sources. This has apparently gone on since 1998 on both Firebirds and Camaros.

• Airbag malfunctions. • Engine seizures. • Sudden acceleration. • Seat belts fail to lock up or retract. • Windshields are seriously distorted. **All models: 1999**— Interestingly, both the Camaro and the Firebird have about one-third fewer safety-related complaints registered against them by NHTSA than the same-year Ford Mustang does. • Cracked fuel tank leaks fuel. • Accelerator pedal sticks. • Many incidents of clutch slippage at low mileage. • Frequent complaints that the stock shifter causes misshifts. • Electrical system shorts cause instrument panel and assorted gauges and lights to operate erratically. • Turn signal lights don't flash, headlights often dim to about 50 percent of their intended brightness, heater slows down, and power windows run slowly. **2000**—Frequent stalling. • Electrical wires melt. • Emergency brake fails to hold vehicle; comes off in driver's hand. • Rear brake lock-ups. • Headlights flicker or suddenly go out. • Horn collects water, which muffles sound. • Front end pulls to the right. • Headrests are set too low (same complaint heard from Mustang owners). • Windows leak water. • Premature power-window motor failures. **2000–01**—T-roof flies off vehicle; one Camaro lost its T-roof while cruising on the highway. **2001**—Airbags fail to deploy. • Engine management computer holds throttle open when foot is lifted off the accelerator. • Premature automatic transmission failure. • Sudden complete brake failure. • The left side mirror often breaks for no reason. **2002**—Fire ignites in the window switch in the door panel. • Turn signal lights burn out and melt the socket wires. • Stalling due to a plugged catalytic converter or faulty fuel-pump and throttle body sensor. • Early headlight and power-window motor failures.

Secret Warranties/Internal Bulletins/Service Tips

All models/years: Eliminate AC odours by applying an evaporator core cooling-coil coating. • Paint delamination, peeling, or fading. • GM guidelines to dealers on troubleshooting exterior light condensation complaints. • Oil leaks between the intake manifold and engine block are most often caused by insufficient RTV bonding between the intake manifold and cylinder block. • Reverse servo cover seal leaks. **All models: 1993–2002**—GM has a special kit to prevent AC odours in warm weather. **1997–2002**—Radio speaker buzz or rattle. **1998–2000**—An engine that loses coolant or runs hot may simply need a new radiator cap or the radiator filler neck to be polished. • Install upgraded after-market disc pads to eliminate rear brake chirp or groan and front brake squeal when braking. • Silence accessory drivebelt chirping or squeaking by installing a double row idler pulley, generator bracket, and serpentine belt. **1998–2002**—Water runs out of front lower corners of rear hatch. • Engine spark, knock remedy. **1999–2001**—Excessive oil consumption. **1999–2002**—Poor transmission performance, slipping. **2000**—Repair tips for fixing an inoperative or erratically operating antenna. **2000–02**—Clogged injectors are the likely cause of poor engine performance. • Delayed shifting. **2001–02**—Tips for troubleshooting an engine that cranks but won't run. • Engine knocking or lifter noise. • Slipping or missing Second, Third, or Fourth gear. • Remedy for harsh upshifts. • Rear brake rattling. **2002**—Intermittent no-start caused by fuel pump and fuel gauge wiring harness short. • Harsh automatic transmission shifts. • Automatic transmission pump leaks. • Quarter trim panels pull away. • Troubleshooting guide for correcting wind noise and water leaks. • Exhaust ping. • Radiator cap may not hold sufficient vacuum. • Rattling door handles. • Noisy, faulty clutch pedal. *Models with 2.5L engines:* **All years:** Frequent stalling may require a new MAP sensor (TSB #90-142-8A). *Models with 3.8L V6 engines:* **1998–2002**—Premature driveshaft wear.

CAMARO, FIREBIRD, TRANS AM PROFILE

	1999	2000	2001	2002
Cost Price ($)				
Camaro/RS	23,100	26,065	26,120	26,995
Z28	28,670	31,630	29,540	30,785
Convertible	30,105	38,270	38,585	39,225
Firebird	24,865	27,605	26,915	27,695
Trans Am	34,750	35,505	35,815	36,365

Used Values ($)

Camaro/RS ▲	4,000	4,500	5,500	7,000
Camaro/RS ▼	3,500	4,000	5,000	6,000
Z28 ▲	6,000	7,000	8,000	9,500
Z28 ▼	6,500	6,000	7,000	8,500
Convertible ▲	9,000	10,000	11,000	13,000
Convertible ▼	8,000	9,000	10,000	11,500
Firebird ▲	4,000	4,500	5,500	7,000
Firebird ▼	3,500	4,000	5,000	6,000
Trans Am ▲	7,500	8,000	9,000	11,000
Trans Am ▼	7,000	7,500	8,000	9,500

Reliability	4	4	5	5
Crash Safety (F) (Camaro)	4	4	4	4
Side (Camaro)	3	3	3	3
Head Restraints	1	—	1	1

CORVETTE ★★★

RATING: Average (1999–2007). Keep in mind that premium fuel and astronomical insurance rates will drive up your operating costs. And don't discount the serious safety-related problems you're likely to experience on all models. They run the gamut of sudden steering lock-ups when underway, electrical shorts causing vehicle shutdowns, nonfunctioning parking brakes, brake failures caused by premature rotor warpage (around 16,000 km), seat belts that jam in the retractor, and, on the 2005, the top suddenly flying off (a 2002 Ford Mustang trait, as well). The locked-up steering is particularly scary because it apparently has carried over to many model years, and traffic accident investigators may simply conclude that a resulting accident was because of driver inexperience or unsafe driving. **"Real" city/highway fuel economy:** *Manual:* 12.3/7.7 L/100 km. *Automatic:* 13.2/7.9 L/100 km. Fuel savings may actually be lower by more than 20 percent. **Maintenance/Repair costs:** Much higher than average, although most repairs can be done by any independent garage. Long waits for recall repairs. **Parts:** Pricey, but easy to find. Surprisingly, it is often easier to find parts for older Corvettes through collectors' clubs than it is to find many of the high-tech components used today. **Extended warranty:** By all means—just saving the diagnostic fees will pay for the warranty. Get a GM-backed supplementary warranty, or look for a recent model that has some of its original warranty left. The frequency of repairs and the high repair costs make maintenance outrageously expensive. **Best alternatives:** Ford Mustang, GM Camaro or Firebird, Mazda Miata, and Toyota Celica or Supra.

Strengths and Weaknesses

Corvettes made in the late '60s and early '70s are acceptable buys, mainly because of their value as collector cars and their uncomplicated repairs (though parts may be rare). Unfortunately, the Corvette's overall reliability and safety have declined over the past 40 years as its price and complexity have increased. GM has chosen to update its antiquated design with complicated high-tech add-ons rather than come up with something original. Consequently, the car has been gutted and then retuned using failure-prone electronic circuitry. Complicated emissions plumbing, braking, and suspension systems have also been added in an attempt to make the Corvette a fuel-efficient, user-friendly, high-performance vehicle—a goal that General Motors has missed by a wide margin.

The electronically controlled suspension systems have always been plagued by glitches. The noisy 5.7L engine frequently hesitates and stalls, there's lots of transmission buzz and whine, the rear tires produce excessive noise, and wind whistles through the A- and C-pillars; these, and the all-too-familiar fibreglass body squeaks and paint delamination (yes, fibreglass delaminates), continue to be unwanted standard features throughout all model years. Also, the electronic dash never works quite right (speedometer lag is one example).

Ownership of more-recent Corvette models does have its positive side. For example, the ABS vented disc brakes, available since 1986, are easy to modulate and fade-free. The standard European-made Bilstein FX-3 Selective Ride Control suspension can be pre-set for touring, sport, or performance. Under speed, an electronic module automatically varies the suspension setting, finally curing these cars of their earlier endemic oversteering, wheel spinning, breakaway rear ends, and other nasty surprises.

Owners admit the redesigned '97 models offer improved performance, better handling, and additional safety features, but they find fault with the stiff ride, poor fuel economy, and excessive interior noise. From a reliability standpoint, these models are much more refined than earlier versions, but they are hell to diagnose and are knuckle-busters to service. And you can expect chronic engine stalling and surging, excessive engine oil consumption, an oily black buildup on the exhaust tips, and catalytic converter failures within the first five years. A real hair-raiser is the tendency of steering columns on 1977–2001 models to suddenly lock while the vehicle is underway or parked. This continues to be a widespread hazard, despite a recall to fix the defect. Says the following Corvette owner:

> This item has failed on an estimated 3,000 Corvettes throughout the U.S. Please see Internet site *www.corvetteforum.com*. As a safety professional, I see this as a hazard that Chevrolet needs to address with more severity. The loss of steering control because the steering wheel locks can lead to property loss, as well as death.

Some performance deficiencies make these cars unsafe: The active handling system often malfunctions and makes the vehicle veer into traffic or spin out of control; faulty electronic and electrical systems cause it to abruptly shut down; the brake, suspension, and AC systems are unreliable; and body accessories and electronics suddenly short out.

Factory-related defects on the post-2000 models are commonplace: The engine is excessively noisy; the cabins overheat; the driver's seat moves while driving; the trunk door warps; seat belts twist easily and tend to pull down uncomfortably against the shoulder; the passenger seat belt jams and won't extend or retract; smelly exhaust fumes enter the cabin, causing watery eyes and dizziness; excessive heat buildup from catalytic converters deforms the rear bumper assembly and heats up the interior even more; the glass rear window limits vision; and front and rear wheel weights sometimes fly off the wheels.

Servicing the different sophisticated fuel-injection systems isn't easy, and this may be the primary reason why so many owners complain of having to take their Corvettes back to the shop repeatedly to correct poor engine and transmission performance.

The 2005–07 redesigned models have produced their own subset of problems, although not as extensive a list as prior models: engine stalling and transmission jerking, electrical short circuits, lousy fit and finish, and squeaky, squealing brakes (see *www.corvetteforum.com* and *www.carreview.com*).

VEHICLE HISTORY: 1997—A substantial redesign is carried out mid-year. The transmission is moved back, creating a roomier cockpit; the interior is much more user-friendly; structural improvements reduce body flexing (a problem with most convertibles) and make for a more-rigid hatchback; and a new aluminum 340 hp LSI V8 engine arrives on the scene. **1998**—Debut of a high-performance hardtop. **2001**—A horsepower boost and an Active Handling performance upgrade, plus the addition of a high-performance Z06 variant. **2002**—The Z06 gets a 20 hp boost to 405 hp, enhanced rear shocks, aluminum front stabilizer-bar links, high-performance brake pads, and new aluminum wheels. **2005**—Revised styling, more power, and new features. The new power top is an instant success. The car's wheelbase is stretched by 3 cm over the 1997–2004 C5, and overall length shrinks by 12.7 cm. The 400 hp 6.0L V8 replaces the C5's 5.7L V8 and adds 50 more horses for good measure. Standard performance safety features still include ABS and traction/anti-skid control. Cars sold with the Z51 package may fetch $1,000 more on the used market due to their firmer, nonadjustable suspension, larger brakes, and automatic transmission that's built for sporty handling. Wheel diameter grows an inch to 18/19. Front side airbags remain standard on the convertible. Thief-magnet xenon headlights are newly standard, along with keyless access and ignition.

 Safety Summary

1999—Sudden, unintended acceleration. • Fuel tank leaks when gassing up; vehicle can catch fire as raw fuel is ignited by the catalytic converter. • Fuel-pump failures. • Parking brake won't hold. • Chronic premature warpage of the brake rotors. • Front lap belts jam in the retractor. • Electrical shorts cause headlights to stick open; rear-view mirror assembly melts; and a plethora of other electronic glitches lead to vehicle shutdown. • Poorly anchored driver's seat and warped trunk door. **1999–2001**—Engine serpentine belt and tensioner failures. **2000–01**—Catalytic converter catches fire. • More reports that when the fuel tank is full, fuel leaks from the top of the vent. • More fuel leaks; this time, owners report leaks from the fuel lines near the firewall inside the engine compartment. • Chronic stalling; fuel-injector failures cause vehicle to shudder and stall. • Engine dies while driving in the rain, and brakes don't work. • If one wheel loses traction, the throttle closes, starving the engine. • Brakes drag and lock up; brake pedal doesn't spring back; overheated rotors are common. • Car is nearly uncontrollable at time of brake lock-up. • Seat belt doesn't retract properly when reeling it out and tightens up progressively when driving. • Driver's seat rocks. • Foot easily slips off clutch and brake pedals. **2002**—Sudden stalling on the highway accompanied by brake failure. • Erratic transmission performance (shifts to Fourth before entering Second gear; won't shift into Second when going uphill). • Horn is hard to access since it's just a small indentation on the steering wheel. **2003**—Very low number of complaints reported. • Sudden engine surge while underway. • When accelerating from a stop, vehicle fails to shift from First to Second gear and then stalls out. • Constant leaking, and failure of rear differential and suspension system. • Leaking oil pan gasket. • Annoying dash reflection onto the windshield. • Inaccurate fuel gauge. • Driver's seat belt locks up. **2004**—Defective steering, despite recall:

> The so-called "fix" GM has for the 1997–2004 Corvette column lock problem does not fix the problem. It merely puts a band-aid on the problem to protect them from lawsuits. I do not understand how this can be allowed by law. I have had to resort to an aftermarket part to fix the problem and chose to ignore the recall.

• Fuel leaks found outside of the car at the fuel-tank, fuel-pump seal, and interconnecting hoses. • Fuel leakage from the crossover pipe and other fuel lines:

> I smelled gas in my garage for approximately 1 week but found no leaks. While filling up at gas station I noticed a large puddle forming under the car and saw gas leaking from the tank. Dealer said gas leak was found in gas tank, crossover fuel line and two other fuel lines. Very dangerous situation. Dealer blamed a manufacturer defect in parts. Took 10 days to repair, as the first time tank was replaced there was no fuel pressure, and it had to be redone.

• Sudden stalling caused by faulty fuel pump. • Steering linkage failure at the steering knuckle. • Power seat pinned driver against the steering wheel. • Clutch won't disengage. • Shifter pops out of Reverse. • Parking brake won't hold car in Neutral on a hill. • Inoperative passenger window regulator. **2005**—Car often throws or shreds the serpentine belt, leading to steering/brake loss and engine overheating. Some owners have experienced the problem several times after it was first repaired. **2005–06**—Corvette also "throws" its top:

> The contact stated the vehicle's roof had separated and flew off while driving 40 mph [65 km/h]. This was the second time the vehicle had problems with the roof. A NHTSA recall #06V181000 was performed in 05/06 regarding structure body: roof and pillars, however the recall did not remedy the problem.

Secret Warranties/Internal Bulletins/Service Tips

All years: A rotten-egg odour coming from the exhaust is probably caused by a defective catalytic converter, which should be covered by the emissions warranty on 2002 and later models. • Clearcoat paint degradation, whitening, and chalking, long a problem with GM's other cars, is a serious problem with the fibreglass-bodied Corvette, says TSB #331708. It too is covered by a secret warranty for up to six years. • Reverse servo cover seal leak. **1993–2002**—GM has a special kit to prevent AC odours in warm weather. **1995–2000**—Guidelines for repairing brake rotor warpage. **1997–99**—A no-start condition can be corrected by reprogramming the power control module (PCM). • TSB #99-06-02-016 has the remedy for a Low Engine Coolant light that comes on at start-up. • Shift-boot squeaking can be silenced by installing a new shift-boot assembly. • Accessory drive squeaks can be corrected by installing a new idler pulley assembly. **1997–2000**—Repair tips for an inaccurate fuel gauge. **1997–2001**—Sound system speakers make the door panel rattle or buzz. **1997–2002**—Tips on correcting water leaks in various areas. • Loose driver's seat. **1997–2003**—Inoperative AC. **1997–2004**—Remedy for a leaking rear differential. **1998–2000**—Tips on correcting a faulty rear window defogger. • An inoperative or noisy window motor can be corrected by replacing the window regulator and motor assembly. **1998–2002**—Engine spark, knock remedy. **1999**—Rattling from the left fuel-tank area can be silenced by installing a fuel-tank foam insulator pad. **1999–2000**—An engine that runs hot or loses coolant may simply need a new radiator cap or polishing of the radiator filler neck. **1999–2001**—Wind noise around the B-pillar. **1999–2002**—Poor transmission performance; SES light lit. • Excessive oil consumption. **2000**—Reducing exhaust boom. • Repair tips on fixing an inoperative or erratically operating antenna. • Left headlight door may not remain closed. **2000–06**—Delayed automatic transmission shifts. **2001**—Incomplete brake pedal return can be fixed by replacing the vacuum brake booster. **2001–02**—Slipping or missing Second, Third, or Fourth gear. **2001–03**—Engine knock or lifter noise. **2001–05**—Harsh upshifts. **2002**—Engine knock. • Erratic fuel gauge or radio operation. • False Service Engine light illumination. • Harsh transmission shifts; 2–4 band and 3–4 clutch damage; transmission pump leaks. • Light brake drag; brake light remains lit. • B-pillar wind noise. **2001–08**—Transmission oil leak; slips in gear. **2002–04**—Exhaust system jingle noise. **2003–06**—Oil leaks from engine's rear cover assembly. **2004**—Erratic idle, idle surge, rough running, and stalling. • Coolant leak from head cup plugs. • Transmission fluid leaks; inoperative Second, Third, and Fourth gears. • Rear axle side cover oil leak. • Poor automatic transmission shifting, slipping. • Transmission squawk, grunt, rattle, growl, or buzz noise. • Intermittent or inoperative fuel gauge addressed in TSB #01659, January 2004. • Wind noise or water leak at top of door glass. • Tire wander. • Seat belt won't release from retractor. • Blotches in all glass. • Inoperative Twilight Sentinel automatic headlight control. **2004–05**—Erratic fuel gauge readings. **2005–06**—Vibration or shudder at idle (replace power-steering inlet pressure hose). • Vehicle's top flies off:

CUSTOMER SATISFACTION—PAINTED ROOF ADHESIVE SEPARATION

2005–06 CHEVROLET CORVETTE WITH PAINTED ROOF

This bulletin is being revised to include Z06 vehicles. A new procedure and labor time have been added.

Discard all copies of bulletin 05112C, issued June 2006.

THIS PROGRAM IS IN EFFECT UNTIL MARCH 31, 2007.

CONDITION: On certain 2005–06 Chevrolet Corvette vehicles, the painted roof panel may separate from its frame in some areas if it is exposed to stresses along with high temperature and humidity. The occupants of the vehicle may notice one or more of these symptoms: a snapping noise when driving over bumps, wind noise, poor roof panel fit, roof panel movement/bounce when a door or hatch is closed, or a water leak in the headliner.

CORRECTION: Dealers are to apply adhesive foam to ensure proper adhesion, or in a small number of vehicles, replace the roof panel.

Ignore GM's cut-off date. The company is negligent and must pay all claims for as long as a provincial court judge decides is reasonable under the implied warranty.

2005–07—Creak or popping noise from the windshield near the front pillar. • Power-steering shudder, vibration at idle. 2005–08—Axle nuts appear loose. • Rear axle chatter, clunk when turning. 2005–09—Tapping or scraping noise from the rear wheel area (replace wheel driveshaft nut). 2007–08—No-shifts, multiple electrical malfunctions. • Erratic power-window operation. 2007–09—Premature headliner wear.

CORVETTE PROFILE

	1999	2000	2001	2002	2003	2004	2005	2006	2007
Cost Price ($)									
Base	53,870	60,050	61,400	62,400	68,120	69,940	67,395	67,805	68,565
Convertible	60,850	66,965	68,315	69,665	74,120	75,940	79,495	79,905	80,665
Used Values ($)									
Base ▲	11,000	13,000	16,000	18,000	21,000	24,000	28,000	31,000	36,000
Base ▼ `	10,000	11,500	14,000	17,000	19,000	22,000	26,000	28,500	34,000
Convertible ▲	14,500	16,000	18,000	20,000	26,000	28,000	34,000	38,000	45,000
Convertible ▼	13,500	14,500	16,500	19,000	24,000	26,000	32,000	35,500	42,000
Reliability	3	3	3	3	3	3	3	3	3
Head Restraints (F)	3	—	3	3	3	3	—	—	—
Rear	—	—	2	2	2	2	—	—	—

Mazda

MX-5 (MIATA) ★★★★★

RATING: Recommended (1999–2007). This is the only sports car *Lemon-Aid* has ever rated Recommended every year from its first model year (1990). For almost 20 years this has been an almost-perfect sports car, except for its poor braking performance on rain-slicked roadways and spotty fit and finish. The redesigned 2006–07 models are the best choices for power and performance. **"Real" city/highway fuel economy:** *5-speed manual:* 10.1/7.6 L/100 km. *6-speed manual:* 10.2/7.7 L/100 km. *6-speed automatic:* 10.6/7.8 L/100 km. Owners say fuel savings may be lower than these estimates by about 10 percent. **Maintenance/Repair costs:** Below-average costs, and most repairs aren't dealer-dependent. **Parts:** Average costs, with good availability. **Extended warranty:** A waste of money. **Best alternatives:** Ford Mustang, GM Camaro or Firebird, Honda S2000, Hyundai Tiburon, Pontiac Solstice, Saturn Sky, and Toyota Celica.

Strengths and Weaknesses

The base engine delivers adequate power and accelerates smoothly. Acceleration from 0–100 km/h is in the high eight-second range. The 5-speed manual transmission shifts easily and has well-spaced gears; the 6-speed adds 27 kg (60 lb.) and isn't that impressive. The vehicle's lightness, precise steering, and 50/50 weight distribution make this an easy car for novice drivers to toss around corners.

VEHICLE HISTORY: 1999—Some handling upgrades and additional standard features. **2001**—A slight horsepower boost, a restyled interior and exterior, 15-inch wheels, seat belt pretensioners, improved ABS, and an emergency trunk release. **2003**—16-inch V-rated tires and strut-tower braces. **2004**—Debut of the MazdaSpeed, equipped with a 178 hp turbocharged engine, 6-speed manual transmission, sport suspension, and 17-inch wheels. **2006**—Name is changed to MX-5. Given about 6.25 cm in wheelbase, 4.25 cm more width, and 4 cm more length while gaining only about 23 kg. Base engine is a 170 hp 2.0L (166 hp with an automatic transmission), in place of the 142 hp 1.8L engine that powered the previous model. An optional 6-speed automatic transmission with steering-wheel shift paddles replaces the 4-speed automatic. Full-torso side airbags, anti-lock four-wheel disc brakes, and a manual-folding soft top with a heated glass rear window are standard features. **2007**—A retractable hardtop adds 35 kg to the car's weight. Mazda continues to offer a removable hardtop for softtop models.

Owners' top performance gripes target the same characteristics that make other sports-car enthusiasts swoon: inadequate cargo space, cramped interior for large adults, excessive interior noise, and limited low-end torque that makes for frequent shifting.

Owners also say that it's important to change the engine timing chain every 100,000 km. Other reported problems include crankshaft failures, leaky rear-end seals and valve cover gaskets, rear differential seal failures, leaking or squeaky clutches, hard starts and stalling, torn drive boots, transmission whining in upper gear ranges, engine and exhaust system rattles, electrical system glitches, brake pulsation, valvetrain clatter on start-up (changing oil may help), prematurely worn-out shock absorbers and catalytic converters, softtop covers that come off or break, and minor body and trim deficiencies. Redesigned 2006s have a few more fit and finish deficiencies due to their redesign. Most of the problems were fixed on the 2007s; however, there are still some reports of rattling from the console area between the seats, convertible-top leaks, and an interior leak that soaks the carpet from the driver's front area to underneath the seat. (See *www.miata.net*, *www.miataforum.com*, and *www.straight-six.com*.)

 ## Safety Summary

All years: Used Miatas will likely have some collision damage; make sure you run a *Carproof.com* check online or by fax. **1999**—Airbags fail to deploy on impact. • While passing another car on the highway, accelerator cable and the cable adjuster assembly disengaged from the horseshoe bracket that holds the cable. • Transmission suddenly failed, causing both rear wheels to seize. • Keizer aluminum wheel cracks, damaging brake caliper, rotor, and fender. • Performs poorly on wet roads. • At highway speeds, vehicle tends to wander all over the road. **2000**—In heavy rain, stepping on the brakes results in a two-second delay before braking; must continually pump the brakes. • Airbags deployed two minutes after collision. • Convertible-top latches may inadvertently open while vehicle is underway. • Hard shifting and stiff shifter at Neutral causes gear hunting, grinding, and rattling. • Gas pump shuts off before tank is full. **2001**—Vehicle rolled downhill despite being parked with emergency brake engaged. **2002**—Interior can heat up to 54°C (130°F) because exhaust system is mounted too close to the centre console. **2003**—When accelerating from a cold start, car lurches and then stalls. • Hard starts. • Wheel rims are easily bent. • Poor headlight illumination. **2004**—Hard starts despite changing the fuel pump. • Seat belt locks up during normal driving. **2006**—While complaints for other years have been nonexistent or in the single digits, the 2006 models logged 10 reports of safety-related failures (still about 40 less than normal). • Constant steering corrections are necessary due to the vehicle wandering all over the road. • In moderately cold temperatures, the power windows won't work. • It is easy to accidentally engage First gear when Reverse is required, or Reverse when First is needed. **2007**—Sudden, unintended acceleration. • "Fix-a-Flat" kit doesn't fix flats caused by a cut tire. • The point where the manual transmission clutch catches keeps moving upward.

Secret Warranties/Internal Bulletins/Service Tips

All years: TSB #006/94 gives all of the possible causes and remedies for brake vibration. • TSB #N00198 addresses complaints that the steering wheel is off-centre. • Other bulletins address the issue of musty AC odours. **1999**—A hard-to-start engine may have debris accumulated at the fuel-pressure regulator valve area, causing the valve to stick open. • Engine rattling may be caused by premature wear of the engine thrust bearing or by the engine harness clips rubbing against the car's frame. **1999–2003**—Clutch chatter on cold start-up. **2000–06**—Troubleshooting body vibration and steering-wheel shimmy. **2002**—Fuelling difficulty caused by gas pump shutting off early. • The 6-speed manual transmission won't shift into Fifth gear or Reverse. **2004**—Door rattling. **2005**—Free replacement of the keyless entry fob. **2006**—Rough idle, hesitation. • Clutch pedal squeaking when depressed. • Abnormal heater performance. • Water leaks from top of door windows and at the front of the convertible top. • Excessive gaps between the header weather stripping and the body above the windshield; windshield adhesive oozes out onto the paint. • Console lid won't stay closed; squeaking noise. • Tire valve stem breaks when removing valve cap. **2006–07**—Manual transmission clutch hard to disengage, excessive pedal free play. • Front brakes produce a low-speed creaking noise. • Convertible-top latch rattling. • Gap in plastic door-trim panel. • Special Program MSP13 allows for the free replacement of the fuel-filler cap. • Poor AM band reception. • Water accumulation in footwells. **2007**—Retractable hard top difficult to open; crunch noise; contacts deck panel.

MX-5 (MIATA) PROFILE

	1999	2000	2001	2002	2003	2004	2005	2006	2007
Cost Price ($)									
Base	26,025	26,995	27,605	27,695	27,695	27,895	27,995	27,995	28,095
Used Values ($)									
Base ▲	5,500	6,000	7,500	9,000	10,500	13,000	15,000	17,000	19,000
Base ▼	5,000	5,500	6,500	8,000	9,000	11,500	13,500	15,500	17,500
Reliability	5	5	5	5	5	5	5	5	5
Crash Safety (F)	—	—	—	4	4	4	4	—	—
Side	—	—	—	3	3	3	3	—	—
Head Restraints (F)	1	—	3	3	3	3	—	—	—
Rear	—	—	2	2	2	—	—	—	—
Rollover Resistance	—	—	—	—	5	5	5	—	—

Note: The Miata's base price has increased only $2,000 in about a decade.

Toyota

CELICA ★★★★

RATING: Above Average (1999–2005). All Celicas handle competently; the extra performance in the higher-line versions does come at a price, but this isn't a problem, given their high resale value. 1997 and later models sacrifice quality for performance. **"Real" city/highway fuel economy:** *5-speed manual:* 8.9/6.5 L/100 km. *5-speed automatic:* 8.3/6.0 L/100 km. *6-speed manual:* 9.6/6.6 L/100 km. *6-speed automatic:* 9.4/7.0 L/100 km. **Maintenance/Repair costs:** Average, and most repairs can be done at any garage. **Parts:** Reasonably priced and usually easy to find, except for body parts. **Extended warranty:** No, you'd be throwing your money away. **Best alternatives:** Ford Mustang, GM Camaro or Firebird, Honda Civic Si, Hyundai Tiburon, and Mazda3 or Miata.

Strengths and Weaknesses

Celicas offer decent reliability and durability, with three major exceptions: engine sludging; an engine-blowing, self-destructing 6-speed gearbox; and the premature, costly replacement of brake calipers, pads, and rotors:

> Toyota has a big problem with their 6-speed in the new Celica. They even told me about it at Toyota. The malfunction is that when trying to shift from Third to Fourth gear, the transmission will slip into Second instead of Fourth. This then causes the engine to be blown.

> This is a very dangerous situation if trying to merge with traffic on interstate at around 70–75 mph [113–120 km/h] and suddenly your car decelerates instantly to around 50 mph [80 km/h]. They need to do something about it before someone gets seriously hurt.

Servicing and repairs are straightforward, and parts are easily found. The front-drive series performs very well and hasn't presented any major problems to owners. Prices are high for Celicas in good condition, but some bargains are available with the base ST model.

The early models saw engine failures caused by engine oil sludge (1997–2001 models), a problem covered by Toyota "goodwill" (see the "Sienna" section); brake pulsations and pulling to one side; rear defroster terminals breaking on convertibles; sunroof leaks; and smelly AC emissions.

Another subset of problems shows up on the redesigned 2000–05 models. This includes engine failures while driving ("weak" valves blamed), not much power when the accelerator is floored, stalling after a cold start, engine knocking, excessive oil consumption, early replacement of the belt tensioner and airflow meter, a failure-prone 6-speed transmission, insufficient AC cooling, lights dimming and heater lagging when shifting into idle, seat belt tabs that damage door panels, interior panels that separate, a driver's window that catches and doesn't go all the way up, a leaky convertible top and sunroof, drivebelt squeaks when turning, a squeaking gearshift lever, a grinding noise emanating from the front wheels and brakes, paint peeling, and limited rear visibility. The audible reverse alarm isn't Toyota's brightest idea: Audible only inside the vehicle, it adds a forklift cachet to your Celica.

VEHICLE HISTORY: 1997—GT is given 5 more horses, and the notchback GT is axed. **1998**—ST is dropped, and GT is given more standard features. **1999**—GT Sport Coupe is dropped. **2000**—Crisper handling, a new 180 hp engine, and a 6-speed gearbox (GT-S), plus lots of factory-related glitches. **2005**—A larger wheelbase, width is narrowed by 1 cm, and the coupe is shortened by almost 10 cm. The convertible is dropped.

Safety Summary

All years: Even if your vehicle has 4×4 capability, it's imperative to fit it with snow tires in order to avoid dangerous control problems on snow and ice. **2000**—A huge increase in safety-related complaints. • Fuel leak caused by a broken hose. • No airbag deployment. • Seat belts didn't hold driver in place in a frontal collision. • Cruise control suddenly slows car without warning. • Constant stalling. • Won't shift into Overdrive. • Clutch and accelerator pedal stick to the floor. • Excessive steering-wheel play. • At 100 km/h, vehicle pulls to one side. • Passenger-side wheel suddenly locked up, causing an accident. • Shield-protecting wires and fuel lines came off and caused extensive AC valve damage. **2000–01**—Without a lockout on the 6-speed gearshift, car can be inadvertently shifted from Fifth to Second gear. **2001**—Engine failures due to weak valves, sludge, says one report. • Steering over-corrects, causing the car to fishtail. **2001–02**—Airbags fail to deploy. • Hatch will not stay up:

> Rear hatch closes by itself. Dealer acknowledges problem but will not replace because it was not reported while still in warranty. The support arms are not strong enough to support the hatch. They have been discontinued and have been replaced with stronger ones. The hatch comes down without warning and could cause injury such as smash[ed] hands or fingers of children especially.

2002—Fuel tank easily punctured. • Gasoline spews out when refuelling. • Total brake failure. • Poor wet road traction. **2003**—Hood latch failure. • Fuel leak because of defective valve clamp. • Fuel splashes out during fill-up, after recall fix. • Inoperative cruise control. • Steering tends to over-correct. • Tire tread separates from the side wall. **2004**—Premature wearout of the brake calipers and rotors.

Secret Warranties/Internal Bulletins/Service Tips

All years: Toyota TSB #TC002-01 confirms misshifts with the 6-speed tranny. • Troubleshooting updates for steering pulling complaints are found in TSB #ST005-01. • Older Toyotas with stalling problems should have the engine checked for excessive carbon buildup on the valves before any extensive repairs are authorized. • Owner feedback and dealer service managers (who wish to remain anonymous) confirm the existence of Toyota's secret warranty that will pay for replacing front disc brake components that wear out before 2 years/40,000 km. **1991–2005**—Loose interior trim. **2000**—GT-S automatic transmission fluid leaks. • Loose outer door handle. • Cruise-control shock can be attenuated by replacing the ECU. • Moonroof creaking. • Squeak-and-rattle service tips. **2000–02**—Insufficient rear hatch support. **2001–04**—Troubleshooting an inoperative AC. **2002–05**—

Diagnosing and correcting vehicle pulling to one side. **2003**—Throttle body motor malfunctions. • Fuel-tank check valve Special Service Campaign. **2003–05**—Ticking noise at the upper and lower windshield areas. **2004–05**—Front-seat squeaking.

CELICA PROFILE

	1999	2000	2001	2002	2003	2004	2005
Cost Price ($)							
Base	34,475	23,980	24,140	24,645	24,645	24,650	24,900
Used Values ($)							
Base ▲	4,500	5,500	6,000	8,000	9,500	11,500	13,500
Base ▼	4,500	5,000	5,500	6,500	8,000	10,000	12,000
Reliability	3	4	4	4	4	4	4
Crash Safety (F)	—	—	4	4	4	4	4
Side	—	—	3	3	3	3	3
Head Restraints (F)	3	—	5	5	5	5	—
Rear	2	—	—	—	—	5	—
Rollover Resistance	—	—	—	—	5	5	5

MINIVANS AND VANS

Minivans

Most Minivans Give Maxi-Headaches

Now that Mazda, Ford, and GM have abandoned the minivan market and may go bankrupt this year, buyers should steer away from any of the Detroit minivans, regardless of how cheap they may be. Gone and best forgotten are Ford's godawful Windstar/Freestar, Mazda's lacklustre MPV, and GM's failure-prone Venture, Montana, Relay, Transport, Terraza, Silhouette, and Outlander. You might get by with a recent-model Chrysler, if you know a garage that does cheap transmission, brake, and AC repairs—year after year.

Your only real choice is Asian: Honda's Odyssey or Toyota's Sienna, followed by Hyundai's fully equipped Entourage, which sells for much less than what Honda and Toyota are asking and has a greater depreciated resale value.

Most minivans are upsized front-drive cars that are mainly "people-movers," meaning they handle like cars and get great fuel economy. The Honda Odyssey and Toyota Sienna are the best examples of this kind of minivan. Following Toyota's 2004 Sienna upgrades and Honda's 2005 Odyssey improvements, their road performance, reliability, and retained value surpass that of the front- and rear-drive minivans built by Detroit.

GM's Astro and Safari minivans are downsized trucks that are dirt-cheap minivan choices, but they haven't held up very well since they were dropped after the 2005 model year. Using rear-drive, 6-cylinder engines, and heavier mechanical components, they handle cargo and passengers equally well. On the negative side, their fuel economy is no match for the front-drives, highway handling is ponderous, with lots of wind buffeting and quirky braking, and parts are getting harder to find. Overall, rear-drive GM minivans are much more reliable performers than the front-drive Ford Windstar/Freestar and rear-drive Aerostar, but this doesn't mean much, because the benchmark is set so low for Detroit's progeny. AWD versions will keep you in the repair bay for weeks.

Rear-drive vans are better suited for towing trailers in the 1,600–2,950 kg (3,500–6,500 lb.) range. Most automakers say their front-drive minivans can pull up to 1,600 kg (3,500 lb.) with an optional towing package (often costing almost $1,000 extra), but don't you believe it. Owners report white-knuckle driving and premature powertrain failures caused by the extra load. It just stands to reason that Ford, Chrysler, and GM front-drives equipped with engines and transmissions that blow out at 60,000–100,000 km under normal driving conditions are going to meet their demise much earlier under a full load.

Chrysler

Chrysler churned out millions of units, paying scant attention to chronic 4-cylinder engine, automatic transmission, ABS, airbag control module, electrical system, and fit and finish deficiencies, or to rust-damaged steering and suspension systems. After all, thought Chrysler, the seven-year bumper-to-bumper warranty would fix the engine and transmission failures, and then Daimler would be stuck with the rest.

Indeed, Chrysler minivans caught on from their debut in 1984, when they were seen as fairly reliable and efficient people-haulers; that is, until the comprehensive warranty expired, or was cut back post-2000. Nevertheless, these minivans have continued to dominate the market despite their well-known mechanical and body problems. In fact, it's amazing how little Chrysler's defect patterns have changed during the past two decades (see *www.geocities.com/plumraptor* (Caravan Sucks!), *www.autosafety.org/autodefects.html*, *www.datatown.com/chrysler*, *terpconnect.umd. edu/~gluckman/Chrysler/index.html* (The Chrysler Products' Problem Web Page), and *www.daimlerchryslervehicleproblems.com* (The Truth Behind Chrysler)).

Ford

Ford's minivans have gone from bad to worse. Its first minivan, the 1985–97 Aerostar, was fairly dependable, although it did have some recurring tranny, brake, and coil-spring problems. Collapsing coil springs have caused tire blowouts on all model years.

Ford's quality decline continued with the mediocre front-drive Mercury Villager, a co-venture that also produced the Nissan Quest. Both vehicles were only so-so highway performers that often resided in dealer repair bays awaiting major engine, transmission, or electrical repairs. The Villager/Quest duo lasted through the 2000 model year. The Quest continued on its own with minimal changes to its 2001–03 models. The 2004 Quest's redesign was both a conceptual and engineering disaster. First-year models were so glitch-prone and stylistically beyond the pale that Nissan sent over 200 engineers to North America to correct the defects and change the interior design. Sales have never recovered.

Then Ford brought out the 1995 Windstar—one of the poorest quality, most dangerous minivans ever built; the year 2000 model has logged 736 safety-related complaints at NHTSA. Renamed the Freestar in 2004, the vehicle's failure-prone powertrain, suspension (broken coil springs), electrical, fuel, and braking systems continue to put owners' wallets and lives at risk.

Ford has compounded the Windstar's failings with its hard-nosed attitude toward customer complaints and by refusing warranty coverage for what are clearly factory-induced defects. Fortunately, there's been a flood of Canadian small claims court decisions that have come to Ford owners' aid when Ford wouldn't. These Canadian courts say Ford and its dealers must pay for engine and transmission repairs, even if the original warranty has expired or the minivan was bought used (see page 86).

General Motors

GM's minivans are even less reliable than Ford's. To begin with, they have more-serious powertrain problems than either Ford or Chrysler, other mechanical components such as fuel gauges and brakes aren't dependable, and fit and finish is so bad that not even the roof can escape developing rust holes, as GM service bulletins confirm.

Asian automakers

Asian competitors don't make perfect machines either, as a perusal of NHTSA-registered safety complaints, service bulletins, and online complaint forums will quickly confirm. Asian companies, looking to keep costs down, have also been bedevilled during the past decade by chronic engine and automatic transmission failures, sliding door malfunctions, catastrophic tire blowouts, and electrical glitches.

There is one big difference, though: Asian companies usually admit to their mistakes. The Detroit automakers cover them up.

A word of warning about Nissan and Toyota: Yes, these importers have made fairly dependable vehicles—including minivans—for the past three decades. However, the newly redesigned Nissan Quest and Toyota Sienna minivans are less reliable than pre-2004 models.

Volkswagen

And, finally, we come back to where we started—Volkswagen. Its vans, including the 1979 Vanagon and 1993 EuroVan/Camper, have never been taken seriously since they came to North America in 1950 with the Transporter cargo van and the nine-seater, 21-window Microbus. A reputation for poor overall quality, puny engines, and insufficient parts and servicing support continues to drive buyers away.

The solution? VW has made a pact with Chrysler to sell 2008–09 Caravans under the VW logo.

Larger and Smaller Alternatives

Most minivans are overpriced for what is essentially an upgraded car or downsized truck. Motorists needing a vehicle with large cargo- and passenger-carrying capacities should consider a Chrysler, Ford, or GM full-sized van, even if it means sacrificing some fuel economy. You just can't beat the excellent forward vision and easy-to-customize interiors that these large vans provide. Furthermore, parts are easily found and are competitively priced because of the great number of independent suppliers.

On the other hand, a minivan may be too large for some shoppers who want the same versatility in a smaller package. For them, the Mazda5 minivan/wagon (about $20,000 new) is a good place to start.

MINIVAN RATINGS

Above Average

Honda Odyssey (2003–07)

Toyota Sienna (2006–07; 1999–2003)

Average

Chrysler PT Cruiser (2001–07)
Honda Odyssey (1999–2002)

Hyundai Entourage (2007)
Toyota Sienna (2005)

Below Average

Chrysler Caravan, Voyager,
    Grand Caravan, Grand Voyager,
    Town & Country (2002–07)
Ford Freestar (2004–07)
Ford Villager/Nissan Quest (1999–2003)

General Motors Astro, Safari
    (1999–2005)
Kia Sedona (2002–07)
Mazda MPV (2002–06)
Nissan Quest (2004–07)
Toyota Sienna (2004)

Not Recommended

Chrysler Caravan, Voyager,
    Grand Caravan, Grand Voyager,
    Town & Country (1999–2001)
Ford Windstar (1999–2003)

General Motors Montana, Montana SV6, Relay,
    Silhouette, Terraza, Uplander, Venture
    (1999–2007)
Mazda MPV (2000–01)

Chrysler

CARAVAN, VOYAGER, GRAND CARAVAN, GRAND VOYAGER, TOWN & COUNTRY

RATING: Below Average (2002–07); Not Recommended (1999–2001). If (when) Chrysler goes bankrupt this year, all warrantees will be worthless and the minivan division will be sold off separately. Do you feel lucky? **"Real" city/highway fuel economy:** *Caravan 2.4L 4-cylinder:* 11.8/8.2 L/100 km. *Caravan 3.0L V6:* 12.7/8.3 L/100 km. *Caravan 3.3L V6:* 12.2/8.2 L/100 km. *Grand Caravan 3.3L V6:* 12.9/8.5 L/100 km. *Grand Caravan 3.8L V6:* 13.2/8.7 L/100 km. *Town & Country:* 13.6/9.1 L/100 km. *Town & Country AWD:* 13.6/9.1 L/100 km. Owners report fuel savings may undershoot these estimates by 20 percent or more. **Maintenance/Repair**

costs: Average during the first three years, and then costs rise dramatically thereafter. **Parts:** Easy to find and reasonably priced when bought from and installed by independent suppliers. **Extended warranty:** Yes, it is essential. Buy the warranty from an insured third party. Why not Chrysler? With Chrysler pinching pennies, how generous do you think it will be in approving your warranty repairs? **Best alternatives:** Honda's Odyssey should be your first choice, followed by Toyota's Sienna (but not the 2004 model). GM and Ford front- and rear-drive minivans aren't credible alternatives because of their failure-prone powertrains; brake, suspension, and steering problems; electrical short circuits; and subpar bodywork. Full-sized GM and Chrysler rear-drive cargo vans are more affordable and practical buys if you intend to haul a full passenger load or do some regular heavy hauling, if you are physically challenged, if you use lots of accessories, or if you take frequent motoring excursions.

Strengths and Weaknesses

Chrysler's minivans continue to dominate the new- and used-minivan markets, though they're quickly losing steam because of the popularity of crossover wagons and better-quality products from Japanese and South Korean automakers. Nevertheless, they offer pleasing styling and lots of convenience features at used prices that can be very attractive. They can carry up to seven passengers in comfort, and they ride and handle better than most truck-based minivans. The shorter-wheelbase minivans also offer better rear visibility and good ride quality, and are more nimble and easier to park than truck-based minivans and larger front-drive versions. Cargo hauling capability is more than adequate.

These minivans can pose maximum safety risks, as well. Owners report bizarre defects such as seat belts that may strangle children, airbags that deploy when the ignition is turned on, transmissions that jump out of gear, and sudden stalling and electrical short circuits when within radar range of airports or military installations.

Other common problems include the premature wearout of engine tensioner pulleys, automatic transmission speed sensors, engine head gaskets, motor mounts, starter motors, steering columns, front brake discs and pads (the brake pad material crumbles in your hands), front rotors and rear drums, brake master cylinders, suspension components, exhaust system components, ball joints, wheel bearings, water pumps, fuel pumps and pump wiring harnesses, radiators, heater cores, and AC compressors. Fuel injectors on all engines have been troublesome, the differential pin breaks through the automatic transmission casing, sliding doors malfunction, door locks often won't lock, engine supports may be missing or not connected, tie rods may suddenly break, oil pans crack, and the power-steering pump frequently leaks. Factory-installed Goodyear and Bridgestone Turanza tires frequently fail prematurely at 40,000–65,000 km.

Chrysler's A604, 41TE, and 42LE automatic transmissions, phased in with the 1991 models, are reliability nightmares that can have serious safety consequences.

Imagine having to count to three in traffic before Drive or Reverse will engage, "limping" home in Second gear at 50 km/h, or suddenly losing all forward motion in traffic.

Fit and finish has gotten worse over the past two decades. Body hardware and interior trim are fragile and tend to break, warp, or fall off (door handles are an example). The premature rust-out of major suspension and steering components is a critical safety and performance concern. Paint delamination often turns these solid-coloured minivans into two-tone models.

And as the minivan takes on its albino appearance, you can listen to a self-contained orchestra of clicks, clunks, rattles, squeaks, and squeals as you drive. Giving new meaning to the phrase "surround sound," these noises usually emanate from the brakes, suspension and steering assemblies, poorly anchored bench seats, and misaligned body panels.

VEHICLE HISTORY: 2001—A small horsepower boost for the V6s, front side airbags, adjustable pedals, upgraded headlights, and a power-operated rear liftgate. **2002**—Fuel-tank assembly is redesigned to prevent post-collision fuel leakage; a tire air-pressure monitor. **2005**—Side curtain airbags and second- and third-row seats that fold flush with the floor; AWD dropped (owners gain; repair bays lose).

Don't buy any minivan with a 4-cylinder engine—it has no place in a vehicle this large, especially when hooked to the inadequate 3-speed automatic transmission. It lacks an Overdrive and will shift back and forth as speed varies, and it's slower and noisier than the other choices. The 3.3L V6 is a better choice for most city-driving situations, but don't hesitate to get the 3.8L if you're planning lots of highway travel or carrying four or more passengers. The sliding side doors are a costly, failure-prone gizmo. Child safety seats integrated into the rear seatbacks are convenient and reasonably priced, but Chrysler's versions have had a history of either tightening up excessively or not tightening enough, allowing the child to slip out. Try the seat with your child before buying it. You may wish to pass on the tinted windshields as well; they seriously reduce visibility. Be wary of models featuring all-wheel drive and ABS brakes: The powertrain isn't reliable and is horrendously expensive to repair, and Chrysler's large number of ABS failures is worrisome. Ditch the failure-prone Goodyear original-equipment tires, and remember that a night drive is a prerequisite, in order to check out headlight illumination, which many call inadequate.

 ## Safety Summary

All models/years: Sudden, unintended acceleration; owners report that cruise-control units often malfunction, accelerating or decelerating the vehicle without any warning. • Airbag malfunctions: Get used to the term "clockspring." It's an expensive little component that controls some parts within the steering wheel and, when defective, can result in the Airbag warning light coming on or the airbag, cruise control, or horn failing. It has been a pain in the butt for Chrysler minivan owners since the 1996 model year. Chrysler has extended its warranty for 1996–2000 minivans in two separate recalls and replaced the clockspring at no charge. Apparently, the automaker has found that the part fails because it was wound too tight or short-circuited from corrosion. • Defective engine head gaskets, rocker arm gaskets, and engine mounts. • Engine sag, hesitation, stumble, hard starts, or stalling. • No steering/lock-up. • Carbon monoxide comes through air vents. • Brakes wear out prematurely or fail completely. • Transmission fails, suddenly drops into low gear, won't go into Reverse, delays engagement, or jumps out of gear when running or parked. • One can move the automatic transmission shift lever without applying brakes. • Several incidents where ignition was turned and vehicle went into Reverse at full throttle, although transmission was set in Park. • ABS failure caused an accident. • Many complaints of front suspension-strut towers rusting then cracking at the weld seams; jig-positioning hole wasn't sealed at the factory. • Brakes activated by themselves while driving. • Seatbacks fall backward. • Rear windows fall out or shatter. • Power window and door lock failures. • Sliding door often opens while vehicle is underway or jams, trapping occupants. • Weak headlights. • Horn often doesn't work. • Several incidents where side windows exploded for no apparent reason. • Adults cannot sit in third-row seat without their heads smashing into the roof as the vehicle passes over bumps. **All models: 2006**—Improperly torqued power-steering hose came loose and sprayed steering fluid throughout the engine compartment. • Turn signals function erratically, and headlights flicker and dim. **2007**—Automatic transmission "bumps" into gear. • Ruptured front brake hoses. • Complete loss of steering because the "roll pin" on the steering shaft was improperly installed at the factory. • Sudden veering to the right.

Secret Warranties/Internal Bulletins/Service Tips

All models: 1996–2006—Rusted, frozen rear brake drums. **1998–2000**—Rusted-out suspensions may cause vehicle to lose steering or suspension and go out of control. **2001–02**—Wind or water leaks at the rear quarter window. **2001–03**—Oil filter leaks with 3.3L and 3.8L engines (confirmed in TSB #09-001-03). **2001–04**—AC water leaks. **2001–06**—Water leaks under passenger-side carpet. **2002–07**—Power liftgate malfunctions. **2003**—Troubleshooting water leaks. • Three bulletins relating to automatic transmission malfunctions: delayed gear engagement, harsh 4–3 downshift, and excessive vibration and transfer gear whine. **2003–05**—Crack, split and/or water leak in the upper body-seam sealer at the B- or C-pillar. **2005**—Engine squeak under light throttle. • Campaign for the free replacement of the rear AC heater tube if it is corroded; another campaign will replace at no charge the underbody heater hose. **2005–06**—AC condenser road debris damage can be prevented by installing a condenser guard supplied by Chrysler (under warranty, of course). **2006–07**—Silencing moonroof noises. **2007**—Troubleshooting body noises.

CARAVAN, VOYAGER, GRAND CARAVAN, GRAND VOYAGER, TOWN & COUNTRY PROFILE

	1999	2000	2001	2002	2003	2004	2005	2006	2007
Cost Price ($)									
Caravan	24,230	24,970	24,885	25,430	25,430	27,620	28,205	27,065	27,445
Grand Caravan	25,890	26,665	29,505	28,875	29,295	30,190	30,740	31,070	29,305
Town & Country	41,260	41,815	41,150	40,815	42,705	44,095	44,595	44,920	42,255
Used Values ($)									
Caravan ▲	2,500	3,500	4,000	4,500	5,500	6,500	8,000	9,500	11,500
Caravan ▼	2,000	3,000	3,500	4,000	4,500	5,500	7,000	8,000	10,000
Grand Caravan ▲	3,000	4,000	4,500	5,000	5,500	6,500	9,000	10,500	12,500
Grand Caravan ▼	3,000	3,500	4,000	4,500	5,000	5,500	7,500	9,000	11,000
Town & Country ▲	3,500	4,000	5,500	6,000	8,000	10,500	13,000	15,000	18,000
Town & Country ▼	3,000	3,500	4,500	5,500	6,500	9,000	11,500	13,500	16,500
Reliability	2	2	2	3	3	3	3	3	3
Crash Safety (F)									
Caravan	—	4	4	4	4	4	4	—	5
Grand Caravan	4	4	4	4	4	4	—	5	5
Town & Country	—	—	—	—	4	4	4	5	—
Town & Country LX	4	4	4	4	4	4	—	5	—
Side									
Caravan	4	4	4	4	4	—	—	—	4
Grand Caravan	5	5	4	5	5	5	—	—	5
Town & Country LX	5	5	4	5	5	4	4	5	—
IIHS Side									
Grand Caravan	—	—	—	—	—	—	—	3	3
Town & Country	—	—	—	—	—	—	—	1	1
Offset (Grand Caravan)	2	2	1	3	3	3	3	3	3
Town & Country	2	2	1	3	3	3	3	3	3
Head Restraints (F)									
Grand Caravan	—	—	—	—	—	1	1	1	1
Town & Country	1	—	3	3	3	1	1	1	1
Town & Country LX	1	—	2	2	2	1	1	1	1
Rollover Resistance	—	—	3	3	3	—	—	4	4

Note: Voyager and Grand Voyager prices and ratings are almost identical to those of the Caravan and Grand Caravan. The $13,000 premium paid out for a 2007 Town & Country over a 2007 Grand Caravan drops to $6,000 a year later, and only $2,500 when the 2003 models are compared.

PT CRUISER ★★★

RATING: Average (2001–07). This mini-minivan has defied all of the odds and shown Chrysler can make a polyester purse out of a sow's ear and Neon parts. Despite its hot-rod flair, this Neon spin-off's popularity is waning, meaning there are many bargains out there. **"Real" city/highway fuel economy:** *Manual:* 9.8/7.5 L/100 km. *Automatic:* 11.0/8.1 L/100 km. *Turbo manual:* 10.4/7.9 L/100 km. *Turbo automatic:* 11.4/8.1 L/100 km. **Maintenance/Repair costs:** Average. **Parts:** Reasonably priced and easily found, except for body parts. **Extended warranty:** A toss-up. **Best alternatives:** Try the Mazda5 or the Subaru Legacy Outback Limited. Sport-utilities worth considering are the Ford Escape, Honda CR-V EX, Hyundai Tucson, Jeep Liberty, Mazda Tribute, and Subaru Forester.

Strengths and Weaknesses

The PT Cruiser is essentially a fuel- and space-efficient small hatchback minivan. It's noted for excellent fuel economy (regular fuel), nimble handling around town, good braking, lots of interior space, easy access, a versatile cargo area, many thoughtful interior amenities, slow depreciation, and unforgettable hot-rod styling.

Forget about hot-rod power with the base engine, though. The 150 hp 2.4L 4-cylinder powerplant is not very smooth-running, and, when matched with the automatic transmission, it struggles when going uphill or merging with highway traffic. This requires frequent downshifting and lots of patience. Costlier turbocharged models will give you plenty of power, but you risk some steep repair bills. The automatic transmission has little low-end torque, forcing early kickdown shifting and deft manipulation of the accelerator pedal. High-speed handling isn't impressive; hard cornering produces an unsteady, wobbly ride because of the car's height. The ride is firm, with lots of interior engine, wind, and road noise. ABS braking is acceptable—when the system functions as it should.

VEHICLE HISTORY: 2002—A CD player and underseat storage bin. **2003**—A 215 hp turbocharged GT and 17-inch wheels. **2004**—A 180 hp 2.4L turbocharged 4-cylinder. **2006**—Revised front ends and dash.

Reliability is problematic for all model years, with frequent drivetrain complaints that include faulty valve cover gaskets, causing oil burning, and automatic transmission control modules, forcing the drivetrain to gear down to "limp home" mode. Power-steering pump units and steering units are also frequently replaced. Fit and finish deficiencies read like an anthology of common Chrysler defects: annoying wind noise when driving with the rear window or sunroof open, drivetrain whine, moisture between the clearcoat and paint that turns the hood a chalky colour, and water leaks through the passenger-side window. (See *www-odi. nhtsa.dot.gov/complaints*, *www.ptcruiserlinks.com*, *www.datatown.com/chrysler*, *terpconnect.umd.edu/~gluckman/Chrysler/index.html* (The Chrysler Products' Problem Web Page), *www.daimlerchryslervehicleproblems.com* (The Truth Behind Chrysler), and *www.autosafety.org/autodefects.html*.)

Safety Summary

All years: Airbag malfunctions. • Sudden, unintended acceleration; chronic stalling. • Steering clockspring failure. • Side-wind instability. • Front axle breaks while vehicle is underway. • Instrument pods are difficult to read in the daylight. • Tall drivers beware: The windshield is uncomfortably close, and overhead traffic lights will disappear. • Wide pillars obstruct one's view. • Headrests are too high, block vision, and are unstable. • Constant short circuits; no lights, gauges. • Lights flicker and dim. • Doors lock and unlock on their own. **2001**—When parked, transmission slipped out of gear and vehicle rolled down driveway. • Engine suddenly shuts down when vehicle passes through a large puddle. • Steering wheel loosens on its shaft. • Headlight failures; low beams may cut out, and only part of the headlight beam illuminates the roadway. **2002**—Gas pedal goes to the floor with no acceleration. • Suddenly shifts into First gear while cruising. • Brake lock-up. **2003**—Chronic engine overheating. • Sudden front axle/bearing seizure threw car out of control and caused $7,000 damage to the drivetrain. • Automatic transmission failures while car is underway. • Self-activating door locks and seat heater. **2004**—Electrical fires. • Steering locks up. **2005**—Power windows can strangle a child due to the location of the button:

> We were parked in a parking lot with the car running talking to another group when my 6 year old stuck her head out the window to join the discussion. When she did, she accidentally kicked the power window button with her foot. The button was located near the floor in the backseat on the middle console. She rolled the window up on her own head and was stuck in the window. She only lived through the event because 1) her head was tilted at the time so the window rolled up on the side of her neck and not on her trachea; and 2) her 8 year old sister in the back seat with her heard her screams and got her foot off the button and rolled the window back down.

• Sunlight reflects off the silver-painted airbag, blinding the driver. **2006**—Cracked engine head gasket. • Early transmission failure. • Side window shattered. • Driver must "pound" the horn. • Driver's power seat has no forward stop; jams driver against the steering wheel. • Light assemblies collect water. **2006–07**—Goodyear Eagle LS side wall blowouts. **2007**—Engine camshaft, crankshaft bearing, and seal failures; head gaskets warp. • Automatic transmission slips in and out of gear. • Brakes failed on wet pavement. • Power-steering fluid leakage. • Exploding rear window. • Driver's seat adjusts when it isn't necessary. • Hazard lights flick on and off. • Horn sticks.

Secret Warranties/Internal Bulletins/Service Tips

2001—A faulty transmission control module (TCM) may cause harsh shifting. • MIL comes on because of a faulty TCM harness connector or a defective evaporator purge flow monitor. • Poor acceleration and spark knock. • Left or right floor latch on rear seat won't release. • Fuel gauge won't indicate full. • Airbag pads fall off. • Wind buffeting with the windows and/or sunroof open or partially open. **2001–02**—Highway speed surge. **2001–03**—Transmission slips in Reverse or

First gears. • High-speed engine surging. **2001–06**—Moisture accumulation in headlights. **2003**—Turbo engine hesitation, loss of boost, and screeching. • Delayed gear engagement. • Harsh 4–3 downshifts. • Warning lights come on for no reason. • Warped rear bumper. **2005–06**—Driveability improvements. **2006–07**—Windshield crack diagnosis (warranty or no warranty). **2006–08**—Starter won't crank; engine doesn't crank. • Harsh shifts.

PT CRUISER PROFILE

	2001	2002	2003	2004	2005	2006	2007
Cost Price ($)							
Base	23,665	23,850	22,500	24,360	21,270	21,670	19,840
Limited	27,180	27,305	27,420	28,800	26,755	27,300	23,835
Turbo	—	—	27,700	31,350	31,665	31,665	30,350
Convertible	—	—	—	—	26,995	27,790	28,220
Used Values ($)							
Base ▲	4,000	5,000	5,500	6,500	7,500	9,000	11,000
Base ▼	3,500	4,500	4,500	5,500	6,500	7,500	9,500
Limited ▲	4,500	5,500	6,000	7,000	8,000	10,000	12,000
Limited ▼	4,000	5,000	5,500	6,000	7,000	8,500	10,500
Turbo ▲	—	—	7,000	8,000	9,000	11,000	13,500
Turbo ▼	—	—	5,500	6,500	7,500	9,500	12,000
Convertible ▲	—	—	—	—	10,000	12,500	15,000
Convertible ▼	—	—	—	—	8,500	11,000	13,000
Reliability	3	3	3	3	3	3	3
Crash Safety (F)	2	4	4	4	4	4	—
Side	4	4	4	—	—	4	—
Offset	—	—	—	—	—	5	5
Head Restraints	5	5	5	4	4	4	4
Rollover Resistance	4	4	4	—	—	4	—

Ford

FREESTAR, WINDSTAR ★★

RATING: *Freestar:* Below Average (2004–07). The Freestar is a Windstar in disguise, with the same poor-quality components and lousy fit and finish that made driving hell for Windstar owners. *Windstar:* Not Recommended (1999–2003). Infamous for atrocious quality control, stonewalled owner complaints, and life-threatening defects. **"Real" city/highway fuel economy:** 11.0/7.1 L/100 km. Owners report fuel savings may undershoot this estimate by at least 15 percent. **Maintenance/Repair costs:** Average while under warranty; outrageously higher than average thereafter. **Parts:** Reasonably priced parts are easy to find. Digital speedometers can cost almost $1,000 to replace at the dealer. Scrounge around. **Extended warranty:** Definitely; a Saint Christopher medallion would also help. **Best alternatives:** The Honda Odyssey and Toyota Sienna (but not the 2004) are the best choices. Some full-sized GM (Chevy Van, Vandura, Express, or Savana) rear-drive cargo/passenger vans are more-affordable and practical buys.

Strengths and Weaknesses

Ford can call it the Windstar or the Freestar; the fact remains that owners call it garbage. Sure, the Windstar combines an impressive five-star crash safety rating, plenty of raw power, an exceptional ride, and impressive cargo capacity. But these minivans have failure-prone engines, self-destructing automatic transmissions, "Do I feel lucky?" brakes, and unreliable electrical systems. Particularly scary is Ford's admission that Windstar's suspension includes poor-quality coil springs that frequently break, blow out the front tire, and make the minivan uncontrollable. As solace, Ford says it will pay for coil breakage up to 10 years on vehicles registered in rust-prone regions.

And, as another counterpoint to Ford's Windstar crashworthiness boasting, there's a frightening archive of Windstar safety-related failures compiled by NHTSA. Besides the many coil-spring failures already noted (these have affected almost all of Ford's vehicles for practically a decade), owners report sudden acceleration, stalling, steering loss, exploding windows, horn failures, wheels falling off, sliding doors that open and close on their own, and vehicles rolling away while parked.

Other safety-related deficiencies include the lack of head restraints for all seats on early Windstars and a digital dash that's often confusing, failure-prone, and expensive to replace. Optional adjustable pedals help protect drivers from airbag injuries. Be careful, though; some drivers have found that these pedals are set too close together and seem loose. Drivers must also contend with mediocre handling, restricted side and rear visibility, and an abundance of clunks, rattles, and wind and road noise (see *www.tgrigsby.com/views/ford.htm* (The Anti-Ford Page), *ca.geocities.com/windstarwoes* (1996 Windstar Head Gasket Issues), and *www.auto safety.org/autodefects.html*).

VEHICLE HISTORY: 1999—A bit more interior space, and the third-row bench gets built-in rollers. Improved steering and brakes are compromised by rear drums. An anti-theft system, ABS, new side panels, a new liftgate, larger headlights and tail lights, and a revised instrument panel. **2001**—The base 3.0L V6 is gone; the Windstar gets an upgraded automatic transmission (still unreliable), a low-tire-pressure warning system, "smart" airbags, and a slight restyling. **2002**—Dual sliding doors. **2003**—An optional anti-skid system. **2004**—Freestar arrives and flops; a two-passenger cargo van arrives.

Freestar: Too little, too late

Built on a modified Taurus platform, the Freestar gives you the same uninspired, though predictable, carlike handling characteristics of Ford's mid-size family sedans. You'll encounter many of the horrific engine, automatic transmission, electrical, suspension, and brake system problems experienced by Taurus and Sable owners.

Ford's denial of owner claims has been blasted in small claims court judgments across Canada over the past few years. Judges have ruled that engines and transmissions (and power-sliding doors) must be reasonably durable long after the warranty expires, whether the vehicle was bought new or used, notwithstanding that it was repaired by an independent or that it had the same problem repaired earlier for free. The three most recent engine judgments supporting Ford owners are *Dufour v. Ford Canada Ltd*, *Schaffler v. Ford Motor Company Limited and Embrun Ford Sales Ltd.*, and *John R. Reid and Laurie M. McCall v. Ford Motor Company of Canada* (see Part Two).

Dangerous doors

We noted previously that the courts have slammed Ford for allowing dangerously defective sliding doors to go uncorrected year after year. Typical scenarios reported by owners include the following: a sliding door slammed shut on a child's head while the vehicle was parked on an incline; passengers are often pinned by the door; the door reopens as it is closing; the door often pops open while the vehicle is underway; a driver's finger was broken when closing a manual sliding door; and the handle is too close to the door jam, which is a hazard that has been reported on the Internet since 1999. Owners also report that the 2003 Windstar's automatic sliding door opens by itself, or the door will not power open, and the door lock assembly freezes.

In *Sharman v. Formula Ford Sales Limited, Ford Credit Limited, and Ford Motor Company of Canada Limited* (Ontario Superior Court of Justice (Oakville), No. 17419/02SR, 2003/10/07), Justice Shepard awarded the owner of a 2000 Windstar $7,500 for mental distress resulting from the breach of the implied warranty of fitness plus $7,207 for breach of contract and breach of warranty. The problem— the Windstar's sliding door wasn't secure and leaked air and water after many attempts to repair it. Interestingly, the judge cited the *Wharton* decision, among other decisions, as support for his award for mental distress (see page 95).

 Safety Summary

All models/years: Severe injuries caused by airbag malfunctions. • While parked, cruising, turning on the ignition, or applying brakes, vehicle suddenly accelerates. • Chronic stalling caused by fuel-vapour lock or faulty fuel pump; engine shuts down when turning. • Control arm and inner tie-rod failures cause the wheel to fall off. • Sudden steering lock-up or loss of steering ability. • Engine head gasket failures. • Frequent transmission failures, including noisy engagement, inability to engage Forward or Reverse, and slipping or jerking into gear. •

Many reports that the vehicle jumps out of Park and rolls away when on an incline, or slips into Reverse with the engine idling. • Transmission and axle separation. • Automatic transmission suddenly seizes. • Steering wheel locks up. • Loose or missing front brake bolts could cause the wheels to lock up or the vehicle to lose control. • Chronic ABS failures. • Faulty fuel pump, sensor, and gauge. • Built-in child safety seat is too easy to get out of; sometimes the securing seat belts are too tight; in one incident, a child was almost strangled. • Faulty rear liftgate latches; trunk lid can fall on one's head. • Rear side windows, liftgate window, and windshield often explode suddenly. • Sliding door opens and closes on its own, sticks open or closed, or suddenly slams shut on a downgrade. • Door locks don't stay locked. • Horn button "sweet spot" is too small. • Interior windows are always fogged up because of inadequate defrosting. • Body seams not sealed; water intrudes into floor seat anchors. • Driver's seat poorly anchored. • Dashboard glare onto the windshield. • Check Tire warning light comes on for no reason. • Tire jack collapses. *Freestar:* **2004**—Sudden, unintended acceleration. • Loss of steering. • Airbag warning light stays on; airbags may not deploy. • A-frame drops out of the tie-rod collar. • Front axle suddenly breaks while underway. • Automatic transmission failure. • Left inner brake pad falls apart and locks up brake. • Sliding door closed on a child in one incident, causing slight injuries; in another incident it crushed an adult's leg. • Plastic running board broke, blocking sliding door operation and locking occupants inside the vehicle. **2005**—A shameful litany of self-destructing automatic transmissions. • Liftgates continue to fall on driver's heads. • Biodegradable brake rotors and pads. • Tire blowouts caused by defective valve stems. • Premature wheel bearing failures preceded by an annoying whine. **2006**—Highway stall-outs. • Transmission here today, gone tomorrow…sigh. • Vehicle suddenly loses power. • Traction control system activates for no reason. **2007**—Van suddenly went out of gear.

Secret Warranties/Internal Bulletins/Service Tips

All models/years: An exhaust buzz or rattle may be caused by a loose catalyst or heat shield. • Sliding-door malfunctions. • Buzzing noise in speakers caused by fuel pump. • A MIL lit for no reason may simply mean that the gas cap is loose. • If the power-sliding door won't close, replace the door controller; if it pops or disengages when fully closed, adjust the door and rear striker to reduce closing resistance. • Front wipers that operate when switched off need a revised multi-function switch (covered under a service program and recall). • Engine oil mixed with coolant or loss of coolant signals the need for revised engine lower intake manifold side gaskets and/or front cover gaskets. Ford's benchmark for refunding repair costs for this problem: 7 years/160,000 km. **All models: 2000–07**—Erratic fluid level readings on the transaxle dipstick; transmission fluid leaks. **2001**—Ford admits automatic transmission defects (slippage, delayed shifts) in Special Service Instruction #01T01. **2001–02**—Service tips for reports of premature engine failures. • Vacuum or air leaks in the intake manifold or engine system, causing warning lights to illuminate. • Concerns with oil in the cooling system. • Hard starts; rough-running engines. • Shudder while in Reverse or during 3–4 shift. • Transmission fluid leakage. • Power-steering fluid leaks. • Brake roughness and pulsation. • Rear brake drum drag in cold weather. • Fogging of the front and side windows. • False low-tire warning. **2001–03**—Remedy for a slow-to-fill fuel tank. **2002**—MIL comes on; vehicle shifts poorly or won't start. • Buzz, groan, or vibration when gear selector lever is in Park. • Some vehicles may run roughly on the highway or just after stopping. • Defective ignition-switch lock cylinders. • Sliding doors rattle and squeak. **2003**—Airbag warning light stays lit. *Freestar:* **2004**—Transmission has no 1–2 upshift (TSB #04-15-12). • False activation of parking assist. • TSB #04-2-3, published 02/09/04, lists ways to find and fix the sliding doors' many failures. **2004–05**—Accelerated rear brake pad wear. • Front brake squeal or squawk. • Excessive vibration. • Faulty, inoperative power door and liftgate. **2004–06**—Seat belts are slow to retract. • Inoperative AC compressor; seal leaks. **2004–07**—Poor engine/transmission response due to water entering the powertrain control module. • Spark knock under light load. • Power-steering hose leak in extreme cold. • Erratic fluid level readings. **2006–07**—Engine intake popping noise.

FREESTAR, WINDSTAR PROFILE

	1999	2000	2001	2002	2003	2004	2005	2006	2007
Cost Price ($)									
Freestar (Base)	—	—	—	—	—	27,295	27,995	22,999	23,299
SE	—	—	—	—	—	29,695	29,695	25,699	26,000
SEL	—	—	—	—	—	37,695	37,020	32,800	33,099
Windstar (Base)	24,295	—	—	24,900	24,901	—	—	—	—
LX	28,195	25,995	26,750	25,995	26,195	—	—	—	—
SEL	36,195	36,195	33,190	33,685	37,015	—	—	—	—
Used Values ($)									
Freestar (Base) ▲	—	—	—	—	—	5,000	6,500	9,000	11,500
Freestar (Base) ▼	—	—	—	—	—	4,000	5,000	7,500	10,000
SE ▲	—	—	—	—	—	6,500	8,000	9,500	12,500
SE ▼	—	—	—	—	—	5,000	6,500	8,000	11,000
SEL ▲	—	—	—	—	—	7,000	9,000	11,500	15,500
SEL ▼	—	—	—	—	—	5,500	7,500	10,000	14,000
Windstar (Base) ▲	1,000	—	—	2,000	3,000	—	—	—	—
Windstar (Base) ▼	700	—	—	1,500	2,500	—	—	—	—
LX ▲	1,500	2,000	2,500	3,000	4,500	—	—	—	—
LX ▼	1,000	1,500	2,500	2,500	3,000	—	—	—	—
SEL ▲	2,000	2,500	3,000	4,000	5,000	—	—	—	—
SEL ▼	1,500	2,000	3,000	3,000	4,000	—	—	—	—
Reliability	1	1	1	1	1	2	2	2	2
Crash Safety (F)	5	5	5	5	5	5	5	5	5
Side	5	4	5	4	4	4	4	4	4
IIHS Side	—	—	—	—	—	—	—	1	1
Offset	3	3	3	3	3	5	5	5	5
Head Restraints (F)	5	5	5	5	5	5	5	5	5
Rear	1	—	3	3	3	5	—	—	—
Rollover Resistance	—	—	4	4	4	4	4	4	4

Ford/Nissan

RATING: *Quest:* Below Average (2004–07). Even though it's larger, more powerful, and better appointed than the old Villager/Quest, the 2004 Quest's redesign was badly done. Engineering goofs and poor-quality body and electrical components still plague the Quest. *Villager/Quest:* Below Average (1999–2003). **"Real" city/highway fuel economy:** *3.0L:* 13.4/9.3 L/100 km. *3.3L:* 13.9/9.0 L/100 km. *3.5L:* 12.4/8.2 L/100 km. Owners report fuel savings may undershoot these estimates by at least 20 percent if the vehicle is equipped with poorly performing Goodyear LS2 tires. **Maintenance/Repair costs:** Higher than average. **Parts:** Best found at Nissan dealers or with independent suppliers. **Extended warranty:** A good idea. **Best alternatives:** Honda's Odyssey and Toyota's Sienna (except the reworked 2004 model, which has quality bugs similar to the Quest's).

Strengths and Weaknesses

1993–2003 Villager/Quest

Smaller and more carlike than most minivans, the pre-2004 Villager and Quest are sized comfortably between the regular and extended Chrysler minivans. These minivans' strongest assets are a 170 hp 3.3L V6 engine plus carlike handling, ride, and cornering, achieved by borrowing Nissan Maxima parts.

These fuel-thirsty minivans are quite heavy, though, and the 3.0L and 3.3L engines have to go all out to carry the extra weight. GM's 2.8L engines produce more torque, and the Villager/Quest powertrain set-up trails the Odyssey in acceleration and passing. Other minuses: The interior looks cheap, the control layout can be a bit confusing, suspension is too soft, and rear-seat access can be difficult.

Most owner-reported problems involve excessive brake noise and premature brake wear, door lock malfunctions, interior noise, and driveline vibrations. There have also been many reports of engine exhaust manifold and crankshaft failures that cost up to $7,000 to repair. Other problems include electrical shorts; brake failures because of vibration, binding, or overheating; premature front disc, rotor, and pad wear; chronic stalling, possibly because of faulty fuel pumps or a shorted electrical system; and loose steering with veering at highway speeds.

Fit and finish is subpar (and remains so up to and including the 2007 models). Owners complain of doors opening and closing on their own and poorly fitted panels that produce a cacophony of wind noise, squeaks, and rattles, as well as water leaks, paint defects, and premature rusting.

2004–07 Quest

A totally different minivan than its predecessor, the 2004–07 Quest is an Altima/Murano spin-off that is larger, more powerful, and better equipped than before. It's also less reliable. Skyroof leaks and dangerous sliding doors are quite common. Owners also complain of malfunctioning engines, transmissions, and brakes. Goodyear tires are notorious for premature wear and poor performance on these minivans (see *www.tirerack.com*).

VEHICLE HISTORY: *Villager:* **1999**—Gains a fourth door, more interior room, a revised instrument panel that's easier to reach, restyled front and rear ends, and improved shifting, acceleration, and braking. The suspension is retuned to give a more carlike ride and handling, and the old climate-control system is upgraded. No more Mercury Nautica. *Quest:* **1999**—A larger platform, standard ABS brakes, a driver-side sliding rear door, upgraded headlights, and rear leaf springs. The second row of seats can be removed, and the third row is set on tracks. **2000**—An improved child safety seat anchoring system; a stabilizer bar on the GLE. **2001**—A slightly restyled exterior and upgraded dashboard. **2004**—Totally redesigned—and made even less reliable. **2005**—A new base model called the 3.5 arrives. **2007**—Restyled interior and exterior.

 Safety Summary

All models: 1993–2003—Airbags malfunction. • Steering wander and excessive vibration. • Chronic ABS failures; brake pads and rotors need replacing every 5,000 km. • Brake failures (extended stopping distances, noisy when applied). • Brake and accelerator pedals are the same height, so driver's foot can easily slip and step on both at the same time. • Cycling or self-activating front-door lock failures; occupants have been trapped in their vehicles. • Weak tailgate hydraulic cylinders. • Instrument panel's white face is hard to read during daylight hours. • Seat belts don't retract properly. • Rear window on liftgate door shattered for unknown reason. • Leaking front and rear struts degrade handling. • Steering wheel may be off-centre to the left. **1993–2004**—Sudden, unintended acceleration. **2004**—Sliding door traps occupants, or continually pops open. • Reflection of dash onto windshield. • Automatic transmission won't downshift. • Faulty tire valve stems. • Excessive tire wear (Goodyear Eagle LS2 224/60/17), and it may be hard to find replacement tires (see *www.tirerack.com/tires/surveyresults/index.jsp*). **2005**—Fire ignited in the tail light housing. • Transmission slippage. • Loss of all electrical power due to alternator failure. • Power windows and locks often malfunction. • Chronic stalling caused by water leaking onto the engine control module. • Defective tire stems leak air. • Sliding door suddenly opened while van was underway; 2004 recall should be extended to the 2005s. • Headlights often blow out. • Goodyear Eagle tires wear out prematurely. **2006**—Premature brake caliper, rotor wearout. • Sliding door inoperative; closes with such force it can seriously injure a child. • Door hinges make opening and closing difficult. • Doors unlock and windows roll down by themselves. • Driver's sun visor falls down. • Gas tank vulnerable to road debris. **2007**—Fire ignited in the wiring. • Engine surging while vehicle stopped at a traffic light. • Windshield is easily cracked. • Sliding door won't open or shut properly; worse on cold days. • Speedometer may be 20 km/h slower than indicated. • Premature wearout of Michelin Pax tires. • Second-row driver-side seat recliner lever breaks easily.

Secret Warranties/Internal Bulletins/Service Tips

All models: 1993–2006—Paint delamination, peeling, or fading. **1996–2002**—Power door locks that intermittently self-activate are a common occurrence that's covered in TSB #98-22-5. **1999–2004**—Troubleshooting abnormal shifting. • Cooling system leaks/overheating. • Side windows pop open. **2002–07**—How to silence engine ticking. **2004**—No-start, hard start remedies. • Tips on correcting an abnormal shifting of the automatic transmission. • Harsh 1–2 shifts. • AC blows out warm air from floor vents. • Guidelines on troubleshooting brake complaints. **2004–05**—Low power, stays in Third gear. • Insufficient AC cooling. • Sliding door squeaks and rattles and is hard to latch. **2004–06**—Skyroof water leaks. **2004–07**—Front brake judder. • Noisy power driver-seat lifter. **2004–08**—Inoperative driver's "power up" window. • Exhaust system buzz, rattle. • Overhead vents come loose, fall from the headliner. • Tire monitor seal leaks.

VILLAGER/QUEST PROFILE

	1999	2000	2001	2002	2004	2005	2006	2007
Cost Price ($)								
Villager GS	24,595	24,595	—	—	—	—	—	—
Villager LS	29,495	29,495	—	—	—	—	—	—
Quest GXE/3.5	27,798	30,498	30,498	30,698	32,900	31,698	31,898	32,498
Quest GXE/SL	32,498	33,498	35,198	35,198	36,600	36,100	36,198	36,998
Used Values ($)								
Villager GS ▲	2,500	3,000	—	—	—	—	—	—
Villager GS ▼	2,500	3,000	—	—	—	—	—	—
Villager LS ▲	3,000	3,500	4,000	—	—	—	—	—
Villager LS ▼	3,000	3,500	3,500	—	—	—	—	—
Quest GXE/3.5 ▲	6,000	7,000	9,000	12,000	18,000	22,000	13,000	15,000
Quest GXE/3.5 ▼	5,000	6,000	7,500	10,500	16,000	20,000	11,500	13,500
Quest GXE/SL ▲	6,500	8,500	10,500	13,500	15,000	24,000	15,500	18,000
Quest GXE/SL ▼	6,000	7,500	9,500	12,500	14,000	22,000	14,000	16,500
Reliability	3	3	3	3	2	2	3	3
Crash Safety (F)	—	—	4	5	5	5	5	5
Side	—	—	5	5	5	5	5	5
IIHS Side	—	—	—	—	—	—	5	5
Offset	1	1	1	1	5	5	5	5
Head Restraints (F)	—	2	—	1	1	1	1	1
Rear	—	1	—	1	1	—	—	—
Rollover Resistance	—	—	—	4	4	4	4	4

General Motors

RATING: Below Average (1999–2005). These run-of-the-mill rear-drive minivans have seen better days, but they aren't as bad as those from the GM and Ford front-drive minivan lemon grove. They have fewer safety-related problems, are easy to repair, and cost little to acquire. Stay away from the unreliable all-wheel-drive models; they're expensive to repair and not very durable. **"Real" city/highway fuel economy:** *Cargo:* 15.0/10.7 L/100 km. *Base:* 16.6/11.9 L/100 km. *AWD:* 17.3/12.6 L/100 km. Owners report fuel savings may undershoot these estimates by more than 20 percent (especially in regard to the AWD model). **Maintenance/Repair costs:** Average. Any garage can repair these rear-drive minivans. **Parts:** Good supply of cheap parts. **Extended warranty:** A powertrain-only warranty is all you'll need. **Best alternatives:** Honda minivans have better handling and are more-reliable and economical people-movers, but they are way overpriced and lack the Astro's considerable grunt, essential for cargo hauling and trailer towing.

Strengths and Weaknesses

More a utility truck than a comfortable minivan, these boxy rear-drives are built on a reworked S-10 pickup chassis. As such, they offer uninspiring handling, average-quality mechanical and body components, and relatively high fuel consumption.

VEHICLE HISTORY: 2000—Only seven- and eight-passenger models available; engine made quieter and smoother, while the automatic transmission has been toughened up to shift more efficiently when pulling heavy loads; a larger fuel tank has been installed. **2001**—Tilt steering wheel; cruise control; CD player; remote keyless entry; power windows, mirrors, and locks. **2003**—Upgraded four-wheel disc brakes.

These minivans suffer from failure-prone automatic transmissions, engine head gasket leaks, poor braking systems, fragile steering components, and failure-prone oxygen sensors. Unloaded, the Astro provides very poor traction, the ride isn't comfortable on poor road surfaces, and interior noise is rampant. Highway performance and overall reliability aren't impressive.

2000–05 models are a bit more reliable and better performing than previous models, inasmuch as they underwent considerable upgrading by GM. Nevertheless, buyers should pay extra attention to the following areas: excessive vibration transmitted through the AWD; automatic transmission clunk; poor braking performance (brake pedal hardens and brakes don't work after going over bumps or rough roads) and expensive brake maintenance; electronic computer module and fuel-system glitches that cause the Check Engine light to remain lit; hard starts, no-starts, or chronic stalling, especially when going downhill; heating and AC performance hampered by poor air distribution; electrical system shorts; and sliding-door misalignment and broken hinges.

 ## Safety Summary

All models: 2000—Airbags fail to deploy. • Brake and gas pedals are too close together. • When brakes are applied, rear wheels tend to lock up while front wheels continue to turn. • Vehicle stalls when accelerating or turning. • Sliding door slams shut on an incline, or hinges break. • Extensive damage caused to bumper and undercarriage by driving over gravel roads. **2000–01**—Vehicle rolls backward when stopped on an incline while in Drive. **2001**—Sudden acceleration. • Chronic stalling. • Brake pedal set too high. • Differential in transfer case locks up while driving; defective axle seals. • Water can be trapped inside the wheels and then freeze, causing the wheels to be out of balance. **2002**—Sticking gas pedal. • Brake pedal goes to floor without braking. • Driver-side window failures. • Sliding-door window blows out. **2003**—Automatic transmission failure. • Harsh, delayed shifting. • ABS engages erratically on dry pavement at slow speeds and increases stopping distances considerably (probable cause is corrosion buildup within the ABS sensors). • Painful harmonic roar from the rear of the vehicle. • On a slight incline, sliding door will unlatch and slam shut. **2004**—Cruise control suddenly shuts off. • Rear driver-side window explodes.

Secret Warranties/Internal Bulletins/Service Tips

All models: 1999–2000—If the engine runs hot, overheats, or loses coolant, try polishing the radiator filler neck or replacing the radiator cap before letting any mechanic convince you that more expensive repairs are needed. **1999–2004**—Automatic transmission malfunctions may be caused by debris in the transmission (TSB #01-07-30-038B). **2000–04**—Automatic transmission delayed shifts. **2001**—Harsh automatic transmission shifts. • 2–4 band and 3–4 clutch damage. • Steering shudder felt when making low-speed turns. • Excessive brake squeal. • Wet carpet/odour in passenger footwell area (repair evaporator case drain to cowl seal/open evaporator case drain). • Delayed shifts, slips, flares, or extended shifts during cold operation (replace shift solenoid valve assembly). **2002**—Automatic transmission slips, incorrect shifts, and poor engine performance. • Service Engine light comes on, no Third or Fourth gears, and loss of Drive. • Slipping or missing Second, Third, or Fourth gears. • Inadequate heating. • Roof panel has a wavy or rippled appearance. • Water leak in the windshield area. **2002–03**—Sliding door difficult to open. **2003**—Hard starts, rough idle, and intermittent misfiring. • Transfer case shudder. **2004**—Measures to silence a suspension pop or sliding-door squeak.

ASTRO, SAFARI PROFILE

	1999	2000	2001	2002	2003	2004	2005
Cost Price ($)							
Cargo	23,290	24,015	24,465	—	—	26,390	26,875
CS/base	23,839	25,675	26,440	27,255	27,600	27,615	28,895
Used Values ($)							
Cargo ▲	2,500	3,000	4,000	—	—	7,000	8,500
Cargo ▼	2,500	2,500	3,500	—	—	6,000	7,000
CS/base ▲	3,500	4,500	5,000	5,500	6,500	8,000	9,000
CS/base ▼	3,500	4,000	4,500	5,000	6,000	6,500	8,000
Reliability	2	2	2	2	2	2	3
Crash Safety (F)	3	3	3	3	3	3	3
Side	—	—	—	—	5	5	5
Offset	1	1	1	1	1	1	1
Head Restraints (F)	2	—	2	2	1	1	1
Rollover Resistance	—	—	3	3	3	—	—

426

MONTANA, MONTANA SV6, RELAY, SILHOUETTE, TERRAZA, UPLANDER, VENTURE ★

RATING: Not Recommended (1999–2007). These minivan orphans should have never left the factory. They are unreliable and dangerous, as evidenced by their automatic transmission and engine head gasket/intake manifold gasket failures and sliding doors that crush and injure children. There is no acceptable model year. **"Real" city/highway fuel economy:** *3.4L:* 12.0/7.8 L/100 km. *3.4L AWD:* 13.7/9.6 L/100 km. Owners report fuel savings may undershoot these estimates by at least 15 percent. **Maintenance/Repair costs:** Average costs, except for engine and tranny glitches that cost $3,000 each to repair. **Parts:** Reasonably priced and not hard to find. **Extended warranty:** Definitely needed for both the engine and automatic transmission. **Best alternatives:** Honda Odyssey and Toyota Sienna (but not the 2004 model).

Strengths and Weaknesses

These minivans have more carlike handling than GM's truck-based Astro and Safari. Seating is limited to five adults in the standard models (two up front, and three on a removable bench seat), but this is increased to seven if you find a vehicle equipped with the additional seats. Seats can be folded down flat, creating additional storage space.

As with most minivans, be wary of vehicles equipped with a power-assisted passenger-side sliding door—it's both convenient and dangerous. Despite an override circuit that should prevent the door from closing when it's blocked, a number of injuries have been reported. Furthermore, the doors frequently open when they shouldn't and can be difficult to close securely.

All ratings on a numbered scale where 5 is good and 1 is bad. See pages 108–109 for a more detailed description.

All models and years have had serious reliability problems—notably engine head gasket and intake manifold defects; electronic module (PROM) and starter failures; premature front brake component wear, brake fluid leakage, and noisy braking; short circuits that burn out alternators, batteries, power door lock activators, and the blower motor; AC evaporator core failures; premature wearout of the inner and outer tie rods; automatic transmission breakdowns; abysmal fit and finish; chronic sliding-door malfunctions; faulty rear-seat latches; a fuel-thirsty and poorly performing automatic transmission; a badly mounted sliding door; side-door glass that pops open; squeaks, rattles, and clunks in the instrument panel cluster area and suspension; and wind buffeting noise around the front doors.

VEHICLE HISTORY: 1999—A 5 hp boost to the base V6 engine (185 hp), depowered airbags, an upgraded automatic transmission, a rear-window defogger, and heated rear-view mirrors. **2000**—Dual sliding rear side doors. **2001**—Slightly restyled with a fold-flat third-row seat and a driver-side power door. **2003**—Optional ABS and front side airbags. **2005**—Venture drops the regular-length model and AWD in a shortened model-year run. Uplander arrives, along with the identical Montana SV6, Relay, and Terraza. **2006**—Optional second-row side airbags; a shorter-length model is introduced; and an upgraded automatic transmission. *Uplander et al:* **2007**—A 240 hp 3.9L V6 replaces the 201 hp 3.5L V6; all-wheel-drive and the load-levelling suspension option are gone.

Fit and finish deficiencies: body panels corrode easily, paint is prone to blistering or delaminating, and the front windshield is particularly prone to leak water from the top portion into the dash instrument cluster (a problem also affecting rear-drive vans and covered by a secret warranty).

Other trouble spots include EGR valve failures; electrical glitches; early wheel bearing failures; blurry front windshields; air being constantly blown through the centre vent; failure-prone AC condensers; and eccentric wipers.

 Safety Summary

All models/years: Fire may ignite around the fuel-filler nozzle or within the ignition switch. • Tie-rod failures may cause loss of steering control. • Sudden steering loss in rainy weather or when passing through a puddle (serpentine belt slippage). • Chronic brake failures or excessive brake fade. • Airbags malfunction. • Sliding doors suddenly open or close, come off their tracks, jam shut, stick open, injure children, and rattle during highway driving. • Transmission failures; slips from Drive into Neutral; won't hold gear on a grade. • Some front door-mounted seat belts cross uncomfortably at the neck, and there's a nasty blind spot on the driver's side that requires a small stick-on convex mirror to correct. • Headlight assembly collects moisture, burns bulb, or falls out. • Seatback suddenly collapses. • Accelerator and brake pedals are too close together. • Fuel slosh/clunk when vehicle stops or accelerates (replacement tank is useless). • Self-activating door locks lock people out or trap them inside. • Faulty fuel pump causes chronic stalling, no-starts, surging, and sudden acceleration. • Rear control arm snaps. •

Steering idler arm falls off because of missing bolt. • Brakes activate on their own, making it feel as if the van is pulling a load. • Electrical harness failures result in complete electrical shutdown. • Headlights, interior lights, gauges, and instruments fail intermittently. • Excess padding around horn makes it difficult to depress horn button in an emergency. • Poorly performing rear AC. • Flickering interior and exterior lights. • Airbag warning light stays lit. • Windshield glass distortion. **All models: 2004**—Engine surging, stalling. • Loss of coolant, engine overheating. • Broken rear sway bar. • Frequent brake failures blamed on faulty brake master cylinder. • Tail lights fail intermittently. • Power-sliding door opens and closes on its own while vehicle is underway. • Two children's wrists were fractured after their elbows and hands were caught between the seat and the sliding-door handle. • Door doesn't lock into position; slides shut and crushes objects in its path. **2005**—Sudden transmission failure. • When underway, vehicle suddenly veers to one side. • Traction control comes on at the wrong time, forcing vehicle to "limp home." • Early failure of the sliding-door motor. • Vehicle stalls if gas tank is half full. • Dash lights are too dim for bright days. • Windshield chips easily. **2006**—Early replacement of the front sway bar links and struts. • Incorrect fuel gauge readings; vehicle runs out of fuel when going downhill. • Sliding doors open on their own. • Headlight failures. • Goodyear tire-tread separation. **2007**— More sliding-door problems.

Secret Warranties/Internal Bulletins/Service Tips

All models: 1993–2005—GM says that a chronic driveline clunk can't be silenced and is a normal characteristic of its vehicles. • Paint delamination, peeling, or fading. **1995–2004**—Engine intake manifold/head gasket failures. GM Canada has settled out of court for about $40 million in claims relating to intake manifold gasket failures, and owners of 1995–2004 V6-equipped models are eligible for refunds of $200–$800. Simply Google "GM Canada" and "intake manifold settlement" to find out how to make your claim. (An excellent law article relative to successfully framing any engine claim for small claims court, John W. Hanson's "New Guidance for *Consumers Legal Remedies Act* Claims," *Trial Bar News*, February 2006, pages 7–8, can be found on California lawyers Rosner and Mansfield's website at *www.rosnerandmansfield.com/pdf/hanson2.pdf*.) **1996– 2001**—Poor heat distribution in driver's area of vehicle (install new heat ducts). **1997–2003**—Rust holes in the roof. **1999–2003**—Incorrect fuel gauge readings caused by a contaminated fuel-tank sensor/sender. If a fuel cleaner doesn't work, GM says it will adjust or replace the sensor/sender for free on a case-by-case basis (*Toronto Star*, June 13 and 14 and December 20, 2003). This failure afflicts GM's entire lineup and could cost up to $800 to repair. **2000–04**—Tail light/brake light and circuit board burn out from water intrusion. Repair cost covered by a "goodwill" policy (TSB #03-08-42-007A) up to five years. **2000–06**—Delayed shifts. **2001–08**—Harsh shifts, slippage. **2003–04**—Power-sliding door binding. **2004–06**—Noisy steering can be silenced by replacing the inner tie-rod boot, says TSB #06-02-32-005. **2005–06**—A defective harmonic balancer may cause severe engine damage. • Hard start/no-start, stalling, inoperative gauges. • Excessive effort to sound horn. • Silencing sliding-door rattles. • Inaccurate temperature and fuel readings. • Poor AC performance. **2005–07**—TSB #07-05-23-003A says a brake pulsation, vibration fix requires rotor variation and new front brake shields (GM should pay for this work). • Remedy for rear brake squeal or squeak. **2006–08**—Guess what? More head gasket leaks to add to the 1995–2004 GM Canada class action settlement (TSB #08-06-01-012, dated June 18, 2008, also includes the 2006–08 Saturn Aura and Chevrolet Monte Carlo, Impala, and Malibu). **2006**—Harsh shifts. **2007–08**—Engine squealing, vibration on start-up.

MONTANA, MONTANA SV6, RELAY, SILHOUETTE, TERRAZA, UPLANDER, VENTURE PROFILE

	1999	2000	2001	2002	2003	2004	2005	2006	2007
Cost Price ($)									
Montana	25,130	26,625	26,755	27,870	28,520	29,380	32,840	—	—
Montana SV6	—	—	—	—	—	—	26,620	24,525	24,550
Relay	—	—	—	—	—	—	27,995	26,995	27,770
Silhouette	29,955	30,630	31,105	33,060	35,695	36,290	—	—	—
Terraza	—	—	—	—	—	—	33,745	32,210	33,025
Uplander	—	—	—	—	—	—	25,405	23,240	23,880
Venture	24,725	24,895	25,230	25,195	25,865	26,680	30,590	—	—
Used Values ($)									
Montana ▲	2,500	3,000	3,500	4,000	4,500	6,000	8,000	—	—
Montana ▼	2,000	3,000	3,500	3,500	4,000	5,000	6,500	—	—
Montana SV6 ▲	—	—	—	—	—	—	6,500	8,500	11,500
Montana SV6 ▼	—	—	—	—	—	—	5,000	7,000	10,000
Relay ▲	—	—	—	—	—	—	15,000	10,500	13,500
Relay ▼	—	—	—	—	—	—	13,500	9,000	12,000
Silhouette ▲	3,000	3,500	4,000	4,500	5,000	7,000	—	—	—
Silhouette ▼	2,500	3,000	3,500	4,000	4,500	6,000	—	—	—
Terraza ▲	—	—	—	—	—	—	8,500	11,500	16,000
Terraza ▼	—	—	—	—	—	—	7,000	10,000	14,500
Uplander ▲	—	—	—	—	—	—	6,500	9,000	11,000
Uplander ▼	—	—	—	—	—	—	5,000	7,500	9,500
Venture ▲	2,000	2,500	3,000	3,500	4,500	6,000	8,000	—	—
Venture ▼	1,500	2,500	3,000	3,500	4,000	4,500	6,500	—	—
Reliability	1	1	1	1	1	1	1	1	1
Crash Safety (F)	4	4	4	4	4	4	4	5	5
Side	5	5	5	5	5	5	5	4	4
IIHS Side	—	—	—	—	—	—	—	1	1
Offset (Venture)	1	1	1	1	1	1	1	—	—
Montana SV6	—	—	—	—	—	—	5	5	—
Relay	—	—	—	—	—	—	—	5	5 5
Terraza	—	—	—	—	—	—	—	5	5 5
Uplander	—	—	—	—	—	—	5	5	5
Head Restraints (F)	2	—	5	5	3	3	1	1	1
Rear	1	—	3	3	2	2	—	—	—
Rollover Resistance	—	—	3	3	3	—	—	3	3

Honda

ODYSSEY ★★★★

RATING: Above Average (2003–07); Average (1999–2002). Odyssey redesigns don't engender as steep a decline in quality as we have seen with Mazda, Nissan, and Toyota redesigns. The upgraded 2005 Odyssey surpassed the Sienna in safety, performance, and convenience features. Nevertheless, from 2005 on, there have been frequent reports of safety- and performance-related failures, hence *Lemon-Aid*'s downgrade of formerly Recommended recent-model Odysseys. Of particular concern are run-flat Pax tire problems, airbag malfunctions, automatic sliding-door failures, damaged AC condensers, transmission breakdowns with erratic shifting, and sudden brake loss. **"Real" city/highway fuel economy:** 2.2L: 11.9/9.2 L/100 km. 2.3L: 10.9/8.3 L/100 km. 3.5L: 13.2/8.5 L/100 km. Owners report fuel savings may undershoot these estimates by about 10 percent. Fuel economy drops dramatically if the rear AC is engaged. **Maintenance/Repair costs:** Average; any garage can repair these minivans. **Parts:** Moderately priced, and availability is better than average because the Odyssey uses many generic Accord parts. **Extended warranty:** Not needed; save your money. **Best alternatives:** If you want something cheaper and reasonably reliable, consider a three-year-old Chrysler minivan or a Hyundai Entourage. If you want handling and dependability, look to Toyota's Sienna (but not the 2004 model). Sadly, GM's front-drive minivans aren't in the running because of their self-destructing engines and malfunctioning automatic transmissions. GM's Astro, Safari, or full-sized van are much more reliable and provide additional towing muscle.

Strengths and Weaknesses

When it was first launched in 1995, the Odyssey was a sales dud. Canadians and *Lemon-Aid* saw through Honda's attempt to pass off an underpowered, mid-sized four-door station wagon with a raised roof as a minivan. In 1999, however, the Odyssey was redesigned, and it now represents one of the better minivans on the Canadian market.

It's easy to see what makes the Odyssey so popular: strong engine performance, carlike ride and handling, easy entry/exit, a second driver-side door, and a quiet interior. Most controls and displays are easy to reach and read, there's a lot of passenger and cargo room and an extensive list of standard equipment, and Honda is willing to compensate owners for production snafus.

This minivan does have its drawbacks, though. A high resale price makes bargains rare, front-seat passenger legroom is marginal because of the restricted seat travel, and third-row seating is suitable only for children. Additionally, power-sliding doors are slow to retract, there's some tire rumbling and rattling and body drumming at highway speeds, premium fuel is required for optimum performance, and rear-seat head restraints impede side and rear visibility.

VEHICLE HISTORY: 1999—A new, more-powerful engine and increased size make this second-generation Odyssey a more-versatile highway performer; still, steering requires fully extended arms, and power-sliding doors operate slowly. **2001**—User-friendly child safety seat tether anchors, upgraded stereo speakers, and an intermittent rear-window wiper. **2002**—A slight restyling, 30 additional horses, disc brakes on all four wheels, standard side airbags, and additional support for front seats. **2003**—Changes include an auto up/down driver-side window, plus new-style keys that Honda says are harder to duplicate. **2005**—Honda updates its minivan for 2005, revising the styling and adding additional safety features. The '05 Odyssey continues with a 255 hp 3.5L V6 and a 5-speed automatic transmission. EX-L and Touring models come with a Variable Cylinder Management system. Standard safety features include anti-lock four-wheel disc brakes, traction control, an anti-skid system, front side airbags, and side curtain airbags for all three seating rows. Most models (except the LX) have power-sliding side doors. 2005s also have a storage compartment in the floor and side windows that power partly down into the sliding doors. **2006**—Horsepower rating cut by 11 (to 244 hp).

Reliability is better than average, but Honda still has a few safety- and performance-related problems to work out. Four examples: failure-prone sliding doors; troublesome, expensive-to-replace Pax run-flat tires; easily damaged AC condensers; and "soft," spongy brakes. The sliding doors open when they shouldn't, won't close when they should, catch fingers and arms, get stuck open or closed, are noisy, and frequently require expensive servicing. The Check Engine light may stay lit because of a defective fuel-filler neck. There's a fuel sloshing noise when accelerating or coming to a stop and an engine pinging when driving up steep hills, and the transmission clunks or bangs when backing uphill or when shifting into Reverse. There are also reports of rattling and chattering when the minivan is in Forward gear. Owners note a loud wind noise and vibration from the left side of the front windshield, along with a constant vibration felt through the steering assembly and front wheels. Passenger doors may also require excessive force to open.

Other problems include transmission breakdowns and transmission gear whine at 90 km/h or when in Fourth gear (the transmission can be replaced under a "goodwill" warranty); front-end clunking that is caused by welding breaks in the front subframe; exhaust that rattles or buzzes; the vehicle pulling to the right when underway; wheel bearings and front brakes that wear prematurely and are excessively noisy, as are the original-equipment tires; frequent sliding side door malfunctions; electrical glitches and defective remote audio controls; leather seats that split, crack, or discolour; and accessory items that come loose, break away, or won't work. Plastic interior panels have rough edges and are often misaligned (*www.carcomplaints.com/Honda/Odyssey/2006/steering*).

 **Safety Summary**

All years: Passenger seatbacks collapsed when vehicle was rear-ended. • Airbag malfunctions. • Sudden, unintended acceleration when slowing for a stop sign or when in Drive with AC turned on. • Stuck accelerator. • Automatic transmission failures. • Transmission doesn't hold when stopped or parked on an incline; gas or brakes have to be constantly applied. • Entire vehicle shakes excessively at highway speeds and pulls to the left or right. • The rear head restraints seriously hamper rear and forward visibility, and it's difficult to see vehicles coming from the right side. • Power-sliding doors are a constant danger. • Static-electricity shocks. **2000**—Many incidents where the driver-side sliding door opens onto the fuel hose while fuelling, damaging gas-flap hinge and tank. • Catastrophic failure of the right-side suspension, causing wheel to buckle. • Protruding bolts in the door assembly are hazardous. **2001**—In a frontal collision, van caught fire because of a cracked brake-fluid reservoir. • Cracked wheel rims. • Passenger-side door window suddenly exploded while driving on the highway. **2002**—Owners say many engines have faulty timing chains. • Loose strut bolt almost caused wheel to fall off. • Axle-bearing wheel failure caused driver-side wheel to fall off. • Head restraints are set too low for tall occupants. • Rear windshield shatters from area where the wiper is mounted. • Rear seat belt unlatches during emergency braking. • Brake line freezes up in cold weather. • Abrupt downshift on deceleration. • Driver-side door came off while using remote control. • Passenger window exploded. • Airbag light comes on for no reason. **2003**—Fire ignited in the CD player. • Fuel spits out when refuelling. • Inaccurate fuel gauge readings. **2004**—Chronic stalling even after recall; repairs to the fuel-pump relay to correct the problem. • Gas pedal will not work due to a broken throttle cable. • Sliding door crushes arms and legs. • Right-hand fingers can get caught in the gap on the steering wheel between the cruise-control buttons and the airbag area. • If vehicle is started and left in idle, the doors lock automatically. This could lock the driver out after a 10-second delay. **2005**—Sudden acceleration while cruising. • Defective power-steering pump and fuel pump. • Front and rear AC temperature varies. • Snow and ice accumulated under the spoiler, causing it to fall off along with the brake light. • Child's hand was crushed in one incident by rear power-sliding door. • Run-flat tire problems:

My wife and I purchased a new Honda Odyssey van in 2005 which was equipped with Pax run-flat tires. At the time, we were told that the tires would wear like regular non run-flat tires, and would be 10–15% more expensive to replace. We were also told that all Honda dealers would have the necessary equipment to service these special tires. None of these statements has proven to be true. The tires are all worn out at 31K miles [50,000 km], and we were quoted a price of $1300 plus tax to have them replaced. Worse yet, our nearest dealer (Flagstaff Honda) does not have the necessary equipment to service them 2 years after their release. To make things worse, we now have a flat and getting it fixed will require us to drive 50 mph [80 km/h] on a busy interstate.

2006—Engine crankshaft and motor mount failures. • Power-steering flywheel fell off. • Loss of power steering and alternator due to belt slipping when driving on rain-soaked roads. • AC condenser damaged by road debris. 2007—Engine surges while brakes feel "soft"—they can be depressed halfway down before any braking effect is felt. • Automatic transmission skips from First to Third gear; sometimes it also jerks into gear. • Brake and gas pedals still mounted too close together. • Vehicle constantly pulls to the left when underway. • Sliding door flew open on the highway; crushed a child's hand in another incident. • Rear window exploded. • AC condensers continue to be destroyed by road debris. • Third-row glove box gets extremely hot. • Tire-pressure monitor alerts driver intermittently as the outside temperature changes.

Secret Warranties/Internal Bulletins/Service Tips

All years: Most of Honda's TSBs allow for special warranty consideration on a "goodwill" basis by the company's District Service Manager or Zone Office. • There's an incredibly large number of sliding-door problems covered by a recall, and a plethora of service bulletins too numerous to print here. Ask Honda politely for the bulletins or "goodwill" assistance. If refused, subpoena the documents through small claims court, using NHTSA's complaint and service bulletin summaries as your shopping list. **1999–2001**—Extended warranty coverage on Odysseys with defective 4- and 5-speed automatic transmissions to 7 years/160,000 km to fix erratic or slow shifting. **1999–2003**—Engine oil leaks. • Deformed windshield moulding. **1999–2006**—Troubleshooting vehicle pull or drift to one side. **2000–01**—Bulletin confirms Honda USA has investigated complaints of pulling or drifting (TSB #99165, Bulletin Sequence #802, September 1999, NHTSA Item #SB608030). **2002**—No-starts; hard starts in cold weather. **2002–03**—Free replacement of the engine timing belt auto-tensioner and water pump under both a recall and "product update" campaign. **2002–04**—Free tranny repair or replacement for insufficient lubrication that can lead to heat buildup and broken gears. **2002–06**—Warranty mileage limitation extended by 5 percent to compensate for defective odometers. • Rear brake noise. **2003**—Engine cranks but won't start. • ABS problems. • Faulty charging system; electrical shorts. • Front door howls in strong crosswind. • Squealing from rear quarter windows and motors. • Fuel-tank leak. • Front damper noise. **2005**—Windshield noise remedy. • Front and rear AC temperature varies. • Correction for middle-row seat that won't unlatch. **2005–06**—Noise remedy for the power steering, front brakes, front wheel bearings, windshield, sliding door, and exhaust system. **2005–07**—Headphones inoperative in DVD mode. • Drivetrain ping, squeal, or rattle. • Power seat won't move forward or backward. **2007**—Delayed First gear engagement. • Insufficient AC cooling at idle.

ODYSSEY PROFILE

	1999	2000	2001	2002	2003	2004	2005	2006	2007
Cost Price ($)									
LX	30,600	30,600	30,800	31,900	32,200	32,400	32,700	33,200	33,300
EX	33,600	33,600	33,800	34,900	35,200	35,400	35,900	36,400	36,900
Used Values ($)									
LX ▲	4,500	6,000	7,000	8,000	10,500	12,500	14,500	17,000	21,000
LX ▼	3,500	5,000	6,000	7,000	9,000	11,000	13,000	16,000	19,500
EX ▲	—	—	8,000	9,500	12,000	13,500	16,500	19,500	23,000
EX ▼	—	—	7,000	8,500	11,000	12,500	15,000	18,000	21,500
Reliability	4	4	4	4	4	4	4	4	4
Crash Safety (F)	5	5	5	5	5	5	5	5	5
Side	—	5	5	5	5	5	5	5	5
IIHS Side	—	—	—	—	—	—	5	5	5
Offset	2	2	2	5	5	5	5	5	5
Head Restraints (F)	2	—	2	2	2	2	2	2	2
Rear	1	—	—	—	—	—	—	—	—
Rollover Resistance	—	—	4	4	4	—	4	4	4

Kia/Hyundai

SEDONA, ENTOURAGE ★★ / ★★★

RATING: *Sedona:* Below Average (2002–07). The Sedona is a very user-friendly, roomy, versatile, and comfortable mid-sized minivan that comes with a comprehensive base warranty; too bad it's so unreliable. *Entourage:* Average (2007). Think of Hyundai's first seven-seat minivan as a slightly better-built Sedona with styling borrowed from the Hyundai Santa Fe SUV. **"Real" city/highway fuel economy:** 15.4/10.9 L/100 km. Owners report fuel consumption may be even worse than this estimate by about 20 percent. **Maintenance/Repair costs:** Average. **Parts:** Likely to be back ordered and cost more than average. Safety recall repairs are often delayed because parts are unavailable. **Extended warranty:** Yes, until these minivans have proved themselves on a long-term basis. **Best alternatives:** Honda Odyssey and Toyota Sienna (excluding the 2004 model).

Strengths and Weaknesses

Used Sedonas cost several thousand dollars less than comparable Detroit-built minivans. Embodying typically bland minivan styling, the front-drive, seven-passenger Sedona is 18 cm shorter than the Honda Odyssey and 11 cm longer than the Dodge Caravan. It comes with a good selection of standard features, including a 195 hp 3.5L V6 engine hooked to an automatic 5-speed transmission, a low step-in height, and a commanding view of the road.

Engine power is drained by the Sedona's heft, giving it a 10–20 percent higher fuel-consumption rate than the V6-equipped Dodge Caravan or Toyota Sienna. The upgraded 2006 V6 engine, however, provides much more power while posting fuel economy numbers that are similar to those of the competition. Handling is compromised by vague steering and a wallowing suspension, owners' ears are assailed by excessive engine and wind noise, braking is mediocre, and overall quality control, especially fit and finish, is embarrassingly bad.

Poor reliability and high fuel consumption are the Sedona's weakest links, especially with its small dealer network. Areas of most concern have been the engine (head gasket leaks and a rattling timing chain), transmission (failures and lock-ups), seat belts, fuel and electrical systems, brake pads and rotors, AC compressor, and overall body construction, especially side window mouldings (see *www.kia-forums.com* and *www.autosafety.org/autodefects.html*).

VEHICLE HISTORY: 2003—New tail lights. The LX adds a standard AM/FM/CD player, central door-lock button, and remote fuel-door release, while the EX version gets additional stereo speakers and a second remote for the keyless entry. **2004**—A new grille, and the LX's centre tray table becomes a standard feature. **2006**—Larger dimensions, more power, and standard side curtain airbags. A more-powerful 244 hp 3.8L V6 hooked to a 5-speed manumatic provides an important 50 hp boost. Comfort and convenience are enhanced through seven-passenger seating, second-row removable bucket seats that slide fore and aft, a third-row bench that splits 60/40 and folds into the floor, and sliding side-door power windows. Standard anti-lock four-wheel disc brakes and traction/anti-skid control are two new standard safety features that distinguish these models from the rest of the pack. Additionally, all Sedonas have front side airbags and side curtain airbags that cover all three seating rows. **2007**—The V6 engine gains 6 hp, and a short-wheelbase model arrives. Kia's owner, Hyundai, launches an identical Entourage minivan.

 Safety Summary

Sedona: **All years:** Airbags fail to deploy. • Sudden, unintended acceleration. • Intermittent stalling. • Poor braking performance due to warped brake rotors and prematurely worn brake calipers and pads. • Parking brake doesn't hold vehicle on an incline. • Defective wheel bearings. • Multiple electrical shorts; electrical system continually blows fuses. • Dash lights fail repeatedly; replacing the instrument-cluster board is only a temporary solution. • Weak rear hatch struts. • Power-sliding door doesn't close properly; opens when vehicle is underway. • AC condenser is vulnerable to puncture from road debris. **2002**—Fuel-tank design could cause fuel to spray onto hot muffler in a collision. • Oil leaks onto the hot catalytic converter. • Fuel leaks from the bottom of the vehicle. • Loose fuel-line-to-fuel-pump clamp. • Fuel-tank filler hose vulnerable to road debris. • Fuel spits back out when refuelling. • Vehicle continues to accelerate when brakes are applied. • Brake failure; pedal simply sinks to the floor. • ABS brake light comes on randomly. • Power-steering pulley breaks. • Windshield may suddenly shatter for no apparent reason. • Windshields have distortion at eye level. • Electrical shorts cause lights, windows, and door locks to fail. • Child safety seat can't be belted in securely. • Child-door safety lock failure. • Inoperative rear seat belts. • Seat belt holding child in booster seat tightened progressively, trapping child. **2003**—Brakes fail because of air in the brake lines. • Broken window regulator. • While reclined, passenger seatback releases upright and slams occupant forward. • Electrical shorts cause door lock malfunctions. **2004**—Fire ignites in the under-hood wiring. • Transmission and TCM replaced because vehicle loses power and gears down constantly. • Loose left rear wheel and suspension struts. • Rear brake assembly and wheel fall off. • Seat belts fail to lock upon impact. • Low-beam headlights burn out repeatedly. **2005**—Engine hesitates for almost five seconds when accelerating. • Rear passenger-side wheel fell off the vehicle due to defective wheel bearings; original recall needs to be extended. • Early replacement of the windshield wiper motor. • Driver left the vehicle running and then found himself locked out. • Toxic mould can grow in the ventilation system because filters were installed beginning only with the 2006 models. **2006**—Engine failure due to sludge buildup. • Transmission suddenly drops out of Drive. • Hole in the fuel tank. **2007**—Front windshield wiper linkage comes loose. • Cruise control doesn't work properly on long hills. *Entourage:* **2007**—No-starts due to a faulty ignition module. • Multiple sliding-door defects similar in nature to the Sedona's. • Water leaks from the roof. • Windshield cracked when driver adjusted the rear-view mirror. • Seat belts lock up and choke passengers. • Many complaints of steering veering to the left and a serious front-end vibration. • Bent wheel rims cause excessive vibration and a poor ride. • Original tires wear out quickly; don't hold their air. • Faulty tire valve stems. • Battery doesn't hold its charge. • Frequent brake light switch failures.

Secret Warranties/Internal Bulletins/Service Tips

Sedona: **2001–05**—Heater pipe corrosion. **2002**—Correction for engine hesitation after cold starts. • Free replacement of seat belt buckle anchor bolts. **2002–03**—Changes to improve alternator output to prevent hard starts or battery drain. **2002–05**—Harsh, delayed shifts. • Insufficient AC cooling, and excessive AC noise. • Sliding door is hard to open. **2004**—Engine head gasket leak. **2006**—Free replacement of the power-sliding door cable (Campaign #SC062); the power-sliding door switch (Campaign #SC063); and the rear-door pinch strip attachment (Campaign #SC066). • Inoperative driver-seat lumbar support. • Fuel-tank humming noise. **2006–07**—Intermittent no-start condition. • Engine runs rough, hesitates. • AC knocking noise. • Remedy for a noisy exhaust. *Entourage:* **2007**—Intermittent no-crank; no-start. • Engine misfire; defective oxygen sensor. • Harsh, delayed shifts, especially when going into Reverse or Drive. • Cannot shift into or out of Park. • Oil leaks from differential seals. • Fuel-pump buzzing, humming. • Front suspension clicking, ratcheting. • Front strut noise. • Tapping noise when AC is activated. • Electromagnetic interference with the Tire Monitor System. • Inoperative driver-seat lumbar support. • Loose roof-assist handles.

SEDONA/ENTOURAGE PROFILE

	2002	2003	2004	2005	2006	2007
Cost Price ($)						
Sedona LX	24,595	24,995	25,595	26,995	29,495	29,495
EX	27,595	28,295	28,995	29,495	31,895	32,495
Entourage GL	—	—	—	—	—	29,995
Used Values ($)						
Sedona LX ▲	3,500	5,000	6,500	8,500	11,000	14,500
Sedona LX ▼	3,000	4,000	5,000	7,000	9,500	13,000
EX ▲	4,000	5,500	7,500	9,000	11,500	15,500
EX ▼	3,500	4,500	6,000	7,500	10,000	14,000
Entourage GL ▲	—	—	—	—	—	16,500
Entourage GL ▼	—	—	—	—	—	15,000
Reliability	1	1	1	1	1	2
Entourage	—	—	—	—	—	4
Crash Safety (F)	5	5	5	5	5	5
Entourage	—	—	—	—	—	5
Side	5	5	5	5	5	5
Entourage	—	—	—	—	—	5
IIHS Side	—	—	—	—	5	5
Entourage	—	—	—	—	—	5
Offset	3	3	3	3	5	5
Entourage	—	—	—	—	—	5
Head Restraints (F)	5	5	5	—	5	5
Entourage	—	—	—	—	—	5
Rear	3	3	3	—	—	—
Rollover Resistance	4	4	—	4	4	4
Entourage	—	—	—	—	—	4

Note: Although the Sedona and Entourage are virtually identical minivans, the 2007 Entourage has posted quality ratings that are a bit better than the Kia Sedona's. It also has a higher resale value.

Mazda

MPV ★ ★

RATING: Below Average (2002–06); Not Recommended (2000–01). Mazda threw in the towel and dropped the MPV after the 2006 model year. The company did accomplish an amazing turnaround when it made the 2002 MPV sportier and more nimble than its more space- and comfort-oriented counterparts. Previous models were underpowered, lumbering, undersized, and overpriced. Now any MPV is a particularly risky buy because it's an orphaned low-volume model serviced by a low-volume, struggling dealership network. **"Real" city/highway fuel economy:** 15.6/10.9 L/100 km. Owners report fuel savings may undershoot this estimate by at least 15 percent. **Maintenance/Repair costs:** Average. **Parts:** Likely to be back ordered and cost more than average. **Extended warranty:** Yes, at least for the powertrain. **Best alternatives:** GM's full-sized Savana/Express, Honda's Odyssey, and Toyota's Sienna (except the 2004 model).

Strengths and Weaknesses

Mazda's only minivan quickly became a bestseller when it first came on the market in 1989, but its popularity fell just as quickly when larger, more-powerful competitors arrived. Early MPVs embodied many of the mistakes made by Honda's first Odyssey: Its 170 horses weren't adequate for people-hauling, and it was expensive for what was essentially a smaller van than buyers expected.

The MPV's most recent engine, a 200 hp 3.0L Duratec V6, gives the Mazda engine better pulling power at lower speeds. Making good use of that power is a smooth-shifting 5-speed automatic transmission. But torque is still less than with the Odyssey's 3.5L, or with the 3.8L engine in top-of-the-line Chryslers.

VEHICLE HISTORY: 1996—A passenger-side airbag, four-wheel ABS, and four doors. **1999**—MPV skips this model year, as Mazda switches it from rear-drive to front-drive. **2000**—Front-drive and sliding side doors. **2002**—A 200 hp V6 and 5-speed automatic transmission, power-sliding side doors, revised suspension settings, and 17-inch wheels.

Engine overheating and head gasket and valve lifter failures are commonplace with the 4-banger. Winter driving is compromised by the MPV's light rear end, mediocre traction, and low ground clearance. Expect some transmission glitches, ABS malfunctions, stalling and surging, and oil leakage. The electronic computer module (ECU), automatic transmission driveshaft, upper shock mounts, front 4×4 drive axles and lash adjusters, AC core, and radiator all fail within the first three to five years. Cold temperatures tend to fry the automatic window motor, and the paint is easily chipped and flakes off early. Brakes are a horror: Premature brake caliper and rotor wear and excessive vibration/pulsation are chronic problem areas.

Safety Summary

2000–01—Engine valve failure. **2000–03**—Airbags fail to deploy. **2001**—Engine surging. • Tranny lever can be shifted out of Park without key in ignition; sometimes it won't shift out of Park when you want it to. • Brake failure. • Brake caliper bolt fell off, causing vehicle to skid. • Sliding doors don't lock in place. • Rear visibility obstructed by high seatbacks. **2002–03**—Engine oil leakage.

2003—Child's neck easily tangled in seat belt. **2004**—Engine seizes when connecting rod fails. • Transmission failure caused by worn shaft solenoid. **2005**—Transmission slippage, then failure. • Rear window shattered when the defroster was turned on.

Secret Warranties/Internal Bulletins/Service Tips

All years: TSB #006-94 looks into all the causes and remedies for excessive brake vibrations, and TSB #11-14-95 gives an excellent diagnostic flow chart for trouble-shooting excessive engine noise. • Serious paint peeling and delamination will be fully covered for up to six years under a Mazda secret warranty, say owners. • Troubleshooting tips for correcting wind noise around doors. • Tips for eliminating a musty, mildew-type AC odour. **2000–06**—More tips on silencing front brake clunk. • Countermeasures for excessive body vibration. **2001**—Rear brake popping, squealing, or clicking. **2002**—Engine tappet noise. **2002–06**—Camshaft ticking noise. • Key won't pull out of the ignition lock. • Power sliding door opens after closing. **2003–04**—Remedies for shift shock (transmission slams into gear). • No warm air from heater. **2005–06**—Idle RPM drop, stalling, rough idle, or hesitation.

MPV PROFILE

	2000	2001	2002	2003	2004	2005	2006
Cost Price ($)							
DX/GX	25,505	25,095	25,975	26,090	26,600	27,595	27,895
LX/GS	29,450	29,450	29,150	29,090	29,995	30,295	30,595
Used Values ($)							
DX/GX ▲	3,000	4,000	4,500	5,000	7,000	9,000	11,500
DX/GX ▼	3,000	3,500	4,000	5,000	6,000	7,500	10,000
LX/GS ▲	4,500	5,000	5,500	6,000	7,500	9,500	13,000
LX/GS ▼	4,000	4,500	5,000	6,000	6,500	8,000	11,500
Reliability	3	3	3	3	3	4	4
Crash Safety (F)	4	4	5	5	5	5	5
Side	5	5	5	5	5	5	5
IIHS Side	1	1	1	1	1	1	1
Offset	3	3	3	3	3	3	3
Head Restraints (F)	3	2	2	2	1	1	1
Rear	—	1	1	1	—	—	—
Rollover Resistance	—	3	3	3	—	—	—

Toyota

RATING: Above Average (2006–07, 1999–2003); Average (2005); Below Average (2004). A resurgence of safety-related defects carried over to the 2005 model following the 2004 Sienna's redesign. **"Real" city/highway fuel economy:** *3.0L:* 12.4/8.8 L/100 km. *3.3L:* 12.2/8.1 L/100 km. *AWD:* 13.1/9.0 L/100 km. Owners report fuel savings may undershoot these estimates by about 10 percent. **Maintenance/Repair costs:** Average; very dealer-dependent. **Parts:** There's an excellent supply of reasonably priced Sienna parts taken from the Camry parts bin. Automatic transmission torque converters on 1998–2000 models are frequently back ordered because of their poor reliability. **Extended warranty:** Yes, for the problematic 2004 and 2005 models. **Best alternatives:** Mazda5 and Hyundai Entourage minivans are catching up to Honda and Toyota in performance and reliability.

Strengths and Weaknesses

The Sienna is Toyota's Camry-based front-drive minivan. It replaced the Previa for the 1998 model year and abandoned the Previa's futuristic look in favour of a more-conservative Chevy Venture styling. Early Siennas seated seven, came with dual power-sliding doors, a V6 powerplant, and lots of safety and convenience features, including side airbags, anti-lock brakes, and a low-tire-pressure warning system.

Some of the Sienna's strong points are standard ABS and side airbags (LE, XLE); a smooth-running V6 engine, and a more-refined transmission; a stable ride, fourth door, and quiet interior; easy entry/exit; and better-than-average fit and finish and reliability. Its weak areas: V6 performance is compromised by the AC and the automatic transmission powertrain, and it lacks the trailer-towing brawn of rear-drive minivans.

The redesigned 2004 Sienna has more interior room than previous models (accommodating up to eight passengers), is better-handling, rides more comfortably, and uses a more-powerful, fuel-efficient 230 hp 3.3L V6 engine. There's less vulnerability to wind buffeting, and minimal road noise. Sienna's interior and exterior have been gently restyled. The third-row seats split and fold away, head restraints don't have to be removed when the seats are stored, and second-row bucket seats are easily converted to bench seats.

Although the rear seats fold flat to accommodate the width of a 4' × 8' board, the tailgate won't close, the heavy seats are difficult to reinstall (it's a two-person job, and the centre seat barely fits through the door), and the middle roof pillars and rear head restraints obstruct rear visibility. Also, there's no traction control, the rear drum brakes are less efficient, fuel economy is mediocre (using premium fuel), the low-mounted radio is hard to reach, and third-row seats lack a fore/aft adjustment to increase cargo space.

Reliability can be problematic, with a large cluster of redesign-related deficiencies appearing around the 2004–05 model years. The most serious concerns are self-destructing, sludge-prone engines (1998–2002 models) and defective automatic transmissions that "lag and lurch" (1998–2007). Many other failure-prone mechanical and body components continue to compromise the Sienna's safety and performance through the 2007 models, including collapsing rear hatch struts and faulty power-sliding doors; engine "piston-slap" and a clunk or banging in the driveline; the vehicle jolting or creeping forward when at a stop, forcing you to keep your foot firmly on the brake; stalling when the AC engages; electrical shorts; premature brake wear and excessive brake noise (mostly screeching); distracting windshield reflections and distorted windshields; sliding-door defects; the window suddenly shattering; easily chipped paint; and various other body glitches, like a hard-to-pull-out rear seat, water leaks, and excessive creaks and rattles.

VEHICLE HISTORY: 1998—Sienna replaces the Previa. **2001**—A rear defroster, some additional horsepower and torque, and a driver-side sliding door. **2004**—New styling, larger dimensions, more power, more safety options, and about 90 extra kilograms. The not recommended optional AWD adds even more weight and includes problematic run-flat tires. A 230 hp 3.3L V6 and 5-speed automatic transmission add 20 more horses. Power windows for the sliding rear side doors are newly standard, and the CE and LE can carry eight with a removable second-row bench seat. A hideaway third-row bench seat folds into the floorwell, à la Honda's Odyssey, but the Sienna's 60/40 split adds to its functionality. **2005**—Dual front power seats.

 Safety Summary

All years: Sudden, unintended acceleration. • Airbag malfunctions. • A multiplicity of sliding-door defects covered by internal bulletins. • Windshield distortion; shatters spontaneously. • Reflection of the dashboard onto the windshield impairs visibility. • Wheel lug nuts shear off. • Chronic transmission failures. • Vehicle rolls down the driveway while in Park. • When proceeding from a rolling stop, acceleration is delayed for about two seconds. • Child can knock gearshift lever into Drive from Park without key in the ignition. • Sluggish transmission downshift; vehicle sometimes seems to slip out of gear when decelerating. • Skid-control system lock-up. • Slope of the windshield makes it hard to gauge where the front end stops. **2004**—Engine surging with minimal pedal pressure. • Fuel-tank leakage after recall repairs; leaking fuel line. • Complete loss of brakes. • Rapid brake degradation (glazed and warped rotors). • Sliding door catches passenger's arm or leg; manual door doesn't latch properly (particularly when windows are open); door opens when turning, jams, or closes when vehicle is parked on an incline:

Our two-year-old son pulled on the sliding door handle, and the door began to open (we thought the child locks were on, but this was not the case). He was surprised and was afraid of falling out of the van, so he just held onto the handle. As the door was opening, his head then was dragged between the sliding door and the side of the van. But the van door did not stop opening. It just continued opening, exerting even more force on our son's head. Fortunately we were able to grab the door and forcefully pull it back closed before our son was horribly injured.

• Small brake lights inadequate. • Foot gets stuck between pedals. • Daytime running lights blind oncoming drivers (2004 Highlander has the same problem). **2005**—Airbag deployed for no reason while vehicle was underway. • Airbag is disabled when passenger seat is occupied. • Hesitation when accelerating, then sudden acceleration. • Laser-controlled cruise control jerks back to former speed when the way seems clear. • Gearshift lever can be accidently knocked from Fourth gear to Reverse. • Vehicle Stability Control (VSC) engages when it shouldn't. • Brake pedal stiffens intermittently. • Premature brake rotor wear leads to longer stopping distances and increased braking noise. • Run-flat tires don't signal driver when they are damaged; may catch fire:

2005 Toyota Sienna has Bridgestone run flat tires and the back right passenger tire went flat, then smoked and caught fire.

• When the rear windows are down, the door will not stay open. • Sliding doors fail to latch when they are opened. • Power-sliding door continues closing even if something is in its way (similar to complaints on previous model-year Siennas). • Rear hatch may fall:

The liftgate on a power liftgate 2005 Toyota Sienna will not stay open. It has come down and wacked my wife and I on the head many times. I found out the replacement is $450.

• Automatic interior light shut-off fails intermittently, draining the battery. • Rear heater core leaks coolant. • Front heater airflow is inadequate. **2006**—Seat belt unbuckled during a collision. • Head restraints cannot accommodate tall people. • Power steering cuts out intermittently. • Increased engine speed when stopped. • Vehicle pulls to the right. • Rear disc clip rust causes the caliper piston to stay extended and keep the disc brake pad in contact with the disc. • Dunlop tires leak air and wear out prematurely. • Windshield optical distortion causes eye strain, headaches, dizziness. • Second-row passengers have no armrests for support and are thrown into the side windows when the vehicle turns. **2006–07**—Tire-pressure monitoring system gives false alerts. **2007**—Hesitation and then sudden acceleration ("lag and lurch") continues. • Engine surges while stopped at a traffic light. • Power-sliding doors are still failing, trapping, and injuring passengers. • Tires often have side wall bulges.

Secret Warranties/Internal Bulletins/Service Tips

All years: Sliding door hazards, malfunctions, and noise are a veritable plague affecting all model years and generating a ton of service bulletins. • Owner feedback confirms that front brake pads and discs will be replaced under Toyota's "goodwill" policy if they wear out before 2 years/40,000 km. • Loose, poorly fitted trim panels (TSB #BO017-03, revised September 9, 2003). • Rusting at the base of the two front doors will be repaired at no cost, usually with a courtesy car included. According to *www.siennaclub.org*, the proper fix is to repaint the insides of the doors (presumably after removing paint and rust), cover with 3M film, and replace and coat inside seals with silicone grease. **1997–2002**—Free engine overhaul or replacement because of engine sludge buildup. The program includes 1997–2002 Toyota and Lexus vehicles with 3.0L V6 or 2.2L 4-cylinder engines. There is no mileage limitation; tell Toyota to shove it if they give you a song and dance about proof of oil changes. **1998–2000**—An 8-year/160,000 km warranty extension for automatic transmission failures. Says Toyota:

> We have recently become aware that a small number of Sienna owners have experienced a mechanical failure in the automatic transaxle, drive pinion bearing. This failure could result in slippage, noise, or a complete lack of movement.
>
> To ensure the continued satisfaction and reliability of your Sienna, Toyota has decided to implement a Special Policy Adjustment affecting certain 1998–2000 Sienna models.... This Special Policy will extend the warranty coverage of the automatic transaxle to 8 years or 160,000 km, whichever occurs first, from the original warranty registration date.

• Outline of various diagnostic procedures and fixes to correct vehicle pulling to one side. **1998–2003**—A new rear brake drum has been developed to reduce rear brake noise. **1999–2001**—Tips on fixing power seat motor cable to prevent a loose seat or inoperative seat adjustment. **2001**—Power windows rattling. • Special service campaign to inspect or replace the front subframe assembly on 2001 models. • Water leaking into the trunk area. **2002**—Troubleshooting complaints that vehicle pulls to one side. **2003–05**—No-start in extreme cold. **2003–07**—Upper, lower windshield ticking noise. **2004**—VSC activates intermittently when it is not needed. • New ECM calibration for a poorly shifting transmission (TSB #TC007-03). • Rear disc brake groan (TSB #BR002-04). • Intermediate steering shaft noise on turns. • Front-door area wind noise (TSB #NV009-03). • Power-sliding door inoperative, rattles (the saga continues). • Backdoor shudder and water leaks. • Seat heaters operate only on high. **2004–05**—Remedy for hard starts in cold weather. • Transmission lag, gear hunting. • Premature brake pad wear. • Fuel-injector ticking. • Inoperative AC light flashing. • AC blower or compressor noise; seized compressor. **2004–06**—Silencing engine ping, knock. • Power-hatch door shudder and leakage. • Power-sliding door rattles. • Excessive steering effort in high road-salt areas. • Upgraded brake pads will extend durability but increase noise. **2004–07**—Back power-sliding doors are hard to close. • Back power-door shudder. **2004–08**—Remedy for front brake pads that wear out prematurely (TSB #T-SB-0044-08). **2007**—Inoperative front, sliding-door windows. • Front-seat squeak.

SIENNA PROFILE

	1999	2000	2001	2002	2003	2004	2005	2006	2007
Cost Price ($)									
Sienna Cargo 3d	24,570	24,570	—	—	—	—	—	—	—
Sienna CE 4d	26,940	27,770	29,535	29,335	29,060	30,000	30,000	30,800	31,200
Sienna LE 4d	29,980	30,705	31,900	32,985	31,925	35,000	35,420	36,255	36,860
Used Values ($)									
Sienna Cargo 3d ▲	3,000	4,500	—	—	—	—	—	—	—
Sienna Cargo 3d ▼	3,000	3,500	—	—	—	—	—	—	—
Sienna CE 4d ▲	4,000	5,500	6,000	7,000	9,000	10,000	11,500	16,500	19,000
Sienna CE 4d ▼	3,500	4,500	5,500	6,000	7,500	9,000	10,500	15,000	17,500
Sienna LE 4d ▲	5,000	6,000	7,000	7,500	9,500	11,500	13,000	19,000	22,000
Sienna LE 4d ▼	4,500	5,000	6,500	6,500	8,000	10,500	12,000	17,500	20,500
Reliability	3	4	4	4	4	4	4	3	3
Crash Safety (F)	4	5	5	5	5	5	4	4	4
Side	—	—	4	4	4	5	3	5	5
Offset	5	5	5	5	5	5	5	5	5
Head Restraints (F)	1	1	2	2	2	5	1	1	1
Rear	—	—	—	—	—	3	—	—	—
Rollover Resistance	—	—	4	4	4	4	4	4	4

Vans

The North American full-sized van is a dying institution. Contractors, electricians, and plumbers use these vans as rolling tool boxes. Campers customize them to travel the country in comfort—canoe or bikes on top and trailer in tow. And, now that gas is about 75 cents a litre, retirees are cruising our nation's highways with large vans chock-full of every safety and convenience feature imaginable, turning their vehicles into mobile condos.

Cheaper than an RV

Sure, they may not be sleek, fuel-efficient, or sexy, their styling is likely decades old, and their popularity has certainly waned, but large vans are relatively cheap, versatile carriers that have more grunt than front-drives and are much more reliable, as well. Okay, they *are* fuel-thirsty. But I'll bet that'll be the last thought in your mind when you pass more fuel-efficient front-drive minivans stuck on the side of the road with cooked engines or burned-out transmissions. There are also some safety reasons for choosing a large van, including superb forward visibility and plenty of room to sit away from the airbag housing. SUVs and other vehicles are also less likely to run up over the frame and crash into the van's passenger compartment.

Handling, though, is definitely not carlike (regardless of hype to the contrary); expensive suspension modifications may be needed to produce a reasonable ride and manoeuvrability. Rear visibility is also problematic. They are susceptible to crosswinds, they wander at highway speeds, and they demand greater driving skills simply to corner safely and to park in the city. They are also not cheap, and in base form, all you get is a steel box on four wheels that is prone to roll over quicker than Fido earning his biscuit reward.

The 15-passenger vans are particularly hazardous. Often used to shuttle sports teams, church groups, and airport passengers, they are three times more likely than regular vans to roll over when carrying 10 or more passengers, according to NHTSA. This is because the van's centre of gravity shifts up and to the back unexpectedly, and excess baggage adds to this instability. Ford paid $37.5 million in a 2004 Kentucky van crash case after a Scott County jury found the automaker's 15-passenger van responsible for two deaths.

GM and Chrysler have substantially redesigned their full-sized vans within the past few years to improve both the handling and the ride, and to add important safety features like stability control, ABS, and additional airbags. Following this redesign, GM has led the Detroit pack with better-handling and smoother-riding models than those available from Ford or Chrysler.

Along with Chrysler's overpriced and underserviced Mercedes-bred rear-drive Dodge Sprinter, Ford and GM are struggling with their vans. GM has hedged its bets, however, by shoehorning the Duramax 6600 diesel engine into its large vans, making the vans less fuel-thirsty and more attractive to frugal buyers. However, this is too little, too late. Many remember the Duramax's poor past performance and are worried that the GM warranty will be worthless once the automaker goes into Chapter 11.

Chrysler's full-sized, American-built rear-drive vans are more reliable than its front-drive minivans. On one hand, this isn't saying much when you consider the expensive repair bills generated by blown transmissions and collapsed ball joints. On the other hand, the problems are well known and easily fixed.

Ford's Econoline joins GM in middle of the pack from a warranty performance standpoint. Both companies are sticking with five-year guarantees, even though they are in serious need of a seven-year powertrain warranty to restore confidence in their lineup.

GM full-sized van quality hasn't improved much over the years (though it isn't as bad as the company's recently dumped front-drive minivans) and is about equal to what Ford and Chrysler offer (except for the Not Recommended Sprinter). Some of the more-common problems shared by all three automakers: engine and drivetrain breakdowns, brake failures, premature brake and suspension/steering wearout, AC failures, electrical and computer module glitches, and both manual- and sliding-door defects.

The reason why there's such similarity in the defect trending among Asian and Detroit van builders is that they all get their key components from a small band of suppliers. And, as they cut supplier profits, quality goes down the drain. Hence, as Toyota and Honda become more skinflint in their supplier payouts, they, too, see a corresponding quality decline, evidenced by engine and transmission defects and sliding-door failures.

VAN RATINGS

Above Average

General Motors Express, Savana (2003–07)

Average

Ford Econoline Cargo Van, Club Wagon (2004–07)   General Motors Express, Savana (1999–2002)

Below Average

Ford Econoline Cargo Van, Club Wagon (1999–2003)

Ford

ECONOLINE CARGO VAN, CLUB WAGON	★★★

RATING: Average (2004–07); Below Average (1999–2003). Easily found at reasonable prices, Econolines don't possess any glaring virtues or vices; they all perform in a manner similar to that of the Chrysler and GM large vans. Overall reliability is on par with similar Chrysler and GM full-sized vans. **"Real" city/ highway fuel economy:** E-150 4.2L: 16.6/11.7 L/100 km. E-150 4.6L: 17.6/12.2 L/100 km. E-150 5.4L: 17.4/12.3 L/100 km. **Maintenance/Repair costs:** Lower than average. **Parts:** Inexpensive and not hard to find. **Extended warranty:** Not needed; invest, instead, in a thorough pre-purchase inspection. **Best alternatives:** Any GM rear-drive, full-sized van, or Dodge Ram Van. Both models are cheaper and more-easily serviced than Chrysler's 2004 and later German-bred Sprinter, a narrow Mercedes-Benz van with a 152 hp turbodiesel used mainly for commercial deliveries. Remember, Chrysler's 2003 and earlier Ram Vans have an edge over Ford and GM vans from a price, performance, and quality standpoint.

Strengths and Weaknesses

First launched in 1961 on the Falcon platform, the rear-drive Econoline has long been a fixture in the commercial delivery market, primarily because of its 4,536 kg (10,000 lb.) carrying capacity. Like Chrysler, Ford has made few changes over the last several decades, figuring that a good thing is best left alone.

The Ford Club Wagon, which is an Econoline dressed up for passenger duty, offers lots of room with capacity to spare for luggage. Nevertheless, full-sized vans have a very high floor, long panelled windows, and seats that are bolted to the floor—unlike most minivans, which feature powered middle windows and seats that stow into the floor or fold to the side.

There are a number of sound reasons for buying a used Ford Econoline: It's more reliable than any Detroit front-drive; all models are reasonably well equipped; it carries a more-refined powertrain and brakes that were phased in with the 2004s; and it has a good control and instrument layout, adequate interior room, and an acceptable ride. Negatives: It's huge and heavy with sloppy handling, similar to the Ram lineup. With earlier vehicles, excessive braking distances and harsh transmission shifting and hunting are the norm. Get used to limited second-row legroom and lots of engine, wind, and road noise. Quality control isn't the best, especially in regards to the failure-prone 6.0L diesel engine, alternators, and AC compressor.

VEHICLE HISTORY: 2004—A 4.6L V8 base engine; the 7.3L diesel is ditched for a problematic 6.0L turbocharged variant; and a new 5-speed automatic transmission is added (turbo models only) along with rear disc brakes on larger wheels. **2006**—Much-needed standard electronic stability control.

Econolines have had fewer quality-control deficiencies than Chrysler and GM, but they are merely the best of an old-tech, bad lot. Admittedly, Ford engine defects are legion, with turbocharger, high-pressure pump, oil pump, and injector malfunctions, and with EGR valve coking, when unburned deposits coat the valve and cause power loss, surging, and stalling. Electrical, fuel, and ignition systems are constantly on the fritz. The 3- and 4-speed automatic transmissions, steering and suspension components (lower steering shaft/tie rods), and brakes (calipers, pads, rotors, and torn rear caliper boots) have also come under considerable criticism.

Body fit and finish are typically below average, and have been that way for the past several decades. Still, squeaks and rattles have been notably reduced on the more-recent models. Premature rusting hasn't been a serious problem since the mid-1980s (except for rusted-out oil pans), but water leaks through the windshield and doors as well as paint delamination and peeling are quite common.

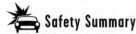

Safety Summary

All models/years: Airbag malfunctions. • Sudden acceleration when idling or when cruise control is activated. • Van rolled away while parked with emergency brake engaged. • Chronic stalling. • Electrical shorts cause fuses to blow and make brakes, turn signals, and transmissions malfunction. • Lots of complaints of road wander, vibration, and premature brake rotor warpage and pad wearout, leading to extended stopping distances and front brake lock-up. • Loss of power steering. • Exhaust fumes enter into the vehicle. • Steering tie-rod end failures. • Sticking or binding ignition lock cylinder. • Tire-tread separation; faulty valve stems cause tires to lose their air. • Windshield stress crack at base of wiper arm. • Horn doesn't work. • Wheel rubs against the torsion bar when turning left. **All models: 2001**—Flat mirrors create a large blind spot. **2002**—Engine damaged because water entered through the air intake. • Loss of power steering. • Fuel tank won't fill up completely. **2003**—Engine stalled and then exploded. • Transmission slipped out of Park into Reverse. **2004**—5.4L slow throttle response. *E-150:* **2005**—When the vehicle stalls going uphill, there are no brakes or steering to maintain control as it backs down. **2006**—Under-hood fire while vehicle was parked. • Throttle sticks. • Brake and gas pedal are mounted too close together. • Sudden stalling while cruising in traffic. • Side door fails to latch properly. **2007**—Passenger-side rear-door lock failure. *E-350:* **2005**—Assorted electrical wiring and alternator problems affect powertrain performance and dash warning lights. • Brake vacuum pump failure caused loss of brakes. • Ambulance firm complained their diesel-equipped ambulance was constantly stalling when sent out on emergency calls:

> 2005 Ford E-350 ambulance had a total engine failure while driving to a 911 call. The Ford dealership service center diagnosed an oil pump failure as the cause and replaced it under warranty. This is compliant #2 of 6. All of the 2005 Ford ambulances we purchased have suffered total engine failures from either the oil pumps or the wiring harness systems, and several have had AC problems as well. Ford is unwilling to replace these parts on the other units until they fail.

E-450: **2005**—Engine surging when foot taken off of the accelerator pedal. • Sticking throttle. • Chronic stalling. • Faulty transmission torque converter.

Secret Warranties/Internal Bulletins/Service Tips

All models: 1993–2003—Paint delamination, peeling, or fading. **1996–2000**—A rear axle whine on E-450 Super Duty with a Dana 80 can be silenced by putting in a dampened rear driveshaft. **1997–2005**—Tips for correcting a rough idle. **1997–2006**—A driveline clunk may signal that the slip yoke needs lubrication. **1997–2007**—Remedy for a brake pedal that kicks back or grabs. **1998–2003**—7.3L diesel engine turbocharger pedestal may leak oil around the exhaust back-pressure actuator; high-pressure oil pump may leak. **1998–2006**—Troubleshooting a no-crank condition. **1999–2000**—To prevent the lower rear brake caliper boots from being damaged from driving over gravel roads, Ford will install a brake caliper shield kit. **1999–2001**—Ford admits to faulty 5.4L engines with defective head gaskets. The April 1, 2002, edition of *Automotive News* says the automaker budgeted up to $4,500 (U.S.) to replace affected engines and $800 to replace the cylinder heads and head gasket. **1999–2003**—Models with the 7.3L diesel engine may have premature oil pan corrosion, or a high-pressure oil pump leak (TSB #04-4-4). **1999–2005**—Troubleshooting broken intake manifold studs. **2000–03**—Poor engine performance. **2001**—Front shaft seal leakage. • Water-pump shaft seal leakage. **2003–04**—6.0L diesel engine runs rough, loses power, or has fuel in the oil (TSB #04-9-3, issued 05/11/04). **2004–06**—TSB #06-9-7, issued 05/15/06, gives more diagnostic and repair tips for poorly performing diesel engines. • Reasons why the AC may not cool properly. **2004–07**—Full tank slow to fill. **2005**—Engine stalls when shifting into Drive or Reverse, or when coming to a stop. **2005–06**—Inadvertent transmission lockup during 1-2 shifts. **2007–08**—Extension housing seal fluid leak.

ECONOLINE CARGO VAN, CLUB WAGON PROFILE

	1999	2000	2001	2002	2003	2004	2005	2006	2007
Cost Price ($)									
Cargo Van	23,295	23,695	25,970	27,273	28,960	28,485	28,740	29,199	29,799
Club Wagon	27,395	27,795	28,195	30,045	30,046	31,120	31,375	31,899	32,400
Used Values ($)									
Cargo Van ▲	3,000	3,500	4,000	4,500	5,000	7,500	9,500	12,000	15,000
Cargo Van ▼	2,500	3,500	4,000	4,000	4,500	6,000	8,000	10,500	13,500
Club Wagon ▲	3,000	4,000	4,500	5,500	7,000	9,000	11,500	14,500	17,500
Club Wagon ▼	3,000	3,500	4,500	4,500	6,000	7,500	10,000	13,000	16,000
Reliability	2	2	2	3	3	3	3	3	3
Crash Safety (F)	4	4	4	4	4	4	4	4	—
Rollover Resistance	—	—	2	2	2	—	3	3	3

General Motors

EXPRESS, SAVANA ★★★★

RATING: Above Average (2003–07); Average (1999–2002). These rear-drive full-sized vans are about as good as the Ford Econoline and cheaper and more easily serviced than Chrysler's 2004 and later German-bred Sprinter. Nevertheless, Chrysler's 2003 and earlier Ram Vans have an edge over Ford and GM vans from a price, performance, and quality standpoint. **"Real" city/highway fuel economy:** *Express 4.3L automatic:* 16.0/11.4 L/100 km. *Express 5.0L automatic:* 16.9/12.5 L/100 km. *Express 5.7L automatic:* 17.3/11.9 L/100 km. **Maintenance/Repair costs:** Lower than average. **Parts:** Inexpensive and found everywhere. **Extended warranty:** A waste of money. **Best alternatives:** Ford Econolines and 2003 or earlier Dodge Ram Vans.

Strengths and Weaknesses

These vans are low-priced bargains because the recent increase in fuel costs drove so many buyers away. Surprisingly, even though gasoline is cheap again, used van prices have stayed in the basement. Passenger versions are usually heavily customized and can mean great savings if you don't pay top dollar for accessories you aren't likely to use.

GM's large full-sized vans come with a large array of powerful engines; multiple wheelbase configurations; a comfortable, soft ride; reasonably good transmission and brakes; plenty of interior room; and dual side-access doors. On the other hand, base models are poorly equipped, and their interior is cheap-looking and difficult to access. The automatic transmission has always been a bit clunky, brakes wear out early, and body fit and finish is bottom-drawer. As with all large vans, handling is ponderous and fuel-economy is nonexistent. No crashworthiness data is available.

The products of GM's 1996 redesign of the Chevy Van and GMC Vandura, the Express and Savana are full-sized cargo-haulers and people-movers that are only a bit better than the vans they replaced. Powered by Vortec engines and a turbocharged diesel, they are built on longer wheelbases and use a ladder-type frame, as opposed to the unit-body construction of their predecessors. This has improved ride quality somewhat, but overall performance remains unchanged. Both vans are a better choice than the average full-size van for hauling capacity, especially if you often need to carry a lot of cargo or large animals. They also out-pull the average full-sized van by a big margin.

VEHICLE HISTORY: 1999—Depowered airbags. **2001**—A powerful 8.1L V8 replaces the 7.4L. **2003**—Optional all-wheel drive, four-wheel disc brakes, a stiffer box frame, enhanced ride and handling, dual side doors that open outward, and a minor facelift. Engines and transmissions are revised, and the suspension retuned. Although the engine-gasket-challenged 200 hp engine remains the base, GM adds the GEN III V8 engines used in full-sized trucks since 1999. **2004**—Standard stability control on 15-passenger models following U.S. government charges that these vans easily roll over. **2005**—Upgraded automatic transmission components. **2006**—Addition of a Duramax 6.6L turbo diesel. **2007**—A 5.3L V8 engine becomes a standard feature on 1500 models.

Owner complaints target diesel injectors and oil cooler lines, turbochargers, and other diesel maladies. Other deficiencies: the electrical system, starter, EMC fuses, fuel pump (black and gray wires fuse together inside the fuel tank), and fuel sending unit; the catalytic converter, suspension, steering gearbox, and power-steering pump; the brake pads and rotors; the ABS sensors; the AC; the tire side walls (they split); the door hinges (they break); and paint (it flakes and delaminates).

 **Safety Summary**

All models/years: Front wheel flies off. • PCM/VCM computer module shorts from water intrusion. • Vehicle won't decelerate when gas pedal is released. • Power-steering and ABS brake failures. • Premature brake pad/rotor wear. • Broken power-seat anchor/brackets, costing $900 to repair. • Broken or weak side-door hinges. • Faulty tire valve stems leak air. • Rear shoulder belts cross too high on the torso. **All models: 2000**—Dashboard fire. • Unnecessary 4–3 downshifts. • Upper ball joint suddenly collapsed. **2001**—Under-hood fire caused by electrical short under dash on passenger side. • Delayed 2–3 transmission shifts. • Brake pedal goes to floor without stopping vehicle. • Vehicle wanders all over the road at 100 km/h. **2002**—Fire ignited at the bottom of driver's door. • Fuel leak. • 5.7L engine loses power when AC is engaged. • Cruise control won't decelerate vehicle when going downhill. • Leaking axle tube seals. • Leaking front grease seals contaminate the front inner disc brake pads, causing loss of braking effectiveness. • Door opened while vehicle was underway. **2003**—Extended stopping distance when brakes are applied; sometimes they fail to hold. • Fire ignited from a short in the right rear door-lock motor. • Horn and wiper failures. **2005**—Seatbelt on a 15-passenger van malfunctioned, and passenger had to be cut free. • Unsafe rear-view mirror design cuts peripheral vision. **2006**—Seat belt design creates a strangulation hazard for 10 of the 15 passengers. • Sudden steering loss. **2007**—Airbags failed to deploy. • Automatic transmission failure.

Secret Warranties/Internal Bulletins/Service Tips

All models/years: GM bulletins say automatic transmission clunks are "normal." • Many diesel engine failures. **All models: 1993–2002**—Paint delamination, peeling, or fading. **1994–99**—Hard starts on vehicles equipped with a 6.5L diesel engine may signal the need to replace the shut-off solenoid. **1996–99**—Engine bearing knocking on vehicles equipped with a 5.0L or 5.7L V8 may be silenced by using a special GM countermeasure kit to service the crankshaft and select-fit undersized connecting rod bearings. **1996–2000**—Poor starts, no-starts, and backfire on starting all point to the need to replace the crankshaft position sensor. **1996–2002**—Cargo door binding requires new hinge pins and bushings. **1997–2008**—Automatic transmission slips, harsh shifts, and delayed shifts. **2001**—Automatic transmission harsh shifting. • Reports of automatic transmission 2–4 band or 3–4 clutch damage. • Inaccurate fuel gauge. **2002**—Check Engine light comes on, followed by poor engine and automatic transmission performance; transmission feels like it has slipped into Neutral. • Leaking engine oil cooler lines. **2003**—Hard starts, rough idle, and intermittent engine misfiring. • Driveshaft may fracture. • Vehicle difficult to fill with fuel. **2003–04**—Suspension clunk and slap. Install a new spring insert and insulator. **2003–05**—Lack of power when the 4.3L engine is hot. **2003–06**—ABS activation at 3 kph. • Ignition key cylinder won't turn.

EXPRESS, SAVANA PROFILE

	1999	2000	2001	2002	2003	2004	2005	2006	2007
Cost Price ($)									
Savana Cargo	25,330	25,495	24,905	25,025	25,125	26,465	26,835	27,080	27,435
Express	29,155	29,330	30,885	29,105	29,215	30,000	26,780	27,080	27,670
Used Values ($)									
Savana Cargo ▲	2,000	2,500	3,000	4,000	5,000	7,000	9,500	12,500	15,000
Savana Cargo ▼	2,000	2,500	3,000	3,000	4,000	5,500	8,000	11,000	14,500
Express ▲	3,000	3,500	4,000	4,500	6,000	8,000	11,000	13,500	16,000
Express ▼	3,000	3,500	3,500	4,000	4,500	6,500	9,500	12,000	14,500
Reliability	3	4	4	4	4	4	4	4	4
Crash Safety (F)	—	—	—	—	—	—	5	5	5
Rollover Resistance	—	—	—	—	—	—	—	3	3

SPORT-UTILITY VEHICLES AND PICKUP TRUCKS

Sport-Utility Vehicles

More than 95 percent of buyers will never need four-wheel-drive capability; it gobbles gas and gets you stuck deeper and farther away from home.

"JOE" THE MECHANIC

Large SUVs—Low Prices

Although insurance premiums and fuel costs have moderated, leasing cutbacks and scarce financing continue to savage full- and mid-sized SUV sales, forcing Detroit's automakers to drop negotiated prices by thousands of dollars and causing the market to shift to downsized and "crossover" models. Automakers say reduced prices are only temporary, but independent industry sources believe lower "real" prices will continue well into the new year, due to deep discounting led by Chrysler, an oversupply of unpopular Chrysler, Ford, and GM models, and shoppers' demands for sweeter rebates and other sales incentives.

Large SUVs, like the Ford Expedition and Excursion, the Jeep Grand Cherokee, and the GM Suburban, Yukon, and Tahoe, are selling for a song; three-year-old vehicles are worth less than 50 percent of their original MSRP. Besides depreciation and steep gas prices, make sure to factor the high insurance costs and increasingly complex mechanical and electronic systems associated with these Goliaths into your purchasing decision.

Dealers are responding with $10,000–$15,000 discounts on leftover 2008 models, while used prices spiral downward to match the incentives. But some behemoths, like the Ford Excursion, GM Suburban, and full-sized Hummer, can't even be given away and, therefore, have been discontinued. Furthermore, the Ford Expedition, Lincoln Navigator and Aviator, and Mercedes M-Class are at the top of the hit list—even though Mercedes is in denial that its SUVs are in peril. In fact, no SUV larger than Honda's CR-V or Toyota's RAV4 has a secure future.

Small sport wagons, like the Ford Escape, Honda CR-V, Hyundai Tucson, Mazda Tribute, and Toyota RAV4, are down, but not by much, because they offer more-reasonable prices, better fuel economy, and easier handling than larger SUVs.

Safety

One of the main reasons buyers choose sport-utility vehicles is the safety advantages they offer. The large windshield and high seating give the driver a commanding view of the road ahead, though rear vision may be obstructed by side pillars, rear head restraints, or the spare tire hanging off the back end. As we react more slowly with age, increased visibility comes in handy (a few extra seconds of warning can make a big difference). Improvements have also been made with three-point seat belts in the front and rear, seat belt pretensioners, optional adjustable brake and accelerator pedals, four-wheel anti-lock brakes, electronic stability control, a high centre brake light, adjustable head restraints on all seatbacks, side head-protecting airbags, side-door beams, and reinforced roofs to protect occupants in rollovers.

Reliability and Quality

In the last decade, many domestic and imported SUVs were rushed to market with serious quality and performance deficiencies. Mercedes' 1997–2005 M-Class luxury sport-utilities, for example, are nowhere near as reliable as Jeep's entry-level Liberty and the SUVs produced by Asian automakers.

Chrysler, Jeep, and Ford have a long way to go to close the quality gap. Dodge's Durango has a barely acceptable reliability score. Jeep's Cherokee and Grand Cherokee have been afflicted by serious powertrain, AC, brake, and body defects, and the 2006 Jeep Commander is mediocre, at best. And don't forget the Ford Explorer, the most popular SUV ever produced. It has a terrible reputation for poor quality control and reliability, plus a plethora of safety-related factory mistakes.

GM's post-2000 SUVs are the best of Detroit's worst. Their relatively recent redesigns (the Acadia, Enclave, and Outlook) have improved overall safety and performance, but reliability is still the pits, with serious engine, transmission, and fit-and-finish defects. After three to five years of use (about when the warranty ends), buyers would be wise to get an extended warranty or dump these vehicles.

What's a "Crossover"?

Advertising hype for a tall wagon, the term describes most family-sized vehicles that incorporate unibody construction, a relatively high seating position, four-wheel drive (usually), a good amount of cargo space, and seating for at least four. Crossover models embrace a wide range of sizes and configurations, from the compact quality- and performance-challenged Dodge Caliber to the seven-passenger Buick Enclave. Some models are styled like traditional SUVs, others may look like downsized SUVs or upsized wagons (Pontiac Vibe and Toyota Matrix), and an emerging type resembles a mini-minivan (Mazda5).

SPORT-UTILITY RATINGS

Recommended

Chrysler TJ Wrangler (2003–07)

Honda CR-V (2002–07)

Above Average

Ford Escape Hybrid (2005–07)
Ford Escape/Mazda Tribute (2005–07)
Honda CR-V (1999–2001)

Hyundai Tucson (2007)
Toyota RAV4 (1999–2007)

Average

Chrysler TJ Wrangler (1999–2002)
Ford Escape/Mazda Tribute (2002–04)
General Motors Escalade, ESV, EXT,
   Denali (2001–07; 1999–2000
   with an extended warranty)

General Motors Suburban, Tahoe, Yukon, XL
   (2002–07)
Hyundai Tucson (2005–06)

Below Average

Ford Escape/Mazda Tribute (2001)

General Motors Suburban, Tahoe, Yukon, XL
   (1999–2001)

Chrysler

TJ WRANGLER ★★★★★

RATING: Recommended (2003–07); Average (1999–2002). **"Real" city/highway fuel economy:** The 5-speed manual and 6-cylinder engine give you the best fuel economy. *2.4L 4-cylinder automatic:* 15.7/12.1 L/100 km. *4.0L 6-cylinder automatic:* 16.8/11.7 L/100 km. **Maintenance/Repair costs:** Average. **Parts:** Inexpensive and not hard to find. **Extended warranty:** Only for the transmission. **Best alternatives:** Honda CR-V or Element, Hyundai Tucson, Subaru Forester, and Toyota RAV4. But remember, none of these other models can follow the Wrangler off-road.

Strengths and Weaknesses

A direct descendent of the original Jeep, the 1941 Willys MB, the Wrangler should be every off-roaders' first car. It's primitive, capable, and fun to drive. Plus the Wrangler's not a bad looker for Saturday night cruising along Yonge or Burrard, and short commutes with the 4-speed automatic are a breeze (2003 and later models).

Best choice: either an improved, second-series 2007 model for both on- and off-roading capability or a 2003–06 version equipped with the 4-speed automatic tranny for better highway performance while burning less fuel. The 2007 model's complete redesign gave it more power, more interior room, better off-road capability, and more on-road refinement. It has more standard features and handles much better than earlier versions.

You will have to take some bad with the good, however: like a rough and noisy ride; vague, imprecise steering; mediocre braking; cramped rear seating; little storage space; a canvas top that is a chore to open; plastic windows that don't stay clean for long; a high step-in; some powertrain and body shortcomings; and mediocre fuel economy.

VEHICLE HISTORY: 2000—Sport and Sahara get a more-refined, quieter 6-cylinder powerplant, along with an upgraded 5-speed manual shifter. **2003**—An optional 4-speed automatic is introduced. SE models use the Liberty's 147 hp 2.4L 4-cylinder engine, and the X, Sport, Sahara, and Rubicon versions now carry a 190 hp 4.0L inline-six powerplant. **2004**—Unlimited gets larger and longer. **2005**—A 6-speed manual transmission replaces the 5-speed. **2007**—A new 205 hp 3.8L V6 with 15 more horses than the 4.0L V6, Electronic Stability Program (ESP), electronic roll mitigation, dual-stage airbags, seat-mounted side airbags and Occupant Classification System (OCS), increased ground clearance, larger wheels and tires, enhanced Dana front and rear solid axles, Command-Trac and Rock-Trac transfer cases, new electric axle lockers, and a revamped front sway bar. Also, a stiffer frame, a 5 cm longer wheelbase, 9 cm wider track, lower spring rates, better brakes, and a retuned suspension. The larger interior gives about 12 cm more hip room and 13 cm more shoulder room, combined with additional legroom of 5 cm in front and 2.5 cm in the rear. The three-piece hardtop is also new.

Factory-related defects have always plagued these vehicles, but not as much now as before. Premature front brake wear is a frequent complaint. Owners say that the 5-speed and 6-speed manual transmissions don't shift smoothly. The 6-speed grinds when going into Reverse, or pops out of Reverse. The 5-speed constantly grinds when shifting or when in Neutral with the clutch depressed; the shifter won't come out of or go into gear, may suddenly pop out of gear, and sticks in Second gear when hot or when accelerating in First or Second; and the Fifth gear suddenly disengages. One dissatisfied owner says:

> There have now been four transmissions in my Jeep, and all have had problems with noise, shifting into and out of gear, and getting stuck in gear.

Another owner had to replace the transmission at 600 km. Watch out for transfer-case malfunctions, engine overheating, engine and transfer-case oil leaks, worn-out suspensions (ball joints, especially) and steering components, and ignition-component malfunctions.

Body welds and seams are susceptible to premature rusting, and there have been frequent complaints about peeling paint and water leaks. The worst leaks occur at the bottom of the windshield frame. An easy way to check for this is to examine the underside of the frame to see if there's excessive rust. This has consistently been a problem area for Jeeps; hence, all of the ads for aftermarket windshield frames. The good news is that you can replace the windshield frame and all of the seals relatively cheaply.

 ## Safety Summary

All years: Insurance industry figures show a much higher-than-average number of accident injury claims, aggravated by a high incidence of sudden rollovers when drivers exceed the Jeep's very low tolerance for sporty driving. • Failures that crop up repeatedly are malfunctioning airbags; fuel-tank leaks; fuel-pump failures; malfunctioning fuel gauges; sudden, unintended acceleration; chronic engine stalling when accelerating or decelerating; clutch master and slave cylinder leaks; premature brake wear; and brake failure—there have been several incidents of sudden brake loss where the pedal goes all the way to the floor with no braking effect (corrected by replacing the master cylinder). Other brake complaints include a seal leak in the power-brake booster that might cause a brake failure; the brake drum not keeping its shape; the vehicle pulling to the left when braking; the rear brakes suddenly locking up while driving in the rain and approaching a stop sign; and the vehicle going into open throttle position when brakes are applied. **1995–2003**—Manual and automatic transmission failures. **2000**—Under-hood fire. • Right rear wheel separated from vehicle. • Vehicle went into Reverse after being shifted into Drive. **2001**—Many engine-related steering column fires. • Sudden steering lock-up. • Camshaft sensor binding and breaking, causing vehicle to stall. • Broken rear axle seal. • Manual tranny pops out of Third gear and grinds as the clutch is let out. • Premature wearout of the rear brake pads. **2003**—Driveshaft fell out while driving. • Vehicle slips into Neutral from Drive. • Sudden axle and steering failure. • Seat belts unlatch too easily. **2004**—Sudden stalling caused by defective crankshaft position sensor. • Left-front axle seal leak. • Gas-line leaks. • Seized front brakes. • Defective steering stabilizer responsible for steering shudder. **2004–05**—Partial loss of control when passing over bumps or railroad tracks. **2005**—Defective steering stabilizer responsible for steering shudder. • Carpet causes accelerator pedal to stick. **2006**—Faulty 6-speed manual transmission:

> The clutch rod comes out of the floor board and attaches to the clutch pedal with a clip/attachment that bolts into the clutch pedal. The problem here is, as part of their new design, the clip or attachment piece can break very easily and disable your Jeep.

• Excessive front shimmy. • Inoperative instrument cluster. • Windshield cracks. **2007**—ABS brakes may suddenly lock up while underway.

Secret Warranties/Internal Bulletins/Service Tips

1997–2005—Tips on repairing a leak in the engine rear main oil seal. **1997–2006**—Tips on plugging door leaks. **1999–2000**—An interior roof sag and water accumulation can be corrected through the installation of foam blocks. **1999–2001**—Tips for correcting windshield/cowl water leaks. **1999–2004**—A rough idle may require the installation of a fuel-injector insulator sleeve. **2001–05**—If the vehicle tends to drift, install upgraded ball joints. **2003**—Manual transmission may have defective Third gear weld. • 4.0L engine crankshaft burr. • Faulty fuel-injector wiring connections. **2003–04**—Automatic transmission leaks. **2003–06**—Drivebelt noise countermeasures. **2005**—Manual 6-speed won't stay in gear. **2007**—Differential squealing. **2007–08**—Oil seepage at front of engine. • No-crank, no-start due to a defective wireless control module. • Water leaks onto dash and console areas. • A squeaking clutch calls for a clutch disc replacement. • Measures to silence windshield wind noise.

TJ WRANGLER PROFILE

	1999	2000	2001	2002	2003	2004	2005	2006	2007
Cost Price ($)									
TJ, SE	19,205	19,445	20,355	21,000	21,340	21,995	22,910	23,230	19,995
Sahara	25,305	26,020	29,285	28,120	28,715	29,950	—	—	26,450
TJ Rubicon	—	—	—	—	29,425	30,420	31,790	32,210	28,150
Unl. Rubicon	—	—	—	—	—	—	33,250	33,160	29,895
Used Values ($)									
TJ, SE ▲	3,500	4,000	4,500	5,000	5,500	7,000	8,000	10,500	11,000
TJ, SE ▼	3,500	4,000	4,000	4,500	5,000	6,000	7,000	9,000	9,500
Sahara ▲	4,000	4,500	5,000	5,500	7,000	9,000	—	—	15,000
Sahara ▼	4,000	4,500	4,500	5,000	5,500	7,500	—	—	13,500
TJ Rubicon ▲	—	—	—	—	7,500	9,500	10,500	12,500	16,500
TJ Rubicon ▼	—	—	—	—	6,500	8,000	9,000	11,000	15,000
Unl. Rubicon ▲	—	—	—	—	—	—	11,500	14,500	17,500
Unl. Rubicon ▼	—	—	—	—	—	—	10,000	13,000	16,000
Reliability	3	3	3	4	4	4	4	4	4
Crash Safety (F)	4	4	4	4	4	4	4	4	5
IIHS Side	2	2	2	2	2	2	2	2	—
Offset	3	3	3	3	3	3	3	3	—
Rollover Resistance	—	—	3	3	3	—	4	4	4

Ford/Mazda

ESCAPE, TRIBUTE, ESCAPE HYBRID ★★★★

RATING: *Escape, Tribute:* Above Average (2005–07); Average (2002–04); Below Average (2001). One of the most improved vehicles in Ford's lineup, but its highway performance cannot match its rivals'. *Escape Hybrid:* Above Average (2005–07). **"Real" city/highway fuel economy:** *2.3L 4-cylinder:* 9.7/7.3 L/100 km. *2.3L Hybrid:* 6.6/7.0 L/100 km (remember, hybrids are more economical in the city). *3.0L V6:* 13.3/9.9 L/100 km. **Maintenance/Repair costs:** Average. **Parts:** Few complaints so far. **Extended warranty:** Only for the transmission. **Best alternatives:** The Honda CR-V, Hyundai Tucson, Jeep Wrangler, Mitsubishi Outlander, Nissan Xterra, Pontiac Vibe, and Toyota RAV4 or Matrix.

Strengths and Weaknesses

Launched as 2001 models, both the Escape and Tribute combine a carlike ride and handling—thanks to an independent rear suspension and front MacPherson struts—with the ability to drive in the snow and carry up to five passengers and their luggage. Neither vehicle is an upsized car or a downsized truck—they're four-doors that sip fuel, look like sport-utilities, and drive like sedans. Improvements on 2005 model-year vehicles correct the quality, power, and performance deficiencies of previous models. Before then, the Escape/Tribute promised a lot but delivered a low-quality SUV that would frequently stall or suddenly accelerate at any time.

VEHICLE HISTORY: *Escape/Tribute:* **2005**—A quieter engine and 26 more horses with the 2.3L Duratec 4-banger. The V6 engine uses upgraded engine mounts and computers to smooth out the idle and improve throttle response. Safety is also enhanced with dual-stage airbags, head restraints and three-point safety belts for all seats, side curtain airbags, "smart" seat sensors, and larger-diameter four-wheel disc and anti-lock brakes. The front structure is reinforced to better protect occupants in offset frontal crashes. Other enhancements include a fully automatic 4×4 system; front shocks that are larger in diameter; a new stabilizer system; a floor-mounted shifter; new headlights, foglights, grille, and front and rear ends; different gauges; upgraded seat cushions; more storage space; additional sound-absorbing materials (though it still lets in excessive wind noise); and alloy wheels. *Escape Hybrid:* **2005**—This gasoline-electric hybrid is equipped with a 2.3L 4-cylinder engine, a 65 kW electric motor, and a 28 kW generator. It has off-road and towing capability, plus acceleration comparable to the Escape's 200 hp V6 engine.

Most owner complaints target powertrain reliability, like chronic stalling and hard starts; engine oil leaks (engine crankshaft out of spec); automatic transmission gear-hunting; loss of Reverse gear; transmission fluid leaks; frequent short circuits; a cruise control that turns itself off; faulty side windows; front wheels that let ice form, causing excessive vibrations; lots of squeaks, rattles, and wind noise; poor fit and finish; and engine hesitation when the AC is engaged.

 ## Safety Summary

Escape/Tribute: **2001**—Fuel leakage around fuel injectors. • Fuel line clip fails, causing loss of power, and fuel sprays onto hot engine. • Vehicle may roll over while driving 25–40 km/h. • CV joints and front axle fall off vehicle. • Automatic transmission pops out of Drive into Neutral while underway. • When going downhill, vehicle often suddenly loses all electrical power and shuts down on the highway with loss of steering and brake assist (faulty EGR valve suspected as the cause of the problem). • Chronic electrical problems. • Left rear wheel suddenly locks up, pulling vehicle into traffic. • Vehicle pulls randomly to the right or left when steering wheel is let go. • Steering is too tight. • Sometimes steering tugs a bit to one side and then freezes. • Rear seats don't lock properly. • Car seatback collapses in collision. • Left rear seat belt frequently jams. **2001–04**—Stalling; sudden, unintended acceleration; airbag and brake malfunctions; and frequent transmission replacements are major problems. **2002**—Gas-tank filler pipe allows fuel to spill out when refuelling. **2002–04**—Cruise control won't deactivate. • Rear window explodes. • Nauseating mildew smell from AC. **2003**—Fire ignites due to faulty fuel injectors. • Throttle cable jams. • Poor starting. • Rainwater leaks at the driver window pillar area, shorting out the electrical system. **2004**—Headlights go on and off. **2005**—Accelerator sticks. • Faulty transmission pump shaft causes vehicle to jump out of gear and not shift. • Excessive steering play. • Constant pulling to the left when underway. • Vehicle nosedives when stopping, due to poorly calibrated suspension. • Passenger-door latch failure causes door to fly open. • Airbag disables when an average-sized passenger occupies the front seat. • Sunroof explodes. • Foglights afflicted with stress cracks. **2006**—Driver's window suddenly shatters. • Brakes fail. **2006–07**—Liftgate fails:

> I was knocked out and pinned by the rear hatch door of our 2006 Ford Escape. I opened the rear hatch and leaned in to remove some items from rear of the Ford Escape and the hatch came slamming down, hitting me in the back of the head and rendering me unconscious (I am not sure as to how long). I came to face-first inside the Ford Escape with the door pinning me down and my feet hanging out the rear.

2007—Fire ignites in the trunk area. • In one incident, driver-side airbag and seat belt failed in a head-on collision. • Passenger-side airbag is disabled even though a small adult occupies the seat. • All four wheels suddenly lock up while the vehicle is underway. • Gas smell permeates the interior. • Excessive Continental tire vibration. *Escape Hybrid:* **2005**—Sudden shutdown while underway, allegedly due to a defective water pump. • Shifter gets stuck in Park. **2005–06**—Loss of power:

> As fleet manager, I have experienced engine failure on all three 2006 Ford Escape Hybrid vehicles. During each failure, the main engine shuts down and the vehicle goes to straight electrical power, which could cause a wreck in situations where a rapid drop in speed could cause an accident. The failure has happened on all three hybrids

at about 15,000 miles [24,000 km] and now again at 36,000 miles [58,000 km]. The dealership replaces the water pump that supplies coolant to the electric motor after each failure. I feel that this situation should be reported due to the fact that I researched *Edmunds.com* and this problem is well documented in their CarSpace automotive [forums]. Ford needs to re-engineer this system.

2005–07—Loss of brakes and steering. **2006**—Fuel tank slow to fill; frequent pump shut-offs.

Secret Warranties/Internal Bulletins/Service Tips

All models/years: Engine hydromount insulator and rear driveshaft replacement. • No forward transmission engagement (yes, the forward clutch piston, the cause of so many Windstar and Taurus/Sable failures, once again rears its ugly head). • Rear axle pinion seal leak. • Driveline grinding and clicking. • Possible leak in the transmission converter housing near the cooler line. • Intermittent loss of First and Second gears. • Manual transmission gear shifter buzz or rattle in Third or Fourth gear is being investigated by Ford technicians. • Possible causes for a lit malfunction indicator light (MIL). • EGR valve failures. • Fuel-pump whine heard through speakers (a Ford problem since 1990). • Vehicles with 3.0L engines may show a false Low Coolant condition. • ABS light may stay lit. • AC temperature-control knob may be hard to turn or adjust. **All models: 2001–02**—Harsh, delayed upshifts • Defective door latches. • Power-steering leaks. **2001–03**—3.0L engine stalling remedy. **2001–04**—Engine misfire troubleshooting tips. • Correction for a sagging rear headliner. **2001–05**—Diagnostic and repair tips for an unstable idle, transmission shuddering, and steering pull and drifting. • Poor shifting in cold weather; install a Cooler Bypass Kit. • Slow-to-retract seat belts. **2001–06**—3.0L engine ticking noise. • Driveline whine. **2001–07**—Heater core leakage. **2002**—Coolant, oil leakage from engine cylinder head area. • Defective Duratec engines. • Brake squealing. • Wheels make a clicking sound. **2003**—Automatic transmission shudder and whine. • Powertrain throttle body service replacement. • Front wheel bearing noise. • Rear shock leak and noise. **2003–04**—False activation of Parking Assist. ("Stop, there's something behind you! Just kidding.") You know what's most worrisome? Ford says this device may be operating as it should. **2003–06**—Inoperative AC; compressor leakage. **2003–08**—Remedy for excessive wheel/tire vibration. **2005**—Engine overheating. • Troubleshooting engine hesitation, miss. • An engine oil leak from the oil dipstick or front/rear crankshaft seals can be fixed by installing a Heated PCV Kit. • Rear brake noise. **2005–06**—Hard starts may require a recalibrated PCM; the half-hour labour charge is covered by the emissions warranty, says TSB #05-26-1. • Excessive steering vibration likely caused by faulty Continental tires, which will be replaced under an extended warranty. **2005–08**—Engine stalling when vehicle is put in gear, likely caused by excessive torque converter wear.

ESCAPE, TRIBUTE, ESCAPE HYBRID PROFILE

	2001	2002	2003	2004	2005	2006	2007
Cost Price ($)							
XLS 4×2	22,895	21,510	21,595	21,895	22,795	23,000	23,000
XLS 4×4	24,795	24,190	30,300	27,825	28,125	28,399	28,399
Tribute 4×2	22,150	22,415	22,790	22,790	24,495	24,595	23,295
Tribute 4×4	24,800	25,065	25,575	25,445	27,295	27,395	26,990
Hybrid 4×2	—	—	—	—	33,195	33,599	33,600
Hybrid 4×4	—	—	—	—	35,925	36,399	36,399
Used Values ($)							
XLS 4×2 ▲	3,500	4,000	4,500	5,500	6,500	8,000	10,000
XLS 4×2 ▼	3,500	3,500	4,500	4,500	5,500	6,500	8,500
XLS 4×4 ▲	4,500	5,000	6,000	7,500	8,500	11,000	13,000
XLS 4×4 ▼	4,000	4,500	5,500	6,500	7,500	9,500	11,500
Tribute 4×2 ▲	4,000	4,500	5,000	6,000	7,500	10,000	13,000
Tribute 4×2 ▼	3,500	4,000	4,500	5,500	6,000	8,500	12,000
Tribute 4×4 ▲	5,500	6,500	7,500	8,500	10,000	12,000	15,000
Tribute 4×4 ▼	4,500	5,500	6,500	7,500	9,000	10,500	13,500
Hybrid 4×2 ▲	—	—	—	—	10,000	14,000	17,000
Hybrid 4×2 ▼	—	—	—	—	8,500	12,500	15,000
Hybrid 4×4 ▲	—	—	—	—	11,000	15,500	19,000
Hybrid 4×4 ▼	—	—	—	—	9,500	14,000	17,500
Reliability	2	2	2	2	2	3	4
Crash Safety (F)	5	5	5	5	4	4	4
Side	5	5	5	5	5	5	5
Offset	2	2	2	2	3	3	3
Rollover Resistance	3	3	3	—	3	3	3

General Motors

ESCALADE, ESV, EXT, DENALI, SUBURBAN, TAHOE, YUKON, XL ★★★

RATING: *Escalade, ESV, EXT, Denali:* Average (2001–07); Average with an extended warranty (1999–2000). *Suburban, Tahoe, Yukon, XL:* Average (2002–07); Below Average (1999–2001). These are brawny, large SUVs for buyers who lack imagination, or for rock stars and politicians with money to burn (unfortunately, with politicians, it's *our* money). **"Real" city/highway fuel economy:** *Tahoe and Yukon 4.8L, with or without 4×4: 16.9/12.7 L/100 km. Tahoe, Suburban, Yukon,*

Yukon Denali, and Yukon XL 5.3L 4×4: 17.1/12.6 L/100 km; *6.0L:* 17.3/12.5 L/100 km. **Maintenance/Repair costs:** Higher than average. The early Suburban's many mechanical and body deficiencies boost its upkeep costs. One saving grace, however, is that it can be serviced practically anywhere. **Parts:** Good supply of inexpensive parts. **Extended warranty:** An extended warranty is a good idea, but it isn't critical. **Best alternatives:** Choose a 2007 GMC Acadia or Saturn Outlook, or an identical 2008 Buick Enclave. If you want to stay with the Tahoe trio, go for the 2007 models, which offer substantial interior and performance upgrades. If you're looking for a cheaper version, opt for the 2005s, which sell for about $13,000 (original price: $45,615). Try to find a Suburban with the 7.4L V8 engine—the 5.7L is barely adequate for this behemoth. Don't become mesmerized by a luxury nameplate on a practically identical model. For example, a 2002 Cadillac Escalade originally retailed for $72,700, or $8,000 more than a Yukon Denali 4×4, but there's only a few thousand dollars separating the two vehicles' resale values today. Alternatively, a full-sized van or extended minivan may be a better choice if off-road capability isn't a priority. If size isn't your primary concern, look to other, more-reliable Asian SUVs that are less costly to operate.

Strengths and Weaknesses

The GMC Yukon and Denali and the Cadillac Escalade share the basic Tahoe/Suburban design but differ in styling, options, and price. Although these models are some of GM's best performing large SUVs, they can't match the Japanese competition in overall reliability and quality control. Plus, over $47,650 (2009 Tahoe 4×2) for the cheapest model in this series is way too much. Used models at about half that price, perhaps. New? You've gotta be kidding—or a former CEO of Nortel.

Don't sell these models short, however. They have a lot to offer, like a good variety of competent engines that are great for trailering, standard stability control, a fuel-saving cylinder-deactivation feature, a lavishly appointed interior, a good selection of instruments and controls, a large and comfortable cabin that adds passenger and cargo space (with the redesigned 2007s), high ground clearance, a rattle-resistant body, and slow depreciation. The Suburban and Yukon XL are the largest heavy-hitters of this group, and they actually acquit themselves quite well, with reasonably predictable handling and more than enough power for most driving needs.

But there is a downside: These vehicles lose value quickly, and the 4-speed automatic transmission wastes fuel and hinders powertrain performance. A high step-up takes some acrobatics, the wide turning circle complicates parking, and braking is barely acceptable. Furthermore, get ready for bizarre electrical short circuits, biodegradable fuel pumps, premature brake wear, excessive suspension and steering vibrations, vague steering, a suspension that provides a too-compliant, wandering ride, and excessive road and engine noise.

VEHICLE HISTORY: The GMC Yukon 4×4 (and its twin, the Tahoe) came on the scene in 1992 when GMC gave the Jimmy name to its smaller sport-utility wagon line and rebadged the big one as the Tahoe/Yukon. **1995**—Blazers become Tahoes, and a four-door version with standard driver-side airbags is added. **2000**—Wider and taller vehicles, the Tahoe and Yukon adopt a new V8 engine, front side airbags, and a seating capacity that grows from six to nine passengers. The familiar two-door version is dropped. **2001**—The 6.0L V8 gains 20 hp. A 340 hp 8.1L V8 for the Suburban 2500. The upscale Yukon Denali (the Cadillac Escalade's big brother) moves to GM's new full-sized platform. **2002**—More standard features, such as AC, power windows, power front seats, heated power mirrors, and rear climate controls. **2003**—An anti-skid system, four-wheel steering, and adjustable pedals. **2005**—The StabiliTrak anti-skid system becomes standard for all Tahoe and 1500 models, and swing-out rear cargo doors are gone. **2006**—No more Quadrastar; Yukons get a 5.3L V8 that uses gasoline and ethanol. Standard stability control. An Active Fuel Management cylinder shutoff system saves gas while cruising. **2007**—More power (the 5.3L V8 comes with 320 hp versus 295 hp), new styling, a larger interior, and additional features like improved second-row seats, a revised navigation system, a power liftgate, and a rear obstacle-detection feature. These models provide more-agile handling, much better steering and braking responses, and a more-comfortable and controlled ride.

Pre-2000 models are set on GM's C/K truck platform and have been available with a variety of V8s over the years. The best choice, though, is the 5.7L gas engine mated to an electronic 4-speed automatic. This matchup provides gobs of torque at low rpm, making these part-time 4×4s great for towing, stump pulling, or mountain climbing.

Except for the Denali's 6-speed automatic, transmission alternatives are limited to your choice of 4-speeds: the manual or the automatic. Standard-equipment hubs must be locked manually before shifting into 4×4 on early models. The diesel provides a good compromise between power and economy, although it has been plagued by malfunctions for decades and has never been the equal of the Cummins used by Chrysler.

As far as highway performance is concerned, these are the best SUVs sold by the Detroit automakers…ho-hum. Overall reliability improved with the 2007 redesign—then it nosedived, with drivetrain, brakes, electrical system, and fit and finish cited as the worst offenders. There have been lots of complaints relative to poor driveability and factory-related defects that include excessive wander and vibration, hesitation when accelerating, transmission failures, wheel bearings wearing out after only a year's use, and incredibly loud, squeaking brakes. Other complaints pertain to the premature replacement of brake rotors, AC squealing, and electrical, fuel, and exhaust system malfunctions. Body assembly and paint application is below standard.

Suburban, Yukon XL

Although it's classed as a full-sized SUV, the Suburban is really a combination of a station wagon, a van, and a pickup. It can carry nine passengers, tow just about anything, and go anywhere with optional 4×4.

These vehicles didn't change much until the launch of the 2000 models. Chevrolet restyled the Suburban by setting it on the Silverado/Tahoe/Yukon platform and using generic parts from the same parts bin. With the changeover, GMC's Suburban name was swapped for the Yukon XL, while the Chevrolet division soldiered on, keeping the Suburban name alive.

The Suburban and Yukon XL are GM's largest sport-utilities: 37.3 cm (14.7 in.) longer than the Ford Expedition but 18.8 cm (7.4 in.) shorter than the Excursion. Handling improves considerably, but fuel economy remains atrocious. Improvements include a wider and taller body; new 5.3L and 6.0L V8 engines that replace the 5.7L and 7.4L engines, and a turbocharged diesel V8; an automatic transmission with tow/haul mode for smoother shifting; standard front side airbags; and four-wheel disc brakes. Rear leaf springs have been replaced by rear coil springs.

Cadillac Escalade

This is GM's pop culture party wagon, favoured by rappers and politicos. Cadillac's first truck, the 1999 Escalade 4×4, was nothing more than a warmed-over GMC Yukon Denali covered with ugly, poorly designed side cladding in an effort to disguise its parentage. The redesigned 2002 Escalade got many improvements, including an EXT version (a Suburban/Avalanche clone with additional luxury features), a 6.0L V8, and a more-refined AWD system.

VEHICLE HISTORY: 2003—A longer ESV and Escalade EXT, an all-dressed version of the Chevrolet Avalanche SUV/pickup truck. Other changes include standard power-adjustable gas and brake pedals and second-row bucket seats for the wagons. **2004**—A tire-pressure monitor, trailering package, and satellite radio are added. A new Platinum Edition offers a standard navigation system and 20-inch wheels. **2005**—An improved cooling system, and upgraded interior trim and gauges. **2006**—Standard electronic stability control.

Safety Summary

All models/years: This SUV will wander and will require constant steering corrections, particularly when buffeted by crosswinds. • Airbags frequently fail to deploy, or deploy when they shouldn't, causing severe trauma. • Braking is terrible—one of the worst in the sport-utility class (100–0 km/h: 50 m). • Sudden, unintended acceleration. • Engine head gasket and exhaust manifold, transmission, steering, ABS brake and brake rotor and pad, tire, and door lock failures. • Vehicle vibrates excessively and jerks to one side when braking. • Seat belt tightens progressively; in one incident, a child had to be cut free from a locked-up seat belt. • Gas tank leaks fuel. • Fuel pumps often need replacing. • Gas fumes permeate the interior. • Rear liftgate window explodes. • Chronic electrical failures. **All models: 2003–07**—Airbags fail to deploy in rollovers or in high-speed frontal collisions, and OnStar fails to activate. *Tahoe, Yukon:* **2001**—Erratic shifting, slipping, jerking, and clunking. **2002**—Loose steering feels unstable, causes vehicle to wander. • Faulty transmission; delayed shifts. **2003**—Faulty steering linkage. • Vehicle can be shifted out of Park without pressing the brake pedal. • Rear passenger doors don't lock properly. **2005**—Overheated fuel-pump wiring. • Wheels intermittently lock up while driving. • Transmission slips from Drive to Neutral. **2006**—Driver's seatback suddenly collapses. • Tread of Goodyear Eagle LS tire splits. **2007**—Automatic transmission failure. • Transmission slips when accelerating after morning start-up. • Brake rotors quickly become deeply grooved. • Auto Start feature doesn't work properly. • Incorrect speedometer. • Instrument panel cannot be read during the day. • Faulty wheel bearings. • Heated seats don't work. • Wipers start on their own (defective wiper module). • Car locks itself, and liftgate opens on its own:

> The electric rear liftgate opens while driving 50 mph [80 km/h]. The failure also occurs while the vehicle is parked. The liftgate opens just enough so that all of the doors continuously lock and unlock and the interior lights illuminate.

• Premature tire wear ("feathering"). *Yukon:* **2005**—Instrument panel gives bizarre readings or simply goes out when vehicle is started. • Chronic stalling. • Headlight fuse burns out constantly. • Spare-tire security device doesn't work as described in manual. *Suburban, Yukon XL:* **2001**—Total electrical shutdown. • Simultaneous failure of steering and brakes. **2002**—Dash lights reflect into mirror and are too bright. • Gas tank hard to refuel, causes premature shutoff. **2003**—Vehicle lunges forward when stopped. • Sudden brake loss. • Premature tie-rod wearout. • Steering shaft failure and differential leaking. • Vehicle registers no gas when the tank is full. • Cab reverberation causes ear pain (not a problem with later models). **2004**—Vehicle fails to accelerate when merging into traffic. • Sharp pull to the right when accelerating, and then vehicle snaps to the left when foot is taken off the accelerator. • Excessive on-road vibration at 110 km/h; vehicle becomes very unstable. • Defroster doesn't clear entire windshield and stops working intermittently. • When using the turn signal, the flashers are activated. • When accelerating from a stop, transmission jumps into gear after a long delay. • Complete transmission replacement followed by chronic electrical system failures. • While driving, tailgate window falls inward. • Inoperative emergency brake. *Suburban:* **2005**—Vehicle rolls backward when parked on a hill. • Sudden brake loss. *Yukon XL:* **2005**—Frequent no-starts. • Transmission shifts harshly when put into Reverse, or is slow to engage Drive. • StabiliTrak fails to activate. • Driver's seat moves on its own; inoperative seat memory. • Rear heater inoperative. *Escalade:* **2006–07**—LED tail lights are annoyingly distracting. **2007**—Inadvertent side airbag deployment. • Hesitation when accelerating. • Retractable steps don't work.

Secret Warranties/Internal Bulletins/Service Tips

All models: 2000–04—Remedies for inoperative power windows. **2000–06**—If the steering column makes a clunking noise, it may signal the need to change the upper intermediate steering-shaft assembly. **2001**—Fuel-tank leakage. • Harsh shifts. • 2–4 band or 3–4 clutch damage. • Rear heater puts out insufficient heat. • Carpet may be wet or have a musty odour. **2004–06**—Automatic transmission shudder due to water intrusion. *Tahoe, Yukon, Escalade:* **1999–2004**—Transmission failure caused by debris in the 2–3 shift solenoid bleed orifice. **2000–03**—Excessive engine noise. **2003–04**—Inoperative AWD. • Noisy, inoperative power windows. **2004–07**—Poor AC performance. *Tahoe, Yukon:* **1999–2004**—Paint delamination, peeling, or fading. **1999–2005**—No Reverse, Second, or Fourth gear may be caused by a defective reaction sun gear. *Suburban, Yukon XL:* **2000–05**—Tips on silencing a differential whine are found in TSB #03-04-17-001E. **2002–03**—Second-row footwell carpet may be wet with dirty water. (TSB #03-08-57-001; May 2003). **2002–04**—Suspension clunk, slap. Replace the spring insert and insulator. **2002–06**—Discoloured cargo covers or body cladding (seen as a chalky colour) will be corrected under a secret warranty. **2003**—Harsh automatic transmission 1–2 shifting, slipping caused by a faulty pressure control solenoid (TSB #03-07-30-020; May 2003). **2003–05**—Faulty AC and audio (replace RSA module). • Front suspension rattle, squeak. *Escalade:* **2006–07**—A Low Oil level indicator light or a visible oil leak may signal the need to reseal the oil-pressure sensor. **2007**—Liftgate malfunctions. • Wind noise from the rear liftgate area. • Inoperative power-assisted running boards. • Steering gear fluid leaks. • Water leak guide. • Silencing buzz, rattles from the instrument panel. • High-pitched whistle heard while driving. • Driver-seat squeak or creak. • Squeak, itching noise heard from the upper door area (replace the roof-drip weather stripping). • Rear suspension rubbing, clunking noise. • Inoperative keyless entry feature. • Front-bumper paint peeling. **2007–08**—Great effort to close hood. • Buzz, rattle heard from the front fender area when accelerating.

ESCALADE, SUBURBAN, TAHOE, YUKON PROFILE

	1999	2000	2001	2002	2003	2004	2005	2006	2007
Cost Price ($)									
Escalade	63,055	63,805	63,805	72,700	74,970	70,675	71,405	71,805	71,730
Suburban	34,620	34,620	37,905	45,875	46,670	46,680	49,820	47,000	46,935
Tahoe, Yukon	31,555	33,305	31,715	42,680	42,530	44,105	45,615	42,795	45,455
4×4	34,555	36,715	35,010	46,895	50,385	42,530	48,870	47,785	47,175
Yukon XL	—	34,620	35,760	46,895	47,290	44,720	50,415	47,665	47,595
Used Values ($)									
Escalade ▲	6,000	8,500	10,500	14,000	18,000	22,000	25,000	32,000	40,000
Escalade ▼	5,000	7,000	9,000	12,000	16,000	20,000	23,000	30,000	38,000
Suburban ▲	4,000	5,500	7,000	8,500	11,000	14,000	16,000	21,500	27,000
Suburban ▼	3,000	4,500	6,000	7,500	9,500	12,500	14,500	20,500	25,000
Tahoe, Yukon ▲	3,500	4,000	5,000	6,000	7,500	10,500	13,000	17,500	23,000
Tahoe, Yukon ▼	3,000	4,000	4,500	5,500	6,000	9,000	11,500	16,000	21,000

4×4 ▲	5,500	6,500	8,500	9,500	11,500	13,000	15,000	19,000	25,000
4×4 ▼	4,500	5,500	7,000	8,000	10,500	11,500	13,500	17,000	23,000
Yukon XL ▲	—	7,500	8,000	9,500	10,500	13,000	15,500	20,500	26,000
Yukon XL ▼	—	6,500	7,500	8,500	9,000	11,000	14,000	18,500	24,000
Reliability									
Tahoe, Yukon	3	3	3	3	3	3	3	4	2
Suburban, Yukon XL	3	3	3	3	3	3	3	4	2
Crash Safety (F)									
Suburban, Yukon XL	4	—	4	4	4	4	4	4	5
Denali 4d	—	4	—	—	—	—	—	—	—
Tahoe/Yukon	4	4	3	3	4	4	4	4	5
Escalade	4	4	—	3	4	4	4	4	5
Rollover Resistance									
Escalade	—	—	—	3	3	—	3	3	3

Honda

CR-V ★★★★★

RATING: Recommended (2002–07); Above Average (1999–2001). Get an upgraded second-series 2002, or a 2007 model, if you can find one. Take solace in knowing that, even if you pay too much, you can drive this bantam 4×4 until you outgrow it and then trade it in for almost as much as you paid originally. **"Real" city/ highway fuel economy:** 10.9/8.9 L/100 km. **Maintenance/Repair costs:** Well below average; easily repaired at independent garages. **Parts:** Parts are easily found and reasonably priced (they come mostly from the Civic parts bin). **Extended warranty:** Honda's impressive quality control makes an extended warranty unnecessary. **Best alternatives:** Good second choices are the Hyundai Tucson or Santa Fe, Subaru Forester, and Toyota RAV4.

Strengths and Weaknesses

Combining sport-utility styling with minivan versatility, this SUV is essentially a restyled Civic with 4×4 capability added. After its '97 launch, the car changed little until the revamped 2002 came out. The small power boost and improved chassis added in 2002 give additional interior space and provide improved functionality. The CR-V's Civic-based platform incorporates a four-wheel independent suspension that shortens the nose and frees up more rear cargo room. The base 160 hp 2.4L I-VTEC 4-cylinder engine is offered with either a 5-speed manual or a 4-speed automatic transmission (through the 2004 models). The 2002–05 versions don't look that different from their predecessors, though they are a bit longer, wider, and higher. The interior, however, underwent a major change, with more space for both passengers and cargo, and more user-friendly features and controls.

Owners laud the CRV's many standard features; impressive steering and handling, particularly around town; easy front entry and exit; top-quality fit and finish; comfortable seating with lots of passenger room; innovative use of storage space; easily storable flip-folding seats; plastic cargo floor panel *cum* picnic table; fair fuel economy; and superior reliability.

Some negatives: Harsh shifting on the 1997–99 models, and high-rev shifting, slipping, pulsing, and surging on the 2000 version. The 1999–2001 CR-Vs also have a history of engine failures caused by defective cylinder heads. Other reported problems include minor body trim defects, premature front brake wear and vibrations, driveshaft popping noises, accessories that malfunction (particularly the sound system and AC), and electrical glitches.

There are some performance deficiencies, as well: Acceleration is somewhat compromised on vehicles equipped with an automatic transmission, though the 2005 4-beater rivals many V6 competitors; no low-range gearing for off-roading; a long history of severe steering pull to the right when accelerating ("torque steer"); jittery ride on less-than-perfect roadways; excessive engine and road noise; 2005 redesign reduces front legroom slightly; on some models, the rear cargo door opens to the street, rather than the curb; and 1999–2001 models may be tippy in a side impact, according to NHTSA crash results. Earlier models have a Marginal IIHS offset crash rating, and head restraints scored poorly. Unlike the Toyota RAV4, there's no third-row seat. Fuel economy is okay, but nowhere near Honda's or Transport Canada's overly optimistic figures.

VEHICLE HISTORY: 1999—Picks up 20 more horses and an Overdrive On-Off switch. **2001**—Standard-issue ABS and user-friendly child-seat tether anchors added to the EX and SE. **2002**—Restyled and given more power, interior room, and features, like a side-hinged tailgate and new interior panels. **2004**—A front-passenger power door lock switch. **2005**—Standard side curtain airbags, skid control, and ABS; an upgraded 5-speed automatic transmission; and minor styling changes. **2007**—A new platform borrowed from the Civic, and a restyled interior and exterior that includes a new swing-up tailgate and a hiding spot underneath the cargo floor for the spare tire. These changes make the car wider and shorter than the previous year's model and enhance ride and handling, especially in turns. Cargo is also easier to load and unload; however, the spare tire is more difficult to access with a full load.

 ## Safety Summary

All years: Sudden acceleration. • Chronic stalling. • ABS lock-up. • Bridgestone tire blowouts. **2000**—Bumper assembly catches fire. • Vehicle rolled over; A-pillar collapsed and killed driver. • Automatic transmission takes an inordinate amount of time to go into First gear and doesn't hold car when stopped in traffic on an incline. • Unacceptable slippage, poor traction of Bridgestone tires on wet pavement. • Excessive shimmying and front suspension vibration when accelerating. • Chronic steering-wheel vibrations. **2001**—Short drivers find airbags point toward their faces. • Rear wheel lock-up while turning caused head-on collision (clutch failure suspected). • Driver's seatback collapsed in rear-ender. • Seat belt tightens uncomfortably. **2002**—Vehicle hesitates when accelerating, or surges and then stalls. **2002–03**—Hood suddenly flies open while cruising. **2003**—Driver-side and rear centre seat belts unbuckled when car was rear-ended. **2003–07**—Airbags fail to deploy, or deploy for no reason. **2004**—Wheel freezes while making a turn. • Stress fractures in windshield. • Wheel lug bolt breaks off. • Removable picnic table caused serious head injuries in a rollover accident. • Gas spews out of filler tube when refuelling. • Water can enter the fuel tank from gas-cap vent. • No seat belt extender available. **2004–05**—Many reports of engine fires after oil has been changed. **2004–06**—Gas pedal sticks. **2005–06**—Dozens of complaints that the vehicle pulls sharply to the right when accelerating:

> Purchased 2005 Honda CR-V for teenaged daughter in December 2004. Her mother drove the car for the first time on March 5, 2005, and was unfamiliar with the severe torque steer present in the vehicle. After making a right turn onto a major highway under hard acceleration, the steering wheel slipped from my wife's hands and the car struck the curb on the right side of the road. This blew both tires on the right side. At my own expense, I had all four tires replaced and a four-wheel alignment done at an independent dealer. Torque steer is still very prevalent.

2006—Vehicle won't hold its alignment settings. • Excessive tire wear. • Seat belt fails to retract. **2007**—Poor acceleration, followed by surging. • Sudden stalling while underway. • Vehicle is unstable when passing over a grooved highway. • Automatic transmission failures. • Defective engine oil seal. • Visibility impaired by windshield lamination. • Frequent AC failures blamed on road debris, but poor quality is suspected. • Hard starts. • False alerts displayed by the tire-pressure warning system.

Secret Warranties/Internal Bulletins/Service Tips

All years: Keep in mind that Honda service bulletins almost always mention that "goodwill" extended warranties may be applied to any malfunction. **1999**—Harsh shifting caused by faulty solenoid; subject to free "goodwill" repair. • Front suspension clunking can be corrected by replacing the upper-arm flange bolts. • Cargo-cover end caps come off. **1999–2007**—Vehicle pulls/drifts to one side. **2000**—Information regarding shudder or vibration upon hard acceleration. • The remedy for differential moan during turns. **2001**—Rear differential noise. • Water leaks into the interior. **2002**—Rattling from the passenger grab handle area and above the doors. **2002–03**—A front brake clicking noise is caused by faulty lower retaining clips on the front brake pad that may be replaced for free under a "goodwill" program. • Engine stumbles or stalls after a stop. **2002–04**—Troubleshooting a rear brake grinding noise. • Correcting harsh or noisy automatic transmission downshifts when slowing down. **2002–05**—Remedy for a rattle, grind, or growl coming from the A-pillar of the front-right side of the vehicle when turning left. **2003**—Coolant in the oil pan. **2007**—Low Tire Pressure light stays on.

CR-V PROFILE

	1999	2000	2001	2002	2003	2004	2005	2006	2007
Cost Price ($)									
LX	26,000	26,000	26,300	26,900	27,300	27,200	28,200	29,300	27,700
Used Values ($)									
LX ▲	5,000	6,000	7,500	8,500	10,500	12,500	14,000	16,000	18,000
LX ▼	4,500	5,000	6,500	7,500	9,000	11,000	13,000	15,000	16,500
Reliability	4	5	5	5	5	5	5	5	5
Crash Safety (F)	4	4	4	5	5	5	5	5	5
Side	5	5	5	5	5	5	5	5	5
IIHS Side	—	—	—	2	2	2	5	5	5
Offset	2	2	2	5	5	5	5	5	5
Rollover Resistance	—	—	3	3	3	—	4	4	4

Hyundai

TUCSON ★★★★

RATING: Above Average (2007); Average (2005–06). With this Kia Sportage twin, you get a lot of features for your money, but a peppy 4-cylinder engine isn't one of them. **"Real" city/highway fuel economy:** *2.0L 4-cylinder: 10.6/7.9 L/100 km. V6: 11.9/8.4 L/100 km.* **Maintenance/Repair costs:** Much lower than average. **Parts:** Easily found and reasonably priced. **Extended warranty:** Not necessary. **Best alternatives:** Ford Escape, Honda CR-V, Jeep Liberty, and Toyota RAV4.

Strengths and Weaknesses

Hyundai's smallest sport-utility is built on a strengthened and stretched Elantra platform powered by the Elantra's engine, and offers the addition of four-wheel drive. The interior looks fairly low-tech and uses cheap-looking plastics everywhere. The optional 2.7L V6 is harnessed to a manumatic 4-speed automatic transmission, a set-up that leads to excessive gear-hunting, imprecise automatic-to-manual shifting, and compromised fuel economy. What's really needed is a conventional 5-speed, or for the Santa Fe's 242 hp 3.3L V6 to handle the Tucson's heft.

While we're on the subject of weight, the Tucson is heavier than either the Honda CR-V or the Toyota RAV4, so true handling enthusiasts will want to throw their lot in with the RAV4 or Ford/Mazda Escape/Tribute to get their performance thrills. Still, the vehicle is fairly cheap, comes well equipped with standard side airbags and stability control, and has earned NHTSA five-star front and side crashworthiness ratings. The Tucson also brakes well, gives a comfortable ride, has a roomy interior, and has few factory defects overall.

Some minuses: It's underpowered and "under-geared," and has a bland interior, mediocre handling, sluggish steering, limited rear visibility, numerous first-year factory-related deficiencies, a noisy suspension, and only average fuel economy. Owners have reported failures related to the cruise control, automatic transmission, manual transmission shift-lever cable assembly, and stability-control module. There's also poor fit and finish; water pours in from behind the glove box:

> Upon removing the glove box and pulling out the cabin filter, I noticed the water coming down through the AC system...similar complaint filed on service bulletins. Car was parked on a 10 degree angle nose end down. Water leak through and near electrical components and near passenger side airbag.

 ## Safety Summary

All years: Airbags fail to deploy. **2005**—A faulty Electronic Stability Program (ESP) module can cause the vehicle to stall and the ABS to suddenly engage, and can result in the vehicle going out of control. This has happened to vehicles that have been recalled and "fixed" for the problem and to cars that aren't included in the recall. • Manual and automatic transmissions suddenly fail to go into gear. • Power steering fails while passing through small pools of water on the road. **2005–06**—The passenger-side airbag is disabled even though an adult occupies the seat. **2007**—Head restraints cause neck stiffness and headaches. • Rear window explodes for no reason.

Secret Warranties/Internal Bulletins/Service Tips

2005—No movement in Drive or Reverse. • Fluid may leak from the area around the automatic transmission torque converter or between the transaxle and the transfer case. • Correcting harsh gear engagement. • Tips on silencing a rattling sunroof. **2006–07**—Troubleshooting complaints relative to a cloudy paint condition.

TUCSON PROFILE

	2005	2006	2007
Cost Price ($)			
GL	19,995	20,596	21,195
V6	24,865	25,695	26,395
GLS	28,725	29,995	30,795

Used Values ($)

GL ▲	9,000	11,000	13,500
GL ▼	7,500	9,500	12,500
V6 ▲	11,000	13,000	15,500
V6 ▼	9,500	11,500	14,000
GLS ▲	11,000	15,500	18,000
GLS ▼	10,000	14,000	16,500

Reliability	4	4	5
Crash Safety (F)	5	5	5
Side	5	5	5
IIHS Side	5	5	5
Offset	3	3	3
Head Restraints (F)	—	1	1
Rollover Resistance	—	4	4

Toyota

RAV4 ★★★★

RATING: Above Average (1999–2007). This small SUV is an impressive performer that carries a remarkable array of standard features suitable for limited off-road tasks. But there is a serious downside: The car's faulty powertrain and erratically functioning cruise control can put your life in danger. **"Real" city/highway fuel economy:** *Pre-2006 models:* 10.7/8.1 L/100 km. *2006–07 models:* 10.1/7.8 L/100 km. *V6:* 11.1/7.7 L/100 km. **Maintenance/Repair costs:** Below average, owing to the proven reliability of Camry and Corolla components used in the RAV4. **Parts:** Moderately priced and fairly easy to find from independent suppliers. **Extended warranty:** Not needed. **Best alternatives:** Ford Escape, Honda CR-V, Hyundai Tucson or Santa Fe, and Mazda Tribute. Other choices worth looking at are the Nissan Xterra or X-Trail, Subaru Forester, and Toyota Highlander.

Strengths and Weaknesses

A cross between a small car and an off-road wagon with a tall roof, the RAV4 is Toyota's entry into the mini-sport-utility market. It has attractive lines, a high profile, and two drivetrains: permanent 4×4 or front-drive (which doesn't include low-range gearing but has a locking centre differential). The car is based on the Camry platform and features a four-wheel independent suspension and unibody construction. The 2005 and earlier models ride and handle like stiffly sprung, small-wheelbase cars; later models are a bit smoother. Like Honda's CR-V, the RAV4 is an upsized car that has been made more rugged with the addition of AWD, larger wheels, more ground clearance, and a boxy body.

Following the car's 2006 redesign, two engines are now offered: a 166 hp 4-cylinder and a 269 hp V6—RAV4's first V6. Both engines come only with an automatic transmission. ABS and traction/anti-skid control are standard. Front-drive RAV4s have a limited-slip differential. Hill ascent/descent control is standard on V6 models and on seven-passenger 4-cylinder models. RAV4s have a side-hinged rear gate that makes for difficult curbside loading. The second-row seat is a split-folding bench that moves fore and aft and has a reclining seatback. The optional third-row seat folds into the floorwell.

VEHICLE HISTORY: 1999–2000—These models aren't much different from their predecessors, except for a minor facelift, the addition of a two-door softtop, and a full-sized spare tire. The two-door convertible is dropped for 2000. **2001**—Restyled and redesigned, growing in size and getting a more-powerful engine, an upgraded suspension, and a more-rigid body. **2004**—Given the Camry's 2.4L engine, rear disc brakes, vehicle skid control, a revised suspension and steering, a tire-pressure monitor, and optional side curtain airbags. **2006**—A major redesign gives the 2006 new styling, a longer wheelbase, additional length, more width, a V6 and a small horsepower boost for the 4-cylinder engine, more cargo room, and third-row seating to carry a total of seven passengers. **2007**—Standard front seat-mounted side airbags and roll-sensing front and rear head/side curtain airbags (side curtain airbags were formerly a $750 option).

The peppy 6-cylinder engine provides excellent acceleration while sipping fuel; it gets about the same fuel economy as the 4-cylinder-equipped competition, which put out 100 fewer horses. The car has adequate 4-cylinder acceleration, good handling, and a smooth ride (the four-door model has a handling advantage over the two-door version); more than enough headroom and legroom for all passengers; more cargo space than most passenger cars with the four-door (but the two-door version reduces that cargo capacity by half); a split rear bench seat that folds for extra cargo space; easy access and a low liftover; a nicely equipped four-door version (the two-door is spartan, though adequate); and an incredibly high resale value.

But owners aren't all happy, and they report the following problem areas: *Pre-2006 models:* Serious throttle delay followed by engine surging, and excessive road and engine noise; an automatic gearbox with 4×4 reduces engine performance (front-drive is faster); and rearward visibility is seriously compromised by the RAV4's convertible top, high headrests, and spare-tire placement. *2006–07 models:* The V6 throttle is super-sensitive and tough to modulate, leading to jerky acceleration and rough low-speed shifts; speed control constantly shifts in and out of gear; tall drivers will find the cockpit cramped; wide rear roof pillars obstruct rearward view; second-row seats give insufficient legroom; third-row seats are hard to access; no manual transmission available; cheap-looking glove box lid and head-liner; and no separately opening hatch glass.

Quality control has declined over the past five years, with countless reports of "lag and lurch" when accelerating. A faulty speed control causes the transmission to shift constantly in a jerky manner, making the engine race:

> When using the cruise control (with the automatic transmission) the vehicle will shift rapidly between 2nd and 3rd gears when climbing small inclines and even sometimes on flat ground. This action starts when the transmission downshifts to maintain current speed. This condition makes for an unstable and dangerous driving condition when the cruise is utilized because you do not know how the vehicle will react during the drive. Currently I am aware of 12 case numbers that have been created with the Toyota customer support center addressing this situation. Some of these cases even involve 2006 models.

There's brake noise and throttle body whine between 2700 and 3000 rpm. The suspension clunks when making slow-speed turns. The brakes screech, squeal, or grind even after the pads have been replaced. Other noises: dash and cowl rattling (worse in low temperatures), rear suspension creaking when accelerating from a stop, and windshield cowling rattles (particularly in cold weather). To a lesser degree, owners tell of rear-view mirror and windshield cowling vibrations as well as minor electrical shorts. The AC and heating display is nearly impossible to read in daylight.

Safety Summary

All years: Airbag malfunctions. • Sudden, unintended acceleration. • Intermittent hesitation when accelerating or making a slow turn ("lag and lurch"). • Frequent brake pad replacement. • Windshield is easily chipped. • Vehicle pulls to one side when accelerating; alignment and tires eliminated as cause. • Rear window suddenly shatters. **2002**—Brake pedal is too small. **2002–04**—Fire ignites in the engine compartment. **2004–05**—Fuel-hose leakage. **2006**—Passenger-side airbag shuts off even though an adult occupies the seat. • More complaints of engine hesitation and surging when accelerating or when coming to a stop:

> My 2006 Toyota RAV4 has a non-responsive throttle. On many occasions, when you give it gas it does nothing, then it takes off like a rocket. I have nearly been in accidents because I pull out from a stop and the throttle is unresponsive while traffic is bearing down on me.

2007—Sudden loss of steering. • Faulty cruise control and engine hesitation when accelerating (a common Toyota problem over the past decade). • Yokohama tire tread disintegrates after only two months of use.

Secret Warranties/Internal Bulletins/Service Tips

All years: Remedy for front brake clicking found in TSB #BR004-00. • Loose, poorly fitted trim panels. **1999–2000**—Delayed upshift to Overdrive with cruise control engaged. **2001**—Windshield creak noise. • Diagnosing noises in passenger-side dash and the A- and C-pillar areas. • Headlight retainer tab broken. •

Improvement to the rear wiper washer nozzle. • Exhaust fumes enter into the interior. • Roof rack rattle or buzz. **2001–02**—Troubleshooting rear brake squeal. • Back door rattles. • Noise from top of instrument panel. **2001–03**—Cowl noise troubleshooting tips. **2001–04**—Fix for a squealing accessory drivebelt and a rattling belt tensioner. **2001–05**—Key sticks in the ignition lock. **2002**—Service campaign to inspect or repair the cruise-control switch. • Wind whistle from front edge of hood. **2002–06**—Correction for vehicles that pull to the right when accelerating. **2003–07**—Windshield ticking noise considered a factory-related problem (TSB #NV009-06, published September 18, 2006). **2004–05**—Tire Pressure warning light may come on for no reason. **2004–07**—Front-seat squeaking. **2006**—Engine timing cover oil leaks. **2006–07**—Automatic transmission shift lever doesn't move smoothly. • Water leaks onto the passenger floorboard. • Whining noise at low speed/idle. • Fuel pump droning noise and vibration at highway speeds (TSB #TC006-07). • Front-door locks may be inoperative in cold weather. **2007**—Paint stains on horizontal surfaces.

RAV4 PROFILE

	1999	2000	2001	2002	2003	2004	2005	2006	2007
Cost Price ($)									
4×2	22,150	—	—	—	—	—	—	—	—
4×4	22,500	24,185	23,260	24,420	24,485	24,485	24,585	28,700	29,300
Used Values ($)									
4×2 ▲	4,000	—	—	—	—	—	—	—	—
4×2 ▼	3,000	—	—	—	—	—	—	—	—
4×4 ▲	4,500	5,000	6,000	7,500	9,000	10,500	13,000	16,500	18,000
4×4 ▼	4,000	4,500	5,000	6,000	7,500	9,000	11,500	15,000	16,500
Reliability	5	4	4	4	4	3	3	3	3
Crash Safety (F)	4	4	4	4	4	4	4	5	5
Side	5	5	—	5	5	5	5	5	5
IIHS Side	—	—	1	1	1	5	5	5	5
Offset	2	2	3	3	3	3	5	5	5
Rollover Resistance	—	—	—	3	3	3	—	4	4

Note: The 2001–05 models were rated Good by IIHS only if they were equipped with side airbags; vehicles without side airbags were rated Poor.

Pickup Trucks

Trucks: Down, but Not Out

Despite a collapsing world economy and Detroit automakers facing bankruptcy (Chrysler will probably be the first to fall), truck sales are bouncing back—helped along by low fuel costs and bargain prices for new and used models.

It's about time we see a turnaround. Canadian truck owners were walloped last summer by the double whammy of fuel that was too expensive to buy, at $1.50 per litre, and trucks that were too depreciated to sell. In fact, three-year-old pickups were worth only about a third of what they originally cost. Many pickup owners owed more money on their trucks than the trucks were worth as trade-ins.

Quality Decline

Over the past decade, American automakers have churned out millions of new pickups equipped with more complicated and hard-to-service safety, performance, and convenience features. At the same time, they squeeze equipment suppliers to give them more for less, and they constantly change part specifications, confounding suppliers even more.

Industry insiders agree that these actions have contributed largely to a dramatic decline in pickup quality over the past decade—a conclusion also reached by J.D. Power and Associates and *Consumer Reports. CR* says their poll results show that American trucks become less reliable as they age and don't match the Asian automakers' trucks for overall quality.

For example, J.D. Power's 2004 Vehicle Dependability Study found that the most fuel-efficient vehicles—diesels and gas-electric hybrids—have more engine problems than similar gasoline-powered vehicles, a conclusion backed by automaker service bulletins and complaints sent to NHTSA. The discrepancies are an eye-opener:

- Ford and Chevrolet diesel pickups were worse than similar gas models, while Dodge and GMC trucks were better overall.
- Owners of 2001 Toyota and Honda hybrids reported twice as many engine problems as did owners of gas-engine Toyotas and Hondas.
- Owners of Volkswagen diesels reported up to twice as many engine problems as did owners of gas-burning VWs.

GM's diesel engine failures primarily affect the 6.6L Duramax engine, which has been plagued by persistent oil leaks, excessive oil burning, and defective turbo-chargers, fuel-injection pumps, and injectors, causing seized engines, chronic stalling, loss of power, hard starts, and excessive gas consumption. To its credit, GM has a Special Policy that extends the warranty to 11 years/193,000 km (120,000 mi.) on injection pumps installed in 1994–2002 models.

Picking a Pickup

When choosing a pickup, consider cost, reliability, size, and style—in that order. Start small with reliable entry-level Mazda, Honda, or Nissan offerings. If you need more brawn and performance and must buy something Detroit-made, go for Chrysler's Ram series. And then consider Ford or GM. But be prepared for subpar reliability, high maintenance costs, rapid depreciation, and abysmally poor fit and finish on all Detroit-bred models.

What do you do if all the full- or medium-sized pickups are still too expensive? Downsize your needs if you can—go down a notch—and buy a cheaper, Japanese-made used compact pickup. Or better yet, wait another year for prices to level out.

PICKUP TRUCK RATINGS

Average

Chrysler Ram (2002–07)

General Motors Sierra, Silverado (2007)

Below Average

Chrysler Ram (1999–2001)
Ford F-Series (1999–2007)

General Motors C/K, Sierra, Silverado (1999–2006)

Chrysler

RATING: Average (2002–07); Below Average (1999–2001). Rams are mediocre buys; however, when equipped with a manual tranny and a diesel powertrain, they are the best truck buy among the Detroit automakers. **"Real" city/highway fuel economy:** *3.9L 4×2:* 15.9/11.0 L/100 km. *5.2L 4×4:* 18.9/13.1 L/100 km. *Hemi V8 with Multi-Displacement System:* 13.9/8.8 L/100 km. *V6:* 12.2/8.1 L/100 km. Pre-2006 models' average real-world fuel consumption has been reported at 21.0 L/100 km. **Maintenance/Repair costs:** Average. **Parts:** With the exception of some Cummins diesels, parts are easily available and reasonably priced. **Extended warranty:** Buy extended coverage if Chrysler's base warranty has expired, particularly after the fourth year, when quality-control problems multiply. **Best alternatives:** A second-series Honda Ridgeline or Nissan Frontier.

 Strengths and Weaknesses

Not a spectacular performer with its weak standard powertrain hookup, the Dodge Ram is a full-sized pickup that mirrors Ford's and GM's truck lineups, but with a bit more reliability. The 2004 and later 1500 series models come with a 3.7L V6 base engine and optional 4.7L and 5.7L V8s. The latter engine is called the Hemi, and it's sold only with a 5-speed automatic transmission. The V6 and 4.7L V8 offer a manual transmission or a 4- or 5-speed automatic, respectively. Automatics include a tow/haul mode for heavy loads. Chrysler plays the nostalgia card with its 345 hp 5.7L Hemi high-performance engine, last seen as an allegedly 425 hp powerhouse offered from 1965 to 1971. It is sold with the 1500 series heavy-duty Ram pickups and the Dodge 300C/Magnum wagon. Drivers can expect to shave about three seconds off the 1500's time of 0–100km/h in 10.5 seconds, all the while praying that the engine doesn't kill the tranny.

The Ram's strong points for the 2006–07 models are mainly bargain resale prices, cylinder deactivation for better fuel economy and more power, and plenty of interior room and convenience features. The 4.7L V8 is a good alternative to the larger, fuel-thirstier Hemi version.

Some of the sore points with the 2006–07 models: You won't get the fuel economy, safety features, or manoeuvrability of other full-sized pickups. The ride is jiggly over rough terrain, the steering is vague, the interior is Kmart kitsch, and the climb up to the lofty cab is a chore. The Mexican plant where these vehicles are made isn't one of Chrysler's best facilities in terms of quality control, and the jury is still out on the Ram's new cylinder deactivation system.

Pre-2006 models are even cheaper to buy, and they offer average quality combined with assertive styling, a high-tech engine, full-time 4×4, adequately sized cabs with good stowage utility, one of the longest and roomiest cargo boxes available, and a comfortable and well-designed interior with easily accessed and understood instruments and controls. The 1500 series models have better handling, improved steering, and fewer rattles. Other pluses: powerful Hemi, V8, and V10 engines; a bit more reliable Cummins diesel; good trailering capability; a smooth-shifting automatic transmission (when it's working right); and four-door versatility.

But there are minuses with pre-2006 models, as well: The 1500 series engines may be outclassed by Ford and GM powerplants. The Hemi V8 is quite fuel-thirsty and has had a few quality problems during the short time it has been on the road. Considering Chrysler's inability to make reliable and safe ball joints, ABS brakes, and automatic transmissions, the 2005's engine cylinder deactivation feature may become a problem as these trucks reach their critical fifth year of use. The 2500 and 3500 models were left in the Jurassic Age until the 2006 redesigned models came on board. Outdated mechanical components, like an inconvenient transfer case and a solid front axle, make for a jittery ride (on 2500s and 3500s only); 4×4 must be disengaged on dry pavement; V6 acceleration is poor; steering response is slow; the ride is bouncy over rough spots; controls aren't easy to calibrate; the 1.8 m (6 ft.) bed looks stubby; and the high hood hides obstacles from view. Very poor fuel economy ties Ford's pickups at a real-world average of about 21.0 L/100 km (11 mpg). And as with Ford and GM trucks, Rams also have had a disturbingly large number of safety- and performance-related defects reported to NHTSA.

VEHICLE HISTORY: 2001—Improved steering and an upgraded rear-suspension system. **2002**—Revamped handling and ride comfort. The 1500 models get more-aggressive styling, two new engines, roomier cabs, and optional side airbags. The two-door extended Club Cab is axed, Quad Cabs are given four front-hinged doors, and short-box models gain 7.6 cm (3 in.) of cabin length at the expense of bed length. The 4×4-equipped Rams get an independent front suspension. **2003**—2500 and 3500 series are revised and given the Hemi 345 hp 5.7L V8 and rack-and-pinion steering. **2004**—An expanded model lineup that includes a Hemi-powered Power Wagon off-roader and the SRT-10 Quad Cab, equipped with the Dodge Viper's 500 hp 8.3L V10 engine. **2005**—More models available with 6-speed manual transmissions (hmm...word must be spreading that the automatics are "fertilizer"). **2006**—The 1500 gets a stiffer frame, a softer front suspension, reduced-drag brake calipers, high-intensity headlights, an electrically operated front-axle disconnect system, a revised interior and body style (Mega Cab), weather seals, and constrained layer (quiet steel) technology in the dash panel area—improvements that should reduce clunks, rattles, and wind noise. There's also a cylinder cut-off system to boost fuel economy—if it functions properly (feeling lucky?). The Mega Cab option can seat six passengers in comfort, which wasn't possible with earlier models. Comfort is enhanced through reclining rear seats that split, fold down, and move forward. Hauling capacity is more than adequate with the Mega's "mega" engine, a 345 hp 5.7L Hemi V8 mated to a heavy-duty 5-speed automatic transmission. **2007**—A new 350 hp 6.7L inline-six Cummins Turbo Diesel (25 more horses than the 2006 version), and the debut of the Class 3 Chassis Cab, equipped with either a 330 hp 5.7L Hemi V8 or a torquier Cummins Turbo Diesel V8.

The Ram 2500, 2500 Heavy Duty, SRT-10, and Mega Cab were all built in Saltillo, Mexico—not a stellar plant. Fit and finish and powertrain, suspension, steering, brake, electrical, and fuel-system components are still not top quality. Hemi engines have had problems with broken valve springs and rear main seal leaks. The Cummins diesel engine has performed exceptionally well, but some serious problems remain.

Other owner-reported problems: Electrical fire at the power disbursement box under the hood; sudden transmission and differential failures; and the accelerator pedal jams while backing up. Be wary of front differential damage caused by road debris striking the unprotected housing. Poorly performing brakes must be adjusted at almost every oil change; premature (5,000 km) wearout of the rear brake hubs and front brake pads; and complete ABS brake failure. The weak stabilizer bar is easily bent when passing over potholes; the lack of an anti-sway bar on the rear axle in the trailer towing package means excessive swaying, causing steering instability; and some trailer hitches are cracked. Very loose steering allows the vehicle to wander all over the roadway, and a defective steering pump causes loss of steering control. Constant pulling to the right on the highway; excessive vibration when approaching 100 km/h; excessive shimmy after hitting a bump or pothole; clunk or rattle felt in the steering wheel after running over a rough surface; and faulty steering gearbox. Inadequate cooling because of AC freeze-up, and an odour comes out of the AC ducts. There's a clunking or rattling noise from the front suspension, a ringing noise from the rear of the vehicle, and a shudder when pulling away from a stop when near maximum gross vehicle weight rating (GVWR). The absence of a baffle in the fuel tank allows gas to slam forward and back in the tank, subjecting connections to stress and causing early failure. The ignition fuse link blows intermittently, shutting down the vehicle. Transmission seal leakage and excessive noise through the 2006 models; obstructive rear door latching mechanism prevents easy access to the rear seat; fragile front ball joints; oil-filter adaptor plate and speed-sensor oil seepage; front disc brake noise on the 3500 series; and the lap belt rides too high on the abdomen, while the shoulder belt lies too close to the neck and jaw.

 Safety Summary

All models/years: Sudden acceleration. • Chronic stalling. • Airbag malfunctions. • Brake pedal goes to floor without any braking effect. • Severe pull to the side when braking. • Warped rotors and worn-out brake pads. • When parked, vehicle rolls down an incline. • Frequent transmission failures and fluid leaks. • Overdrive engages poorly in cold weather. • Vehicle wanders excessively at highway speeds. **All models: 2001**—Many reports of electrical shorts causing under-hood fires. • Power-steering line blows out. • Front suspension bottoms out on speed bumps. • Rear window shatters. • Hood flies up and shatters windshield. **2002**—Front end jumps from side to side when vehicle passes over uneven pavement, or it easily hydroplanes when passing over wet roads. • Premature brake master cylinder failure. • Differential and rear axle bearing fail prematurely. **2003**—Accelerator pedal falls off. • Stalling and hard starting. • Front suspension collapse. **2004**—Fire ignites in the driver-side rear wheelwell. • Stalling Hemi engine (EGR valve on national back order). • Wheel bearing failure. • Rear axle breaks. **2005**—Electrical fire ignites in the engine compartment. • Vehicle speeds up when going downhill. • Early ball joint failure. **2006**—Tie-rod failures. • Gas and brake pedals are mounted too close together. **2006–07**—Automatic transmission slips out of Reverse and grinds. **2007**—Front control arm (suspension/steering) breaks:

> This caused the tire to dislocate from the vehicle. The tire, ball joint, brake system and hoses stayed attached to the rim of the tire. This caused the vehicle to drop and surge to the right, then collide with another vehicle.

• Engine oil sensor failures. • Dashboard cracks may impair airbag deployment. • Michelin tire failures. *2500, 3500:* **2003–04**—Vehicles with automatic transmissions might roll backward when shifted into the Park position.

Secret Warranties/Internal Bulletins/Service Tips

All models: 1999–2007—Paint delamination, peeling, or fading. • An erratically shifting automatic transmission may only require a recalibrated PCM or TCM. Check out this solution before spending big bucks. **2001**—Engine may not crank because of a blown starter-relay circuit fuse. • Engine cranks but won't start, or starts and stalls. • Low fuel output from the transfer pump may be the cause of hard starts or no-starts. • Troubleshooting tips for complaints of poor diesel engine performance. • Low engine power when transmission is in Overdrive. • Harsh transmission engagement when the torque converter clutch is applied. • Rear may sit too high to attach a fifth wheel. **2001–04**—Water leaks on passenger-side floor (Dakota also affected). **2002–04**—Water leaks at grab handle. **2003**—Low start-up oil pressure with the Hemi engine requires the replacement of the oil-pump pick-up tube. • Brake vibration or shudder requires the replacement of many major brake components, says TSB #05-008-03, published November 28, 2003. • Instrument panel whistle. • Poor idle and coasting. • Lack of air from floor vents. • Buzzing, vibration from front of vehicle. **2003–04**—Dirt accumulates in door opening area; install an improved secondary door seal. **2003–05**—Steering snaps or ticks. **2004**—Brake kit should be installed to eliminate brake shudder, vibration. • Power-window binding or slow operation. *1500:* **2001**—Remedy for steering wander.

RAM PROFILE

	1999	2000	2001	2002	2003	2004	2005	2006	2007
Cost Price ($)									
D-150, 1500	20,345	20,630	18,750	23,255	23,865	24,910	26,975	26,020	26,395
Quad Cab	—	—	—	27,280	26,900	—	—	—	—
SRT-10	—	—	—	—	—	61,000	58,465	61,555	—
Used Values ($)									
D-150, 1500 ▲	2,000	2,500	4,000	5,000	6,500	8,500	10,500	12,000	14,500
D-150, 1500 ▼	1,500	2,000	3,000	4,000	5,500	7,000	8,500	10,500	12,500
Quad Cab ▲	—	—	—	6,000	8,000	—	—	—	—
Quad Cab ▼	—	—	—	5,000	6,500	—	—	—	—
SRT-10 ▲	—	—	—	—	—	20,000	23,000	30,500	—
SRT-10 ▼	—	—	—	—	—	18,000	21,000	28,500	—
Reliability	2	2	2	3	3	3	3	3	3
Crash Safety (F)	—	—	5	4	4	5	5	5	5
Ext. cab	4	4	4	—	—	—	5	5	—
Quad cab	3	3	4	—	—	—	5	5	—
Side	5	5	—	—	—	3	—	—	—
Quad Cab	—	—	—	4	5	3	—	—	—
Offset	1	1	1	5	5	5	5	5	5
Rollover Resistance	1	1	3	3	3	—	4	4	4

Ford

RATING: Below Average (1999–2007). Without question, the F-Series trucks are versatile and brawny haulers, with much-improved handling, a quieter ride, and a more-comfortable interior incorporated into the 2005 model's redesign. Quality control, however, remains abysmally poor. Over the past two decades, owners have had to put up with poor-quality powertrain components that were practically biodegradable and serious safety-related defects like sudden tie-rod separation, torsion bar failures, unintended acceleration, and the complete loss of braking. **"Real" city/highway fuel economy:** Very poor; average real-world fuel economy hovers around 21.0 L/100 km—equal to the Dodge Ram's. *4.2L 4×2:* 15.1/11.1 L/100 km. *4.6L 4×2:* 16.2/11.3 L/100 km. *5.4L 4×2:* 17.4/12.3 L/100 km. *4.2L 4×4:* 15.9/12.2 L/100 km. *4.6L 4×4:* 17.4/12.9 L/100 km. *5.4L 4×4:* 18.6/13.6 L/100 km. **Maintenance/Repair costs:** Higher than average, but easily repaired by independent garages. **Parts:** With the exception of Power Stroke diesels, parts are generally widely available from independent suppliers and are of average cost. **Extended warranty:** An extended powertrain warranty is a must to counter Ford's poor quality control. **Best alternatives:** Honda, Mazda, and Nissan pickups are a lot safer and more reliable.

Strengths and Weaknesses

In Ford's glory days, it and GM were the only pickup games in town and relations with parts suppliers were cordial. Now, Chrysler, Honda, Nissan, and Toyota are gobbling up Ford's market share and supplier relations are testy at best. Buyers are clamouring for more versatile and reliable trucks that mix high-tech features with dependability and are covered by stronger warranties. Unfortunately, Ford's F-Series revamp in 2005 was too little, too late, and wasn't corrected until the latest redesign of the 2009 models, which gave these pickups more power, passenger room, and features.

The most obvious changes on the 2005s are a new angular styling, a four-door configuration (a first for entry-level trucks), a deeper bed box, an upgraded interior, and a bigger, quieter cab. Ride comfort was improved by creating a roomier interior and adding a new rear suspension. SuperCab models gained 15 cm in cab length plus larger rear doors and entry and exit handles. Other nice touches include a power-sliding rear window controlled by a button on the overhead console, power rear side windows, and an easier-to-lift tailgate that houses a built-in torsion-bar-assist mechanism.

The Ford 4.2L V6 is rated better in fuel economy than the 4.6L V8, but the V8 gets better mileage in the real world. The V6 also was known for oil pump problems, so it has been dropped from the reworked F-150. An engine Ford should have dropped, but didn't—the 300 hp 5.4L V8, known for chronic production glitches—was added a few years ago. It features three valves per cylinder, variable-cam timing, and an electronic throttle control that dealer mechanics are still trying to master.

Safety features on the 2005 and later F-150s were augmented to include multi-stage front airbags; a sensor to determine if the front passenger seat is empty; five three-point seat belts, with the front shoulder belts integrated into the seats; and a LATCH (lower anchors and tethers for children) system to facilitate the installation of child safety seats.

2007 and later F-150s have easy and predictable handling; a pleasant ride on bad roads; well-thought-out ergonomics, instruments, and controls; and fourth-door access. With a few exceptions (like tacky cloth seats), base models are nicely appointed, with lots of handy convenience features and a classy interior. The F-Series offers a commanding view of the road, lots of cab space, and excellent interior ergonomics. The front bench holds three in relative comfort, though there's insufficient footroom for the front centre passenger. They're some of the quietest pickups available.

The 2006 and earlier F-150s' underpowered base V6 engine and 4.6L V8 don't have sufficient passing power. Other pre-2007 problems: questionable engine, transmission, suspension/steering, and brake performance and reliability; poor braking performance with four-wheel ABS; and an uncomfortable rear seat. The climate-control system is a bit slow in warming up the cabin. There's no left footrest on some models, and the cramped and upright rear seats can't match GM's for comfort. Cargo flexibility is compromised by the second-row layout. An inordinate number of serious safety-related complaints have been collected by NHTSA, with cruise-control switch fires, tie-rod end and front torsion bar failures, and steering vibration and drivetrain shudder heading the list. Watch out for violent body shaking when passing over a bumpy highway and for severe dash glare onto the front windshield. Warranty payouts have been unacceptably Scrooge-like in the past, and fuel economy is astoundingly poor.

Apparently, Ford's '97 and '05 redesigns created more bugs than they fixed. In fact, the company's flagship 6.0L diesel engines, introduced in December 2003, were so badly flawed that Ford had to initiate a service program to fix them and buy back over 500 trucks. Their problems included a rough idle, loss of power, stalling, excessive exhaust smoke, leaky fuel injectors, high fuel consumption, and engine seizures. Ford says the engines are fine now, but there are many skeptics. Non-diesel engines aren't very durable, either, and they have severe engine knock through the 2005s.

Another serious defect, afflicting 1996–2004 models, is the collapsing tie rods/torsion bars in the steering/suspension system that throw the truck out of control when they fail. Ford has sent a letter to owners asking them to *please* have their vehicles inspected and repaired—at their own cost, of course. That's just another example of Ford's crappy customer relations attitude. Engine and automatic transmission breakdowns top the list of owners' complaints, which extends to failure-prone engine gaskets, timing belt tensioners, oil pumps, fuel injectors, fuel and ignition systems, and drivelines (principally clutches). If that weren't enough, owners have also been burdened with poor-quality front and rear brake components that include premature pad and caliper replacement and chronic rotor warping; faulty powertrain control modules that cause sudden stalling at full throttle; excessive vibration felt throughout the vehicle; front suspension and steering problems; and inadequate AC cooling. There are also body defects up the wazoo, including door cracks on 1997–2000 models (see "Not What It's Cracked Up to Be," *www.F150online.com/articles/cracks.html*).

VEHICLE HISTORY: 1999—A restyled front end, upgraded front seats, and the arrival of a four-door SuperCab. **2001**—The F-150 Crew Cab debuts with four full-sized doors and a full rear-passenger compartment; the 4.6L V8 gains 20 additional horses; the F-250 and F-350 get a horsepower upgrade for the 7.3L Power Stroke turbodiesel engine; the Trailer Tow package becomes standard on all models, as does four-wheel ABS; and the Lightning gets a slight increase in power and a shorter final drive ratio. **2002**—The mid-year return of the Harley-Davidson Edition; SuperCrew models receive 20-inch wheels and special trim; and the 260 hp 5.4L V8 is joined by a 340 hp supercharged variant. **2003**—Lightning models receive a stiffer rear suspension to support a 635 kg (1,400 lb.) payload. **2004**—The entry-level Heritage debuts. **2005**—Redesigned. **2007**—F-250 and F-350 pickups offer a new 350 hp 6.4L V8 diesel engine to replace the quality-plagued 6.0L diesel.

 Safety Summary

All models/years: Tie-rod and front torsion-bar failures send the truck out of control. • Dangerous front-end bounce. • Sudden acceleration and chronic stalling. • Sticking accelerator pedal. • Frequent automatic transmission failures; transmission slippage. • Airbag malfunctions. • Brake failure as pedal goes to the floor. • Wheel lug nut failures. • Firestone and Goodrich tire-tread separation. • Gas and brake pedals are mounted too close together. **All models: 2000**—A driver's face was burned when airbags deployed and gases caught on fire. • Steering loss because of shearing of the sector shaft. • Loss of brakes caused by prematurely worn calipers and pads. • Transmission torque converter may lock up without warning. • Halogen lights look like high beams to other drivers. • Metal cable breaks, allowing spare tire to fall off while underway. • Left rear tire flies off truck. • Radio heats up to the point where tapes melt. **2000–01**—Truck parked with emergency brake set rolls down incline. **2000–02**—Windows suddenly shatter while vehicle is underway. **2001**—Owners cite most of the aforementioned defects, plus a host of new safety-related failures. **2001–02**—High seats positioned so that driver stares into the tinted top part of the windshield, and inside rear-view mirror blocks forward visibility. **2001–03**—Driver's seat belt buckle won't fasten. **2002**—Fire ignites under the power-adjusted seat mechanism. • Automatic transmission jerks when vehicle accelerates. • Headlights and dash lights fail intermittently. • Small wheel hubs cause vehicle to vibrate excessively. **2003**—Faulty EGR valve causes throttle to stick wide open and brakes to fail. • Rear axle failure; wheel comes off. • One truck's left front wheel separated, and the truck ran into a wall. • Harley Truck Owners Club (*www.nhtoc.com*) reports that rubber strips on stainless steel gas pedals peel off, making the pedal too slippery. • Fuel-tank leakage. **2004**—Driving with rear window open makes the cabin vibrate violently. • Painful, high-pitched noise comes from the dash area. • Tire chains cannot be used. • Wiper leaves a 15 cm blind spot near the driver's side pillar. **2004–05**—Tailgate falls off. • Excessive vibration and rear-end shudder at highway speeds. **2005**—Many complaints of sudden, unintended acceleration with complete loss of braking capability. • Airbags continue to fail when needed. • When parked, vehicle slips out of gear and goes into Reverse. • Tire jack won't raise truck high enough to allow the mounting of a fully inflated spare. • Faulty ignition keys. **2006**—Many complaints of 5.4L V8 engine hesitating or stalling when accelerating. • Other complaints of unintended acceleration when the brakes are applied. • Reports of faulty fuel pumps leaking fuel onto the exhaust system. • Poorly designed suspension causes the vehicle to jump and shake wildly when passing over a small bump in the road. • Rack-and-pinion steering falls apart. • Sudden brake loss. • Ice accumulates in the wheels. • Many complaints relative to prematurely worn Hankook DynaPro original-equipment tires. **2007**—Unintended acceleration when braking, or when the cruise control is enabled. • Steering failure in rainy conditions. • Fuel gauge shows empty when the tank is full. • Vision hampered by dash reflection (glare) onto front windshield. *F-250:* **2005**—Faulty diesel engine fuel injectors and exhaust system cause sickening exhaust fumes to enter the cabin. • When the diesel engine is turned off for fuelling, it cannot be restarted. • Engine blows because of a faulty camshaft fuse. • Frequent fuel-pump failures. • Truck will not shift down automatically when carrying a load. • On the highway, the truck vibrates excessively and sways uncontrollably. **2006**—Automatic transmission gear slippage and stalling. • Transmission suddenly downshifts into 4×4 mode, abruptly slowing the truck down. • Recessed gauges and windshield glare impair visibility. • Vehicle stalls just as the accelerator pedal is released. **2007**—Truck is easily stolen:

> All it took for a thief to break into my Ford F-250 was, what the police officer determined, a flat-head screwdriver. It is extremely disturbing to think that all a person has to do is jam a screwdriver under the plate, for the door handle/lock plate, pry down and the door pops open.

• Engine goes to idle with no response to the accelerator. • Violent shaking when passing over a bumpy highway. • Severe dash glare onto the front windshield. *F-350:* **2007**—Diesel exhaust fumes enter into the cabin. • Long delay when accelerating. • Converter/transmission snap ring and solenoid failures. • Multiple brake failures. • When towing a trailer, the brakes don't work at low speeds (10–15 km/h). • Defective brake booster and engine oil pump. • Weak coil springs won't support a plow.

Secret Warranties/Internal Bulletins/Service Tips

All models: 1999–2002—High idle speeds; throttle sticks in cold weather. 1999–2005—Ford will install a special axle kit to stop rear axle noise. Ford's bulletin admission of this defect is actionable in small claims court if the company won't pay for the six-hour repair. • Water leaks from the roof flange area and accumulates in the headliner, or the leak may occur at the cab floor pan area. • Drivetrain drive-away shudder or vibration. 1999–2006—A driveline clunk may signal that the slip yoke needs lubrication. Check this out before spending money on more-involved tests or repairs. • Tips for correcting a rough idle. • Paint delamination, peeling, or fading. • Troubleshooting broken intake manifold studs. 2000–05—Seat belts slow to retract. 2002—Throttle may stick in cold weather. • Engine power loss in hot weather. • Vacuum or air leaks in the intake manifold and engine. • Faulty ignition switch lock cylinder. 2003–06—Inoperative AC; compressor leakage. 2004—Faulty handle cables could make it impossible to open the doors from the inside. 2004–05—Remedy for warm engine knocking or ticking. • Correction of axle chatter, shudder, or vibration during low-speed turning manoeuvres. • Remedies for steering-wheel and body vibrations. • Upgraded brake rotors will be installed to stop brake shudder and vibration. • Cooling fan noise on trucks equipped with 4.6L and 5.4L engines. • Free butyl bed pad removal to prevent corrosion. 2004–07—Vibration on hard acceleration. • Aluminum body panel corrosion. 2004–08—Power-steering-line fluid seepage in cold weather. • Excessive steering-wheel vibration (80–105 km/h). • High-speed driveline vibration. 2005—Hard starts or rough running, or engine won't crank. • Excessive steering-wheel shimmy after passing over bumps. 2005–07—Power rear sliding window may need a new motor. • Slow power-window upward travel. *Diesels:* 2003–04—Remedies for 6.0L diesel engines that have fuel in oil, lose power, or run roughly are covered in TSB #03-14-6. 2003–05—Troubleshooting tips for misfire, lack of power, excessive smoke, and excessive cranking to start. Keep in mind that Ford *must* pay for this troubleshooting and repair under the little-publicized, though much-longer, emissions warranty. Don't take no for an answer. 2003–06—TSB #06-9-7, issued May 15, 2006, gives more diagnostic and repair tips for poorly performing diesel engines. 2005—Engine stalls when shifting into Drive or Reverse, or when coming to a stop. 2005–06—Inadvertent transmission lock-up during 1–2 shifts.

F-SERIES PROFILE

	1999	2000	2001	2002	2003	2004	2005	2006	2007
Cost Price ($)									
XL	22,995	22,295	22,710	23,310	23,380	22,850	23,840	22,499	22,499
Used Values ($)									
XL ▲	3,000	3,500	4,000	5,000	6,500	8,000	9,000	11,000	12,500
XL ▼	2,500	3,000	3,500	4,000	5,000	7,000	8,000	9,500	11,000
Reliability	2	2	2	2	2	2	2	2	2
Crash Safety (F)	4	4	5	5	—	5	5	5	5

Side	5	5	5	5	5	—	—	—	—
Ext. cab	—	—	4	4	4	—	—	—	—
IIHS Side	—	5	5	5	5	—	—	—	—
SuperCrew	—	—	—	5	5	—	—	—	—
Offset	**1**	**1**	**1**	**1**	**1**	5	5	5	5
Rollover Resistance	—	—	—	—	3	4	4	4	4
4×4	—	—	—	—	**2**	4	4	4	4

General Motors

C/K, SIERRA, SILVERADO ★★★

RATING: Average (2007); Below Average (1999–2006). Both the Sierra and Silverado are living on borrowed time. **"Real" city/highway fuel economy:** *4.3L V6 manual: 14.1/9.5 L/100 km. 4.3L V6 automatic: 14.6/10.6 L/100 km. 4.8L V8 automatic: 14.6/10.5 L/100 km. 5.3L V8 automatic: 16.2/12.0 L/100 km. 5.3L V8 automatic hybrid: 10.4/13.2 L/100 km.* **Maintenance/Repair costs:** Upkeep costs for these trucks are high; use independent garages to keep costs down. **Parts:** Mechanical parts are widely available and reasonably priced due to the proliferation of independent suppliers. The 2007 model's body parts may be costly and in short supply due to that year's changes. **Extended warranty:** A good idea for the powertrain, judging by consumer complaints and the high incidence of diesel engine deficiencies. **Best alternatives:** A used Dodge Ram (mainly for the warranty and the less-troublesome, but not perfect, Cummins diesel), a Honda Ridgeline, a Mazda B-Series, or a Nissan Frontier V6.

Strengths and Weaknesses

Similar to Detroit's other pickups, these models are classed as 1500 half-ton, 2500 three-quarter-ton, and 3500 one-ton models. They come with a wide range of engine options, body styles, and bed sizes. The "C" designation refers to 4×2, and the "K" designation to 4×4. The 3500 series offers a four-door cab with a full rear seat. The variety of cab and cargo bed combinations, along with a choice of suspensions, makes these pickups adaptable to just about any use. Standard features include one of the biggest cabs among pickups, a fourth door, a three-piece modular truck frame, rack-and-pinion steering, and four-wheel disc brakes with larger pads and rotors.

An AutoTrac AWD drivetrain allows the driver to select an automatic mode that delivers full-time 4×4 (particularly useful if you live in a snowbelt area), while a 4-speed automatic features an innovative tow/haul mode that stretches out the upshifts to tap the engine's power at its maximum. There's also a potent family of four Vortec V8s in addition to a 6.6L turbodiesel (360 hp), 16-inch tires and wheels, and the highest minimum ground clearance among the Detroit pickups.

Chevy and GMC full-sized pickups are good domestic workhorses—when they're running. Of course, that's the problem: They're not dependable. On the one hand, they have a large, quiet cabin and give relatively easy access to the interior. On the other hand, their size and heft make for lousy fuel economy, a mediocre ride, and subpar handling and braking. Resale value? Don't ask.

For over a decade, Sierras and Silverados have been plagued with severe vibrations that GM has routinely ignored. Owners have nicknamed their trucks "Shakerados," and they say that the new frame braces added to the 2001s to stop the shakes haven't worked (see *agmlemon.freeservers.com/index.html*).

Powertrain and brake repairs and troubleshooting complaints of excessive vibration often sideline the vehicle for days at a time, and dealer repair suggestions often don't make any sense. GM plant workers claim that the porous frame on both Sierras and Silverados cracks behind the cabin and near the tow hook. Original-equipment springs are also failing en masse:

> The front springs on 2003 Chevrolet 1500 [Silverado] Quad Cab trucks are collapsing and GMC/Chevrolet knows about problem and says...the owners [are] responsible to fix their mistake in designing and engineering the truck. They sent out a technical service bulletin to all dealers about [the] problem and [it] says...the owners need to pay $18.00...for rubber bushing to push up spring and $380.00 in labor.

The 1999–2006 models got many new features that make them more powerful, versatile, and accommodating, and they're safer than previous models. However, these changes also make them less reliable than the pickups they replaced. Major powertrain, brake, suspension, electrical system, and body deficiencies have turned these "dream machines" into motoring nightmares.

The 6.0L Duramax diesel has serious reliability and performance problems. The base 4.3L V6 needs more grunt, the transmission hunts for the right gear and produces an incessant whine, the base suspension provides a too-compliant ride, and there's insufficient room for the driver to reach between the door panel and seat to access the seat-adjusting mechanism. And an incredibly high number of performance- and safety-related complaints regarding 2006 and earlier models have been reported to NHTSA and confirmed through confidential bulletins, whistle-blowers, and disappointed owners.

2007 Sierra and Silverado

GM's latest redesign of Sierra and Silverado, for 2007, produced mediocre trucks with only marginally improved performance and reliability. The new diesel engines are expected to have serious performance and quality failings during their first few years on the market, judging by the Duramax's prior performance.

Nevertheless, the 2007–08 models do have a number of improvements that include a large cabin, high ground clearance, good noise insulation, and a rattle-resistant body. You will also find a more-stylish interior; user-friendly instruments and controls; large, supportive seats; lots of leg clearance; and wide-opening doors with useful pull-lever handles.

On the other hand, there are many minuses with the newer models: Hybrid systems and cylinder deactivation haven't produced promised fuel savings. You still get a mediocre ride, problems with brakes and steering are omnipresent, and handling continues to be compromised by lots of body roll and under-steer when cornering, and by serious chassis shake when going over potholed roads. Quality control is only slightly better than with previous models.

VEHICLE HISTORY: 2000—An optional fourth door on extended-cab models, and a small power boost for the Vortec 4800 and 5300 V8 engines. **2001**—Debut of three-quarter-ton and one-ton versions of the Silverado. They offer two engines: the 6.6L Isuzu-built Duramax V8 diesel and GM's homegrown 8.1L Vortec V8. A traction-assist feature becomes available on rear-drive V8 automatics. The Sierra C3 luxury truck offers a number of new features, including a 325 hp 6.0L Vortec V8, full-time all-wheel drive (no 2-speed transfer case for serious off-roading, though), upgraded four-wheel disc anti-lock brakes, an increased-capacity suspension system, and a luxuriously appointed interior. The Sierra HD truck lineup comes with stronger frames; beefed-up suspensions, axles, brakes, and cooling systems; new sheet metal; bigger interiors; and three new V8s: a 6.6L Duramax turbodiesel and two gas engines, a hefty 8.1L and an improved 6.0L. **2003**—Quadrasteer expanded to other models, improved electrical system and passenger-side airbag sensor, a new centre console, and dual-zone temperature and steering-wheel controls. **2004**—Standard cruise control, power door locks, and a CD player. **2006**—A new 360 hp 6.6L V8 turbodiesel engine late in the model year; Quadrasteer option dropped. **2007**—Active Fuel Management cylinder deactivation with the 5.3L V8; more-powerful engines (the 4.8L V8 gets 10 more horses, the 5.3L gets five more, and the 6.0L gets 22 more); a 980 kg (2,160 lb.) payload rating; and towing capability boosted to 4,763 kg (10,500 lb.). Also a reinforced chassis, upgraded suspension and steering systems, a larger cabin and bed, and new exterior and interior styling. Standard stability control on Crew Cabs.

Safety Summary

All models/years: Sudden, unintended acceleration. • Airbag fails to deploy. • Intermittent loss of power steering. • Brake failures (pedal goes to the metal with no braking effect) with ABS light lit constantly. • Brake pad failure and warped rotor. • Parking brake doesn't hold. • ABS doesn't engage; results in extended stopping distances and wheel lock-up. • Chronic stalling. **All models: 1999**—Inability to shut off headlights without shutting down vehicle. • Delayed transmission shifting in cold weather. • Broken spare-tire cable allows spare to fly off. **2000**—A very common problem appears to be that the rear frame breaks from the bottom up to about 5 cm in front of the tow hook attachment. • Transmission jumps from Park into Reverse. • Several cases relating to a broken power-steering pump shaft. • Rear left emergency brake shoe and drum allow salt and debris to get into drum and drum elbow. **2000–01**—Fuel line leakage; allows fuel to spray out rear. **2001**—Loose lug nuts cause left rear wheel to fall off. • Spongy brakes lead to extended stopping distances. • After driving in snow and parking vehicle, brakes won't work. • When accelerating from a stop, vehicle momentarily goes into Neutral. • Transmission suddenly shifts from Fifth down to Third or Second gear while cruising on the highway. • Defective transmission valve body results in transmission jumping out of gear. • Drifting all over the highway. • Driver's seat belt causes pain in the shoulder. • Upper ball joint and right sway bar ends may be missing nuts and cotter keys. **2002**—Fire ignites in the dash. • Throttle sticks. • Chronic engine surging when braking. • Automatic transmission suddenly downshifts when accelerating, as engine surges then clunks into gear. • Passenger-side front end suddenly collapses (replaced outer tie-rod end). • Steel wheel collects water that freezes and throws wheel out of balance. • Steering-column bolt comes apart. • Interior rear-view mirror distortion. • Dimmer switch overheats. • Driver's seatback will suddenly fall backwards. • Head restraint blocks vision to right side of vehicle. **2002–04**—Steering wheel locks up while driving. **2003**—Fire ignites in the engine compartment. • Cracked transmission transfer case. • Automatic transmission slips when shifting from First to Second gear. • 4×4 shifts erratically, causing serious highway instability. • Seat belts lock up. • Tailgate pops open. **2004**—Front axle assembly collapses. • Sway bar mounting bracket breaks, causing the frame and mounting bar to come off. • Brakes are too soft and set too close to the accelerator pedal. • Cruise control surges when going downhill. • Transmission suddenly jumps from Second gear to Reverse. • Tailgate falls apart. • Doors won't unlock in cold weather. • Driver's door window shatters for no reason. • Hood coil spring fails. • Jack slips off the vehicle. • Side mirrors constantly vibrate and are easily scratched when wiped clean. **2005**—Airbag warning light comes on, even when seat is occupied by an adult. • Sudden acceleration and chronic stalling:

> Diesel system has a problem transferring fuel into the truck for use. It runs out while the front fuel tank is still full of fuel. The fuel tank never reads over half full.

• Transmission slips when accelerating, making the truck an easy target when turning into an intersection. • Sudden driveshaft failure:

> GMC Sierra 1500 Crew Cab; while driving at interstate speed, the drive shaft fell off the vehicle and shattered. There was substantial damage to the underside of the vehicle, including muffler, yoke, heat shield, and drive shaft.

• The 4.3L engine and 4-speed automatic transmission work poorly together, constantly downshifting and gear hunting when going up an incline. • On diesels, fuel gauge and transfer pump fail repeatedly. • Rear diesel tank sprays fuel on the highway. • Vehicle is hard to move from a stopped position; feels like the rear brakes are locked up (master cylinder was changed). • Front brakes seem to stick, then overheat and catch fire. • Leaf springs aren't very durable. • Wheel hubcap nuts overheat, and the hubcaps fly off. • Interior door handles easily snag clothes or purse straps when opening the door. • Front doors won't close properly. • Outside rear-view mirrors don't show the rear bumper area when backing up and are useless when hauling a trailer. • Jack bends under weight of vehicle and collapses. **2006**—Erratic cruise-control performance:

> When you are driving using the cruise control and start up a hill the truck slows down at least 10 miles an hour [16 km/h] then suddenly without warning the cruise control system jolts the truck forward trying to compensate for the loss of speed.... It has happened to us going up hills and around hilly curves. If I did not keep both hands on the wheel I very well could have lost control and crashed.

• Rear drum brakes perform poorly. • Loose steering:

> The intermediate shaft on the steering wheel column is loose. The dealer and manufacturer have told me that they are aware of this problem, but there is no fix for it. The front end on the vehicle will feel loose and bounce while driving over uneven pavement and bumps and more so while driving on freeways.

• Out-of-round General tires; Goodyear Wrangler tire-tread separation. • Front tires rub against the suspension when the steering wheel is turned. • Automatic door lock cannot be overridden. • Headliner falls down. **2006–07**—Hard-shifting manual transmission. **2007**—Passenger-side airbag is disabled even though an adult is seated. • The 5.3L V8 with Active Fuel Management will not idle properly or slow down in a timely manner. • Steering, brake lock-up. • Dash gauges are hard to read in daylight (especially the speedometer). • Truck bounces all over the road. • Failed welds under the front seat. • Windshield distortion. • Windshield wiper and washer fluid come on for no reason. • Prematurely worn Bridgestone Dueler tires. • Inoperative tire-pressure monitor system. • Cracked tow hitch receiver. *1500:* **All years:** Regular-cab model vibrates excessively at highway speeds ("beam shake"), rendering mirrors useless:

> The vehicle shimmied in the front and rear at 40–60 mph [64–96 km/h]. The contact was unable to see out of the rear view and passenger side mirrors due to the severe vibration. The dealership informed the contact there was a problem with the frame on the 1999–2006 model years.

Secret Warranties/Internal Bulletins/Service Tips

All models: 1999—If the 4×4 won't engage, you may need to install a new transfer-case actuator and shift detent plunger. • Before you spend big bucks overhauling the transfer case, remember that a bump or clunk heard on acceleration may be silenced by simply changing the transfer-case fluid. • If the front wheels slip while in 4×4, consider replacing the transfer-case clutch plates and front drive axle lubricant. • A steering-column squeak may be silenced by replacing the steering-wheel SIR module coil assembly. **1999–2000**—Wind noise coming from the side may be silenced by replacing the quarter window assembly under warranty. **1999–2003**—An exhaust moan or vibration can be corrected by installing an exhaust-system flex pipe kit. **1999–2004**—Chronic engine knock or piston slap. • Prematurely worn and noisy brake rotors and pads may be replaced with higher-quality aftermarket parts for about half the price. • GM says in TSB #00-05-23-005B that owners should invest in a GM mud flap kit (Part #15765007) to make their rear brakes last longer. Again, save money by shopping at independent retailers. • Inoperative power windows. • Remedy for steering-wheel clunk. • Suspension clunk, slap. GM will do this repair for free as "goodwill" up to 3 years/60,000 km, and will offer a 50 percent refund thereafter. **1999–2005**—Install an exhaust system flex pipe kit to stop an exhaust moan, vibration. **1999–2007**—Engine misfire may be due to an ECM ground terminal that has corroded with rust over time. Inspect the main engine wiring harness ground terminal (G103) for this condition. **1999–2008**—Silencing rear leaf spring noise. **2000–04**—Troubleshooting delayed gear engagement. **2000–05**—Rattle, squeak from front of vehicle. **2001**—Loose engine connecting-rod bolts may cause engine knock and complete engine failure. • Loss of turbo boost accompanied by thick black smoke. • No-starts or hard starts. • Harsh shift remedies. • When in 4×4 and in Reverse gear, engine won't go over 1000–1300 rpm. • Transmission slips when placed in 4×4. • 6-speed manual transmission clutch fluid may be contaminated by water entering through the reservoir cap. • Automatic transmission 2–4 band or 3–4 clutch damage. • Inoperative wiper motor; fuse blows repeatedly. • Windows are slow to defrost. • Steering-column lock shaft doesn't lock. **2001–02**—Troubleshooting tips to correct slow or no automatic transmission engagement, no-starts, or a blank PRNDL. **2001–03**—The torque converter relief spring and lube regulator spring may need to be changed to correct automatic transmission delayed shifts or loss of power. • TSB #01-07-30-043 and 03-07-30-031 explain why the automatic transmission may slip or leak. **2001–05**—Fuel gauge reads empty on trucks with a spare tank. **2002**—Check Engine light comes on as automatic transmission begins shifting erratically. • 1–2 shift shudder. • Clunk noise from under the hood. • Clunk, bump, or squawk heard when accelerating or coming to a stop. • Shudder or vibration when accelerating from a stop. • Driveline growl or prop shaft ring noise. • Steering shaft clunk. • Noisy brakes. • Water leak at the roof centre clearance light. • Inability to control temperature setting. • Intermittent failing of the tail lights, backup lights, or trailer harness. **2003**—Harsh automatic transmission 1–2 shifting; slipping caused by a faulty pressure control solenoid (TSB #03-07-30-020, May 2003). **2003–04**—Remedies for buzz noise or vibration felt in floor or throttle pedal. • Inoperative front power window. **2003–05**—AC blower motor won't shut off. **2004–05**—Front end pop or snap. **2004**—Cold engine rattling. **2004–06**—Automatic transmission shudder due to water intrusion. **2005**—Poor automatic transmission performance troubleshooting tips. • Free replacement of the powertrain/engine control module; courtesy transportation available. • Loose, rattling hubcaps. **2005–06**—Troubleshooting a steering-column shaft clunk. **2006–07**—AC doesn't cool; noisy compressor. • V8 engine oil leaks. **2007**—No-starts; loss of power. • Power-steering leaks. • Water leaks into the rear footwell area. • Steering whistle. • Exhaust system noise. • Turn signals get an increased flash rate. •

Vertical lines show up on the rear door outer panel (extended-cab rear door). • Some 1500 Series, 4×4, regular-cab, long-box Chevrolet Silverado, and GMC Sierra vehicles have an incorrect GVWR on the Certification Label and an incorrect capacity shown on the Tire and Loading Information Label. Both of these numbers should be increased by 181 kg (400 lb). **2007–08**—Front fender buzz, rattle. *Diesel engines:* **1999–2002**—Special policy covers fuel injection pump failure up to 11 years/193,000 km. **2001**—Excessive vibration and surging. **2001–02**—"Goodwill" warranty will pay for faulty fuel injectors:

SPECIAL POLICY ADJUSTMENT (REPLACE INJECTOR)

BULLETIN NO.: 04039   **DATE: JUNE 2004**

2001–02 SILVERADO/SIERRA (6.6L DURAMAX DIESEL)
CONDITION: Some customers of 2001–02 model year Chevrolet Silverado and GMC Sierra vehicles, equipped with a 6.6L Duramax Diesel (RPO LB7—VIN Code 1) engine, may experience vehicle service engine soon (SES) light illumination, low engine power, hard start, and/or fuel in crankcase, requiring injector replacement, as a result of high fuel return rates due to fuel injector body cracks or ball seat erosion.
SPECIAL POLICY ADJUSTMENT: This special policy covers the condition described above for a period of 7 years or 200,000 miles (320,000 km), whichever occurs first, from the date the vehicle was originally placed in service, regardless of ownership. The repairs will be made at no charge to the customer.

2001–04—Free O-ring replacement:

DIESEL ENGINE OIL LEAK

BULLETIN NO.: 02-06-01-023C   **DATE: JULY 20, 2004**

OIL LEAK AT OIL COOLER TO 6.6L DIESEL ENGINE BLOCK MATING SURFACE (REPLACE O-RINGS, APPLY SEALANT)
2001–04 Chevrolet Silverado 2500/3500
2001–04 GMC Sierra 2500/3500
2003–04 Chevrolet Kodiak C4500/5500
2003–04 GMC Topkick C4500/5500
CAUSE: Minor imperfections in the engine block machined surfaces at the oil cooler interface may allow oil seepage past the oil cooler O-rings.

2001–06—Troubleshooting a turbocharger failure. **2004–07**—Noisy engine drivebelt.

C/K, SIERRA, SILVERADO PROFILE

	1999	2000	2001	2002	2003	2004	2005	2006	2007
Cost Price ($)									
C/K	21,735	—	—	—	—	—	—	—	—
Sierra, Silverado	21,895	22,100	22,060	22,410	23,240	24,070	24,925	24,900	24,900
Hybrid	—	—	—	—	—	—	—	—	33,025
Used Values ($)									
C/K ▲	1,500	—	—	—	—	—	—	—	—
C/K ▼	1,500	—	—	—	—	—	—	—	—
Sierra, Silverado ▲	3,000	3,500	4,000	4,500	6,000	7,500	9,500	11,000	17,000
Sierra, Silverado ▼	2,500	3,000	3,500	4,000	4,500	6,000	8,000	9,500	15,000
Hybrid ▲	—	—	—	—	—	—	—	—	18,000
Hybrid ▼	—	—	—	—	—	—	—	—	16,500
Reliability	2	2	2	2	2	3	3	3	3
Crash Safety (F)	—	—	—	—	—	4	4	4	5
Ext. cab	—	3	3	3	4	4	4	—	5
Side	—	—	—	—	—	4	4	4	5
Offset	2	2	2	2	2	2	2	2	—
Rollover Resistance	—	—	—	—	—	4	4	4	4
Ext. cab	—	3	3	3	4	4	4	4	4
Ext. cab 4×4	—	3	3	3	3	4	4	4	4

BEGINNERS AND BEATERS

Here, we include thumbnail sketches of some of the vehicles we passed over in Part Three. "Beginners" are recent models, were discontinued after only a few model years, or sell only in small numbers in Canada, so they haven't generated enough owner feedback or manufacturer service bulletins to be reviewed thoroughly. "Beaters" are vehicles that are 10 years old or older, and many are no longer built—they're inexpensive wheels that will tide you over until you can get that more-expensive dream machine you've always wanted.

Phil's Beginners

Cars

The mid-sized 2003 **Acura CL** is an Above Average buy; the 1997–2002s are Average, due to serious first-year factory glitches and powertrain problems. A 2003 CL is now worth about $10,500 (new models sold for $37,800); 1997–2002 prices vary from $3,500 to $8,000. Good alternative vehicles are the BMW 318, Honda Accord, Lexus SC 300, and Toyota Camry.

CLs are stylish front-drive, five-passenger luxury coupes that are American-designed and built. And while other Japanese automakers took content out of their vehicles, Acura made the CL one of the most feature-laden cars in its class. Sure, we all know that the coupe's mechanicals and platform aren't that different from the Accord's, but when you add up all of its standard bells and whistles, you get a fully loaded medium-sized car that costs thousands of dollars less than competing luxury coupes.

CLs have changed little since they were launched as 1997 models. 1998 saw the debut of the 2.3L engine; 2003 CLs have plenty of power from the quiet, smooth-running 3.2L V6. And handling is better than average, thanks to an upgraded suspension, variable assisted steering, and 16-inch wheels.

On the downside, this is not a car designed with rear-seat passengers in mind. Adults will likely find their heads pressed against the top of the back-light glass, and legroom and footroom are at a premium. Rear access is a crouch-and-crawl affair. In the trunk, lid hinges intrude into the trunk area and risk damaging cargo when the trunk is closed. The CL hasn't been crash tested by NHTSA; IIHS says the head restraints are Poor for protecting occupants from serious crash-related injuries.

Here are some of the problems reported with the 1997–2002 models: faulty transmission control unit; transmission downshift problems; chronic brake rotor pulsation and other brake problems, leading to resurfacing of brake rotors and the early replacement of brake pads, rotors, calipers, and springs; repeated front-end realignments; and door and wind noise, leading to the replacement of the door.

Owners have reported that the 2003 models equipped with either manual or automatic gearboxes can also be troublesome. Sudden, unintended acceleration and hesitation problems are thought to be transmission-related also. Premature brake pad and caliper wear and warped brake rotors continue to be a serious problem.

Most Honda/Acura TSBs allow for special warranty consideration on a "goodwill" basis, even after the warranty has expired or the car has changed hands. In September 2002, Honda extended its warranties to 7 years/256,000 km (160,000 mi.) on automatic transmissions on about 1.2 million cars and minivans because the components may fail or wear out early. The retroactive warranty includes 2000–01 model year Accords, Preludes, and Odysseys; 2000–02 Acura 3.2L TLs; 2001–02 Acura 3.2L CLs; and some 2003 models of both Acuras, spokesman Kurt Antonius says.

Chrysler's 2004–07 **Crossfire** is an expensive, low-volume luxury sports coupe that gets a Below Average rating. This low-slung, sleekly styled two-door, two-passenger coupe offers a cramped interior, high windowsills, and a low roofline that combine to create a claustrophobic cabin. Service bulletins and owner feedback indicate serious reliability problems during the car's first year on the market.

Depreciation has also been brutal: A $47,745 base 2004 model is now worth only $11,000–$12,000—a good price for a bad car. 2007s sold originally for $40,000 and have a resale value of $16,000–$18,000. Crashworthiness ratings for the 2004–06s are quite good, with five stars given for frontal occupant protection, side protection, and rollover resistance; 2007s got similar marks, except that frontal protection wasn't tested.

Very few owner complaints have surfaced relative to 2005–07 model Crossfires; nevertheless, many safety-related incidents logged by NHTSA are particularly frightening:

> Lack of power when at a stop, even though you might be mashing in the gas pedal (pedal to the metal). So if you fear for your life when you're in the middle of an intersection and your car won't move, don't worry because it's normal.

There's also sudden acceleration when the brakes are applied, high-performance tires and a low-slung body that impair safe handling in inclement weather, airbags that fail to deploy, chronic stalling, transmission breakdowns, a manual transmission that abruptly slips out of First gear into Neutral, defective wheel bolts that lead to the wheel separating from the car, a short circuit in the dash wiring harness that poses a fire risk, original-equipment Continental tires with weak side walls, $400 wheel rims that are easily bent in normal driving, front and rear strut failures, headlights that don't adequately illuminate the road, lights that dim at stoplights and at idle, and erratic voltage (faulty voltage regulator?) that fries powertrain computer modules and other electronic components.

Bland but solid-looking, the spacious 2005–07 **Ford Five Hundred** and **Freestyle** (an SUV wagon clone) have not captured buyers' hearts, due to a combination of high gas prices, mediocre highway performance, and early reports of poor-quality components. Now that fuel prices have reached new lows, used prices haven't yet recovered. Both models are rated Below Average and are priced similarly. Although originally priced at $29,295, used 2005 versions are selling for only $8,000; 2006 versions are worth barely $9,500; and 2007s cost $11,500–$12,500.

A spin-off of the Volvo S80, the Five Hundred will eventually replace the Crown Victoria to become Ford's flagship sedan. It uses a modified Volvo XC90 SUV and S80 wagon/sedan platform capable of giving the car some SUV advantages such as higher seating, increased interior space, and optional four-wheel or all-wheel drive. There is more interior space and trunk capacity than in the full-sized Crown Victoria. Additionally, crash test scores are impressive: Frontal and side crash protection are rated at five stars, and rollover resistance scored four stars.

There are plenty of performance shortcomings with this large car, though. For example, the 203 hp V6 isn't powerful enough for a 1,860 kg vehicle; it has a very limited towing capability of approximately 907 kg (2,000 lb.); the self-levelling shocks are unproven; the optional all-wheel-drive system is part Volvo, part Ford (not the best combination for trouble-free performance); front occupants will want more legroom; and the 18-inch tires make for a stiff, choppy ride.

Owners are most unhappy about a number of serious factory-related defects, affecting primarily the automatic transmission, fuel supply, and ignition (hard starts, stalling, and dieselling). They report that the transmission jumps out of Park into Reverse, has no intermediate or Second gear for descending mountains, and often hunts for the right gear. Also, battery acid may eat away the plastic transmission cable; the engine loses power when accelerating; various rear brake and suspension problems crop up; there's insufficient dash lighting, and the dash reflects onto the windshield; the fuel gauge gives incorrect readings; rear seat belts cross at children's necks; doors leak water into the interior; and Continental tires may fail prematurely.

Ford's 2000–07 **Jaguar S-Type** is a Not Recommended buy, primarily because of its persistent factory-related and design deficiencies, compounded by a small dealer network, chaotic Ford mismanagement, and its acquisition last year, along with Land Rover, by Tata, an Indian conglomerate. Volvo and Saab will likely be the next auto marquees to be dumped by Ford and General Motors.

The car itself is an attractively styled, small rear-drive luxury sedan that shares its platform with the Lincoln LS. Resale prices reflect a stunningly high depreciation rate. A 2003 model originally selling for $59,950 is now worth barely $11,500; the $62,795 2005 version is now worth $16,000; and the $62,000 2007 is now $29,000.

The S-Type's V8 engine provides plenty of power, and the car handles well. Nevertheless, it's a terrible buy due to its clunky, failure-prone automatic transmission; limited cargo room; unreliable engine and electronics and fuel delivery systems; and frequently needed brake repairs. The 3.0L V6 is derived from a Ford design, while the 4.0L V8 is Jaguar-bred. Both engines are mated to a Ford/Jaguar 5-speed automatic transmission, which explains their overall poor performance.

An Average buy, **GM**'s 2005–07 **Allure** (called the **LaCrosse** in the United States) is a substantially upgraded and stiffened version of the Century and Regal, resulting in improved ride and handling qualities. The rack-and-pinion steering is revised for a better response, and the four-wheel disc braking system is completely new. Nevertheless, the Allure isn't that much different from the cars it replaces, and it has been selling poorly, with 2005–07 models selling between $9,000 and $14,000. The car has a full complement of standard safety features, along with optional Ultrasonic Rear Parking Assist (of doubtful value) and a factory-installed remote starting system. Crash test scores have been acceptable, with frontal crash protection rated at five stars, side protection given three stars, and rollover resistance earning four stars.

The 2005–07 GM **Cobalt** and **Pursuit** are Below Average buys that replace the Cavalier and Sunfire with what GM calls a "premium" small car, though there is little that merits that designation. For example, all-important side curtain airbags and traction control are optional, while many automakers include them as standard features. Set on the Saturn Ion Delta platform for increased body rigidity, structural integrity, and crashworthiness, the Cobalt sedan is about 5 cm shorter in length and about the same width, and has a slightly shorter wheelbase, than the Cavalier it replaces. A trio of noisy, fuel-thirsty 4-cylinder engines provides power: a 140 hp 2.2L, a 170 hp 2.4L, and a 205 hp 2.0L supercharged version.

These small cars offer mediocre handling, vague steering, an unacceptably small rear seat, and subpar fit and finish. The 2005's $15,495 base price has been reduced to about $5,000 for a used version; a 2005 LS sedan that first sold for $19,795 now costs $7,000; an LT sedan that first sold for $22,995 now sells for $8,000; and the supercharged SS coupe, once priced at $24,995, has lost $16,000 in value and can now be bought for $9,000. Crash test scores are mixed for the 2005s and 2006s—frontal crash protection and rollover resistance are rated at four stars, and side protection is given between two and four stars.

Owner complaints target the premature wearout of the front brakes, poor fit and finish, assorted powertrain glitches, and suspension, electrical, and fuel system malfunctions.

GM's 2006–07 **Lucerne** is another also-ran that gets only a Below Average rating. It's a competent front-drive family car that replaced the venerable LeSabre. Two engines are offered with the 2006 model: a 197 hp 3.8L V6 and a 275 hp V8. With a list price of $30,995, the base 2006 model is barely worth $13,500 today. Smart used-car shoppers may wish to consider a 2007 Lucerne ($17,000 used) to escape first-series 2006 model glitches (over 100 reported so far) like the following: no airbag deployment; sudden acceleration when the cruise control is engaged; light steering that allows the car to wander, pulling to the right once underway; dash gauges that can't be read in daylight; a trunk lid that closes too easily on one's head; a driver's mirror that cannot be adjusted to compensate for the rear blind spot and that often fogs up; and a fuel gauge that gives incorrect readings (such as indicating Full when the tank isn't).

GM's 2005–07 **G6** is also rated Below Average. A 2005 sold for $24,670 new and now sells for about $8,500 used (a 2006 is now $12,500). It's a mid-sized replacement for the Grand Am and is built on GM's 2004 Chevy Malibu platform. The G6 comes with a weak, fuel-thirsty 2.4L 4-cylinder engine and a barely competent 3.5L V6, which is rated at 219 hp—much less power than with most of the family-sedan competition. Crash test scores vary considerably: 2005–06 frontal and side crash protection are rated at five and three stars, and rollover resistance scored between four and five stars; however, the 2007s garnered five stars in all three categories.

These cars have major reliability problems that put both your life and your wallet in danger. Foremost of these is the steering system, which can suddenly lock up, throwing your car out of control:

> This has happened in cold weather and mainly in low speed situations immediately after starting my vehicle. The failure prevents you from turning the wheel at all and you are unable to steer the vehicle for a limited amount of time.

The ABS module can overheat and catch fire; brake pads and rotors are in constant need of replacement; and an intense, painful noise occurs if the car is driven with the rear window open. An owner reported that, when pulling into a sloped driveway, the chassis was bent back due to the I-beam structure catching the concrete driveway slope. This caused the entire engine cradle to shift, requiring thousands of dollars in repairs. Other concerns include brake lights that remain lit, automatic transmissions that shift erratically, an instrument panel that can be hard to read in daylight, a sun visor that shorts out, a windshield that chips easily, and dash rattles and noisy struts. And, as if all that isn't enough to worry about, how about staining your clothes? Yep, when the seat material is wet, it transfers its colour to any other material that it contacts...ugh.

The 2006–07 **Hyundai Azera** is an Average luxury, mid-sized, front-drive sedan that replaced the XG350 for 2006. Larger than the XG350 and Sonata, the Azera also has more power (a 263 hp 3.8L V6 coupled to a 5-speed manumatic transmission), and it competes with the Honda Accord, Nissan Maxima, and Toyota

Avalon. The engine is smooth and quiet, fuel economy is fair, the interior is roomy, and handling is first class, providing a comfortable ride. Standard safety features include anti-lock brakes, an anti-skid system, front and rear torso side airbags, and head-protecting side curtain airbags. Used prices are more reasonable than what you would find with the Accord, Avalon, or all-dressed Camry. A $34,495 2006 base Azera is now worth $15,000—less than half its original price. A 2007 version will cost $20,000. Owner reliability complaints have targeted engine head gaskets; rough shifting; electrical short circuits; suspension thumping; Airbag warning light false alerts, and passenger-side "disabled" alerts when the seat is occupied by an adult; and poor headlight illumination, with dimming when stopped and flickering.

Hyundai's 1997–2007 Above Average **Tiburon** is a steal for buyers who want some high-performance features without spending much money. Essentially a sportier variant of the Elantra, this is a fun-to-drive budget sport coupe with a good overall reliability record. Since dealer maintenance and repair costs can be a bit higher than average, owners usually get inspections and repairs done cheaply by independent garages. Used prices vary from $2,500–$11,000 for 1997–2007 models. On early models, the base 16-valve 1.8L 4-cylinder engine is smooth, efficient, and adequate when mated to the 5-speed manual transmission. Put in an automatic transmission, and performance suffers somewhat, plus engine noise increases proportionally. Overall handling is crisp and predictable. The 1998 versions use a stronger 145 hp 2.0L engine, and the $8,000 2003 GT is powered by a sizzling 2.7L V6.

Crashworthiness and rollover resistance as tested on the 2004 model have been outstanding: five stars for frontal and side occupant protection, and four stars for rollover resistance. 2007 models did almost as well, with five-star frontal and four-star side and rollover ratings. Head restraints have been judged Poor up to the 2003 models but Above Average thereafter. Standard brakes are adequate, though sometimes difficult to modulate. As with most sporty cars, interior room is cramped for average-sized occupants. Although no serious defects have been reported, be on the lookout for body deficiencies (fit, finish, and assembly), harsh shifting, slipping with the automatic transmission, clutch failures, oil leaks, and brake glitches (premature front brake wear and excessive brake noise).

Mitsubishi sold the following 2005–06 models in Canada: the compact **Lancer** ES ($15,998); the mid-sized **Galant** DE ($23,948 and $23,998); and the **Eclipse** GS ($25,498), GT ($32,998), and Spyder ($35,148 only for the 2005 version). A convertible Spyder GS version returned as a $31,998 2007 model and is now worth about $19,000. Earlier 2005–06 Spyder GS versions can be found for $11,000–$12,000. As for the Lancer and Galant versions, the 2007 Galant ES (no Lancer was sold) sells for $13,500. 2005–06 Galants are worth $9,000 and $10,500; the cheaper 2005–06 Lancers go for $5,500 and $7,500.

There's not much to dislike with the Lancer, and that's why we give it an Above Average rating. You get spirited acceleration with the OZ Rally's turbocharged engine, excellent frontal and offset crashworthiness scores, and good overall quality. The only drawbacks: the base engine is a bit horsepower-challenged, especially with the automatic transmission; you can expect some parts delays; and front side crashworthiness is below average.

These entry-level front-drive econocars offer an incredible choice of vehicles that run the gamut from the cheap and mundane ES to the high-performance street racer called the OZ Rally. Yes, Mitsus depreciate faster than most Japanese vehicles, but if you're shopping for used models, that's an important advantage. For example, a 2003 base Lancer that retailed originally for $15,998 is now worth $3,500, a 2004 sells for $5,000, and a 2005 goes for $5,500. And don't forget that Mitsubishis are just as reliable as other Asian makes and can be serviced practically anywhere. Crash test scores are both good and bad: Frontal crash protection and rollover resistance got four stars, and side protection earned two stars. The few owner complaints received by NHTSA deal with engine stalling and stumbling; automatic transmissions that lurch, jerk, and slip; clutch failures; broken axles; windshield creaking; frequent paint defects that include swirls, scratches, and peeling; and rear bumper-support rusting.

The Galant is another Above Average buy sold by Mitsubishi. It's reasonably priced, carries competent 4- and 6-cylinder powerplants, handles very well, enjoys good crashworthiness scores, and is fairly reliable, as was its Colt predecessor over a decade ago. Depreciation is rather steep: A $23,097 2003 model now sells for $5,500; a $23,498 2004 is now worth $7,500; and a $23,948 2005 now goes for $9,000.

Surprisingly, first-year glitches haven't plagued the redesigned 2004 models, which came out with more-powerful engines, handling enhancements, larger interiors, and sleeker styling. Crash test scores are better than average on the 2004 and 2005 versions: Frontal and side crash protection were given five stars, and rollover resistance scored four stars. Overall quality control is impressive, generating few owner complaints.

On the downside, some model years don't have a manual transmission to make full use of the car's spirited engine, and rear-seat entry and exit can take some acrobatics. Some of the reported problems are engine hesitation; transmission and brake malfunctions; noisy, squeaking front brakes; an AC that may not provide an even flow of cool air through the lower vents; and a loose driver's seat. Technical service bulletins cover rear suspension rattling, seat adjustments, window glass freezing to the moulding, and tips on reducing brake noise.

The Eclipse is an Above Average, beautifully styled, reasonably priced sporty coupe. Its on-road performance lags behind its looks. As with other Mitsubishis, early models quickly lose their value, making the car a bargain if bought used. A $23,857 2003 model sells for $5,500; a $23,998 2004 is now worth $7,500; and a $35,148 2005 Spyder (the cheapest model available) is now worth almost $12,000.

There are two engine choices available: a 162 hp 2.4L 4-banger and a 263 hp V6. A manual 5-speed is standard, but the optional automatic 5-speed and the 6-speed manual are better performers. Both engines have plenty of grunt throughout their power range when mated to a manual gearbox, but much less when hooked to an automatic transmission. Handling is exceptionally good on all models, but the sportier GT and Spyder are better than the rest. Front-seat occupants get a firm, comfortable ride with fairly supportive seats and adequate room. Crash test scores are mixed: Frontal crash protection is rated at four stars, side protection gets three stars, and rollover resistance gets four stars.

Some of the Eclipse's deficiencies include an automatic transmission that doesn't have the quickness needed for confident highway merging; frequent shifting with the manual transmission; real-world fuel economy that's much less than promised with the automatic tranny; the V6 engine's thirst for premium fuel; so-so steering with the base sedan; a larger-than-expected turning radius for the coupe; considerable torque steer (a pulling to the side on acceleration) felt with the GT; brakes that are overly aggressive; excessive engine, tire, and wind noise; difficult rear entry and exit; and rear seating that's adequate only for children or small adults.

Porsche's 1999–2007 **911** Carrera Coupe and Turbo are Above Average buys. The 911 was redesigned in 1999, gaining additional length and width, and 8 cm to the wheelbase. The 3.4L engine switched from air-cooling to water-cooling and produced 296 hp—more than the previous 3.6L powerplant. A 6-speed manual transmission, side airbags, and ABS were standard. 2007 models saw the return of the glass-roof Targa coupes. Although originally sold for $100,400, a 2003 911 Carrera is now worth about one-third of that amount, or about $36,000. A 2005 now sells for $46,000; and a 2007 model will run you $60,000. The 2000 models got four more horses; 2001 models came with a 415 hp 3.6L twin-turbo engine; and 2002 models adopted the 320 hp 3.6L engine and upgraded the 5-speed automatic transmission.

These cars are famous for high-performance acceleration and handling, impressive braking, and excellent fit and finish. As with most sports cars, you can expect lots of engine and road noise, acrobatic entry and exit, cramped rear seating, and limited storage space. *Consumer Reports* says there are a higher-than-average number of factory-related problems, highlighted by engine, transmission, fuel system, and fit and finish deficiencies affecting principally the 1999 through 2005 model years of Porsche's entire model lineup.

The 1999–2007 rear-drive **Boxster** is a Recommended roadster that competes with the Mercedes-Benz SLK, the BMW Z3, and the Mazda Miata. It's powered by a 201 hp 2.5L dual-overhead-cam 6-cylinder engine coupled to either a 5-speed manual or an optional 5-speed automatic gearbox. The car offers all of the same advantages and disadvantages as the more-refined 911. A 2004 commands almost $47,000.

Sport-Utilities

An Above Average buy, the **Acura RDX** is marketed as the SUV version of Acura's sporty TSX. This $41,400 ($33,195 in the States) luxury crossover combines an innovative powertrain (tur bocharger, etc.), lots of safety gear and high-tech standard features, a sporty platform, and a versatile, plush interior. It was launched as a 2007 model, and returns in 2009 relatively unchanged, except for an engine upgrade (likely trading the turbocharged 4-banger for a V6) and a $1,775 freight fee. The Mazda CX-7 represents a better buy as a much cheaper alternative with similar horsepower, torque, drivetrain, and body styling. Both the 2007 and 2008 RDX have earned five-star ratings for front and side crashworthiness and four stars for rollover resistance. IIHS safety ratings are Good for offset and side occupant protection and head-restraint effectiveness. A 2007 version can be found for about $27,000, or about $14,000 less than its original selling price.

Some complaints: Road noise is omnipresent, and the ride is stiff. You get the impression that the RDX is trying too hard to target the BMW "sporty" SUV market, especially since the 42 buttons and knobs mounted in the centre console area seem zo be copying BMW's confusing iDrive cockpit controls.

Chrysler's **Aspen** is a Not Recommended model that's essentially a $49,995 Dodge Durango with a different front grille. Chrysler says the 2009 Aspen lineup may include a hybrid model. *Lemon-Aid* says the vehicle may not be around that long. A 2007 Aspen will cost about $28,000. The Aspen hasn't been crash tested by NHTSA, but the identical Durango was rated five stars for frontal collision occupant protection and three stars for rollover protection. IIHS also gave the 2007 1998–2003 Durango an Average score for passenger protection in frontal/offset collisions.

The 2007 **Ford Edge** and **Lincoln MKX** are Not Recommended buys that sold new for $34,999 and $42,399, respectively. A 2007 Edge is now worth $18,500; an MKX goes for $25,500. These practically identical small, car-based SUVs use the Mazda6 platform, share Volvo CX-7 parts, and take their styling cues from the Ford Fusion. In the past, an infusion of Mazda parts has always helped bring up the quality of Ford's cars and trucks, including the Escort/Tracer, Probe/MX6, and Escape/Tribute. However, mixing in Volvo components when Ford has Volvo on the auction block presents added risks. Prudent buyers may wish to wait another year to get a better fix on quality and servicing. The 3.5L V6 (265 hp) mated to a 6-speed automatic transmission makes both vehicles better-than-average performers. Big minuses, though, are the absence of third-row seating, unlike the Taurus X, and mediocre fit and finish. Crash test scores are excellent, however. Competitors worth considering: the Honda CR-V, Hyundai Tucson or Santa Fe, Nissan Murano, and Toyota RAV4.

The Ford **Taurus X** is no more than a renamed Ford Freestyle. It is rated an Above Average buy and sells for $33,999 for the 2008 SEL and $41,999 for the AWD

Limited. Unfortunately, the 2008 SEL has already depreciated to a worth of $16,000; the AWD Limited's resale value is $22,500. With the Taurus X, you get all of the attributes of a minivan, an SUV, and a station wagon but few of the disadvantages inherent in each category. There's plenty of interior room for passengers and pets, and the third-row seat can actually accommodate adults. Ride and handling are first class, and the inclusion of electronic stability control as a standard feature has eliminated the fishtailing instability sometimes felt with the Freestyle. Although real-world fuel economy is about 10 percent less than advertised, the 3.5L V6 has plenty of power for most driving activities. NHTSA crashworthiness scores are also quite good: five stars for front- and side-impact occupant protection and four-star rollover resistance. Finally, as the most financially stable of the Detroit automakers, Ford has an edge.

GM Acadia, **Enclave**, and **Outlook**—These are practically identical mid-sized models that are Recommended buys. The trio sold new for $36,495 (2007), $40,895 (2008), and $33,990 (2007), respectively. Today, the models are worth $22,000 (2007), $28,500 (2008), and $20,500 (2007) used. They all offer front-drive/all-wheel-drive powertrains and use a car-based platform that incorporates a third-row seat, which allows for a maximum of eight passengers. Power is provided by a 3.6L V6 mated to 6-speed automatic transmission. GM says the upgraded powertrain set-up gives 8 percent improved performance and up to 4 percent improved fuel economy when compared with current front-drive 4-speed automatics. Competing models worth considering are the Honda Pilot, Nissan Murano, Mazda CX-9, and Toyota Highlander.

Saturn's Outlook replaced the Relay minivan for the 2008 model year. It rides on a unibody platform, which cuts weight by eliminating the usual hefty trucklike frame and other heavy-duty chassis components. The user-friendly interior resembles GM's Yukon and Tahoe cabins, with roomy and easily accessed seating. Furthermore, an innovative second-row seat can be pushed forward and folded against the front row, thereby enlarging the pathway to the third-row seating area. Entry and exit height is low, and the rear tail light design isn't to everyone's taste.

As with most of GM's recent SUVs, standard safety features abound. A wide stance and low centre of gravity reduce the threat of a rollover. NHTSA crashworthiness scores are quite good: five stars for front- and side-impact occupant protection and four stars for rollover resistance.

Some of the minuses inherent in GM's new crossover trio: Outlook servicing may be problematic if GM dumps the Saturn brand in mid-2009, third-row seating is a bit cramped, the new 6-speed tranny has yet to prove itself, and the V6 powerplant is a mixed-breed design from Australia, Germany, Sweden, and North America that was first introduced on Cadillac's CTS sedan and SRX SUV crossover. CTS and SRX complaints logged by NHTSA and others frequently mention engine and transmission/differential failures. Furthermore, GM's touted fuel economy savings associated with its new powertrain (*front-drive*: 13.8/9.4 L/100 km; *AWD*: 14.7/9.8 L/100 km) may be illusory when compared to real driving reports.

The Cadillac **SRX**, a Below Average buy, is a mid-sized rear-drive or all-wheel-drive luxury crossover. It has been on the Canadian market since 2004, when the car originally sold for $52,250 as a front-drive SUV, $54,875 with AWD, and $63,965 for a V8 AWD. Today, the same vehicles are worth $13,000, $14,000, and $15,000, respectively.

SRX owners report frequent transmission and differential breakdowns in addition to brake and electrical failures and fit and finish deficiencies. The 2004–07 models earned four stars for front crashworthiness and five stars for side-impact protection. The 2008 models got similar ratings, but they also scored three stars for front-drive rollover resistance and four stars for AWD rollover protection.

First launched as a 2003 model, the 2003–08 GM **Hummer H2** SUV and SUT (SUT is the pickup version, launched as a 2005 model) are Not Recommended due to their overall poor reliability, mediocre highway performance, and mind-spinning depreciation. A 2003 H2 SUV that originally sold for $71,000 is now barely worth $18,000; a 2007 SUV or SUT that sold for $67,700 new has already lost $30,000 of its trade-in value. Outward visibility is severely compromised by the small windshield and wide roof pillars, and NHTSA hasn't crash tested the H2 yet. Still, the H2 is a good off-road performer (it uses the Tahoe's previous generation platform), and it appeals to those who like ultra-macho styling.

The more-moderately priced 2006–07 **Hummer H3** is also Not Recommended, mainly because its mechanicals are derivative of the poor-quality GM Canyon/Colorado and it has been on the market only a few years. Depreciation is unusually rapid: a $40,000 2006 H3 now fetches $21,000. Like its big brother, the H3 is a good off-roader, but for this attribute you must sacrifice access, visibility, a quiet interior, and a comfortable ride. The base engine is noisy, has little grunt, and is a gas-guzzler. It was replaced by a 3.7L engine in late 2007. A 300 hp 5.3L V8 powers the new 2008 H3 Alpha variant. NHTSA has given the H3 its top five-star rating for frontal and side crashworthiness, beginning with the 2006 model, although passenger protection is rated only four stars in side impacts.

Isuzu's 1993–2004 **Ascender**, **Axiom**, **Rodeo**, **Rodeo Sport**, and **Trooper** are competent SUVs for light city commuting. However, Isuzu's decision to abandon the North American truck market in 2009 means all of the automaker's vehicles are destined to become automotive orphans; for this reason, these SUVs are Not Recommended buys. Although they look tacky and feel outdated, Isuzus are good performers with powerful V6s, shift-on-the-fly capabilities, versatile transmissions, predictable rear-drive handling, spacious interiors, and very few complaints of safety-related defects. Less attractive characteristics are a wimpy 4-cylinder engine, part-time 4×4 that can't be used on dry pavement, a harsh ride over bumpy terrain, excessive body lean when cornering, obstructed rear visibility, narrow rear doors, excessive road and engine noise, and poor fuel economy. Some of the safety-related failures tabulated by NHTSA include brake loss, automatic transmission failures, and sudden, unintended acceleration.

Used **Jeeps** (Liberty and Wrangler excepted) are Not Recommended. To be fair, the Jeep's tendency to roll over isn't as high as that of other small sport-utilities; parts aren't yet hard to find; and servicing, if not given with a smile, at least isn't accompanied by a snarl or head-scratching. Nevertheless, Chrysler's string of money-losing years and its penny-pinching owners make the Jeep division a prime candidate for the auction block in 2009. And if the company is sold, there will be fewer dealers, warranties will be worthless, parts will be hard to find, and resale values will plummet even more. Early Cherokees, CJs, and Wagoneers have been known for their rattle-prone bodies, air and water leaks, electrical glitches, and high-cost brake maintenance. Expect to spend $1,500, tops, for a decade-old entry-level CJ, and a thousand more for an even older Wagoneer.

As predicted last year by *Lemon-Aid*, **Land Rover** was sold on March 26, 2008, to Tata Motors, an Indian conglomerate that also picked up Jaguar for about $2.3 billion (U.S.). News of the deal sent Tata shares down when it was learned that the purchase was financed by a $3 billion 15-month loan. (Tata also owns the Taj Mahal Palace & Tower hotel, which was hit hard by a terrorist attack in late 2008.) This sale means Tata will have the unenviable position of paying the annual $2 billion losses Land Rover and Jaguar are expected to incur, judging by past performance. Our prediction: Ta-ta, Land Rover; ta-ta, Jaguar.

Land Rover's **Discovery** was replaced by the Not Recommended2005 and 2006 **LR3** SE/HSE ($61,900/$67,900), a much more refined vehicle that was completely reengineered by Ford and given a Jaguar-sourced 300 hp 4.4L V8 along with decent disc/disc brakes. It is now worth $22,000–$26,000.

According to J.D. Power's 2006 Initial Quality Study (IQS), Land Rover anchored the bottom of the quality heap with 204 problems per 100 vehicles—more than two problems per vehicle, and a far cry from the industry average of 124 problems. Land Rover also tied for last with Hummer and Porsche in *Consumer Reports*' 2006 car reliability survey, and it was one of only six makes that didn't have a model with reliability of "Good" or above, a "distinction" shared with Mercedes-Benz, Volkswagen, and Jaguar.

The following year, Land Rover placed second-last in the same *Consumer Reports* reliability survey. (Mercedes-Benz took the bottom spot.) The V8-equipped LR3/Discovery was ranked the second-least reliable mid-sized SUV. (The Mercedes-Benz M-Class SUV took last place.)

Range Rover launched a sportier-looking $77,800–$93,800 Sport for the 2006 model year, which is also Not Recommended. Equipped with the LR3's V8 engine (an optional supercharger adds 25 horses) and loaded with performance features, the Sport targets the FX45 and Porsche Cayenne crowd. However, Sport sales have been underwhelming, and 2006 models have lost so much of their original value that they sell for as little as $34,000.

Rapid depreciation has spared none of the Land Rover lineup over the past few decades. Range Rover and Discovery versions have been particularly hard hit. A 1996 $42,000 Discovery is now worth about $5,000, and the same-year Range Rover, originally priced at $80,000, *may* fetch $8,000 on a good day.

The cheapest of the Not Recommended Land Rovers is the **Freelander**, launched in 2002 with an entry-level price of $34,800; its resale value is now about $6,000. It survived only four model years. The 2005 versions included the SE and SE3 (now worth $22,000/$24,000). They carry a wimpy 174 hp 2.5L V6 engine, feature a removable hardtop that takes a two-man crew to install, and use antediluvian disc/drum brakes.

More softly styled than its larger, squared-off Discovery brother, the Freelander is a small, underpowered, cramped truck with luxury SUV pretensions. Headroom is at a premium for tall drivers (don't look for the seat height-adjustment control—there isn't one), and storage space behind the back seats is clearly inadequate. Ground clearance is also quite low when compared with the competition. When pushed, the 174 hp V6 engine whines and struggles to hold its own. A stick shift isn't available, so there's no way to improve the mediocre 15.0 L/100 km average fuel economy.

On paper, the latest rendition of these models looks impressive indeed, with a long list of standard safety, performance, and convenience features. But, as with other Land Rovers, when you buy one of these entry-level British imports, you are buying into a make that's unreliable, outclassed by most other automakers, and served by a limited, chaotic dealer network that was poorly administered by Ford and is now Tata Motors' headache.

Mazda's **CX-7** and **CX-9** are Above Average buys that were sold in Canada as 2007s for $32,095 and $39,995, respectively (an AWD version costs about $2,000 more); they are now worth $20,000 and $25,000. The sporty five-passenger CX-7 is a promising new unibody, four-door crossover SUV based on the Mazda5 and Mazda6. It isn't suitable for off-roading, even though it looks like it could go anywhere. The turbocharged 4-cylinder engine is taken from the MazdaSpeed6 and hasn't accumulated enough road time to determine its long-term durability. Electronic stability control is a standard feature. A longer version, the CX-9, is equipped with a V6 and a third-row seat. Both models have earned high crashworthiness rankings for the 2007–08 models: five-star occupant protection in front and side impacts, and four stars for rollover resistance.

Next, we come to **Mercedes-Benz** and its problem-racked foray into luxury sport-utilities, first launched in 1997. Known collectively as the **M-Class**, these SUVs are Not Recommended buys from 1998 to 2007. ML320, ML350, ML430, and ML500 models are a far cry from being cheap wheels, even though they depreciate about 50 percent after five years (a $48,600 2001 ML320 is now worth about $9,000). The main drawbacks of these luxury lemons are poor quality control; unreliable, limited servicing; and so-so parts availability. Owners report automatic transmission failures, frequent engine oil leaks and engine oil sludge, and electrical system shorts. Other problems afflict brake pads, rotors, master cylinders, fuel pumps, oxygen sensors, mass airflow sensors, and fit and finish.

Mercedes-Benz redesigned the 2006 M-Class to make it longer, lower, and wider. It handles and rides in a more-carlike fashion because of the retuned suspension and the removal of its truck frame. Power is supplied by a 268 hp 3.5L V6 or by a 302 hp 5.0L V8. The ML350 was launched as a 2003 model and sold for $50,600; it's now worth about $14,500. A 2005 ML500 that originally sold for $68,690 is now worth approximately $24,500.

Is the redesigned 2006 and later M-Class more reliable and glitch-free? No, nothing indicates that this is the case. In fact, consumer complaints are still highlighting electronic, brake, and powertrain problems as the car's more common failings.

The same caveat applies to Mercedes' **R-Class**, launched in 2006. It fills the gap between wagons and the M-Class with a six-passenger crossover reminiscent of the Chrysler Pacifica. It's available with a 268 hp 3.5L V6, a 302 hp 5.0L V8, and an incredibly powerful and totally inappropriate 360 hp 5.5L V8 AMG engine. On- and off-road driving is aided by the electronically controlled 4ETS four-wheel-drive system used in the M-Class and G-Class, an Airmatic air suspension system, and a high-pressure brake system. A 2006 R350 sold for $64,400 and can now be bought used for $33,000. A used 2006 R500 takes a harder hit: Sold originally for $75,950, it is now worth about $40,000.

Is the Mercedes cachet worth the headache of constant repairs and adjustments, and the requirement that you see your service manager more than your spouse? Again, no matter how low their prices, these SUVs, like Mercedes' other vehicles, are mainly for buyers with more money than common sense.

Porsche's **Cayenne** is a Below Average buy, mainly due to its limited servicing network, mediocre performance, and outrageously high retail price—reserved for Canadians who are too naive to know they're being scammed. In fact, we're paying a retail price that is still way too high, even after having been cut by more than $10,000 following *Lemon-Aid*'s criticism of Porsche's greed in late 2007. For example, Canadian dealers sold the 2006 for $60,100, $80,100, and $126,900 (for the V6, V8, and AWD V8 Turbo, respectively). Meanwhile, this luxury SUV sells for $43,400, $57,900, and $93,700 in the States. Incidentally, a used 2006 Canadian version of the above models costs $36,000, $41,000, and $62,000.

First launched as a 2003 model, the Cayenne skipped the 2007 model year and returned as a 2008 model. A mid-sized unibody SUV, the Cayenne shares many of the VW Touareg's parts (remember, VW, Audi, and Porsche are all under the same corporate umbrella); hence, reliability has been subpar. Cayenne does have some limited off-road capability, thanks to its low gearing, sophisticated electronics, and Touareg-sourced V6 engine, plus Porsche V8 and twin-turbo variants—a 3.2L V6

(247 hp), 4.5L V8 (340 hp), 4.5L Twin-Turbo V8 (450 hp), and another, more-powerful 4.5L Twin-Turbo V8 (520 hp). Transmissions consist of a 6-speed manual and a 6-speed automatic. On-road capability is a big disappointment, however, since the vehicle lacks Porsche's usual handling prowess. Furthermore, many of the cabin controls are needlessly complex and confusing. Crashworthiness has not yet been rated.

The 2003–06 **Subaru Baja** is a Below Average all-wheel-drive crossover that provides the handling and passenger-carrying characteristics of a car with its open-bed versatility, and, to a lesser degree, the load capacity of a pickup truck (think of a small 1959–60 Chevrolet El Camino, or a mini GM Avalanche). Baja's unibody platform borrows heavily from Subaru's Legacy and Outback.

The car is too small to offer much that is useful or fun. Still, poor sales mean deeply discounted used prices. For example, a 2006 version that sold new for almost $30,000 is now available for about $14,500. Some of the Baja's minuses: uncomfortably upright rear seating; the bed is too short to carry a bike without extending the tailgate into part of the bed; there's no 5-speed automatic transmission; and the absence of a folding midgate means the flip-and-fold versatility isn't as practical as Subaru pretends. Head restraints are ranked Marginal by IIHS, and no crashworthiness tests were carried out by NHTSA, although the Legacy Outback was awarded five stars for front- and side-impact occupant protection and four stars for rollover resistance.

The **Toyota FJ Cruiser** takes its inspiration from the Toyota FJ40 Land Cruiser, built between 1956 and 1983. First model year 2007s sold for $30,000 and are now worth $20,000; 2008 used prices are only a couple of thousand dollars more. The Cruiser is an Above Average buy that competes especially well off-road against the Ford Escape, Honda Element, Jeep Liberty or Wrangler, and Nissan Xterra. It is powered by a competent 239 hp 4.0L V6 that can be used for either two- or four-wheel drive. A 5-speed automatic transmission comes with both versions, and a 6-speed manual gearbox is available with the all-wheel drive. Although the FJ's turning circle is about 1.5 m larger than those of similar-sized SUVs, off-roading should be a breeze if done carefully, thanks to standard electronic stability control, short overhangs, and better-than-average ground clearance.

Interestingly, NHTSA crashworthiness scores for front and side impacts have been five stars; however, the rollover rating was only three stars. This is disappointing, and it's almost never seen with vehicles that are equipped with electronic stability control.

The rear side doors are taken from the Honda Element, which means rear and side visibility is severely limited. There is also some side-wind vulnerability, and annoying wind noises are generated by the large side mirrors. Although touted as a five-passenger conveyance, an average-sized adult fifth passenger in the back seat won't be comfortable. Plus, the rear seats are hard to access, forcing front occupants to unbuckle every time a rear occupant gets in or out. Front-seat head-rests may be uncomfortably positioned for short occupants.

Of course, if you don't mind driving a really old Toyota, there's nothing wrong with a 1987–89 Toyota **Land Cruiser**, which sells for about $2,500. Just be sure to pull the wheels off to examine the brakes, to check for undercarriage corrosion, and to make sure the engine head gasket is okay.

VW's **Touareg** is a Not Recommended buy that is living on borrowed time due to poor sales and quality-control deficiencies. Restyled in 2007, it's now cleaner-burning and more fuel-efficient. But the Touareg has already earned a bad reputation for poor reliability and expensive servicing ever since it was first launched as a 2005 luxury SUV listed at $55,010 (now worth $20,000); a new 2006 sold for almost 10 percent less at $50,790, The 2004 is now worth about $16,500.

Despite its sharing of some parts with the Porsche Cayenne, all you get as a trade-off are befuddled mechanics; long waits for parts; complicated controls; a modest cargo area; myriad electrical, powertrain, and brake problems; premature tire wear; and performance and handling that's abysmal. A 276 hp 3.6L V6 became the standard engine in the summer of 2006; however, it is just as thirsty as, and only slightly less lethargic than, the earlier 3.2L V6. An optional 4.2L V8 offers a bit better performance, but only the turbocharged V10 diesel is adequate to give this beast the grunt it requires, especially when used for off-roading.

Crashworthiness ratings are fairly impressive. The 2005 and 2006 models scored four stars for frontal collision occupant protection and five stars in side-impact tests. The 2007 and 2008 models were judged to give five-star protection in both tests. Rollover resistance was rated four stars.

Pickups

All of the small Japanese pickups are good performers. **Mazda**'s **B-Series** trucks, though, are the weakest brand for reliability and durability when compared with Nissan and Toyota. Mazdas are particularly vulnerable to powertrain, suspension, brake, and fuel system failures. But interestingly, fit and finish is better with Mazda than with other Asian automakers.

Nissan's small trucks are the most reliable, although body fit and finish and accessories (AC, sound system, and electrical systems) are problem-prone.

Toyota's small pickups have the second-worst reliability record, but come nowhere near Mazda's dismal reputation. Most of Toyota's glitches mirror Nissan's, except for one major rusting problem: Toyota will repair or buy back 1995–2000 **Tacoma** pickups affected by rust-damaged structural frames. An estimated 813,000 Tacomas from that era are still on North American roads and may be affected, especially if driven in areas where snow and road salt are found. The excessive rusting is caused by inadequate anti-corrosion undercoating applied at the factory.

As for larger trucks, the Toyota **Tundra** beats out Nissan's **Titan**. Although Toyota has had a number of powertrain, brake, suspension, and fuel delivery problems, the scope of these deficiencies doesn't come close to the Nissan Titan's deficiencies, which comprise all of the above plus accessories and body fit and finish.

Although information is still sketchy, service bulletins and a small number of owner complaints show that the **Honda Ridgeline** has far fewer performance and reliability/durability complaints than do either Mazda or Toyota trucks.

Phil's Beater Beat

There are plenty of cheap, reliable used cars, vans, and trucks out there that will suit your driving needs and budget. In the 1970s, the average car was junked after around seven years or 160,000 km; two decades later, the average car was driven for almost eight years or 240,000 km. Industry experts now say that most new models should last 10 years or 300,000 km before they need major repairs. This means you can get good high-mileage vehicles for less than one-quarter to one-half of their original price, and expect to drive them for five years or more.

But having said that, it can be tough to find a 10-year-old vehicle that's safe and reliable. Personally, I'd be reluctant to buy any decade-old vehicle from someone I didn't know, or one that has been brought in from another province. All of that accumulated salt is a real body killer, and it's just too easy to fall prey to scam artists who cover up major mechanical or body problems resulting from accidents or environmental damage.

Nevertheless, if you know the seller and an independent mechanic gives you the green light, you might seriously consider a 10-year-old, beat-up-looking car, pickup, or van (but heed my advice about old SUVs, following). Look for one of those listed in this appendix, or, if you have a bit more money to spend and want to take less of a risk, look up the 1999–2003 Recommended or Above Average models found in Part Three.

Warning: No matter what you buy or how much you spend later on, you will remember your first "beater" as one of the best cars you ever owned.

Old Sport-Utilities

Anyone buying a sport-utility that's a decade old or more is asking for trouble, because many SUVs are worked hard off-road. The danger of rollovers for vehicles not equipped with electronic stability control is also quite high, particularly with Ford, Isuzu, and Suzuki versions; safety features are rudimentary, dangerous, and unreliable (especially airbags and ABS); overall quality control is very poor; and performance and handling cannot match today's models.

It's no wonder that many buyers are opting for new or almost-new SUVs manufactured during the past three years. During that time, prices came down considerably because more products were in the supply line, electronic stability control and full-torso side airbags were more widely available as standard features, and crashworthiness scores climbed higher.

Depreciation Quirks

Depreciation varies considerably among different vehicle types and models. For example, minivans depreciate a bit more slowly than cars, and diesel cars and trucks hold their value better than gas-powered vehicles do.

Gas-electric hybrids, which have been on the market since 1999, apparently lose their values at about the same rate as conventional cars. Undoubtedly, this is because used-car buyers are afraid to replace the costly high-tech components (imagine paying $8,000 for a replacement battery once the eight-year warranty has expired).

10 Beater Rules

1. Try to buy a vehicle that's presently being used by one of your family members. Although you may risk a family squabble somewhere down the road, you'll likely get a good buy for next to nothing, you will have a good idea of how it was driven and maintained, and you can use the same repair facilities that have been repairing your family's vehicles for years. Don't worry if a vehicle is almost 10 years old—that's becoming the norm for Canadian ownership, particularly the farther west you go.

2. Buy from a private seller—prices are usually much cheaper and sales scams less frequent.

3. Cut insurance and fuel costs. Use the Internet (*www.insurancehotline.com*) to compile a list of models that are the cheapest to insure. Be wary of diesel-equipped or hybrid cars that may require more-expensive dealer servicing and thus wipe out any fuel-consumption savings. Also, pay attention to the quality and performance of your fuel-efficient choice: A 2001–03 fuel-sipping Ford Focus will likely have higher repair bills than gas bills, and a 4-cylinder minivan, though cheap to run, can make highway merging a nightmare.

4. Find out the vehicle's history through a franchised dealer, CarProof, or provincial licensing authorities and then have an independent garage (preferably CAA-affiliated) check out the body and mechanical components.

5. Look for high-mileage vehicles sold by rental agencies like Budget Rent A Car—a company that offers money-back guarantees and reasonably priced extended warranties.

6. Refuse all preparation or "administration" fees and 50/50 warranties where the repair charges are submitted by the seller.

7. Stay away from vehicles or components known for having high failure rates. American front-drives, for example, have more-frequent failures and costlier repairs than rear-drives. "Orphaned" American models like the Ford Taurus/ Sable and Windstar or GM front-drive minivans are also poor choices because

of low-quality components and inadequate servicing support from dealers who wish these cars were never made. Other sinkholes: any vehicle equipped with a turbocharger or supercharger, or multiple computers (BMW's 7 Series, for example); Cadillacs with 4.1L engines and/or front-drive; and Chryslers with sludge-prone 2.7L engines or 4-speed automatic transmissions. If the engine has a timing chain instead of a belt, you will save a fortune. Timing chains frequently survive the lifespan of the engine, whereas timing belts must be replaced every 70,000–100,000 km.

8. Steer clear of European models. They are often money pits. Parts and competent, reasonably priced servicing will likely be hard to find, and quality control has declined considerably over the past decade.

9. Buy three-year-old Hyundais, but stay away from Excels or early Sonatas and early Kias or Daewoos. Also look for five- to 10-year-old single-owner Japanese models.

10. Shop for used rear-drive full-sized wagons or vans instead of front-drive American minivans.

Beaters You Will Love

Acura—The 5-cylinder **Vigor** is a 1992–94 Honda Accord sedan spin-off that sells for $3,000–$4,500 and is rated an Above Average buy. This compact has power to spare, handles well, and has an impressive reliability/durability record. Problem areas: excessive brake noise and premature brake wear in addition to fit and finish deficiencies. The 1992 Vigor turned in below-average crash test scores.

The 1989–95 **Legend** is an Above Average $3,000–$3,500 buy, but the 1986–88 model years are Not Recommended. Resale values are high on all Legend models, especially the coupe. Shop for a cheaper 1989 or later base Legend with the coupe's upgraded features and fewer reports of sudden, unintended acceleration. Pre-1990 Legends were upscale, enlarged Accords that were unimpressive performers with either of the two 6-cylinder powerplants. The 3.2L V6 that appeared in 1991 is by far a better performer.

Chrysler Dart, **Valiant**, **Duster**, **Scamp**, **Diplomat**, **Caravelle**, **Newport**, rear-drive **New Yorker Fifth Avenue**, and **Gran Fury**—Problem areas are electrical systems, suspensions, brakes, body and frame rust, and constant stalling when humidity is high. The Caravelle, Diplomat, and New Yorker Fifth Avenue are reasonably reliable and simple-to-repair throwbacks to a time when rear-drive land yachts ruled the highways. Powered with 6- and 8-cylinder engines, they will run practically forever with minimal care. The fuel-efficient "slant 6" powerplant was too small for this type of car and was changed to a gas-guzzling but smooth and reliable V8 after 1983. Handling is vague and sloppy, though, and emergency braking is often accompanied by rear-wheel lock-up. Still, what do you want for a $500–$750 1984–89 "retro rocket"? Other problem areas include the carburetor (don't ask what that is; your dad knows), ignition, and suspension (premature idler-arm wear). It's a good idea to adjust the torsion bars frequently for better suspension performance. Doors, windshield pillars, the bottoms of both front and rear fenders, and the trunk lid rust through more quickly than average.

The **Stealth** is a serious, reasonably priced sports car that's as much go as show. Although 1995 was its last model year in Canada, it was still sold in the United States as the Mitsubishi 3000GT. Prices range from $2,500–$3,500 for the 1991–93 base or ES model. A '95 high-performance R/T will go for about $4,000— not a bad price for an old "orphaned" sports car, eh? Problem areas are engine, transmission, front brake, and electrical failures. The 1993 model excelled in crash tests.

Chrysler's 1999–2001 **Prowler** is a Recommended fast, sporty rear-drive coupe that handles well and is attractively styled to resemble a hot-rod roadster from the '50s. On the minus side, it has little interior room, entry and exit is a chiropractor's delight, and overall visibility is less than ideal. Its 253 hp 3.5L V6 was borrowed from Chrysler's 300M and LHS. A 1999 Prowler costs about $18,000; the 2001 model is worth about $25,000.

Ford Maverick, **Comet**, **Fairmont**, **Zephyr**, **Tracer**, **Mustang**, **Capri**, **Cougar**, **Thunderbird** V6, **Torino**, **Marquis**, **Grand Marquis**, **LTD**, and **LTD Crown Victoria**—Problem areas are trunk, wheelwell, and rocker panel rusting as well as brake, steering, and electrical system failures.

The 1990–97 **Probe** is essentially a Mazda MX-6 sporty two-door coupe in Ford garb. It's quite reliable and gives better-than-average highway performance. Problem areas are AC, CV joints, and electrical and body glitches. Good crashworthiness ratings, but limited servicing support. Prices range from $1,000 to $2,500.

GM's 1982–96 **Caprice**, **Impala SS**, and **Roadmaster** are Above Average-rated, comfortable, and easy-to-maintain large cars that have been off the market since the 1996 model year. Overall handling is acceptable, but expect a queasy ride from the too-soft suspension. The trunk is spacious, but gas mileage is particularly poor. Despite the many generic deficiencies inherent in these rear-drives, they still score higher than GM's front-drives for overall reliability and durability. The Impala SS is basically a Caprice with a 260 hp Corvette engine and high-performance suspension. Good, cheap cars for first-time buyers, the 1991–93 models can be bought for $700–$1,000, while later models will cost $1,500–$2,000. Maintenance is inexpensive and easy to perform, and any corner garage can do repairs. Average parts costs can be cut further by shopping at independent suppliers, who are generally well stocked.

The 1991–96 models have shown the following deficiencies: AC glitches; prematurely worn brake (lots of corrosion damage), steering, and suspension components, especially shock absorbers and rear springs; serious electrical problems; and poor-quality body and trim items. Body assembly is not impressive, but paint quality and durability is fairly good, considering the delamination one usually finds with GM's other models. Wagons often have excessive rust around cargo-area side windows and wheelwells, and hubcaps on later models tend to fly off.

GM's 1984–96 rear-drive Cadillac **Brougham** and **Fleetwood** are Above Average-rated luxury "land yacht" buys that sell for $2,000–$4,000. Originally front-drives, these big sedans adopted the rear-drive, stretched platform used by the Buick Roadmaster and Chevrolet Caprice in 1993. Equipped with a 185 hp V8 mated to a 4-speed automatic transmission, all models came with standard traction control and anti-lock brakes. The rear-drive configuration is easy to repair and not hard to diagnose, unlike the cars' front-drive brethren. Other cars worth considering are Cadillac's DeVille and a fully loaded Ford Crown Victoria or Mercury Grand Marquis. The most serious problem areas are the fuel-injection system, which frequently malfunctions and costs an arm and a leg to repair; engine head gasket failures; automatic transmissions that shift erratically; a weak suspension; computer module glitches; brakes that constantly need rotor and pad replacement; poor body assembly; and paint defects. From a reliability/durability standpoint, the rear-drives are much better made than their front-drive counterparts.

Pontiac's 1991–95 **Sunbird** was GM's smallest American-built car, along with its twin, the Chevrolet **Cavalier**. Available as two-door coupes, four-door sedans, and two-door convertibles, both models are Average buys. Nearly all Sunbirds were powered by a wimpy 96 hp 2.0L 4-cylinder engine as standard equipment, mated to a clunky, performance-sapping, fuel-wasting 3-speed automatic tranny. GT models featured a 165 hp turbocharged version of the same engine. Neither engine was very dependable. A better-quality, optional 140 hp 3.1L V6 came on the scene in 1991. In 1992, ABS became a standard feature, increasing the complexity and cost of brake maintenance for years to come. The 2.0L engine gained 14 more horses.

Honda's 1984–91 **CRX** is a highly Recommended and seriously quick two-seater sports car—a Honda Civic spin-off that was replaced in 1991 by the less sporty and much less popular Honda del Sol. Prized by high-performance "tuners," a well-maintained CRX is worth between $2,000 and $3,000.

The 1985–2001 **Prelude** is an Above Average buy. It's unimpressive as a high-performance sports car, but instead it delivers a stylish exterior, legendary reliability, and excellent resale value. Preludes are, nevertheless, a bit overpriced and over-hyped; cheaper, well-performing makes such as the Ford Mustang or Probe, GM Camaro or Firebird, Mazda Miata, and Toyota Celica should be checked out first. Prelude repair costs are average, though some dealer-dependent repairs to the steering assembly and transmission can be quite expensive.

The year for big Prelude changes was 1997, while 1998–2001 models just coasted along with minor improvements (their prices vary from $4,000 to $10,000, while earlier models run about $3,000 to $3,500). The '97 was restyled and repowered, and given handling upgrades that make it a better-performing, more comfortably riding sports coupe. There's no crashworthiness data, though head-restraint protection has been given a Marginal designation. On these more-recent models, owners report that the engine tends to leak oil and crank bolts often loosen (causing major engine damage). AC condensers frequently fail after a few years and often need cleaning to eliminate disagreeable odours. Most corner mechanics are poorly equipped to service these cars, and the Automatic Torque Transfer System (ATTS) won't make their job any easier. Owners also report that a poorly designed clutch disc causes harsh shifting, and there have been clutch-spring failures.

Mazda—Sports-car thrills, minus the bills: The 1992–96 **MX-3**'s base 1.6L engine supplies plenty of power for most driving situations, and it's reasonably priced at $2,000. When equipped with the optional 1.8L V6 powerplant (the smallest V6 on the market at the time) and high-performance options, the car transforms itself into a 130 hp pocket rocket. In fact, the MX-3 GS easily outperforms the Honda del Sol, Toyota Paseo, and Geo Storm on comfort and high-performance acumen. It does fall a bit short of the Saturn SC because of its limited low-end torque, and fuel economy is disappointing. Reverse gear is sometimes hard to engage, and brake and wheel bearing problems are commonplace. Most of the MX-3's parts are used on other Mazda cars, so their overall reliability should be outstanding. Crash safety ratings have been average. Also consider the **MX-6**.

Toyota—All '80s and early '90s models are Above Average buys, except the **LE Van**, which has a history of chronic brake, chassis, and body rusting problems. Chassis rusting and V6 engine head gasket failures are common problems with the 1988–95 sport-utilities and pickups (Toyota has paid for the engine repairs up to eight years). The **Celica** is an especially fine buy, combining smooth engine performance and bulletproof reliability with sports-car thrills.

From its humble beginnings in 1979, the **Supra** became Toyota's flagship sports car by 1986, and it took on its own unique personality—with the help of a powerful 3.0L DOHC V6 powerplant. Supra prices range from a low of $4,000 for a '90 model up to $17,000 for a '97. It's an attractively styled high-performance sports car that had been quite reliable up until it caught the Corvette/Nissan 300ZX malady in 1993. Early models (pre-'93) are more reasonably priced and are practically trouble-free, except for some premature front brake wear and vibrations. On later models, owners report major turbocharger problems; frequent rear differential replacements; electrical short circuits; AC malfunctions; and premature brake, suspension, and exhaust system wear. The 3.0L engine is an oil-burner at times, and cornering is often accompanied by a rear-end growl. Seat belt guides and the power antenna are failure-prone. Body deficiencies are common.

Toyota's 1991–99 **Tercel** and **Paseo** models are Above Average buys, while the 1987–90 Tercel remains a good Average pick. Prices vary little: A 1992–1995 Tercel will cost $1,000–$2,000, while the 1996–99 versions sell for $2,000–$3,000. These economy cars are dirt cheap to maintain and repair, inexpensive parts are everywhere, and repairs can be done by almost anybody. Tercels are extraordinarily reliable, and the first-generation improvements provided livelier and smoother acceleration and made the interior space feel much larger than it was. Owners report these early models had hard-shifting automatic transmissions, premature brake and suspension component wearout, brake pulsation, leaking radiators, windshield whistling, and myriad squeaks and rattles. Be careful with very early models (1985–90). Updated 1995–99 Tercels are noted for sporadic brake, electrical system, suspension, and body/accessory problems. Frontal crashworthiness was rated two stars on the 1992 Tercel, four stars on the 1993–94, and three stars on the 1995–97. Head restraints were always rated Poor.

The Recommended 1996–99 Paseo is a baby Tercel. Its main advantages are a peppy 1.5L 4-cylinder engine, a smooth 5-speed manual transmission, good handling, a supple ride, great fuel economy, and above-average reliability. This light little sportster is quite vulnerable to side winds; there's lots of body lean in turns; there's plenty of engine, exhaust, and road noise; front headroom and legroom are limited; and there's very little rear-seat space. Generally, safety problems and defects affecting the Tercel are also likely to affect the Paseo.

Beaters You Will Hate

These cars will keep you eternally poor but healthy from your daily walks, and they'll quickly teach you humility—and mechanics.

Audi Fox, **4000**, and **5000**—Engine, transmission, and fuel-system problems; a combination of sudden acceleration and no acceleration.

British Leyland Austin Marina, **MG**, **MGB**, and **Triumph**—Electrical system, engine, transmission, and clutch problems; chassis rusting.

Chrysler—**Cricket**, **Omni/Horizon**, and **Volaré/Aspen**: Engine, brakes, and steering problems; chassis rusting. **Charger**, **Cordoba**, and **Mirada**: Brake, body, and electrical system problems. The 1985–89 **Lancer** and **LeBaron** GTS may cost only $500–$700, but they're no bargain. In fact, they suffer from many of the same problems as the Aries and Reliant K cars and their 1989 replacements, the Spirit and Acclaim. Poor reliability causes maintenance costs to mount quickly. Turbo models are especially risky buys. Head gaskets are prone to leaks on all engines. Shock absorbers, MacPherson struts, and brakes wear out quickly. Front brake rotors are prone to rusting and warping. Crash test scores are below average.

Although they don't cost much—$300–$700, depending on the year—steer clear of 1983–89 **Aries** and **Reliants**. Uncomplicated mechanical components and roomy interiors made these cars attractive buys when new, but they quickly deteriorated once in service. Both cars use dirt cheap, low-tech components that tend to break down frequently. They have also performed poorly in crash tests. Serious corrosion generally starts along the trunk line, the edges of the rear wheelwells, and the front fenders.

The 1990–98 **Laser** and **Talon** are Not Recommended, although the sporty Talons gave true high-performance thrills, just before they broke down.

Maintenance and repair costs are much higher than average, mainly because of a scarcity of parts and a failure-prone and complicated-to-repair powertrain and emissions system.

Datsun/Nissan 210, 310, 510, 810, F-10, and 240Z—Electrical system and brake problems; rusting. Not worth buying at any price.

Eagle Medallion, Monaco, and Premier—These bargain-priced French American Motors *cum* Renault *cum* Chrysler imports—$500 for the Medallion and $1,000 for the Premier—had a 1988–92 model run. Sold through Chrysler's Renault connection, they're some of the most failure-prone imports to ever hit our shores.

Fiat—"Fix it again, Tony." All Fiat models and years are known for temperamental fuel and electrical systems and disintegrating bodies. Alfa Romeos have similar problems.

Ford Cortina, Pinto, Festiva, Fiesta, Bobcat, and Mustang II—These over three-decade-old cars are disasters. Watch out for electrical system, engine, and chassis rusting—fire-prone Pintos and Bobcats are mobile Molotov cocktails. The German import Fiesta and the South Korean–built Festiva are two small imports that survived only a few years in Canada. Parts are practically unobtainable for both vehicles.

The 1994–97 Korean-built Ford/Kia **Aspire**'s size, engine, and drivetrain limitations restrict it to an urban environment, and its low quality control restricts it to the driveway. Be wary of brake, electrical, and fuel system failures. Parts are also hard to find. That said, you can pick up an Aspire dirt cheap for less than $1,500. In its favour, the car has consistently posted higher-than-average crash test scores.

Stay away from the Ford **Contour** and **Mystique** (1995–99); they're two of the most failure-prone, hazardous vehicles you can buy—industry insiders call the Mystique the "Mistake." The reason these cars are an even worse buy than the Taurus and Sable is that they've been taken off the market, drying up a minuscule parts supply and driving up parts prices (try $700 for an alternator). Resale values vary between $1,000 and $1,500.

General Motors—**Vega, Astre, Monza, and Firenza**: Engine, transmission, body, and brake problems. Cadillac **Cimarron, Allanté, and Catera**: All gone; all bad. Overpriced, with poor-quality components. All front-drives suffer engine, automatic transmission, electronic module, steering, and brake problems, not to mention rust/paint peeling. **Citation, Skylark, Omega, and Phoenix**: Engine, brake, and electronic module problems; severe rust canker.

The Pontiac **Fiero**, sold from 1984 to 1988, snares lots of unsuspecting first-time buyers with its attractive sports-car styling, high-performance pretensions, and $500–$1,000 price. However, one quickly learns to both fear and hate the Fiero as it shows off its fiery disposition (several safety recalls for engine compartment fires) and its "I'll start when I want to" character.

Hyundai Pony and **Stellar**—Two of the worst South Korean small cars ever imported into Canada. Their most serious problems involve electrical and fuel-system failures that cause fires, no-starts, stalling, and chronic engine hesitation. Stellars have irreparable suspension, steering, and brake deficiencies that make them dangerous to drive. Cost: $300–$500.

The **Excel** is a low-tech and low-quality economy car that was orphaned in 1995. Resale prices are low ($300 for an '88; $1,000 for a '94). Likely problem areas are defective constant velocity joints, water pumps, oil-pan gaskets, oil pressure switches, and front struts as well as leaking engine head gaskets. An Excel cross-dressing as a sports car, the 1991–95 **Scoupe** ($2,000–$2,500) is essentially a cute coupe with an engine more suited to high gas mileage than hard driving.

Worth between $1,500 and $2,000, the **Mercedes-Benz** 1990–93 **190E** "Baby Benz" was a flop from the very beginning. It was the company's smallest and cheapest sedan, powered by a 158 hp 2.6L 6-cylinder gasoline engine borrowed from the mid-size 260E sedan. A 5-speed manual transmission was standard, but most models were bought with the optional 4-speed automatic. A less-powerful, 130 hp 2.3L 4-cylinder engine was added to the 1991 model. Standard safety features were a driver-side airbag and ABS. Owners found the car to be both unreliable (automatic transmission, electrical and fuel system, and brake problems) and hard to service. Now, parts are almost impossible to find and mechanics run away when a 190E pulls into their service bay.

The 1989–96 **300ZX**, **Nissan**'s answer to the Corvette, has everything: high-performance capability, a heavy chassis, complicated electronics, and average depreciation, resulting in a price range of $3,000–$4,000. Turbocharged 1990 and later models are much faster than previous versions and better overall buys. This weighty rear-drive offers a high degree of luxury equipment along with a potent 300 hp engine. Traction is poor on slippery surfaces, though, and the rear suspension hits hard when going over speed bumps. Crashworthiness scores have been average. The complexity of all the bells and whistles on the 300ZX translates into a lot more problems than you'd experience with either a Mustang or a Camaro—two cars that have had their own reliability problems but are far easier and less costly to repair. The best example of this is the electrical system, long a source of recurring, hard-to-diagnose shorts. Fuel injectors are a constant problem and guarantee sustained poor engine performance. The manual transmission has been failure-prone, clutches don't last long, front and rear brakes are noisy and wear out quickly, and the aluminum wheels are easily damaged by corrosion and road hazards. The exhaust system is practically biodegradable. The weird spongy/stiff variable shock absorbers and the glitzy digital dash with three odometers are more gimmicky than practical. Body assembly is mediocre.

Saab 900, 9000, 9-3, and 9-5 models sold from 1985 to 2003 are Not Recommended buys. Maintenance and repair costs can be quite high and must be done by a GM or Saab dealer. The 1996–2003 used prices range from $2,500 to $12,000. The 900 and 9000 series have similar deficiencies affecting the engine, cooling (disintegrating water pumps), and electrical systems; brakes; automatic transmissions (clutch O-rings); and body hardware. Interestingly, the upscale 9000 series isn't as crashworthy as the cheaper 900 versions, nor is it more reliable, exhibiting similar generic deficiencies to its entry-level brother. The 9-5 models have garnered a five-star crash protection rating. On more-recent models, chronic stalling can make these vehicles extremely dangerous to drive. Short circuits are legion and run the gamut from minor annoyances to fire hazards. Electrical glitches in the traction control system's relay module shuts the engine down, and engine sludging affects 9-3 and 9-5 models (covered by a "goodwill" warranty). Turbo-equipped models should be approached with extra caution because owner abuse or poor maintenance can make them wallet-busters. Air conditioners and exhaust system parts have a short lifespan, and leaky seals and gaskets are common. Rust perforations tend to develop along door bottoms and the rocker panels.

The original **Volkswagen Beetle** was cheap to own but deadly to drive. Its main deficiencies were poorly anchored, unsafe front seats; a heater that never worked (fortunately, we were young and hot-blooded enough in those days to generate our own heat); fuel-tank placement that was dangerous in collisions; and poorly designed wheels and seat tracks. The **Camper** minivan was safer but less reliable, with engine, transmission, fuel-system, and heater failings. VW's 1987–93 **Fox** was the company's cheapest small car, combining good fuel economy with above-average road handling. An upgraded 5-speed manual transmission was added to the 1993 model year. This Brazilian-made front-drive never caught on because of its notoriously unreliable engine and transmission; quirky electronics; excessive road, wind, and body noise; atrocious fit and finish; and cramped interior (in the sedan). Parts are especially hard to find. Crashworthiness is way below average. Priced between $300 and $500, these cars are more skunk than fox.

VW's **Scirocco** is fun to drive but risky to own. Chronic breakdowns, parts shortages, and poor crashworthiness are just the beginning. Electrical short circuits, chronic fuel-supply problems, premature front brake wear, and fragile body parts are common owner complaints. Expect to pay $1,000. Selling for $2,000 to $2,500, the 1990–95 **Corrado** gives good all-around performance, with the accent on smooth acceleration, a firm but not harsh ride, and excellent handling with little body roll. So why is it Not Recommended? Poor reliability, hard-to-find parts, limited servicing outlets, and undetermined crashworthiness.

The 1989–93 **Volvo 240 Series** is a Below Average buy, costing approximately $2,000. Avoid the turbocharged 4-cylinder engine and failure-prone air conditioning system. Diesels suffer from cooling system breakdowns and leaky cylinder head gaskets. The brakes on all model years need frequent and expensive servicing, and exhaust systems are notorious for their short lifespans. When a '79 Volvo 240 was crash tested, researchers concluded that both the driver and passenger would have sustained severe head traumas. The 1992–93 models, however, received excellent NHTSA crashworthiness scores.

Selling for $2,000 to $2,500, the 1986–92 **700 Series** models are more spacious, luxurious, and complicated to service than the entry-level 240. The standard engine and transmission perform well but aren't as refined as the 850's. The 700 Series suffers from some electrical, engine cooling, air conditioning, and body deficiencies. Brakes tend to wear rapidly and can require expensive servicing. The 1988 model performed poorly in crash tests, while the 1991–92 versions did quite well.